T0074654

Human-Computer Interaction

An Empirical Research Perspective

Second Edition

I. Scott MacKenzie
York University
Toronto, ON, Canada

MORGAN KAUFMANN PUBLISHERS

ELSEVIER   AN IMPRINT OF ELSEVIER

ISBN: 978-0-443-14096-9

For information on all Morgan Kaufmann publications
visit our website at https://www.elsevier.com/books-and-journals

Publisher: Mara E. Conner
Acquisitions Editor: Craig Smith
Editorial Project Manager: Isabella Silva
Production Project Manager: Fahmida Sultana
Cover Designer: Greg Harris

Typeset by VTeX

Working together
to grow libraries in
developing countries

www.elsevier.com • www.bookaid.org

In memory of Torsten Felzer

Contents

Preface to second edition

Following publication of the first edition of this book in 2013 . . . My gosh, where to begin! A lot has happened. Covid-19 hit in 2020, climate calamity is now daily news, there is war, foreign malfeasance, and political unrest everywhere. Oops, wrong book. Yes, the world has changed. This book's focus, luckily, is a narrower world: human-computer interaction (HCI). In HCI, change is continual, fast, and expected. There is a revolving door of computing products, interfaces, and interaction techniques. Contemporary smartphones have multiple cameras, and include ever-more memory, higher resolution displays, expanding computing power, fingerprint and other new sensors, and so on. Head-mounted displays (HMDs) for virtual reality (VR) are no longer a niche product. New HMDs are many users' preferred choice for games and often include built-in eye tracking. Smartwatches, Fitbits, Garmins, and Stravas count our every step, time the steps, measure the distances, map the routes, and motivate us to workout and share our accomplishments. There's an app for this, a device for that. Yes, there's a lot to unpack. And let's not forget the mainstream emergence of artificial intelligence (AI). The next edition of this book might just have a new author: Chat-something-or-other.

The Covid-19 pandemic changed many aspects of our lives, including our use of computers. The pandemic brought a shift in the way we interact, with a move to remote work and online socializing. In February 2020 I had never heard of Zoom. Fast forward a few months and Zoom was part of my daily routine. Socializing from a distance became the new normal for all of us. We are now returning to pre-pandemic norms, but what lies ahead is anyone's guess.

Notably, the role for empirical research in human-computer interaction is the same today as it was when the first edition of this book was published. The difference only lies in the new possibilities for products and ideas that inspire and challenge us today. The value in exploring new ideas with research that is empirical and experimental remains.

This second edition contains the same eight chapters as the first, but dozens of new topics appear, with existing themes and examples updated. More than 20 new students exercises are added. There is now a glossary for the most common terms in empirical research. A rigorous treatment of errors and outliers is added in Chapter 2 (The Human Factor) with additional and contemporary interaction methods added in Chapter 3 (Interaction Elements). Chapter 4 (Scientific Foundations) now includes deeper analyses on the nature of research and its relationship to engineering and design. Ethics concerns and questionnaire design are more thoroughly represented in Chapter 5 (Designing HCI Experiments). A change in Chapter 6 (Hypothesis Testing) is the use of single GUI tool to demonstrate and implement the most common statistical procedures for hypothesis testing in HCI user studies. GoStats is a single easy-to-use `.jar` file that will run on any computer capable of running Java programs. It is available on this book's web site as a free download. An additional procedure is also included, the Lilliefors test for normality. Chapter 7 (Modelling Interaction) adds the circumplex model of affect with ratings quantified using the self-assessment manikin. Chapter 8 (Writing and Publishing a Research Paper) moves forward with new practice for citations and references and promotes contemporary environments such as Overleaf.

A website supplements the book, primarily to host downloadable files containing the data and analyses in the book:

www.yorku.ca/mack/HCIbook2e

The downloads on the book's web site include SPSS, R, MATLAB, and StatView implementations for all the statistical tests in Chapter 6 (Hypothesis Testing). For each application, there is a downloadable ZIP file containing the necessary files and a readme.txt file that explains how to do the analyses in SPSS, R, MATLAB, or StatView.

Scott MacKenzie
Toronto, 2023

Preface to first edition

A few years ago, my son approached me with a problem. It was November, daylight savings time had ended, and his watch was an hour fast. He was having trouble adjusting the time. Could I help? "Sure," I said. He gave me the watch. By most measures, I am an expert in user interfaces. Modern watches have many features and just a few buttons. They have modes. I understand modes. Repeatedly press one button to cycle through the modes. Press and hold another button and the device is ready for change. That sort of thing. It might take some trial and error, but the task seemed simple enough. I was wrong. Try as I may, the watch resisted. I couldn't change the time! I borrowed the watch and brought it to work. At the time I was teaching a course called Advanced Human-Computer Interaction. The students, all MSc or PhD candidates, are more tech-savvy than their instructor. After all, these students were born in the digital age. Technology to them is like food or air. They consume it! I explained the situation and gave the watch to the closest student. A few minutes later the watch was passed to the next student, then the next. About 30 minutes later, the watch was returned to me. The time was unchanged. Not a single student was able to change the time.

I am thankful for stories like this. They give you and me something to do – something to think about and work on. Human-computer interaction (HCI) as a field of research and practice extends back to the 1980s. Despite the accomplishments, we still confront technology that utterly perplexes and frustrates us. Yes, there is work to do.

This book is not about designing a better watch. Of course, the end game is better designs and products, but the focus here is on the ideas – ideas for new and improved user interfaces or interaction techniques. The journey from idea to product is long, however. Before embedding in a product, an idea must be implemented, refined, tested, refined again, tested again, and so on. Testing is key: Is the idea any good? How good? Does it improve on current practice? According to what criteria and by how much? Do users like it? Is it intuitive, efficient, even fun, or will users find it awkward or frustrating? This book is about answering questions like these. The questions above are expressions of curiosity. They capture the true and unstructured spirit of innovative thought. But answering these questions is a challenge. Terms like "any good" and "improve on" are subjective. To answer with clarity and assurance, the questions must be recast and narrowed – to make them answerable, so to speak. Well-formed questions about new ideas for user interfaces invite observation and measurement of human interaction with the technology of interest. In the narrowed form, the questions are "research questions." Furthermore, questions that are pursued through observation and measurement are empirical. With this, we arrive at this book's theme: human-computer interaction, with an empirical research perspective.

This book's study of empirical research in HCI is admittedly narrow. The reader is implored not to view this as dismissive of research methods in HCI that are also empirical but with a qualitative or non-experimental emphasis. HCI is a tremendously broad field with a considerable amount of empirical research, particularly in the social sciences, that uses observational methods as opposed to experimental methods. The emphasis on experimental methods in the pages ahead is a by-product of the book's single-author design. To expand the treatment of observational methods here, giving them equal space with experimental methods, would be a disservice to the substantial community of researchers skilled in these methods. This book reflects one researcher's perspective and that perspective has more to do with the author's personal experience and expertise than with any suggestion that certain methods are superior to others. For this reason, the "empirical research" label is delegated to the book's subtitle, or secondary title. Bracketing empirical research with "perspective" and the indefinite article "an" is deliberate. The book presents one perspective on empirical research in HCI. Often, the focus is broad (What is empirical? What is research?), but, still, the emphasis on research that is empirical and experimental. If there is one deliverable in this book, it is the knowledge and skills required to design and conduct a "user study" – a factorial experiment with human participants where two or more facets of a user interface are empirically and quantitatively compared.

The book has eight chapters. It begins with a historical context of the field in Chapter 1, chronicling significant work leading to the emergence in the 1980s of HCI as a field of research and practice. This is followed with an overview of the human factor in Chapter 2, where the sensory, motor, and cognitive characteristics of the human are introduced and summarized. Chapter 3 presents the core elements of human interaction with computers. The examination focuses on human actions and the responses they invoke in the computer. Of course, the goal is to distinguish action-response pairings that work well from those that are awkward or confusing. The scientific foundations of research and, in particular, experimental research are elaborated in Chapter 4. Here we learn how to craft narrow and testable research questions. The underlying principles of science and research are studied, as well. Following this, Chapter 5 provides a step-by-step guide on how to design and conduct an HCI experiment, or user study. The focus is on controlled experiments, with independent variables, dependent variables, within- and between-subjects assignment of conditions, counterbalancing, etc. Chapter 6 is on hypothesis testing; answering research questions in a statistical sense. The review is introductory, cookbook-like, and is limited to the analysis of variance (causal relationships), the chi-square test (circumstantial relationships), and non-parametric tests on ordinal data.

One important theme in HCI research is building and testing models of interaction. This is the subject of Chapter 7, where two approaches to modeling are presented. Descriptive models partition a problem space, usually with visual aids, to help understand an aspect of human interaction with technology. Predictive models are equations that predict human performance from task characteristics. The final and essential step in research is publishing the results, so the book concludes in Chapter 8 with tips and discussions on writing and publishing a research paper.

In style, the book has several approaches. It is not a research monograph, although some original and unpublished research is included. An example is the experiment on visual search, leading to a predictive model. The model gives the time to scan n items on a display while searching for a particular item. The task is common in HCI. For example, soft keyboards on touchscreen devices often include word completion. As entry progresses, the system offers candidates completing the current key sequence. If there are n candidates in the list, how much time is needed for a user to determine if the desired word is present? The cost of viewing the list can be traded against the cost of not viewing it. Design choices follow. Herein is the essence of predictive modeling, a subject well-traveled in HCI (and in this book).

The book is not a work of fiction, but stories and anecdotes help frame many of the discussions (with an HCI motivation). In the pages ahead, you will read about the sitcom character Dobie Gillis' pensive moments by The Thinker (how to find a research topic), the unusual definition of a false start in the 100 meter dash in the Olympics (human reaction time to an auditory stimulus), the danger in feeding a digital pet while driving (visual attention; secondary tasks), the use of duct tape to fix a bad user interface (importance of tactile feedback; form versus function) and the framing of important achievements in science, such as microbiologist Louis Pasteur's development of a standardized research methodology (research must be reproducible; the importance of a consistent methodology for user studies). And the writing style occasionally slips into the first person, where a personal experience seems relevant. An example is my experience in 1981 at the National Computer Conference (NCC) in Chicago. The event of note was the introduction of the Xerox Star – the first computer system to use a graphical user interface (GUI) and a mouse.

Mostly this book is a textbook, though it also serves as a handbook. The intended audience is students of HCI, but anyone undertaking empirical or experimental research in HCI will likely find interest within. Many topics are presented with a pedagogical intent, such as designing and conducting experiments (user studies), building a regression model from experimental data, or performing and explaining an analysis of variance. As well, there are student exercises to hone one's skill on the topics within.

A website supplements the book. The primary purpose is to host downloadable files supporting topics in the book. There is Java-based software, including full source code and detailed APIs. An analysis of variance application (Anova2) and other statistics utilities are included as are several complete packages for HCI experiments. Here's the URL:

www.yorku.ca/mack/HCIbook

The website will evolve as more resources become available. The software is intended for desktop computing environments or devices running the Android operating system. More will be added later.

Scott MacKenzie
Toronto, 2013

Historical context

Human-computer interaction. Humans, then computers, then interaction. Yes, that's it. In the beginning, there were humans. In the 1940s came computers. In the 1980s came interaction. Wait! What about 1940 to 1980? Were humans *interacting* with computers then? Well, yes, sort of, but not just any human. Computers in those days were too precious, too complicated, to allow just your average human to mess with them. Computers were carefully guarded. They lived a secure and secluded life in corporate or university research labs or government facilities. They lived in large air-conditioned rooms with raised floors and locked doors. The rooms often had glass walls to show off the unique status of the behemoths within. Yes, it was a special time.

If you were of that breed of human permitted access, you were probably an engineer or scientist – a computer scientist. And you knew what to do. Whether it was connecting relays with patch cords on an ENIAC (1940s), changing a magnetic memory drum on a UNIVAC (1950s), adjusting the JCL stack on a System/360 (1960s), or *greping* and *awking* around the unix command set on a PDP-11 (1970s), you were on home turf. Unix commands like "grep," for "global regular expression print," were obvious enough. Why consult the manual? You wrote it! And unix's vi editor. If some poor soul was stupid enough to start typing text while in command mode, well, he got what he deserved.[1] Who gave him a login account, anyway? And what's all this talk about *make the state of the system visible to the user?* User! What user? Sounds a bit like ... well ... socialism!

Interaction was not on the minds of the engineers and scientists who designed, built, configured, and programmed early computers. But, by the 1980s, interaction arrived. The new computers were not only powerful, they were usable – by anyone! With usability added, computers moved from secure confines onto people's desks throughout the workplace and, critically, into people's homes. One reason human-computer interaction is so exciting is that the field's emergence and progress is aligned with, and in good measure responsible for, this dramatic shift in computing practices.

This book is about research in human-computer interaction. As in all fields, research in HCI is the force underlying advances that migrate into products and pro-

---

[1] One of the classic UI foibles – told and re-told by HCI educators around the world – is the vi editor's lack of feedback when switching modes. Many a user has provided input while in *command mode* or entered a command while in *input mode*.

cesses that people use, whether for work or pleasure. While HCI is broad and with a substantial applied component – most notably in design – the focus in this book is narrow. The focus is research – the what, the why, and the how – with a few stories along the way.

Many people associate research in HCI with developing a new or improved inter-action or interface and testing it in a user study. And that's fine. But, this book takes a more formal approach, where a user study is "an experiment with human partici-pants." HCI experiments are discussed throughout the book. The word "empirical" is added simply to add weight to some valuable properties of experimental research. The research espoused here is empirical because it is based on observation and expe-rience and is carried out and reported on in a manner that allows results to be verified or refuted through the effort of other researchers. In this way, each item of HCI re-search joins a large body of work that, taken as a whole, defines the field and sets the context for applying HCI knowledge in real products or processes.

We begin with a historical context for HCI.

1.1 Background

Although only emerging in the 1980s, the field of HCI owes a lot older disciplines. The most central of these is *human factors*, also called *ergonomics*. Indeed, the pre-eminent conference in HCI is the annual forum sponsored by a special interest group of the Association for Computing Machinery (ACM).[2] The full name of the event reflects this connection: The ACM SIGCHI Conference on Human Factors in Com-puting Systems. SIGCHI is the special interest group on computer-human interaction.

Human factors is both a science and a field of engineering. It is concerned with human capabilities, limitations, and performance, and with the design of systems that are efficient, safe, comfortable, and even enjoyable for the humans that use them. It is also an art in the sense of respecting and promoting creative ways for practitioners to apply their skills in designing systems. One need only change systems to *computing systems* to make the leap from human factors to HCI. HCI, then, is human factors, but narrowly focused on human interaction with computing technology of some sort.

"Narrowly focused" is not typically associated with HCI. On the contrary, HCI is broad in scope and draws upon interests and expertise in disciplines such as psy-chology (particularly cognitive psychology and experimental psychology), sociology, anthropology, cognitive science, computer science, and linguistics.

---

[2] The Association of Computing Machinery (ACM), founded in 1947, is the world's leading educational and scientific computing society, with over 100,000 members. The ACM is organized into over 150 special interested groups, or "SIGs." Among the services offered is the ACM Digital Library, a repository of over one million publications which includes 45+ ACM journals, 85+ ACM conference proceedings, and numerous other publications from affiliated organizations. See www.acm.org.

As a backdrop to our historical context, Fig. 1.1 presents a timeline of notable events leading to the birth and emergence of HCI as a field of study. We begin in the 1940s.

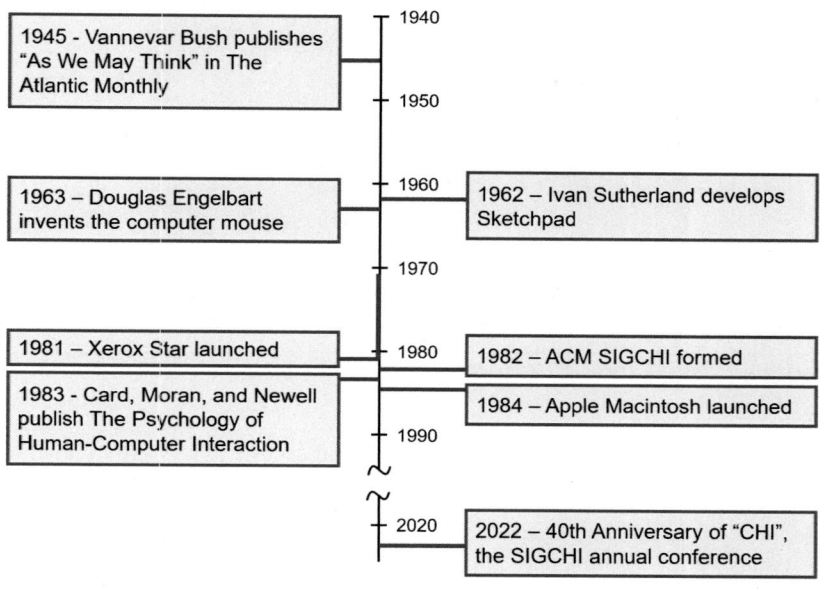

FIGURE 1.1

Notable events in the history of human-computer interaction (HCI).

1.2 **Vannevar Bush's "As We May Think" (1945)**

Vannevar Bush's prophetic essay "As We May Think" was published in the *Atlantic Monthly* in July, 1945 [47]. It is required reading in many HCI courses, even today. The article has garnered 10000+ citations in scholarly publications.[3] Attesting to the importance of Bush's vision to HCI is the 1996 reprint of the entire essay in the ACM's *interactions* magazine, complete with annotations, sketches, and biographical notes.

Bush, seen in Fig. 1.2, was the U.S. government's Director of the Office of Scientific Research and a scientific advisor to President Franklin D. Roosevelt. He was charged with leading some 6,000 American scientists in the application of science to warfare. It was 1945. But, Bush was keenly aware of the hope and possibilities that lay ahead in peacetime in applying science to more lofty and humane pursuits.

---

[3] Google Scholar search using "author:bush as we may think."

FIGURE 1.2

Vannevar Bush at work (circa 1940-1944).

His essay concerned the dissemination, storage, and access, to scholarly knowledge. Bush wrote:

> *The summation of human experience is being expanded at a prodigious rate, and the means we use for threading through the consequent maze to the momentarily important item is the same as was used in the days of square-rigged ships.*
>
> **[47, p. 37]**[4]

Aside from the reference to square-rigged shits, Bush's words are relevant today, especially his mention of the *expanding human experience* in relation the HCI. For most people, nothing short of Olympian talent is needed to keep abreast of the latest advances in this, the information age. Bush's *consequent maze* is today's *information overload* or *lost in hyperspace*. Bush's *momentarily important item* sounds like a blog posting or a tweet? Although blogs and tweets didn't exist in 1945, Bush clearly anticipated them.

Bush proposed navigating the knowledge maze with a device he called *memex*. Among the features of memex is *associative indexing*, whereby points of interest are connected and joined so that selecting one item automatically selects another: "When the user is building a trail, he names it, inserts the name in his code book, and taps it out on his keyboard." [47, p. 44]. Sounds like hyperlinks and bookmarks. Although today it is easy to equate memex with hypertext and the World Wide Web, Bush's inspiration came from the contemporary telephone exchange, which he described as a "spider web of metal, sealed in a thin glass container" (viz. vacuum tubes) [47, p. 38]. The maze of connections in a telephone exchange gave rise to Bush's more

---

[4] For convenience, page references are to the March 1996 reprint in the ACM's *interactions*.

general theme of a spider web of connections for the information in one's mind, one's experiences.

It is not surprising that some of Bush's ideas today seem naïve; e.g., *dry photography*. Yet, the ideas are naïve only when juxtaposed with Bush's brilliant foretelling of a world we are still struggling with and are still tuning and perfecting.

1.3 Ivan Sutherland's Sketchpad (1962)

Ivan Sutherland developed Sketchpad in the early 1960s as part of his PhD research in electrical engineering at the Massachusetts Institute of Technology (MIT). Sketchpad was a graphics system that supported the manipulation of geometric shapes and lines (objects) on a display using a light pen. To appreciate the complete absence of usability in the computers available to Sutherland at the time of his studies, consider these introductory comments in a paper he published in 1963:

> *Heretofore, most interaction between man and computers has been slowed by the need to reduce all communication to written statements that can be typed. In the past we have been writing letters to, rather than conferring with, our computers.*
> **[478, p. 329]**

With Sketchpad, commands were not typed. Users did not "write letters to" the computer. Instead, objects were drawn, resized, grabbed and moved, extended, deleted – directly, using the light pen. See Fig. 1.3. Object manipulations worked with constraints to maintain the geometric relationships and properties of objects.

The use of a pointing device for input makes Sketchpad the first *direct manipulation* interface – a sign of things to come. The term "direct manipulation" was coined many years later by Ben Shneiderman at the University of Maryland to provide a psychological context for a suite of related features that naturally came together in this new genre of human-computer interface [449]. These features include visibil-

 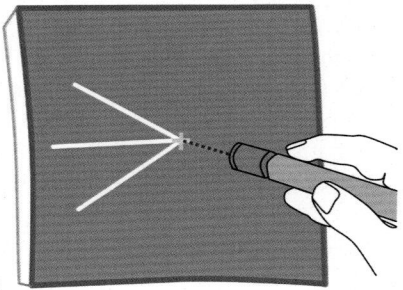

(a)   (b)

FIGURE 1.3

(a) Demo of Ivan Sutherland's Sketchpad. (b) A light pen dragging ("rubber banding") lines, subject to constraints.

ity of objects, incremental action, rapid feedback, reversibility, exploration, syntactic correctness of all actions, and replacing language with action. While Sutherland's Sketchpad was one of the earliest examples of a direct manipulation system, others soon followed, most notably the Dynabook concept system by Alan Kay of the Xerox Palo Alto Research Center (PARC) [241]. We will say more about Xerox PARC throughout this chapter.

Sutherland's work was presented at an IEEE conference in Detroit in 1963 [478]. The article is available in the ACM Digital Library.[5] Demos of Sketchpad are viewable on YouTube.[6] No user study of Sketchpad was conducted. This is not surprising, since Sutherland was a student in electrical engineering. Had his work proceeded in industrial engineering (where human factors is studied), testing with users might have occurred.

1.4 Invention of the Mouse (1963)

If there is one computing device above all others that symbolizes the emergence of HCI, it is the computer mouse. Invented by Douglas Engelbart in 1963, the mouse was destined to fundamentally change the way humans interact with computers.[7] Instead of typing commands, a user could manipulate a mouse to control an on-screen tracking symbol, or cursor. With the cursor positioned over a graphic image representing the command, the command is issued with a select operation – pressing and releasing a button on the mouse.

Engelbart was among a group of researchers at the Stanford Research Institute (SRI) in Menlo Park, California. The project for which an improved pointing device was needed was NLS (oN-Line System), an early hypertext system. The specific need was to replace the light pen. The light pen was an established technology, but it was awkward. The user held the pen in the air in front of the display. After a few minutes of interaction, fatigue sets in. What would a more natural and comfortable device look like? Perhaps something on the desktop, something in close proximity to the keyboard. The keyboard is where the user's hands are normally situated, so perhaps a device beside the keyboard makes the most sense. Engelbart's invention meets this requirement.

The first prototype mouse is seen in Fig. 1.4a. The device included two potentiometers positioned at right angles to each other. Large metal wheels were attached to the shafts of the potentiometers and protruded slightly from the base of the housing. As the device was manoeuvred on a surface, the wheels rotated. Side-to-side motion

---

[5] http://portal.acm.org/.

[6] http://www.youtube.com/.

[7] The actual date of invention is subject to speculation. Notably, Engelbart's patent for the mouse was filed on June 21, 1967 and issued on November 17, 1970 [114]. U.S. patent laws allow one year between public disclosure and filing; thus, we can assume that Engelbart's invention was not publicly disclosed prior to June 21, 1966.

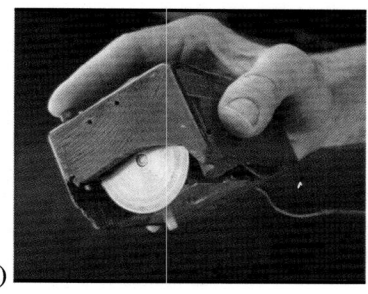 

(a)　　　　　　　　　　　　　　　　(b)

FIGURE 1.4

(a) The first mouse. (b) Inventor Douglas Engelbart holding his invention (left hand) and an early three-button variation (right hand).

rotated one wheel; to-and-fro motion rotated the other. With diagonal movement, both wheels rotated, in proportion to the amount of movement in each direction. For each wheel, the rotation altered the voltage at the wiper terminal of the potentiometer. The voltages were passed on to the host system for processing. The x and y position of an on-screen object or cursor were controlled, indirectly, by the two voltage signals. A button for selection is seen in the figure under the user's index finger. Engelbart is seen in Fig. 1.4b with his invention (left hand) and a three-button version of a mouse developed much later (right hand).

Initial testing focused on selecting and manipulating text, rather than drawing and manipulating graphic objects. Engelbart was second author of the first published evaluation involving a mouse. This was, arguably, HCI's first user study, so a few words are in order here. With English and Berman, a controlled experiment was conducted comparing several input devices capable of both selection and x-y position control of an on-screen cursor [115]. Besides the mouse, the comparison included a light pen, a joystick, a knee-controlled lever, and a Grafacon. The joystick (Fig. 1.5a) was isotonic (i.e., with a moving stick) and was operated in two control modes. In absolute or position-control mode, the cursor's position on the display had an absolute correspondence to the position of the stick. In rate-control mode, the cursor velocity was determined by the amount of stick deflection, while the direction of cursor motion was determined by the direction of the stick. An embedded switch was included for selection and was activated by pressing down on the stick.

The light pen (Fig. 1.5b) was operated much like the pen used by Sutherland (see Fig. 1.3). The device was picked up and moved to the display surface with the pen pointing at the desired object. A projected circle of orange light indicated the target to the lens system. Selection involved pressing a switch on the barrel of the pen.

The knee-controlled lever (Fig. 1.5c) was connected to two potentiometers. Side-to-side knee motion controlled side-to-side (x-axis) cursor motion; up-and-down knee motion controlled up-and-down (y-axis) cursor movement. Up-and-down knee motion was achieved by a "rocking motion on the ball of the foot" [115, p. 7]. The de-

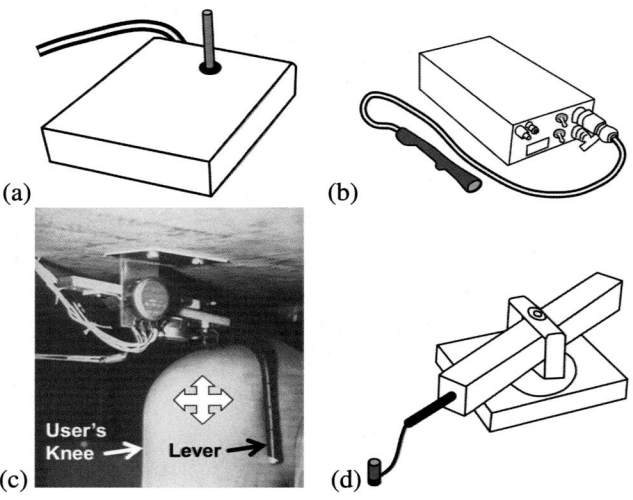

FIGURE 1.5

Additional devices used in the first comparative evaluation of a mouse. (a) Joystick. (b) Lightpen. (c) Knee-controlled lever. (d) Grafacon (Source, a, b, d adapted from [115]; c, 1967 IEEE Reprinted with permission.)

vice did not include an integrated method for selection. Instead, a key on the system's keyboard was used.

The Grafacon (Fig. 1.5d) was a commercial device for curve tracing. The device consisted "of an extensible arm connected to a linear potentiometer, with the housing for the linear potentiometer pivoted on an angular potentiometer" [115, p. 6]. Originally, there was a pen at the end of the arm; however, this was replaced with a knob-and-switch assembly (see figure). The user gripped the knob and moved it about to control the on-screen cursor. Pressing the knob caused a selection.

The knee-controlled lever and Grafacon are interesting alternatives to the mouse. They illustrate and suggest the processes involved in empirical research. It is not likely Engelbart simply woke up one morning and invented the mouse. While it may be true that novel ideas sometimes arise through eureka moments, there is more. Refining ideas – deciding what works and what doesn't – is an iterative process that involves a good deal of trial and error. No doubt, Engelbart and colleagues knew from the outset that they needed a device that would involve some form of human action as input and would produce two channels (x-y) of analog positioning data as output. A select operation was also needed to produce a command or generate closure at the end of a positioning operation. Of course, we know this today as a *point-select*, or *point-and-click*, operation. And, operating the device away from the display meant an on-screen tracker (e.g., an arrow) was needed to establish correspondence between the *device space* and the *display space*. It all seems so obvious today. But, it was new and emerging form of human-to-computer interaction in the 1960s.

In the comparative evaluation, English et al. [115] measured users' *access time* (the time to move the hand from the keyboard to the device) and *motion time* (the time from the onset of cursor movement to the final selection).[8] The evaluation included 13 participants (8 experienced, 3 inexperienced). For each trial, a character target (with surrounding distractor targets) appeared on the display. The trial began with the participant pressing and releasing the SPACEBAR on the system's keyboard, whereupon a cursor appeared on the display. The participant moved their hand to the input device and then manipulated the device to move the cursor to the target. With the cursor over the target, a selection was made using the method associated with the device. Examples of the results are shown in Fig. 1.6 for the inexperienced participants. Each bar is the mean for 10 sequences of 8 target-patterns each. Results are shown for the mean task completion time (Fig. 1.6a) and error rate, where the error rate is the ratio of missed target selections to all selections (Fig. 1.6b).

While it might appear that the knee-controlled lever is the best device in terms of time, each bar in Fig. 1.6a includes both the access time and the motion time. The access time for the knee-controlled lever is, of course, zero. The authors noted that considering motion time only, the knee-controlled lever "no longer shows up so favourably" [115, p. 12]. At 2.43 seconds per trial, the light pen had a slight advantage over the mouse at 2.62 seconds per trial; however, this must be viewed considering the discomfort in continued use of a light pen, which is operated in the air at the surface of the display. Besides, the mouse was the clear winner in terms of accuracy. The mouse error rate was less than half that of any other device condition in the evaluation (see Fig. 1.6b).

The mouse evaluation by English et al. [115] marks a milestone in HCI research. The methodology was empirical and the write-up included most of what we expect today in a user study destined for presentation at a conference and publication in a conference proceedings. For example, the write-up contained a detailed description of the participants, the apparatus, and the procedure. The study could be reproduced if other researchers wished to verify or refute the findings. Of course, reproducing the evaluation today would be difficult, as the devices are no longer available. The evaluation included an independent variable, input method, with six levels: mouse, light pen, joystick (position-control), joystick (rate-control), light pen, and knee-controlled lever. There were two dependent variables, task completion time and error rate. The order of administering the device conditions was different for each participant, a practice known today as counterbalancing. While testing for statistically significant differences using an analysis of variance (ANOVA) was not done, it is important to remember that the authors did not have at their disposal the many tools we take for granted today, such as spreadsheets and statistics applications.

The next comparative evaluation involving a mouse was by Card, English, and Burr [60], about ten years later. Card et al.'s work was carried out at Xerox PARC and was part of a larger effort that eventually produced the first windows-based graphical

---

[8] Access time, as used here, is also called *homing time*.

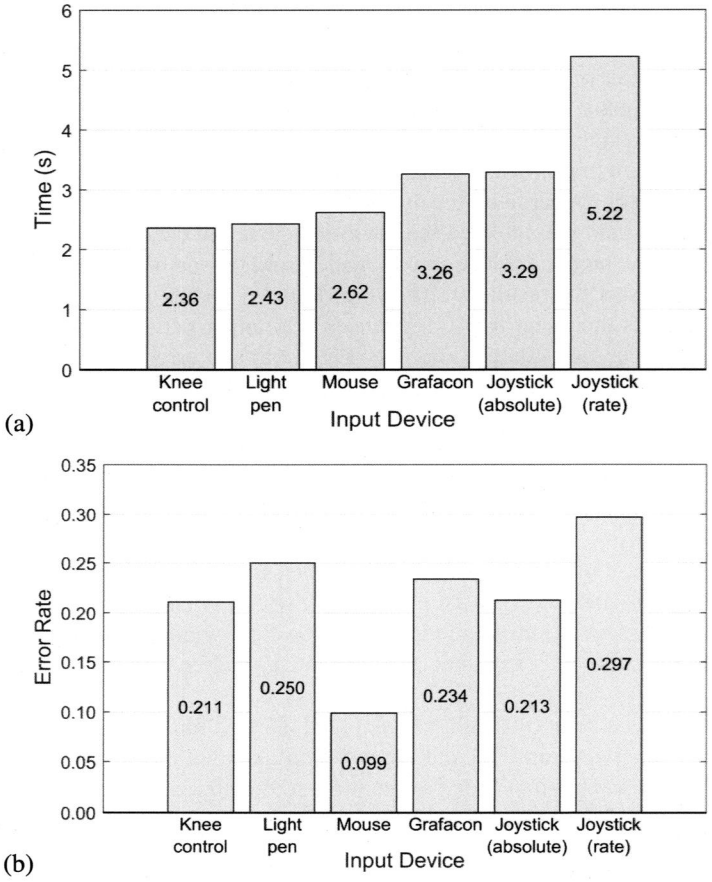

FIGURE 1.6

Results of the first comparative evaluation including a computer mouse. (a) Task completion time in seconds. (b) Error rate as the ratio of missed selections to all selections (adapted from [115]).

user interface, or GUI (see next section). Among other things, the mouse underwent considerable refining and re-engineering at PARC. Most notably, the potentiometer wheels were replaced with a rolling ball assembly, as developed by Rider [414]. The advantage of the refined mouse over competing devices was re-confirmed by Card et al. [60] and has been demonstrated in countless comparative evaluations since and throughout the history of HCI. It was becoming clear, that Engelbart's invention was about to change the face of computing.

Years later, Engelbart would receive the ACM's Turing Award (1997) and the ACM SIGCHI Lifetime Achievement Award (1998; first recipient). It is interesting that Engelbart's seminal invention dates to the early 1960s, yet commercialization of the mouse did not occur until 1981, when the Xerox Star was launched.

1.5 Xerox Star (1981)

There was a buzz around the floor of the NCC in Chicago in May 1981. In those days, the NCC, for National Computer Conference, was *the* yearly conference for computing. It was a gathering of researchers (sponsored by AFIPS, the American Federation of Information Processing Societies) and a trade show. The event was huge, with attendance of 73,000 in 1981 [417]. All the players were there. There were big players, like IBM, and little players, like Qupro Data Systems of Kitchener, Ontario, Canada. I was there, working the booth for Qupro. Our main product was a small desktop computer system based on a single-board computer known as the Pascal MicroEngine. But, that's another story.

The buzz at the NCC wasn't about Qupro. It wasn't about IBM, either. The buzz was about Xerox. "Have you been to the Xerox booth?" I would hear. "You gotta' check it out. It's really cool." And, indeed it was. The Xerox booth had a substantial crowd mulling around throughout the conference. There were scripted demos every hour or so, and the crowd was clearly excited by what they saw. The demos were of the Star, or the Xerox 8100 Star Information System, as it was formally called. The excitement was well deserved, as the 1981 launch of the Xerox Star at the NCC marks a watershed moment in the history of computing. The Star was the first commercially released computer system with a GUI and mouse. It had windows, icons, menus, and a pointing device (WIMP). It supported direct manipulation and what-you-see-is-what-you-get (WYSIWYG) interaction. The Star had what was needed to bring computing to the people.

The story of the Star began around 1970, when Xerox established its Palo Alto Research Centre, PARC, in California. The following year, Xerox signed an agreement with SRI licensing Xerox to use Engelbart's invention, the mouse [230, p. 22]. Over the next ten years, development proceeded along a number of fronts. One was the development beginning in 1973 of the Alto, the Star's predecessor. The Alto also included a graphical user interface and mouse. It was used widely within Xerox and in a few external test sites. However, the Alto was never released commercially – a missed opportunity on a grand scale, according to some [458].

Fig. 1.7 shows the Star workstation. It is unremarkable by today's standards, but the image shows graphical information on the system's display. This was novel at the time. The display was bit-mapped, meaning images were formed by mapping bits in memory to pixels on the display. Most systems at the time used character-mapped displays, meaning the screen image was composed of sequences of characters, each limited to a fixed pattern (e.g., 7×10 pixels) retrieved from read-only memory. Character-mapped displays required considerably less memory, but limited the richness of the display image. The mouse – a two-button variety – is seen by the system's keyboard.

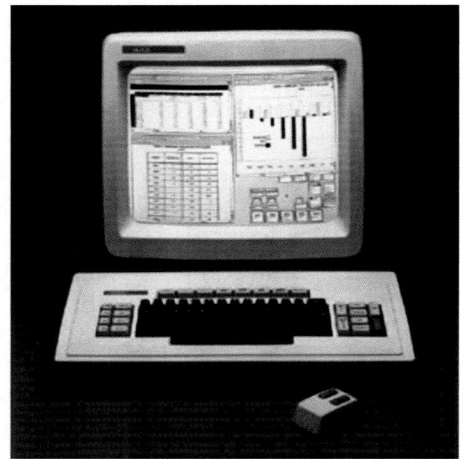

FIGURE 1.7

Xerox Star workstation.

As the designers noted, the Star was intended as an *office automation system* [230]. Business professionals would have Star workstations on their desks and would use them to create, modify, and manage documents, graphics tables, presentations, etc. The workstations were connected via high-speed Ethernet cables and shared centralized resources, such as printers, file servers, etc. A key tenet in the Star philosophy was that workers wanted to get their work done, not fiddle with computers. Obviously, the computers had to be easy to use, or *invisible* so to speak.

One novel feature of Star was the *desktop metaphor*. Metaphors are important in HCI. When a metaphor is present, the user has a jump-start on knowing what to do. The user exploits existing knowledge from another domain. The desktop metaphor brings concepts from the office desktop to the system's display. On the display the user finds pictorial representations (icons) for things like documents, folders, trays, and accessories such as a calculator, printer, or notepad. A few examples of the Star's icons are seen in Fig. 1.8. By using existing knowledge of a desktop, the user has an immediate sense of what to do and how things work. The Star designers, and others since, pushed the limits of the metaphor, where it is more an office metaphor than a desktop metaphor. There are windows, printers, and a trashcan on the display, but, of course, these artefacts are not found on an office desktop. But, the metaphor seemed to work, as we hear even today that the GUI is an example of the "desktop metaphor." We will say more about metaphors in Chapter 3.

In making the system usable ("invisible") the Star developers created interactions with files, not programs. So, users *open a document*, rather than *invoke an editor*. This means files are associated with applications, but these details are hidden from the user. Opening a spreadsheet document launches the spreadsheet application, while opening a text document opens an editor

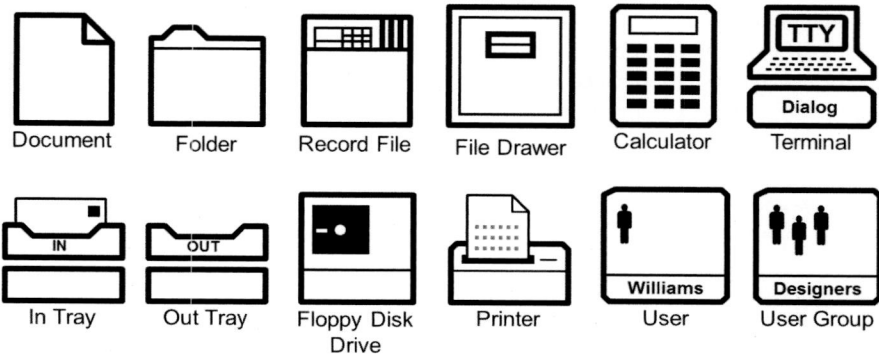

FIGURE 1.8

Examples of icons appearing on the Xerox Star desktop (adapted from [457]).

With a GUI and point-select interaction, the Star interface was the archetype of direct manipulation. The enabling work on graphical interaction (e.g., Sutherland) and pointing devices (e.g., Engelbart) was complete. By comparison, previous command-line interfaces had a single channel of input. Every action required a command. The user had to learn and remember the syntax of the system's commands and type them in to get things done. Direct manipulation systems, like the Star, have numerous input channels, and each channel has a direct correspondence to a task. Furthermore, interaction with the channel is tailored to the properties of the task. A continuous property, such as display brightness or sound volume, has a continuous control, such as a slider. A discrete property, such as font family or text alignment, has a discrete control, such as a multi-position switch or a menu item. Each control also has a dedicated location on the display and is engaged using a direct point-select operation. Johnson et al. [230, p. 14] compare direct manipulation to driving a car. A gas pedal controls the speed, a lever controls the wiper blades, a knob controls the radio volume. Each control is a dedicated channel, each has a dedicated location, and each is operated according to the property it controls.

When operating a car, the driver can adjust the radio volume, and then turn on the windshield wipers. Or, the driver can first turn on the windshield wipers, and then adjust the radio volume. The car is capable of responding the driver's inputs in any order, according to the driver's wishes. Direct manipulation, in computing, brings the same flexibility. This is no small feat. Command-line interfaces, by comparison, are simple. They follow a software paradigm known as *sequential programming*. Every action occurs in a sequence under the system's control. When the system needs a specific input, the user is prompted to enter it.

Direct manipulation interfaces require a different approach, because they must accept the user's actions, according the user's wishes. While manipulating *hello* in a text editor, for example, the user might change the font to Courier (hello) and then change the style to bold (hello). Or, the user might first set the style to bold (**hello**) and then change the font to Courier (hello). The result is the same, but the order of actions differs. The point here is that the user is in control, not the system. To support this, direct manipulation systems are designed using a software paradigm known as *event-driven programming*, which is more complicated than sequential programming. Although event-driven programming was not new (it is used in process-control to respond to *sensor events*), designing systems that responded asynchronously to *user events* was new in the early 1970s when work began on the Star. Of course, from the user's perspective, this detail is irrelevant (remember the "invisible" computer). We mention it here only to give credit for the Herculean effort that was invested in designing the Star and bringing it to market.

Designing the Star was not simply a matter of building an interface using windows, icons, menus, and a pointing-device (WIMP), it was about designing a system on which these components could exist and work. A team at PARC led by Alan Kay developed such a system beginning around 1970. The central ingredients were a new object-oriented programming language known as Smalltalk and a software architecture known as *model-view controller*. This was a complex programming environment, and it evolved in parallel with the design of the Star. It is not surprising, then, that the development of Star spanned about ten years, since the designers were not only inventing a new style of human-computer interaction, they were inventing the architecture on which this new style was built.

In the end, the Star was not a commercial success. While many have speculated on why (e.g., [458]), probably the most significant reason is that the Star was not a personal computer. In the article by the Star interface designers Johnson et al. [230], there are numerous references to the Star as a personal computer. But, they had a different view of "personal." They viewed Star as a beefed-up version of a terminal connected to a central server, "a collection of personal computers" [230, p. 12]. In another article, designers Smith and Irby call the Star "a personal computer designed for office professionals" [456, p. 17]. Personal? Not by today's standards.

Fundamentally, the Star was a networked workstation connected to a server and intended for an office environment. And it was expensive: $16,000 for the workstation alone. That's a distant world from personal computing, as we know it today. It was also a distant world from personal computing, as it existed in the late 1970s and early 1980s. Yes, even then, personal computing was flourishing. The Apple II, introduced in 1977 by Apple Computer, was hugely successful. It was the platform on which VisiCalc, the first spreadsheet application was developed. VisiCalc eventually sold over 700,000 copies and became known as the first *killer app*. Notably, the Star did not have a spreadsheet application, nor could it run any spreadsheet or other application available in the market place. The Star architecture was *closed* – it could only run applications developed by Xerox.

Other popular personal computer systems at the time were the PET, VIC-20, and Commodore 64, all by Commodore Business Machines, and the TRS-80 by Tandy Corp. These systems were truly personal. Most were located in people's homes. But, the user interface was terrible. These systems worked with a traditional command-line interface. The operating system – if you could call it that – usually consisted of a

BASIC-language interpreter and a console prompt. LOAD, SAVE, RUN, EDIT, and a few other commands were about the extent of it. Although these systems were indeed personal, a typical user was a hobbyist, computer enthusiast, or anyone with enough technical skill to connect components together and negotiate the inevitable software and hardware hiccups. But, hobbyists loved them, and they were cheap. However, they were tricky to use. So, while the direct manipulation user interface on the Star may have been intuitive and had the potential to be used by people with no technical skill (or interest!), the system just didn't reach the right audience.

1.6 **Birth of HCI – 1983**

Nineteen eighty-three is a good year to peg as the birth of human-computer interaction. There are at least three key events as markers:

1. The first ACM SIGCHI conference
2. Publication of Card, Moran, and Newell's *The Psychology of Human-Computer Interaction* [64]
3. Announcement of the Apple Macintosh (the Mac)

Although the Mac was launched in January 1984, it was announced with flyers in December 1983. So, we include it here.

1.6.1 **First ACM SIGCHI Conference (1983)**

Human-computer interaction has its roots to at least 1969 with the formation of the ACM's Special Interest Group on Social and Behavioral Computing (SIGSOC) [36]. Initially, SIGSOC focused on computers in the social sciences. However, emphasis soon shifted to the needs and behavioural characteristics of the users, with talk about the user interface or the human factors of computing. Beginning in 1978, SIGSOC lobbied the ACM for a name change. This happened at the 1982 *Conference on Human Factors in Computing Systems* in Gaithersburg, Maryland, where the formation of the ACM Special Interest Group on Computer-Human Interaction (SIGCHI) was first publicly announced. Today, the ACM provides the following statement of SIGCHI and its mission:

> *The ACM Special Interest Group on Computer-Human Interaction (SIGCHI) is the world's largest association of professionals who contribute towards the research and practice of human-computer interaction (HCI). We are an interdisciplinary group of computer scientists, software engineers, psychologists, interaction designers, graphic designers, sociologists, multi-media designers, information scientists, and anthropologists, just to name some of the domains whose special expertise come to bear in this area. What brings us together is a shared un-*

derstanding that designing useful and usable technology is an interdisciplinary process, and when done properly it has the power to transform lives.[9]

In the following year, 1983, the first SIGCHI conference was held in Boston. Fifty-nine technical papers were presented. The conference adopted a slightly modified name to reflect its new stature: *ACM SIGCHI Conference on Human Factors in Computing Systems.* "CHI," as it is known (pronounced with a hard "k"), has been held yearly since and in recent years has attendance around 3000.[10]

The CHI conference brings together both researchers and practitioners. The researchers are there for the technical program (presentation of papers), while the practitioners are there to learn about the latest themes of research in academia and industry. Actually, both groups are also there to network (meet and socialize) with like-minded HCI enthusiasts from around the world. Simply put, CHI is *the* event in HCI, and the yearly pilgrimage to attend is often the most important entry in the calendar for those who consider HCI their field.

The technical program is competitive. Research papers are peer reviewed, and acceptance reveals a high bar for quality. Statistics compiled from 1984 to 2021 indicate a total of 36,042 paper submissions with 8,581 acceptances, for an overall acceptance rate of 23.8%. Fig. 1.9 shows the breakdown by year.[11] The technical program is growing rapidly. For example, the number of accepted contributions in 2021 (747) exceeded the number of submissions in 2010 (714).

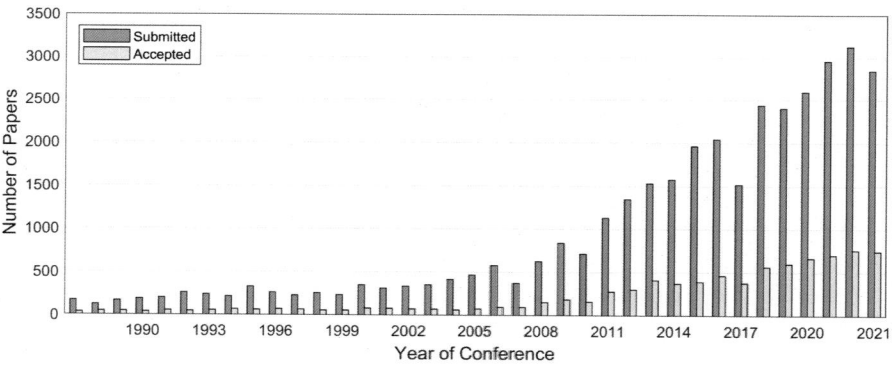

FIGURE 1.9

Number of papers submitted and accepted by year for the ACM SIGCHI Conference on Human Factors in Computing Systems ("CHI").

With acceptance, researchers get to present their work at the conference, usually in a 15-20 minute talk augmented with visual slides and perhaps a video demo of the

---

[9] Retrieved from https://sigchi.org/about/ on March 28, 2023.

[10] Due to the Covid-19 pandemic, CHI in 2020 was fully virtual with about 3200 "attendees." Since 2022, attendance is a mixture of virtual and in-person.

[11] Data retrieved from https://sigchi.org/conferences/conference-history/chi/.

research. Acceptance also means the final submitted paper is published in the conference proceedings and archived in the ACM Digital Library. Some tips on writing and publishing a research paper are presented in Chapter 8.

CHI papers have high visibility, meaning they reach a large community of researchers and practitioners in the field. One indication of the quality of the work is impact, the number of citations to a paper. Since the standards for acceptance are high, one might expect CHI papers to have high impact on the field of HCI. And, indeed, this is the case [299]. We will say more about research impact in Chapter 4.

1.6.2 The Psychology of Human-Computer Interaction (1983)

If two HCI researchers are overheard speaking of "Card, Moran, and Newell," there is a good chance they are talking about *The Psychology of Human-Computer Interaction* – the book published in 1983 and co-authored by Stuart Card, Tom Moran, and Allen Newell. See Fig. 1.10. The book emerged from work at Xerox PARC. Card and Moran arrived at PARC in 1974 and they soon after joined PARC's *Applied Information-Processing Psychology Project* (AIP). Newell, who was the 1975 recipient of the ACM's Turing award, was a professor of computer science and cognitive psychology at Carnegie Mellon University in Pittsburgh, PA. He was a consultant to the project. The AIP mission was "to create an applied psychology of human-computer interaction by conducting requisite basic research within a context of application" [64, p. ix].

FIGURE 1.10

Card, Moran, and Newell's *The Psychology of Human-Computer Interaction*, published by Erlbaum in 1983.

The book contains 13 chapters organized roughly as follows:

- Scientific foundation (100 pages)

- Text editing examples (150 pages)
- Modelling (80 pages)
- Extensions and generalizations (100 pages)

So, what is an "applied psychology of human-computer interaction?" To begin, applied psychology is built upon basic research in psychology. The first 100 or so pages in the book provide a comprehensive overview of core knowledge in basic psychology, as it pertains to the human sensory, cognitive, and motor systems. Many computer science students (and professionals) in the 1980s were challenged with building simple and intuitive interfaces for computer systems, particularly in view of emerging interaction styles based on a graphical user interface. For many, Card, Moran, and Newell's book was their first formalized exposure to human perceptual input (e.g., visually perceiving a stimulus), cognition (e.g., deciding on the appropriate reaction), and motor output (e.g., reacting and moving the hand or cursor to a target). Of course, research in human sensory, cognitive, and motor behaviour was well developed at the time. Card noted that the challenge was in how to apply this knowledge:

> Anyone who has had the task of trying to obtain from the literature psychological guidance for the design of an interactive computer system is aware of the great frustrations engendered by the jumble of empirical results and micro-theories, tightly bound to experimental paradigms.

[59, p. 301]

What Card, Moran, and Newell did was make the connection between low-level human processes and the seemingly innocuous interactions humans have with computers, such as typing or using a mouse. The framework for this was the *model human processor* (MHP). See Fig. 1.11. The MHP had an eye and ear (for sensory input to a perceptual processor), a brain (with a cognitive processor, short-term memory, and long-term memory), and an arm, hand, and finger (for motor responses).

The application selected to frame the analyses in the book was text editing. This might seem odd today, but it is important to remember that 1983 predates the World Wide Web and most of today's computing environments, such as mobile computing, touch-based input, virtual reality, texting, tweeting, and so on. Text editing seemed like the right framework to develop an applied psychology of human-computer interaction.[12] Fortunately, all the issues pertinent to text editing are applicable across a broad spectrum of human-computer interaction.

An interesting synergy between psychology and computer science – and it is well represented in the book – is the notion that human behaviour can be understood, even

---

[12] At a panel session at CHI 2008, Moran noted that the choice was between text editing and programming.

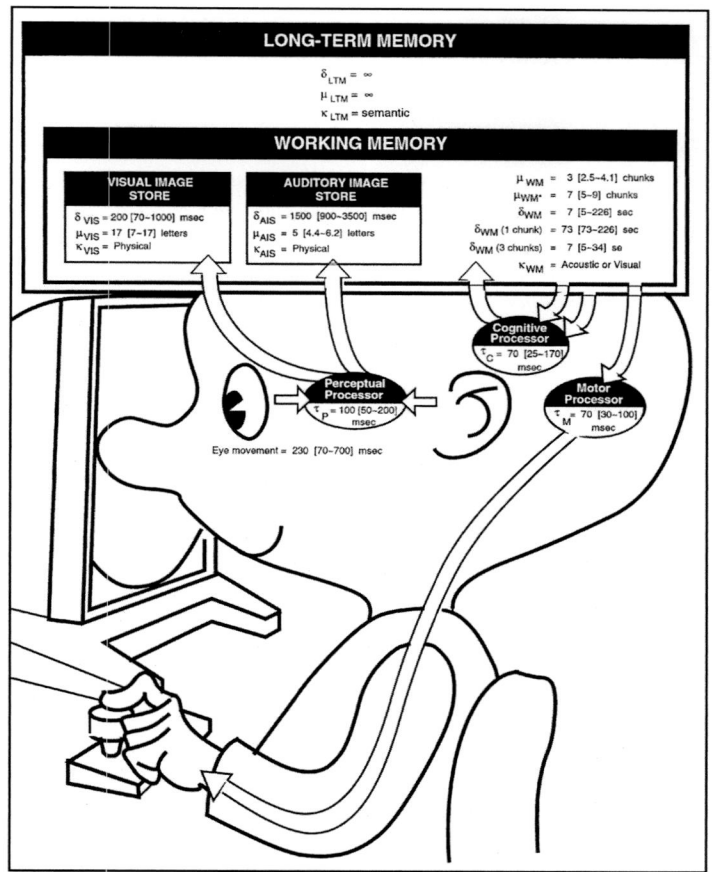

FIGURE 1.11

The model human processor (MHP) [64, p. 26].

modelled, as an information processing activity. The work of Claude Shannon [444], Huffman [203], and others, in the 1940s and 1950s on the transmission of information through electronic channels was quickly picked up by psychologists like Miller [358], Fitts [125], Welford [514], and others, as a way to characterise human perceptual, cognitive, and motor behaviour. Card, Moran, and Newell adapted information processing models of human behaviour to interactive systems. The two most prominent examples in the book are the Hick-Hyman law for choice reaction time [189] and Fitts' law for rapid aimed movement [125]. We will say more about these in Chapter 7, Modelling Interaction.

Newell reflected later on the objectives of *The Psychology of Human-Computer Interaction* and wrote the following:

We had in mind the need for a theory for designers of interfaces. The design of the interface is the leverage point in human-computer interaction. The classical emphasis of human factors and man-machine psychology on experimental analysis requires that the system or a suitable mock-up be available for experimentation, but by the time such a concrete system exists, most of the important degrees of freedom in the interface have been bound. What is needed are tools for thought for the designer – so at design time the properties and constraints of the user can be brought to bear in making the important chooses. . . . Our objective was to develop an engineering-style theory of the user that permitted approximate, back-of-the-envelope calculations of how the user would interact with the computer when operating at a terminal.

[369, pp. 29-30]

Here, Newell astutely identifies a dilemma in the field: Experimentation can't be done until it's too late. As he put it, the system is built and the degrees of freedom are bound. This is an overstatement, perhaps, but it is true that novel interactions in new products always seem to inspire a flurry of research papers identifying weaknesses and suggesting and evaluating improvements. There is more to the story, however. Consider the Apple iPhone's two-finger gestures, the Nintendo Wii's acceleration sensing flicks, the Microsoft IntelliMouse's scrolling wheel, or the Palm Pilot's text-input gestures (aka Graffiti). These innovations were not fresh ideas born out of engineering or design brilliance. The context for these breakthroughs is the milieu of basic research in human-computer interaction and related fields.[13] For the examples just cited, the research preceded commercialization. Research by its very nature requires dissemination through publication. It is not surprising then, that conferences like CHI and books like *The Psychology of Human-Computer Interaction* are fertile ground for discovering and spawning new and exciting interaction techniques.

Newell also notes that the book aimed to generate tools for thought. This is a casual reference to models – models of interaction. The models may be quantitative and predictive or qualitative and descriptive. Either way, they are tools, the carver's knife, the cobbler's needle, call them what you may. Whether generating quantitative predictions across alternative designs or delimiting a problem space to reveal new relationships, a model's purpose is to tease out strengths and weaknesses in a hypothetical or prototype design and to elicit opportunities for improvement. The book includes exemplars, such as the keystroke-level model (KLM) and the goals, operators, methods, and selection rules model (GOMS). Both of these models were presented in earlier work [62,63], but were re-presented in the book, with additional discussion and analysis. The book's main contribution on modelling, however, was

---

[13] Of the four examples cited, research papers anticipating each are found in the HCI literature. On multi-touch finger gestures, there is Rekimoto's pick-and-drop [410], Dietz and Leigh's DiamondTouch [102], or, much earlier, Herot and Weinzapfel's two-finger rotation gesture on a touchscreen [187]. On acceleration sensing, there is Harrison et al.'s *tilt me!* [177]. On the wheel mouse, there is Venolia's Roller Mouse [499]. On single-stroke handwriting, there is Goldberg and Richardson's Unistrokes [148].

to convincingly demonstrate why and how models are important and to teach us how to build them. For this, HCI's debt to Card, Moran, and Newell is considerable. We will discuss descriptive and predictive models further in Chapter 7, Modelling Interaction.

Newell also suggests using approximate "back of the envelope" calculations as a convenient way to describe or predict user interaction. In *The Psychology of Human-Computer Interaction*, these appear, among other ways, through 19 interaction examples in Chapter 2 [64, pp. 23-97]. The examples appear as questions about a user interaction. The solutions use rough calculations but are based on data and concepts gleaned from basic research in experimental psychology. Example 10 [64, p. 66] is typical:

> A user is presented with two symbols, one at a time. If the second symbol is identical to the first, he is to push the key labelled YES. Otherwise he is to push NO. What is the time between signal and response for the YES case?

Before giving the solution, here's a modern context. Suppose a user with a smartphone is texting a friend using the phone's soft keyboard. Interaction with the soft keyboard includes "word completion." After each letter is entered, candidate words appear above the keyboard. If the user looks at the candidates, the interaction involves a choice: If the word appears, select it; if the word does not appear, enter the next letter.[14] An example is shown in Fig. 1.12 for a user entering "computer." After entering "com," "computer" does not appear (left). The user enters the next letter "p" and "computer" appears (right). Tap "computer" and the word is automatically completed. That sort of thing.

As elaborated by Card, Moran, and Newell, the interaction just described is a type of *simple decision* known as *physical matching*. The reader is walked through the solution using the model human processor to illustrate each step, from stimulus, to cognitive processing, to motor response. The solution is approximate. There is a nominal prediction accompanied by a *fastman* prediction and a *slowman* prediction. The user's reaction time (RT) is calculated as follows:

$$\begin{aligned}
RT &= t_P + 2 \times t_C + t_M \\
&= 100[30 \sim 200] + 2 \times (70[25 \sim 170]) + 70[30 \sim 100] \qquad (1.1) \\
&= 310[130 \sim 640] \text{ ms}
\end{aligned}$$

[64, p. 69]. There are four low-level processing cycles: a perceptual processor cycle (t_P), two cognitive processor cycles (t_C), and a motor processor cycle (t_M). For

---

[14] This description is an over-simplification, since there is an additional decision on whether to look at the candidate list in the first place.

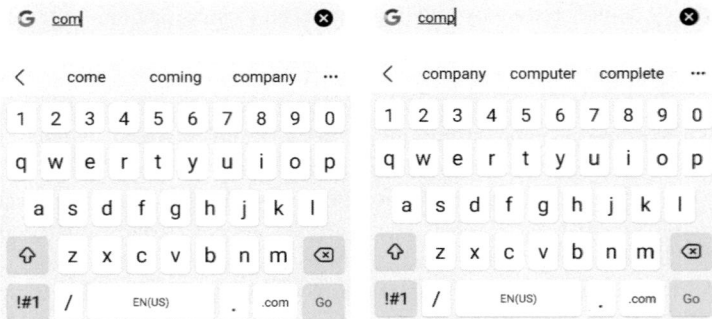

FIGURE 1.12

Entering "computer" on a soft keyboard with word completion. The interaction requires simple decisions. See text for discussion.

each, the nominal value is bracketed by an expected minimum and maximum. The values in Eq. (1.1) are obtained from basic research in experimental psychology, as cited in the book. The fastman-slowman range is large and demonstrates the challenge in accurately predicting human behaviour. The book has other examples like this. And there are modern contexts for the examples, just waiting to be found and applied.

It might not be apparent that predicting the time for a task that takes only one third of a second is relevant to the bigger picture of designing interactive systems. But, don't be fooled. If a complex task can be deconstructed into primitive actions, there is a good chance the time to do the task can be predicted by dividing the task into a series of motor actions interlaced with perceptual and cognitive processing cycles. This idea is presented in Card, Moran, and Newell's book as a keystroke-level model (KLM), which we meet in Chapter 7.

The Psychology of Human-Computer Interaction is still available (e.g., see http://www.amazon.com) and is regularly and highly cited in research papers (9000+ citations according to Google Scholar). At the ACM SIGCHI conference in Florence Italy in 2008, there was a panel session celebrating the book's 25th anniversary. Both Card and Moran spoke on the book's history and on the challenges they faced in bringing a psychological science to the design of interactive computing systems. Others spoke on how the book affected and influenced their own research in human-computer interaction.

1.6.3 Launch of the Apple Macintosh (1984, January)

January 22, 1984 was a big day in sport. It was the day of Super Bowl XVIII, the championship game of the National Football League in the U.S. It was also a big day in advertising. With an audience in the millions, companies were jockeying (and paying!) to deliver brief jolts of hype to viewers who were hungry for entertainment

FIGURE 1.13

The Apple Macintosh.

and primed to purchase the latest must-have products. One ad – played during the 3rd quarter – was a 60-second stint for the Apple Macintosh (the "Mac"). The ad, which is viewable on YouTube,[15] used Orwell's *Nineteen Eighty-Four* as a theme, portraying the Mac as a computer that would shatter the conventional image of the home computer. The ad climaxed with a female athlete running toward and tossing a sledgehammer through the face of Big Brother. The disintegration of Big Brother signalled the triumph of the human spirit over the tyranny and oppression of the corporation. Directed by Ridley Scott,[16] the ad was a hit and was even named the 1980s Commercial of the Decade by *Advertising Age* magazine.[17] It never aired again.

The ad worked. Soon after, computer enthusiasts scooped up the Mac. The Mac was sleek and sported the latest input device, a computer mouse. See Fig. 1.13. The operating system and applications software heralded the new age of the graphical user interface (GUI) with direct manipulation and point-select interaction. The Mac was not only cool, the interface was simple and intuitive. Anyone could use it. Part of the simplicity was the one-button mouse. With one button, there was no confusion on which button to press.

There are plenty of sources chronicling the history of Apple and events leading to the release of the Mac [280,287,359]. Unfortunately, along with the larger-than-life

---

[15] Search using "1984 Apple Macintosh commercial."

[16] Known for a striking visual style, Scott directed many off-beat feature-length films, such as "Alien" (1979), "Blade Runner" (1982), "Thelma and Louise" (1991), "Gladiator" (2000), and "House of Gucci" (2021).

[17] http://en.wikipedia.org/wiki/1984_(advertisement).

Year	Event
1976	April – Apple Computer, Inc. founded in Cupertino, California
1977	Launch of Apple II. Sells for $1300 U.S. with 4KB RAM. Hugely successful "hobby" computer. VisiCalc, the first "killer app," was developed on the Apple II.
1978	Lisa project started. Goal of producing a powerful high-end personal computer.
1979	September – Macintosh project started. Goal of producing a low-cost easy-to-use computer for the average consumer.
	December – Apple and Xerox sign an agreement that allows Xerox to invest in Apple. In return Apple's engineers visit Xerox PARC and see the Xerox Alto. The GUI ideas in the Alto influence Lisa and Macintosh development.
1980	December – Apple goes public through initial public offering (IPO) of its stock.
1981	May – Xerox Star launched at the National Computer Conference (NCC) in Chicago. Members of the Lisa design team are present and see the Star demo. They decide to re-vamp the Lisa interface to be icon-based.
	August – IBM PC announced. Highly successful, but embodies traditional text-based command-line interface.
1982	Lisa and Macintosh development continue. Within Apple, there is an atmosphere of competition between the two projects.
1983	January – Lisa released. Lisa incorporates a GUI and mouse input. Sells for $10,000 U.S. In the end, Lisa is a commercial failure.
	December – brochures appear in magazines (e.g., *Time*) pre-announcing the Macintosh
1984	January 22 – Macintosh ad plays during Super Bowl XVIII.
	January 24 – Macintosh released. Sells for $2500 U.S.

FIGURE 1.14

Timeline of events within Apple leading to the release of the Macintosh.

stature of Apple and its flamboyant leaders comes plenty of folklore to untangle. A few notable events are listed in Fig. 1.14.[18] Names of the key players are deliberately omitted.

1.7 Growth of HCI and graphical user interfaces

With the formation of ACM SIGCHI in 1983 and the release and success of the Apple Macintosh in 1984, human-computer interaction was off and running. GUIs entered the mainstream and, consequently, a much broader community of users and researchers were exposed to this new genre of interaction. Microsoft was a latecomer in graphical user interfaces. Early versions of Microsoft Windows appeared in 1985, but it was not until the release of Windows 3.0 (1990) and, in particular, Windows 3.1 (1992) that Microsoft Windows was considered a serious alternative to the Mac-

---

[18] Sources: http://www.theapplemuseum.com/, http://en.wikipedia.org/wiki/History_of_Apple, and http://www.guidebookgallery.org/articles/lisainterview, with various other sources to confirm dates and events.

intosh operating system. Microsoft increased its market share with improved versions of Windows, most notably Windows 95 (1995), Windows 98 (1998), Windows XP (2001), Windows 7 (2009), Windows 10 (2014), and perhaps Windows 11 (2021). Reports in 2022 on operating systems for desktop computers cite about 76% market share for Windows compared to about 15% for MacOS.[19]

With advancing interest in human-computer interaction, all major universities introduced courses in HCI or user interface design, with graduate students often choosing a topic in HCI for their thesis research. Many such programs of study were in computer science departments; however, HCI also emerged as a legitimate and popular focus in other areas, such as psychology, cognitive science, industrial engineering, information systems, and sociology. And not just universities. Companies soon realized that designing good user interfaces is good business. But, it wasn't easy. Stories of bad UIs are legion in HCI (e.g., [87,229,376]). So, there was work to be done. Practitioners – that is, specialists applying HCI principles in industry – are important members of the HCI community, and they form a significant contingent at many HCI conferences today.

1.8 Empirical research in HCI

Research interest in human-computer interaction, at least initially, was in the quality, effectiveness, and efficiency of the interface. How quickly and accurately can people do common tasks using a GUI versus a text-based command-line interface? Or, given two or more variations in a GUI implementation, which is quicker or more accurate? These or similar questions formed the basis of much empirical research in the early days of HCI. And the same is true today.

A classic example of an early research topic in HCI is the design of menus. With a GUI, commands to the computer are largely a matter or selecting an item in a menu. Menus require *recognition*; typing requires *recall*. It is known that recognition is preferred over recall in user interfaces [17, p. 144] [196,201], at least for novices, but a new problem surfaces. If there are numerous commands in a menu, how should they be organized?

One approach is to organize menu commands in a hierarchy that includes depth and breadth. The question arises: What is the best structure for the hierarchy? Consider the case of 64 commands organized in a menu. The menu could be organized with depth = 8 and breadth = 2, or with depth = 2 and breadth = 6. Both structures provide access to 64 menu items. The breadth-emphasis case gives $8^2 = 64$ choices (Fig. 1.15a). The depth-emphasis case gives $2^6 = 64$ choices (Fig. 1.15b). Which organization is better? Is another organization better still (e.g., $4^3 = 64$)? Given these questions, it is not surprising that menu design was actively researched in the early days of HCI (e.g., [58,245,271,357,459,494]).

---

[19] https://www.statista.com.

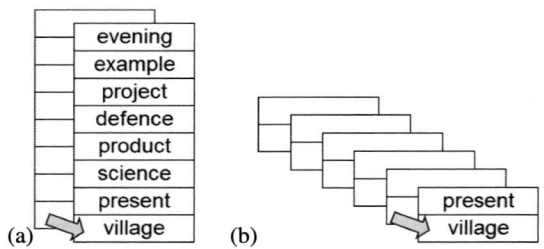

FIGURE 1.15

Breadth vs. depth in menu design. (a) 8 × 8 choices in a broad hierarchy. (b) 2 × 2 × 2 × 2 × 2 × 2 choices in a deep hierarchy.

Depth vs. breadth is not the only research issue in menu design. Research questions involving menu design and access include the following:

- Should items be ordered alphabetically or by function [58,354]?
- Does the presence of a title on a sub-menu improve menu access [154]?
- Is access improved if an icon is added to the label [186]?
- Do people in different age groups respond differently to broad vs. deep menu hierarchies [543]?
- Is there a depth vs. breadth advantage for menus on mobile devices [141]?
- Does auditory feedback improve menu access [553]?
- Can the tilt of a mobile phone be used for menu navigation [411]?
- Can menu lists be pie shaped, rather than linear [55]?
- Can pie menus be used for text entry [501]?

Above, research questions are posed but not answered. The answers are in the papers cited. The goal here is not to review and critique research in menu design. The point is to present research problems of relevance to HCI and to frame the questions as opportunities for empirical research.

1.8.1 Conferences – the backbone of HCI

In celebrating the 40th anniversary of SIGCHI in 2022, the ACM's *interactions* magazine published a chronology of the launch of 24 SIGCHI-sponsored conferences [260]. See Fig. 1.16. Except for CHI itself, each of these is considered a "specialized conference" – focusing on a sub-topic within the broad spectrum of human-computer interaction.

The topics suggested in the names of the conferences in Fig. 1.16 are vast. Whether working with children (IDC), robots (HRI), or cars (AUTOMOTIVE), if the interaction involves computers, there's an HCI conference to explore novel ideas. And attending the conference to present and share one's work with like-minded researchers is what motivates all researchers in human-computer interaction. As Kumar et al. note,

First Year	In Short	Full Name
1983	CHI	Human Factors in Computing Systems
1988	UIST	User Interface Software and Technology
1988	CSCW	Computer-Supported Cooperative Work and Social Computing
1993	IUI	Intelligent User Interfaces
1994	VRST	Virtual Reality Software and Technology
1995	DIS	Designing Interactive Systems
1997	GROUP	Supporting Group Work
1999	C&C	Creativity and Cognition
2000	ETRA	Eye Tracking Research & Applications
2003	ICMI	Multimodal Interaction
2006	HRI	Human-Robot Interaction
2007	RECSYS	Recommender Systems
2009	EICS	Engineering Interactive Computing Systems
2009	ISS	Interactive Surfaces and Spaces
2009	UBICOMP	Pervasive and Ubiquitous Computing
2010	TEI	Tangible and Embedded Interaction
2012	MobileHCI	Human-Computer Interaction with Mobile Devices and Services
2013	SUI	Spatial User Interfaces
2014	IMX	Interactive Media Experiences
2014	CHI PLAY	Computer-Human Interaction in Play
2015	IDC	Interaction Design and Children
2017	AUTOMOTIVE	Automotive User Interfaces and Interactive Vehicular Applications
2018	CI	Collective Intelligence
2022	COMPASS	Computing and Sustainable Societies
2022	CUI	Conversational User Interfaces

FIGURE 1.16

Chronology of SIGCHI-sponsored conferences beginning with CHI in 1983 (from [260]).

Conferences form the backbone of SIGCHI. They are the reason we exist as a collective entity and a special interest group. They connect us and bring us together as a community of human-computer interaction (HCI) researchers, educators, students, and practitioners.

[260, p. 35]

Besides conferences on specialized topics, there are regional conferences such as NordiCHI (the Nordic Conference on Computer-Human Interaction), OzCHI (Australia), IndiaHCI, or AfriCHI. Other conferences of note include ASSETS (sponsored by the ACM's Special Interest Group on Accessible Computing, SIGACCESS), INTERACT (sponsored by IFIP, the International Federation for Information Processing), HCII (Human-Computer Interaction International), and GI (Graphics Interface, the Canadian conference on computer graphics and human-computer interaction).

GI, which was held jointly with CHI in 1987 as CHI+GI, holds the bragging rights as the oldest running conference in human-computer interaction; it was first held in Ottawa in 1969.[20] And there are numerous HCI-related conferences sponsored by other organizations, such as the IEEE[21] and the Human Factors and Ergonomics Society.[22]

1.9 Other readings

The following papers in the literature are notable contributions to the history of HCI.

- "Personal Dynamic Media," 1977, by A. Kay and A. Goldberg [241] – This article describes Dynabook. Although never built, Dynabook provided the conceptual basis for laptop computers, tablet PCs, and E-books.
- "The Computer for the 21st Century," 1991, by M. Weiser [513] – the essay that presaged ubiquitous computing. Weiser begins "The most profound technologies are those that disappear. They weave themselves into the fabric of everyday life until they are indistinguishable from it" [513, p. 94].
- "A Brief History of Human-Computer Interaction Technology," 1998, by B. Myers. [364] – reviews early HCI user interfaces and interaction techniques, including gesture recognition.
- "The Evolution of HCI and Human Factors: Integrating Human and Artificial Intelligence," 2023, by M. Chignell et al. [76] – a historical look at HCI's emergence from and relationship with human factors and psychology, with perspectives on many of the events and people noted in this chapter and book. Anticipates future challenges with the emergence of data science and artificial intelligence (AI).

Other sources taking a historical view of human-computer interaction include publications by Baecker et al. [16], Erickson and McDonald [118], and Grudin [163,164].

1.10 Resources

Below are useful online resources for conducting research in human-computer interaction.

- Google Scholar: http://scholar.google.ca/
- ACM Digital Library: http://portal.acm.org/
- HCI Bibliography: http://hcibib.org/
- Wikipedia: http://en.wikipedia.org/

---

[20] https://graphicsinterface.org/about/.
[21] https://www.ieee.org/conferences/.
[22] https://www.hfes.org/.

A web site is available as a resource accompanying this book's second edition:

• http://www.yorku.ca/mack/HCIbook2e

Many downloads are available to accompany the examples presented herein.

*****

With this historical introduction, we now proceed to specific topics in empirical research in human-computer interaction. Our first stop – the next chapter – is the human factor.

Student exercises

1-1 The characteristics of direct manipulation include visibility of objects, incremental action, rapid feedback, reversibility, exploration, syntactic correctness of all actions, and replacing language with action. For each characteristic consider and discuss an example task performed with modern graphical user interfaces. Contrast the task with the same task, as performed in a command-line environment such as unix, linux, or DOS.

1-2 What is the difference between sequential programming and event-driven programming? Frame your answer in terms of the two types of user interfaces described in this chapter. Elaborate using examples (which are not presented in this chapter).

1-3 There is a time-gap in Fig. 1.1 from 1984, when the Apple Macintosh was launched, to 2022, when SIGCHI celebrated its 40th anniversary. Pick five significant events (e.g., product releases) in this time frame that significantly impacted computing and, in particular, human-computer interaction. Ensure at least one event is in each decade in the 1990s, 2000s, and 2010s. Prepare a brief report or slide show presentation, highlighting the event and its importance to the field. Aim to juxtapose the significance of the event with computing practice around the time of the event. Perhaps include statistics, such as sales or other data, that confirm the significance of the event.

The human factor

2

The deepest challenges in human-computer interaction (HCI) lie in the human factor. Humans are complicated. Computers, by comparison, are simple. Computers are designed and built and they function in rather strict terms according to their programmed capabilities. There is no parallel with humans. Human scientists (including those in HCI) confront something computer scientists rarely think about: variability. Humans differ. We're young, old, female, male, gay, straight, trans, experts, novices, left-handed, right-handed, English-speaking, Spanish-speaking, from the North, from the South, tall, short, strong, weak, fast, slow, able-bodied, challenged, sighted, blind, motivated, lazy, creative, bland, tired, alert, and on and on. The variability humans bring to the table means our work is never precise. It is always approximate. Designing systems that work well – period – is a lofty goal, but, unfortunately, this is not possible in a precise way. A system might work well for a subset of the human condition but venture to the edges along any dimension (see list above), and the system might work poorly, or not at all. It is for this reason, that HCI designers have precepts like "know thy user" [450, p. 66].

Researchers in HCI have questions, lots of them. We are good at the small ones, but the big ones are difficult: Why do humans make mistakes? Why do humans forget how to do things? Why do humans get confused while installing "apps" on their computer? Why do humans have trouble driving while talking on a mobile phone? Why do humans enjoy Facebook or Twitter so much? Obviously, the human part is hugely important and intriguing. The more we understand humans, the better are our chances of designing interactive systems – interactions – that work as intended. So, in this chapter we will examine the human, but the computer and the interaction are never far off.

The questions in the preceding paragraph begin with why. They are big questions. Unfortunately, they do not lend themselves to empirical inquiry – the focus of this book. Take the first question: *Why do humans make mistakes?* From an empirical research perspective, the question is too broad. It cannot be answered with any precision. Our best bet is to narrow in on a defined group of humans (a *population*) and ask them to do a particular task on a particular system in a particular environment. We observe the interaction and measure the behaviour. Along the way, we log the mistakes, classify them, count them, and take note of where and how the mistakes occurred. If our methodology is sound, we might assimilate enough information to put forth an answer the why question – in a narrow sense. If we do enough research

Human-Computer Interaction. https://doi.org/10.1016/B978-0-44-314096-9.00008-7

like this, we might develop an answer in a broad sense. But, a grounded and rigorous approach to empirical research requires small and narrowly focused questions.

Descriptive models, which we discuss in Chapter 7, seek to delineate and categorize a problem space. They are tools for thinking, rather than tools for predicting. A descriptive model for "the human" would be useful indeed. It would help us get started in understanding the human, to delineate and categorize aspects of the human that are relevant to HCI. In fact there are many such models, and we will meet several in this chapter.

2.1 Time scale of human action

Newell's *time scale of human action* is a descriptive model of the human [369, p. 122]. It delineates the problem space by positioning different types of human actions in timeframes within which the actions occur. See Fig. 2.1. The model has four bands, a *biological band*, a *cognitive band*, a *rational band*, and a *social band*. Each band is divided into three levels. Time is ordered by seconds and appears on a log scale with each level a factor of ten longer than the level below. The units are microseconds at the bottom, months at the top. For nine levels, Newell ascribes a label for the human system at work (e.g., *operations* or *task*). Within these labels, we see a connection with HCI. The labels for the bands suggest a worldview or theory of human action.

The most common dependent variable in experimental research in HCI is time – the time for a user to do a task. In this sense, Newell's time-scale model is relevant to HCI. The model is also appropriate because it reflects the multidisciplinary nature of the field. HCI research is both *high level* and *low level*, and we see this in the model. If desired, we could select a paper at random from an HCI conference proceedings or journal, study it, then position the work somewhere in Fig. 2.1. For example, research on selection techniques, menu design, force or auditory feedback, text entry, gestural input, and so on, is within the cognitive band. The tasks for these interactions typically last on the order of a few hundred milliseconds to a few dozen seconds. Newell characterises these as deliberate acts, operations, and unit tasks.

Up in the rational band, users are engaged in tasks that span minutes, tens of minutes, or hours. Research topics here include web navigation, user search strategies, user-centred design, collaborative computing, ubiquitous computing, social navigation, and situated awareness. Tasks related to these research areas occupy users for minutes or hours.

Tasks lasting days, weeks, or months, are in the social band. HCI topics here might include workplace habits, groupware usage patterns, social networking, online dating, privacy, media spaces, user styles and preferences, design theory, and so on.

Another insight in Newell's model pertains to research methodology. Research at the bottom of the scale is highly quantitative in nature. Work in the biological band, for example, is likely experimental and empirical – at the level of neural impulses. At the top of the scale, the reverse is true. In the social band, research methods tend

Scale (seconds)	Time Units	System	World (theory)
10^7	Months	-	SOCIAL BAND
10^6	Weeks	-	
10^5	Days	-	
10^4	Hours	Task	RATIONAL BAND
10^3	10 min	Task	
10^2	Minutes	Task	
10^1	10 s	Unit Task	COGNITIVE BAND
10^0	1 s	Operations	
10^{-1}	100 ms	Deliberate act	
10^{-2}	10 ms	Neural circuit	BIOLOGICAL BAND
10^{-3}	1 ms	Neuron	
10^{-4}	100 μs	Organelle	

FIGURE 2.1

Newell's time scale of human action (from [369, p. 122]).

to be qualitative and non-experimental. Techniques researchers employ here include interviews, observation, case studies, scenarios, and so on. Furthermore, the transition between qualitative and quantitative methods moving from top to bottom in the figure is gradual. As one methodology becomes more prominent, the other becomes less prominent. Researchers in the social band primarily use qualitative methods, but often include some quantitative methods. For example, research on workplace habits, while primarily qualitative, might also quantify the number of personal e-mails sent each day while at work. Thus, qualitative research in the social band may also include quantitative assessments. Conversely, researchers in the cognitive band primarily use quantitative methods, but typically include some qualitative methods. For example, an experiment on human performance with pointing devices, while primarily quantitative, might include an interview at the end to gather comments and suggestions on the interactions. Thus, quantitative, experimental work in the cognitive band includes some qualitative assessment as well.

Newell speculates further on bands above the social band: a *historical band* operating at the level of years to thousands of years, and an *evolutionary band* operating at the level of tens of thousands to millions of years [369, p. 152]. We will forgo interpreting these in terms of human-computer interaction.

2.2 **Human factors**

There are many ways to characterise the human in interactive systems. One is the model human processor of Card et al. [64], which we met in Chapter 1. But, other characterizations exist. Human factors researchers often use a model showing a hu-

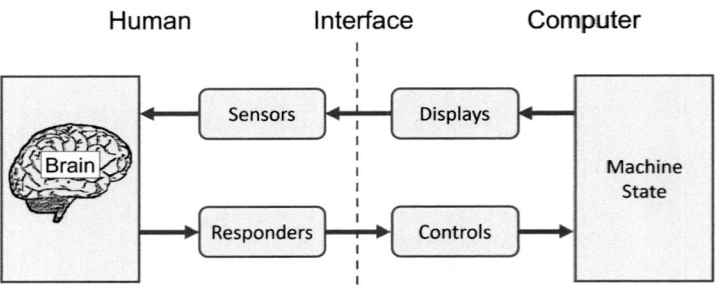

FIGURE 2.2

Human factors view of the human operator in a work environment (after [238, p. 4]).

man operator confronting a machine, like the image in Fig. 2.2. The human monitors the state of the computer through sensors and displays and controls the state of the computer through responders and controls. The dashed vertical line is important since it the interface where interaction takes place. This is the location where researchers observe and measure the behavioural events that form the interaction.

Fig. 2.2 is a convenient way to organize this section, since it simplifies the human to three components: sensors, responders, and a brain.

2.3 Sensors

Rosa: You deny everything except what you want to believe. That's the sort of man you are.

Bjartur: I have my five senses, and don't see what need there is for more.

Halldór Laxness, *Independent People*

The five classical human senses are visual (seeing), auditory (hearing), gustatory (taste), olfactory (smell), and tactile (touch). Each brings distinctly different physical properties of the environment to the human. One feature the senses share is the reception and conversion into electrical nerve signals of physical phenomena such as sound waves, light rays, flavours, odours, or physical contact. The signals are transmitted to the brain for processing. Sensory stimuli and sense organs are physiological. Perception, discussed later, includes both the sensing of stimuli and use of the brain to develop identification, awareness, and understanding of what is being sensed. We begin with the first of the five senses just noted – vision.

2.3.1 Visual (seeing)

Vision, or sight, is the human ability to receive information from the environment in the form of visible light. The visual sensory channel is hugely important, as most

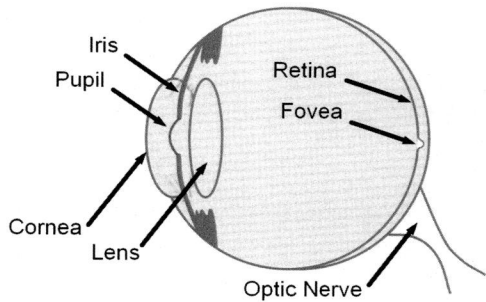

FIGURE 2.3

The eye.

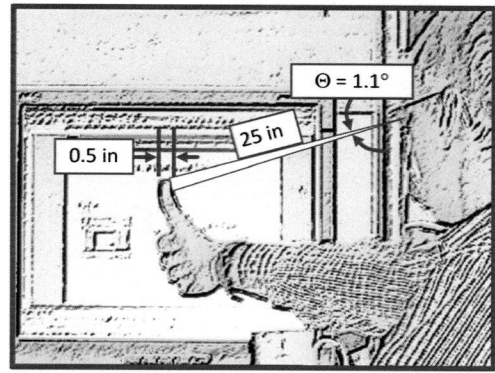

FIGURE 2.4

The fovea image spans a region a little more than 1° of visual angle.

people obtain about 80% of their information though the sense of light [14]. The act of seeing begins with the reception of light through the eye's lens. The lens focuses the light into an image projected on to the retina at the back of the eye. See Fig. 2.3. The retina is a transducer, converting visible light into neurological signals sent to the brain via the optic nerve.

Near the centre of the retina is the fovea, which is responsible for sharp central vision, such as reading or watching television. The fovea image in the environment encompasses a little more than 1° of visual angle, approximately equivalent to the width of one's thumb at arm's length (see Fig. 2.4). Although the fovea is only about 1% of the retina in size, the neural processing associated with the fovea image engages about 50% of the visual cortex in the brain.

As with other sensory stimuli, light has properties such as intensity, frequency, and so on.

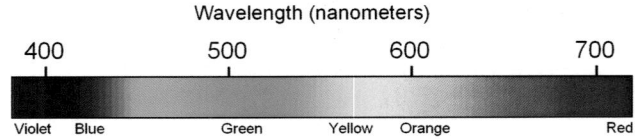

FIGURE 2.5

The visible spectrum of electromagnetic waves.

2.3.1.1 Frequency

Frequency is the property of light leading to the perception of colour. Visible light is a small band in the electromagnetic spectrum, the latter including everything from radio waves to x-rays. Different colours are positioned within the visible spectrum of electromagnetic waves, with violet at one end (390 nanometers) and red at the other (750 nm). See Fig. 2.5.

2.3.1.2 Intensity

Although the frequency of light is a relatively simple concept, the case is different for intensity. Quantifying light intensity, from the human perspective, is complicated because the eye's light sensitivity varies by the wavelength of the light and also by the complexity of the source (e.g., a single frequency vs. a mixture of frequencies). Related to intensity is *luminance*, which refers to the amount of light passing through a given area. With luminance comes *brightness*, a subjective property of the eye that includes perception by the brain. The unit for luminance is candela per square meter (cd/m^2).

2.3.1.3 Fixations and saccades

Vision is more than the human reception of electromagnetic waves having frequency and intensity. Through the eyes, humans look at and perceive the environment. In doing so, the eyes engage in two primitive actions: fixations and saccades. During a fixation, the eyes are stationary, taking-in visual detail from the environment. Fixations can be long or short, but typically last at least 200 ms. Changing the point of fixation to a new location requires a saccade – a rapid repositioning of the eyes to a new position. Saccades are inherently quick, taking only 30-120 ms.

Early and influential research on fixations and saccades was presented in a 1965 publication in Russian by Alfred Yarbus, translated as *Eye Movements and Vision* (reviewed in [482]). Yarbus demonstrated a variety of inspection patterns for people viewing scenes. One example used *The Unexpected Visitor* by painter Ilya Repin (1844-1930). Participants were given instructions and asked to view the scene, shown in Fig. 2.6a. Eye movements (fixations and saccades) were recorded and plotted for a variety of tasks. The results for one participant are shown in Fig. 2.6b for the task "remember the position of people and objects in the room" and in Fig. 2.6c for the task "estimate the ages of the people." Yarbus provided many diagrams like this, with analyses demonstrating differences within and between participants, as well as

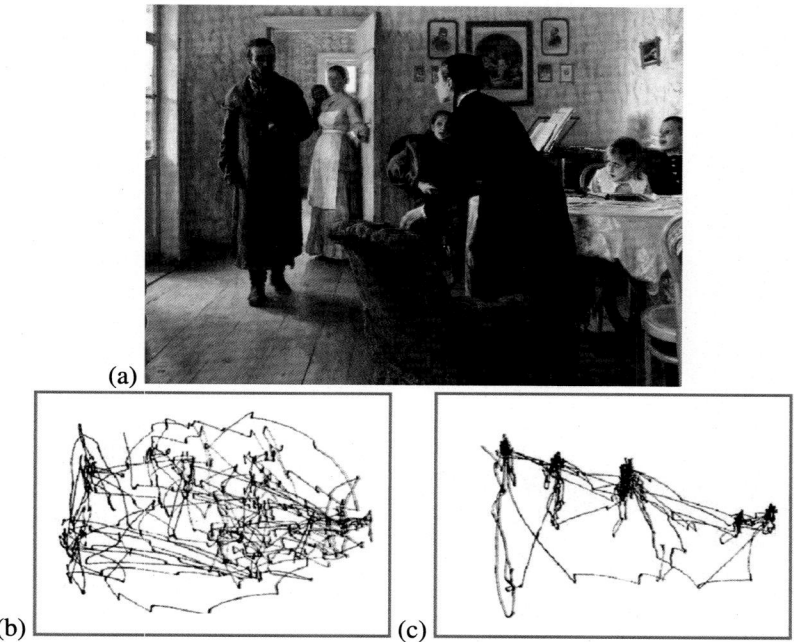

FIGURE 2.6

Yarbus's research on eye movements and vision [482]. (a) Scene: Repin's *The Unexpected Visitor*. (b) Task: Remember the position of the people and objects in the room. (c) Task: Estimate the ages of the people.

changes in viewing patterns over time and for subsequent viewings. He noted, for example, that the similarity of inspection patterns for a single viewer was greater than the patterns between viewers.

HCI research in eye movements has several themes. One is analysing how people read and view content on web pages. Fig. 2.7 shows an example of a scanpath (a sequence of fixations and saccades) for a user viewing content at different places on a page. (See also [149, Figure 2].) There are implications for design. For example, advertisers and product designers are interested in viewing patterns [382] and, for example, how males and females differ in viewing content. There are gender differences in eye movements [385], but it remains to be demonstrated how low-level experimental results can inform and guide design.

2.3.2 Auditory (hearing)

Hearing, or audition, is the detection of sound by humans. Sound is transmitted in the environment as sound waves – cyclic fluctuations of pressure in a medium, such as air. Sound waves are created when physical objects are moved or vibrated, thus

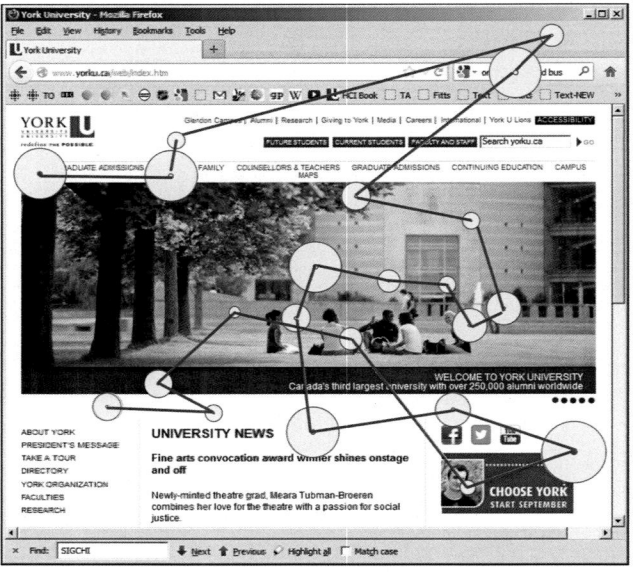

FIGURE 2.7

Scanpath for a user locating content on a web page.

Attribute	Extremes
Intensity	Soft – Loud
Frequency	Low – High
Timbre	Plain – Rich
Shape	Impulsive – Reverberant
Rhythm	Rhythmic – Irregular
Speed	Slow – Fast
Organization	Ordered – Chaotic

FIGURE 2.8

Attributes of sound and qualities at the extremes.

creating fluctuations in air pressure. Examples include plucking a string on a guitar, slamming a door, shuffling cards, or a human speaking. In the latter case, the physical object creating the sound is the larynx, or vocal cords, in the throat.

Hearing occurs when sound waves reach a human's ear and stimulate the ear drum to create nerve impulses that are sent to the brain. Sounds bring forth many qualities that can be categorized [463, p. 65]. Seven attributes of sound and their subjective qualities are listed in Fig. 2.8.

A single sound from a single source has at least four physical properties: intensity (loudness), frequency (pitch), timbre (richness), and envelope (shape). As a simple example, consider a musical note played from an instrument, such as a trumpet. The note may be loud or soft (intensity), high or low in pitch (frequency). We hear and recognize the note as from a trumpet, as opposed to a flute, because of the note's timbre (richness) and envelope (shape). Let's examine each of these properties.

2.3.2.1 Loudness (intensity)

Loudness is the subjective analog to the physical property of intensity or volume. It is quantified by *sound pressure level*, which expresses the pressure in a sound wave relative to the average pressure in the medium. The unit of sound pressure level is the decibel (dB). Human hearing begins with sounds of 0-10 dB. Conversational speech is about 50-70 dB in loudness. Pain sets in when humans are exposed to sounds of approximately 120-140 dB.

Hearing loss can occur when humans are exposed to sound that is too loud for too long, for example, music that exceeds 80 dB for 40 hours over a 7-day period. Devices with headphones, such as the Apple iPhone, offer notifications of such with loudness reduced accordingly.

2.3.2.2 Pitch (frequency)

Pitch is the subjective analog of frequency, which is the reciprocal of the time between peaks in a sound wave's pressure pattern. The unit of pitch is cycles per second, or Hertz (Hz). Humans can perceive sounds in the frequency range of about 20 Hz to 20,000 Hz (20 kHz), although the upper limit tends to decrease with age.

Notes on a standard 88-key piano keyboard range in pitch from 27.5 Hz for low-A (A_0) up to 4186 Hz for high-C (C_8). Middle-C (C_4) is 261.1 Hz. The tuning standard for musical instruments is "A440" corresponding to 440 Hz, or A above middle C.

The speech of typical adults has frequency range from about 85 to 155 Hz for males and 165 to 255 Hz for females. However, due to the presence of harmonics (see below) and to achieve reasonable fidelity, systems generating speech output typically include frequencies up to about 3000 Hz.

2.3.2.3 Timber (richness)

Timber (aka richness or brightness) results from the harmonic structure of sounds. Returning to the example of a musical note, harmonics are integer multiples of a note's base or fundamental frequency. For example, a musical note with a fundamental frequency of 200 Hz includes harmonics at 400 Hz, 600 Hz, 800 Hz, and so on. The relative amplitudes of the harmonics create the subjective sense of timbre, or richness. While the human hears the note as 200 Hz, it is the timbre that distinguishes the tone as being from a particular musical instrument. For example, if notes of the same frequency and loudness are played from a trumpet and an oboe, the two notes sound different, in part, because of the unique pattern of harmonics created by each instrument. The purest form of a note is a sine wave, which includes the fundamental frequency, but no harmonics above the fundamental frequency. The musical notes created by a flute are close to sine waves.

Quality/Ability	Eyes	Ears
Frequency sensitivity	$(4 \text{ to } 7.2) \times 10^{14}$ Hz	20 to 20,000 Hz
Wavelength sensitivity	$(4 \text{ to } 7.6) \times 10^{-7}$ meters	16.5 mm to 16.5 meters
Speed of light/sound	300,000,000 m/s	343 m/s
Can distinguish ratios	No	Yes
Primary brain processing	Intellectual, reason	Emotional, intuition
Focus	Narrow, pointed	Broad, omnidirectional
Open or closed	Either	Only open
Habitat	Space	Time
Transmission	Time	Space

FIGURE 2.9

Comparison of the eyes (seeing) and ears (hearing) along common dimensions for quality and ability [463, p. 151].

2.3.2.4 Envelope (shape)

Envelope or shape is the way a sound and its harmonics build up and transition in time – from silent to audible to silent. There is considerable information in the on-set envelope, or attack, of musical notes. In the example above of the trumpet and oboe playing notes of the same frequency and same loudness, the attack also assists in distinguishing the source. If the trumpet note and oboe note were recorded and played back with the attack removed, it is surprisingly difficult to distinguish the instruments. The attack results partly from inherent properties of instruments (e.g., brass vs. woodwind), but also from the way notes are articulated (e.g., staccato vs. legato).

Besides physical properties, sound has other properties. These have to do with human hearing and perception. Sounds, complex sounds, can be harmonious (pleasant) or discordant (unpleasant). This property has to do with how different frequencies mix together in a complex sound, such as a musical chord. Sounds may also convey a sense of urgency or speed.

Humans have two ears, but each sound has a single source. The slight difference in the physical properties of the sound as it arrives at each ear helps humans in identifying a sound's location (direction and distance). When multiple sounds from multiple sources are heard through two ears, perceptual effects such as stereo emerge.

Sounds provide a surprisingly rich array of cues to humans, whether walking about while shopping or sitting by a computer typing an e-mail message. Not surprisingly, sound is crucial for blind users, for example, in conveying information about the location and distance of environmental phenomena [481].

Before moving on, it is instructive to compare the two primary human senses of seeing and hearing. Fig. 2.9 positions the eyes and ears along several common dimensions, including conditions in the environment and perceptual and cognitive processing in the brain [463].

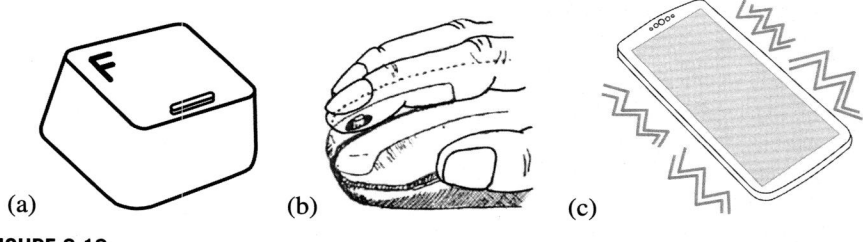

FIGURE 2.10

Tactile feedback. (a) Identifier on key top. (b) Solenoid-driven pin under the index finger (adapted from [5]). (c) Vibration signalling an in-coming call.

2.3.3 **Tactile (touch)**

Touch, or tactition, is one of the five traditional human senses.[1] The sense of touch occurs through cutaneous sensors in the skin. But touch is just one component of the somatosensory system, which also includes proprioception (the ability to sense the *position* of the body and limbs) and kinesthesis (the ability to sense the *movement* of the body and limbs) [150]. The somatosensory system works through the skin, muscles, bones, joints, and organs that provide information on physical or environmental phenomena, including touch, temperature, pain, and body and limb position.

Tactile feedback, in HCI, refers to information provided through the somatosensory system from a body part, such as a finger, when it is in contact with (touching) a physical object. Additional information, such as temperature, shape, texture, or position of the object or the amount of resistance, is also conveyed.

All user interfaces that involve physical contact with the user's hands (or other body parts) include tactile feedback. Simply grasping a mouse and moving it brings considerable information to the human operator – the smooth or rubbery feel of the mouse chassis, slippery or sticky movement on the desktop. Interaction with a desktop keyboard is also guided by tactile feedback. The user senses the edges and shapes of keys and experiences resistance as a key is pressed. Tactile identifiers on key tops facilitate eyes-free touch-typing. Identifiers are found on the 5-key for numeric keypads and on the F and J keys for alphanumeric keyboards. Sensing the identifier informs the user that the home position is acquired. See Fig. 2.10a.

Augmenting the user experience through active tactile feedback is a common research topic. Fig. 2.10b shows a mouse instrumented with a solenoid-driven pin below the index finger [5]. The pin is actuated (pulsed) when the mouse cursor crosses a boundary, such as the edge of a soft button or window. The added tactile feedback helps inform and guide the interaction and potentially reduces the demand on the visual channel. A common use of tactile feedback in mobile phones is vibration, signalling an incoming call or message. See Fig. 2.10c.

---

[1] The term "haptic," meaning "relating to or based on the sense of touch," is used interchangeably with "touch."

2.3.4 **Olfactory (smell) and gustatory (taste)**

Smell, or olfaction, is the ability to perceive odours. For humans, this occurs through sensory cells in the nasal cavity. Taste, or gustation, is a direct chemical reception of sweet, salty, bitter, and sour sensations through taste buds in the tongue and oral cavity. Flavour is a perceptual process in the brain that occurs through a partnering of the smell and taste senses. Although smell and taste are known intuitively by virtually all humans – and with expert-like finesse – they are less understood than the visual and auditory senses.

Smells are commonly associated with memory. In fact, the associations are often emotionally loaded and vivid, with power autobiographical connections to past events and experiences [380]. Furthermore, humans can discriminate thousands of smells. But, among the thousands, there are as few as ten categories: fragrant, body/resinous, fruity (non-citrus), chemical, minty/peppermint, sweet, popcorn, lemon, pungent, decayed [416].

Complex smells and tastes can be built up from simpler elements, but the perceptual processes for this remain a topic of research. For example, classifications schemes have been developed for specific industries (e.g., perfume, wine) but these do not generalize to human experiences with other smells and tastes.

While humans use smell and taste without effort all the time, these senses are not generally "designed in" to systems. There are a few examples in HCI. Brewster et al. [40] studied smell as an aid in searching digital photo albums. Users employed two tagging methods, text and smell, and then used the tags later to answer questions about the photos. Since smell has links to memory, it was conjectured that smell cues might aid in recall. In the end, recall with smell tags was poorer than with word tags. Related work is reported by Bodnar et al. [34] who compared smell, auditory, and visual modalities for notifying users of an interruption by an incoming message. They also found poorer performance with smell. Notable in both examples, though, is the use of an empirical research methodology to explore the potential of smell in a user interface. Both studies included all the hallmarks of experimental research, including independent variables, dependent variables, statistical significance testing, and counterbalancing for a within-subjects independent variable.

Smell and taste, along with the other senses and the mind, are the formative pillars in Ericsson's Internet of Senses, a futuristic look at computing [119]. The 2019 report was based on an online poll of users from 15 cities worldwide, with at least 500 respondents from each city. Users were asked about their hopes and dreams for computing, looking forward, with scenarios presented. As an example, 59% of respondents believed it will be possible in the future to see map routes on VR glasses by simply thinking of a destination. Many scenarios assume that smell and taste will be realized through digital means for future interactions. For smell, 60% of respondents predict it will be possible to digitally visit forests or the countryside and experience the natural smells of those places. For taste, 40% anticipate a revolution in online shopping, with the ability to digitally taste samples from the comfort of their devices. Not surprisingly, the report is long on ideas, but short on details.

2.3.5 **Other senses**

The word "sense" appears in many contexts apart from the five senses discussed above. We often hear of a sense of urgency, a sense of direction, musical sense, intuitive sense, moral sense, or even common sense. The value of these and related senses to HCI cannot be overstated. Although operating at a higher level than the five primary senses, these additional senses encapsulate how humans feel about and experience their interactions with computers. Are there receptors that pick up these senses, like cells in the naval cavity? Perhaps. It has been argued and supported with experimental evidence that humans may have a moral sense that is like our sense of taste [157]. We have natural receptors that pick up sweetness and saltiness. In the same way, we may have natural receptors that help us recognize fairness or cruelty. Just as a few universal tastes can grow into many different cuisines, a few moral senses can grow into different moral cultures.

2.4 **The brain**

The brain is the most complex biological structure known. With billions of neurons, the brain provides humans with a multitude of capacities and resources, including pondering, remembering, recalling, reasoning, deciding, and communicating. While sensors (human inputs) and responders (human outputs) are nicely mirrored, it is the brain that connects them. Without sensing or experiencing the environment, the brain would have little to do. However, upon experiencing the environment through sensors, the brain's task begins.

2.4.1 **Perception**

Perception is the first-stage of processing in the brain. Perception occurs when sensory signals are input from the environment. It is at the perceptual stage that associations and meanings take shape. An auditory stimulus is perceived as harmonious or discordant. A smell is pleasurable or abhorrent. A visual scene is familiar or strange. Touch something and the surface is smooth or rough, hot or cold. With associations and meaning attached to sensory input, humans are vastly superior to the machines they interact with. Norman explains:

> *People excel at perception, at creativity, at the ability to go beyond the information given, making sense of otherwise chaotic events. We often have to interpret events far beyond the information available, and our ability to do this efficiently and effortlessly, usually without even being aware that we are doing so, greatly adds to our ability to function.*

[376, p. 136]

Since the late 19th century, perception has been studied in a specialized area of experimental psychology known as psychophysics. Psychophysics examines the relationship between human perception and physical phenomena. In a psychophysics

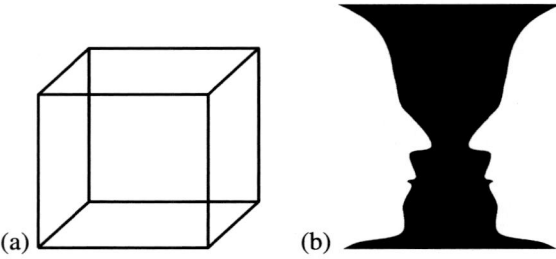

(a)　　　　　　　　　　　(b)

FIGURE 2.11

Ambiguous images. (a) Necker cube. (b) Rubin vase.

experiment, a human is presented with a physical stimulus and then is asked about the sensation felt or perceived. The link is between a measurable property of a real-world phenomenon that stimulates a human sense and the human's subjective interpretation of the phenomenon.

A common experimental goal is to measure the *just noticeable difference* (JND) in a stimulus. A human subject is presented with two stimuli, one after the other. The stimuli differ in a physical property, such as frequency or intensity, and the subject is asked if the stimuli are the same or different. The task is repeated over a series of trials with random variations in the magnitude of the difference in the physical property manipulated. Below a certain threshold, the difference between the two stimuli is so small it is not perceived by the subject. This threshold is the JND. JND has been highly researched for all the human senses and in a variety of contexts. Does the JND depend on the absolute magnitude of the stimuli (e.g., high intensity stimuli vs. low intensity stimuli)? Does the JND on one property (e.g., intensity) depend on the absolute value of a second property (e.g., frequency)? Does the JND depend on age, gender, or another property of the human? These are basic research questions that, on the surface, seem far afield from research relevant to human-computer interfaces. But, over time and with new research extending results from previous research, there is indeed an application. For example, basic research in psychophysics is used in algorithms for audio compression in MP3 audio encoding.

Another property of perception is ambiguity – the human ability to develop multiple interpretations of a sensory input. Ambiguous images provide a demonstration of this for the visual sense. Fig. 2.11a shows the Necker wire-frame cube. Is the top-right corner on the front surface, or the back surface? Fig. 2.11b shows the Rubin vase. Is the image a vase, or two faces? The very fact that we sense ambiguity in these images reveals our perceptual ability "to go beyond the information given."

Related to ambiguity is illusion, the deception of common sense. Fig. 2.12a shows the Ponzo lines. The two black lines are the same length; however, the black line near the bottom appears shorter, because of the 3D perspective. The Müller-Lyer arrows are shown in Fig. 2.12b. In comparing the straight-line segments in the two arrows, the one in the top arrow appears longer when in fact both are the same length. Our intuition has betrayed us.

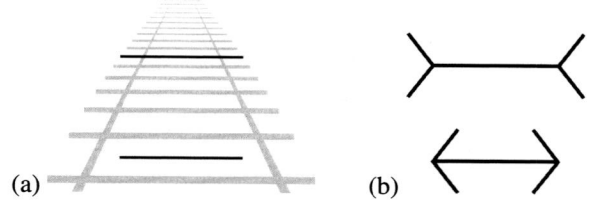

FIGURE 2.12

Visual illusion. (a) Ponzo lines. (b) Müller-Lyer arrows.

FIGURE 2.13

Munker illusion of colour. The two circles are the same colour. See text for discussion.

Besides length or size, visual illusions of colour are possible. These serve as a reminder that the subjective interpretation of a stimulus is separate from its physical structure. Fig. 2.13 shows a Munker illusion (from [248]). There are two filled circles, each with a foreground grating and a background grating. Both circles are the same colour. The effect of the grating is to shift the apparent tinting of the circle in the same direction as the foreground grating and in a direction opposite the background grating. Since the foreground and background gratings are reversed in the two images, the shift has the opposite effect for the left and right circles.

The visual illusion in Fig. 2.13 demonstrates a common cause of frustration for users of standard, ubiquitous colour picker interfaces. Users pick a colour that they perceive as appropriate, but find it looks incorrect when viewed in context [219]. For this reason, tools are needed to manipulate colours directly via a hardware interface to allow colour adjustments within context [56].

If illusions are possible in visual stimuli, it is reasonable to expect illusion in the other senses. An example of an auditory illusion is the Shepard musical scale. It is perceived by humans to rise or fall continuously, yet somehow stay the same. A variation is a continuous musical tone known as the Shepard-Risset glissando – a tone that continually rises in pitch while continuing also to stay at the same pitch. Fig. 2.14 illustrates. Each vertical line represents a sine wave. The height of each line

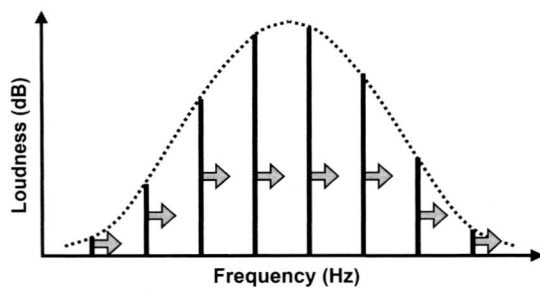

FIGURE 2.14

Auditory illusion. A collection of equally spaced sine waves rise in frequency within a loudness profile. The human hears a tone that apparently rises in frequency, but at the same time stays the same.

is the perceived loudness of the sine wave. Each wave is displaced from its neighbour by the same frequency; thus, the waves are harmonics of a musical note with a base frequency equal to the displacement. This is the frequency of the single tone that a human perceives. If the sine waves collectively rise in frequency (block arrows in figure), there is a sense that the tone rises. Yet, because the sine waves are equally spaced, there is a competing sense that the tone remains the same (because the frequency perceived is the distance between harmonics). Sine waves at the high end of the frequency distribution fade out, while new sine waves enter at the low end. Examples of the Shepard scale and the Shepard-Risset glissando can be heard on YouTube.

Tactile or haptic illusions also exist. A well-documented example is the "phantom limb." Humans who have lost a limb through amputation often continue to sense that the limb is present and that it moves along with other body parts as it did before amputation [172].

Beyond perception, sensory stimuli are integrated into a myriad of other experiences to yield ideas, decisions, strategies, actions, and so on. The ability to excel at these higher-levels capabilities is what powers humans to the top tier in classification schemes for living organisms. By and large it is the human ability to think and reason that affords this special position.

2.4.2 **Cognition**

Among the brain's vital faculties is cognition – the human process of conscious intellectual activity, such as thinking, reasoning, or deciding. Cognition spans many fields – from neurology to linguistics to anthropology – and, not surprisingly, there are competing views on the scope of cognition. Does cognition include social processes, or is it more narrowly concerned with deliberate goal-driven acts such as problem solving? It is beyond the reach of this book to unravel the many views of cognition.

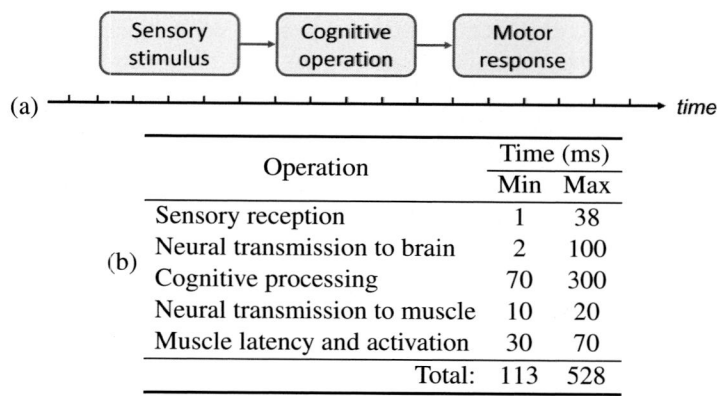

(a)

Operation	Time (ms)	
	Min	Max
Sensory reception	1	38
Neural transmission to brain	2	100
Cognitive processing	70	300
Neural transmission to muscle	10	20
Muscle latency and activation	30	70
Total:	113	528

(b)

FIGURE 2.15

Cognitive operations in a reaction time task. (a) Problem schematic. (b) Sequence of operations [17, p. 41].

The task is altogether too great and in any case is aptly done in other references, many in human factors (e.g., [238,431,515]).

Sensory phenomena, such as sound or light, are easy to study because they exist in the physical world. Instruments abound for recording and measuring the presence and magnitude of sensory signals. Cognition occurs within the human brain; so studying cognition presents special challenges. For example, is not possible to directly measure the time for a human to "make a decision." When does the measurement begin and end? Where is it measured? On what input is the human deciding? Through what output is the decision conveyed? The latter two questions speak to a sensory stimulus and a motor response that bracket the cognitive operation. Fig. 2.15a illustrates. Since sensory stimuli and motor responses are observable and measurable, the figure conveys, in a rough sense, how to measure a cognitive operation.

Still, there are challenges. If the sensory stimulus is visual, the retina converts the light to neural impulses that are transmitted to the brain for perceptual processing. This takes time. So, the beginning of the cognitive operation is not precisely known. Similarly, if the motor response involves a finger pressing a button, neural associations for the response are developed in the brain with nerve signals transmitted to the hand – before movement begins. So, the precise ending of the cognitive operation is also unknown. The sequence of events is shown in Fig. 2.15b, noting the operations and the time range for each. The most remarkable observation here is the wide range of values – an indication of the difficulty in pinpointing where and how the measurements are made. Despite these challenges, techniques exist for measuring the duration of cognitive operations. These are discussed shortly.

The range of cognitive operations applicable to Fig. 2.15 is substantial. While driving a car, the decision to brake in response to a changing signal light is simple enough. Similar scenarios abound in HCI. While using a mobile phone, one might decide to press the REJECT-CALL key in response to an incoming call. While reading the morning news online, one might decide to click the CLOSE button on a popup ad. While editing a document, one might switch to e-mail in response to an audio alert of a new message. These examples all involve, in sequence, a sensory stimulus, a cognitive operation, and a motor response.

Other decisions are more complicated. While playing the card game 21 (aka Blackjack), perhaps online,[2] if a card is drawn and the hand is then 16, the decision to draw another card is likely to produce a cognitive pause. What is the chance the next card will bring the hand above 21? Which cards 6 to KING are already dealt? The decision in this scenario goes beyond the information in the sensory stimulus. There are strategies to consider, as well as the human ability to remember and recall past events – cards previously dealt. This ability leads us to another major function of the brain – memory.

2.4.3 Memory

Memory is the human ability to store, retain, and recall information. The capacity of our memory is remarkable. Experiences, whether from a few days ago or from decades past, are collected together in the brain's vast repository known as *long-term memory*. Interestingly enough, there are similarities between memory in the brain and memory in a computer. Computer memory often includes separate areas for data and code. In the brain, memory is similarly organized. A declarative/explicit area stores information about events in time and objects in the external world. That's similar to a data space. An implicit/procedural area in the brain's memory stores information about how to use objects or how to do things. That's similar to a code space.[3]

Within long-term memory is an active area for *short-term memory* or working memory. The contents of working memory are active and readily available for access. The amount of such memory is small, about seven units, depending on the task and the methodology for measurement. A study of short-term memory was published in 1956 in a classic essay by Miller, aptly titled "The magic number seven plus or minus two" [358].[4] Miller reviewed a large number of studies on the absolute judgement of stimuli, such as pitch in an auditory stimulus or salt concentration in water in a

---

[2] "perhaps online" is a reminder that many activities humans do in the physical world have a counterpart in computing, often on the Internet.

[3] The reader is asked to take a cautious and loose view of the analogy between human memory and computer memory. Attempts to formulate analogies from computers to humans are fraught with problems. Cognitive scientists, for example, frequently speak of human cognition in terms of operators, operands, cycles, registers, and the like, and build and test models that fit their analogies. Such reverse anthropomorphism, while tempting and convenient, is unlikely to reflect the true inner workings of human biology.

[4] Miller's classic work is referred to as an *essay* rather than a *research paper*. The essay is casual in style and, consequently, written in the first person, for example, "I am simply pointing to the obvious fact that …" [358, p. 93]. Research papers, on the other hand, are generally plain in style and avoid first-person narratives (cf. "This points to the fact that …").

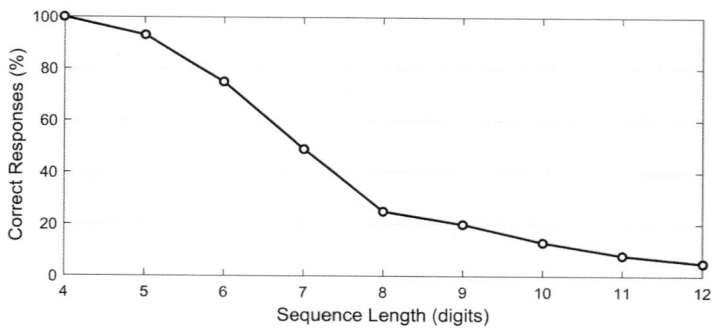

FIGURE 2.16

Results of a short-term memory test. See text for discussion.

taste stimulus. Humans are typically able to distinguish about seven levels of a uni-dimensional stimulus.[5]

Miller extended this work to human memory, describing an experiment where participants viewed a sequence of items and were asked to recall the items. He found that the human ability with such tasks is, similarly, about seven items (±2). A simple demonstration of Miller's thesis is shown in Fig. 2.16. For this "mini experiment," log sheets were distributed to students in a class on human-computer interaction ($n \approx$ 60). The instructor dictated sequences of random digits, with sequences varying in length from 4 digits to 13 digits. After each dictation, students copied the sequence from short-term memory onto the log sheet. The percentage of correct responses by sequence length is shown in the figure. At length 7, the number of correct responses was about 50%. At lengths 5 and 9 the values were about 90% and 20%, respectively.[6]

Miller extended his work by revealing and analysing a simple but powerful process within the brain: our ability to associate multiple items as one. So-called chunking is a process whereby humans group a series of low-level items into a single high-level item. He described an example using binary digits. For example, a series of 16 bits, such as

1000110001110010

is difficult to commit to memory. However, if collected into groups of four

1000 1100 0111 0010

---

[5] The human ability to distinguish levels is greater if the stimulus is multidimensional; that is, the stimulus contains two or more independent attributes, such as a sound that varies in pitch and intensity.

[6] A response was deemed correct only if all the items were correctly recalled. For the longer sequences, many responses were "mostly correct." For example, at sequence length = 7, many of the responses had 5 or 6 items correct.

and chunked into decimal numbers or hexadecimal digits, the pattern is smaller and easier to remember:

```
8 12 7 2
8  C 7 2
```

Card et al. [64, p. 36] give the example of BSCBMICRA. At 9 units, the letter sequence is beyond the ability of most people to repeat back. But, the sequence is similar to the following three 3-letter sequences CBS IBM RCA. Shown like this, the sequence contains three chunks, and is relatively easy to remember provided the person can perform the recoding rapidly enough. The process of chunking is mostly informal and unstructured. Humans intuitively build up chunked structures recursively and hierarchically, leading to complex organizations of memory in the brain.

2.5 Responders

Through movement, or motor control, humans are empowered to affect the environment around them. Control occurs through *responders*. Whether using a finger to text[7] or point, the feet to walk or run, an eyebrow to frown, vocal chords to speak, or the torso to lean, movement provides humans with the power to engage and affect the world around them. Penfield's *motor homunculus* is a classic illustration of human responders [392]. See Fig. 2.17. The illustration maps areas in the cerebral motor cortex to human responders. The lengths of the underlying solid bars show the relative amount of cortical area devoted to each muscle group. As the bars reveal, the muscles controlling the hand and fingers are highly represented compared to the muscles responsible for the wrist, elbow, and shoulders. Based partially on this information, Card et al. hypothesized that "those groups of muscles having a large area devoted to them are heuristically promising places to connect with input device transducers if we desire high performance," although they rightly caution that "the determinants of muscle performance are more complex than just simple cortical area" [61, p. 111]. (See also [19]).

See also student exercise 2-1.

2.5.1 Limbs

Human control over machines is usually associated with the limbs, particularly the upper-body limbs. The same is true in HCI. With fingers, hands, and arms we type on keyboards, manoeuvre mice and press buttons, hold mobile phones and press keys, touch and swipe the surface of touchscreen phones, and wave game controllers in

---

[7] "Text" is now an accepted verb in English. "I'll text you after work," although strange in the 1980s, is understood today as sending a text message on a mobile phone.

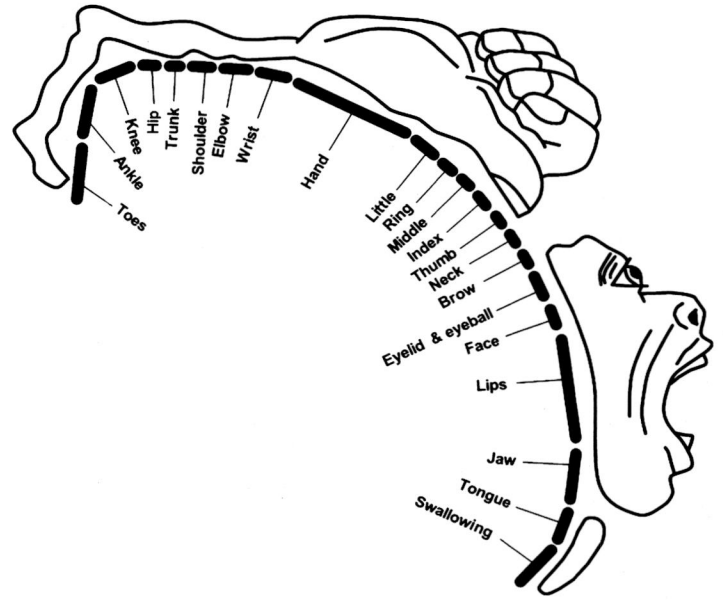

FIGURE 2.17

Motor homunculus showing human responders and the corresponding cortical area (adapted from [392]).

front of displays. Of course, legs and feet can also act as responders and provide input to a computer. For users with limited use or no use of their arms, movement of the head can control an on-screen cursor. Some example scenarios are seen in Fig. 2.18.

Movement of the limbs is tightly coupled to the somatosensory system, particularly proprioception, to achieve accuracy and finesse as body parts move relative to the body as a whole. Grasping a mouse without looking at it and typing without looking at the keyboard are examples.

In Fig. 2.18a, the user's left hand grips the mouse. Presumably this user is left-handed. In Fig. 2.18b, the user's right index finger engages the surface of the touch-pad. Presumably, this user is right-handed. Interestingly enough, handedness, or hand preference, is not an either-or condition. Although 8-15% of people are deemed left-handed, hand preference exists along a continuum, with people considered, by degree, left-handed or right-handed. Ambidextrous people are substantially indifferent in hand preference.

A widely used tool to assess hand preference is the Edinburgh Handedness Inventory, dating to 1971 [381]. The inventory is a series of self-assessments of the degree of preference one feels toward the left or right hand in doing common tasks, such as throwing a ball. The inventory is shown in Fig. 2.19 along with the instructions,

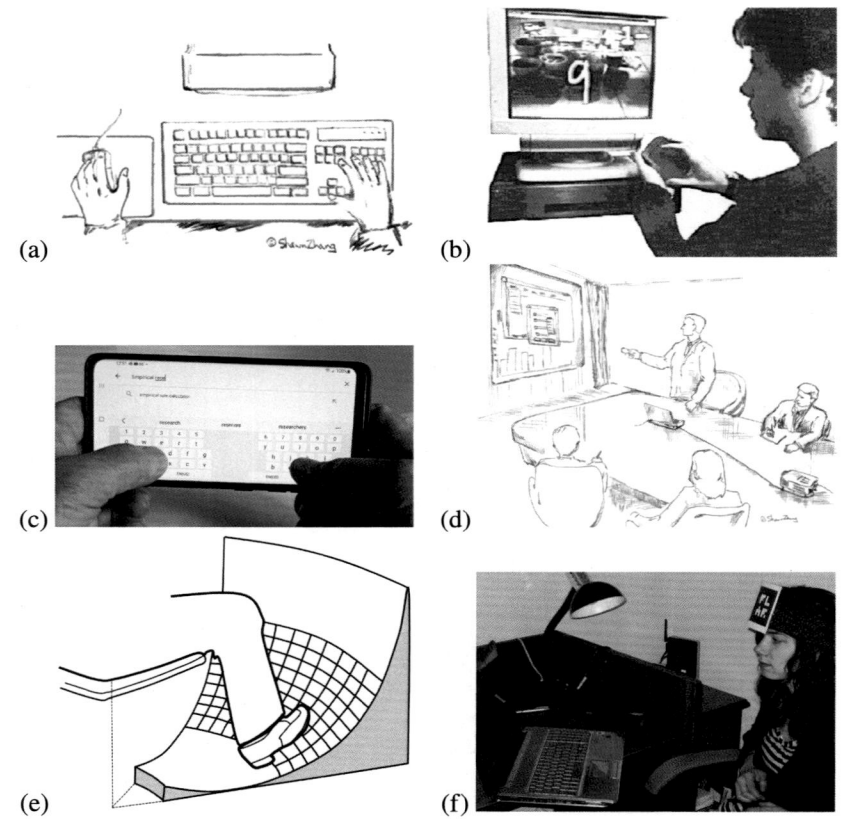

FIGURE 2.18

Use of the limbs in HCI. (a) Hands (sketch courtesy of Shawn Zhang). (b) Fingers [116]. (c) Thumbs. (d) Arms (sketch courtesy of Shawn Zhang). (e) Feet (adapted from [390]). (f) Head [221].

scoring, and interpretation.[8] Scores range from −100 to +100 with the following interpretations:

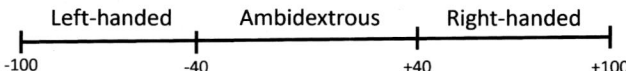

There are many examples in HCI where the Edinburgh Handedness Inventory was administered to participants in experiments [27,75,81,82,101,233,235,346]. In many

---

[8] Dragovic [104] presents an updated version of the Edinburgh Handedness Inventory, using more contemporary and widely-understood tasks.

	Left	Right
1. Writing	□□	□□
2. Drawing	□□	□□
3. Throwing	□□	□□
4. Scissors	□□	□□
5. Toothbrush	□□	□□
6. Knife (without fork)	□□	□□
7. Spoon	□□	□□
8. Broom (upper hand)	□□	□□
9. Striking a match	□□	□□
10. Opening box (lid)	□□	□□
Total (count checks)		

Difference   Cumulative Total   **RESULT**

Instructions

Mark boxes as follows:
x   preference
xx   strong preference
blank no preference

Scoring

Add up the number of checks in the "Left" and "Right" columns and enter in the "Total" row for each column. Add the left total and the right total and enter in the "Cumulative Total" cell. Subtract the left total from the right total and enter in the "Difference" cell. Divide the "Difference" cell by the "Cumulative Total" cell (round to 2 digits if necessary) and multiply by 100. Enter the result in the "RESULT" cell.

Interpretation of RESULT
-100 to -40   left-handed
-40 to +40   ambidextrous
+40 to 100   right-handed

FIGURE 2.19

Edinburgh Handedness Inventory for hand dominance assessment [381].

cases, the degree of hand preference is reported. For example, Hinckley et al. [191] reported that all participants in their study were "strongly right-handed," with a mean score of 71.7 on the inventory.

Another example is research by Annett et al. [9] on stylus behaviour while inking on tablets. For the user study, they recruited 16 right-handed participants and 14 left-handed participants. The inventory was given to both groups. The mean scores were 73.7 and −57.4 for the right-handed and left-handed participants, respectively.

Joshi et al. [233] researched the intersection of hand preference, hand used, and finger vs. thumb input for target selection on a touchscreen smartphone. They pre-screened participants using the Edinburgh Handedness Inventory and settled on 32 participants, equally split by hand preference. Those deemed left-handed or right-handed had scores below −28 or above +48, respectively. The imbalance was likely a practical consideration due to the preponderance of right-handed people in society.

Hand preference is clearly relevant in situations involving touch- or pressure-sensing displays. If interaction requires a stylus or finger on a display, then the user's hand may occlude a portion of the display. Occlusion may lead to poorer performance [133] or to a "hook posture" where users contort the arm position to facilitate inter-action [507]. This can be avoided by positioning UI elements in a different region on the display [173,508]. Of course, this requires sensing or determining the hand preference of the user, since the occlusion is different for a left-handed user than for a right-handed user.

As well as different hand preferences, users also have different hand sizes and finger sizes. Hand size is a potential influence on user performance and preference in using game controllers. Brown and MacKenzie [44] investigated the relationship between hand size and usability of game controllers. They found a significant rela-

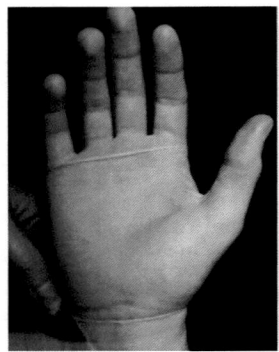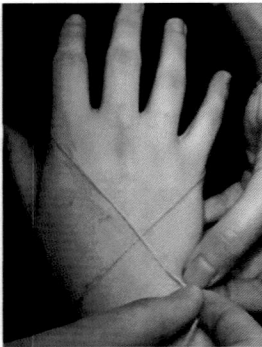

FIGURE 2.20

Figure-of-eight method for measuring hand size (from [44, Fig. 6]).

tionship between hand size and ease of use with four controllers. Participants with larger hands were able to easily operate a larger number of controls than those with smaller hands. There was no effect of hand size on user preference, however. Hand size was measured using the figure-of-eight method [391]. See Fig. 2.20. The participants in the study had a mean hand size of 15.9 in ($SD = 1.2$ in). Individual measurements ranged from 13.0 in to 18.3 in. (Note: 1 inch = 25.4 mm)

Finger size is potentially relevant when interacting with small devices, such as smartphones or tablets. For devices with a touch screen, users frequently select small UI elements with the touch of a finger. This challenge is often referred to as the "fat finger problem" [518]. Is selection accuracy affected by finger size? This was investigated in a user study seeking to measure Fitts' throughput for touch-based target selection on a smart phone [302]. The study also examined the relationship between the width of participants' fingers and error rates. Using the caliper in Fig. 2.21, participants' index fingers were measured at the distal joint. Finger widths ranged from 12.0 mm to 16.5 mm (mean = 14 mm, $SD = 1.4$ mm).

The task involved selecting targets of two widths: 78 pixels (6.2 mm) and 130 pixels (10.4 mm). The device was an LG Nexus 4. The target sizes might seem odd, since even the largest target (10.4 mm) was smaller than the mean finger width (14.0 mm). In fact, this is not unusual. Fig. 2.22 puts this in perspective by comparing a typical user's finger with the small and large targets. The image in the centre shows application icons as rendered on the device's display. As seen, the target widths bracket the size of application icons.

Accurate touch-based target selection is a challenge since the point of selection is digitized from the contact area of the finger on the display surface. The shape and size of the contact area will vary with the angle of finger contact, the contact pressure, and the size of the finger. The error rate in the study was 7.4%. Further examination revealed that the error rate was more than 4× higher for the small targets (12.2% compared to only 2.7% for large targets). This is not surprising given the size of the targets relative to a user's fingertip – compare the left and right images in Fig. 2.22.

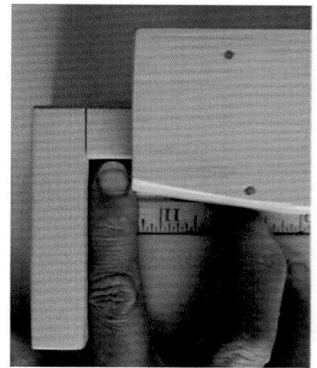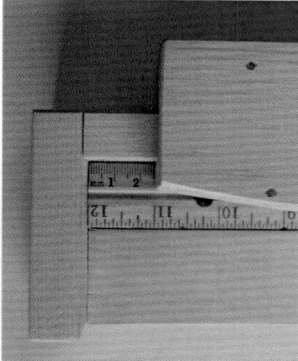

FIGURE 2.21

Caliper to measure finger width (from [302, Fig. 5]).

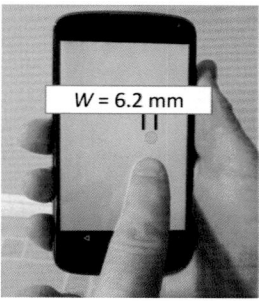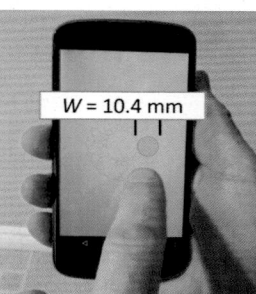

FIGURE 2.22

Size comparison between index finger, targets, and application icons on the device's display.

Fig. 2.23 shows the error rates by target width for each of the 16 participants in the study. There is a positive trend by finger width, particularly for the small targets. For the small targets, the participant with the widest finger (16.5 mm) had an error rate of 19.8% whereas the participant with the narrowest finger (12 mm) had an error rate less than half that, at 9.3% (see figure). It is not surprising then, that finding creative ways to improve touch-based target selection is a common theme in HCI research. We will return to this point in Chapter 3 (section 3.7, Mobile Context).

2.5.2 Voice

The human vocal cords are responders. Through the combination of movement in the larynx, or voice box, and pulmonary pressure in the lungs, humans can create a great a variety of sounds. The most obvious form of vocalized sound is speech

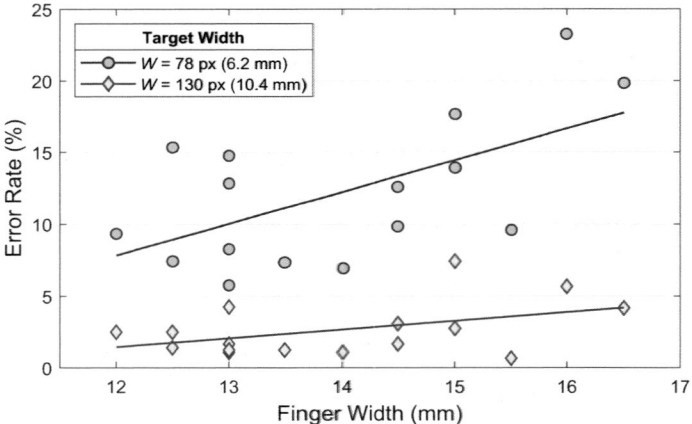

FIGURE 2.23

Error rate by target width and finger width (from [302, Fig. 11]).

– the primary channel for human communication. As an input modality, speech is recognized by algorithms implemented in software on the host computer. With this, the computer interprets spoken words as though the same words were typed on the system's keyboard. Vertanen and Kristensson [502] describe a system for mobile text entry using automatic speech recognition. They report entry rates of 18 words per minute while seated and 13 wpm while walking.

Computer input is also possible using non-speech vocalized sounds, a modality known as *non-verbal voice interaction* (NVVI). In this case, acoustic parameters of the sound signal, such as pitch, volume, or timbre, are measured over time and the data stream is interpreted as an input channel. The technique is particularly useful to specify analog parameters. For example, the user articulates "*volume up, aaah*" and the system increases the volume of the TV as long as the user sustains "*aaah*" [207]. Harada et al. [176] describe the *vocal joystick* – a system using NVVI to simulate a joystick and control an on-screen cursor (e.g., "*eee*" = move cursor left). Zinck and Vogel [557] extend NVVI to users vocalizing musical sounds, such as a musical interval or a three-note melody.

Applications here are often in accessible computing for users without a manual alternative.

2.5.3 **The eye as a responder**

In the normal course of events, the human eye receives sensory stimuli in the form of light from the environment. In viewing a scene, the eyes combine fixations, to view particular locations, and saccades, to move to different locations. This is the role of the eye as a sensory organ. However, the eye is also capable of acting as a responder, to provide input to a computer through fixations and saccades. In this

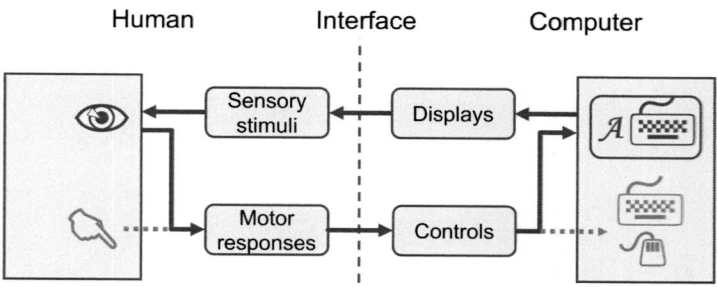

FIGURE 2.24

The human-computer interface using an eye tracker for computer input. The eye serves double duty, processing sensory stimuli from computer displays and providing motor responses to control the system.

capacity, the eye is called upon to do "double duty" since it acts both as a sensor and as a responder. The idea is illustrated in Fig. 2.24, which is a modified view of the human-computer interface in Fig. 2.2 (p. 34). The normal path from the human to the computer is altered. Instead of the hand providing motor responses to control the computer through physical devices (set in gray), the eye provides motor responses that control the computer through soft or virtual controls on the system's display.

For computer input control using the eye, an eye tracking apparatus is required to sense and digitize the gaze location and the movement of the eyes. An eye tracker is often configured to emulate a computer mouse. Much like point-select operations with a mouse, the eye can "look-select," and thereby activate soft controls, such as buttons, icons, links, or text (e.g., [551]). The most common method for selecting with the eye is by fixating, or dwelling, on a selectable target for a predetermined period of time, such as 700 ms. A widely noted downside to dwell-time selection is inadvertent selections which occur if the user casually looks at a selectable on-screen object. This is known as the "Midas touch problem" [215].

One of the earliest research studies using the eyes for computer input was presented by Ware and Mikaelian at CHI+GI in 1987 [510].[9] As well as a computer and display, the apparatus included a Gulf+Western TV camera and an image processing sub-system to digitize the position of the pupil and the display coordinates of the point of fixation. They conducted a user study with four participants using a task similar to Fitts' law, referring to the targets as "menu items." Three selection methods were tested: an on-screen button, a hardware button on the keyboard, and dwell. For dwell, they settled on 400 ms after pilot testing. Noting the inherent jitter in eye fixations and with error rates above 15% when targets subtended less than 1°

[9] In 1987, the annual ACM SIGCHI conference (CHI) was held in Toronto jointly with the Canadian Graphics Interface conference (GI).

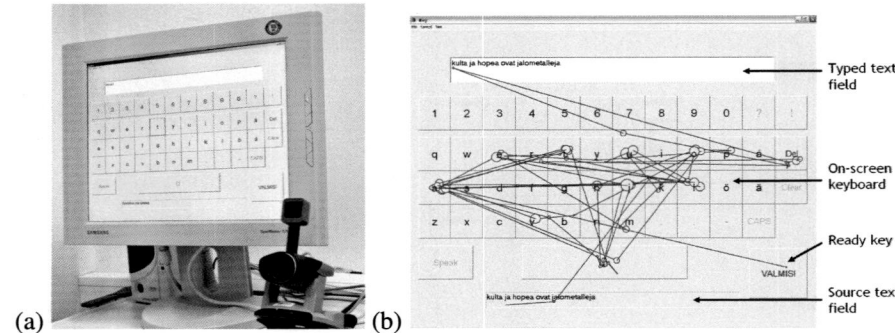

(a)   (b)

FIGURE 2.25

Eye typing. (a) Apparatus. (b) Example sequence of fixations and saccades [334].

of visual angle, they concluded, "the results show that an eye tracker can be used as a fast selection device providing that the target size is not too small" [510, p. 183].

A common application of eye tracking for input control is text entry. So-called "eye typing" uses an on-screen keyboard [335]. The user looks at soft keys, fixating for a prescribed dwell time to make a selection. An example setup using an iView X RED-III eye tracking device by SensoMotoric Instruments[10] is shown in Fig. 2.25a. Fig. 2.25b shows a sequence of fixations and saccades (a scanpath) for one user while entering a phrase of text [334]. Straight lines indicate saccades. Circles indicate fixations, with the diameter indicating the duration of the fixation. Bear in mind that the fixations are conscious, deliberate acts for controlling a computer interface. This is different from the fixations shown in Fig. 2.7 (p. 41), where the user was simply viewing content on a web page. In Fig. 2.25b, the interaction includes numerous fixations meeting the required dwell-time criterion to select soft keys. There is also a fixation (with two corresponding saccades) to view the typed text.

Although not engaging the eye per se, eye blinks can be detected and used for computer control [257]. See Fig. 2.26a. Detection is possible using an eye tracker or other apparatus that senses the closing and opening of an eye lid. This is simpler than sensing the point of fixation of the eye on a display.

An example of "blink input" is BlinkWrite, seen in Fig. 2.26b [308]. The setup uses an EyeTech Digital System[11] TM3 eye tracker situated below a computer display. Although intended primarily for full-fledged eye tracking, the TM3 software also detects blinks. In the figure, the user is entering text using a *scanning ambiguous keyboard* (SAK) which uses just one "key" for input [311]. Key-selections are implemented by the detection of deliberate blinks. A threshold setting distinguishes deliberate blinks from involuntary blinks. In an experimental evaluation, a text entry

---

[10] www.smivision.com.

[11] http://www.eyetechds.com/.

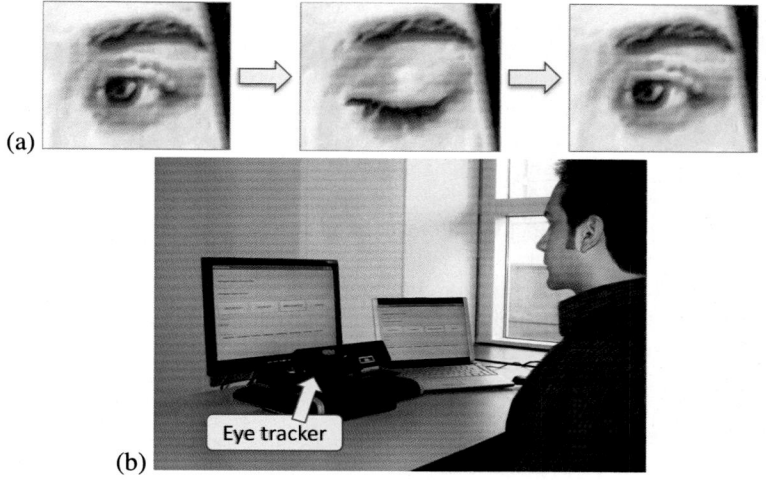

(a)

(b)

FIGURE 2.26

(a) The blink of an eye can serve as a responder for computer control (b) BlinkWrite text entry using an eye tracker to detect blinks [308].

rate of 7.9 wpm was attained with a 700 ms scanning interval. If the eye-tracking apparatus is located within a head-mounded display, then blinks can be used for text entry in a VR setting [293]. See also student exercise 2-7.

2.5.4 The brain as a responder

An active area of research in HCI is brain-computer interaction (BCI). The goal of BCI is to use signals generated by the brain to control a user interface. There are a few approaches to this. One approach is "motor imagery," whereby the user consciously thinks of certain actions, such as clenching a fist or raising a foot, while the signals emitted by the brain coincident with that action are measured and identified. Once identified, events are generated in software as computer inputs. This idea is elaborated further in Chapter 3 (section 3.1.4.2, Brain Signals).

2.6 Language

Language – the mental faculty that allows humans to communicate – is universally available to virtually all humans. Remarkably, language as speech is available without effort. Children learn to speak and understand speech without conscious effort as they grow and develop. Writing, as a codification of language, is a much more recent phenomenon. And learning to write demands effort, considerable effort, spanning years of study and practice. Daniels and Bright distinguish language and writing as follows: "Humankind is defined by language; but civilization is defined by writing." [98, p. 1]. These words are a reminder that the cultural and technological status associated with civilization is enabled by systems of writing. Indeed, the term *prehistory*, as applied to humans, dates from the arrival of human-like beings, millions of years ago, to the emergence of writing. It is writing that presaged *recorded history*, beginning a mere six thousand years ago.

Our HCI interest in language is primarily in methods of writing and in the technology that enables communication in a written form. Text is the written material on a page or display. How it gets there is a topic that intrigues and challenges HCI researchers, as well as the engineers and designers that create products that support text creation, or text entry. Although text entry is hugely important in HCI, our interest here is language itself – in a written form.

One way to characterise and study a language in its written form is through a corpus – a large collection of text samples gathered from diverse and representative sources, such as newspapers, books, e-mails, and magazines. Of course, it is not possible for a corpus to broadly yet precisely represent a language. The sampling process brings limitations: During what timeframe were the samples written? In what country? In what region of the country? On what topics are the samples focused and who wrote them? A well-known corpus is the British National Corpus (BNC), which includes 100 million words.[12] The sources are British English from the late 20th century. So, analyses gleaned from the BNC, while generally applicable to English, may not precisely apply, for example, to American English, to present-day English, or to the language of teenagers sending text messages.

To facilitate study and analysis, a corpus is sometimes reduced to a word-frequency list, which tabulates unique words and their frequencies in the corpus. One such reduction of the BNC includes about 64,000 unique words with frequencies totalling 90 million [454]. Only words occurring three or more times in the original corpus are included. The most frequent word is "the," representing about 6.8% of all words.

Fig. 2.27 gives excerpts from several corpora, showing the five most frequent words and the words at ranks 1000-1004. The English entries are from the British National Corpus. There are additional columns for French [367], German [467], Finnish, SMS English, and SMS Pinyin [289].[13] The Finnish entries are from a database of text from a popular newspaper in Finland, *Turun Sanomat*. The SMS English entries are from a collection of about 10,000 text messages, largely from students at the University of Singapore.[14] SMS text messaging is a good example of the dynamic and context-sensitive nature of language. Efforts to characterise SMS English are prone to the limitations noted above. Note that there is no overlap in the entries 1-5 under English and SMS English.

---

[12] http://www.natcorp.ox.ac.uk/.

[13] SMS (short messaging service), introduced in 1992, is a text messaging service used with telephone, Internet, and mobile device systems.

[14] https://www.kaggle.com/datasets/rtatman/the-national-university-of-singapore-sms-corpus.

Word Rank	English	French	German	Finnish	SMS English	SMS Pinyin
1	the	de	der	ja	u	wo (我)
2	of	la	die	on	i	ni (你)
3	and	et	und	ei	to	le (了)
4	a	le	in	että	me	de (的)
5	in	à	den	oli	at	bu (不)
...	...	...		...	...	...
1000	top	ceci	konkurrenz	muista	ps	jiu (舅)
1001	truth	mari	stieg	paikalla	quit	tie (贴)
1002	balance	solution	notwendig	varaa	rice	ji (即)
1003	heard	expliquer	sogenannte	vie	sailing	jiao (角)
1004	speech	pluie	fahren	seuran	sale	ku (裤)
...	...	...	...	...	...	...

FIGURE 2.27

Sample words from word-frequency lists in various languages. See text for discussion.

The right-hand column in Fig. 2.27 is for SMS Pinyin. Pinyin has been the standard coding system for Mandarin Chinese since 1958. The entries are pinyin marks, not words. Each mark maps to the Chinese character shown in parentheses. The entries are from a corpus of 630,000 text messages containing over nine million Chinese characters.

A notable feature of some corpora is part-of-speech (POS) tagging, where words are tagged by their category, such as noun, verb, or adjective. Importantly, the part of speech is contextual, reflecting a word's use in the original text. For example, paint is sometimes a verb (*Children paint with passion*), sometimes a noun (*The paint is dry*). Part of speech tagging can be important in predictive systems where knowing a word's part of speech limits the possibilities for the next word [153].

2.6.1 Redundancy in language

Native speakers of a language innately possess an immense statistical understanding of the language. We automatically insert words that are omitted or obscured (*ham and ____ sandwich*). We anticipate words (*a picture is worth a thousand ____*), letters (*questio__*), or entire phrases (*to be or __ __ __*). We might wonder: Since humans can fill-in missing letters or words, perhaps the unneeded portions can be omitted. Let's consider this further. The example in Fig. 2.28 gives three variations of a paragraph of text. The original excerpt contains 243 characters. In part (a), all 71 vowels are removed, thus shortening the text by 29.2%. Many words are easily guessed (e.g., smmr → summer, thrgh → through) and with some effort the gist of the text is apparent. It has something to do with summer [smmr], gardens [grdn], and scent [scnt]. Part (b) is similar except the first letter of each word is intact, even if it is a vowel.

(a)	Th std ws flld wth th rch dr f rss, nd whn th lght smmr wnd strrd mdst th trs f th grdn, thr cm thrgh th pn dr th hvy scnt f th llc, r th mr dlct prfm f th pnk-flwrng thrn.
(b)	Th std ws flld wth th rch odr of rss, and whn th lght smmr wnd strrd amdst th trs of th grdn, thr cm thrgh th opn dr th hvy scnt of th llc, or th mr dlct prfm of th pnk-flwrng thrn.
(c)	The studio was filled with the rich odour of roses, and when the light summer wind stirred amidst the trees of the garden, there came through the open door the heavy scent of the lilac, or the more delicate perfume of the pink-flowering thorn.

FIGURE 2.28

First paragraph of Oscar Wilde's *The Picture of Dorian Gray.* (a) Vowels removed. (b) Vowels intact at beginning of words. (c) Original.

Still, 62 vowels are missing. The meaning is slightly easier to decipher. The original text is in part (c). It is the first paragraph from Oscar Wilde's *The Picture of Dorian Gray.*

There are other examples, as above, where portions of text are removed, yet comprehension remains. Characters are frequently removed in SMS text messages. Recoding is an option, for example, using sound (th@s → that's, gr8 → great) or inventing acronyms (w → with, gf → girlfriend, x → times) [161]. One anecdote tells of a 13-year-old student submitting an entire essay written in SMS shorthand.[15] Although the teacher was not impressed, the student's rationale was direct and honest: "It is easier to write in shorthand than in standard English." An example from the essay is shown in Fig. 2.29. Part (a) gives the shortened text. There are 26 words and 102 characters (including spaces). The expanded text in (b) contains 39 words and 199 characters. The reduction is dramatic: 48.7% fewer characters in the SMS shorthand. Of course, there are differences between this example and Fig. 2.28. For one, punctuation and digits are introduced for recoding. As well, the shortened message is tailored to the language of a particular community of users. It is likely the 13-year-old's teacher was not of that community.

There is, unfortunately, a more insidious side to redundancy in written text. A common fault in writing is the presence of superfluous words, with their eradication promoted in many books on writing style. Strunk and White's Rule 17 is to Omit Needless Words, and advises reducing, for example, "he is a man who ..." to "he

---

[15] http://news.bbc.co.uk/2/hi/uk_news/2814235.stm.

(a)	My smmr hols wr CWOT. B4, we used 2go2 NY 2C my bro, his GF & thr 3 :- kids FTF. ILNY, it's a gr8 plc.
(b)	My summer holidays were a complete waste of time. Before, we used to go to New York to see my brother, his girlfriend and their three screaming kids face to face. I love New York. It's a great place.

FIGURE 2.29

Shortening English. (a) SMS shorthand. (b) Standard English.

..." or "this is a subject that ..." to "this subject ..." [474, p. 23]. Tips on writing style are given in Chapter 8.

2.6.2 Entropy in language

If redundancy in language is what we inherently know, entropy is what we don't know – the uncertainty about forthcoming letters, words, phrases, ideas, concepts, and so on. Clearly, redundancy and entropy are related: If we remove what we know, what remains is what we don't know. A demonstration of redundancy and entropy in written English was provided in the 1950s by Shannon in a letter-guessing experiment [443]. See Fig. 2.30. The experiment proceeds as follows. The participant is presented with a series of dashes representing the letters in a phrase and is asked to guess the letters, starting at the beginning. As guessing proceeds, the phrase is revealed to the participant, letter by letter. The results are recorded as shown in the line below each phrase in the figure. A dash ("-") is a correct guess; a letter is an incorrect guess. Shannon called the second line the "reduced text." In terms of redundancy and entropy, a dash represents redundancy (what is known), while a letter represents entropy (what is not known). Among the interesting observations in Fig. 2.30 is that errors are more common at the beginning of words, less common as words progress. Within words, the statistical nature of the language and the participant's inherent understanding of the language facilitate guessing.

The letter-guessing experiment in Fig. 2.30 is more than a curiosity. Shannon was motivated to quantify the entropy of English in information-theoretic terms. He pointed out, for example, that both lines in a phrase contain the same information in that it is possible, with a good statistical model, to recover the first line from the second. Because of the redundancy in printed English (viz. the dashes), a communications system need only transmit the reduced text. The original text can be recovered using the statistical model. Shannon also demonstrated how to compute the entropy of printed English. Considering letter frequencies alone, the entropy is about 4.25 bits

```
THE ROOM WAS NOT VERY LIGHT A SMALL OBLONG
--------ROO-----------NOT-V---------I------------SM--------OB-------

READING LAMP ON THE DESK SHED GLOW ON
REA-------------------O-----------D--------SHED-GLO----O-

POLISHED WOOD BUT LESS ON THE SHABBY RED CARPET
P-L-S----------O------BU----L-S----O------------SH--------RE----C----------
```

FIGURE 2.30

Shannon's letter-guessing experiment (adapted from [443]).

per letter.[16] Including previous letters in the analysis reduces the entropy because there is less uncertainty about forthcoming letters. Considering long-range statistical effects (up to 100 letters), Shannon estimated the entropy of printed English at about 1 bit per letter with a corresponding redundancy of about 75%.

See also student exercise 2-3 at the end of this chapter.

2.6.3 Language modelling for text creation

The most common form of text creation is user input on a conventional Qwerty keyboard. Each key press generates a character of text. Simple enough. However, text creation often exploits the statistical properties of a language using a dictionary or language model, and includes features such as word prediction, word completion, or auto-correct. An example of word completion was given earlier in Fig. 1.12 (p. 22). The goal is to improve and potentially fast-track the creation process. There are clear benefits in term of keystroke reduction and these can be quantified analytically using metrics such as KSPC (keystrokes per character) [303,325].

However, other factors emerge such as the need for increased vigilance. While there is a certain appeal and benefit to having words – even entire phrases – automatically completed, language models are imperfect. Thus, during text creation the user's attention must switch between different areas of the display to monitor and participate in the process. Inattention bears a cost. As a personal example, while using my phone to send an email to a friend, I was horrified to discover after clicking "send" that my intended text, "[name] has finally got back to me …", was sent as "[name] has finally got bacteria to me …". Apparently, distraction and inaccurate tapping overcame the need for due diligence.

User performance combining mental operators (for attention) with keystrokes (for input) can be modelled using Card et al.'s keystroke-level model (KLM), which we meet in Chapter 7. Section 7.2.4.5 (The KLM and Predictive Text Entry, p. 331) explores text creation with word prediction and completion.

---

[16] The data set and calculation are given in Chapter 7 (see Fig. 7.25, p. 321).

Language models are also used in *machine translation* – translating text from one language to another. Machine translation is like text creation, except the process begins with text in another language, rather than with keystrokes or gestures. Google Translate is the predominant example, with capability to convert text between more than 100 languages and with an estimated 200 million users daily.[17] There are many applications, such as the translation of menus [136], social media [89], and websites [226]. Difficulties arise in converting meaning in general purpose translation, especially with unstructured or poorly formed text and with minority languages [8]. Critics of machine translation note a bias towards English and a potential for misuse [533]. Even so, machine translation has revolutionized the way adults on an international stage manage language. Applications with children are interesting in that children are highly forgiving when confronted with mistranslations. Mistakes often generate interest, create humour, and inspire additional conversation [269].

The bigger picture for language modelling is the emergence of AI chatbots – products that mimic human conversation using text or an artificial voice. An example is ChatGPT by OpenAI.[18] Chatbots go well beyond word or phrase prediction: They are generative, spawning entire conversations and full text narratives through large language models based on deep learning, natural language processing, and so on. At the time of this writing, it is not clear where language modelling in next-generation AI products is headed. The text narratives just mentioned are often both accurate and well intended; at other times, they are neither. So, the future for language modelling holds hope and promise, yet also concern and unease.

2.7 **Human performance**

Humans use their sensors, brain, and responders to do things. When the three elements work together to achieve a goal, human performance arises. Whether tying shoelaces, folding clothes, searching the web, or entering a text message on a smartphone, human performance is present. Better performance is typically associated with faster or more accurate behaviour, and this leads to a fundamental property of human performance – the *speed-accuracy trade-off*: Go faster and errors increase; slow down and accuracy improves. Reported in academic papers dating back more than a century (see [479] for a review), mundane and proverbial ("Haste makes waste"), and steeped in common sense (we instinctively slow down to avoid errors), it is hard to imagine a more banal feature of human performance. Clearly, research on human performance using a new interface or interaction technique must consider both the speed in doing a task and the overall accuracy.

Humans position themselves on the speed-accuracy trade-off in manner that is both comfortable and consistent with their goals. Sometimes we act with haste, even

---

[17] https://en.wikipedia.org/wiki/Google_Translate.
[18] https://openai.com/.

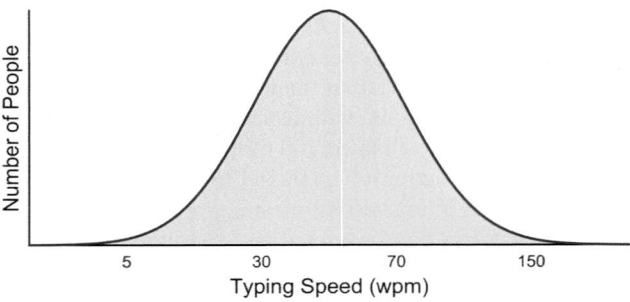

FIGURE 2.31

Variability of people in performing a task such as typing.

recklessly, at other times with great attention to detail. Furthermore, we may act in the presence of a secondary task, such as listening to the radio, conversing with a friend, or driving a car. Clearly, context plays an important role, as do the limits and capabilities of the sensors, the brain, and responders.

With human performance, we see complexities and challenges in HCI that are absent in traditional sciences, such as physics or chemistry. Humans bring diversity and variability, and these characteristics bring imprecision and uncertainty. Some humans perform tasks better than others. As well, a particular human may perform a task better in one context and environment than when performing the same task in a different context and environment. Furthermore, if that same human performs the same task repeatedly in the same context and environment, the outcome will likely vary.

Human diversity in performing tasks is sometimes illustrated in a distribution resembling a normal distribution. See Fig. 2.31. Here, the distribution reveals the number of people performing a task (y-axis) vs. their proficiency in doing it (x-axis). The example assumes computer users as the population and illustrates typing as the task. Most people fall somewhere in the middle, with typing speeds of, say, 30 to 70 words per minute (wpm). Some people are slower, some faster. However, a small number of people will be exceedingly fast, say, 150 wpm or faster. Yet others, a small number, exhibit difficulty in achieving even a modest speed, such as 5 wpm, equivalent to one word every 12 seconds.

2.7.1 Reaction time

One of the most primitive manifestations of human performance is *simple reaction time*, defined as the delay between the occurrence of a single fixed stimulus and the initiation of a response assigned to it [127, p. 95]. An example is pressing a button in response to the onset of a stimulus light. The task involves the three elements of the human shown in Fig. 2.15 (p. 47). And the cognitive operation is trivial, so the task is easy to study. While the apparatus in experimental settings is usually simple,

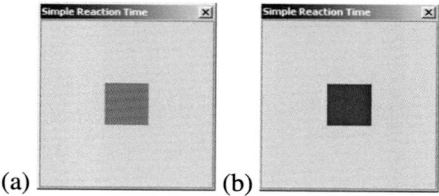

(a)   (b)

FIGURE 2.32

Simple reaction time. (a) The user fixates on the gray box. (b) After a delay, the box turns red whereupon the user presses a key as quickly as possible.

humans react regularly in everyday pursuits and in a variety of contexts, such as reacting to the ring of a phone, reacting to a traffic light, or reacting to water in a bath (hot!). These three examples all involve a motor response. But, the sensory stimuli differ. The ring of a phone is an auditory stimulus; a changing traffic light is a visual stimulus; hot water touching the skin is a tactile stimulus. It is known that simple reaction times differ according to the stimulus source, with approximate values of 150 ms (auditory), 200 ms (visual), 300 ms (smell), and 380 ms (pain) [17, p. 41] [402, Figure 3].

To explore visual reaction times further, an application named ReactionTimeExperiment was developed to experimentally test and demonstrate several reaction times tasks.[19] After describing each task, the results of an experiment are presented. For *simple reaction time*, the interface is shown in Fig. 2.32. A trial begins with the appearance of a gray box in a GUI window. Following a delay, the box turns red. This is the sensory stimulus. The goal is to press a key on the system keyboard as a quickly as possible after the stimulus appears. The delay between the gray box appearing and the box turning red varies from trial to trial to prevent the user from anticipating the onset of the stimulus.

The software implements three extensions of simple reaction tasks: *physical matching*, *name matching*, and *class matching*. Each adds a layer of complexity to the cognitive operation. The tasks were modelled after descriptions by Card et al. [64, pp. 65-71]. For physical matching, the user is presented with a five-letter word as an initial stimulus. After a delay a second stimulus appears, also a five-letter word. The user responds as quickly as possible by pressing one of two keys: a "match" key if the second stimulus matches the first stimulus, or a "no-match" key if the second stimulus differs from the first stimulus. Matches occur with 50% probability. An example experimental setup is shown in Fig. 2.33.

Obviously, physical matching is more complicated than simple reaction, since the user compares the stimulus to a code in working memory. An example in HCI is predictive text entry on a mobile phone, where the user has an intended word in working memory. After each letter entered, candidate words appear. At each juncture,

---

[19] The software, API, and related files are on this book's web site.

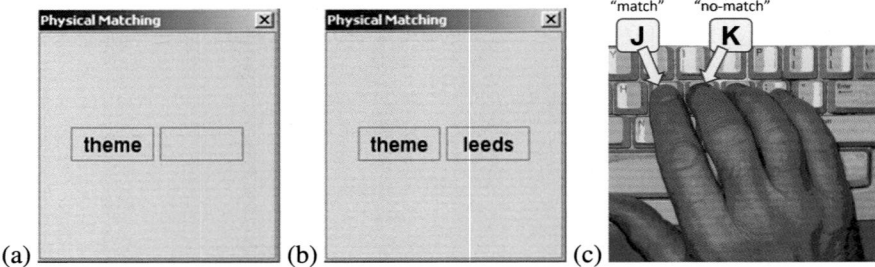

FIGURE 2.33

Physical matching. (a) Initial stimulus. (b) After a delay, a second stimulus appears. (c) Setup. See text for discussion.

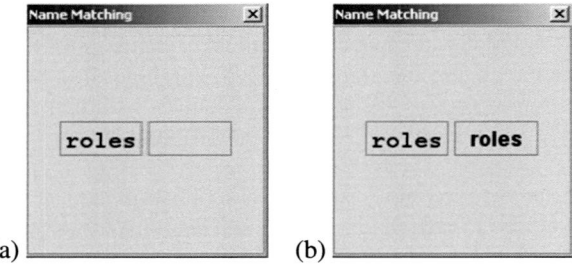

FIGURE 2.34

Name matching. (a) Initial stimulus. (b) Second stimulus. See text for discussion.

the user has two choices: accept a candidate word or enter the next letter.[20] (Details vary depending on the phone.)

Name matching is the same as physical matching except the words vary in appearance: uppercase or lowercase, mono-spaced or sans serif, plain or bold, 18 pt or 20 pt. A match is deemed to occur if the words are the same, regardless of the look. See Fig. 2.34. Name matching should take longer than physical matching because "the user must now wait until the visual code has been recognized and an abstract code representing the name of the letter is available" [64, p. 69].

For class matching, the initial stimulus contains a letter or digit. After a delay a second stimulus appears, also containing a letter or digit. The font is mono-spaced or sans serif, plain or italic, 18 pt or 20 pt. A match is deemed to occur if both symbols are of the same class; that is, both are letters or both are digits. Class matching takes longer still because, "the user has to make multiple references to long-term memory"

---

[20] This assumes the user inspects the candidate words. The user might not look at the candidates or perhaps only look after two or three letters are entered.

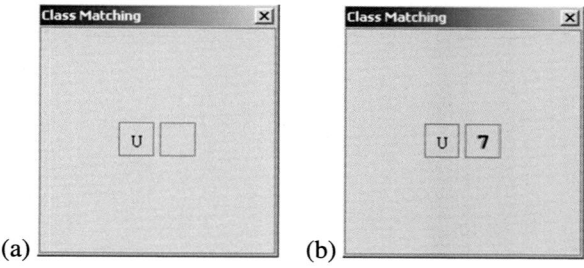

FIGURE 2.35

Class matching. (a) Initial stimulus. (b) Second stimulus. See text for discussion.

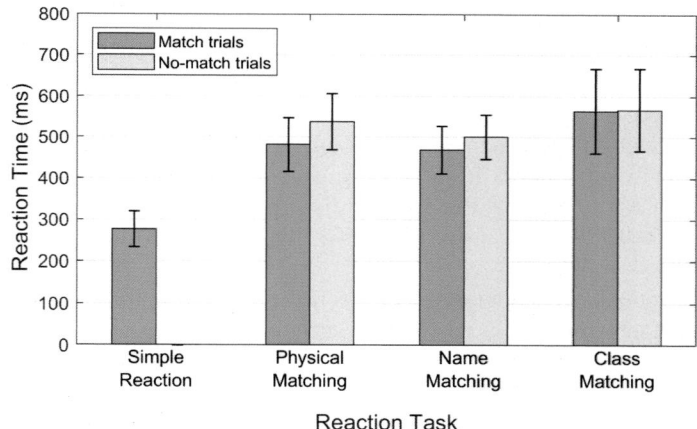

FIGURE 2.36

Results of an experiment comparing several reaction tasks. Error bars show ±1 *SD*.

[64, p. 70]. To avoid confusion, 0 (digit) and O (letter) are not included, nor are 1 (digit) and I (letter). See Fig. 2.35.

The interfaces described above were tested in the lab component of a course on HCI. Fourteen students served as participants and performed 3 blocks of 10 trials for each condition. The first block was considered practice and discarded. To offset learning effects, participants were divided into two groups of equal size. One group preformed the simple reaction task first, followed in order by the physical, name, and class matching tasks. The other group performed the tasks in the reverse order.

The results are shown in Fig. 2.36. The mean time for simple reaction was 276 ms. This value is nicely positioned in the 113 to 528 ms range noted earlier for reaction time tasks (see Fig. 2.15). Note that the time measurement began with the arrival of the second stimulus and ended with the key-event registered in software when a key was pressed; thus, the measurement includes the time for the motor response.

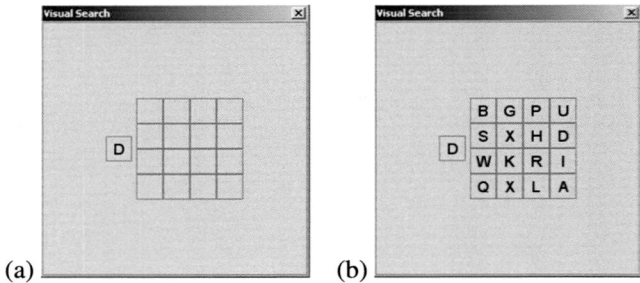

(a)   (b)

FIGURE 2.37

Visual search. (a) Initial stimulus. (b) A collection of letters appears after a delay. See text for discussion.

Physical matching took about twice as long as simple reaction, depending on whether the second stimulus was a match (482 ms) or a no-match (538 ms). Interestingly enough, name matching did not take longer than physical matching. An explanation is that the words in the name-matching task had insufficient variability in appearance to require additional cognitive processing. Class matching was the hardest of the tasks, with means of about 565 ms for both the match and no-match conditions.

Choice reaction is yet another type of reaction time task. In this case, the user has n stimuli, such as lights, and n responders, such as switches. There is a one for one correspondence between stimulus and response. Choice reaction time is discussed in Chapter 7 on modelling.

2.7.2 **Visual search**

A variation on reaction time is *visual search*, where the user scans a collection of items searching for a desired item. Obviously, the time increases with the number of items to scan. The software described above includes a mode for visual search, with the search space configurable for 1, 2, 4, 8, 16, or 32 items. An example for $N = 16$ is shown in Fig. 2.37. The initial stimulus is a single letter. After a random delay of 2 to 5 seconds, the squares on the right are populated with letters selected at random. The initial stimulus appears on the right with 50% probability. The user presses a "match" or "no-match" key, as appropriate.

A small experiment was conducted with the same 14 students from the experiment described above, using a similar procedure. The results are shown in Fig. 2.38 in two forms. In (a), reaction time (RT) vs. number of items (N) is plotted. Each marker reveals the mean of $14 \times (10 + 10) = 280$ trials. The markers are connected and a linear regression line is superimposed. At $R^2 = .9932$, the regression model is an excellent fit. There is clearly a linear relationship between reaction time and the number of items to scan in a visual search task. This is well known in the HCI literature, particularly from research on menu selection (e.g., [85,198,271]). For this

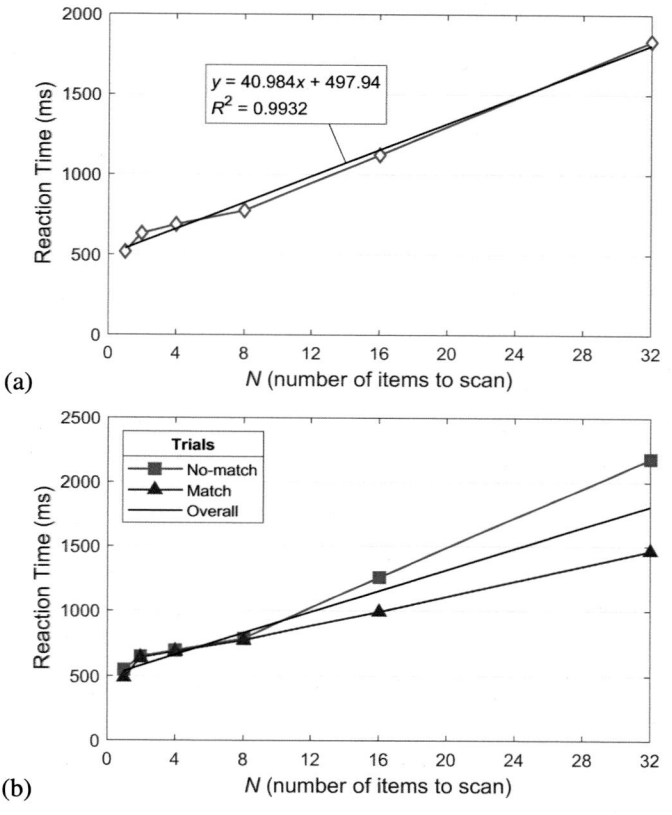

FIGURE 2.38

Results of visual search experiment. (a) Overall result with linear regression model. (b) Results by no-match and match trials.

experiment,

$$RT = 498 + 41N \text{ ms}, \tag{2.1}$$

where N is the number of items to scan. $N = 1$ is a special case since there is only one item to scan. The task is reduced to physical matching. This is slightly different than in the physical matching experiment, since the user is matching a letter rather than a word. Nevertheless, the result is consistent with Fig. 2.38a ($RT \approx 500$ ms).

In Fig. 2.38b, the results appear separately for the match trials and the no-match trials. The no-match trials take longer. The reason is simple. If the initial stimulus is not present, an exhaustive search is required to determine such – before pressing the no-match key. If the initial stimulus is present, the user presses the match key immediately upon locating the initial stimulus in the right-side stimuli. The effect only surfaces at $N = 16$ and $N = 32$, however.

Before moving on, here is a reaction time situation, and it bears directly on the title of this section, Human Performance. Consider an athlete competing in the 100-meter dash in the Olympics. Sometimes at the beginning of a race, there is a "false start." The definition of a false start is interesting: A false start occurs if an athlete reacts to the starter's pistol before it is sounded or *within 100 ms after*.[21] Clearly, an athlete who reacts before the starter's pistol sounds is anticipating, not reacting. Interesting in the definition, however, is the criterion that a false start has occurred if the athlete reacts within 100 ms *after* the starter's pistol is sounded. One hundred milliseconds is precariously close to the lower bound on reaction time, which is cited in Fig. 2.15 as 113 ms. Card et al. peg the lower bound at 105 ms [64, p. 65]. World records are set by humans at the extreme tails of the normal distribution. Is it possible that a false start is declared occasionally, very occasionally, when none occurred (e.g., honestly reacting, say, 95 ms after the starter's pistol is sounded)?[22]

There are slight differences between the lower-bound reaction times cited above and the false-start scenario, however. The values cited are for pressing a key with a finger in response to a visual stimulus. The motor response signals in the 100-meter dash must travel farther to reach the feet. This tends to lengthen the reaction time. Also, the stimulus in the 100-meter dash is auditory, not visual. Auditory reaction time is less than visual reaction time; so, this tends to shorten the reaction time. Nevertheless, the example illustrates the application of low-level research in experimental psychology to human performance and to the design of human-machine systems.

2.7.3 Skilled behaviour

The response time tasks in the previous section are simple: A sensory stimulus initiates a simple cognitive operation, which is followed by a simple motor response. It takes just a few trials to get comfortable with the task and with additional practice there is little if any improvement in performance. However, in many tasks, human performance improves considerably and continuously with practice. For such tasks, the phenomenon of learning and improving is so pronounced that the most endearing property of the task is the progression in performance and the level of performance achieved, according to a criterion such as a speed, accuracy, degree of success, and so on. *Skilled behaviour*, then, is a property of human behaviour whereby human performance necessarily improves through practice. Examples include playing darts, playing chess or, in computing scenarios, gaming or programming. One's ability to do these tasks is likely to bear significantly on the amount of practice.

The examples just cited were chosen for a reason. They delineate two categories of skilled behaviour: *sensory-motor skill* and *mental skill* [514, p. 21]. Proficiency in

---

[21] Rule 162.6 of the IAAF (International Association of Athletics Federations) deems a false start to occur "when the reaction time is less than 0.100 second" [206, p. 107].

[22] A possible example is the false start attributed to Devon Allen in the final of 110-meter hurdles at the 2022 IAAF World Championships. Allen was disqualified, having recorded a reaction time of 99 ms after the gun. He was shocked: "I know for a fact that I didn't react until I heard the gun" [158].

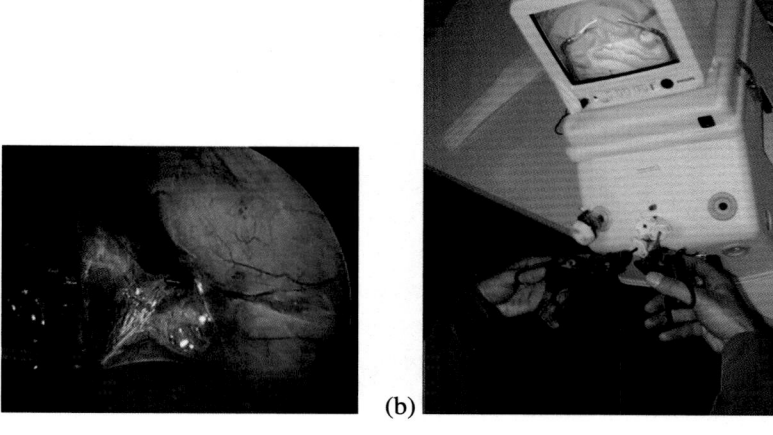

(a)   (b)

FIGURE 2.39

Sensory-motor skill combined with mental skill during laparoscopic surgery. (a) Tips of tools for grasping and cutting. (b) Exterior view of tools and monitor in a training simulator (photos courtesy of The Centre of Excellence for Simulation Education and Innovation at Vancouver General Hospital).

darts or gaming is likely to emphasize sensory-motor skill, while proficiency in chess or computer programming is likely to emphasize mental skill. Of course, there is no dichotomy. All skilled behaviour requires mental faculties, such as perception, decision, and judgement. Similarly, even the most contemplative of skilled tasks requires co-ordinated, overt action by the hands or other organs.

While tasks such as gaming or computer programming may focus on sensory-motor skill or mental skill, respectively, other tasks involve considerable elements of both. Consider a physician performing minimally invasive surgery, as common for abdominal procedures. To access the abdominal area, a camera and light mounted at the end of a laparoscope are inserted through a small incision, with the image displayed on an overhead monitor. Tools are inserted through other incisions for convenient access to an internal organ. The surgeon views the monitor and manipulates the tools to grasp and cut tissue. In Fig. 2.39a, the tips of the surgeon's tools for grasping (left) and cutting (top) are shown as they appear on a monitor during a cholecystectomy, or gallbladder removal. The tools are manually operated, external to the patient. Fig. 2.39b shows examples of such tools in a training simulator. The tools are complex instruments. Note, for example, that the tips of the tools articulate, or bend, thus providing an additional degree of freedom for the surgeon [188,344]. Clearly, the human-machine interaction involves both sensory-motor skill (operating the tools while viewing a monitor) and mental skill (knowing what to do and the strategy for doing it).

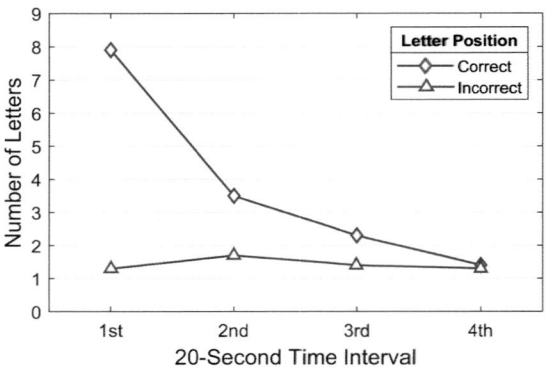

FIGURE 2.40

Positioning letters on a Qwerty layout by skilled typists (from [460]).

With skilled behaviour comes *implicit knowledge*. A task becomes over-learned and automatic. Buttoning a shirt and tying shoelaces are examples. Most adults are experts, having "practiced" for many years. Implicit knowledge is contrasted with *explicit knowledge*. Novices use explicit knowledge to perform the same task that experts perform automatically. A person learning to tie shoes laces will think through, and visually attend to, the steps. An expert proceeds automatically.

A good example in computing is typing. Novices move their fingers to find and press keys while exercising deliberate and explicit knowledge of the task. An expert – a touch typist – acts implicitly. An interesting consequence of this for typing is that experts are less aware of the layout of the Qwerty keyboard than novices. There is empirical evidence to support this. Synder et al. [460] tested users' knowledge of the layout of a Qwerty keyboard. Skilled typists' ability to recall and identify the letter positions was incomplete and inaccurate. One hundred typists with a mean typing speed of 72 wpm were only able to correctly position 15 of 26 letters during an 80-second test. See Fig. 2.40. With the acquisition of skill – over years of practice – their knowledge had migrated from the explicit to the implicit. See also student exercise 2-2.

One way to study skilled behaviour is to record and chart the progression of skill over a period of time. The level of skill is measured in a dependent variable, such as speed, accuracy, or some variation on these. The time element is a convenient procedural unit such as trial, block or session number, or a temporal unit such as minutes, hours, days, months, or years. There are, of course, practical considerations in designing an experiment to measure and record the acquisition of skill. True mastery takes on the order of 10,000 hours of practice [145, Chap. 2]. Clearly, such a timeline is beyond the reach of experimental research.

Measuring and modelling the progression of skill is common in HCI research, particularly where users confront a new interface or interaction technique. The methodology for evaluating skilled behaviour is presented in Chapter 5 (see Longitudinal

Studies) with the mathematical steps for modelling presented in Chapter 7 (see Skill Acquisition). See also student exercise 2-4.

2.7.4 **Attention**

Texting while driving. It's hard to imagine a more provocative theme to open our discussion on attention. Although driving a car is relatively easy, even the most experienced driver is a potential killer if he or she chooses to read and send text messages while driving. The problem lies in one's inability to attend to both tasks simultaneously. Much like the bottleneck posed by working memory (7 ± 2 items), the human ability to attend is also limited. But, what is the limit? More fundamentally, what is attention? Which tasks require attention? Which don't? How is human performance impacted? According to one view, attention is a property of human behaviour that occurs when a person who is attending to one thing cannot attend to another [243, p. 4]. Typing, for example, requires attention because while typing we cannot engage in conversation. On the other hand, walking requires very little attention since we can think, converse, and do other things while walking. One way to study attention is to observe and measure humans performing two tasks separately and then to repeat the procedure with the two tasks performed simultaneously. A task with performance that degrades in the simultaneous case is said to require attention.

Attention is often studied along two themes: *divided attention* and *selected attention* [238, p. 179]. Divided attention is the process of doing and concentrating on more than one task at time. Texting while driving is an example, and the effect is obvious enough. In other cases, divided attention poses no problem, as in walking and talking. Selected attention (aka *focused attention*) is attending to one task to the exclusion of others. For example, we converse with a friend in a crowded noise-filled room, while blocking out extraneous chatter. But, there are limits. In that same conversation we are occasionally unable to recall words just spoken because our attention drifted away or was pulled away by a distraction. Selective attention, then, is the human ability to ignore extraneous events and to maintain focus on a primary task.

One theory of selective attention holds that our ability to selectively attend bears on the importance of the events to the individual. A person listening to a speech is likely to stop listening if the person's name is spoken from another location [243, p. 140]. One's own name is intrinsically important and is likely to intrude on the ability to selectively attend to the speech. Clearly, importance is subjective. Wickens describes the crash of an airplane where the flight crew was preoccupied with a malfunction in the cockpit that had no bearing on the safety of the flight [515, p. 249]. The crew attended to the malfunction while failing to notice critical altimeter readings showing that the airplane was gradually descending to the ground. The malfunction was of salient importance to the flight crew.

The distinction between divided and selected attention is often explained in terms of channels [515, p. 254]. Events in a single channel (e.g., visual, auditory, motor) are processed in parallel, whereas events in different channels are processed in serial.

When processing events in parallel (single channel) one event may intrude on the ability to focus attention on another event. When processing events in serial (different channels), we strive to focus on one event to the exclusion of others or to divide attention in a convenient manner between the channels.

Analysing accidents is an important theme in human factors, as the aviation example above illustrates. And there is no shortage of incidents. Accidents on the road, in the air, on the seas, or in industry are numerous and in many cases the cause is at least partly attributable to the human element – to distractions or to selectively attending to inappropriate events. One such accident involving a driver and cyclist occurred because a Tamagotchi digital pet distracted the driver.[23] Evidently, the pet developed a dire need for "food" and was distressed: *bleep, bleep, bleep, bleep, bleep*. The call of the pet was of salient importance to the driver, and with a horrific and fatal outcome [67, pp. 255-259]. More likely today, it is the lure of the mobile phone that brings danger. And the statistics are shocking. In the U.S. in 2020, 3,142 deaths on the road were attributed to distracted driving.[24]

Attention has relevance in HCI, for example, in office environments where interruptions that demand task switching affect productivity [96]. The mobile age has brought a milieu of issues bearing on attention. Not only are attention resources limited, these resources are engaged while users are on the move. There is a shift toward immediate brief tasks that demand constant vigilance and user availability, and with ever-demanding expectations in response times. So-called psychosocial tasks compete for and deplete attention resources, with evidence pointing to an eventual breakdown of fluency in the interaction [383].

2.7.5 Human error

Human error has different perspectives. When a user interacts with a computer to perform a task, errors of some sort are inevitable. If the user is a participant in an HCI experiment and is performing tasks with a new interface, perhaps using a new interaction technique, then the logging and analysis of errors is important. The goal is to assess the merits of, or problems in, the interface. Perfection is desirable, but rarely attainable. A single trial might be correctly done, but over the course of many trials, errors – at least some – are likely. On the surface, the term *error* leaves little room for interpretation: Something was done, and it was done wrong! This leads to a simple definition:

> *An error is a discrete event where the outcome of a task is incorrect, having deviated from the correct and desired outcome.*

In experimental research, events are logged and analysed as a component of human performance, along with task completion time and other measurable properties of the interaction. Most commonly, errors are reported as *error rate* as a percent:

---

[23] See Wikipedia for details on the Tamagotchi digital pet.

[24] https://www.nhtsa.gov/risky-driving/distracted-driving.

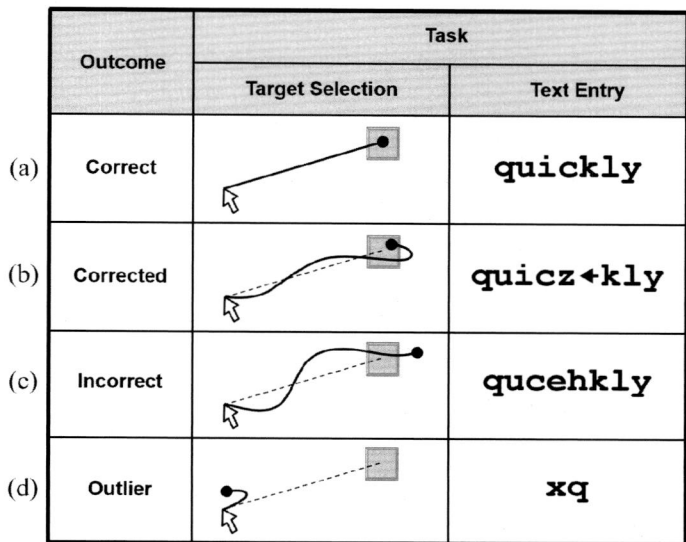

	Outcome	Task	
		Target Selection	**Text Entry**
(a)	Correct		quickly
(b)	Corrected		quicz◂kly
(c)	Incorrect		qucehkly
(d)	Outlier		xq

FIGURE 2.41

Computing tasks with different outcomes. See text for discussion.

the ratio of incorrectly completed trials to all trials ($\times 100$). Sometimes *accuracy* is reported – the ratio of correctly completed trials to all trials.

Discussions that followed refer the examples in Fig. 2.41 for target selection tasks and text entry tasks. For each, the goal is simple. For target selection, the goal is to operate an input device to manoeuvre a tracking symbol – a cursor – from a starting position to a target and select the target. Perhaps a button on the input device is used for selection. For text entry, the goal is to use a device such as a keyboard or a technique such as handwriting to enter the word "quickly." In (a), the tasks were performed correctly: The target was selected, the word was entered.

In Fig. 2.41b, the task was also performed correctly, but only after corrective actions. For the target selection task, the cursor path wavered and travelled through the target, with an adjustment at the end to select the target. For the text entry task, "z" was entered instead of "k." There was a corrective action (BACKSPACE) followed by entry of the correct letter.

In Fig. 2.41c the task was performed incorrectly – an error was committed. For the target selection task, the cursor ventured through the target, with the final selection outside the target. For the text entry task, the wrong combination of letters was entered. Fig. 2.41d is discussed in the next section, Outliers.

The behaviours in Fig. 2.41 parts (b) and (c) are rich in detail. In a discrete-error sense, the tasks in (b) were correct, albeit corrected, while the tasks in (c) were in error. However, a deeper look is needed. Why did the interactions waiver from the ideal scenario in part (a)? In experimental research, leveraging such insight into plausible explanations is critical. By its very nature, experimental research seeks to compare two or more conditions.[25] Observing that one condition is better than another (e.g., faster, fewer errors) is fine, but understanding and explaining why is also important. The goal is to inform, guide, and inspire new ideas that move the state of the art forward.

Consider again the target selection tasks in Fig. 2.41 parts (b) and (c). The tracking symbol veered off a direct path to the target. But why? Was there a grip or stability problem in the way the user held or controlled the input device? Was the device's gain setting too sensitive? Was the device a mouse, a touchpad, an eye tracker, a game controller, or something else? Note in (b) that the tracking symbol entered then exited the target. Was there a particular problem in the final target acquisition phase of the task?

Now consider the text entry tasks in (b) and (c). What went wrong? If input involved a keyboard, were the errors due to the user pressing keys adjacent to correct keys? Perhaps the keys were small. If entry involved gestural input using a finger or stylus, did the user enter the wrong gesture or an ill-formed gesture?[26] Was the digitizing surface too small, awkwardly positioned, or unstable? Clearly, there are many questions that arise to fully understand how and why errors occur. Note as well that the questions are not simply about the human. They question aspects of the device or the interaction.

A broader perspective in analysing errors may consider the environmental circumstances coincident with the tasks. Were users disadvantaged due to noise, vibration, lighting, or other environmental conditions? Were users walking, talking, driving, or performing a secondary task? Were they adversely influenced by the presence of other people, as might occur in a social or collaborative work setting?

Fig. 2.41 depicts single trials. In an HCI experiment, there are likely dozens, perhaps hundreds, even thousands of such trials. Although generating and critiquing visualizations of interaction is useful and important, the assignment is painstaking for a large number of trials. It would be convenient to have a way to collect together and summarize the pertinent behaviours. This, in itself, is interesting and valuable. Improving the methodology of HCI research can be as important as finding a novel and useful interaction technique. A research contribution, then, is to develop and demonstrate measurements of behaviour that capture subtle aspects of the interaction. One benefit of computers is their willingness to tirelessly collect, store, and summarize data. Rather than examining potentially thousands of visualizations of behaviours, the researcher can examine summary measurements of the behaviours. Of course, this is done across test conditions to find differences. But, as important as

---

[25] An experiment must have at least one independent variable, which in turn must have at least two levels. The levels of the independent variable are the conditions compared. Further details are given in Chapter 5 (Designing HCI Experiments).

[26] There is a subtle but important distinction between a wrong gesture and an ill-formed gesture. A wrong gesture is a *mistake* – the intent was wrong. An ill-formed gesture is a *slip* – the intent was right, but the action was wrong [376, Chap. 5].

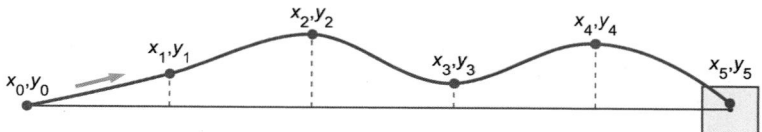

FIGURE 2.42

Digitized cursor path.

finding differences is explaining differences – through measures that capture nuances of the behaviour. Let's examine some candidate measurements for the behaviours in Fig. 2.41.

For the target selection tasks, the cursor wavered from a direct path to the target. There are likely several control issues to consider. Whatever they are, the first challenge is to quantify "wavered." One such measure is movement variability (MV). In Fig. 2.42a, the cursor path is digitized in a series of x-y points.

Capturing these data is relatively straight forward, provided the apparatus embeds software for the interaction under investigation. Given a set of points, as in Fig. 2.42, movement variability is calculated as

$$MV = \sqrt{\frac{\Sigma(y_i - \bar{y})^2}{n-1}}. \tag{2.2}$$

Movement variability can also be calculated in 3D. An example is a virtual reality (VR) setting where a virtual hand moves toward and acquires a target. Does the hand move directly to the target, or does the path vary along the way? An example is shown in Fig. 2.43 where the ideal path – the task axis – appears as a black straight line. The movement path appears in red as solid line segments. For each sample point, a dashed line of minimum length is projected on to the task axis. In the figure, the projected distances are 0, 12.3, 14.1, 22.6, and 7.3.[27] The calculation for movement variability is the same except the projected distances are substituted for the y-data in Eq. (2.2). For the example, MV = 8.39.

In the target selection task in Fig. 2.41b, the cursor entered the target, exited, then re-entered before the final selection. This behaviour might indicate a control problem during final selection, as noted earlier. A measure to capture this is target re-entries (TRE), which is simply the number of times the cursor re-entered the target (having already entered it once). Obviously, a count of zero is preferred. Fig. 2.44 shows an example trial from an experiment investigating target selection on a tablet computer [326, Fig. 9]. The interaction used device tilt to control the cursor. Selection required the cursor to enter and remain within the target for 500 ms. In the example, TRE = 3.

As evident in Fig. 2.44, there are a variety of cursor control issues at play in the interaction. If measures like MV or TRE are high – or, rather, higher in one condition

---

[27] Calculations for 3D projected distances with the help of Rob Teather.

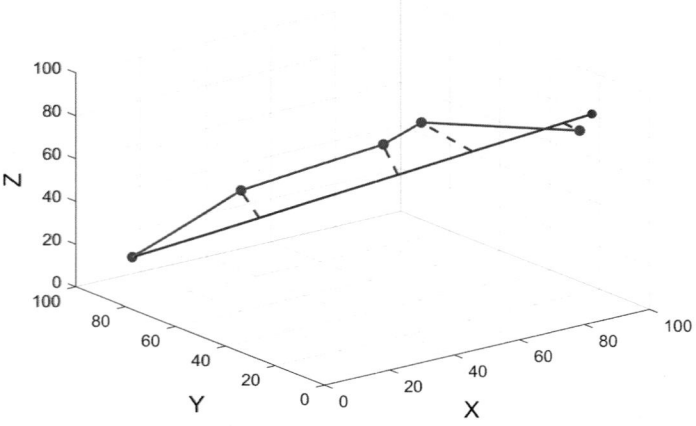

FIGURE 2.43

Digitized path for 3D interaction. See text for discussion.

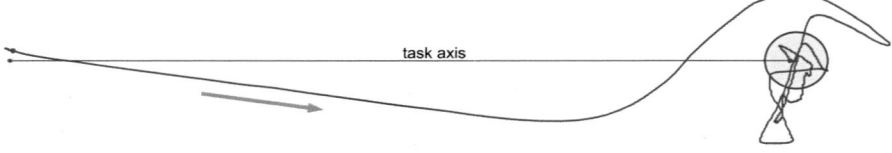

FIGURE 2.44

Digitized cursor path for a target selection task using tilt input on a tablet computer [326, Fig. 9]. There were three target re-entries.

than in another – this is relevant in distinguishing the methods of interaction. The values measured, in view of overt and known properties of the interaction, are important in finding plausible explanations. This is critical for research – to understand why some test conditions work well and others not so well.

Examples of additional measures for target selection tasks are movement offset (MO), movement error (ME), task axis crossings (TAC), movement direction changes (MDC), and orthogonal direction changes (ODC) [314]. These measures, like MV and TRE, are potential dependent variables in an experiment, as elaborated further in Chapter 5 (section 5.5, Dependent Variables). Examples where these measures were used in HCI experiments are found in the work of Long and Gutwin [290], Murthy et al. [362], Keates and Trewin [242], Herring et al. [188], Pandey et al. [386], Wobbrock and Gajos [523], and Pino et al. [401]. See also student exercise 2-9.

Let's turn to the text entry tasks in Fig. 2.41. In part (b) the final text is correct, but only after corrective actions. So, considering only the final text misses important aspects of the interaction. One measure to capture the behaviour in part (b) is keystrokes per character (KSPC) [303,325]. KSPC is both an analytic metric and an empirical measure. Analytic metrics or models are calculations by analysis, without observing actual interaction.[28] Empirical measures are calculated by observing interaction and gathering relevant data. As an empirical measure, KSPC is calculated as the number of keystrokes entered divided by the number of text characters produced. For Fig. 2.41b,

$$\text{KSPC} = \frac{\text{len}(quicz < kly)}{\text{len}(quickly)} = \frac{9}{7} = 1.286 \tag{2.3}$$

Here, we assume input was via a Qwerty keyboard or some other method where one action produces one character. With this, the baseline for error-free input is KSPC = 1.000. The extent KSPC rises above the baseline is a measure of the overhead of making and correcting errors.

Eq. (2.3) is for a single word of entry. KSPC is more useful as an empirical measure of performance if the mean is computed over multiple units of input where each unit is (typically) a phrase of text drawn at random from a collection [321]. Furthermore, calculations across two or more test conditions have potential to expose differences that distinguish the test conditions. For additional examples in the HCI literature where KSPC was used as an empirical measure, see Abdrabou et al. [1], Hassan et al. [181], Jain and Balakrishnan [218], Kuang et al. [258], and Palin et al. [384].[29]

In Fig. 2.41c, the final text was incorrect: "qucehkly" instead of "quickly," At the word-level, this amounts to one error. At the character-level, the situation is different because the input is partly correct. Once again, there is value in going beyond visualizations – to quantify a property of the observed behaviour. Let's study this idea with two questions. First, how many character-level errors are there in the final text ("qucehkly")? This is a bit tricky. A close inspection of the actual vs. desired text suggests three errors. A measure that captures this is the minimum string distance (MSD) [464]. The MSD algorithm recursively traverses the two strings and builds a matrix tabulating differences between the strings. The final entry is an integer equal to the minimum number of primitive operations required to convert one string into the other. For the example, MSD = 3. See Fig. 2.45a. Of course, error-free input yields MSD = 0. MSD rises with the number of errors.

The error rate (ER) for the example is

$$\text{ER} = \frac{\text{MSD}(A, B)}{\max(\text{len}(A), \text{len}(B))} = \frac{3}{8} = 0.125 = 12.5\% \tag{2.4}$$

---

[28] The analytic application of KSPC is discussed in Chapter 7 (section 7.2.4.5, The KLM and Predictive Text Entry).

[29] Jain and Balakrishnan [218] used KSPC but preferred the term *gestures per character* (GPC) since the interaction involved finger gestures on a touchscreen.

```
        q u c e h k l y
      0 1 2 3 4 5 6 7 8        quic--kly
   q  1 0 1 2 3 4 5 6 7        qu-cehkly
   u  2 1 0 1 2 3 4 5 6
   i  3 2 1 1 2 3 4 5 6        quic-kly
   c  4 3 2 1 2 3 4 5 6        qucehkly
   k  5 4 3 2 2 3 3 4 5
   l  6 5 4 3 3 3 4 3 4        qui-ckly
(a) y  7 6 5 4 4 4 4 4 3 ◄ MSD (b) qucehkly
                                   qu-ickly
                                   qucehkly
```

FIGURE 2.45

Character-level errors. (b) MSD matrix and statistic. (b) Alignments.

The denominator uses a max-function to ensure the error rate never exceeds 100%. As with Eq. (2.3) (for KSPC), the calculation in Eq. (2.4) is for a single word. Of course, error rate analyses are most useful if the mean is computed over larger units of input (e.g., phrases) and across multiple test conditions. Examples in the HCI literature where the MSD error rate was used include the work of Castellucci et al. [72], Hedeshy et al. [185], Mutasim et al. [363], Nicolau and Jorge [372], and Tominaga et al. [492].[30]

Developing a comprehensive understanding of what went wrong and why is important in exposing subtle aspects of the interaction – properties that may impede input and compromise the user experience. This leads to our second question: What are the errors? It may be useful to know what errors occurred, as opposed to just counting them. The question posed may not have a simple answer, however. For the text entry example in Fig. 2.41c, there are at least four answers. These are shown in Fig. 2.45b as *alignments*, which reveal the errors – the operations needed to convert one string into the other [319]. There are four possible scenarios, each contrasting the desired (top) and actual (bottom) text. Where characters differ in the top and bottom strings, a *substitution* is shown. Where a dash appears in the top string, an *insertion* is shown. Where a dash appears in the bottom string, a *deletion* is shown. Of course, it is not possible to know what happened simply by looking at the data. Unless there is a particular reason to consider one of the scenarios correct, an approach is to equally weight the possibilities. As more data are collected, patterns may emerge. These analyses are important since they can determine effects such as which keys are error prone for keyed entry or which strokes are frequently misrecognized for gestural entry. Let's turn to part (d) in Fig. 2.41.

---

[30] The MSD error rate is sometimes called the "uncorrected error rate" or the "not-corrected error rate." An additional error rate metric is the corrected error rate, which can be calculated for text entry methods where the baseline KSPC = 1.000 [465].

2.7.6 **Outliers**

One important category of human error is an *outlier*. See Fig. 2.41d. Yes, something went horribly wrong. The target selection task had an early and abrupt end. The text entry task yielded nothing remotely similar to the intended word. These outcomes are so egregious they deserve special attention and classification.

Classifying a trial as an outlier is both a qualitative and quantitative process. Qualitatively, an outlier is an event that is situated away from or classed differently from the main collection of events. The event is different, substantially different. The process involves observation and assessment, rather than measurement. The goal is to uncover and explain what went wrong (rather than simply measure that something deviates from an expected value). Quantitatively, an outlier is a measure that is markedly different in value from the other measures in the sample. Quantitative assessment is straight forward because it is based on numbers. Of course, the criterion is set by the researcher and the criterion is not necessarily quantitative.

In Fig. 2.41d, a measurement criterion for target selection might be "trials where the movement distance was less than one half the expected distance." A criterion for text entry might be "trials where the error rate exceeded 50%." These criteria would capture the example trials. It is important to accompany a quantitative assessment with a qualitative explanation. What went wrong? Classifying trials as outliers demands a plausible account. Earlier, we suggested a few such explanations for the variant behaviours in Fig. 2.41 parts (b) and (c). Similar explanations may hold for outliers.

It is also possible the participant, broadly speaking, is an outlier because of not understanding or lacking skill due to physiological or other reasons. For example, in an eye tracking experiment there may be severe calibration difficulties for a participant wearing eye glasses. Let's continue looking at outliers with a hypothetical example.

2.7.6.1 Example

Fifteen participants are recruited and given a demonstration of a new search engine interface. They use the interface to perform 20 search tasks. The success of each task is accessed on a scale from 0 (*not successful*) to 100 (*very successful*). The scores are summarized. See Fig. 2.46. The mean (not shown) was 66.4 with a standard deviation (*SD*) of 13.4. The mean and standard deviation are the most common statistical measures for central tendency (mean) and variability (*SD*). In a set of normally distributed data, for example, about 68.2% of the values should lie within one *SD* of the mean, 95.4% within two *SD*s of the mean, and 99.7% within three *SD*s of the mean. Let's examine the raw scores in view of the mean and standard deviation.

Scanning the data in Fig. 2.46, most participants had a score close to the mean. However, some scores deviated substantially from the mean. P06 and P11 had low scores, 50 and 25, respectively. P13 had a high score, 85. These are shown in Fig. 2.47 along with a normal distribution curve using the mean and *SD* for this data set. The cited values are outside the range of ± 1 *SD*, which extends from 53.0 to 79.8. Of course, it is reasonable that some values are outside this range. So, perhaps there is

Participant	Score
P01	71
P02	70
P03	69
P04	67
P05	70
P06	50
P07	71
P08	69
P09	71
P10	67
P11	25
P12	67
P13	85
P14	75
P15	69

FIGURE 2.46

Participant scores for the success of search tasks.

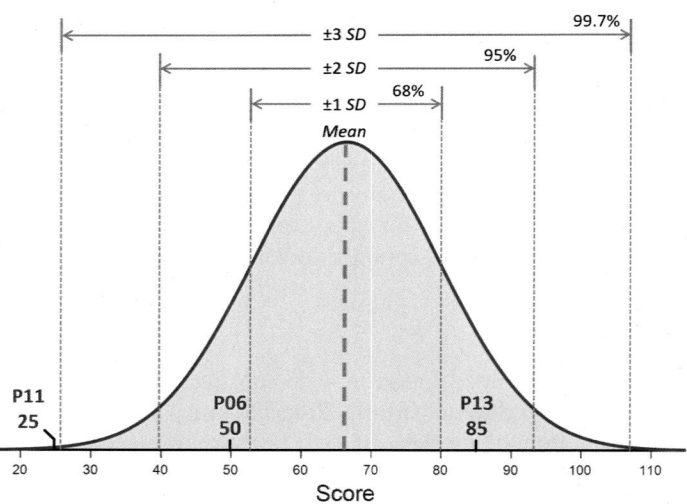

FIGURE 2.47

Normal distribution with mean = 66.4, *SD* = 13.4. Scores are positioned for three participants in Fig. 2.46.

nothing untoward in the data. However, P11's score of 25 is below 26.2, which is three *SD*s below the mean. This value is highly unusual. Perhaps P11's score is an outlier.

At this juncture, excluding the data for P11 is an option. Although the red flag is in the data, which are quantitative, categorizing a data point as an outlier merits a deeper examination. What went wrong? Did P11 understand the instructions? Did the participant complete the tasks or were some interrupted or abandoned along the way? An explanation is needed. Provided there is a clear criterion (quantitative) and a rationale (qualitative), the choice to label some data as outliers and discard them is reasonable. See also student exercise 2-8.

2.7.7 **Accidents**

Human factors researchers often examine human error in relation to commercial or industrial accidents, where the outcome caused substantial damage or loss of life. Such events rarely occur simply because a human operator pressed the wrong button, or committed an interaction error with the system or interface. Usually, the failures are systemic – the result of a confluence of events, many having little to do with a specific human.

To the extent a significant accident is deemed to result from human error, a deeper analysis is often more revealing. Casey's retelling of dozens of such accidents leads to the conclusion that the failures are often *design-induced errors* [66,67]. This point is re-cast as follows: If a human operator mistakenly flicked the wrong switch or entered an incorrect value, and the action resulted in a serious accident, is the failure due to human error? Partly so, perhaps, but clearly the accident was enabled by the design. A design that can lead to catastrophic outcomes purely on the basis of an operator's interaction error is a faulty design. For safety-critical systems, interaction errors by an operator must be considered and accounted for. Such errors are not only possible, they are, in time, likely. Designs of safety-critical systems must accommodate such vagaries in human behaviour.

*****

In this chapter, we examined the human factor in HCI. The topics were organized focusing on the human. Where necessary, examples and context relating to technology were provided. The topics in the next chapter are directed specifically at interaction.

A web site is available as a resource accompanying this book's second edition:

- http://www.yorku.ca/mack/HCIbook2e

Student exercises

2-1 Penfield's motor homunculus in Fig. 2.17 (p. 51) illustrates the area in the cerebral cortex devoted to human responders. The sketch uses solid bars for the cortical area for each responder. The length of each bar is a quantitative indicator. Reverse engineer the motor homunculus to determine the length of each bar. Organize the data in a spreadsheet. The general idea is shown in Fig. 2.48

	A	B	C	D	E	F	G	H
1	Responder	x1	y1	x2	y2	dx	dy	Length
2	Toes	52	153	55	111	-3	42	42.1
3	Ankle	56	106	64	58	-8	48	48.7
4	etc.							

FIGURE 2.48

Student exercise on Penfield's motor homunculus.

FIGURE 2.49

Student exercise on memory recall for key positions on a keyboard.

for the toes and ankles. The shaded cells contain values digitized from an image processing application. The toes bar, for example, extends from (52, 153) to (55, 111). Using the Pythagorean theorem, the length is 42.1 pixels. Of course, the scale and units are arbitrary. Evidently, there is about 15.7% more cortical area devoted to the ankle than to the toes. This is also evident in the figure.

For all responders, digitize the end-points of the corresponding bars and enter the values in a spreadsheet, as in Fig. 2.48. Create a bar chart showing the relative amounts of cortical area for each responder. It might be useful to collect together the values for the leg, arm, and head, with each shown as the sum of contributing responders. Prepare a brief report or slide show presentation on the motor homunculus and the empirical data for the various responders.

2-2 Conduct an experiment on memory recall as follows. Find an old discarded keyboard and remove the key-tops for the letters (Fig. 2.49, left). Using a drawing application, create and print an outline of the letter portion of a Qwerty keyboard (Fig. 2.49, right). (Alternatively, just use 26 small cardboard squares and print a letter on each square.) Find five computer users (participants). Ask each to position the key-tops in the printout. Limit the time for the task to three minutes. Record the number of key-tops correctly positioned. (Suggestion: Photograph the result and do the analysis afterward.)

Then, assess each participant's typing style and typing speed as follows. Open a blank document in an editor and enter the 43-character phrase "the quick brown fox jumps over the lazy dog." On the next line, ask the participant to correctly

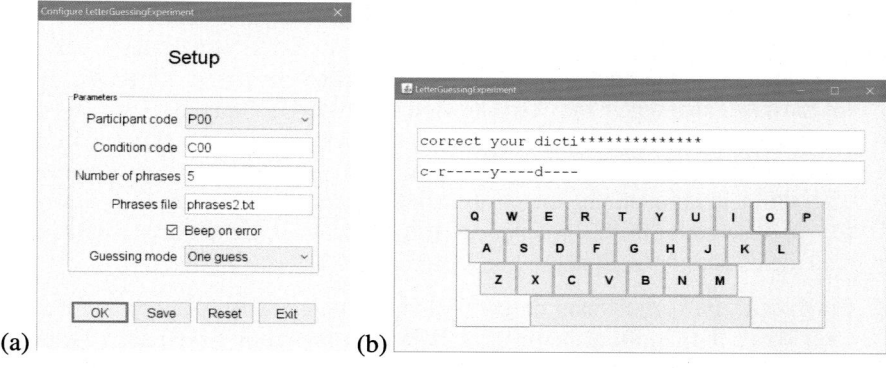

(a)   (b)

FIGURE 2.50

Student exercise using Shannon's letter guessing experiment. (a) Setup dialog. (b) Experiment task.

type the same phrase. Measure and record the time in seconds. Repeat five times. For each participant, observe and record whether the typing style is touch or hunt-and-peck. Enter the data into a spreadsheet. Convert the time to enter the phrase (t, in seconds) to typing speed (s, in words per minute)[31] using

$$s = \frac{(43/5)}{(t/60)}. \tag{2.5}$$

Prepare a brief report or slide show presentation on your findings for "number of key-tops correctly positioned." Consider participants overall as well as by typing speed and by typing style. Discuss other relevant observations.

2-3 Conduct a small experiment on redundancy and entropy in written English, similar to Shannon's letter guessing experiment described earlier. See Fig. 2.30 (p. 64). Use 5-10 participants. For the experiment, use the LetterGuessingExperiment software on this book's web site. Use five trials (phrases) for each participant. The setup dialog and a screen snap of the experiment procedure are shown in Fig. 2.50. Data collection is automated in the software. Analyse the results for the number of letters correctly guessed (redundancy) and the number incorrectly guessed (entropy). Examine the results overall and by participant. Investigate, as well, whether the responses differ according to the position of letters in words and in phrases. Prepare a brief report or slide show presentation on your findings.

---

[31] It has been a convention since about 1905 to standardize the computation of text entry speed in "words per minute," where "word" is defined as five keystrokes [530]. This includes letters, spaces, punctuation, and so on.

2-4 Construct a chart on skilled behaviour showing sensory-motor skill on one axis and mental skill on the other. For both axes, add the label "little" near the origin, and "lots" near the end. An example of a similar chart is given in Fig. 3.67 (p. 154). Add markers in the chart showing at least five computing skills. Position the markers according to the relative emphasis on sensory-motor skill and mental skill in each task. Prepare a brief report or slide show presentation, describing each skill and rationalizing the position of the marker in the chart. For guidance, see the discussion in this chapter on Skilled Behaviour. For further guidance, read the discussion in Chapter 7 on Descriptive Models.

2-5 Conduct a small experiment on gestural input, human performance, and human error using the GraffitiExperiment software on this book's web site. There is both a Windows version and an Android version. Recruit about 10 participants. Divide the participants into two groups and use a different input method for each group. Consider using a mouse and touchpad (Windows) or a finger and stylus (Android). The software uses Graffiti gestures for text entry. For the experiment, the participants are to enter the alphabet 10 times. The setup dialog and a screen snap of the experimental procedure are shown in Fig. 2.51 for Windows (top) and for Android (bottom).

One of the options in the setup dialog is "Phrases file." Use `alphabet.txt`. Set the "Number of phrases" to 10. Leave "Show gesture set" checked. The gestures are viewable in the experiment screen (see Fig. 2.51). Participants may correct errors using the BACKSPACE stroke (←). However, instruct participants not to attempt more than three corrections per symbol.

Data collection is automated. Consult the API for complete details. Analyse the data to reveal the progress over the 10 trials for both groups of participants. Analyse the entry speed (wpm), error rate (%), and keystrokes per character (KSPC). (A "keystroke," here, is a gesture stroke.) Prepare a brief report or slide show presentation on your findings.

2-6 Conduct a small experiment on human reaction time using the ReactionTime-Experiment software on this book's web site. Recruit about 10 participants. The setup dialog is shown in Fig. 2.52. Examples of the experiment procedure were given earlier (see Reaction Time, p. 66). Consider modifying the software in some way, such as using words instead of letters for the visual search task, or using an auditory stimulus instead of a visual stimulus for the simple reaction time task. The modification can serve as a point of comparison (e.g., visual search for words vs. letters, or reaction time to an auditory stimulus vs. a visual stimulus). Prepare a brief report or slide show presentation on your findings.

2-7 Conduct a small experiment on one-key text entry using 5-10 participants. Use the scanning ambiguous keyboard software on this book's web site, SAKExperiment. The setup dialog and a screen snap of the experiment procedure are shown in Fig. 2.53. Prepare a brief report or slide show presentation on your findings.

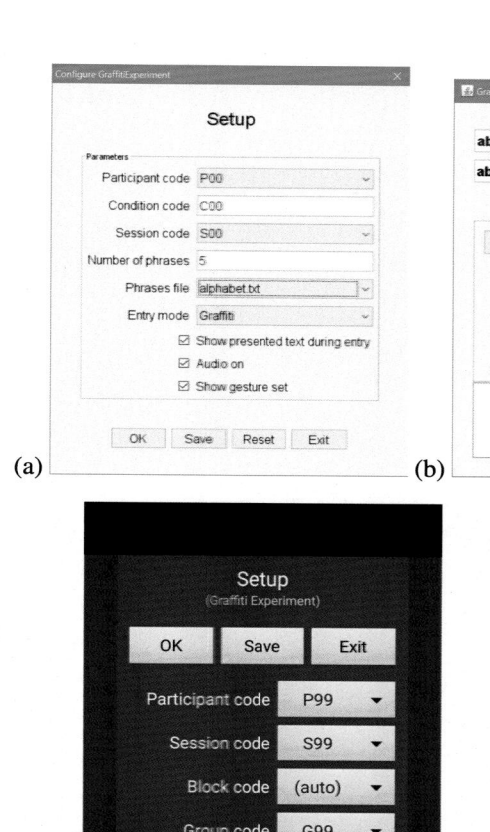
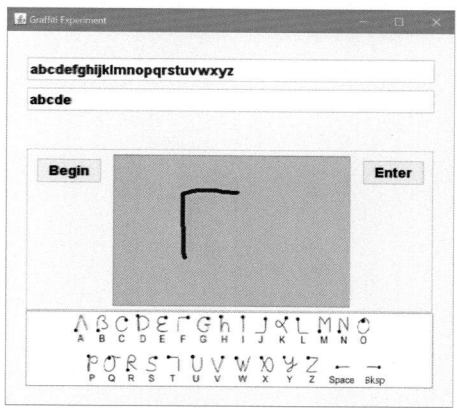
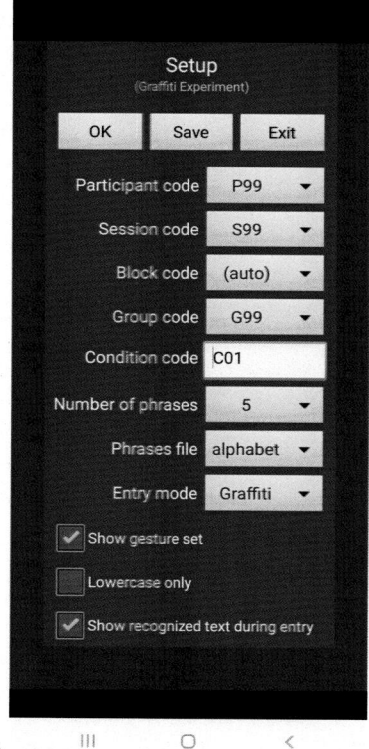
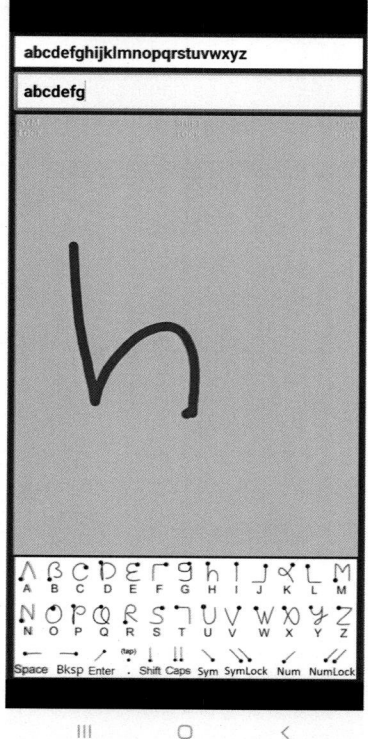

FIGURE 2.51

Student exercise on Graffiti gestural input. (a) Setup dialog (Windows). (b) Experiment task (Windows). (c) Setup dialog (Android). (d) Experiment task (Android).

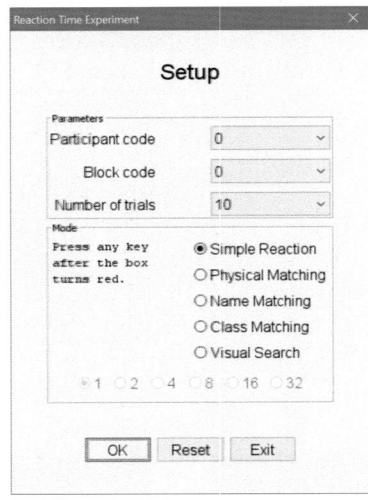

FIGURE 2.52

Student exercise on human reaction time.

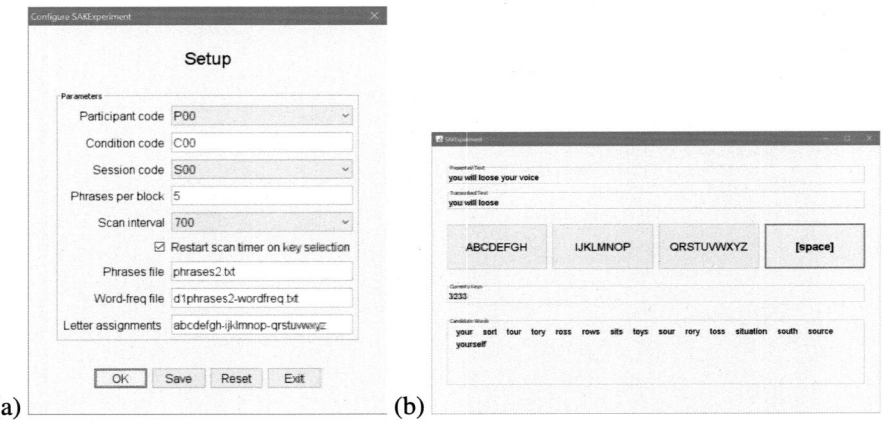

(a)   (b)

FIGURE 2.53

Student exercise using a scanning ambiguous keyboard (SAK). (a) Setup dialog. (b) Experiment task.

2-8 The following 48 data points are the x-axis selection coordinates in pixels for a series of trials in an experiment on target selection. The data are on this book's web site in the file StudentExercise2-8.txt. The target was 16 pixels wide, centred at $x = 0$.

-6, 5, 1, 7, 4, 10, -4, 0, -15, 16, -4, 9
-3, 2, -1, 5, -5, 2, 6, -34, 0, 4, 1, -1
-38, 2, 0, 1, -16, 0, 1, 0, -2, -30, -67, 3
-2, 11, -4, 4, 0, -45, -7, 3, -4, 3, 0, -2

Analyse the data to examine if there are any outliers in the set. Prepare a brief report or slide show presentation on your findings. Include an appropriate chart showing the distribution of the selection coordinates.

2-9 The following data are from a target selection task:

From (x/y):	765, 592.5
To (x/y):	640, 126
Width:	100
Px:	762, 764, 766, 766, 767, 768, 769, …
Py:	626, 628, 629, 630, 631, 631, 631, …

The task was to move a cursor from the "From" coordinate to the "To" coordinate and select a circular target of "Width" diameter centred at the "To" coordinate. The actual cursor path is given in a series of points with coordinates P_x and P_y. The complete path was digitized in a series of 224 points. The full data set is on this book's web site in the file StudentExercise2-9.txt. Analyse the data to compute the movement variability (MV) and number of target re-entries (TRE). The calculations can be done either in a spreadsheet or using a programming language of your choice. Include additional measures that might reveal performance issues in the interaction. Prepare a brief report or slide show presentation on your findings. Include visual aids, as appropriate.

Interaction elements

Interaction occurs when a human performs a task using computing technology. The task is often goal-oriented, such as sending e-mail, cropping a photo, warming food in a microwave oven, or entering a destination in a car's GPS tracking system. But, sometimes there is no specific goal. Just reading the morning news, browsing the web, or chatting with friends on a social networking site is sufficient. If the user is engaged in any activity with computing technology, interaction is taking place.

In this chapter, elements of human-computer interaction are examined. The topics do not comprehensively span the field of HCI. Instead, the topics are selective and focus on low-level aspects of interaction. Most of the tasks are in the cognitive band in Newell's time scale of human action in Chapter 2 (p. 33). The interactions involve deliberate acts ($\sim$ 100 ms), operations ($\sim$ 1 s), and unit tasks ($\sim$ 10 s). With duration from 100 ms to 10 s, the tasks are well suited to empirical research. Indeed, most experimental research in HCI focuses on tasks of this sort. Due to the brevity of the tasks, extraneous behaviours are easy to control. Thus, experiments with high *internal validity* are possible. (Internal validity is discussed in the next chapter.) Although it is possible to experimentally study higher-level tasks – those in the rational band and social band – difficulties arise due to the duration of the tasks. Operations in these bands take from minutes to months (see Fig. 2.1, p. 33), and therefore include extraneous behaviours, such a pausing, task switching, pondering, decision-making, and secondary and unrelated tasks. Although such behaviours are germane to the HCI experience, they present challenges for experimental study. So, we focus on interaction elements in the cognitive band.

At a stripped-down level, interaction involves humans using their sensors and responders to monitor and control devices, machines, or systems that include computing technology. We saw a typical human factors view of this in Chapter 2 (see Fig. 2.2, p. 34). The internal states of the human and machine interact in a closed-loop system through controls and displays (the machine side) and motor-sensory behaviours (the human side). By convention, the terms "input" and "output" are with respect to the machine. So, inputs, or input devices, are inputs to the machine that are controlled or manipulated by human outputs. Most commonly, human outputs are limbs – the fingers, hands, arms, legs, feet – but speech, articulated sounds, eye motions, blinks, winks, head nods, breath, brain signals, and so on, can also serve as human outputs. Some of these communication channels are extremely important for users with special needs, for example.

Human-Computer Interaction. https://doi.org/10.1016/B978-0-44-314096-9.00009-9

There is a long history of human factors research following a classical "knobs and dials" view [73,495]. Using responders, the human operator manipulates knobs (controls), perhaps with a goal in mind, while engaging senses to perceive the status of a system on dials (displays).[1] This work is important in HCI too. Relevant examples are numerous, particularly when things go wrong: terminating an application when minimizing a window, putting food in a microwave and heating it for three seconds instead of three minutes, or putting a smartphone in sleep mode when grabbing a screenshot. These are all knobs and dials issues, and they perplex and frustrate us, even today.

We begin with the basic interactions between humans and computers (the knobs or controls). With the arrival of the graphical user interface in the 1980s, the most common interactions involve pointing and selecting, perhaps with a mouse. Setups are more varied today with the proliferation of smartphones and tablets, and environments such as gaming, virtual reality, eye tracking, and even brain-computer interfaces (BCI).

3.1 Techniques

Many interactions on computer systems exhibit a pattern of "forming an intent" followed by "confirming an intent." These expressions nicely map into the more common yet narrower terms "pointing" (forming an intent) and "selecting" (confirming an intent). Indeed, throughout the history of HCI, devising novel point-select methods and evaluating them in user studies is a common research theme. This research flourished after the introduction of the graphical user interface (GUI) and the computer mouse in the early 1980s, as detailed in Chapter 1.[2] And it continues to flourish today. The pre-GUI equivalent for command-line input is typing a command (forming an intent) followed by pressing ENTER on the system's keyboard (confirming an intent).

The possibilities for point-select operations are vast. Fig. 3.1 provides a coarse summary while opening the door for deeper examination. In the table, an SOI is a "selectable object of interest," such as a button, icon, or other target of interest.

The most common point-select methods fall within the first three rows of Fig. 3.1. Other methods are included to acknowledge the breadth of possibilities.

It is worth noting that form-confirm (FC) actions exist in a hierarchy. At a high-level, an FC action might be a task such as booking a hotel online. This involves considering alternative hotels (forming an intent) and then narrowing in on or choosing a hotel to book (confirming an intent). The task contains lower-level FC operations,

---

[1] The term "display," as used here, is any form of computer output. This includes visual displays as well as auditory displays and tactile displays.

[2] We again acknowledge the important earlier research on point-select operations using a mouse by English, Engelbart, and Berman in 1967 [115] and Card, English, and Burr in 1978 [60].

Input Method	Pointing (Forming an Intent)	Selecting (Confirming an Intent)
Mouse (indirect)	Position a tracking symbol inside SOI	Press and release a button on the device
Touchpad (indirect)	Position a tracking symbol inside SOI	Finger tap on touchpad or press down
Finger on display (direct)	Move finger to SOI	Brief touch followed by lift on SOI
Eye gaze	Look at SOI	Gaze dwell on SOI for a pre-defined period
Keyboard	Use TAB or SHIFT-TAB to move "focus" to SOI	Press and release ENTER
Single-switch scanning	Wait for scanning highlight to reach SOI	Activate switch when highlight is on SOI

FIGURE 3.1

Example methods for pointing and selecting. Note: SOI = selectable object of interest.

such as viewing and confirming rooms options (e.g., "breakfast included"), entering email or phone contact information, or entering a credit card number. And each button that is clicked or character that is entered requires an even lower-level FC action, such as positioning a finger on a key, then pressing the key. This multi-level view of FC actions potentially maps into Newell's time scale of human action presented in Chapter 2 (p. 33).

The most common evaluation techniques for point-selection operations follow a Fitts' law paradigm, which we present in Chapter 7.

3.1.1 Pointing

The archetype device for pointing is the computer mouse. Pointing involves manoeuvring the device to control the position of a pointer or tracking symbol (e.g., ⟍, ✛, 🖑) on a display. The interaction is "indirect" because a tracking symbol is required as an intermediary, connecting the device movement or position to the selectable object of interest.

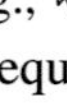

Besides the mouse, there are other indirect pointing devices and these often use different methods for pointing and selecting. As a general rule, if a cursor or pointer is involved, the interaction is indirect. Laptop computers typically include a touchpad, also an indirect pointing device. The touchpad is built-in: Pointing occurs by moving a finger on the touchpad surface.

For all indirect pointing techniques, it is important to consider the relationship between interaction with the input device – the control – and movement of the on-screen tracking symbol – the display. Such control-display relationships are presented in greater detail later in this chapter.

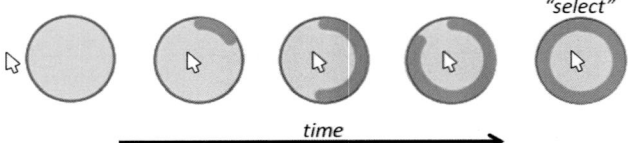

FIGURE 3.2

Dwell-time selection feedback.

For direct pointing, there is no need for a tracking symbol or cursor. The most obvious example is finger input on touchscreen devices such as tablets or smartphones. Another example is eye tracking input where the eye looks directly at an object and it is selected, typically using dwell-time selection.

3.1.2 Selecting

Selection typically occurs by pressing and releasing a button on or near a device, such as a mouse, touchpad, or game controller. For touchpads, there are at least three selection methods: (i) press a button situated near the touchpad, (ii) lift the finger from the touchpad and quickly tap on the surface, or (iii) keep the finger intact on the surface while pressing firmly down. The emergence of the latter technique is chronicled in Chapter 7 (see Fig. 7.14, p. 307).

If a button is not available, dwell-time selection is possible. The user acquires an object for a pre-determined time interval whereupon selection occurs. In this case, feedback is needed to inform the user of the dwell progress. See Fig. 3.2.

3.1.3 Point-select improvements

Many ideas have been proposed and evaluated for improving the point-select experience. These often involve changing properties of the interaction in real time, during the pointing or selecting actions. The goal is to make point-select operations faster or more accurate.

3.1.3.1 Spatial hysteresis

One possibility to improve selection is *spatial hysteresis*. Using spatial hysteresis, a larger virtual target is added around a target. The mouse pointer is deemed to enter the target when it enters the "real target." The pointer leaves the target when it exits the hysteresis zone. Thus, a target can be selected if the pointer enters the target, then leaves the target but remains in the hysteresis zone. See Fig. 3.3.

Spatial hysteresis was used by Hansen et al. [175] in a study on target selection using eye tracking within a head-mounted display (HMD). The spatial hysteresis zone was $2\times$ the nominal target width. When the gaze point entered the target, the target doubled in size, while visually remaining constant. A variation of spatial hysteresis, also for eye tracking, is Elmadjian and Morimoto's GazeBar [113]. A target in the

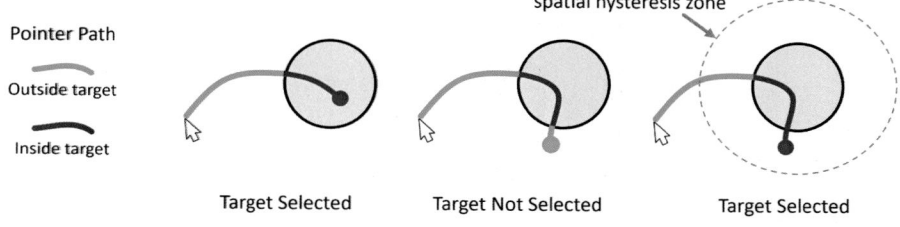

FIGURE 3.3

Spatial hysteresis. On the right, spatial hysteresis is used. The target is selected since the pointer enters the target, then leaves the target but remains in the spatial hysteresis zone. Note: The dashed line showing the spatial hysteresis zone does not appear on the display.

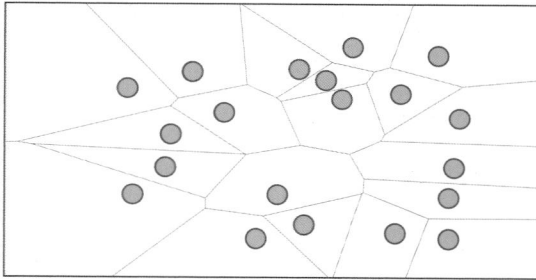

FIGURE 3.4

Target size expands to an effective size determined by Voronoi regions.

GazeBar is only acquired when the gaze point enters a threshold region inside the target. The inner threshold region is smaller than the actual target. The target continues to be acquired until the gaze point exists an outer threshold which delimits the actual target. The goal with GazeBar is to mitigate the Midas touch problem, which is common in eye tracking systems.

Spatial hysteresis is just one example of "expanding targets" – techniques that increase the actual or apparent size of targets to improve selection [350,545]. Another example is bubble cursor.

3.1.3.2 Bubble cursor

If there are many targets closely spaced, spatial hysteresis is of limited value, since the hysteresis zone may overlap other targets. Grossman and Balakrishnan's *bubble cursor* technique [162] respects neighbouring targets by using the Voronoi region around each target as the effective size of the target. See Fig. 3.4. This increases each target's size to the maximum possible extent without encroaching on neighbouring targets. They found a 28% reduction in selection error rates, from 3.2% for a standard point cursor to 2.3% using the bubble cursor.

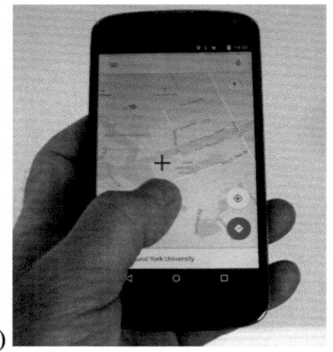 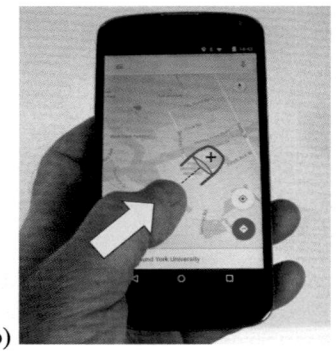

(a)   (b)

FIGURE 3.5

Improving touch selection. (a) Concept image for Potter et al.'s offset cursor introduced in 1988. (b) ExtendedThumb is offset from the real thumb in the direction of thumb movement (from [268, Fig. 1b]).

The bubble cursor technique also extends to targets in 3D virtual environments [100,496]. In this case, the effective volume of each target is maximized in consideration of neighbouring targets.

3.1.3.3 Offset cursor

For touch input, finger occlusion is problem for target selection. A selection enhancement for touchscreens is the *offset cursor*, originally presented by Potter et al. [405] at the ACM SIGCHI conference in 1988.[3] See Fig. 3.5a. When the finger contacts the display surface, a crosshair cursor appears just above the fingertip. The user manoeuvres her finger along the display surface, positions the crosshair within a selectable target, then lifts the finger to select the target. Potter et al. [405] called the method *take-off* selection. They described an experimental evaluation to compare take-off selection with two alternate methods, first-contact, where selection occurs immediately when the contact point enters a target, and land-on, where selection occurs only if the initial contact point is on a target. Of the three methods, they found take-off most accurate, but first-contact fastest. The main point here is that Potter and colleagues choose a methodology that was both empirical and experimental to present and evaluate a novel interaction method and to compare it with alternatives.

A variation of Potter et al.'s offset cursor is ExtendedThumb proposed by Lai and Zhang [268]. ExtendedThumb is an offset cursor that appears as virtual thumb extending from the user's real thumb (or finger) as it moves on the display surface. An interesting feature is that the virtual thumb appears offset from the real thumb in the

---

[3] Unfortunately, an image of the offset cursor was not included in the cited paper, or in related papers. However, a video by Sears and Shneiderman from 1991 shows the offset cursor (search YouTube using "1991 touchscreenkeyboards.mpg").

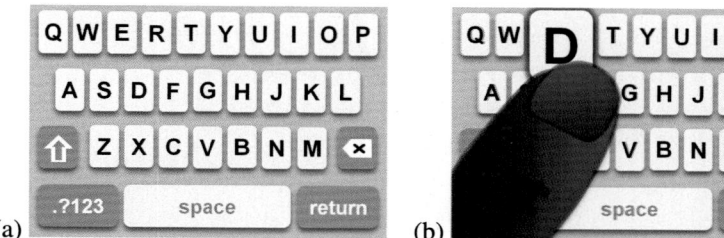

(a)   (b)

FIGURE 3.6

Enhancing touchscreen selection. (a) Smartphone soft keyboard. (b) User finger on D-key with offset animation. Selection occurs on finger lift.

direction of thumb movement. See Fig. 3.5b. Selection occurs at the highlighted red cross in the virtual thumb when the real thumb is lifted off the display surface. In an empirical test, ExtendedThumb was slower but more accurate compared to direct touch. However, there were benefits in the user experience. ExtendedThumb significantly out-performed direct touch in perceived ease of use, perceived effectiveness, and overall satisfaction.

There are other variations of the offset cursor. The most common is on soft keyboards with smartphones and tablets. Fig. 3.6a shows a portion of the keyboard, including the D-key. In Fig. 3.6b, the user's finger is in contact with the D-key. The key is occluded. However, an offset animation alerts the user that the D-key is tentatively selected. The user may slide her finger to another key or lift the finger to enter D.

3.1.4 Alternate inputs

While most user input to computers is through touch (e.g., on a tablet surface) or a device (e.g., a mouse or stylus), alternate inputs are common in certain contexts, such as accessible computing.

3.1.4.1 Skin surface electrical signals

In accessible computing, users often have insufficient motor control to operate a conventional computer input device. One possibility for input is surface electromyography (sEMG) which uses electrical signals produced by muscles measured at the surface of the skin. In O'Meara's study [378], participants had electrodes attached to their forearm and used strategies to generate signals for computer control. See Fig. 3.7.

During training, participants observed the sEMG signals on an oscilloscope while practising different hand or wrist movements. They self-selected movements that worked best for them. These included flexing their wrist, making a fist, or raising one or two fingers. The signals generated were used as input commands to control the movement and direction of a cursor in a Fitts' law target selection task. Selection

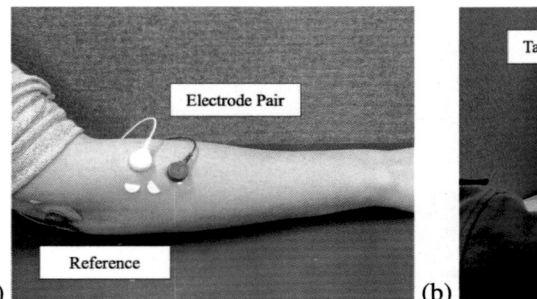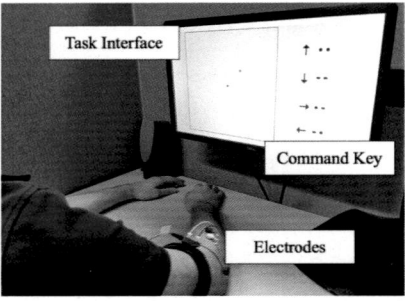

FIGURE 3.7

Surface electromyography (sEMG) interface [378]. (a) Electrode placement. (b) Experiment setup (photos courtesy of Sarah O'Meara).

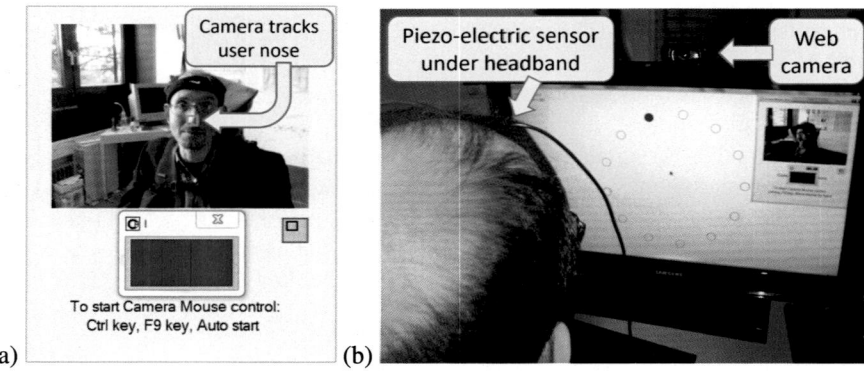

FIGURE 3.8

Interaction using Camera Mouse + ClickerAID [331]. (a) Camera Mouse setup. (b) ClickerAID setup.

was performed using dwell-time selection – maintaining the cursor inside the target for one second. In a user study, results for throughput reached 3.6 bits/s. For users without arm control, a different strategy is needed.

Magee et al. [331] used an sEMG setup on a user's forehead. They used the Camera Mouse + ClickerAID system which uses a web camera to track face movement and control the position of a cursor (Fig. 3.8a). Click selections occurred though an sEMG signal received from a piezo-electric sensor. The sensor was positioned on the user's forehead under a headband and was activated by raising the eye brow (Fig. 3.8b). The setup was used in a case study with one disabled participant with the neuromuscular disease Friedreich's Ataxia. In a Fitts' law target selection task, the participant had considerable difficulty controlling the cursor position and achieved a throughput of only 0.45 bits/s.

It is important to distinguish the use of body sensors for computer input control (see above) from the more traditional application of monitoring a person's physiology. As an example of the latter, Mandryk et al. [338] used sensors to measure emotional responses while participants played NHL 2003 by EA Sports. Two sensors were positioned on the face, one for smiling and one for frowning. Additional sensors monitored participants' galvanic skin response (GSK) and heart rate via electrocardiography (EKG) electrodes. The data were fed to a fuzzy logic system which calculated participants' emotional state in a 2D valence-arousal space according to Russell's circumplex model of affect (CMA) [424]. (The CMA is discussed in Chapter 7.) The user study included three play conditions, with participants playing against either a co-located friend, a co-located stranger, or the computer. Their setup was able to significantly distinguish the emotional state of players across the play conditions, with strong correlations between the measured and subjective assessments.

3.1.4.2 Brain signals

Brain signals, or brain-computer interfaces (BCI), have been studied for use in accessible computing and other applications, such as gaming. Hou et al. [200] tested one such commercial device, NextMind,[4] a head-mounted sensor with nine comb-shaped dry electrodes to pick up electroencephalogram (EEG) signals and send them to a host computer. Unlike many BCI setups, NextMind is inexpensive and relatively easy to setup for non-professionals, such as gamers or home users [200]. See Fig. 3.9.

Like camera-based eye tracking, a brain-computer interface (BCI) may provide information on where a user is looking, and thereby enable gaze interaction. Thus, BCI is a potential alternative to camera-based eye tracking, which is sensitive to ambient light and other sources of interference.

Wong [527] describes a BCI system tested with participants wearing a skullcap with 31 sensors detecting brain signals. Three participants with paralysis in all four limbs were able to control the movement of a wheelchair using motor imagery. To move right, the participants imagined moving both arms. To move left, they imagined moving both legs. Accuracy was a challenge, however. During the first 10 training sessions, "Person 1," only delivered correctly interpreted commands 37% of the time. Accuracy increased to 87% for the last 10 sessions.

3.1.4.3 Fogscreen interaction

An example of direct pointing using the finger is an interactive fogscreen. A fogscreen is an immaterial mid-air display formed from a flowing sheet of light-scattered particles (like fog). Users can reach into or even walk through the display. See Fig. 3.10a.

In one fogscreen setup [412,433], interaction was added using a Microsoft Kinect gesture detecting sensor. See Fig. 3.10b. There is no cursor: The user "touches" the

---

[4] https://www.next-mind.com/.

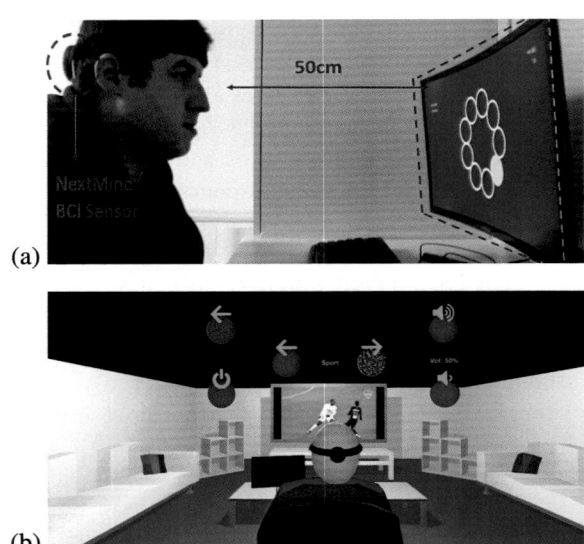

FIGURE 3.9

NextMind BCI system [200]. (a) Experiment setup. (b) Simulation for TV control.

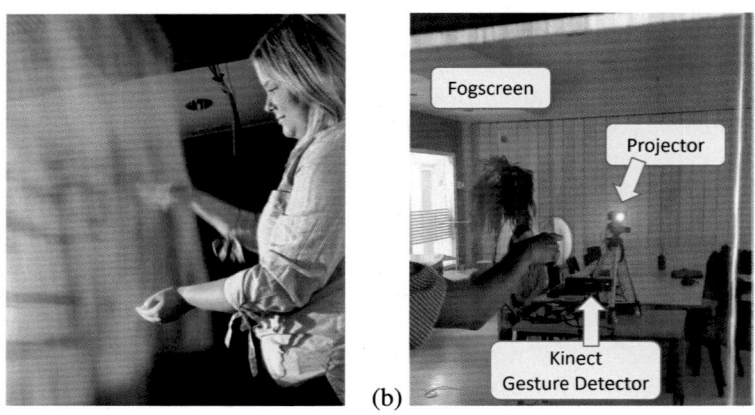

FIGURE 3.10

Fogscreen interaction [412]. (a) Reaching into the fog display. (b) User interaction is possible using a Kinect gesture detecting sensor. (photos used with permission).

display directly. The system was evaluated for target selection using the GoFitts software. An example target is seen in the figure. Two methods of selection were tested: mid-air tapping (moving a finger into and out of a target) or dwell-time selection (holding a finger inside a target for one second). Since, the user's actions are not on a

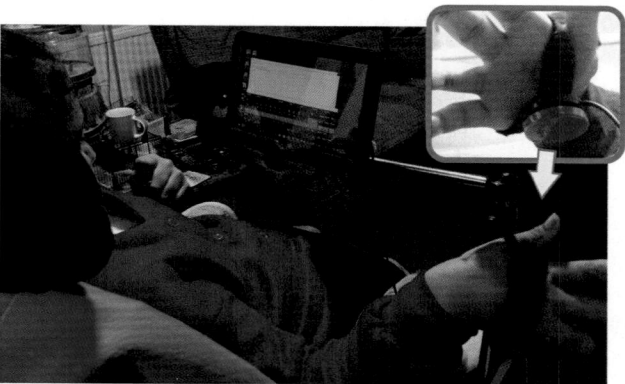

FIGURE 3.11

Single-switch scanning with an input button in the palm of the user's hand.

hard surface, feedback is needed. This occurred through a graphic animation depicting the progression of the dwell interval, as depicted earlier in Fig. 3.2. Throughput was 2.18 bits/s for tap selection and 1.43 bits/s for dwell-time selection.

3.1.5 Single-switch scanning

A common method of interaction in accessible computing is *scanning*, often called *single-switch scanning*. The method is of particular interest, and sometimes essential, for users with a motor control limitation. Instead of two hands operating a keyboard and pointing device, the user operates a single input switch or button by whatever means are available. Fig. 3.11 shows interaction using single-switch scanning with the user operating a button mounted in the palm of their hand. Other input possibilities include eye blinks, a foot switch, breath, head nods, or an sEMG sensor, as noted earlier.

A common application for single-switch scanning is text entry using a virtual or on-screen keyboard. Keys are highlighted in sequence ("scanned") with the input switch activated when the key bearing the desired letter is highlighted. The idea is shown in Fig. 3.12 for linear scanning. The method is clearly slow, as numerous scanning intervals – "scansteps" – are needed to reach letters beyond the first few in the alphabet. The timing interval will vary according to a user's capabilities. Rates in the range of 700 ms to 1200 ms are common for testing.

To speed-up entry, a two-tier scanning pattern is often used, such as row-column scanning. Fig. 3.13 shows an example with letters arranged alphabetically in a rectangle. Scanning proceeds row by row. When the row bearing the desired character is highlighted, it is selected. Scanning then proceeds within the row, column by column. When the key bearing the desired character is highlighted, it is selected. The character is appended to the text message with scanning starting anew at the top row.

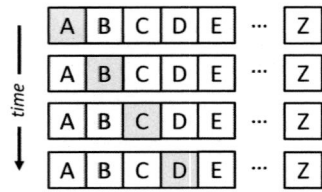

FIGURE 3.12

Linear scanning. Virtual keys are highlighted in a linear scanning sequence according to a timer. Selection occurs by activating a switch when the highlight reaches the key bearing the desired character.

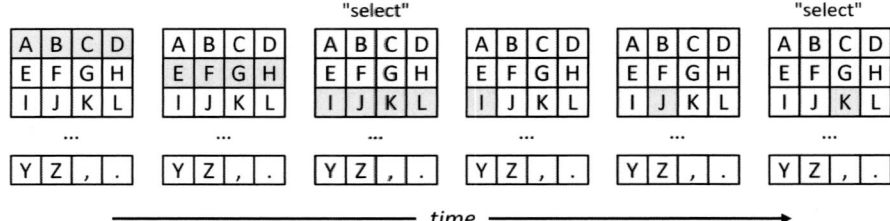

FIGURE 3.13

Row-column scanning. Input of "K". The 1st selection is for row "I J K L", the 2nd selection is for column "K" within the row.

Scanning is cyclic, so if the user misses an opportunity, selection can occur on the next pass. Note that two-tier scanning, although potentially faster, is more physically demanding since two selections are required for each character generated.

An example scanning keyboard is the On-Screen Keyboard (OSK) embedded in Microsoft Windows. See Fig. 3.14. This is a full-feature Qwerty keyboard, providing access to all the capabilities of a conventional desktop keyboard. Input by default uses the SPACEBAR on the system's physical keyboard, although other input options are possible. Instead of row-column scanning, OSK uses three-tier row-group-key scanning. Scanning proceeds row-by-row, then by groups in a selected row, then by keys in the selected group. In the figure, the user is about to enter "r" which is in the second group in the third row. The intended phrase is "hello world."

Note in Fig. 3.14 that OSK includes word prediction along the top row, which is included in the scanning sequence. For the example, instead of entering "r", the user could select along the top row and choose "world" with immediate effect. Clearly, selecting "world" at this juncture reduces the number of scansteps and creates a performance advantage. This is shown in Fig. 3.15 which contrasts the letter-by-letter interaction with interaction using word prediction. The difference is dramatic: 41 scansteps for letter-by-letter interaction versus just 18 scansteps if word prediction is used.

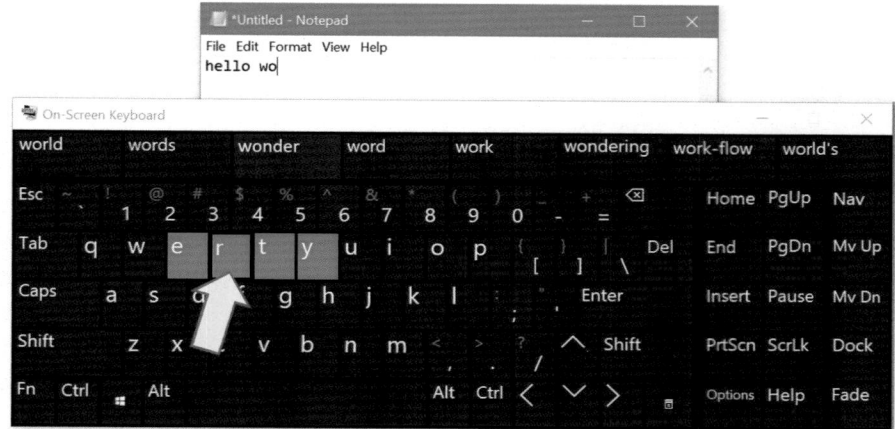

FIGURE 3.14

Entry of "hello world" on Microsoft's On-Screen Keyboard (OSK) in single-switch scanning mode. The keyboard uses three-tier row-group-key scanning. The user is about to enter "r" in "hello world."

	Letter	Input	Scansteps
	w	..RG..w	7
	o	..R..G..o	9
(a)	r	..R.G.r	7
	l	...R..G..l	10
	d	...R.G.d	8
		Total:	41

	Letter	Input	Scansteps
	w	..RG..w	7
(b)	o	..R..G..o	9
	rld	RW	2
		Total:	18

FIGURE 3.15

Analysis for input of "world" on Microsoft On-Screen Keyboard using scanning. (a) Letter by letter. (b) With word prediction. Under Input, "." is a passive scanstep, "R" is a row selection, "G" is a group selection, "W" is a word selection, and a lowercase character is a letter selection.

The analysis in Fig. 3.15 can assist more broadly in considering alternative designs using "scansteps per character" (SPC) as an analytic metric. For "world" with 5 characters, SPC is $\frac{41}{5} = 8.2$ using letter-by-letter interaction and $\frac{18}{5} = 3.6$ using word prediction.

Comparing the interactions for a single word, while interesting, is of limited value. With the addition of a corpus in the form of a letter-frequency list or a word-frequency list, the calculations in Fig. 3.15 can generalize to a language (e.g., English) with a weighted average computed over the entire corpus. The result is an overall average SPC for English text entry using a particular keyboard and interaction

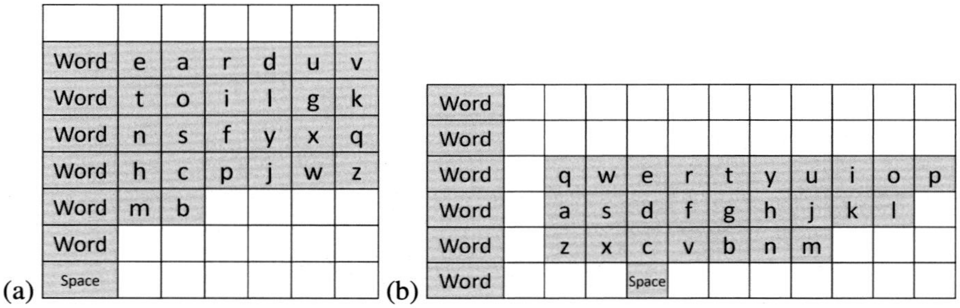

(a)

Word	e	a	r	d	u	v
Word	t	o	i	l	g	k
Word	n	s	f	y	x	q
Word	h	c	p	j	w	z
Word	m	b				
Word						
Space						

(b)

Word										
Word										
Word	q	w	e	r	t	y	u	i	o	p
Word	a	s	d	f	g	h	j	k	l	
Word	z	x	c	v	b	n	m			
Word		Space								

FIGURE 3.16

WiViK scanning keyboard. (a) Optimized letter arrangement. (b) Qwerty letter arrangement. Images show the letter arrangements and position of words for word prediction (from [304]). Blank keys are for other inputs.

strategy [304]. Using a letter-frequency list, SPC is calculated as

$$SPC = \frac{\Sigma(S_c \times F_c)}{\Sigma(N_c \times F_c)} \qquad (3.1)$$

where

- S_c is the number of scansteps to enter character c
- F_c is the frequency count for character c in the corpus
- $N_c = 1$ (the number of characters in c)

The calculations leading to SPC are similar to those for calculating KSPC (keystrokes per characters) as an analytic metric for physical keyboards, such the ambiguous phone keypad [303,325]. Although $N_c = 1$ in Eq. (3.1), if a word-frequency list is used, the calculations can proceed at the word-level, substituting w (word) for c (character) in the formula. In this case, N_w is the number of characters in the word +1 for a space following the word.

Another way to speed-up entry, is to position high-frequency letters, such as "e", "a", or "t", for English, near the beginning of the scanning sequence. This reduces the number of scansteps to reach letters. One example is Shein et al.'s WiViK keyboard [445]. Fig. 3.16 shows the WiViK letter arrangement and the position of words for word prediction. The user can choose between an optimized letter arrangement or a Qwerty letter arrangement. For the optimized arrangement, common letters are at the top-left, thus reducing the number of scansteps to reach them. The result is an overall performance advantage for English text entry: SPC = 2.64 compared to SPC = 3.80 for the Qwerty letter arrangement [304].[5]

---

[5] These metrics for SPC assume word prediction is used and with the intended word selected at the earliest opportunity [304].

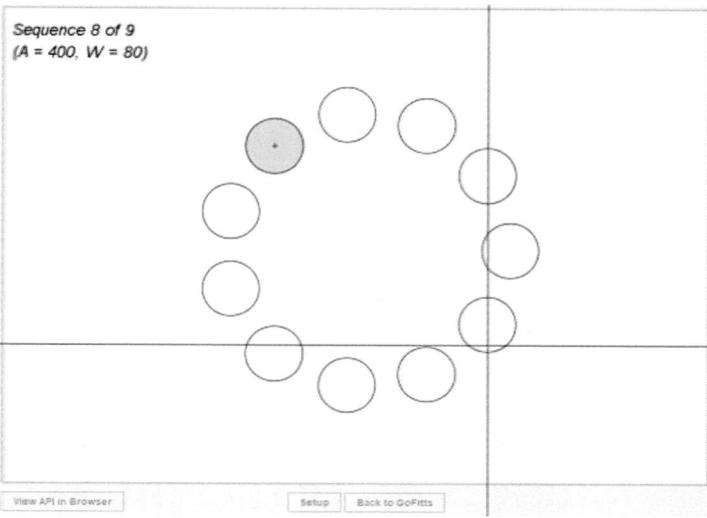

FIGURE 3.17

TBS[3] (two-bar single-switch scanning) [408]. Single-switch selections control the movement of horizontal and vertical bars. The intersection marks the location for target selection.

There are other possibilities to model and potentially improve scanning keyboards
for text entry. Some alternative designs with and without word prediction are implemented in the ScanningKeyboardExperiment software available on this book's web
site. The app also supports custom designs.

Generally, a low SPC implies efficient input. MacKenzie and Felzer's scanning
ambiguous keyboard (SAK), for example, has SPC = 1.56 for English text entry
[311, Figure 6]. One implementation is BlinkWrite, which uses eye blinks for the
input switch (see Chapter 2, Fig. 2.26, p. 59).

Scansteps per character (SPC), although useful as a point of comparison, must
be viewed in a larger picture that also considers the cognitive and physical demands
on the user. Other design issues for scanning keyboards abound [32,252,279,340,
434,472,480]. See as well the letter arrangement in Fig. 5.16a (p. 234) and student
exercise 3-1 at the end of this chapter.

Single-switch scanning can also serve as an interaction method for general purpose target selection. Raynal and MacKenzie [408] describe TBS[3], two-bar single-
switch scanning, a technique using horizontal and vertical lines that traverse a display
with their intersection marking a point for selection. The method is slow but interaction does not require operating a pointing device such as a mouse or touchpad.
Input is through a single input switch. In the empirical evaluation, participants used
the SPACEBAR on the system's physical keyboard to select targets in a 2D Fitts' law

target selection task. See Fig. 3.17. Fitts' law is presented in greater detail in Chapter 7.

3.1.6 Gesture input

Gestures are movements to communicate. They are germane to human communication, whether through eye, face, or head movement during conversation or through finger, hand or arm motions to provide context or emphasis.

Described so broadly (*movements to communicate*), gestures encompass all human interactions with computers.[6] Even in the 1960s, Sutherland's Sketchpad (Chapter 1) used a light pen for gesture input. The light beam was moved across a display. The movement communicated the user's intent, such as creating or editing graphical shapes, terminating commands, and so on.

An example from 1980 of gestures is the "Put That There" demonstration by Bolt [35]. The user makes mid-air gestures, moving their hand to point to objects or locations on a large display and then issues voice commands. Bolt's system was a room with a large projection screen and a instrumented chair for the user. The system included voice recognition for simple commands and a Polhemus 6 DOF tracker mounted on the user's hand or wrist. It was, perhaps, the first VR "Cave." An "x" cursor appeared on the display as visual feedback for pointing. Because of the cursor, Bolt's system is an example of indirect pointing; the cursor is a intermediary between the user's hand position and a position on the display. But, the pointing movements are gestures, specifying a location or object as the target for a voice command.

Often, the intent or purpose of a gesture is a matter of the gesture location and shape. Classic non-computing examples are the marks a copy editor puts on a document. Kurtenbach and Buxton's GEdit extended the idea to gestures for graphics editing using a tablet and stylus [264]. See Fig. 3.18. The operations, such as copying or deleting objects, normally require the use of both hands with a combination of keyboard and mouse or stylus input. Notably, GEdit gestures only require stylus input and so only involve the use of one hand.

For text entry, there are Goldberg and Richardson's Unistrokes for English letters [148]. Each letter is formed by a single gesture stroke; thus, the "segmentation problem" is avoided and eyes-free input is possible.[7] A well known commercial variant is Graffiti, which was the primary text entry method on the Palm Pilot personal digital assistant (PDA), introduced in 1997 by US Robotics. Fig. 3.19 shows four Graffiti gestures, each with a shape corresponding to a letter. The gestures are made with a finger or stylus on a digitizing surface [310]. Although the gestures are shown in a sequence in the figure, they typically occur on top of one another on the digitizing surface.

---

[6] A possible exception is interaction using a brain-computer interface (BCI).

[7] The "segmentation problem" refers to a challenge with natural handwriting recognition whereby the spatial relationship between strokes is important. A "t", for example, has two strokes, a horizontal stroke positioned on top of and aligned near the centre of a vertical stroke.

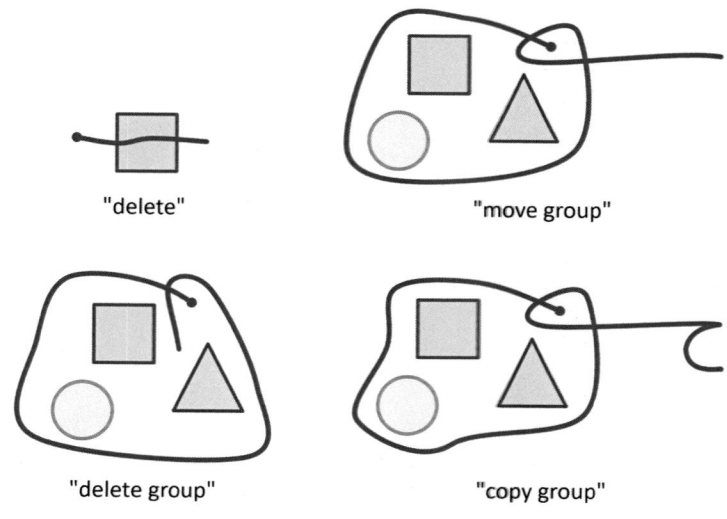

FIGURE 3.18

GEdit graphics editing gestures (from [264]).

FIGURE 3.19

Gestures for "easy" in Graffiti strokes.

Sometimes the meaning or purpose of a gesture depends on articulation points within the path of the gesture. There are many examples, including Quikwriting [393], EdgeWrite [524], Cirrin [339], WatchMI [537], and MojiBoard [7]. A widely-used example is *shape writing* where words are entered on a soft keyboard by gesturing through the keys bearing the letters in the word [256,547,548]. The gesture for "easy" is shown in Fig. 3.20a. When viewed with the underlying Qwerty keyboard, as in Fig. 3.20b, the association of the gesture with the word is revealed. The gesture starts on "e", transitions through "a" and "s", and finishes on "y". Note in the figure that word prediction is used with "way" and "ready" offered as alternatives. Shape writing gestures for text entry are also possible for entire sentences [503] or on other keyboard layouts, such as an ambiguous phone keypad [258].

See Dube et al. [106, Table 1], Fallah and MacKenzie [121, Table 1], or Remizova et al. [412, Table 1] for reviews of additional gesture-based input techniques.

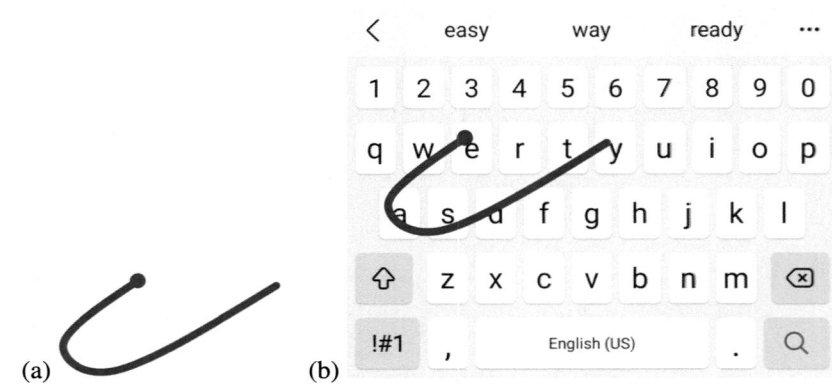

FIGURE 3.20

Shape writing on a Qwerty keyboard. (a) "easy." (b) Gesture superimposed on keyboard.

3.2 Hard controls and soft controls

Before computers infiltrated every aspect of our homes and workplaces, displays and controls tended to be physical single-purpose devices. Controls like joysticks, switches, arrays of switches, push buttons, keys, keyboards, mice, steering wheels, handles, knobs, levers, and so on, arrived through an involved process of design, engineering, and manufacturing. Once built, they were fixed for life. And this meant their behaviours were constrained to a small set of relationships with the displays they accompanied. Even an aircraft's cockpit had a relatively small number of controls and displays. Because they were physical and single-purpose, there was a limited set of relationships that existed between them.

The advent of computers with software, graphical displays, and point-select interactions changed this. Through *soft interfaces*, the way humans interact with technology changed, and changed everywhere. The malleability of a display, through software, brings unlimited possibilities to a relatively small physical space. The result is *soft controls*. A soft control can be born out of little more than a programmer's whim – a few lines of computer code and a quick round or two of code-compile-test – all done between the morning coffee break and lunch. Before you know it, there is a new button on a toolbar, a new "Options ... " popup dialog, or a new drawing mode invoked with CTRL-*something*. The possibilities are limitless.[8]

Human-computer interfaces contain lots of controls. Most are soft controls manipulated by physical controls (the mouse, finger, or keyboard). Desktop computer

---

[8] On the programmer's whimsical role in creating overly complex and unusable interfaces, Cooper is less kind [87]. Others also note the undue influence of technical staff. In one case, management's inability to challenge the judgement of engineering staff is cited as contributing to the failure of an entire project [458, p. 160].

FIGURE 3.21

Many soft controls are also displays. See text for discussion.

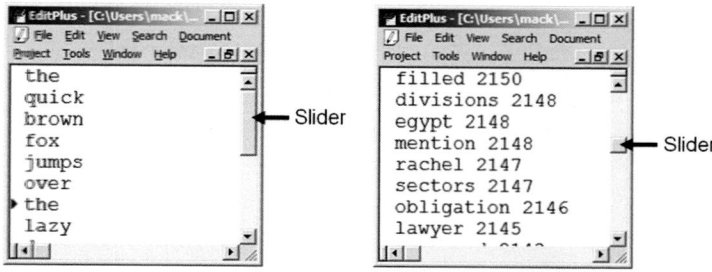

FIGURE 3.22

A scrollbar slider is both a control and a display. See text for discussion.

applications, for example, have thousands of control-display arrangements. Every conceivable action one might make with a soft control that produces a displayed response on the system is an example. Controls invoke different responses (displays) depending on the context, so the combinations multiply rapidly.

The distinction between controls and displays is blurred with soft controls. Since a soft control is rendered on a display through software, its size, shape, or appearance, can change dynamically to convey information to the user. Thus, soft controls often have properties of displays. Toolbar buttons and widgets are typical examples. Fig. 3.21 shows an example from a word processor. The image contains three combo boxes and nine buttons. Each is both a control and a display. The combo boxes reveal that the style is Body Text, the font is Times, and the font size is 12 point. The buttons reveal the state of the text at the insertion point. The text is italicised, underlined, left justified.

A scrollbar slider, or elevator, is another example.[9] See Fig. 3.22. The slider is both a control and a display. As a control, it is moved to change the view in the document. As a display, the slider's size reveals the magnitude of the view relative to the entire document and its position reveals the location of the view within the document. Most soft controls are also displays.

Soft controls need little space. Fig. 3.23 shows a small area of a GUI application. It is only 40 cm^2, but it contains a bewildering array of soft controls – more than 20. Or, are they displays? Each is a world unto itself and identifies or suggests its purpose by its shape, position, a label, or an icon. Each of these soft controls is manipulated

---

[9] The scrollbar slider has a variety of names, depending on the platform. Other names include thumb, box, knob, scroller, wiper, and grip.

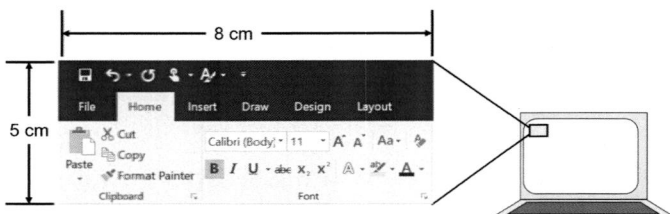

FIGURE 3.23

A small physical space on a graphical display. There are more than 20 soft controls and displays in a 40-cm^2 area. A single user action can initiate a complete re-definition of the space.

by a hard control, by clicking. Or is double-clicking? Or is it SHIFT-clicking? Or dragging? What about right-clicking? What about keyboard access? And there are presumptions that somehow it all makes sense to the user. As well, each control is precariously close to a neighbour. Many users of this application (Microsoft Word) will invest hundreds of hours working this 40 cm^2 interface. The users are, by all accounts, experts. Yet, hundreds of times users, even expert users, commit errors working this same space. Sometimes, they act in haste. At other times, they're just not sure what to do. It's a complex space, this 40 cm^2. And all it takes is one user action – a key press or button click – and the entire 40 cm^2 morphs into a completely different interface. See also student exercise 3-2 at the end of this chapter.

The hard-control / soft-control distinction is similar to *space multiplexing* vs. *time multiplexing* [50]. With space multiplexing, there is a dedicated physical control for each parameter that is controlled. Each has a separate physical location. With time multiplexing, there are fewer controls than parameters, and so, a single device (e.g., a small region of a display) is reconfigured to control different parameters at different stages of an operation.

In the next section, we examine controls and displays by their spatial relationships. We begin with hard controls, such as a mouse, and typical displays as found on desktop computer systems.

3.3 Control-display relationships

When a user grasps a computer mouse and moves it to the right, the pointer on the system's display moves to the right. This *control-display relationship* is not something users think much about. This is human-computer interaction as it should be – where the relationship between what a user does and what is experienced is natural, seamless, intuitive, efficient, and so on. Control-display relationships are sometimes called *mappings*, since the relationships attribute how a controller property maps to a display property.

The example describes a *spatial relationship*. There are also *dynamic relationships*, describing how a controller affects the speed of the response, and *physical relationships*, describing whether the response is to a movement or a force in the controller. We will examine each of these in this section, beginning with spatial relationships.

3.3.1 Spatial relationships

The mouse-pointer spatial relationship described above is illustrated in Fig. 3.24a. The mapping is *congruent* because there is an exact spatial correspondence between the controller input and the display output. Move the mouse right, and the pointer moves right. The situation in Fig. 3.24b is different. Move the mouse *forward* and the pointer moves *up*. As with side-to-side movement, users likely don't think much about this. Yet, the first time someone encounters a mouse, there is likely some uncertainty on how it works. What does it do? What is it controlling? Where is the effect seen? No doubt, the spatial relationship between mouse and pointer is quickly learned.[10] We will say more about learned vs. natural relationships later.

It is useful at this juncture to introduce labels to further examine the spatial mappings between input controls and output displays. Fig. 3.25a and Fig. 3.25b show the display and mouse pad surfaces in a Cartesian coordinate space with an x-axis, y-axis, and z-axis.[11] Left-right motion is along the x-axis. Up-down motion is along the y-axis. Forward-backward motion is along the z-axis. Of course, a cursor cannot move along the z-axis, nor is mouse motion sensed on the y-axis. The arrows show positive motion along each axis.

The mouse-to-pointer mapping is shown in Fig. 3.25c. Here we see the slight disjoint noted above. Mouse x-axis motion maps to pointer x-axis motion, but mouse z-axis motion maps to pointer y-axis motion. The plus (+) symbols indicate that positive motion of the control yields positive motion in the display along each axis.

The y-axis pointer motion is an example of a *transformed spatial mapping*. In this case the transformation is 90° if viewed along the y-z plane. We might expect an effect on user performance in the presence of a spatial transformation. And that is the case. Aiming error is known to be higher for 90° to 135° transformations and lower for 0° or 180° transformations [93]. It is also known that adaptation occurs for all transformations, in as few as 50 trials [519]. So, while initial exposure to a mouse might pose a problem (and yield inaccurate pointing), with practice the relationship is learned and accuracy improves.

Describing mouse-pointer mappings in a three-dimensional (3D) space, as above, invites a deeper analysis of other control-display relationships. This is justified at the very least since HCI is more than desktop interaction. Whether using a thumb-controlled wheel to scroll through a calendar or using a handheld controller to an-

---

[10] A student once told me of his experience teaching his mother how to use a computer. At one point he told his mother to move the cursor *up* to the menu bar. She raised the mouse *up* off the mousepad.

[11] The choice of labels is, of course, arbitrary.

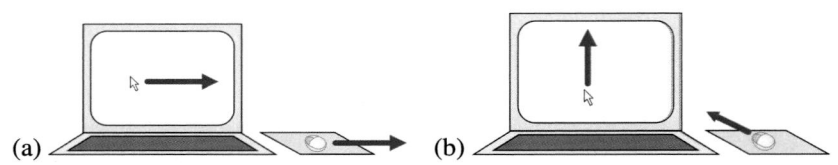

FIGURE 3.24

Control-display relationships for a mouse and pointer. See text for discussion.

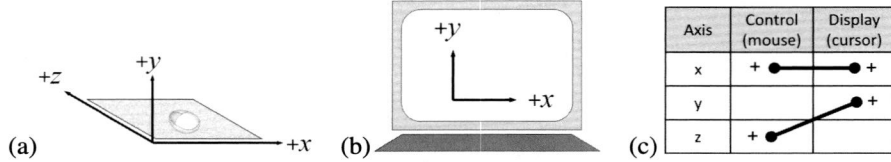

Axis	Control (mouse)	Display (cursor)
x	+	+
y		+
z	+	

FIGURE 3.25

Axis labels. (a) Control space. (b) Display space. (c) Control-display mapping for a mouse and pointer.

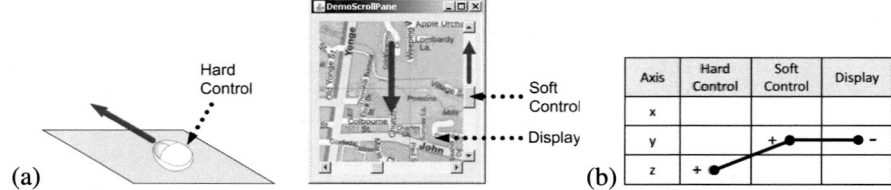

Axis	Hard Control	Soft Control	Display
x			
y		+	−
z	+		

FIGURE 3.26

A three-tier control-display relationship. (a) Moving the hard control forward moves the soft control up, which in turn moves the display (the view's content) down. (b) control-display mappings. See text for discussion.

nihilate the enemy in a first-person shooter game, the relationship between what we do and what we get is of utmost importance in designing interfaces and interaction techniques that are efficient and transparent.

Now consider scrolling the view of an image or document. A scroll pane includes scrollbars with sliders to move the view. Interaction involves manipulating a physical controller, such as a mouse (a hard control), to move a pointer to the slider (a soft control) and acquiring it with a button-down action. The slider is then dragged up or down to produce a change in the view. This scenario adds a third tier to the control-display mappings. Fig. 3.26a shows a mouse and an image of a map displayed in a GUI window. Scrollbars with sliders appear on the right and bottom of the window. There is a spatial transformation between the hard control and soft control and between the soft control and the view on the display. See Fig. 3.26b.

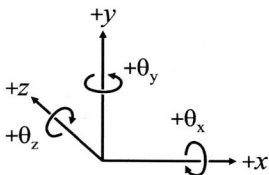

FIGURE 3.27

Axis labels for a three-dimensional space. See text for discussion.

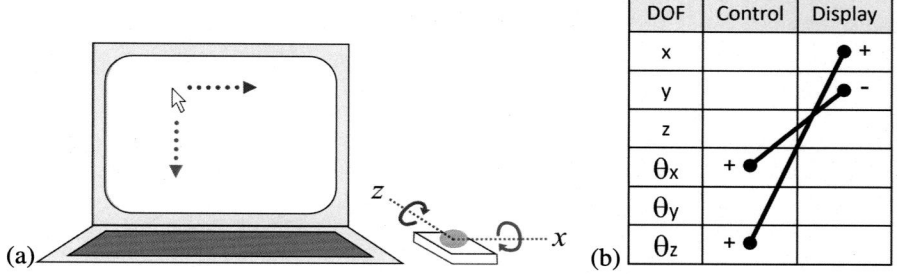

DOF	Control	Display
x		+
y		−
z		
θx	+	
θy		
θz	+	

(a) (b)

FIGURE 3.28

Trackball example. (a) Ball rotation about the x-axis (blue) moves the display pointer along the y-axis (blue). Rotation about the z-axis (red) moves the pointer along the x-axis (red). (b) Control-display correspondence in 6 DOF space. See text for discussion.

Most computer users are adept in scrolling through documents, and have no trouble with the spatial transformations in Fig. 3.26. The $+/−$ reversal in the control-display relationship along the z-axis is interesting, however. What if the relationship between the soft control (scrollbar slider) and display (map image) was reversed? Would this be OK? Yes, but the relationship must be learned.

The next step in examining spatial relationships is to expand the 3D space to include rotation about each axis. This is shown in Fig. 3.27 using theta (θ) to designate angle or rotation. For translation, the arrows indicate right (x), up (y), and back (z) movement relative to the origin. For rotation, the arrows indicate clockwise movement as viewed looking out from the origin along each axis. In all, there are six parameters, or *degrees of freedom* (DOF). "Degrees of freedom" means that each parameter may be manipulated independently of the others. To fully place an object in 3D space, six parameters are required: three for the object's *position* in space (x, y, z), and three for the object's *orientation* in space (θ_x, θ_y, θ_z). In aeronautics, the rotation terms are known as pitch (θ_x), roll (θ_z), and yaw (θ_y).

With rotation added, let's consider the trackball. Although trackballs are commonly used in gaming and other specialized contexts, they are also many users' preferred choice over a mouse for desktop systems. When emulating a mouse, rotating the ball controls the movement the pointer on the display. Fig. 3.28a shows the

DOF	Control	Display
x	+ ●————● +	
y	+ ●————● +	
z	+ ●————● +	
θx	+ ●————● +	
θy	+ ●————● +	
θz	+ ●————● +	

(a)   (b)

FIGURE 3.29

Spatial congruence in 3D. (a) 6 DOF input controller and 6 DOF display (sketch courtesy of Bartosz Bajer). (b) 6 DOF control-display correspondence. See text for discussion.

relationship between ball rotation and pointer translation. In the figure, red and blue colours reveal the correspondence between the control and the display. Fig. 3.28b shows the control-display mappings using the 6 DOF labels in Fig. 3.27. Note that movement control involves a transformed spatial mapping for both axes. Also, there is a sign reversal for x-axis clockwise rotation. This is needed in the figure since clockwise ball rotation about the x-axis moves the pointer down on the display.

Fig. 3.29a shows 3D interaction with *spatial congruence*. Each degree of freedom in the control space is correctly matched with the corresponding degree of freedom in the display space (see also [556]). Of course, the depth, or z-axis, is simulated on the display. Nevertheless, the figure illustrates the goal of facile 6 DOF interaction. The figure shows a 6 DOF input glove (a controller) in exact spatial correspondence with a simulated glove on the display. The fluidity of the interaction is clearly evident: The mappings are congruent for all 6 DOF, as illustrated in Fig. 3.29b.

Most interactive systems support a subset of the 6 DOF available in 3D. And in most cases, spatial transformations encumber the user with small challenges to learn and overcome, like the mouse-pointer or trackball-pointer interactions examined earlier. Rotation is a challenge with the mouse since the device only senses translation along the x-axis and z-axis. Control-display spatial congruence is not possible; so, creative mappings are needed to facilitate interaction. The typical solution is modes, which we examine in more detail later.

Now consider Street View in Google Maps, which provides panoramic views of streets in major cities around the world.[12] A simulated street scene showing the city hall in Toronto is seen in Fig. 3.30a along with facsimiles of the controls for viewpoint control. The most common manipulations are *panning*, *zooming*, and *positioning*. Panning involves rotating the camera view, left-right, up-down. Zooming involves changing the magnification of the view. Positioning is a change in the camera position. In the case of Google Street View, the camera position is constrained to points

---

[12] http://maps.google.com/streetview.

DOF	Control	Display
x	+	
y		
z	+	
θx		+
θy		-
θz		

(a)  (b)

FIGURE 3.30

Rotating a 3D scene. (a) Street scene in Toronto with pan and zoom controls. (b) Mapping of mouse control for panning if the scene is dragged.

along the street from which the images were captured. So, while it is possible to zoom in to the city hall, it is not possible to walk toward it.

Scene manipulations are supported through a variety of interactions using the keyboard or mouse. One way to pan with the mouse is to drag the image – position the pointer anywhere on the image, press and hold the primary mouse button, then move the pointer. Left-right, or x-axis, linear movement of the mouse effects rotation of the scene about the y-axis. Forward-backward, or z-axis, linear movement of the mouse rotates the scene about the x-axis. These mappings are illustrated in Fig. 3.30b. Although the mappings look convoluted, the interaction is reasonably simple (i.e., quickly learned).

Another way to pan with the mouse is through the soft control labelled Pan in the figure. Clicking an arrow effects a discrete pan in the expected direction. Left-right continuous panning is possible by dragging the circle that surrounds the arrows. This interaction is tricky, and of questionable merit. It requires a tight coupling of left-right, up-down linear movement of the mouse and it requires the user's visual attention on the soft control! Of course, the user would prefer to look at the scene.

Zooming is performed by clicking on the plus (+) and minus (–) soft controls seen in the figure. The effect is to zoom the view in and out along the z-axis. It is interesting to consider zooming via z-axis movement of the mouse, since the result is a spatially congruent control-display mapping.[13] Unfortunately, z-axis mouse movement is committed to x-axis scene rotation (i.e., up-down panning; see Fig. 3.30b). Perhaps a modifier key, such a shift, could be used to map mouse z-axis movement to z-axis zooming.

Another congruent mapping to consider is using y-axis rotation of the mouse to control y-axis rotation of the camera, to create left-right panning. y-axis rotation amounts to rotating the mouse on the mouse pad or desktop surface. Of course, such

---

[13] Zooming is possible using the mouse wheel, but the detents in the wheel motion make the interaction feel jerky.

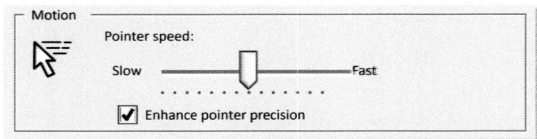

FIGURE 3.31

Controlling the CD gain (pointer speed) from the mouse control panel.

movement is not sensed. But, with some careful re-engineering, it can be (as discussed later in this chapter).

Using y-axis rotation with a mouse is a potentially interesting and new interaction technique – worth investigating through empirical research. Can user interaction with Google Street View be improved using other input controllers or other mappings? If so, how is a conjectured improvement evaluated? What is the task? What user performance measurements are relevant? The spatial mappings between input controls and output displays are numerous in HCI, and the relationships are often complex. These complexities invite thinking about the problem space, searching out new and potentially facile interactions, and then testing and comparing them through experimental research. See also student exercise 3-4 at the end of this chapter.

3.3.2 **CD gain and transfer function**

There is more to mouse-pointer movement than spatial mappings. Another property is *CD gain* – the amount of movement in a display object, such as a pointer, for a given amount of movement in a control.[14] For example, if a mouse is moved 3 cm and the pointer also moves 3 cm, then the CD gain is 1. If the pointer moves 6 cm, the CD gain is $\frac{6}{3} = 2$. CD gain for a mouse and pointer is typically set in a control panel, as seen in Fig. 3.31. Moving the slider to the slow end of the scale reduces CD gain, meaning more controller movement is required for each unit of pointer movement.

Often the relationship between controller motion and pointer motion is non-linear and uses a *power function*. In this case, the amount of pointer motion depends also on the velocity of mouse motion. This is enabled in Fig. 3.31 by selecting "Enhance pointer precision." If the mouse moves quickly, CD gain increases. If the mouse moves slowly, CD gain decreases. Lowering the CD gain for slow controller movements is useful to enhance the precision of target selection at the end of a point-select operation. The term *transfer function* is sometimes used since non-linear relationships are more elaborate. To ensure the pointer is responsive to mouse movement, with no perceivable delay, the software implementation of a non-linear relationship typically uses a lookup table to map controller movement to display movement. See also student exercise 3-5.

---

[14] CD gain is sometimes called C:D ratio. A CD gain of 2 is equivalent to a C:D ratio of 1:2; that is, one unit of control (mouse) movement yielding two units of display (pointer) movement.

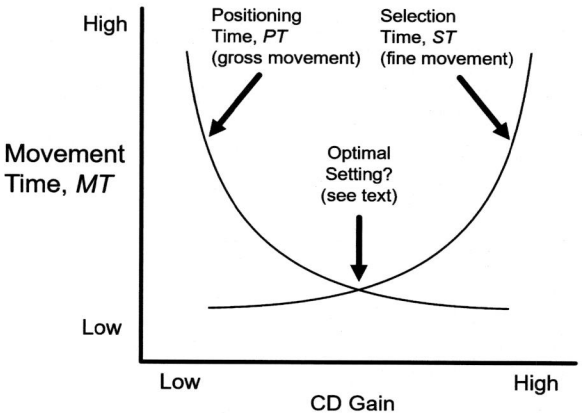

FIGURE 3.32

Trade-off between positioning time (PT) and selection time (ST) as a function of CD gain.

Research on optimizing CD gain dates at least to the 1940s, when the first electronic joysticks were developed [224]. Optimization is trickier than it seems, however. For each point-select task the overall time is movement time (MT) which combines the positioning time (PT) and the selection time (ST):

$$MT = PT + ST \qquad (3.2)$$

In Eq. (3.2), PT is for gross movements (getting to the general vicinity of the target) and ST is for fine movements (making the final selection).[15] The timing for ST begins when the pointer first enters the target or a region around the target.

Varying CD gain exposes a trade-off between PT and ST. See Fig. 3.32. In a simplistic sense, the optimal setting minimizes the movement time – the combined gross and fine movement times. However, a CD gain that minimizes movement time might not minimize the error rate. Other factors such as display size or scale (independent of CD gain) also bring into question the optimization of this common input device parameter [13,33].

Since the 1980s, CD gain has been highly researched for interaction with GUIs on desktop computing systems (e.g., [24,223,237]). Most studies found that significant performance benefits are not achieved by adjusting CD gain. One challenge is in defining optimal performance. Is the goal to maximize speed or to maximize accuracy? The goal of optimizing both speed and accuracy is problematic, because of the speed-accuracy trade-off. What improves speed tends to worsen accuracy, and vice versus. A useful metric that combines speed and accuracy is Fitts' throughput

---

[15] Gross movements are sometimes characterised as open-loop or ballistic, whereas fine movements are said to be closed-loop or guided by feedback.

[300,312], but the calculation of throughput is subject to considerable variation in the literature, and this exacerbates forming a comprehensive understanding of CD gain and human performance.

Optimizing CD gain is of on-going interest, with a focus in diverse settings. Examples in the HCI literature include the following:

- Very large displays [251,348]
- Very small displays [178]
- Accessible computing [522]
- Remote pointing [255]
- 3D interaction [11]
- Mouse-based pointing in VR [554]
- Auto-adjusting CD gain based on cursor trajectory [274]

In each example, the research brought a new idea to the problem of tuning the relationship between an input control and interaction on an output display. Since human performance is the main criterion for optimization, research on CD gain is well suited to empirical inquiry and experimentation. See also student exercises 3-5 and 3-6 at the end of this chapter.

3.3.3 **Latency**

Human interaction with computers is two-way. As participants in a closed-loop system, we issue commands through input controllers and process responses on output displays. Subsequent input depends on the latest output. Not surprisingly, human performance and the interaction experience are adversely affected when feedback is delayed. The delay between an input action and the corresponding response on a display is called *latency* or *lag*. Fortunately, latency is negligible in many interactive computing tasks, such as typing or pointer positioning.

The opposite extreme is remote manipulation, where the human operator is physically displaced from the machine under control. The latency may be due to mechanical linkages or to transmission delays in the communications channel. For example, in controlling a space vehicle on a distant moon or planet (as viewed on a display), transmission delays – latency – are on the order of several minutes or longer.

Latency is often present with Internet connections – click on a link and wait a few seconds or longer for a page to appear. The research issues here are more about user experience and frustration than about human performance. Frustration is reduced, for example, if the interface includes feedback informing the user that the network is processing the request [37].

Virtual reality relies heavily on the tracking of hand, head, or body motion in a simulated 3D environment. The pretense of reality requires a tight link between the user's view of the environment and the actions – usually hand, head, or body motions – that set the view. When changes in the environment lag behind input motions, the loss of fidelity is dramatic.

FIGURE 3.33

Polhemus G^4 6 DOF tracking system. The 6 DOF sensor is identified by the arrow (photo courtesy of Polhemus).

Latency is attributable to properties of input devices, output devices, and software. Input devices are usually sampled at fixed rates in the range of 10 to 60 samples per second. At 60 Hz sampling, for example, an input movement may not be sensed for $\frac{1}{60} = 16.7$ ms. Latency increases further due to software overhead – a loose expression for a variety of system-related factors. Communication modes, network configurations, number crunching, and application software all contribute.

Latency will increase dramatically when output requires substantial computation for graphics rendering. A display frame rate of 10 Hz is considered minimal to achieve real time animation. Since the rendering of the frame only begins when the position is known, the potential for parallel processing is limited. Using standard double buffering (where the frame is only presented once fully drawn), there is 100 ms minimum latency to the start of the frame display interval and a latency of 150 ms to the middle of the frame display interval.

Note that it is not possible to accurately measure latency from within the target system. Using software to log timestamps for input and output operations within a system misses the actions and responses at the human interface. To reflect the user's experience as a whole, a proper latency measurement is done externally [415,471]. Teather et al. [486] describe a pendulum apparatus for measuring latency. The input controller swings in front of the output display with a high-speed camera recording the temporal relationship between input motion and the output response.

Latency in virtual reality is associated mostly with 6 DOF tracking devices attached to the hand, head, or body as well as the latency caused by the low frame rates. Typical tracking devices include the Polhemus[16] G^4 (Fig. 3.33) and the Ascension[17] MotionStar. These devices and their interfaces transmit six degree-of-freedom position and orientation data to the host computer at a high rate while acting in concert with competing processes in the complete VR environment. Maintaining negligible

---

[16] http://www.polhemus.com/.
[17] http://www.ascension-tech.com/.

latency is usually not possible. The Polhemus G^4, for example, is sampled at 120 Hz, meaning one sample every $\frac{1}{120} = 0.00833$ s $= 8.33$ ms. According to the device specification, latency is less than 10 ms, meaning the three position and three orientation coordinates are available no later than 10 ms after each sample. Of course, this only applies to the input sub-system. From an HCI perspective, this value is irrelevant. The user experiences the system as a whole.

Although latency is known as a compromising parameter in VR systems [284], and its effect on human performance is considerable, the evidence is mostly anecdotal. On intuitive grounds, Pausch noted that low-latency is significantly more important than high-quality graphics or stereoscope [388]. His low-end VR system emphasized presence (i.e., low latency) over output graphics by maintaining seven screen updates per second with wire-frame images. In an experiment with force feedback, Brooks et al. [43] concluded that screen updates are needed 15 times per second minimum to maintain the illusion of continuous change in the force sensed. Even at this rate, subjects noted the sponginess of the feel. Others cite motion sickness as a by-product of lag with head-mounted displays [105,131,273,415].

Empirical measurements across levels of latency on human performance are rare. There was some research in the 1960s (e.g., [142,446]) on the design of controllers for remote manipulation systems; however the latency tested was extremely long (up to several seconds). In one instance, the apparatus was mechanical [446], and in another latency was programmed as an exponential time constant preventing the pointer from fully reaching a target unless a deliberate overshoot was programmed [142]. In both cases movement time increases due to latency were dramatic – well in excess of the amount of latency. Since latency is on the order of a few hundred milliseconds in VR, its effect on human performance is less apparent.

MacKenzie and Ware [327] systematically introduced latency in a system and measured the effect on human performance in simple point-select tasks. With 75 ms latency, movement time increased by 16% and error rate by 36%. At 225 ms, the effect was dramatic, with movement time increasing by 64% and error rate by 214%.

Gaming is an obvious example were low latency is important. In a study with five participants, Eg et al. [111] injected delays in a chase-and-catch game where players had to catch a bouncing puck. They systematically varied puck speed and latency. At a puck speed of 1550 pixels/s, the time to catch the puck was about 3 seconds at low or negligible latency. This increased to over 25 seconds at 440 ms latency. Halbhuber et al. [171] studied latency in a first person shooter game. They demonstrated the potential to compensate for latency using an artificial neural network that predicts user inputs and anticipates output responses.

3.3.4 Property sensed and order of control

When a human engages an input controller, the actions involve touching, tapping, grasping, moving, pushing, flicking, squeezing, and so on. The input controller senses the interaction and coverts a *property sensed* into data that are transmitted to the host computer for processing. For pointing devices, the most common properties sensed are *position, displacement,* or *force.* In this section, we examine both the property sensed and the way the property is used to control an object or view on an output display. Does the property sensed control the position or velocity of the object or view? This question speaks to the *order of control,* which we present shortly.

With a graphics tablet, touchpad, or touchscreen, the property sensed is the position of a stylus or finger on a digitizing surface. Position is sensed as an absolute coordinate at the point of contact along the x-axis and z-axis. (Discussions here use the axis labelling in Fig. 3.27.) A mouse is different. It is not possible to know where a mouse is situated on a mouse pad or desktop. With a mouse, the property sensed is the *displacement* – the amount of movement along the x-axis and z-axis. Each sample is reported relative to the last sample. Touchpads in laptop computers typically operate in mouse-emulation mode. Even though the property sensed is the absolute position of the finger on the touchpad surface, the value is reported to the host in relative terms – the amount of finger displacement relative to the last sample. Graphics tablets typically support either absolute or relative modes of reporting.

The most common orders of control are *position-control* and *velocity-control* with latter also called *rate-control* [249,291,528], With position-control, the sensed property of the input device controls the position of the object or view on a display. A mouse is typical example since mouse displacement controls the position of the pointer. With velocity-control, the sensed property controls the velocity of the object or view. Alternate terms for position-control and velocity-control are *zero-order control* and *first-order control,* respectively. If the velocity function is a non-linear power function, as described earlier, the term *second-order control* applies.

Order of control is often associated with joysticks. Joysticks are either *isotonic* or *isometric.* With an isotonic joystick, the user manipulates the stick handle, which, in turn, swivels about a pivot-point. The property sensed is the movement of the stick. Isotonic joysticks are also called *displacement joysticks.* The output signal represents the position of the stick as the amount of displacement (i.e., rotation) from the neutral or home position, about the x and z axes. An example is the Premium II from Kraft Systems, a common joystick for computer games in the 1980s. See Fig. 3.34a.[18]

With an isometric joystick, the stick does not move. The property sensed is the force applied to the stick. The output signal represents the amount of force along the x-axis and z-axis. An example is the joystick between the G, H, and B keys on many notebook computer keyboards. See Fig. 3.34b.

The order-of-control mappings for isotonic (position sensing) and isometric (force sensing) joysticks are illustrated in Fig. 3.35. These possibilities raise the question of performance: Which mappings are best in terms of speed and accuracy for common point-select tasks. Kantowitz and Elvers [237] evaluated an isometric joystick in both position-control and velocity-control modes. Velocity-control performed best. A full investigation of the possibilities in Fig. 3.35 requires evaluation with two independent variables: property sensed and property controlled. In other words, both position-sensing and force-sensing input controllers must be tested in both position-control

---

[18] From the Buxton Collection (https://www.microsoft.com/buxtoncollection).

(a) (b)

FIGURE 3.34

Joysticks. (a) Isotonic (displacement sensing). (b) Isometric (force sensing).

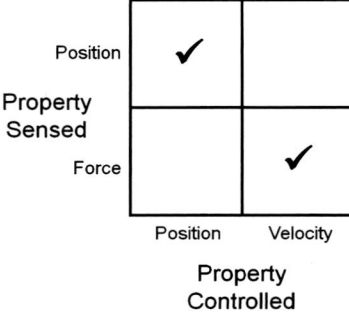

FIGURE 3.35

Order of control mapping for property sensed vs. property controlled. Checks indicate the preferred mappings.

and velocity-control modes. Zhai conducted such an experiment and observed that position control is best for a position-sensing device and that velocity control is best for a force-sensing device [544, p. 35]. These mappings are indicated in the figure.

Velocity control was used with a virtual joystick by Teather et al. [487] to control player movement in a game. The joystick was implemented using touch on a tablet display. See Fig. 3.36. Sliding the finger away from the joystick centre increased the velocity of the player movement. Position control was not tested as it did not work well in pilot testing. This is contrary to Zhai's observation (noted above), since the preferred interaction occurred when the position of the finger was mapped to the velocity of the player.[19]

Order of control is also relevant to tilt-based interaction. In some applications, the tilt of a device is used as a input primitive, for example to control a rolling ball in a marble maze game. Does tilt control the velocity of the ball or the position

---

[19] It is important to note: For a virtual joystick, there is no equivalence to isometric behaviour with a physical joystick. That is, it is not possible to sense horizontal finger force on a tablet surface.

FIGURE 3.36

Velocity control used with a virtual joystick to control player movement in a game (from [487]).

of the ball? Either is possible. Teather and MacKenzie [484] investigated this using tablet tilt to control the movement of a paddle in the game Pong. Position control performed better: Participants reached a criterion score roughly twice as fast using position control compared to velocity control.

3.4 Mental models and metaphor

There is more to learning or adapting than simply experiencing. One of the most common ways to learn and adapt is through *physical analogy* [376, p. 23] or *metaphor* [65]. Once we latch on to a physical understanding of an interaction, based on experience, it all makes sense. We've experienced it, we know it, it seems natural. With a scroll pane, moving the slider *up* moves the view *up*. If the relationship were reversed, moving the slider up would move the *content* up. We could easily develop a physical sense of *slider up → view up* or *slider up → content up*. The up-up in each expression demonstrates the importance of finding a spatially congruent physical understanding. These two analogies require opposite control-display relationships, but either is fine and we could work with one just as easily as the other, provided implementations were consistent across applications and platforms.

Physical analogies and metaphors are examples of the more general concept of *mental models*, also known as *conceptual models*. Mental models are common in HCI. The idea is simple enough: "What is the user's mental model of . . . ?" An association with human experience is required. HCI's first mental model was perhaps that of the office or desktop. The desktop metaphor helped users understand the graphical user interface (GUI). Today, it is hard to imagine the pre-GUI era, but in late 1970s and early 1980s, the GUI was strange. It required a new way of thinking. Designers exploited the metaphor of the office or desktop to give users a jump-start on the interface [230]. And it worked. Rather than learning something new and unfamiliar,

FIGURE 3.37

Bookshelf metaphor. E-books organized on a bookshelf give the user a sense of purpose and possibility.

users act out with concepts already understood: documents, folders, filing cabinets, trashcans, the top of the desk, pointing, selecting, dragging, dropping, and so on. This is the essence of mental models.

Another example is the bookshelf or bookcase. It's an artifact in the physical world that we all understand. For an e-book collection, the entries could be organized and presented to the user as set of files, for example via a browser. After all, e-books are files. But, to the user, these are e-books, not files. We can do better. The user interface can organize the entries using a bookshelf metaphor [497]. See Fig. 3.37. The UI provides an immediate sense to the user of purpose and possibility – of what the items are and how they are accessed and used.

Implementation models are to be avoided. These are systems that impose on the user a set of interactions that follow the inner workings of an application. Cooper and Reimann give the example of a software-based fax product where the user is paced through a series of agonizing details and dialogs [88, p. 25]. Interaction follows an implementation model, rather than the user's mental model of how to send a fax. The user is prompted for information when it is convenient for the program to receive it, not when it makes sense to the user. Users often have pre-existing experiences with artefacts like faxes, printers, calendars, media players, and so on. It is best to exploit these at every opportunity in designing a software-based product. Let's visit a few other examples in human-computer interfaces.

Toolbars in GUIs are fertile ground for mental models. To keep the buttons small and of a consistent size, they are adorned with an icon rather than a label. An icon is a pictorial representation. In HCI, icons trigger a mental image within the user, a clue to a real-world experience related to the action associated with the button or tool. Drawing or painting applications provide good examples. Fig. 3.38a shows the Tool

FIGURE 3.38

Icons create associations. (a) Array of toolbar buttons from Corel's Paint Shop Pro. (b)
Tooltip help for Picture Tube icon.

Palette in Corel's Paint Shop Pro,[20] a painting and image manipulation application.
The palette contains 21 buttons, each displaying an icon. Each button is associated
with a function and its icon is carefully chosen to elicit the association within the
user's mind. Some are clear, like the paintbrush. Some are less clear. Have a look.
Can you tell what action is associated with each button? Probably not. But, expert
users likely know.

Preparing this example gave me pause to consider my experience with this toolbar.
I use this application frequently, yet some of the buttons are strange to me. In 1991
Apple introduced a method to help users like me. Hover the mouse pointer over a
GUI button and a field pops up providing a terse elaboration on the button's purpose.
Apple called the popups *balloons*, although today they are more commonly known
as *tooltips* or *screen tips*. Fig. 3.38b gives an example for a button in Paint Shop Pro.
Apparently, the button's purpose is related to a picture tube. I'm still in the dark, but
not alone: "Each user learns the smallest set of features that he needs to get his work
done, and he abandons the rest" [87, p. 33].

Another example of a mental model is a clock face or compass as a metaphor
for direction or location. Most users have an ingrained understanding of a clock or
compass. The labels can serve as a mental model for direction. Once there is an
understanding that the metaphor is present, the user has a mental model and uses it
efficiently and accurately for direction: *12 o'clock* or *north* for straight ahead or up,
9 o'clock or *west* for left, and so on.

This was demonstrated in Cassidy et al.'s radar interface for locating objects [69].
See Fig. 3.39a. Four interfaces were compared including a clock face (Fig. 3.39b)
and compass (Fig. 3.39c). The radar sweep traversed 180° and emitted beeps at the
tick points in the clock face or compass. A separate distinguishing sound was heard
within the beep sequence to identify the location of an object. Users were able to
identify the location of objects within about 10° of the actual location.

With twelve divisions, a clock provides finer granularity than a compass ("obsta-
cle ahead at 2 o'clock!"). Examples in HCI include numeric entry [151,211,352] and
locating people and objects in an environment [429,440]. Using a clock metaphor for

---

[20] https://www.paintshoppro.com.

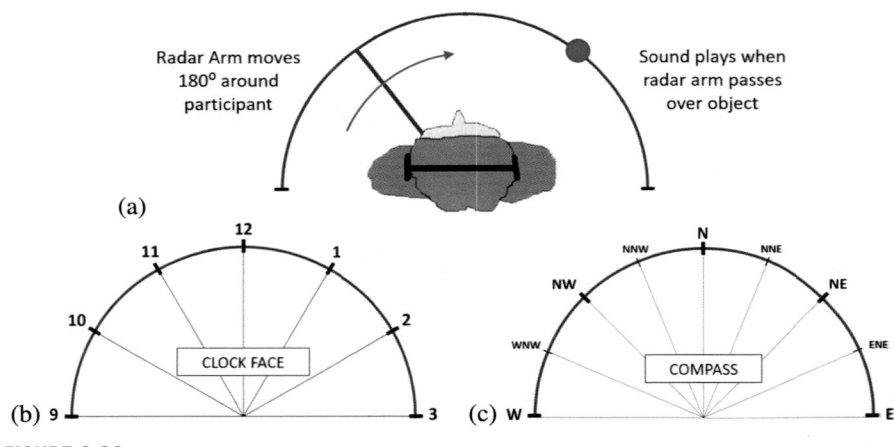

(a)

(b)

(c)

FIGURE 3.39

Mental model example. (a) Radar sweep combined with (b) clock metaphor or (c) compass metaphor (from [69]).

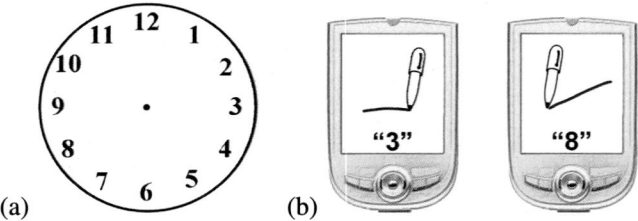

(a)

(b)

FIGURE 3.40

Mental model example. (a) Clock face. (b) Numeric entry with a stylus.

numeric entry with a stylus is shown in Fig. 3.40. Instead of scripting numbers using Roman characters, the numbers are entered using straight-line strokes. The direction of the stroke is the number's position on a clock face. In a longitudinally study, McQueen et al. [352] found that numeric entry was about 24% faster using straight-line strokes compared to handwritten digits. The 12 o'clock position was used for 0. The 10 o'clock and 11 o'clock positions were reserved for system commands.

Sáenz and Sánchez describe a system to assist the blind [429]. Users carried a mobile locating device that provided spoken audio information about the location of nearby objects (see Fig. 3.41a). For the metaphor to work, the user is assumed to be facing the 12 o'clock position. The system allowed users to navigate a building eyes-free (Fig. 3.41b). Users could request position and orientation information from the locator. Auditory responses were provided using the clock metaphor and a text-to-speech module (e.g., "door at 3 o'clock").

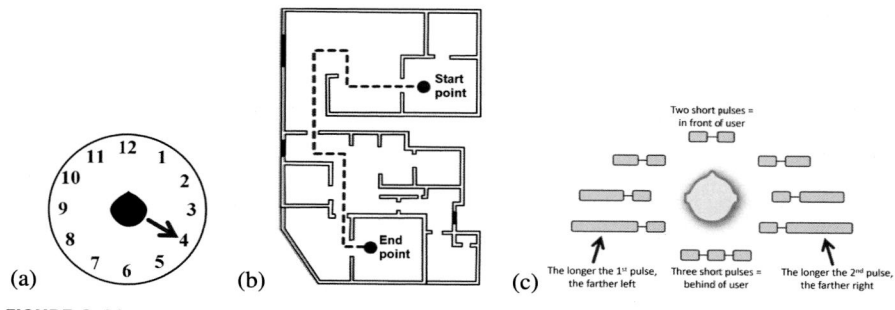

FIGURE 3.41

Spatial metaphor. (a) Auditory feedback provides information for locating objects, such as "object at 4 o'clock." (b) Navigation task (adapted from [429]). (c) NaviRadar (adapted from [423]).

A similar interface is Rümelin's NaviRadar [423], which uses tactile feedback rather than auditory feedback. Although not specifically using the clock metaphor, NaviRadar leverages users' spatial sense of their surroundings to aid navigation. Users receive combinations of long and short vibratory pulses to indicate direction (Fig. 3.41c). Although the patterns must be learned, the system is simple and avoids auditory feedback, which may be impractical in some situations.

The systems described by Cassidy et al. [69], Sáenz and Sánchez [429], and Rümelin et al. [423] have similar aims yet were presented and evaluated in different ways. Sáenz and Sánchez emphasized and described the system architecture in detail. Although this is of interest to some in the HCI community, from the user's perspective, the system architecture is irrelevant. A user test was reported, but the evaluation was not experimental. There were no independent or dependent variables. Users performed tasks with the system and then responded to questionnaire items, expressing their level of agreement to assertions such as "The software was motivating" or "I like the sounds in the software." While qualitative assessments are an essential component of any evaluation, the navigation and locating aides described in this work are well suited to experimental testing. Alternative implementations, even minor modifications to the interface, are potential independent variables. Speed (e.g., the time to complete tasks) and accuracy (e.g., the number of wrong turns, retries, direction changes, wall collisions) are potential dependent variables.

Cassidy et al. [69] and Rümelin et al. [423] took an empirical and experimental approach. The research included both the technical details of the radar interfaces and an evaluation in a formal experiment with independent variables, dependent variables, and so on. The main independent variable included different radar sweep interfaces in the case of Cassidy et al. [69] or difference intensities, durations, and rhythms in the tactile pulses in the case of Rümelin et al. [423]. Since the approach was empirical, important analyses were possible, for example, on the deviation of indicated and reported direction or location or how this varied according to the radar sweep interface or the direction and type of tactile information. The approach enables other

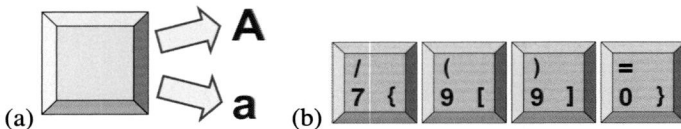

FIGURE 3.42

Keys and modes. (a) Key with two modes. (b) Keys on a German keyboard with three modes.

researchers to study the strengths and weaknesses in the interfaces – in empirical terms – and consider methods of improvement.

3.5 Modes

A common and sometimes frustrating property of user interfaces is modes. A mode is "a functioning arrangement or condition." The soft controls in Fig. 3.23 (p. 112) demonstrate modes, since every new application brings a new functioning arrangement of controls and displays. Usually, though, modes are viewed in a more limited sense, such as lowercase mode vs. uppercase mode. Either way, it is a simple fact that systems of all stripes have modes.

We confront modes everywhere, often without realizing it. For example, office phones have modes: light = on means "message waiting." Electric staplers have modes: LED = on means "add staples." Complex physical systems, such as lawn mowers, stoves, traffic intersections, washing machines, and so on, are more challenging. If computers are involved, all bets are off. For example, some lights at traffic intersections – under computer control – include a time-of-day mode to control the advance green signal. There is an advance green signal, but only during rush hours. Or, is it non-rush hours? Traffic flow may improve, but other problems may arise, such as pedestrians or motorists incorrectly anticipating a mode.

For interactive systems, challenges with modes occur because there are fewer controls than tasks. A computer keyboard is an example. A standard desktop keyboard has about 100 keys, yet can produce more than 800 key variations, using the modes afforded by modifier keys, such as SHIFT, CTRL, and ALT. For example, a key might produce *a* in one mode, *A* in another. See Fig. 3.42a. Most users are fully aware of a keyboard's SHIFT mode. Keyboards for European languages, such as German, include three modes for some keys. See Fig. 3.42b. No doubt, local users are comfortable with the arrangement; however, operating such a keyboard for the first time is a challenge. Still, mode problems with standard keyboards do arise. An example is CAPS_LOCK mode, which we'll visit later.

Is it over-reach to ascribe modes to the A-key on a keyboard? Not at all. Taking a research perspective in HCI involves, among other things, finding simple ways to explain the complex. If keys on a computer keyboard have modes, this is worth thinking about. Taking a broad view of modes, or other elements of HCI, is a powerful

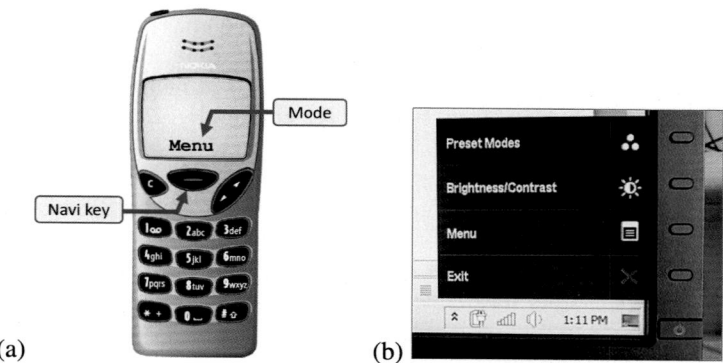

FIGURE 3.43

Physical keys with modes. (a) Navi key on the Nokia 3210 mobile phone. (b) Image adjust buttons on computer monitor.

approach to developing a comprehensive understanding that includes the intricate, the common, and the banal. This idea underpins *descriptive models*, where the goal is to delineate and categorize a problem space. Descriptive models are described in more detail in Chapter 7 (Modelling Interaction).

Function keys have many modes. Help for Microsoft Word lists six interpretations of the F9 key. Pressed alone, it means "update selected fields." With combinations of SHIFT, CTRL, or ALT, there are five additional interpretations.

Some mobile phones have physical keys with modes. The idea first appeared in 1997 as the Navi key, introduced by Nokia [286, p. 24]. The Nokia 3210 implementation is shown in Fig. 3.43a. The Navi key was embossed only with a blue horizontal line, leaving its interpretation unclear. The trick – novel at the time – was a creative use of the display. The current action (mode) of the Navi key was revealed by the word on the display immediately above the key. So, the possibilities explode. A quick look in the 3210 User Guide reveals at least fourteen interpretations of the Navi key: Menu, Select, Answer, Call, End, OK, Options, Assign, Send, Read, Use, View, List, Snooze, and Yes. The word displayed above the key provides feedback – a feature that is crucial for systems with modes. The close proximity of the display (the word) with the control (the Navi key) alerts the user of the current mode of the Navi key and the action associated with pressing the key.

A contemporary version of the same concept is shown in Fig. 3.43b. The figure shows a portion of a computer monitor. There are four physical buttons above the power button (right side of image). In a general sense the buttons adjust the image or configure the display. However, unlike the power button, there is no icon or label embossed on the buttons, leaving their purpose unclear. Press any button and a set of associations appears on the display. Since the associations are created in software, the purpose of the buttons can change with the context of use.

If we combine the ideas above with the discussion earlier on soft controls, there is the possibility of a *mode model for keys*. Physical keys on standard keyboards are *hard keys*. They have a few modes. The Navi key and image adjust buttons just described are *soft-hard keys*, since they involve both a physical key and a purpose for the key created through software. They have lots of modes. The small regions on graphical user interfaces, shown in Fig. 3.23 (p. 112), are the full embodiment of *soft keys*. The size, shape, location, and function are entirely malleable. Soft keys have an infinite number of modes.

Designing modeless interactions is desirable [209]; but, in most cases, modes can't be avoided. A car, for example, has at least three transmission modes: neutral, drive, and reverse. Good luck designing a modeless car. The same is true of computer systems where modes are unavoidable, as demonstrated above. From a design perspective, the main issues with modes are (a) switching modes, and (b) feedback, or making the mode apparent to the user. Let's examine each of these.

3.5.1 Mode switching

Fig. 3.44a shows five soft controls for switching view modes in Microsoft PowerPoint. The controls persist on the display, so they are discoverable. They are clearly apparent to the user. That's good. Furthermore, tooltips (as per Fig. 3.38b) help the user, if necessary. Good, also. Changing modes is a simple matter of clicking the desired soft button. It's all quite simple, and it works reasonably well. But, still, problems lurk. For example, with five view modes, there are $5 \times 4 = 20$ mode transitions. Most of these transitions are accomplished using the soft buttons in Fig. 3.44a. However, transitioning from Slide Show mode to another mode cannot, because the buttons are hidden during Slide Show mode. The user must press the Esc key on the system's keyboard. Pressing Esc transitions from Slide Show mode to the previous mode. While many users know this, not all will. Can you think of an occasion when you were stuck in a mode and had to take drastic to get out of it, like exiting an application or, worse yet, restarting the system?[21] Probably.

Small devices, such as media players, handheld games, watches, radios, thermostats, and so on, are more limited. They have a small display, if any, and just a few physical controls. There are lots of modes. Fig. 3.44b demonstrates the method of switching modes on a sport watch. The buttons are physical, but there are only five. Changing modes requires cycling through the modes using a single button.

Physical buttons are absent or awkward on most smartphones or tablets. Mode switching can use a soft control. For example, a region on the display is touched with a finger on one hand to evoke a mode-switch while a finger on the other hand interacts according to the new mode. With pressure-sensing, multi-touch, gesture capabilities, and built-in sensors, smartphones and tablets provide a rich space for modes and mode switching. Surale et al. [477] explored this space, describing several

---

[21] Applications that include a full screen view mode typically use Esc to transition out of full-screen mode. But, this is not always the case. Users of Mozilla Firefox are invited to investigate this.

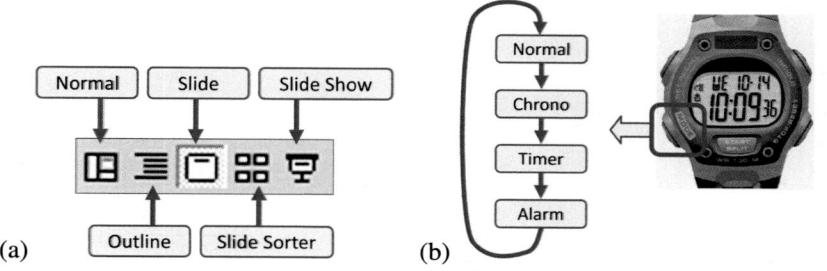

FIGURE 3.44

Mode switching. (a) Dedicated soft buttons on Microsoft PowerPoint change the view mode. (b) A single physical button on a sport watch cycles through watch modes.

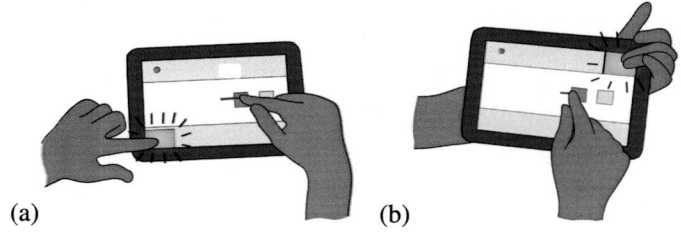

FIGURE 3.45

Touch-based mode-switching. A mode-switch region (green) is positioned for activation by the user's non-dominant hand [477]. (a) Location if the device is in a supported position. (b) Location if the user is standing (figure courtesy of Hemant Surale).

mode-switching possibilities for touch-based interfaces. Fig. 3.45 shows an example. In the figure, a mode-switching soft button is located conveniently for the user's non-dominant hand. Furthermore, the region is automatically positioned according to whether the user is (a) operating the device in a seated position (i.e., supported) or (b) standing.

3.5.2 Feedback and mode errors

Making the mode apparent to the user is a long-standing principle in user interface design. The issue is feedback. Shneiderman and Plaisant advise to "offer informative feedback" [450, p. 74]. Norman argues to "make things visible" [376, pp. 17-25]. Obviously, problems arise if the user doesn't know what mode or state the system is in.

A classic example is the vi editor in the unix operating system. There are two modes: command mode and insert mode. vi launches in command mode. This is interesting in itself. If a user launches vi and immediately types "hello," look out! The letters typed are interpreted as commands. The first key the user must type is "i"

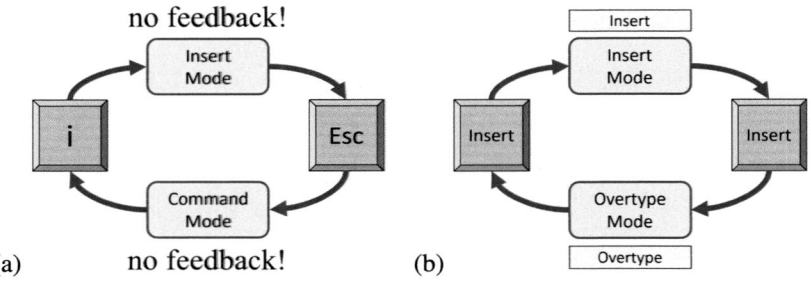

FIGURE 3.46

Changing modes and mode visibility. (a) vi editor. (b) Microsoft Word. See text for discussion.

to enter INSERT mode. Hitting the ESC key switches back to command mode. See Fig. 3.46a. Remarkably, there is no feedback indicating the current mode, nor the transition between modes. Consequently, the vi editor is susceptible to mode errors, a phenomenon that is well documented in the HCI literature (e.g., [41,276,375,403, 439]).

The vi text editor is a legacy application emblematic of pre-GUI text-based sequential programming and command-line interaction. Most vi users were computer specialists – expert users. GUI-based systems necessitate a higher standard of usability, since they are targeted at a broad base of users, many of whom are not computer professionals per se. This was argued in Chapter 1. Yet, problems still exist. Similar to the vi example is INSERT vs. Overtype mode on Microsoft Word. See Fig. 3.46b. Word's default mode is INSERT. In INSERT mode, typed text appears within existing text. In Overtype mode, typed text overwrites existing text. There are two problems: changing modes and mode visibility. Changing modes uses the INSERT key. Simple enough, but a quick look at keyboard images reveals considerable variability in the location of the INSERT key.[22] Seems the INSERT key is not important enough to have entrenched itself in a consistent location. And, for good reason. Many users rarely, if ever, use this key. Furthermore, INSERT is sometimes on a key with modes. In "normal mode" the key means something (perhaps INSERT), in "function-lock mode," it means something else. So, the INSERT key may be pressed by accident, if there is confusion on the current mode of the key. This amounts to a "mode within a mode."

So, changing modes is a potential problem with the INSERT key. Mode visibility is also a problem. There is feedback (see Fig. 3.46b), but it is in a status bar along the bottom of the screen. It is so subtle that many users are not likely to notice. Furthermore, a user who inadvertently enters Overtype mode may not have a linguistic

---

[22] Many keyboard layouts can be found at http://images.google.com/. The INSERT key may appear (a) along the top row of function keys, (b) in the numeric keypad, (c) in the block above the arrow keys, or (d) along the bottom row in the main keyboard.

association of "overtype" with the problem they are experiencing. This is an example of a *gulf of evaluation* – a disconnect between what the system provides and what the user intends and expects [376, p. 51].[23]

From an empirical research perspective, it is worth thinking about ways to improve interaction that involves modes. Feedback is the critical issue. Can audio feedback improve a user's awareness of mode transitions? Can a larger visual indication help, and, if so, what are the trade-offs? Is mode awareness improved if a large visual indication appears in the centre of the screen when a mode is entered, and then shrinks to a small persistent mode display at the bottom of the screen? See also student exercise 3-7 at the end of this chapter.

3.5.3 Graphics and 3D

Modes are common in graphics and 3D interaction. Consider the control-display operations in Fig. 3.47. In (a) the hand+mouse movement combines side-to-side and forward-backward motion. The object manipulated on the display moves similarly. Of course, the hand-mouse motion is on the desktop, or x-z plane, while the object motion is on the display, or x-y plane, using the labelling in Fig. 3.25. Despite the spatial incongruence, users are accustomed to this (learned) relationship. In Fig. 3.47b the hand-mouse action includes a sweeping or rotating motion. There is an additional deficiency here. Note that the final position of the triangle is the same in (a) and (b). Yet the hand-mouse movements were different. Let's examine this in more detail.

If the user wanted the triangle to move as the hand moves, then there is a breakdown in the interaction. This occurs because of a gap between the capabilities of 2D pointing devices, such as a mouse, and the characteristics of a 2D surface. The typical fix is a *rotate mode*. To rotate the triangle in a typical graphics application, a few steps are involved: (1) select the triangle, (2) select the application's rotate tool, (3) acquire a handle on the triangle, (4) drag the handle. This is shown in Fig. 3.48. Part (a) shows the Microsoft PowerPoint rotate tool, with instructions below on using it. Part (b) shows the triangle being rotated. Side-to-side x-axis motion or forward-backward z-axis motion of the mouse rotates the triangle. There is clearly a disconnect. We manage, but the interaction is awkward and difficult. For one, translation of the triangle is prevented while in rotate mode. This control-display relationship is anything but natural.

---

[23] User frustration with INSERT vs. Overtype mode in Microsoft Word is well-travelled in online help forums. With Office 2010, the INSERT key is disabled by default but is enabled through a setting in the Options → Advanced dialog. If enabled, the INSERT key toggles between INSERT mode and Overtype mode; however, there is no feedback indicating the current mode.

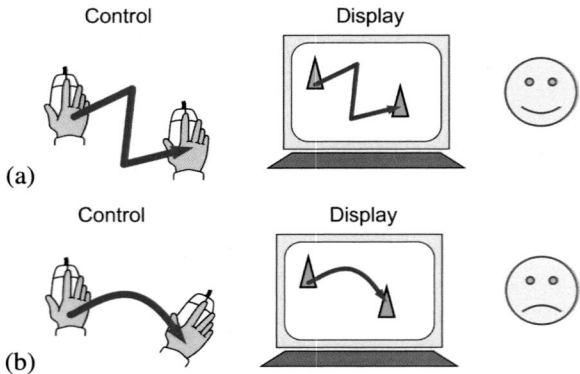

FIGURE 3.47

Two-dimensional movement with the hand+mouse. (a) x and y displacement only. (b) z-axis rotation of the hand+mouse is not sensed, so the object on the display undergoes x and y displacement only.

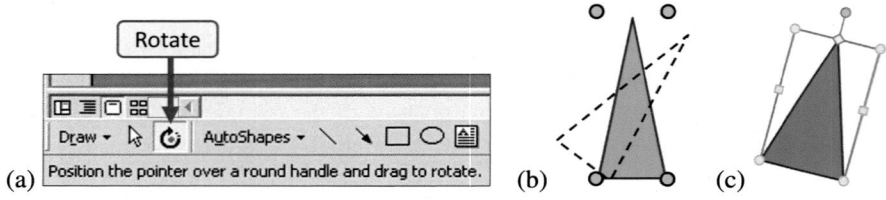

FIGURE 3.48

Rotate mode. (a) Microsoft PowerPoint's rotate tool is selected, with instructions below on using it. (b) The selected triangle enters rotate mode. The x and y displacement of the mouse with the button down (dragging) is used to rotate the triangle. (c) Newer version of PowerPoint. Rotate handle appears when triangle is selected.

In newer versions of PowerPoint, a rotate handle appears when an object is selected. See Fig. 3.48c. This eliminates the need for a rotate mode. However, the control-display relationships are the same – one mapping for rotation, another for translation.

Another way to eliminate the rotate mode in 2D is to re-engineer a mouse to sense rotation. Several configurations are possible. Almeida and Cubaud [6] glued two small mice together. See Fig. 3.49a. MacKenzie et al. [323] put the mechanical and electrical components of two mice into a single chassis. Their "two-ball mouse" is shown in Fig. 3.49b. Contemporary designs are more likely to use camera technology. Hannagan and Regenbrecht's [174] TwistMouse in Fig. 3.49c is an example. The latter two configurations are advantageous from the user's perspective, since the device has the look and feel of a conventional mouse.

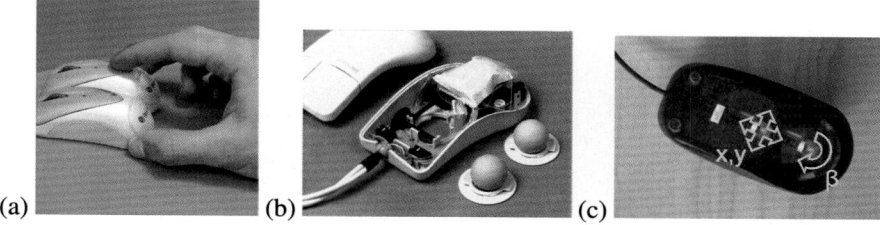

FIGURE 3.49

Mouse configurations sensing rotation. (a) Two small mice glued together [6] (photo courtesy of Rodrigo Almeida). (b) The components from two mice assembled in a single chassis [323]. (c) Optical mouse with additional camera for rotation [174] (photo courtesy of Holger Regenbrecht).

For all the examples in Fig. 3.49, the prototype is equivalent to two mice and requires a custom driver to handle both data streams. If the device is manoeuvred with x- and z-axis displacement only, the two data streams are the same. If movement includes y-axis rotation, the two data streams are slightly different. With a little trigonometry, the driver is able to produce y-axis rotation data coincident with x- and z-axis translation. Thus, an acquired object can undergo translation and rotation at the same time.

There are interesting design issues for a 3 DOF mouse. Usually the extra DOF is not needed; so, the rotation data can be ignored most of the time. When a task requires both translation and rotation, a modifier key can engage the third DOF. This in itself is interesting. Recall that our analysis began as an effort to eliminate the rotate mode in graphics applications. Yet, the solution includes modes: a 2 DOF translate-only mode and a 3 DOF translate-rotate mode.

Another challenge is in accommodating the biomechanics of the lower arm. It is difficult to effect the required wrist movement if an on-screen object is rotated through a wide angle, such as 200°. A solution is to use another modifier key to amplify the angular mapping of mouse rotation. This is analogous to CD gain, except the gain is applied to rotation. Hinckley et al. [193] take a different approach. Their system is camera-based, with a mouse pad serving as the ground plane for the camera image. They propose a two-handed technique: One hand manipulates and rotates the mouse, while the other hand counter-rotates the mouse pad. Large rotation angles are thereby possible.

Although a 3 DOF mouse demos well, a complete bottom-up redesign is necessary for deployment as a product. Today's optical mice are well suited to this. Since the built-in camera captures 2D images (e.g., 18 × 18) of the desktop surface at 1000+ frames per second, it is relatively easy to determine the rotational component of mouse movement without a second camera (as used in the TwistMouse; see Fig. 3.49c). However, turning such initiatives into products is easier said than done. Besides re-engineering the hardware and firmware, a new driver protocol is needed

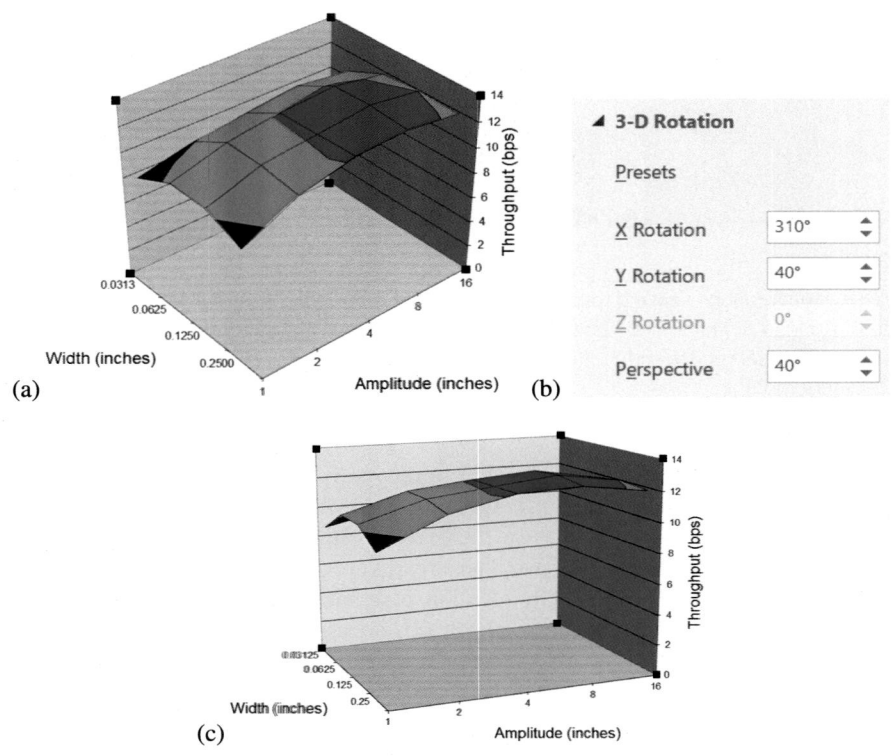

FIGURE 3.50

Two views of the same data in the same chart. (a) Original chart. (b) Pop-up dialog for 3D-Rotation. (c) Rotated view, following awkward and unnatural interaction.

(with y-axis rotation data) along with modifications to applications to effectively use the full potential of 3 DOF data.

The situation is more complicated in 3D environments, since there are six degrees of freedom (see Fig. 3.27, p. 115). If the input controller has fewer than six degrees of freedom, then modes are needed to fully access the environment. A particularly unnatural interaction is shown in Fig. 3.50. The figure shows a 3D surface plot in Microsoft Excel.[24] Part (a) shows one view. To alter the view, the user must right-click on the chart to access a popup dialog, then select "3D-rotation" to bring up a rotation panel (b). There is no interactive method to change the view. Obtaining the view in part (c) requires clicking arrow buttons in the rotation panel. The interaction is clumsy and degrades to trial and error.

---

[24] The data are from the pin-transfer task in Fitts' 1954 paper [125, Table 3]. Fitts included a hand-drawn 3D plot similar to that shown here [125, Figure 4].

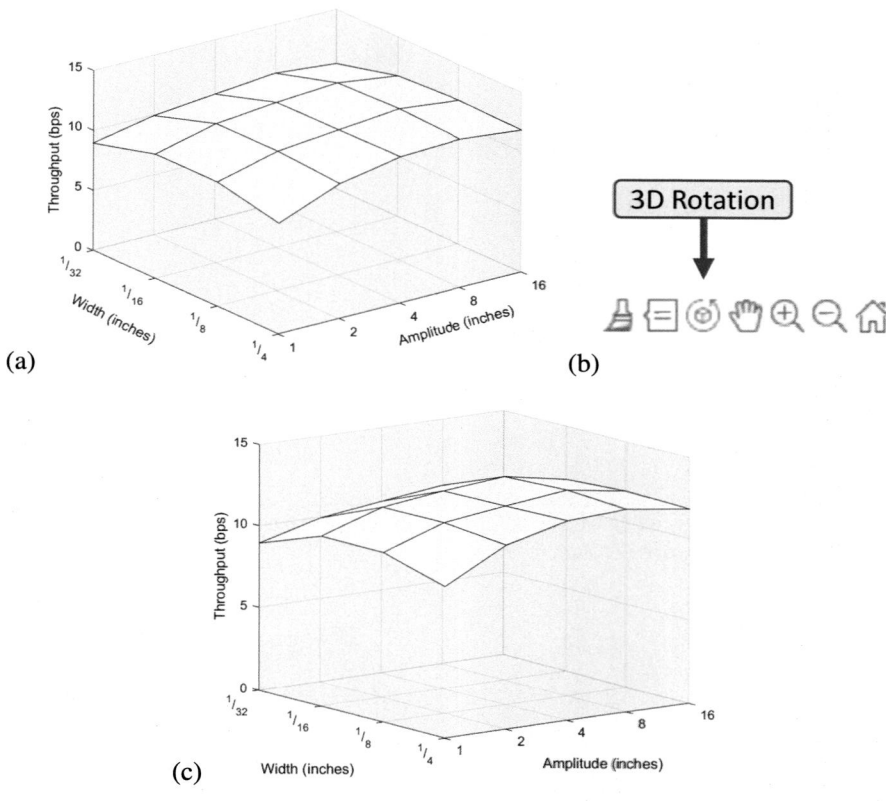

(a)

3D Rotation

(b)

(c)

FIGURE 3.51

Rotating a 3D chart in MATLAB. See text for discussion.

A slight improvement is shown in Fig. 3.51. Part (a) shows a chart for the same data rendered in MATLAB®. Part (b) shows interactive tools that appear when the chart is selected. With the 3D rotation tool active, the user can interactively rotate the image by dragging the mouse. Mouse translation along the x-axis rotates the image about the y-axis and mouse translation along the y-axis rotates the image about the x-axis. Image rotation about the z-axis is not possible.

Desktop systems are simply inappropriate for this sort of interaction. If 3D is the goal, then a more sophisticated setup is needed. Typically, different or additional devices are added to provide more natural control-display relationships. These systems may include a head-mounted display and a 6 DOF motion tracker to provide an improved view of 3D objects in 3D space. Not only is the head position tracked with six degrees of freedom, the image provided to each eye is altered slightly to provide depth cues, making the virtual scene appear three-dimensional. With the addition of

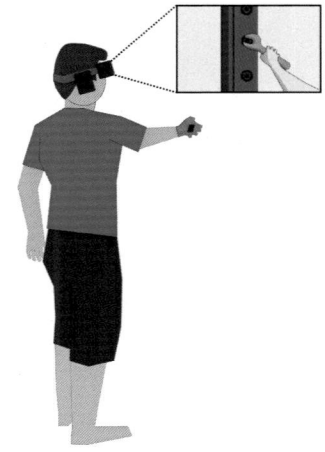

FIGURE 3.52

A head-mounted display along with 6 DOF head and hand trackers provides 3D viewing and control (sketch courtesy of Bartosz Bajer).

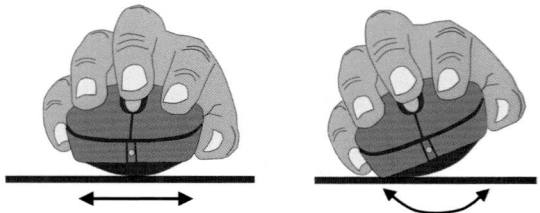

FIGURE 3.53

The Rockin'Mouse works like a mouse but also senses side-to-side (θ_z) rotation (shown) and forward-backward (θ_x) rotation [18]. Rotation about the z-axis is not sensed (sketch courtesy of Bartosz Bajer).

a 6 DOF hand tracker, more powerful 3D control is possible. An example setup is shown in Fig. 3.52 (see also [138]).

3.6 More about degrees of freedom

The research literature in HCI has numerous examples of devices engineered to provide additional sensing capabilities. The Rockin'Mouse is a 4 DOF mouse with a curved bottom [18]. It senses planar x-z movement, like a regular mouse, but also senses rocking side-to-side (θ_z) and to-and-fro (θ_x). Fig. 3.53 illustrates.

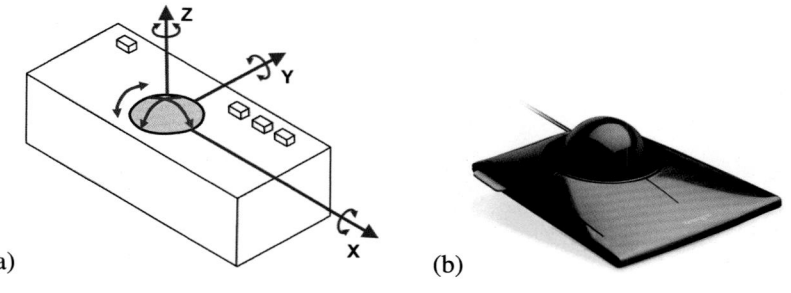

(a)   (b)

FIGURE 3.54

Three-axis trackball. (a) Concept from 1981 [120]. (b) SlimBlade trackball by Kensington.

The prototype operated on the surface of a tablet. A cordless sensor was mounted in the centre of the Rockin'Mouse. The sensor was extracted from the tablet's stylus. From the tablet's perspective, the Rockin'Mouse is a stylus. From the user's perspective, it looks and feels like a mouse, except for the rounded bottom. The tablet senses and reports the x and z positions of the sensor as well as tilt (θ_x and θ_z). Balakrishnan et al. [18] evaluated the Rockin'Mouse in a 3D positioning task using tilt for the up-down movement of the object. In the mouse comparison condition, participants had to select a handle on the object to switch movement modes. Overall, the Rockin'Mouse was about 30% faster than the mouse.

Evans et al. [120] in 1981 anticipated a three-axis trackball that senses rotation about each of the x, y, and z axes. See Fig. 3.54a. Even though the usual operation of a trackball is x-y planar control of a pointer, the ball freely rotates; so, the labelling of the degrees of freedom in Fig. 3.54a is appropriate. A device like this has potential to perform well in controlling the view of the 3D surface plot in Fig. 3.50. Spatial congruence is clearly possible between the three-axis rotation of the ball and similar rotation of the surface plot. Of course, it is relatively easy to include modes, allowing mouse-emulation.

A commercial example of a three-axis trackball is the SlimBlade by Kensington.[25] See Fig. 3.54b. Canham et al. [56] used the device for colour space navigation. Their setup used ball rotation about the x, y, and z axes to control a colour's brightness, saturation, and hue, respectively.

There is more to degrees of freedom than simply counting them. It is important to consider the relationship between device properties, such as degrees of freedom, and task requirements. Jacob et al. [217] speak of the *integrality* and *separability* of degrees of freedom. With a regular mouse, controlling one degree of freedom in isolation of the other is difficult. Consider drawing a horizontal line with a mouse using the drawing mode of an application. The task is difficult because the x and y degrees of freedom are integrated. Of course, degrees of freedom can be separated. A classic

---

[25] https://www.kensington.com/.

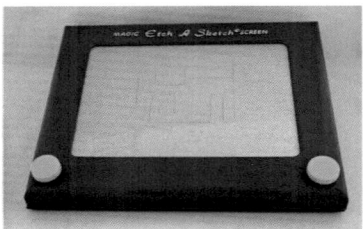

FIGURE 3.55

Etch-A-Sketch children's toy with separate controls for the x and y degrees of freedom.

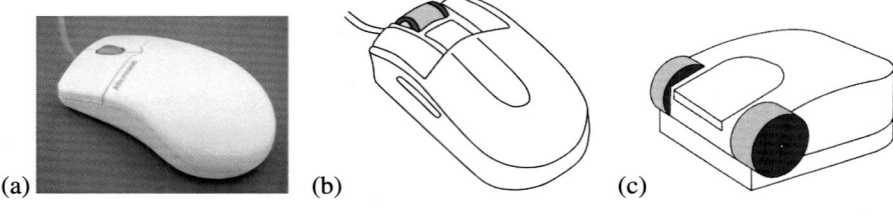

(a)   (b)   (c)

FIGURE 3.56

Wheel mice. (a) Microsoft's IntelliMouse. (b) Mouse Systems' ProAgio (adapted from [144]). (c) Roller Mouse research prototype (adapted from [500]).

example for x-y positioning is the children's toy Etch-A-Sketch introduced in the 1950s by the Ohio Art Company. See Fig. 3.55. There are separate 1 DOF controllers to move the drawing instrument along the x and y axes. Drawing a horizontal line is easy. Drawing a diagonal line is a challenge, however. See Buxton [50] for additional discussion on input using the Etch-A-Sketch and other toys.

Another example is the wheel mouse, released in 1996 as Microsoft's IntelliMouse. See Fig. 3.56a. The rotating wheel gives the mouse an extra – and separate – degree of freedom. A less successful version was Mouse System's ProAgio, released about a year earlier. See Fig. 3.56b. Even earlier was Venolia's Roller Mouse [499], presented at the annual ACM SIGCHI conference in 1993. See Fig. 3.56c. The Roller Mouse had two wheels. The intended use was controlling degrees of freedom in 3D graphics applications.

Additional, but separate, degrees of freedom are evident in Balakrishnan and Patel's PadMouse [20]. See Fig. 3.57a. A touchpad was added to the surface of a regular mouse. The intent was to support pie menu access with gestures on the touchpad while the mouse operated as usual, controlling an on-screen pointer. Clearly, combining interaction in this manner requires separating the degrees of freedom for pie menu access and pointer control.

Silfverberg et al. [453] describe a display screen that allows the displayed image to be zoomed and panned by two touch sensors positioned underneath the device (Fig. 3.57b). Occlusion is avoided since the fingers act below the display. As well,

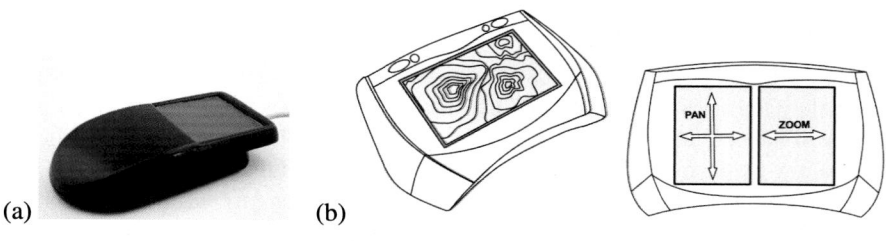

FIGURE 3.57

Adding degrees of freedom with a touchpad. (a) PadMouse [20]. (b) Zooming and panning display screen [453], top view (left), bottom view (right).

FIGURE 3.58

Multi-touch sensing input devices [504] (photo courtesy of Nicolas Villar).

the 1 DOF zooming and 2 DOF panning operations are separated and, thus, do not interfere.

Villar et al. [504] describe a variety of mouse configurations instrumented to detect touch, including multi-touch. The devices use IR transmitters that inject light into the edge of an acrylic surface. An IR camera below the surface receives an image of the surface. When fingers contact the surface, the light is scattered at the points of contact. Image processing software determines the location and pressure of the points of contact. Some of the device configurations are shown in Fig. 3.58. The devices support multi-touch gestures as well as regular mouse operations.

One configuration is the CapMouse (second from left in Fig. 3.58). It uses a capacitive sensor, rather than an IR transmitter and camera. The setup is similar to Balakrishnan and Patel's PadMouse (Fig. 3.57a), except the touch-sensing surface is contoured and seamlessly integrates with the device chassis.

The message in this section is that degrees of freedom (DOF) is a property that spans a rich complement of tasks and interaction techniques. User interactions are plentiful, and they are juxtaposed in complex ways, such as overlapping, sequential, or in parallel. The degrees of freedom in the interactions merit deeper consideration. Opportunities for empirical research are plentiful. Let's move on to the unique interactions in the world of mobile computing.

3.7 Mobile context

Mobile computing dates to the 1980s, with the emergence of pocket organizers and personal digital assistants (PDAs). This was followed in the early 1990s with the first pen-based tablet computers and mobile phones supporting text messaging. A significant follow-on event from a user interface standpoint was the release in 2007 of the Apple iPhone. With the arrival of the iPhone and follow-on products, such as touch-based tablet computers, the landscape of HCI experienced a dramatic shift. Pressing keys on small keyboards or gesturing with a stylus gave way to finger actions: swiping, flicking, pinching, tapping, and so on. Furthermore, devices in this genre include additional components to enhance the user experience. Cameras, light sensors, vibrotactile actuators, accelerometers, gyroscopes, GPS trackers, and so on, work together in broadening the experience for users. With the prefix "smart," these devices are full-fledged media players, providing unprecedented connectivity to users, through both 5G and Internet access.

Many of the interaction elements noted above for desktop environments don't even exist in the mobile context. This follows from the distinction between *indirect input* and *direct input*, as elaborated earlier (see Fig. 3.1). Cursor or pointer control using a mouse or touchpad is an example of *indirect input* because the system response is spatially displaced from the input device. Finger input on a touch-sensitive display uses *direct input* because the system response is located at the point of touch. On a touch-sensitive display, a pointer, or on-screen tracking symbol, is not needed. Properties like control-display mappings and CD gain do not exist for direct input. Mouse-based systems, on the other hand, require an on-screen tracking symbol such as a cursor or pointer. Of course, this is a by-product of indirect input. Direct touch input is the full embodiment of WYSIWYG interaction – *what you see is what you get*. A simple example on a tablet computer appears in Fig. 3.59. A slider to control screen brightness appears on the tablet's display (left). The finger directly interacts with the slider (right).

However, direct touch input has an unfortunate side effect: Precise pixel-level selection is difficult. On a desktop system, the tip of the on-screen pointer visually identifies the selection point. With touchscreens, users typically do not know, and cannot control, the precise location of the contact point. There are two reasons: (i) the finger occludes the location of contact, and (ii) finger contact forms an area, not a point. This is the "fat finger problem" [518] noted earlier and follows from the physiology of the human finger. The size and shape of the contact area varies by user and also by usage patterns, such as the force applied or the reach of the arm. See also Chapter 2 (section 2.5.1, Limbs).

New technologies bring possibilities, which in turn bring challenges. With challenges come ideas for solutions. Early research on touchscreens focused on their use in information kiosks. Improving the precision of pointing was a key challenge. How can occlusion and precision be accommodated for touch input? Are there alternate methods to consider and, if so, which ones perform better? These are the sorts of questions that underpin empirical research in HCI.

FIGURE 3.59

Direct input. A slider GUI element to control the display brightness (expanded, left) is engaged directly by the user's finger (right).

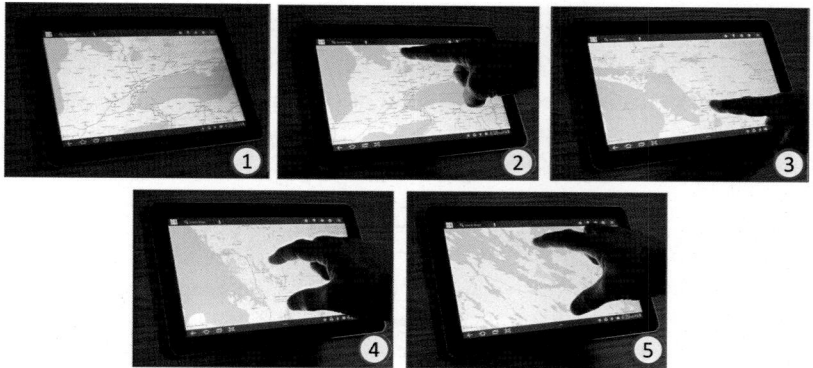

FIGURE 3.60

Touch example. A map image (1) is moved by touching the map (2) and dragging the finger (3). The image is zoomed in by touching with two fingers (4) and widening the distance between the fingers (5).

Yet another difference between touch input and mouse input is the ability of touch-sensing technologies to sense multiple contact points. Multi-touch, indeed, is one of the most provocative interaction techniques to enter mainstream computing. An example is shown in Fig. 3.60 where a map is manoeuvred by a sliding gesture, then resized with a two-finger reverse pinching gesture.

Multi-touch does not end at two. Contemporary devices can sense several contact points. Fig. 3.61a is a multi-touch demonstration on a tablet computer. Although the thumb contacts are partly occluded in the image, ten contact points are sensed. They appear as coloured circles. Beginning with the pinkie contact on the right, the circles follow the colour coding for numbers on electronic resistors: black (0), brown (1), red (2), orange (3), yellow (4), green (5), blue (6), violet (7), gray (8), and white (9).

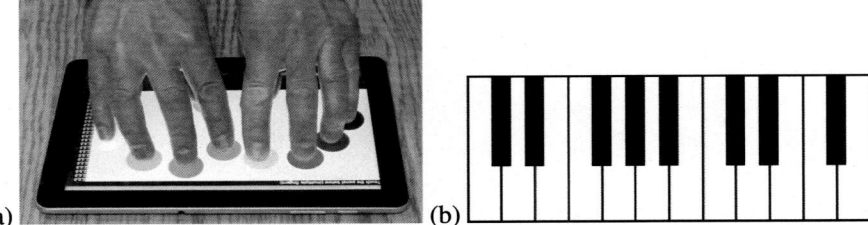

(a)   (b)

FIGURE 3.61

Multi-touch demonstration. (a) Ten contact points are sensed. Markers, beginning with the user's pinkie finger on the right, follow the colour codes for electronic resistors. (b) Piano keyboard application.

It is easy to imaging applications for input using multiple contacts points (> 2). A simple example is the piano keyboard in Fig. 3.61b. This was suggested as early as 1985 as an application of multi-touch input system described by Lee et al. [275]. Their system also sensed pressure (as do contemporary touch-sensitive displays). With added pressure data, both the pitch and loudness of notes can be controlled upon finger contact. Multi-touch piano keyboard applications are readily downloadable for Android tablets.

Besides multi-touch, today's mobile devices include a host of additional components. A good example is the accelerometer. The technology has matured in terms of pricing, size, data speed, precision, and power consumption to the point where accelerometers are now standard on smartphones and tablet computers. An accelerometer allows the angle or tilt of the device to be sensed. And so, tilt as an input primitive has entered the mainstream of interaction techniques in mobile computing.

Early research on tilt, dating to the 1990s, examined its potential for tasks such as document scrolling [25,177,455], panning and zooming [455], menu navigation [411], and changing screen orientation [192]. As with any new technology, research initially focused on *what can be done* rather than *how well it can be done*. The focus was on the technology and its integration in prototype devices. Test results with users tended to be anecdotal, not empirical. In fact, tilt is a user input primitive that is well suited to empirical inquiry. For each of the tasks just cited, several input methods either currently exist or can be envisioned as alternatives. Implementing the tasks using tilt is novel and exciting. But, how well can the tasks be executed? How does tilt input compare to alternative methods in terms of human performance? What aspects of tilt influence human performance? These questions are well suited to empirical inquiry. One such evaluation compared four settings of tilt gain: 25, 50, 100, 200 [326].[26] The experiment used a position-select task similar to the multi-direction task in ISO 9241-

---

[26] Tilt gain is a multiplier that maps the magnitude of device tilt (degrees) to the velocity of an object on the display (pixels per second).

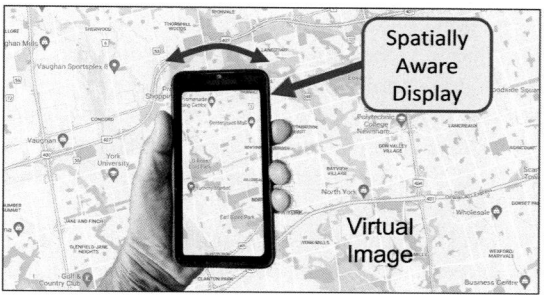

FIGURE 3.62

Spatially aware display. As the device moves, the view into the virtual image moves.

411 [210,466].[27] Results suggest that performance is best (i.e., lower task completion time, higher throughput) for a tilt gain setting in the range of 50 to 100.

In another application, the tilt of a smartphone was used to control the movement of a robot [542]. Other applications used tilt input in games, for example to control the movement of a ball in a marble maze game [86] or the movement of a paddle in Pong [484].

Another application of accelerometer input is a spatially aware display. In this case, a view on the display moves as the device moves, as sensed by the accelerometer. See Fig. 3.62. A variety of new issues arise. For planar 2D movement, the interaction is straightforward. But, what if the device rotates, or moves in and out. How should the view change? Is the interaction fluid and natural? These issues are well-suited to empirical inquiry. Experimental studies of spatially aware displays are reported by Fitzmaurice [128], Rohs and Oulasvirta [419], Cao et al. [57], and others.

If there is one observation that emerges from the annual ACM SIGCHI conference, it is that the pace of innovation in HCI is increasing. New technologies and new ideas for interactions are plentiful and they are emerging quickly. They are often presented, like tilt was initially, as possibilities. Prototypes, demos, videos, posters, work-in-progress contributions, and so on, get the ideas out there. But, sooner or later, plausible ideas need testing with users. Testing that is empirical and experimental is recommended. The results will add to the knowledge base that engineers and designers draw upon in bringing to market new and cool products.

3.8 Interaction errors

Most of analyses in this chapter were directed at the physical properties of the human-machine interface, such as degrees of freedom in 2D or 3D or spatial and temporal

---

[27] ISO 9241-411, reaffirmed in 2022, is an updated version of ISO 9241-9. With respect to performance evaluation, the two versions of the standard are the same.

relationships between input controllers and output displays. Human performance, although elaborated in Chapter 2, has not entered into discussions here, except through secondary observations that certain interactions are better, worse, awkward, or unintuitive. At the end of the day, however, human performance is what counts. Physical properties, although instructive and essential, are secondary. Put another way, human performance is like food, while physical properties are like plates and bowls. It's good and nutritious food we strive for.

Empirical research in HCI is largely about finding physical properties and combinations that improve and enhance human performance. We conclude this chapter on interaction elements with comments on that nagging aspect of human performance that frustrates: interaction errors. Although the time to complete a task can enhance or hinder by degree, errors only hinder. Absence of errors is, for the most part, invisible. As it turns out, errors – interaction errors – are germane to the HCI experience. The big errors are the easy ones – they get fixed. It's the small errors that are interesting. Let's see.

As the field of HCI matures, a common view that emerges is that the difficult problems (in desktop computing) are solved, and that researchers should focus on new frontiers – mobility, surface computing, virtual reality, ubiquitous computing, online social networking, gaming, and so on. This view is partly right. Yes, the emerging themes are exciting and fertile ground for HCI research. And many frustrating UI problems from the old days are gone. But desktop computing is still fraught with problems, lots of problems. Let's examine a few of these. Although the examples below are from desktop computing, there are counterparts in mobile computing. See also student exercise 3-10.

The four examples developed below were chosen for a specific reason. There is a progression. In severity, they range from serious problems causing a loss of information to innocuous problems that most users rarely think about and may not even notice. In frequency, they range from rarely if ever occurring anymore, to occurring perhaps multiple times every minute while users engage in computing activities. The big, bad problems are well-travelled in the literature, with sources providing deep analyses on what went wrong and why (e.g., [66,67,87,229,238,376]). While the big problems get lots of attention, and generally get fixed, the little ones tend to linger. We'll see the effect shortly. Let's begin with one of the big problems.

3.8.1 Lost information

Most users have, at some point, lost information while working on their computer. Instead of saving new work, it was mistakenly discarded, overwritten, or lost in some way. Is there any user who has not experienced this? Of course, everyone has a story of losing data in some silly way. Perhaps there was a distraction. Perhaps we just didn't know. It doesn't matter. It happened. An example is shown in Fig. 3.63. A dialog pops up and the user responded a little too quickly. Press ENTER, with the "Save changes?" dialog (Fig. 3.63a) and all is well, but the same response with the "Discard changes?" dialog spells disaster (Fig. 3.63b). The information is lost. This

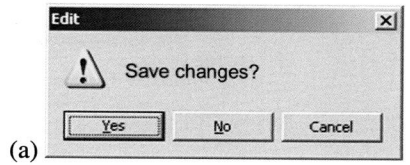 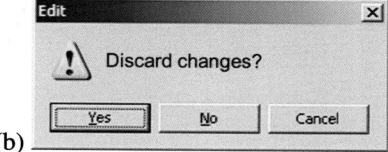

(a)   (b)

FIGURE 3.63

HCI has come a long way. (a) Today's UIs consistently use the same, predictable dialog to alert the user to a potential loss of information. (b) Legacy dialog, rarely seen today.

scenario, told by Cooper [87, p. 14], is a serious UI design flaw. The alert reader will quickly retort, yes, but if the "Discard changes?" dialog defaulted to "No," the information is safe. But, that misses the point. The point is that a user expectation is broken. Broken expectations sooner or later cause errors.

Today, systems and applications consistently use the "Save changes?" dialog in Fig. 3.63a. With time and experience, user expectations emerge and congeal. The "Save changes?" dialog is expected and we act without hesitation. All is well. But new users have no experiences, no expectations. They will develop them sure enough, but there will be some scars along the way. Serious flaws like the "Discard changes?" dialog are rare in desktop applications today.

3.8.2 Caps_Lock error

Another example is entering passwords. If prompted to enter a password, and CAPS_LOCK mode is in effect, logging on will fail and the password must be re-entered. The user may not know CAPS_LOCK is on. Perhaps a key-stroking error occurred. The password is re-entered, slowly and correctly, with the CAPS_LOCK mode still in effect. Oops! Commit the same error a third time and further log-on attempts may be blocked. This is not as serious as loosing information by pressing ENTER in response to a renegade dialog, but, still, this is an interaction error. Or, is it a design flaw? It is completely unnecessary, it is a nuisance, it slows our interaction, and it is easy to correct. Today, many systems have corrected this problem (Fig. 3.64a), while others have not (Fig. 3.64b).

The CAPS_LOCK error is not so bad. But, it's bad enough that it occasionally receives enough attention to be the beneficiary of the few extra lines of code necessary to popup a CAPS_LOCK alert.

3.8.3 Hyper-scrolling

Let's examine another small problem. In editing a document, the user might wish to move some text to another location. The task is easy. With the pointer positioned at the beginning of the text, the user presses and holds the primary mouse button and begins dragging. But, the text spans several lines and extends past the viewable region. As the dragging extent approaches the edge of the viewable region, the user is

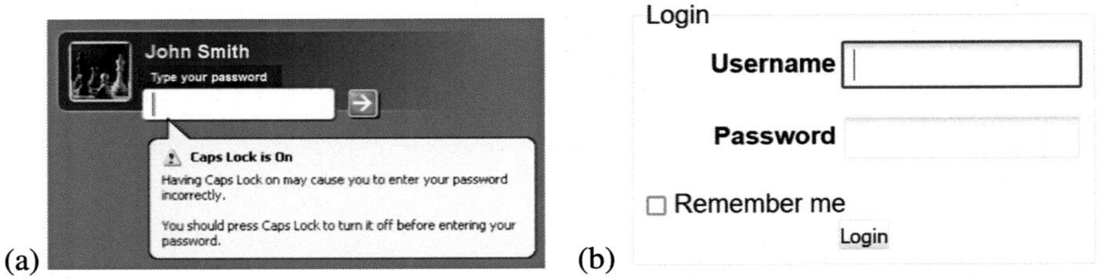

(a) (b)

FIGURE 3.64

Entering a password. (a) Some systems alert the user if CAPS_LOCK is on. (b) Others do not.

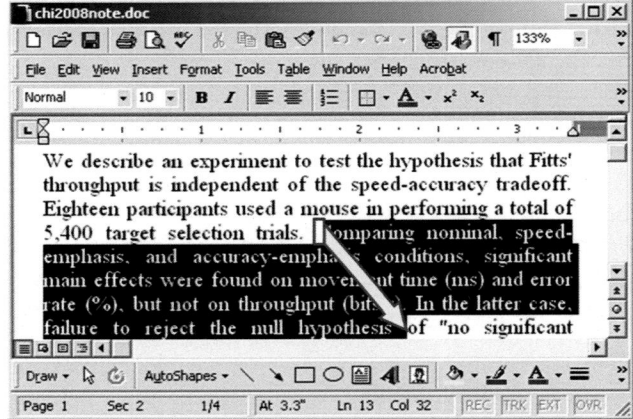

FIGURE 3.65

On the brink of hyper-speed scrolling. As the mouse pointer is dragged toward the edge of the viewable region, the user is precipitously close to losing control over the speed of dragging.

venturing into to a difficult situation. The interaction is about to change dramatically. See Fig. 3.65. Within the viewable region, the interaction is position-control – the displacement of the mouse pointer controls the *position* of the dragging extent. As soon as the mouse pointer moves outside the viewable region, scrolling begins and the interaction becomes velocity-control – the displacement of the mouse pointer controls the velocity of the dragging extent. User beware!

In velocity-control mode, it is anyone's guess what will happen. This is a design flaw. A quick check of several applications while working on this example revealed dramatically different responses to the transition from position control to velocity control. In one case, scrolling was so fast, the dragging region extended to the end of the document in less than the time one could react ($\sim$ 200 ms). In another case, the velocity of scrolling was controllable, but it was frustratingly slow. Can you think of a way to improve this interaction? A two-handed approach, perhaps. Any technique that gets the job done and allows the user to develop an expectation of the interaction is an improvement. Perhaps there is some empirical research waiting in this.

Whether the velocity-control is too sensitive or too sluggish really doesn't matter. What matters is that the user experience is broken or awkward. Any pretence to the interaction being facile, seamless, or transparent is gone. The user will recover, and no information is lost, but the interaction has degraded to error recovery. This is a design error or, at the very least, a design-induced error. Let's move on to a very minor error.

3.8.4 Focus uncertainty

When an application or dialog is active, one of the UI components has focus and receives an event from the keyboard if a key is pressed. For buttons, focus is usually indicated with a dashed border (see "Yes" button in Fig. 3.63). For input fields, it is usually indicated with a flashing insertion bar ("|"). "Focus advancement" refers to the progression of focus from one UI component to the next. There is wide-spread inconsistency in the way UI widgets acquire and lose focus and in the way focus advances from one component to the next. The user is in trouble most of the time. Here's a quick example. When a login dialog pops up, can you immediately begin to enter your username and password? Sometimes, yes. Sometimes, no. In the latter case, the entry field does not have focus. The user must click in the field with the mouse pointer or press TAB to advance the focus point to the input field. Fig. 3.64 (above) provides examples. Both are real interfaces. The username field in (a) appears with focus; the same field in (b) appears without focus. The point is simply that users don't know. This is a small problem (or is it an interaction error?), but it is entirely common. Focus uncertainty is everywhere in today's user interfaces. Here's another more specific example.

Many online activities, such as reserving an airline ticket or booking a vacation, require a user to enter data into a form. The input fields often require very specific information, such as a two-digit month, a seven-digit account number, and so on. When the information is entered, does focus advance automatically or is a user action required? Mostly, we just don't know. So, we remain "on guard." Fig. 3.66 gives an example, a real example, from a typical login dialog. The user is requested to enter an account number. Account numbers are 9 digits, in three 3-digit segments. After seeing the dialog, the user looks at the keyboard and begins entering: 9, 8, 4, and then what? Chances are the user is looking at the keyboard while entering the numeric account number. Even though the user can enter the entire nine digits at once, interaction is halted after the first group because the user doesn't know whether focus will automatically advance to the next field. There are no expectations here, because this example of GUI interaction has not evolved and stabilized on a consistent behaviour. Data entry fields have not reached the evolutionary status of, for example, dialogs for saving vs. discarding changes (Fig. 3.63a). The user either acts, with 50% likelihood of committing an error, or pauses, switching their attention to the display (*Has the focus advanced to the next field?*).

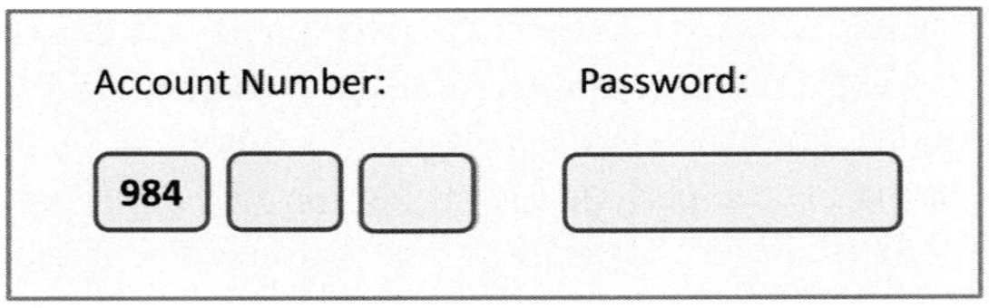

FIGURE 3.66

Inconsistent focus advancement keeps the user "on guard." What to do next?

Strictly speaking, there is no gulf of evaluation here. Although not shown in the figure, the insertion point is present. After entering 984, the insertion point is either after the 0 in the first field, if focus did not advance, or at the beginning of the next field, if focus advanced. So, the system does indeed "provide a physical representation that can be perceived and that is directly interpretable in terms of the intentions and expectations of the person" [376, p. 51]. That's not good enough. The user's attention is on the keyboard while the physical presentation is on the system's display. The disconnect is small, but, nevertheless, a shift in the user's attention is required.

The absence of expectations keeps the user on guard. The user is often never quite sure what to do or what to expect. The result is a slight increase in the attention demanded during interaction, and this produces a slight decrease in transparency. Instead of engaging in the task, attention is diverted to the needs of the computer. The user is like a wood carver who sharpens tools, rather than creating works of art.

3.8.5 Little errors linger

Where the consequences of errors are small, such as an extra button click or gaze shift, errors tend to linger. For the most part, these errors aren't on anyone's radar. The programmers who build the applications have bigger problems to focus on, like working on their checklist of new features to add to version 2.0 of the application before an impending deadline.[28] The little errors persist. Often, programmers' discretion rules the day [87, p. 47]. An interaction scenario that makes sense to the programmer is likely to percolate through to the final product, particularly if it is just a simple thing like focus advancement. Do programmers ever discuss the nuances of focus advancement in building a GUI? Perhaps. But, was the discussion famed in terms of the impact on the attention or gaze shifts imposed on the user? Not likely.

Each time a user shifts his or her attention (e.g., from the keyboard to the display and back), the cost is two gaze shifts. Each gaze shift, or saccade, takes from

---

[28] The reader who detects a modicum of sarcasm here is referred to Cooper [87, pp. 47-48 and elsewhere] for a full frontal assault on the insidious nature of feature bloat in software applications. The reference to version 2.0 of a nameless application is in deference to Johnson's second edition of his successful book where the same tone appears in the title: *GUI Bloopers 2.0*. McGrenere and Moore provide more sober and academic look at software bloat, feature creep, and the like [349].

10 to 100 ms [107, p. 40].[29] These little bits of interaction add up. They are the fine-grained details – the microstructures and microstrategies used by, or imposed on, the user. "Microstrategies focus on what designers would regard as the mundane aspects of interface design; the ways in which subtle features of interactive technology influence the ways in which users perform tasks" [155, p. 232]. Designers might view these fine-grained details as a mundane sidebar to the bigger goal, but the reality is different. Details are everything. User experiences exist as collections of microstrategies. Whether booking a vacation online or just hanging out with friends on a social networking site, big actions are collections of little actions. To the extent possible, user actions form the experience, our experience. It is unfortunate that they often exist simply to service the needs of the computer or application.

Another reason little errors tend to linger is that they are often deemed *user errors*, not design, programming, or system errors. These errors, like most, are more correctly, *design-induced errors* [67, p. 12]. They occur "when designers of products, systems, or services, fail to account for the characteristics and capabilities of people and the vagaries of human behaviour" [66, p. 11]. We should all do a little better.

Fig. 3.67 illustrates a trade-off between the cost of errors and the frequency of errors. There is no solid ground here – it's just a sketch. The four errors described above are shown. The claim is that high-cost errors occur with low frequency. They receive a lot of attention and they get dealt with. As systems mature and the big errors get fixed, designers shift their efforts to less costly errors, like the CAPS_LOCK design-induced error, or a consistent implementation of velocity-controlled scrolling. Eventually more and more systems include reasonable and appropriate implementations of these interactions. Divergence in the implementations diminishes and, taken as a whole, there is an industry-wide coalescing toward the same, consistent implementation (e.g., a popup alert for CAPS_LOCK). The ground is set for a user expectation to take hold.

Of the errors noted in Fig. 3.67, discard changes is ancient history (in computing terms), CAPS_LOCK is still a problem but is improving, scrolling frenzy is much better in new applications, and focus uncertainty is, well, a mess. The cost is minor, but the error happens frequently.

Here is another example of a little error. Actually, it's not an error. It's just a small annoying disconnect. Consider Fig. 3.68. The user knows what's going on, but isn't sure what to do. The figure shows a field in an online form supporting "auto complete" (aka "type ahead").[30] The user is entering "Canada." After "Ca" some options appear. How to select "Canada?"

Answering the question above isn't the point. The point is that the user isn't sure what to do. TAB doesn't work, neither does ENTER. The user must type down-arrow ($\downarrow$) followed by ENTER. The user will likely to get through this without any serious

---

[29] An eye movement involves both a saccade and fixation. A saccade – the actual movement of the eye – is fast, about 30 ms. Fixations take longer as they involve perceiving the new stimulus and cognitive processing of the stimulus.

[30] The UI in the figure appears while creating an account with precisionconference.com/~sigchi/.

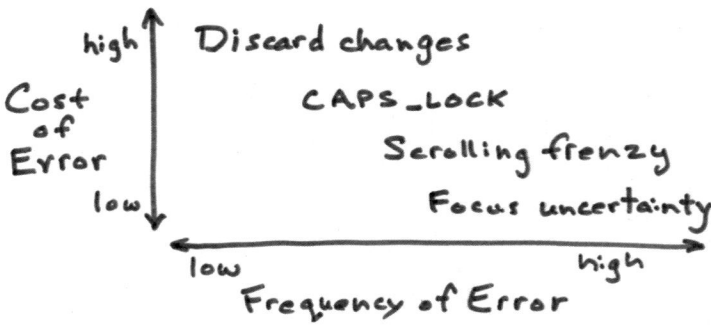

FIGURE 3.67

Trade-off between the cost of errors and the frequency of errors.

Country | Ca
Canada
Cambodia
Cameroon
Cape Verde
Cayman Islands

FIGURE 3.68

Auto complete. What to do next?

misstep. The problem is that the interaction is not standardized: it's hit and miss, trial and error. Play with a few examples online, and you'll experience the same issues. See also student exercise 3-11.

Graphical user interfaces have matured for more than forty years. Surely... Again, you get my point. Let me finish with a small observation. There are many ACM conferences with the word "Intelligent" in the title. One is called the International Conference on Intelligent User Interfaces, or IUI for short. It's an annual conference dating to 1993. I suspect the researchers attending this conference are working on "big problems." My example here is by all accounts a "small problem." Is it too small to bother with? What do you think?

In many ways, the little errors are the most interesting, because they slipped past designers and programmers. A little self-observation and reflection goes a long way. What were you trying to do? Did it work the first time, just as expected? The small interactions are revealing. What were your hands and eyes doing? Were your interactions quick and natural, or were there unnecessary or awkward steps? Could a slight reworking of the interaction help? Could an attention shift be averted with the judicious use of auditory or tactile feedback? Is there a "ready for input" auditory signal that could sound when an input field receives focus? Could this reduce the need for an attention shift? Would this improve user performance? Would it improve the user experience? Would users like it, or would it be annoying? The little possibilities add up. Think of them as opportunities – opportunities for empirical research in HCI. See also student exercises 3-11 and 3-13.

*****

This chapter examined the basic human interactions with computer systems. The next chapter explores the foundations of scientific research.

A web site is available as a resource accompanying this book's second edition:

- http://www.yorku.ca/mack/HCIbook2e

Student exercises

3-1 Using a spreadsheet, compute the average scansteps per character (SPC) for English text entry for two single-switch scanning keyboards: the linear arrangement in Fig. 3.12 and the row-column arrangement in Fig. 3.13. For this analysis, we are only considering the 26 letters of the English alphabet. Use Eq. (3.1) (p. 106) and the letter-frequency data given in Fig. 7.25 (p. 321). The data are also available on this book's web site.

Begin by determining the number of scan steps required to enter each letter. Do this for both keyboards. Using the linear layout, for example, "A" is entered in 1 scanstep, "B" in 2 scansteps, and so on. Using the row-column layout, "A" is entered in 2 scansteps (1 to select the row + 1 to select "A") and "L" is entered in 7 scansteps (3 to reach and select the correct row + 4 to reach "L", see Fig. 3.13).

Which letter arrangement is faster (i.e., requires fewer scansteps per character)? Propose a third letter arrangement that is even faster still.

3-2 Conduct a small experiment on icon recognition, as follows. Find 15 computer users (participants) and inquire as to their computer experience. Find users with different levels of computer experience (e.g., <10 hr/week, 10-25 hr/week, >25 hr/week). Preferably, find an equal number of participants for each experience level. Prepare a handout sheet with the six toolbar buttons (soft controls) shown in Fig. 3.23a (p. 112). The general idea is shown in Fig. 3.69. Ask each participant to identify the purpose of the buttons. Record the responses. Write a brief report on the findings, showing and discussing the responses for participants overall and for participants by button and by experience level.

3-3 Conduct a small experiment on icon recognition, as follows. Find 15 participants. Divide them into groups A, B, and C, five participants per group. Give each participant a copy of the sheet for their group (see Fig. 3.70), and ask them

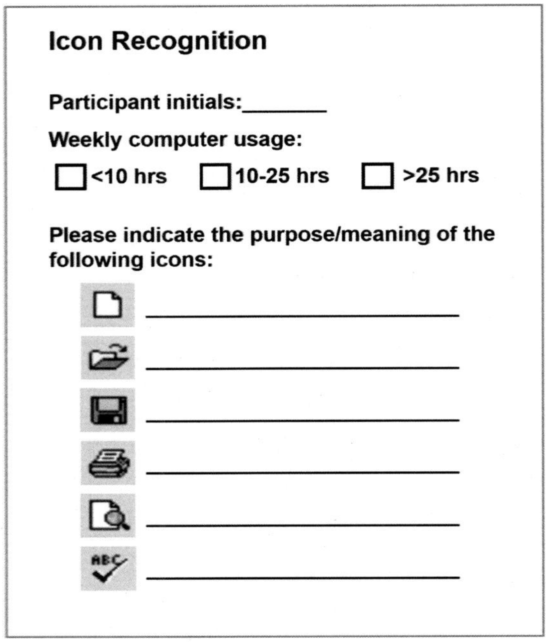

FIGURE 3.69

Student exercise on icon recognition.

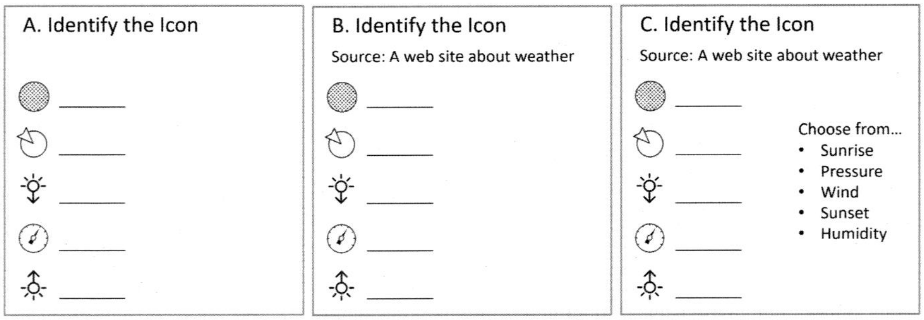

FIGURE 3.70

Student exercise on icon recognition.

to fill in the name or meaning of each icon in the space provided. Score the answers by number of correct responses. Most likely, the results will differ by group. The groups are "unknown subject matter" (A), "known subject matter" (B), and "select from set" (C). Prepare a brief report or slide show presentation on your findings.

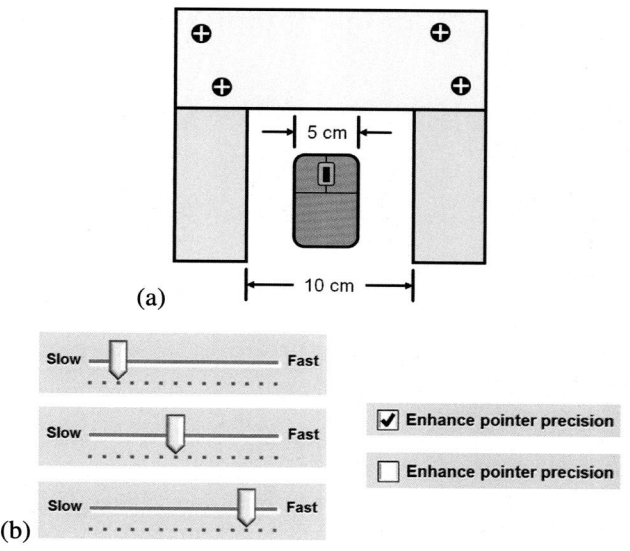

FIGURE 3.71

Student exercise on CD gain. (a) Apparatus. (b) Mouse speed settings.

Save the data from this mini-experiment. After studying Chapter 6 on hypothesis testing, analyse the data to determine if the responses are significantly different by group.

3-4 Conduct a small experiment on panning and zooming using Google Street View. Devise three tasks and measure users' performance using two input methods (e.g., keyboard vs. mouse, touchpad vs. mouse). As an example task, see Fig. 3.30a (p. 117). For this scene, a reasonable task is to pan and zoom to the clock tower (right side of image), determine the time on the clock, then pan and zoom back to the starting position. User performance may be measured a variety of ways, such as task completion time, accuracy in the final scene position, number of steps or corrective actions, etc. Use five participants. Prepare a brief report or slide show presentation on your observations and measurements.

3-5 Conduct a small experiment to measure the CD gain of the mouse and cursor on a computer system. Build an apparatus, perhaps using wood, with an opening for a mouse. See Fig. 3.71a. Measure the width of the opening and the mouse, as in the figure, and determine the span of mouse movement in the opening. Set the pointer speed in the control panel to the centre of the slider position. See Fig. 3.71b. Position the system pointer (cursor) near the left side of the display and position the mouse on the left side of the opening. Move the mouse at a nominal speed across the opening. Measure and record the amount of pointer movement on the display. Repeat five times. Repeat the above exercise for slow

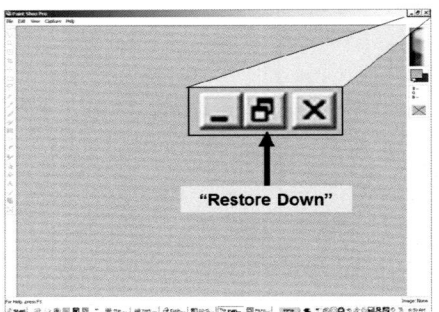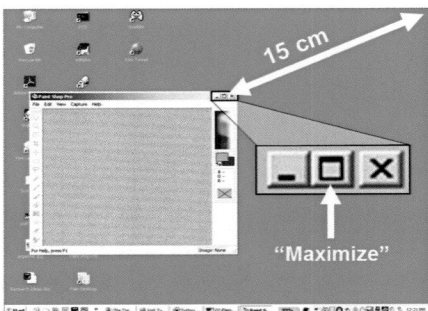

FIGURE 3.72

Student exercise on cursor positioning and CD gain.

and fast mouse movement. As well, repeat for two other pointer speed settings in the control panel and for two pointer precision settings. Tailor according to the control panel options on the computer system used.

The total number of measurements is 90 (5 repetitions × 3 mouse movement speeds × 3 pointer speed settings × 2 enhance pointer precision settings). Prepare a brief report or slide show presentation on your observations and measurements.

3-6 Conduct a small experiment investigating speed and accuracy in cursor positioning as a function of CD gain. Find five computer users (participants). Prepare a computer system as follows. Set the pointer speed in the system control panel to the middle position. Open any application in full screen mode (Fig. 3.72, left). Click the Restore Down button. Position the window by dragging the title bar so that the button (now Maximize) is about 15 cm away from the initial position (Fig. 3.72, right). Ask the participants to use the mouse (or other pointing device) to alternately restore down and maximize the window ten times. Measure and record the time to do the task. Observe and record behaviours (e.g., miss-selections) that represent accuracy. Repeat using a lower and higher pointer speed setting. Prepare a brief report or slide show presentation on your observations and measurements.

3-7 Conduct a small experiment on mode switching, as follows. Find five computer users (participants) who are familiar with Microsoft PowerPoint. Seat them in front of a computer system with a set of slides open in PowerPoint in Slide View mode (aka Normal mode). Have each participant do the following two tasks. First, ask them to use the system's pointing device to switch modes (e.g., to Outline mode or to Slide Sorter mode). Record the time to do the task and whether they used the buttons or menu method (buttons method = soft buttons on the display; menu method = view pull-down menu or ribbon). Return the mode to Slide/Normal. Second, ask them to again change the mode, but this time tell them to use another method, without telling them about the other method. Prepare a brief report or slide show presentation on your observations.

3-8 Many companies use the Word Wide Web to sell their products (e.g., amazon.com). To assist users in making purchases, these sites often use a metaphor borrowed from the user experience in a grocery store. What is this metaphor? With reference to at least two such web sites, discuss the implementation of the metaphor. Describe the metaphor's presentation and the actions supported. Use screen snaps or other aides to support the analysis. Present your findings in a brief report or slide show presentation.

3-9 This chapter includes several analyses comparing the mappings of an input controller with the movement of a cursor on an output display. For example, see the control-display mappings in Figs. 3.24, 3.25, 3.29, and 3.30. Perform a similar analysis for each of the six device conditions in the study by English et al. [115] discussed in Chapter 1 (section 1.4, Invention of the Mouse). The devices are shown in Fig. 1.4a and Fig. 1.5.

3-10 Consider the trade-off between the cost of errors and the frequency of errors shown in Fig. 3.67. The examples are from desktop computing. For each of the four errors, identify a corresponding error from mobile computing using a touchscreen device such as a phone or tablet computer. "Corresponding," in this sense, is the severity in the error, not the interaction per se. Position the errors in a similar chart and develop discussion to justify the choice of error and its placement in the chart. Present your findings in a brief report or slide show presentation.

3-11 Find and analyse five examples of "auto complete" (aka "type ahead") similar to Fig. 3.68. Find examples that demonstrate inconsistency in the interactions. Use an input word or phrase of your choice and describe how the example responds to keypresses such as TAB, ENTER, or arrow keys. Prepare a brief report or slide show presentation. Show screenshots of the interfaces and identify and discuss the interactions that work or don't work to complete the input. Include a table identifying the possibilities and the outcomes for each interface.

3-12 After entering a food order on a mobile app, the button in Fig. 3.73 appears. What is the purpose of this button? If you think the button leads to a screen to pay for the order, you are wrong. The button leads to a screen for setting or changing the method of payment. This is an example of "button uncertainty" – a button with a purpose other than what is reasonably suggested.[31] Find five examples of button uncertainty in mobile or web-based apps for purchasing food or merchandise. Use screen snaps to illustrate the problem and mock-ups to suggest improvements. Prepare a brief report or slide show presentation on your findings.

---

[31] Thanks to Aleks Oniszczak for providing this example.

FIGURE 3.73

Student exercise on button uncertainty.

Double-click on computer and type Ctrl+U for underline.

Double-click on computer and type Ctrl+U for underline.

Double-click on computer and type Ctrl+U for underline.

FIGURE 3.74

Student exercise on click uncertainty.

3-13 This student exercise explores "click uncertainty." What happens when you "click" or "double-click" on a UI element? While entering text in an email or some other application, if a user wishes to underline a word, a common method is to double-click on the word and type Ctrl+U. But, the result is inconsistent among applications. See Fig. 3.74. A common problem is that the underline extends past the word into the SPACE following the word. Most likely, that's not what the user intended. Explore this interaction in some applications. Find at least three examples that demonstrate this problem and three that don't. Prepare a brief report or slide show presentation on your findings. Include screenshots or other visuals to demonstrate the interactions observed.

3-14 In the spirit of the preceding student exercise, find a small problem in a user interface or in how a user interacts with technology of some sort. Find an example where the interaction can be compared in different settings and where the results differ. Prepare a brief report or a slide show presentation describing the problem and demonstrating the inconsistency in different settings.

Scientific foundations

4

In the last chapter, we examined a variety of interaction topics in HCI. By and large, the research methodology for studying these topics is empirical and scientific. Ideas are conceived, developed, and implemented and then framed as hypotheses that are tested in an experiment. This chapter presents the enabling features of this methodology. Our goal is to establish the what, why, and how of research, with a focus on research that is both empirical and experimental. While much of the discussion is general, the examples are directed at HCI. We begin with the terminology surrounding research and empirical research.

4.1 What is research?

Research means different things to different people. "Being a researcher" or "conducting research" carries a certain elevated status in universities, colleges, and corporations. Consequently, the term "research" is bantered around in a myriad of situations. Often, the word is used simply to add weight to an assertion ("Our research shows that . . ."). While writing an early draft of this chapter, a television ad for an Internet service provider was airing in southern Ontario. The ad proclaimed, "Independent research proves our Internet service is the fastest and most reliable – period."[1] One might wonder about the nature of the research, or of the independence and impartiality of the work. Of course, forwarding assertions to promote facts, observations, hypotheses, and the like, is often the goal. But what is research? Surely, it is more than just a word to add weight to a statement or opinion. To rise above conjecture, we demand evidence – evidence meeting a standard of credibility such that the statement is beyond dispute. Providing such credibility is the goal of research.

Returning to the word itself, research has at least three definitions.[2] First, conducting research can be a simple exercise:

> 1. Research is careful or diligent search.

---

[1] Advertisement by Rogers Communications, Inc. airing on television in southern Ontario during the winter of 2008/2009.

[2] http://www.merriam-webster.com/.

Human-Computer Interaction. https://doi.org/10.1016/B978-0-44-314096-9.00010-5

So, carefully searching one's garden to find and remove weeds meets one standard of conducting research. Or, perhaps one undertakes a search on a computer to locate all files modified on a certain date. That's research. It's not the stuff of MSc or PhD theses, but it meets one definition of research.

Here's a second definition:

> 2. Research is collecting information about a particular subject.

So, surveying voters to collect information on political opinions is conducting research. In HCI we might observe people interacting with an interface and collect information about their interactions, such as the number of times they consulted the manual, clicked the wrong button, re-tried an operation, or uttered an expletive. That's research.

The third definition is more elaborate:

> 3. Research is investigation or experimentation aimed at the discovery and interpretation of facts, revision of accepted theories or laws in the light of new facts.

In this, we find several key elements of research that motivate discussions in this book. We find the idea of *experimentation*. Conducting experiments is a central activity in a lot of HCI research, and we will say more about this in the next chapter. In HCI, an experiment is often called a *user study*. The methodology is sometimes formal, sometimes ad hoc (unfortunately). A formal and standardized methodology is preferred because it brings consistency to a body of work and facilitates the review and comparison of research from different studies. One objective of this book is to promote the use of a consistent methodology for experimental research in HCI.

To be fair, the title of this book changed a few times on the way to press. Is the book about *experimental research*? Well, yes, a lot of it is, but there are important forms of HCI research that are non-experimental. So as not to exclude these, the focus shifted to *empirical research*, a broader term that encompasses both experimental and non-experimental methodologies. Among the latter is building and testing models of interaction, which we present in Chapter 7.

Returning to research, the third definition speaks of *facts*. Facts are the building blocks of evidence, and it is evidence we seek in experimental research. For example, we might observe that a user committed three errors while entering a command with an interface. That's a fact. Of course, context is important. Did the user have prior experience with the interface, or with similar interfaces? Was the user a child or a computer expert? Perhaps we observed and counted the errors committed by a group of users while interacting with two different interfaces over a period of time. If they committed 15 percent more errors with one interface than with the other, the facts are more compelling (but, again, context is important). Collectively, the facts form an outward sign leading to evidence – evidence that one interface is better, or less error prone, than the other. Evidence testing is presented in more detail in Chapter 6, Hypothesis Testing. Note that *prove* or *proof* is not used here. In HCI research we do not prove things, we gather facts and formulate and test evidence. Our conclusions always bear the burden of probabilities.

The third definition mentions *theories* and *laws*. Theory has several common meanings, some rather loose, such as *a hypothesis assumed for the sake of argument*[3] or *abstract or speculative thought*.[4] In the sense of Darwin's *theory of evolution* or Einstein's *theory of relativity*, the term "theory" is synonymous with hypothesis. Of course, through experimentation, theories advance beyond argument, investigation, or speculative thought. The stringent demands of scientific inquiry confirmed the hypotheses of these great scientists. When confirmed through research, a theory becomes *a scientifically accepted body of principles that explain phenomena*.

A law is different from a theory. A law is more specific, more constraining, more formal, more binding. In the most exacting terms, a law is a relationship or phenomenon that is *invariable under given conditions*. Since variability is germane to human behaviour, laws are of questionable relevance to HCI.

Of course, HCI has laws. Take HCI's best-known law as an example. Fitts' law refers to a body of work, originally in human motor behaviour [125], but now widely used in HCI. Fitts' work pertained to rapid-aimed movements, such as rapidly moving the hand to acquire an object or, in more recent contexts, rapidly moving a cursor to an object and selecting it in a graphical user interface. Fitts, himself, never proposed a law. He proposed a model of human motor behaviour. And, by all accounts, that's what Fitts' law is – a model, a behavioural, descriptive, and predictive model. It includes equations and such, for predicting the time to do point-select tasks. It is a law only in that other researchers took-up the label as a celebration of the generality and importance of Fitts' seminal work. We should all be so lucky. Fitts' law is presented in more detail in Chapter 7.

Research, according to the third definition, involves *discovery*, *interpretation*, and *revision*. Discovery is obvious enough. That's what we do – look for, or discover, things that are new and useful. Perhaps the discovery is a new style of interface or a new interaction technique. Interpretation and revision are central to research. Research does not proceed in a vacuum. Today's research builds on what is already known or assumed. We interpret what is known, we revise and extend through discovery.

There are additional characteristics of research that are not encompassed in the dictionary definitions. Let's examine a few of these.

4.1.1 Research must be published

Publication is the final step in research. It is also an essential step. Never has this rung as true as in the edict *publish or perish*. Researchers, particularly in academia, must

---

[3] https://www.merriam-webster.com/dictionary.

[4] https://dictionary.apa.org.

publish. A weak or insufficient list of publications might spell disappointment when applying for research funds or for a tenure-track professorship at a university. Consequently, developing the skill to publish begins as a graduate student and continues throughout one's career as a researcher, whether in academia or industry. The details and challenges in writing research papers are elaborated in Chapter 8.

Publishing is crucial, and for good reason. Until it is published, the knowledge gained through research cannot achieve its critical purpose – to extend, refine, or revise the existing body of knowledge in the field. This is so important, that publication bearing a high standard of scrutiny is required. Not just any publication, but publication in archived peer-reviewed journals or conference proceedings. Research results are "written up," submitted, and reviewed for their integrity, relevance, and contribution. The review is by peers – other researchers doing similar work. Are the results novel and useful? Does the evidence support the conclusions? Is there a contribution to the field? Does the methodology meet the expected standards for research? If these questions are satisfactorily answered, the work has a good chance of acceptance and publication. Congratulations. In the end, the work is published and archived. *Archived* implies the work is added to the collection of related work accessible to other researchers throughout the world. This is the "existing body of knowledge" referred to earlier. The final step is complete.

Research results are sometimes developed into bona fide inventions. If an individual or company wishes to profit from their invention, then patenting is an option. The invention is disclosed in a patent application, which also describes previous related work (prior art), how the invention addresses a need, and the best mode of implementation. If the application is successful, the patent is granted and the inventor or company thereafter owns the rights to the invention. If another company wishes to use the invention for commercial purpose, they can enter into a license agreement with the patent holder. This sidebar is included only to make a small point: A patent is a publication. By patenting, the individual or company is both retaining ownership of the invention and making it public through publication of the patent. Thus, patents meet the must-publish criterion for research.

4.1.2 Citations, references, impact

Imagine the World Wide Web without hyperlinks. Web pages would live in isolation, without connections between them. Hyperlinks provide the essential pathways that connect web pages to other web pages, thus providing structure and cohesion to a topic or theme. Similarly, it is hard to imagine the world's body of published research without *citations* and *references*. Citations, like hyperlinks, connect research papers to other research papers. Through citations, a body of research takes shape. The insights and lessons in early research inform and guide later research. The citation itself is just an abbreviated tag that appears in the body of a paper, for example,

> . . . as noted in earlier research (Smith & Jones, 2020).

or

> . . . as confirmed by Green et al. [5].

These two examples are formatted differently, and follow the requirements of the conference or journal. The citation is expanded into a full bibliographic entry in the reference list at the end of the paper. Formatting of citations and references is discussed in Chapter 8.

Citations serve many purposes, including intellectual honesty. By citing previous work, researchers acknowledge that their ideas continue, extend, or refine ideas in earlier research. Citations are also important to back-up assertions that are otherwise questionable, for example, "the number of tablet computer users worldwide now exceeds two billion [9]." In the Results section of a research paper, citations are used to compare the current results with those from earlier research, for example, "the mean time to formulate a search query was about 15 percent less than the time reported by Smith and Jones [5]."

Fig. 4.1 is a schematic of a collection of research papers. Citations are shown as arrows. There is a timeline, so all arrows are to the left, to earlier papers. One of the papers seems to have quite a few citations to it. The number of citations to a research paper is a measure of the paper's *impact*. If many researchers cite a single paper, there is a good chance the work described in the cited paper is both of high quality and significant to the field. This point is often echoed in academic circles: "The only objective and transparent metric that is highly correlated with the quality of a paper is the number of citations."[5] Interestingly enough, citation counts are only recently available with ease. Before services like Google Scholar emerged, citation counts were difficult to obtain.

Since citation counts are available for individual papers, they are also easy to compile for individual researchers. Thus, impact can be assessed for researchers as well as for papers. The most accepted single measure of the impact of a researcher's publication record is the H-index. If a researcher's publications are ordered by the number of citations to each paper, the H-index is the point where the rank equals the number of citations. So, a researcher with H-index $= n$ has n publications each with n or more citations. Physicist J. Hirsch first proposed the H-index in 2005 [195]. H-index quantifies in a single number both research productivity (number of publications) and overall impact of a body of work (number of citations). Some of the strengths and weaknesses of H-index, as a measure of impact, are elaborated elsewhere [299]. A common theme is exploring research impact and citations using visualizations [345,470,509].

---

[5] Dianne Murray, past editor of *Interacting with Computers*. Posted to chi-announcements@acm.org on Oct 8, 2008.

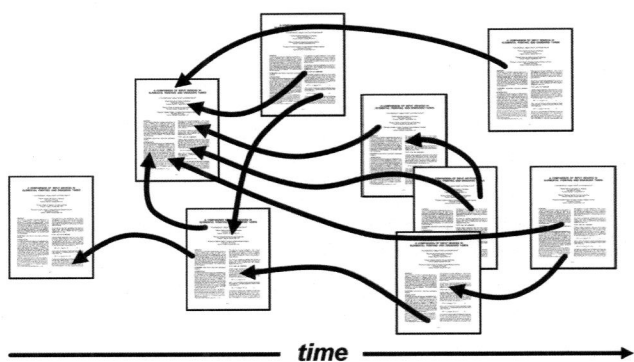

time

FIGURE 4.1

A collection of research papers. Arrows indicate citations to earlier papers.

4.1.3 **Research must be replicable**

Research that cannot be replicated is useless. Achieving an expected standard of re-producibility, or repeatability, is therefore crucial. This is one reason for advancing a standardized methodology: It enforces a process for conducting and writing about the research that ensures sufficient detail is included to allow the results to be replicated. If a skilled researcher cares to test the claims, he or she will find sufficient guidance in the methodology to reproduce, or replicate, the original research. This is an essential characteristic of research.

Many great advances in science and research pertain to methodology. A significant contribution of Louis Pasteur (1822-1895), for example, was his use of a consistent methodology for his research in microbiology [99, pp. 8-9]. Pasteur's experimental findings on germs and diseases were, at the time, controversial. As Pasteur realized, the best way to fend off scepticism was to empower critics – other scientists – to see for themselves. Thus, he adopted a methodology that included a standardized and meticulous description of the materials and procedure. This allowed his experiments and findings to be replicated. A researcher questioning a result could re-do the experiment and thereby verify or refute the result. This was a crucial advance in science. Today, reviewers of manuscripts submitted for publication are often asked to critique the work on this very point: "Is the work replicable?" "No" spells certain rejection.

One of the most cited papers in publishing history is a method paper. Lowry et al.'s 1951 paper "Protein Measurement With the Folin Phenol Reagent" has garnered in excess of 220,000 citations [292].[6] The paper describes a method for measuring proteins in fluids. In style, the paper reads much like a recipe. The method is easy to read, easy to follow, and, importantly, easy to reproduce.

---

[6] See http://scholar.google.ca.

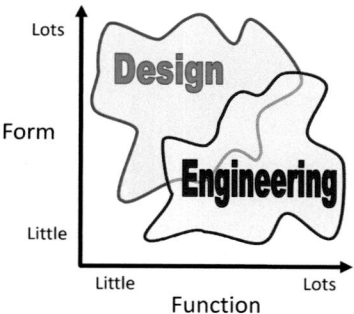

FIGURE 4.2

Design and engineering comparison in terms of form vs. function.

4.1.4 **Research vs. engineering vs. design**

There are many ways to distinguish research, engineering, and design. Researchers in the corporate world often work closely with engineers and designers, but the skills and contributions each brings are different. Engineers and designers are in the business of building things. They create products that strive to bring together the best in *form* (design emphasis) and *function* (engineering emphasis). Dating to the late 1900s, the expression "form follows function" emerged in architecture, where a building must first meet requirements of purpose (function), then achieve aesthetic qualities of beauty (form). Today, function generally refers to how well a product performs its intended task and form reflects the experience the product creates for those using the product. Fig. 4.2 is a loose expression of this in a 2D chart, showing form emphasis for design and function emphasis for engineering (from [307]).

One can imagine that there is certain tension, even a trade-off, between form and function. Finding the right balance is key. However, sometimes the balance tips one way or the other. When this occurs, the result is a product or a feature that achieves one (form or function) at the expense of the other. An example is shown in Fig. 4.3a. The image shows part of a laptop computer, manufactured by a well-known computer company. By most accounts, it is a typical laptop computer. The image shows part of the keyboard as well as the built-in pointing device, a touchpad. The touchpad design (or is it engineering?) is interesting. It is seamlessly embedded in the system chassis. The look is elegant – smooth, shiny, metallic. But, something is wrong. Because the mounting is seamless and smooth, tactile feedback at the sides of the touchpad is missing. While positioning a cursor, the user has no sense of when his or her finger reaches the edge of the touchpad, except by observing that the on-screen pointer stops moving. This is an example of form trumping function. One user's solution is shown in Fig. 4.3b. Tape added on each side of the touchpad provides the all-

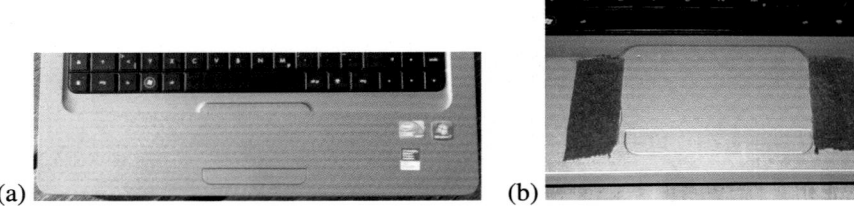

FIGURE 4.3

Form trumping function. (a) Notebook computer with touchpad. (b) Duct tape provides tactile feedback indicating the edge of the touchpad.

important tactile feedback.[7] You are asked to further consider form vs. function in student exercise 4-4.

Engineers and designers work in the world of products. The focus is on designing complete systems or products. Research is different. Research tends to be narrowly focused. Small ideas are conceived of, prototyped, tested, then advanced or discarded. New ideas build on previous ideas and, sooner or later, good ideas are refined into the building blocks – the materials and processes – that find their way into products. But, research questions are generally small in scope. Research tends to be incremental, not monumental.

Engineers and designers also work with prototypes, but the purpose is to assess alternatives at a relatively late stage: as part of product development. A researcher's prototype is an early mock-up of an idea, and is unlikely to directly appear in a product. Yet, the idea of using prototypes to inform or assess is remarkably similar, whether for research or for product development. The following characterisation by Tim Brown (Chair of design firm IDEO) is directed as designers, but is well aligned with the use of prototypes for research:

> *Prototypes should command only as much time, effort, and investment as are needed to generate useful feedback and evolve an idea. The more "finished" a prototype seems, the less likely its creators will be to pay attention to and profit from feedback. The goal of prototyping isn't to finish. It is to learn about the strengths and weaknesses of the idea and to identify new directions that further prototypes might take.*

[46, p. 3]

One facet of research that differentiates it from engineering and design is the timeline. Research precedes engineering and design. Furthermore, the march forward for research is slow, without the shackles of deadlines. Fig. 4.4 shows the timeline

---

[7] For an amusing example of function gone crazy, visit Google Images using "Rube Goldberg simple alarm clock."

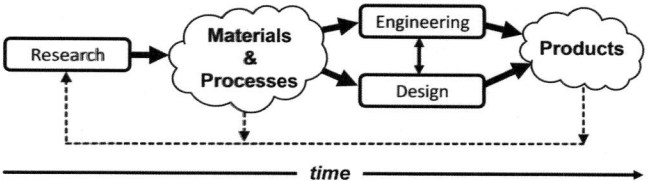

FIGURE 4.4

Timeline for research, engineering, and design.

for research, engineering, and design. Products are the stuff of deadlines. Designers and engineers work within the corporate world, developing products that sell, and hopefully sell well. The raw materials for engineers and designers are the knowledge – materials and processes – that already exist or emerge through research. Put another way, research involves the creation of knowledge, whereas design and engineering involve the creative use of knowledge (see also [122]).

4.1.5 The nature of research

Research is not a product-driven exercise. Where the connection is claimed, we might question whether the work is research. Perhaps the work is really just, well, work. In this context, the term *applied research* is often heard. But, is applying the fruits of research itself research? Or, is this just what engineers and designers do: apply and combine what is already known in creative and efficient ways to build products that appeal to consumers.

There are at least two facets of research that are at odds with engineering and design. One is the timeline. The computer mouse, once again, is a good example. Although the mouse first appeared in a commercial product in 1981, the research began nearly 20 years earlier with the goal of improving user interaction with a graphical interface. The research leading to the first prototype mouse occurred over a brief time period – in the 1960s. But, bringing the mouse to market was a long and iterative process. This is characterised in Buxton's *Long Nose of Innovation* [48]. See Fig. 4.5. The chart begins with innovation – the emergence of new ideas. The march forward is slow and requires substantial refinement. In the case of Engelbart's mouse, this involved, among other things, replacing perpendicular potentiometers with a rolling ball. We might ask whether the effort in refining an idea is research or engineering? People with different perspectives differ on this point. But, it is likely that refining an innovation is not deadline-driven. Germane to the process is that points of refinement are tried and discarded before a final form is reached. The final form is not known a priori; it arrives with a good deal of trial and error, and even serendipitous good fortune. This brings us to the second distinction.

The second distinction between research and its counterparts engineering and design is less tangible but equally important. The term "traction" in Fig. 4.5 celebrates the final and desired goal – a material or process that gains traction and achieves

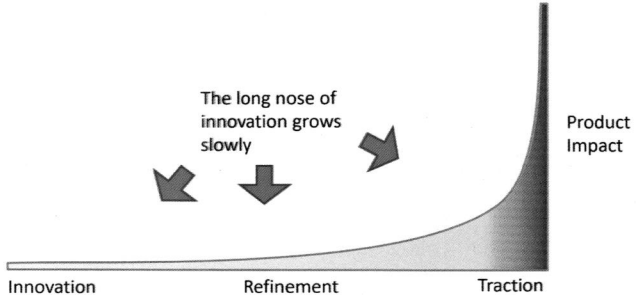

The long nose of
innovation grows
slowly

Product
Impact

Innovation   Refinement   Traction

FIGURE 4.5

The long nose of innovation (after [48]).

impact in the market place. The computer mouse is an example, an easy example. It is easy because we are using hindsight to pull a success story – a homerun – from the milieu of research. But, the vast majority of research amounts to a bunt, not a homerun. Let's push the baseball metaphor a bit further.[8] Most research outcomes are modest: hits, walks, pop flies, outs, or even strikeouts. Yes, strikeouts. Remember, this is just an analogy! The point is that most research never arrives in products in any tangible or directly identifiable form. This simple truth is easily verified. Just pull a paper at random from a 10-year-old conference proceedings. Peruse the paper and try to identify the product where the research result appears. Most likely, there is no such product. This is not only a simple truth, it's an inconvenient truth. Such results do not make headlines (or are acknowledged in a proposal for research funding!). But, it is a simple reality: Most research nips away at the edges. Are the small nips, tucks, and modest efforts a waste of time? Not at all. Importantly, the small contributions create the context and enabling methods and materials (see Fig. 4.4) that inspire and guide more compelling advances.

At this juncture, it is instructive to consider the words of John Wanamaker on his substantial investment in advertising:

> *Half the money I spend on advertising is wasted. The problem is, I don't know which half.*[9]

Wanamaker's insight has a straight line to research: One cannot simply *choose* to do research that generates high-impact results. The entirety of the effort is needed, lest no high-impact results are forthcoming.

Of course, the fruits of research do not simply crystallise from the ether. Researchers and consumers live in the same material world. Returning to Fig. 4.4, consider the dashed line from "products" to "materials and processes" and "research."

---

[8] Readers are invited to re-frame the analogy in the language of cricket, football, or some other sport.

[9] John Wanamaker (1838-1922) was an early proponent of advertising and marketing. His ads directed consumers to goods sold in his successful department stores in Philadelphia and elsewhere.

View this line in the broadest sense. It is the "empirical" in empirical research (i.e., relying on experience or observation; see section 4.2).

Similar stories to the computer mouse are heard today. The mouse was a hugely successful product that, in many ways, defines a generation of computing, post 1981, when the Xerox Star was introduced. But, in the 1960s the mouse was just an idea. As a prototype it worked well as an input controller to manoeuvre a tracking symbol on a graphics display. Engelbart's invention [115] took nearly 20 years to be engineered and designed into a successful product.

Let's not forget Apple Computer Inc., long known as a leader in innovation and always building a better mousetrap. An example is the iPhone, introduced in June 2007. And, evidently, the world has beaten a path to Apple's door.[10] Notably, "with the iPhone, Apple successfully brought together decades of research" [438]. Many of the raw materials of this successful product came by way of low-level research, undertaken well before Apple's engineers and designers set forth on their successfully journey. Among the iPhone's interaction novelties is a two-finger *pinch* gesture for zooming in and out. New? Perhaps, but Apple's engineers and designers no doubt were guided or inspired by research that came before them. For example, multi-touch gestures date at least to the 1980s [51,183]. What about changing the aspect ratio of the display when the device is tilted? New? Perhaps not. Tilt, as an interaction technique for user interfaces, dates to the 1990s [177,192,410]. These are just two examples of research ideas that, taken alone, are small scale. While engineers or designers strive to build better systems or products, in the broadest sense, researchers provide the raw materials and processes engineers or designers work with: stronger steel for bridges, a better device for pointing, a faster algorithm for searches, a more natural touch interface for mobile phones.

4.2 What is empirical research?

By prefixing research with *empirical*, powerful new ideas are added. According to one definition, empirical means *originating in or based on observation or experience*. Empirical research, then, is research that is built upon observation or experience – the human experience. Empirical research is contrasted with *theoretical research* which explores the inherent structure and relationships of phenomena in the physical world.

By another definition, empirical means *relying on experience or observation alone, often without due regard for system and theory*. This suggests that empirical research is guided by direct observations and experiences about phenomena, without prejudice to, or even consideration of, existing theories. This powerful idea is a guiding principle in science – not to be blinded by dogma or preconceptions. As

---

[10] The entire quotation is "build a better mousetrap and the world will beat a path to your door" and is attributed to American essayist Ralf Waldo Emerson (1803-1882). See http://en.wikipedia.org/wiki/Mousetrap.

an example, prior to the 15th century there was prevailing *system* or *theory* that celestial bodies revolved around the earth. The Polish scientist Nicolas Copernicus (1473-1543) found evidence to the contrary. His work was empirical. It was based on observation without bias toward, influence by, or due regard to, existing theory. He observed, he collected data, he looked for patterns and relationships in the data, and he found evidence within the data that cut across contemporary thinking. His empirical evidence led to one of the great achievements in modern science – a heliocentric cosmology that placed the sun, not the earth, at the centre of the solar system. Now that's a nice discovery (see the third definition of research at the beginning of this chapter). In HCI and other fields of research, discoveries are usually more modest.

By another definition, empirical means *capable of being verified or disproved by observation or experiment*. These are strong words. An HCI research initiative is framed by hypotheses – assertions about the merits of an interface or an interaction technique. The assertions must be sufficiently clear and narrow to enable a hypothesis to be verified or disproved by gathering and testing evidence. This means using language in an assertion that speaks directly to empirical, observable, quantifiable aspects of the interaction. We will dwell on this later in this chapter in our discussion on research questions.

4.3 Research methods

There are three common approaches, or methods, for conducting research in HCI and other disciplines in the natural and social sciences: the *observational method*, the *experimental method*, and the *correlational method*. All three are empirical as they are based on observation or experience. But, there are differences and these follow from the objectives of the approach taken. Let's examine each method.

4.3.1 Observational method

Observation is the starting point. In conducting empirical research in HCI, it is essential to observe humans interacting with computers or computer-embedded technology of some sort. The observational method encompasses a collection of common techniques in HCI research. These include interviews, field investigations, contextual inquiries, case studies, field studies, focus groups, think aloud protocols, storytelling, walkthroughs, cultural probes, and so on. The approach is qualitative rather than quantitative. As a result, observational methods achieve *relevance* while sacrificing *precision* [447, p. 76]. Behaviours are studied by directly observing phenomena in a natural setting, as opposed to crafting constrained behaviours in an artificial laboratory setting. Real world phenomena are high in relevance, but lack the precision available in controlled laboratory experiments.

Observational methods are generally concerned with discovering and explaining the reasons underlying human behaviour. In HCI, this is the *why* or *how* of the interaction, as opposed to the *what*, *where*, or *when*. The methods focus on human thought, feeling, attitude, emotion, passion, sensation, reflection, expression, sentiment, opinion, mood, outlook, manner, style, approach, strategy, and so on. These human qualities can be studied through observational methods, but they are difficult to measure. The observations likely involve note-taking, photographs, videos, or audio recordings, rather than measurement. Measurements, if gathered, tend to use categorical data or simple counts of phenomena. Put another way, observational methods tend to examine and record the quality of interaction rather than quantifiable human performance.

The most common HCI example of research following the observational method is a *usability evaluation*. A usability evaluation seeks to assess the usability of a system's user interface (UI) to identify specific problems [103, p. 319]. Although there are more than 100 different usability evaluation methods [214], the general approach is to engage users to do tasks with the UI. The goal is to find problems that compromise usability. Some usability evaluation methods involve expert users who make observations about the interface.

4.3.2 **Experimental method**

With the experimental method (also called the *scientific method*), knowledge is acquired through controlled experiments conducted in laboratory settings. Acquiring knowledge may imply gathering new knowledge, but it may also mean studying existing knowledge for the purpose of verifying, refuting, correcting, integrating, or extending. In the relevance-precision trade-off, it is clear where controlled experiments lie. Since the tasks are artificial and occur in a controlled laboratory setting, relevance is diminished. However, the control inherent in the methodology brings precision, since extraneous factors – the diversity and chaos of the real world – are reduced or eliminated. In HCI, a controlled experiment is typically called a *user study*.

A controlled experiment requires at least two variables: a *manipulated variable* and a *response variable*. In HCI, the manipulated variable is typically a property of an interface or interaction technique that is presented to participants in different configurations. Manipulating the variable refers to systematically exposing participants to different configurations of the interface or interaction technique. A manipulated variable is also called an *independent variable* or *factor*.

A response variable is a property of human behaviour that is observable, quantifiable, and measurable. The most common response variable is *time*, often called *task completion time* or some variation thereof. Given a task, how long do participants take to do the task under each of the configurations tested? There are, of course, a multitude of other behaviours that qualify as response variables. Which ones are used depend on the characteristics of the interface or interaction technique studied in the research. A response variable is also called a *dependent variable*. Independent variables and dependent variables are explored in greater detail in Chapter 5.

HCI experiments involve humans. And so, the methodology employed is borrowed from experimental psychology, a field with a long history of research involving humans. In a sense, HCI is the beneficiary of this more mature field. The circumstances manipulated in a psychology experiment are often quite different from those manipulated in an HCI experiment, however. HCI is narrowly focused on the interaction between humans and computing technology, while experimental psychology covers a much broader range of the human experience.

It is naïve to think we can simply choose to focus on the experimental method and ignore qualities of interaction that are outside the scope of the experimental procedure. A full and proper user study – an experiment with human participants – involves more than just measuring and analysing human performance. We engage observational methods by soliciting comments, thoughts, and opinions from participants. Even though a task is performed quickly and with little or no error, if participants experience fatigue, frustration, discomfort, or another quality of interaction, we want to know about it. These qualities of interaction may not appear in the numbers, but they are important.

One final point about the experimental method deserves mention. A controlled experiment, if designed and conducted properly, supports a powerful form of conclusion from the data and analyses. The relationship between the independent variable and the dependent variable is one of *cause and effect*. That is, the manipulations in the interface or interaction techniques are said to have *caused* the observed differences in the response variable. This point is elaborated in greater detail shortly. Cause-and-effect conclusions are not possible in research using the observational method or the correlational method.

4.3.3 Correlational method

The correlational method involves looking for relationships between variables. For example, a researcher might be interested in knowing if users' privacy settings in a social networking application are related to their personality, IQ, level of education, employment status, age, gender, income, and so on. Data are collected on each item (privacy settings, personality, etc.) and then relationships are examined. For example, it might be apparent in the data that users with certain personality traits tend to use more stringent privacy settings than users with other personality traits.

Quantifying phenomena is the defining step in correlational research. The possibilities for variables are limitless: age, gender, hours per day playing computer games, number of privacy settings, etc. For nominal-scale variables, categories are established (e.g., personality type, gender) and then counts are collected. The data may be collected through a variety of methods, such as observation, interviews, on-line surveys, questionnaires, or measurement. Correlational methods often accompany experimental methods, if questionnaires are included in the experimental procedure. Do the measurements on response variables suggest relationships by gender, by age, by level of experience, and so on?

Data collected using a survey are often subject to self-selection bias. If the survey was disseminated using a mass-distribution process, such as automated phone calls, an e-mail list, or the Internet, the number of responses is usually less than the number

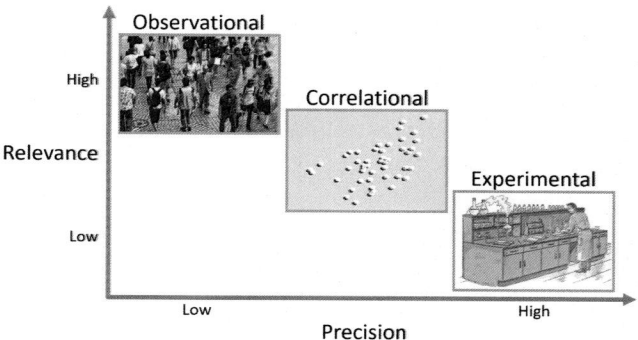

FIGURE 4.6

Relationship between precision, relevance, and research methodology [307, Fig. 1].

of people contacted. Some people respond, others don't. Those who respond may have a particular or vested interest in the topic and may wish to share their opinion on the topic. The result is bias, since the respondents are not a random sample from the population of interest.

Correlational methods provide a balance between relevance and precision. Since the data were not collected in a controlled setting, precision is sacrificed. However, data collected using informal techniques, such as interviews, bring relevance – a connection to real-life experiences. Finally, the data obtained using correlational methods are circumstantial, not causal. We will return to this point shortly.

This book is primarily directed at the experimental method for HCI research. However, it is clear in the discussions above that the experimental method will often include observational methods and correlational methods.

4.3.4 Precision and relevance in experimental methodology

Let's summarize the issues of precision and relevance as they relate to research methodology. Fig. 4.6 provides a visual summary of points noted above.

Observational methods are high in relevance since the observations are gathered in real-world settings. They are low in precision, however, since real-world settings inherently reflect the diversity of the human experience. Such diversity brings variability which in turn compromises precision. Experimental methods are positioned at the low end of the relevance axis since data are collected in an artificial and controlled laboratory setting. They are high in precision, however, since the diversity of real-world situations is eliminated or controlled. Correlational methods bring compromise in the relevance and precision they bring to the research.

The point here is that any attempt to describe one methodology as better or worse than another is misguided. Each methodology brings something the others cannot.

4.3.5 **User study vs. usability evaluation**

We noted in section 4.3.2 that a controlled experiment in HCI is typically called a *user study*. A user study (or controlled experiment) requires at least one manipulated variable (aka independent variable) which in turn must have at least two levels or configurations. Users are exposed to the different levels of the manipulated variable while their performance is observed and measured. Thus, comparison is germane to a user study. This point deserves further elaboration.

In HCI, we often hear of researchers or practitioners doing a *usability evaluation*. By and large, a usability evaluation is an assessment of a particular user interface (UI). The UI might be a commercial product, but frequently it is a prototype. The goal is to find faults or weaknesses in the UI, often with reference to accepted UI design principles.

Clearly, usability evaluation is hugely important for companies bringing products to market. But, it is important to differentiate a usability evaluation from a user study. In a usability evaluation, there is no manipulated variable. Users do a variety of tasks while problems are noted; but the different tasks are not levels of a manipulated variable. The tasks are chosen simply to encompass the range of activities supported and for which a usability assessment is sought.

Another distinction is the level of inquiry. A user study is low-level. The goal is to assess and compare two or more interaction details to determine which works better. The details studied and compared are the minutiae of interaction – for example, examining whether a particular task or operation is performed better with tactile feedback vs. popup animation. A usability evaluation is high-level. The goal is to assess a UI or application as a whole, and to uncover potential problems that an end-user might confront. This is a higher level of inquiry, since the evaluation involves complete tasks done on a complete (perhaps prototype) UI or application.

Yet another distinction is the position in the research-engineering-design timeline discussed in section 4.1.4 (p. 167). User studies occur early in the timeline, usability evaluations late. This is illustrated in Fig. 4.7, which augments Fig. 4.4 (p. 169) to show the position for these activities. A user study is a concluding step in research, while a usability evaluation follows engineering and design and is closer to an end product.

From Fig. 4.7, it is clear why a user study is associated with research: It is the final step. The figure suggests that a usability evaluation is far removed from research, since it is further along the timeline. Of course a usability evaluation is research, since it aligns with the first definition of research ("collecting information about a particular subject," section 4.1, p. 161). As for research methods, a usability evaluation is an example of observational research while a user study is an example of experimental research.

Fig. 4.8 summarizes the features distinguishing a user study from a usability evaluation.

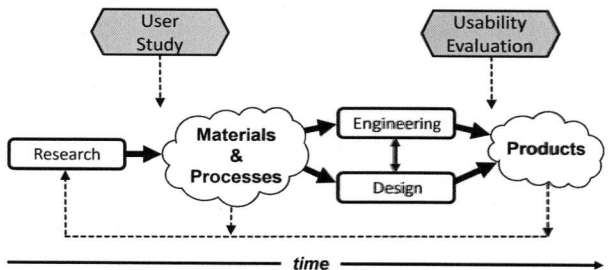

FIGURE 4.7

Research-engineering-design timeline. A user study follows research, whereas a usability evaluation follows engineering and design [307, Fig. 11].

Feature	User Study	Usability Evaluation
Manipulated variables	Yes	No
Research method	Experimental	Observational
Place in timeline	Early	Late
Level of inquiry	Low	High

FIGURE 4.8

Distinction between a user study and a usability evaluation.

4.4 Observe and measure

Let's return to the foundation of empirical research: observation.

4.4.1 Observation

The starting point for empirical research in HCI is to observe humans interacting with computers. But, how are observations made? There are two possibilities. Either another human is the observer or an apparatus is the observer. A human observer is the experimenter or investigator, not the human interacting with the computer. Observation is the precursor to *measurement*, and if the investigator is the observer, then measurements are collected manually. This could involve using a log sheet or notebook to jot down the number of events of interest observed. Events of interest might include clicking a button, moving a hand from the keyboard to the mouse, or rotating a smartphone. It might involve observing users in a public space and counting those who are using a smartphone or tablet in a certain way, for example, while walking, while driving, or while paying for groceries at a checkout counter. The observations may be broken down by gender or some other attribute of interest.

Manual observation could also involve hand timing the duration of activities, such as the time to type a phrase of text or the time to enter a search query. One can imagine the difficulty in manually gathering measurements as just described, not to mention the inaccuracy in the measurements. Nevertheless, manual timing is useful for preliminary testing, sometimes called *pilot testing*.

More often in empirical research, the task of observing is delegated to the apparatus – the computer. Of course, this is a challenge in some situations. As an example, if the interaction is with a digital sports watch or automated teller machine (ATM), it is not possible to embed data collection software in the apparatus. Even if the apparatus is a conventional desktop computer, some behaviours of interest are difficult to detect. For example, consider measuring the number of times the user's attention switches from the display to the keyboard while doing a task. The computer is not capable of detecting this behaviour. In this case, perhaps an eye tracking apparatus or camera could be used, but that complicates the experimental apparatus. Another example is clutching – lifting and repositioning a mouse. The data transmitted from a host computer do not include information on clutching, so a conventional host system is not capable of observing and recording this behaviour. Again, some additional apparatus or sensing technology may be devised. Or, a human observer can be used. So, depending on the behaviours of interest, some ingenuity is needed to build an apparatus and collect the appropriate measurements.

If the apparatus includes custom software implementing an interface or interaction technique, then it is straightforward to log events, such as key presses, mouse movement, selections, finger touches, or finger swipes and the associated timestamps. These data are stored in a file for follow-up analyses.

4.4.2 Measurement scales

Observation alone is of limited value. Consider observations about rain and flowers. In some locales, there is a lot of rain but very few flowers in April, followed by less rain and a full bloom in May. The observations may inspire anecdote – *April showers bring May flowers* – but a serious examination of patterns for rain and flowers requires measurement. In this case, an observer located in a garden would observe, measure, and log the amount of rain and the number of flowers in bloom. The measurements are recorded each day during April and May and perhaps by several observers in several gardens. The measurements are collected together, summarized by month, and analysed for "significant differences" (see Chapter 6). With measurement, anecdotes turn to empirical evidence. The observer is now in a position to quantify the amount of rain and the number of flowers in bloom, separately for April and May.

The added value of measurement is essential for science. In the words of engineer and physicist Lord Kelvin (1824-1907), after whom the Kelvin scale of temperature is named,

Without measurement your knowledge is of a meager and unsatisfactory kind.[11]

---

[11] The full quote, according to several online sources, is "When you can measure what you are speaking about, and express it in numbers, you know something about it, but when you cannot measure it, when you cannot express it in numbers, your knowledge of it is of a meager and unsatisfactory kind, it may be the beginning of knowledge, but you have scarcely, in your thoughts, advanced it to the stage of science."

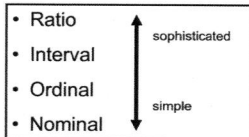

FIGURE 4.9

Scales of measurement: nominal, ordinal, interval, and ratio. Nominal measurements are considered simple, while ratio measurements are sophisticated. See text for discussion.

As elaborated in many textbooks on statistics, there are four scales of measurement. Organizing our discussion by these scales will help. Fig. 4.9 shows the scales along a continuum with nominal-scale measurements as the least sophisticated and ratio-scale measurements as the most sophisticated. This follows from the types of computations possible with each measurement, as elaborated below.

The nature, limitations, and abilities of each scale determine the sort of information and analyses possible in a research setting. Each is briefly defined below.

4.4.2.1 Nominal data

A measurement on the nominal scale involves arbitrarily assigning a code to an attribute or category. The measurement is so arbitrary that the code needn't be a number (although it could be). Examples are automobile licence plate numbers, loyalty card numbers, student ID numbers, codes for postal zones, job classifications, military ranks, etc. Clearly, mathematical manipulations on nominal data are meaningless. It is nonsense, for example, to compute the mean of several license plate numbers. Nominal data identify mutually exclusive categories. Membership or exclusion is meaningful, but little less. The only relationship that holds is equivalence, which exists for entities in the same class. Nominal data are also called *categorical data*.

If there is interest in knowing whether males and females differ in their use of mobile phones, the investigation might begin by observing people and assigning each a code of "M" for male, "F" for female. Here, the attribute is gender and the code is M or F. If there is interest in hand preference, the writing habits of users might be observed. Users are assigned codes of "LH" for left-handers and "RH" for right-handers. If there is interest in scrolling strategies, perhaps users are observed interacting with a GUI application and are categorized accordingly to their scrolling method, for example as "MW" for mouse wheel, "CD" for clicking and dragging the scrollbar, or "KB" for keyboard.

Nominal data are often used with frequencies or counts – the number of occurrences of each attribute. In this case, the research is likely concerned with the difference in the counts between categories: "Are males or females more likely to ...," "Do left handers or right handers have more difficulty with ...," or "Are Mac or PC users more inclined to ..." Bear in mind that while the attribute is categorical, the count is a ratio-scale measurement (discussed shortly).

Gender	Mobile Phone Usage		Total	%
	Not Using	Using		
Male	683	98	781	51.1%
Female	644	102	746	48.9%
Total	1327	200	1527	
%	86.9%	13.1%		

FIGURE 4.10

Two examples of nominal scale data: gender (male, female) and mobile phone usage (not using, using).

Here's an example of nominal scale attributes using real data. Attendees of an HCI research course were dispatched to several locations on a university campus. Their task was to observe, categorize, and count students walking between classes. Each student was categorized by gender (male, female) and by whether he or she was using a mobile phone (not using, using). The counts are shown in Fig. 4.10. A total of 1,527 students were observed. The split by gender was roughly equal (51.1% male, 48.9% female). By mobile phone usage, 13.1% of the students (200) were observed using their mobile phone while walking.

The research question in Fig. 4.10 is this: Are males or females more likely to use a mobile phone as they walk about a university campus? We'll demonstrate how to answer this question in Chapter 6 on Hypothesis Testing.

4.4.2.2 Ordinal data

Ordinal scale measurements provide an order or ranking to an attribute. The attribute can be any characteristic or circumstance of interest. For example, users might try three vehicle GPS trackers for a period of time, and then rank the systems by preference: 1st choice, 2nd choice, 3rd choice. Or, users could consider properties of a mobile phone, such as price, features, cool-appeal, and usability, and then order the features by personal importance. One user might choose usability (1st), cool-appeal (2nd), price (3rd), then features (4th). The main limitation of ordinal data is that the interval is not intrinsically equal between successive points on the scale. In the example just cited, there is no innate sense of how much more important usability is over cool-appeal or whether the difference is greater or less than that between, for example, cool-appeal and price.

If we are interested in studying e-mail habits, we might use a questionnaire to collect data. Fig. 4.11 gives an example of a questionnaire item soliciting ordinal data. There are five rankings according to the number of e-mail messages received per day. It is a matter of choice whether to solicit data in this manner or, in the alternative, to ask for an estimate of the number of e-mail messages received per day. It will depend on how the data are used and analysed.

Ordinal data are slightly more sophisticated than nominal data since comparisons of *greater than* or *less than* are possible. However, it is not valid to compute the mean of ordinal data.

> How many email messages do **you receive?**
>   1. None (I don't use email)
>   2. 1-5 per day
>   3. 6-25 per day
>   4. 26-100 per day
>   5. More than 100 per day

FIGURE 4.11

Example of a questionnaire item soliciting an ordinal response.

4.4.2.3 Interval data

Moving up in sophistication, interval data have equal distances between adjacent values. However, the zero point is arbitrary. A value of zero does not imply the absence of the property measured. The classic example of interval data is temperature measured on the Fahrenheit or Celsius scale. Unlike ordinal data, it is meaningful to compute the mean of interval data, for example, the mean mid-day temperature during the month of July. Ratios of interval data are not meaningful, however. For example, it is little more than opinion to say that 20° C is twice as warm as 10° C.

In HCI, interval data are commonly used in questionnaires where a response on a linear scale is solicited. An example is a Likert scale[12] (see Fig. 4.12), where verbal responses are given a numeric code. In the example, verbal responses are symmetric about a neutral, central value with the gradations between responses more-or-less equal. It is this last quality – equal gradations between responses – that validates calculating the mean of the responses across multiple respondents.

There is some disagreement among researchers on the assumption of equal gradations between the items in Fig. 4.12. Do respondents perceive the difference between 1 and 2 (*strongly disagree* and *mildly disagree*) the same as the difference between 2 and 3 (*mildly disagree* and *neutral*)? Attaching verbal tags to numbers may bring a personal interpretation to the responses. There is evidence that respondents perceive items at the extremes of the scale as farther apart than items in the centre [240]. Nevertheless, the graduation between responses is more similar here than between the five ordinal responses in Fig. 4.11. One remedy for non-equal gradations in Likert-scale response items is simply to instruct respondents to interpret the items as equally spaced.

Examples of Likert Scale questionnaire items in HCI research papers are hereby cited [272,285,294,371,413,428].

4.4.2.4 Ratio data

Ratio-scale measurements are the most sophisticated of the four scales of measurement. Ratio data have an absolute zero. Zero implies the absence of the property mea-

---

[12] The scale is named after its inventor, American psychologist Rensis Likert (1903-1981).

Please indicate your level of agreement with the following statements.

	Strongly disagree	Mildly disagree	Neutral	Mildly agree	Strongly agree
It is safe to talk on a mobile phone while driving.	1	2	3	4	5
It is safe to read a text message on a mobile phone while driving.	1	2	3	4	5
It is safe to compose a text message on a mobile phone while driving.	1	2	3	4	5

FIGURE 4.12

Questionnaire items using a Likert scale. The responses are examples of interval scale data.

sured. With ratio data a myriad of calculations are possible to summarize, compare, and test the data. The data can be added, subtracted, multiplied, divided, averaged, with standard deviations and variances computed. In HCI, the most common ratio-scale measurement is time – the time to complete a task. But, generally, all physical measurements are also ratio-scale, such as the distance or velocity of a cursor as it moves across a display, the force applied by a finger on a touchscreen, the angular movement of the eye in changing the point of gaze, and so on. Many social variables are also ratio-scale, such as a user's age or years of computer experience.

As well as time, a common ratio-scale measurement is a count (noted above). Often in HCI research, we count the number of occurrences of certain human activities, such as the number of button clicks, the number of corrective button clicks, the number of characters entered, the number of incorrect characters entered, the number of times an option is selected, the number of gaze shifts, the number of hand movements between the mouse and keyboard, the number of task re-tries, the number of words in a search query, etc. Although we tend to give *time* special attention, it too is a count – the number of seconds or minutes elapsed as an activity takes place. These are all ratio-scale measurements.

The expressive nature of a count is improved through *normalization*, that is, expressing the value as a count *per something*. So, for example, knowing that a 10-word phrase was entered in 30 seconds is less revealing than knowing that the rate of entry was $\frac{10}{0.5} = 20$ words per minute (wpm). The main benefit of normalizing counts is to improve comparisons. It is easy to compare 20 wpm for one method with 23 wpm for another method – the latter method is faster. It is much harder to compare 10 words entered in 30 seconds for one method with 14 words entered in 47 seconds for another method.

As another example, let's say two errors were committed while entering a 50-character phrase of text. Reporting the occurrence of two errors reveals very little, unless we also know the length of the phrase. Even so, comparisons with results from another study are difficult. What if the other study used phrases of different lengths? However, if the result is reported as a $\frac{2}{50} = 4\%$ error rate, there is an immediate sense of the meaning, magnitude, and relevance of the human performance measured, and, as convention has it, the other study likely reported error rates similarly. So, where possible, normalize counts to make the measurements more meaningful and to facilitate comparisons.

An example in the literature is an experiment comparing five different text entry methods [332]. On speed, results were reported in "words per minute" (that's fine), however, for accuracy, results were reported as the number of errors committed. Novice participants, for example, committed 24 errors while using multi-tap [332, Table 2]. While this number is useful for comparing results within the experiment, it provides no insight on how the results compare with related research. A better approach is to normalize for the amount of text and report "error rate" – the number of character errors / the total number of characters entered × 100.

Another example in the literature is research on foot movement for computer input. Velloso et al. [498] investigated foot input for tasks commonly performed using the hand (e.g., with a mouse). In their literature review, five foot-movement studies were compared. Not surprisingly, the experiment tasks were quite different among the studies. Because of this, it was not possible to compare task completion time between studies. To facilitate the between-study comparison, Velloso et al. first normalized the data. For each study, they formed the ratio of the task completion time for foot movements to the task completion time for hand movements. A comparison of the ratios was then possible. For example, the foot:hand ratio of task completion times was 2.32 in one study and 1.58 in another study [498, Table 1].

4.5 **Research questions**

In HCI, we conduct experimental research to answer (and raise!) questions about a new or existing user interface or interaction technique. Often, the questions pertain to the relationship between two variables, where one variable is a circumstance or condition that is manipulated (an interface property) and the other is an observed and measured behavioural response (task performance).

The notion of posing or answering questions seems simple, but, this is tricky because of the human element. Unlike an algorithm operating on a data set, where the time to search, sort, or whatever, is the same with each try, people vary in their actions. This is true from person to person and for a single person repeating a task. The result is always different. This variability affects the confidence with which we can answer *research questions*. To gauge the confidence of our answers, we use statistical techniques, as presented in Chapter 6 (Hypothesis Testing).

Research questions emerge from an inquisitive process. The researcher has an idea and wishes to see if it has merit. Initial thoughts are fluid and informal:

- Is it viable?
- Is it as good as or better than current practice?
- What are its strengths and weaknesses?
- Which of several alternatives is best?
- What are the human performance limits and capabilities?
- Does it work well for novices, for experts?
- How much practice is required to become proficient?

These questions are clearly relevant, since they capture a researcher's thinking at the early stages of a project. However, the questions above are deficient: They are not testable. The goal, then, is to move forward from loose and informal thinking to testable questions suited for empirical and experimental inquiry.

Let's use an example to see how this is done. Perhaps a researcher is interested in text entry on smartphones. "Texting" is something people do a lot. The researcher is experienced with the Qwerty soft keyboard on smartphones, but finds it error prone and slow. With some thought invested, an idea emerges for a new technique for entering text. Perhaps it's a good idea. Perhaps it's really good, better than the basic Qwerty soft keyboard (QSK). Motivated to do research in HCI, the researcher builds a prototype of the technique, and fiddles with the implementation until it works fine. The researcher decides to undertake some experimental research to evaluate the idea. What are the research questions? Perhaps the following capture the researcher's thinking:

- Is the new technique any good?
- Is the new technique better than QSK?
- Is the new technique faster than QSK?
- Is the new technique faster than QSK after a bit of practice?
- Is the measured entry speed (in words per minute) higher for the new technique than for a QSK after 15 minutes of practice?

From top to bottom, the questions are progressively narrower and more focused. Expressions like "any good" or "better than" are well intentioned, but problematic. How does one measure "better than?" Farther down the list, the questions address qualities that can be observed and measured. Furthermore, they are expressed across alternative designs, so comparisons are possible. The last question speaks very specifically to entry speed measured in words per minute, to a comparison between two methods, and to a criterion for practice. This is a testable research question.

One way to assess research questions is to ensure they pass the "ROT" test [342, p. 49] – that they are *repeatable*, *observable*, and *testable*. These words appear in the preceding paragraphs. More specifically, "repeatable" or "replicable" is the need to describe the experimental apparatus and procedure with sufficient detail that other researchers could pose and answer the same research question. (See also section 4.1.3, Research must be Replicable.) "Observable" implies texting human responses that are directly measurable through observation, such as the time to complete a task. (See also section 4.4.1, Observation.) "Testable" is the need to pose questions about numbers; for example, is the time to complete a task less for one technique than another?

Meeting the testable criterion is more difficult for questions of a qualitative nature, since users' feelings, opinions, or attitudes are not directly observable and measurable. In this case, the approach is to solicit user responses via a questionnaire. If the responses use a numeric rating scale, for example, from 1 (*strongly disagree*) to 5 (*strongly agree*), then the testable criterion is met by analysing the coded responses. The testing of research questions is the focus of Chapter 6 (Hypothesis Testing).

4.6 Internal validity and external validity

At this juncture, we are in a position to consider two important properties of experimental research: *internal validity* and *external validity*. Let's use the research questions above to frame the discussion. Two of the questions appear in Fig. 4.13. The *x*-axis is labelled Breadth of Question or, alternatively, External Validity. The *y*-axis is labelled Accuracy of Answer or, alternatively, Internal Validity.

The question,

> Is the new technique better than QSK?

is positioned as high in breadth (that's good!) yet answerable with low accuracy (that's bad!). As noted, this question is not testable in an empirical sense. Attempts to answer it directly are fraught with problems, because we lack a methodology to observe and measure "better than" (even though finding better interfaces is the final goal).

The other more detailed question,

> Is the measured entry speed (in words per minute) higher with the new technique than with QSK after 15 minutes of practice?

is positioned as low in breadth (that's bad!) yet answerable with high accuracy (that's good!). The question is testable, which means we can craft a methodology to answer it through observation and measurement. Unfortunately, the narrow scope of the question brings different problems. Focusing on entry speed is fine, but what about other aspects of the interaction? What about accuracy, effort, comfort, cognitive load,

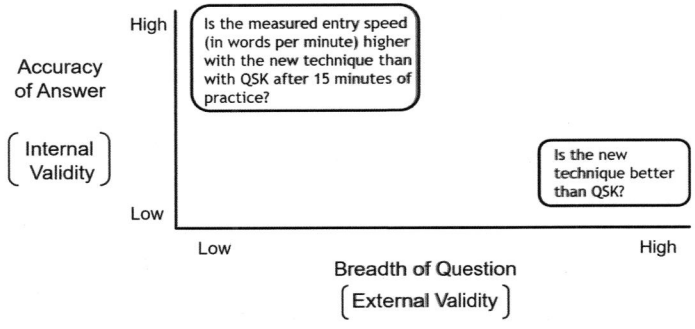

FIGURE 4.13

Graphical comparison of internal validity and external validity.

user satisfaction, practical use of the technique, and so on? The question excludes consideration of these, hence, the low breadth rating.

The alternate labels for the axes in Fig. 4.13 are internal validity and external validity. The figure was designed to setup discussion on these important terms in experimental research.

Internal validity is the extent that an effect observed is due to the test conditions. For the example, an *effect* is simply the difference in entry speed between the new technique and QSK. If we conduct an experiment to measure and compare the entry speed for the two techniques, we want confidence that the difference observed was actually due to inherent differences between the techniques. Internal validity captures this confidence. Perhaps the difference was due to something else, such as variability in the responses of the participants in the study. Humans differ. Some people are pre-disposed to be meticulous, while others are carefree, even reckless. Furthermore, human behaviour – individually or between people – can change from one moment to the next, for no obvious reason. Were some participants tested early in the day, others late in the day? Were there any distractions, interruptions, or other environmental changes during testing? Suffice it to say that any source of variation beyond that due to the inherent properties of the test conditions tends to compromise internal validity. High internal validity means the effect observed really exists.

External validity is the extent that experimental results are generalizable to other people and other situations. *Generalizable* clearly speaks to *breadth* in Fig. 4.13. To the extent the research pursues broadly framed questions, the results tend to be broadly applicable. But there is more. Research results that apply to "other people" imply that the participants involved were representative of a larger intended population. If the experiment used 18- to 25-year-old computer literate college students, the results might generalize to middle-aged computer literate professionals. But, they might not generalize to middle-aged people without computer experience. And they likely would not apply to the elderly, to children, or to users with certain disabilities. In experimental research, random sampling is important for generalizability, that is,

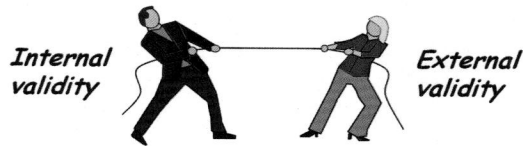

FIGURE 4.14

Tension between internal validity and external validity. Improving one comes at the expense of the other. See text for discussion (sketch courtesy of Bartosz Bajer).

the participants selected for testing were drawn at random from the desired population.

Generalizable to "other situations" means the experimental *environment* and *procedures* were representative of real world situations where the interface or technique will be used. If the research studied the usability of a GPS tracker for taxi drivers or delivery personnel and the experiment was conducted in a quiet, secluded research lab, there may be a problem with external validity. Perhaps a different experimental environment should be considered. Research on text entry where participants enter pre-determined text phrases with no punctuation symbols, no uppercase characters, and without any ability to correct mistakes, may have a problem with external validity. Again, a different experimental procedure should be considered.

The scenarios above are overly dogmatic. Experiment design is an exercise in compromise. While speaking in the strictest terms about high internal validity and high external validity, in practice one is achieved at the expense of the other, as characterized in Fig. 4.14.

To explore the tension between internal and external validity, two additional examples are presented. The first pertains to the experimental environment. Consider an experiment that compares two remote pointing devices for presentation systems. To improve external validity, the experimental environment mimics expected usage. Participants are tested in a large room with a large presentation-size display, they stand, and they are positioned a few meters from the display. The other participants are engaged to act as an audience by attending and sitting around tables in the room during testing. There is no doubt this environment improves external validity. But, what about internal validity? Some participants may be distracted or intimidated by the audience. Others might have a tendency to show off, impress, or act out. Such behaviours introduce sources of variation outside the realm of the devices under test, and thereby compromise internal validity. So, our effort to improve external validity through environmental considerations may negatively impact internal validity.

A second example pertains to the experimental procedure. Consider an experiment comparing two methods of text entry. In an attempt to improve external validity, participants are instructed to enter whatever text they think of. The text may include punctuation symbols, uppercase and lowercase characters, and participants can edit the text and correct errors as they go. Again, external validity is improved since this is what people normally do when entering text. However, internal validity is compromised because behaviours are introduced that are not directly related to the text entry techniques – behaviours such as pondering (*What should I enter next?*) and fiddling with commands (*How do I move the cursor back and make a correction? How is overtype mode invoked?*). Furthermore, since participants generate the text, errors are difficult to record since there is no "source text" with which to compare the entered text. So, here we again see the compromise. The desire to improve external validity through procedural considerations may negatively impact internal validity.

Unfortunately, there is no universal remedy for the tension between internal and external validity. At the very least, one must acknowledge the limitations. Formulating conclusions that are broader than what the results suggest is sure to raise the ire of reviewers. We can strive for the best of both worlds with a simple approach, however. Posing multiple narrow (testable) questions that cover the range of outcomes influencing the broader (untestable) questions will increase both internal and external validity. For example, a technique that is faster, more accurate, easy to learn, easy to remember, and considered comfortable and enjoyable by users is generally better. Usually, there is a positive correlation between the testable and untestable questions; that is, participants generally find a UI better if it is faster, more accurate, takes fewer steps, more enjoyable, more comfortable, and so on.

Before moving on, it is worth mentioning *ecological validity*, a term closely related to external validity. The main distinction is in how the terms are used. Ecological validity refers to the methodology (using materials, tasks, and situations typical of the real-world), whereas external validity refers to the outcome (obtaining results that generalize to a broad range of people and situations). High ecological validity implies that the testing took place in a manner that mimics real-world conditions.

Obviously, ecological validity and external validity are correlated: Testing in a natural setting (ecological validity) fosters results that are generalizable (external validity).

4.7 Comparative evaluations

Evaluating new ideas for user interfaces or interaction techniques is central to research in human-computer interaction. However, evaluations in HCI sometimes focus on a single idea or interface. The idea is conceived, designed, implemented, and evaluated – but not compared. The research component of such an evaluation is questionable. Or, to the extent the exercise is labelled research, it is more aligned with the second definition of research noted earlier: "collecting information about a particular subject."

From a research perspective, our third definition is more appealing, since it includes the ideas of experimentation, discovery, and developing theories of interaction. Certainly, more meaningful and insightful results are obtained if a comparative evaluation is performed. In other words, a new user interface or interaction technique is designed and implemented and then compared with one or more alternative designs to determine which is faster, more accurate, less confusing, more preferred by users,

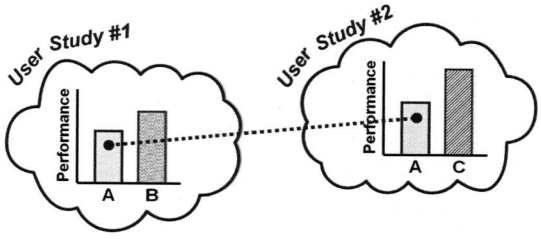

FIGURE 4.15

Including a baseline condition serves as a check on the methodology and facilitates the comparison of results between user studies.

etc. The alternatives may be variations in the new design, an established design (a baseline condition), or some combination of the two. In fact, testable research questions above are crafted as comparisons (e.g., "Is Method A faster than Method B for ..."). And for good reason. A controlled experiment must include at least one independent variable and the independent variable must have at least two levels or test conditions. Comparison, then, is inherent in research following the experimental method discussed earlier. The design of HCI experiments is elaborated further in Chapter 5.

The idea of including an established design as a baseline condition is particularly appealing. There are two benefits. First, the baseline condition serves as a check on the methodology. Baseline conditions are well travelled in the research literature, so, results in a new experiment should align with previous results. Second, the baseline condition allows results to be compared with other studies. The general idea is shown in Fig. 4.15. Results from two hypothetical user studies are shown. Both studies are comparative evaluations and both included condition A as a baseline. Provided the methodology was similar, the performance results for condition A should also be similar. This serves not only as a check on the methodology but also facilitates comparisons between the two user studies. A quick look at the charts suggests that condition C out-performs condition B. This is an interesting observation because condition C was evaluated in one study, condition B in another.

Consider the idea cited earlier of comparing two remote pointing devices for presentation systems. Such a study would benefit by including a conventional mouse as a baseline condition.[13] If the results for the mouse are consistent with those found in other studies, then the methodology was probably OK, and the results for the remote pointing devices are likely valid. Furthermore, conclusions can often be expressed in terms of the known baseline condition, for example, "Device A was about 8% slower than a conventional mouse."

---

[13] The example cited earlier on remote pointing devices included a conventional mouse as a baseline condition [313].

The value in conducting a comparative study was studied in research by Tohidi et al. [491], who tested the hypothesis that a comparative evaluation yields more insight than a one-of evaluation. In their study, participants were assigned to groups and were asked to manually perform simple tasks with climate control interfaces (i.e., thermostats). There were three different interfaces tested. Some of the participants interacted with just one interface, while others did the same tasks with all three interfaces. The participants interacting with all three interfaces consistently found more problems and were more critical of the interfaces. They were also less prone to inflate their subjective ratings. While this experiment was fully qualitative – human performance was not measured or quantified – the message is the same: a comparative evaluation yields more valuable and insightful results than a single-interface evaluation.

4.8 Relationships: causal and circumstantial

We noted above that looking for and explaining interesting relationships is part of what we do in HCI research. Often a controlled experiment is designed and conducted specifically for this purpose, and if done properly a particular type of conclusion is possible. We can often say that the condition manipulated in the experiment *caused* the changes in the human responses that were observed and measured. This is a *cause-and-effect relationship*, or, simply, a *causal relationship*.

In HCI, the condition manipulated is often a nominal-scale attribute of an interface, such as device, entry method, feedback modality, selection technique, menu depth, button layout, and so on. The property measured is typically a ratio-scale human behaviour, such as task completion time, error rate, or the number of button clicks, scrolling events, gaze shifts, etc.

Finding a causal relationship in an HCI experiment yields a powerful conclusion. If the human response measured is vital in HCI, such as the time to do a common task, then knowing that a condition tested in the experiment reduces this time is a valuable outcome. If the condition is an implementation of a novel idea and it was compared with current practice, there may be reason to celebrate. Not only has a causal relationship been found, the new idea improves on existing practice. This adds valuable knowledge to the discipline, it moves the state of the art forward.[14] This is what HCI research is all about!

Finding a relationship does not necessarily imply a causal relationship. Many relationships are *circumstantial*. They exist, and they can be observed, measured, and quantified. But, expressing the relationship as causal is wrong. The classic example is the relationship between smoking and cancer. Suppose a research study tracked the

---

[14] Reporting a non-significant outcome is also important, particularly if there was reason to believe a test condition might improve an interface or interaction technique. Reporting a non-significant outcome means, at the very least, other researchers needn't pursue the idea further.

habits and health of a large number of people over many years. The methodology is correlational, not experimental. In the end, a relationship is found: Cancer is more prevalent in the people who smoked. Is it correct to conclude from the study that smoking *caused* cancer? No. The relationship is circumstantial, not causal. Consider this: On a closer examination of the data, it is discovered that people who developed cancer also had a higher tendency to drink alcohol, eat fatty foods, stay up late, listen to rock music, etc. Perhaps the cancer was caused by the increased consumption of alcohol or fatty foods, or some other factor. The relationship is circumstantial, not causal.

Of course, it might be possible to conduct a controlled experiment looking for a causal relationship between smoking and cancer. But, such an experiment has never been conducted. The sticking point is ethics. Experiments with human participants must undergo ethics approval before proceeding. Approval is not forthcoming if participants are likely to be harmed during the experiment. (See also section 5.2, Ethics Approval.) This is not to say that *circumstantial relationships* are not useful. Looking for and finding a circumstantial relationship is often the first step in further research, in part because it is relatively easy to collect data and look for circumstantial relationships.

Causal relationships emerge from controlled experiments. Looking for a causal relationship requires a study where, among other things, participants are selected randomly from a population and are randomly assigned to test conditions. A random assignment ensures that each group of participants is approximately the same in all respects except for the conditions under test. Thus, the differences that emerge are more likely due to (*caused by*) the test conditions than to environmental or other circumstances. Sometimes participants are balanced into groups where the participants in each group are screened so the groups are equal in terms of other relevant attributes. For example, an experiment testing two input controllers for games could randomly assign participants to groups or balance the groups to ensure the range of gaming experience is approximately equal.

Here is an HCI example similar to smoking versus cancer: A researcher wishes to compare tapping and gesturing for text input on a Qwerty soft keyboard. Tapping is the usual method: Use a finger to tap on soft keys to enter letters. Gesturing involves inputting each word by sliding through the soft keys bearing the desired letters.[15] The researcher ventures into the world and approaches users of Android smart phones, asking for five minutes of their time. Many agree. They answer a few questions about experience and usage habits, including their preferred method of entering text messages. Fifteen tap-typing users and 15 gesture-typing users are found. The users are asked to enter a prescribed phrase of text while they are timed. Back in the lab, the data are analysed. Evidently, the gesture-typing users were faster, entering at a rate of 27 words per minute, compared to 18 words per minute for the tap-typing

---

[15] Gesture typing has other names, such as Shape Writing, SHARK, T9 Trace, FlexT9, or Swype. The idea was first explored by Kristensson and Zhai [256,548].

users. That's 50 percent faster for the gesture-typing users! What is the conclusion? There is a relationship between method of entry and text entry speed; however, the relationship is circumstantial, not causal. It is reasonable to report what was done and what was found, but it is wrong to venture beyond what the methodology gives.

Concluding from the example above gesture-typing is faster than tap-typing would be premature. Upon inspecting the data more closely, it is discovered that the gesture-typing users were more tech-savvy, reporting considerably more experience using smart phones. They also reported sending considerably more text messages per day than the tap-typing users who, by and large, said they didn't like sending text messages and did so very infrequently. So the difference observed may be due to experience or usage habits, rather than inherent differences in the methods compared. If there is a genuine interest in determining if one text entry method is faster than another, a controlled experiment is required. This is the topic of the next chapter.

One final point deserves mention. Cause and effect conclusions are not possible in certain types of controlled experiments. If the variable manipulated is a *naturally occurring attribute* of people, then cause and effect conclusions are unreliable. Examples of naturally occurring attributes include gender (female, male), personality (extrovert, introvert), hand preference (left, right), first language (e.g., English, French, Spanish), political viewpoint (left, right), and so on. These attributes are legitimate independent variables, but they cannot be manipulated, which is to say, they cannot be assigned to participants. In such cases, a cause and effect conclusions are unreliable because is not possible to avoid confounding variables (defined in Chapter 5). Being a male, being an extrovert, being left handed, and so on, brings forth other attributes germane to the attribute of interest. Cause and effect conclusions should be avoided because it is not possible to know whether the experimental effect was due to the independent variable or to the confounding influence of other attributes.

As an example, Hinckley et al. [194] treated *sex* as an independent variable in an evaluation of rotation tasks with 3D input devices. They found a statistically significant difference in task completion time between males and females. While it is possible that the difference was caused by perceptual or cognitive processing differences in males vs. female for object rotation, it is also possible that the difference is due to other non-sex issues, such as previous use of certain software applications or input devices.

4.9 Research topics

Most HCI research is not about designing products. It's not even about designing applications for products. In fact, it's not even about design or products. Research in HCI, like in most fields, tends to nip away at the edges. The march forward is incremental. The truth is, most research ideas build on existing ideas and do so in modest ways. A small improvement to this, a little change to that. Big changes when they do arise, usually involve bringing to market, through engineering and design,

FIGURE 4.16

A two-finger gesture on a touch-sensitive display is used to rotate a virtual knob (adapted from [187]).

ideas that already exist in the research literature. Examples are the finger flick and two-finger gestures used on touchscreen phones. Most users likely first encountered these with the Apple iPhone, introduced in June 2007. The gestures seemed like bold new advances in interaction, but, of course, they were not. The flick gesture dates at least to the 1960s. They were used by Sutherland to terminate drawing gestures in his Sketchpad system [478]. Two-finger gestures date at least to the 1970s. Fig. 4.16 shows Herot and Weinzapfel's two-finger gesture used to rotate a virtual knob on a touch-sensitive display [187]. As reported, the knob can be rotated to within 5° of a target position. So, what might seem like a bold new advance is often a matter of good engineering and design, using ideas that already exist.

Finding a *research topic* is often the most challenging step for graduate students in HCI (and other fields). The expression "ABD" for "all but dissertation" is a sad reminder of this predicament. Graduate students sometimes find themselves in a position of having finished all degree requirements (e.g., coursework, a teaching practicum) without nailing down the big topic for dissertation research. Students might be surprised to learn that seasoned researchers in university and industry also struggle for that next "big idea." Akin to "writer's block," the harder one tries, the less likely is the idea to appear. Below, we offer four tips to overcome "researcher's block." First, we present a few observations on ideas and how and where they arise.

4.9.1 Ideas

In the halcyon days after World War II, there was an American television show, a situation comedy, or sitcom, called *The Many Loves of Dobie Gillis* (1959-1963). Much like *Seinfeld* many years later, the show was largely about, well, nothing. Dobie's leisurely life mostly focused on getting rich or on endearing a beautiful woman to his heart. And each episode began with an idea, a scheme. The opening scene often placed Dobie on a park bench beside *The Thinker*, the bronze and marble statue by French sculpture Aguste Rodin (1840-1917). See Fig. 4.17. After some pensive moments by the statue, Dobie's idea, his scheme, would come to him. Voila! It would be nice if research ideas in HCI were similarly available, and with such assurance as Dobie's ideas. That they are not is no cause for concern, however. Dobie's plans usually failed miserably, so, we might question his approach to formulating his plans. Is it possible that *The Thinker*, in his pose, is more likely to inspire "writer's block"

FIGURE 4.17

The Thinker appeared in the opening scenes of the American sitcom *The Many Loves of Dobie Gillis.*

than the idea so desperately sought? The answer may be yes, but there is little science here. We are dealing with human thought, inspiration, creativity, and a milieu of other human qualities that are highly variable and poorly understood, at best.

If working hard to find a good idea doesn't work, perhaps a better approach is to relax and just get on with one's day. This seems to have worked for the ancient Greek scholar Archimedes (287-212 BC) who is said to have effortlessly come upon a brilliant idea as a solution to a problem. As a scientist, Archimedes was called upon to determine if King Hiero's crown was pure gold or if it was compromised with a lesser alloy. One solution was to melt the crown, separating the constituent parts. This would destroy the crown – not a good idea. Archimedes idea was simple, and he is said to have discovered it while taking a bath. Yes, taking a bath, rather than sitting for hours in *The Thinker*'s pose. He realized – in an instant – that the volume of water displaced as he entered the bathtub must equal the volume of his body. Immersing the crown in water would similarly yield the crown's volume, and this combined with the crown's weight would reveal the crown's density. If the density of the crown equalled the known density of gold, the King's crown was pure gold – problem solved. According to the legend, Archimedes was so elated at his moment of revelation that he jumped from his bath and ran nude about the streets of Syracuse shouting "Eureka!" ("I found it!").

While legends make good stories, we are unlikely to be as fortunate as Archimedes in finding a good idea for an HCI research topic. Inspiration is not always the result of single moment of revelation. It is often gradual, with sources unknown or without a conscious and recognizable connection to the problem. Recall Vannevar Bush's memex, described in the opening chapter of this book. Memex was a concept. It was never built, even though Bush described the interaction with memex in considerable detail. We know memex today as hypertext and the World Wide Web. But, where and how did Bush get his idea? The starting point is having a problem to solve. The problem of interest to Bush was coping with ever-expanding volumes of information. Scientists, like Bush, needed a convenient way to access this information. But how? It

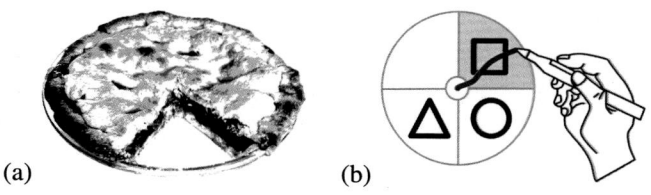

(a)   (b)

FIGURE 4.18

Pie menus in HCI. (a) The inspiration? (b) HCI example (adapted from [262]).

seems Bush's inspiration for memex came from ... Let's pause for a moment, lest we infer Bush was engaged in a structured approach to problem solving. It is not likely that Bush went to work one morning intent on solving the problem of information access. More than likely, the idea came without deliberate effort. It may have come flittingly, in an instant, or gradually, over days, weeks, or months. Who knows? What is known, however, is that the idea did not arise from nothing. Ideas come from the human experience. This is why in HCI we often read about things like "knowledge in the head and knowledge in the world" [376, chap. 3] or metaphor and analogy [65]. The context for inspiration is the human experience. So, what was the source of Bush's inspiration for memex? The answer is in Bush's article, and also in Chapter 1.

Are there other examples relevant to HCI? Sure. Twitter co-founder Jack Dorsey is said to have come up with the idea for the popular blogging site while in a park and sitting on a children's slide eating Mexican food.[16] What about pie menus in graphical user interfaces? Pie menus, as an alternative to linear menus, were first proposed by Don Hopkins at the University of Maryland in 1988 (cited in Callahan et al. [55]). We might wonder about the source of Hopkin's inspiration (see Fig. 4.18).

See as well student exercise 4-2 at the end of this chapter.

4.9.2 Finding a topic

It is no small feat to find an interesting research topic. In the following paragraphs, four tips are offered on finding a topic suitable for research. As with the earlier discussion on the cost and frequency of errors (see Fig. 3.67, p. 154), there is little science to offer here. The ideas follow from personal experience and from working with students and other researchers in HCI.

4.9.2.1 Tip #1: think small!

At a conference recently, I had an interesting conversation with a student. He was a graduate student in HCI. "Have you found a topic for your research," I asked. "Not really," he said. He had a topic, but only in a broad sense. Seems his supervisor had funding for a large research project related to aviation. The goal was to develop an

---

[16] New York Times, Oct. 30, 2010, page BU1.

improved user interface for an air traffic control system. He was stuck. Where to begin? Did I have any ideas for him? Well, actually, no I didn't. Who wouldn't be stuck? The task of developing a UI for an air traffic control system is huge. Furthermore, the project mostly involves engineering and design. Where is the research in designing an improved system of any sort? What are the research questions? What are the experimental variables? Unfortunately, graduate students are often saddled with similar big problems, because a supervisor's funding source requires it. The rest of our discussion focused on narrowing the problem – in a big way. Not to some definable sub-system, but to a small aspect of the interface or interaction. The smaller, the better.

The point here is to think small. On finding that big idea, the advice is . . . forget it. Once you shed that innate desire to find something really significant and important, it's amazing what will follow. If you have a small idea, something that seems a little useful, it's probably worth pursuing as a research project. Pursue it and the next thing you know, three or four related interaction improvements come to mind. Soon enough, there's a dissertation topic in the works. So, don't hesitate to think small.

4.9.2.2 Tip #2: replicate!

An effective way to get started on research is to replicate an existing experiment from the HCI literature. This seems odd. Where is the research in simply replicating what was already done? Of course, there is none. But, there is a trick. Having taught HCI courses many times over many years, I know that students frequently get stuck finding a topic for the course's research project. Students frequently approach me for a suggestion. If I have an idea that seems relevant to the student's interests, I'll suggest it. Quite often (usually!) I don't have any particular idea. If nothing comes to mind, I take another approach. The student is advised just to study the HCI literature – research papers from the CHI proceedings, for example – and find some experimental research on a topic of interest. Then, just replicate the experiment. Is that OK, I am asked? Sure, no problem.

The trick is in the path to replicating. Replicating a research experiment requires a lot of work. The process of studying a research paper and precisely determining what was done, then implementing it, testing it, debugging it, doing an experiment around it, and so on, will empower the student – the researcher – with a deep understanding of the issues, much deeper than simply reading the paper. This moves the line forward. The stage is set. Quite often, a new idea, a new twist, emerges. But, it is important not to *require* something new. The pressure in that may backfire. Something new may emerge, but this might not happen until late in the process, or after the experiment is finished. So, it is important to avoid a requirement for novelty. This is difficult, because it is germane to the human condition to strive for something new. Self-doubt may bring the process to a standstill. So, keep the expectations low. A small tweak here, a little change there. Good enough. No pressure. Just replicate. You may be surprised with the outcome.

Study (1st author)	Number of Keys[a]	Direct/ Indirect	Scanning	Number of Participants	Speed[b] (wpm)	Notes
Bellman [2]	5	Indirect	No	11	11	4 cursors keys + SELECT key. Error rates not reported. No error correction method.
Dunlop [4]	4	Direct	No	12	8.90	4 letter keys + SPACE key. Error rates reported as "very low."
Dunlop [5]	4	Direct	No	20	12	4 letter keys + 1 key for SPACE/NEXT. Error rates not reported. No error correction method.
Tanaka-Ishii [25	3	Direct	No	8	12+	4 letters keys + 4 keys for editing, and selecting. 5 hours training. Error rates not reported. Errors corrected using CLEAR key.
Gong [7]	3	Direct	No	32	8.01	3 letter keys + two additional keys. Error rate = 2.1%. Errors corrected using DELETE key.
MacKenzie [16]	3	Indirect	No	10	9.61	2 cursor keys + SELECT key. Error rate = 2.2%. No error correction method.
Baljko [1]	2	Indirect	Yes	12	3.08	1 SELECT key + BACKSPACE key. 43 virtual keys. RC scanning. Same phrase entered 4 times. Error rate = 18.5%. Scanning interval = 750 ms.
Simpson [24]	1	Indirect	Yes	4	4.48	1 SELECT key. 26 virtual keys. RC scanning. Excluded trials with selection errors or missed selections. No error correction. Scanning interval = 525 ms at end of study.
Koester [10]	1	Indirect	Yes	3	7.2	1 SELECT key. 33 virtual keys. RC scanning with word prediction. Dictionary size not given. Virtual BACKSPACE key. 10 blocks of trials. Error rates not reported. Included trials with selection errors or missed selections. Fastest participant: 8.4 wpm.

[a] For "direct" entry, the value is the number of letter keys. For "indirect" entry, the value is the total number of keys.
[b] The entry speed cited is the highest of the values reported in each source, taken from the last block if multiple blocks.

FIGURE 4.19

Table showing papers (rows) and relevant conditions or results (columns) from research papers on text entry using small keyboards (from [306, Table 1]; consult for full details on studies cited).

4.9.2.3 Tip #3: know the literature!

It might seem obvious, but the process of reviewing research papers on a topic of interest is an excellent way to develop ideas for research projects. The starting point is identifying the topic, in a general sense. If one finds gaming of interest, then gaming is the topic. If one finds social networking of interest, that's the topic. From there the task is to search out and aggressively study and analyse all published research on the topic. If there are too many publications, then narrow the topic. What, in particular, is the interest in gaming or social networking? Continue the search. Use Google Scholar, the ACM Digital Library, or whatever resource is conveniently available. Download all the papers, store them, organize them, study them, make notes, then open a spreadsheet and start tabulating features from the papers. Use one row for each paper. In the columns, tabulate aspects of the interface or interaction technique, conditions tested, results obtained, and so on. Organize the table in whatever manner seems reasonable.

The process is chaotic at first. Where to begin? What are the issues? The task is daunting, at the very least, because of the divergence in reporting methods. But, that's the point. The gain is in the process – bringing shape and structure to the chaos. The table will grow as more papers are found and analysed. There is an example in this book. See Fig. 7.23 (p. 319).

There are also many examples in published papers. Fig. 4.19 is from a research paper on text entry using small keyboards. The table is a literature review summary. Although neat and tidy, don't be fooled. It emerged from a difficult and chaotic process of reviewing a collection of papers and finding common and relevant issues. The collection of notes in the right-hand column is evidence of the difficulty: pointing out issues that complicate comparisons of the data in the other columns.

Are there research topics lurking within Fig. 4.19? Probably. But the point is the process, not the product. Building such a table shapes the research into relevant categories of inquiry.

Similar tables are presented in the literature, for example, by Hafizi et al. [169, Table 1], Ivory and Hearst [214, Table 1], Choi et al. [79, Table 1], Soukoreff and MacKenzie [466, Table 3 & Table 4], Teather and MacKenzie [485, Table 1], Al-Megren [353, Table 1], Dube et al. [106, Table 1], and Griffiths et al. [160, Table 1].

See also student exercise 4-3 at the end of this chapter.

4.9.2.4 Tip #4: think inside the box!

The common expression "think outside the box" is a challenge to all. The idea is to dispense with accepted beliefs and assumptions (in the box) and to think in a new way that assumes nothing and challenges everything. However, there is a problem with the challenge. Contemporary, tech-savvy people, clever as they are, often believe they in fact do think outside the box, and everyone else is confined to mundane life in the box. With this view, the challenge is lost before starting. There is an unsavoury precept in tip #4: You are inside the box! All is not lost, however. Thinking inside the box, then, is thinking about and challenging one's own experiences – the experiences inside the box. The idea is simple. Just get on with your day, but at every juncture, every interaction, think and question. What happened? Why did it happen? Is there an alternative? Play the role of both a participant (this is unavoidable) and an observer. Observe others, of course, but more importantly observe yourself. You are in the box, but have a look, study, and reconsider.

Here's an example, which on the surface seems trivial (but see tip #1). While at work at York University, I was walking to my class on Human-Computer Interaction. Being a bit late, I was in a hurry. The class was in a nearby building on the 3rd floor and I was carrying some equipment. I entered the elevator and pushed the button – the wrong button. Apparently, for each floor the control panel has both a button label and a button. See Fig. 4.20a. I pushed the button label instead of the button. A second later I pushed the button, and my journey continued. End of story.

Of course, there is more. Why did I push the wrong button? Yes, I was in a hurry, but that's not the full reason. With a white number on a black background, the floor is identified more prominently by the button label than by the button. And the button label is round, like a button. On the button, the number is recessed in the metal, and is barely visible. The error was minor, only a *slip* (right intention, wrong action, see [376, chap. 5]). Is there a research topic in this? Perhaps. Perhaps not. But, experiencing, observing, and thinking about one's interactions with technology can generate ideas and promote a humbling yet questioning frame of thinking – thinking that moves forward into research topics. The truth is, I have numerous moments like this every day, and so do you! Most amount to nothing, but the small foibles in interacting with technology are intriguing and worth thinking about. See also student exercise 4-5.

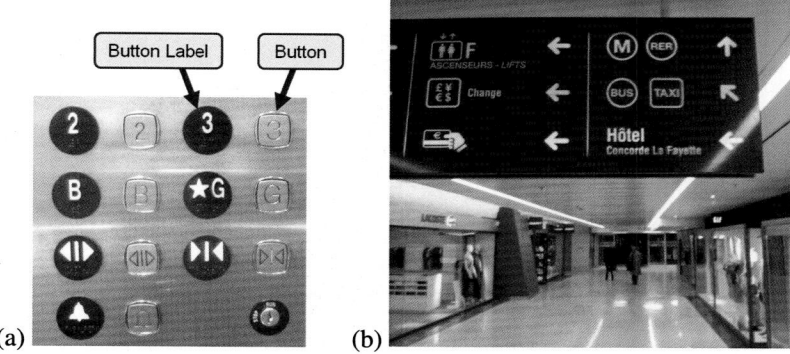

FIGURE 4.20

Thinking about one's experiences. (a) Elevator control panel. The button label is more prominent than the button. (b) A sign directing pedestrians to their destinations.

As another example, while at the ACM SIGCHI conference in 2013, I was in a maze of corridors below the conference centre, trying to find the Metro station. There were numerous signs directing people to their destination. One such sign is shown in Fig. 4.20b. It includes a Metro icon (a capital M in a circle) and an arrow. I followed the arrow – the wrong arrow! I turned left, instead of continuing straight. It's so obvious now, but I was rushed and only looked briefly. The sign seems well designed. There is a vertical bar separating groups of items. But, in that brief moment of stimulus and response, the proximity of the left arrow to M clearly trumped the separation of the vertical line. What's the lesson here? As with the elevator-button example the point is not about deep analysis but simply to think inside one's personal experiences – inside the box.

*****

In this chapter, we examined the scientific foundations for research in human-computer interaction. The next challenge is in designing and conducting experiments using human participants (users) to evaluate new ideas for user interfaces and inter-action techniques. We meet these topics in Chapter 5.

A web site is available as a resource accompanying this book's second edition:

- http://www.yorku.ca/mack/HCIbook2e

Student exercises

4-1 Examine some published papers in HCI and find examples where results were reported as a raw count (e.g., number of errors) rather than as a count per some-thing (e.g., percent errors). Find three examples and prepare a brief report or

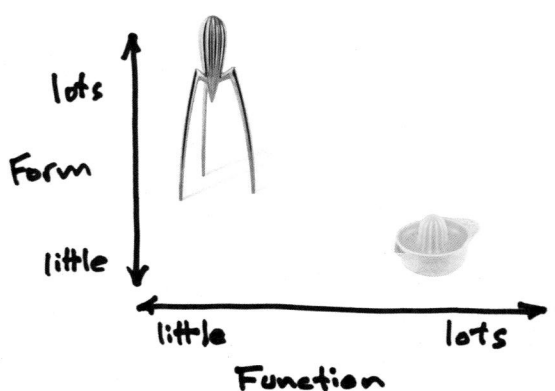

FIGURE 4.21

Student exercise on form vs. function.

slide show presentation detailing how the results were reported and the weakness or limitation in the method. Propose a better way to report the same results. Use charts or graphs, where appropriate.

4-2 What in Vannevar Bush's "human experience" formed the inspiration for memex? (If needed, review Bush's essay "As We May Think," or see the discussion in Chapter 1.) What are the similarities between his inspiration and memex?

4-3 Here are some research themes: 3D console gaming, VR gaming, mobile phone use while driving, privacy settings in social networking, location-aware user interfaces, tactile feedback in gaming, multi-touch tabletop interaction. Choose one of these topics (or another) and build a table similar to that in Fig. 4.19. Narrow the topic, if necessary (e.g., mobile phone texting while driving), and find at least five relevant research papers to include in the table. Organize the table with one row per paper and columns holding research details that can be compared between the papers. Prepare a brief report or slide show presentation about the table. Include citations and references to the selected papers.

4-4 The form vs. function comparison for design and engineering in Fig. 4.2 (p. 167) is recast in Fig. 4.21 showing two juice squeezers positioned according to their possible form vs. function. Create three diagrams similar to Fig. 4.21, each with two implementations of something, anything. Ensure at least one of the diagrams uses computer-based items and at least one uses non-computer-based items. Prepare a brief report or slide show presentation describing the artefacts, the implementations, and rationalizing their placement in the chart.

4-5 Find a small interaction problem based on your personal experience with computing technology. Prepare a brief report or slide show presentation that identifies and describes the problem. No matter how small the problem, describe it in as much detail as possible. Suggest a way to solve the problem. Use visual aids, as appropriate. As examples, review the problems elaborated in Tip #4 in section 4.9.2.4. For this student exercise, interpret "computing technology" broadly. Items such as a microwave oven or a sports watch apply (but please, don't use these for your example).

4-6 Repeat the student exercise above using an example of an artefact or situation that is not related to computing technology.

Designing HCI experiments

Learning how to design and conduct an experiment with human participants is a skill required of all researchers in human-computer interaction. In this chapter we describe the core details of designing and conducting HCI experiments. One way to think about experiment design is through a signal and noise metaphor. In the metaphor, we divide our observations and measurements into two components: signal and noise. See Fig. 5.1. The source shows a time series. A slight upward trend is apparent; however, the variability or noise in the source makes this difficult to detect. If we separate the source into components for signal and noise, the trend in the signal is clear.

In HCI experiments, the signal is related to a variable of interest, such as input device, feedback mode, or an interaction technique under investigation. The noise is everything else: the random influences. These include environmental circumstances, such as temperature, lighting, background noise, a wobbly chair, or glare on the computer screen. As well, the people or participants in the experiment are a source of noise or variability. Some participants may be having a good day, while others are not. Some people are predisposed to behave a certain way; others behave differently. The process of designing an experiment is one of enhancing the signal while reducing the noise. This is done by carefully considering the setup of the experiment in terms of the variables manipulated and measured, the variables controlled, the procedures, the tasks, and so on. Collectively, these properties of an experiment establish the methodology for the research.

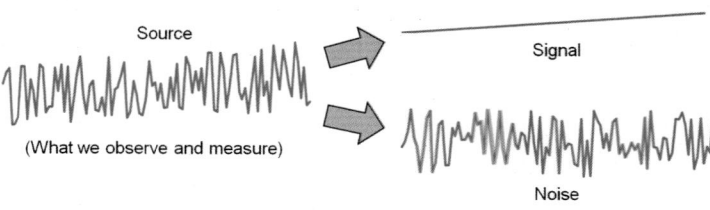

FIGURE 5.1

Signal-to-noise concept for experiment design.

Human-Computer Interaction. https://doi.org/10.1016/B978-0-44-314096-9.00011-7

5.1 What methodology?

The term *method* or *methodology* refers to the way an experiment is designed and carried out. This involves deciding on the people (participants), the hardware and software (materials or apparatus), the tasks, the order of tasks, the procedure for briefing and preparing the participants, the variables, the data collected and analysed, and so on. Having a sound methodology is critical. On this point, Allen Newell did not hesitate:

Science is method. Everything else is commentary.[1]

These are strong words. Why did Newell apply forceful yet narrow language to a topic as broad as science? The reason is that Newell, and others, understand that methodology is the bedrock of science. If the research methodology is weak or flawed, there is no science forthcoming. What remains is little else than commentary.

In the preceding chapter, we advocated the use of a standardized methodology to strengthen experimental research. The flip side is that an ad hoc, or made-up, methodology weakens research. There is little sense in contriving a methodology simply because it seems like a good way to test or demonstrate an idea.

So, what is the appropriate methodology for research in human-computer interaction? The discussions that follow pertain only to experimental research and in particular to *factorial experiments*, where participants are exposed to levels of factors (aka independent variables) while their behaviour (human performance) is observed and measured. By and large, the methodology is plucked from one of HCI's parent disciplines: experimental psychology.

Just as the Association for Computing Machinery (ACM) is the dominant organization overseeing computer science and related special interests, such as HCI, the American Psychological Association (APA) is the dominant organization overseeing experimental psychology. Their *Publication Manual of the American Psychological Association*, first published in 1929, is a must-have resource for researchers undertaking experimental research involving human participants [10]. The manual, now in its 7th edition, is used by over 1000 journals across many disciplines [29]. These include HCI journals. The APA guidelines are recommended by journals such as the ACM's *Transactions on Computer-Human Interaction* (TOCHI) [4] and Taylor and Francis's *Human-Computer Interaction* [483].

The APA's *Publication Manual* is about more than publishing style; the manual lays out many methodological issues, such as naming and referring to independent and dependent variables, recruiting participants, reporting the results of statistical tests, etc. The totality of the work is commonly referred to as "APA style." As well, the important link between research and publication is reflected in the title.

---

[1] These words from Allen Newell were offered and elaborated on by Stuart Card in an invited talk at the ACM's SIGCHI conference in Austin, Texas (May 10, 2012).

The proceedings of the ACM SIGCHI's annual conference ("CHI") are also an excellent resource. CHI papers are easily viewed and downloaded from the ACM Digital Library or Google Scholar. Of course, many research papers in the CHI proceedings do not present experimental research. And that's fine. HCI is multidisciplinary. The research methods brought to bear on human interaction with technology are equally diverse. However, of those papers that do present a *user study* – an experiment with human participants – there are, unfortunately, many where the methodology is ad hoc. The additional burden of weaving one's way through an unfamiliar methodology while simultaneously trying to understand a new and potentially interesting idea, makes studying these papers difficult. This is all too common, and unfortunate.

Fortunately, there are many CHI papers that follow the standard methodology for experiments with human participants. It is relatively easy to spot examples. If the paper has a section called Method or Experiment (or something similar) and the first sub-section within is called Participants, there is a good chance the paper and the research it describes follow the standards for experimental research, as laid out in this chapter and book.[2] Examples from the CHI proceedings are papers by Elkin et al. [112], Hafizi et al. [169], Hedeshy et al. [185], Jamil et al. [220], Sengupta et al. [441], Surale et al. [477], and Zhang et al. [550].

5.2 **Ethics approval**

A crucial step preceding every HCI experiment is *ethics approval*. Since HCI research involves humans, researchers must respect the safety, welfare, and dignity of human participants and treat them equally and fairly. The approval process is governed by the institution or funding agency overseeing the research. At this author's institution, research projects must be approved by the Human Participant Review Committee (HRPC). Other committee names commonly used are the Institutional Review Board (IRB), Ethics Review Committee (ERC), and so on.

Typically, the review committee ensures ethical guidelines are acknowledged and adhered to. These include the right of the participant to be informed of the following:

- the nature of the research (hypotheses, goals and objectives, etc.),
- the research methodology (e.g., medical procedures, questionnaires, participant observation, etc.),
- any risks or benefits,
- the right not to participate, not to answer any questions, or to terminate participation at any time without prejudice (e.g., without academic penalty, withdrawal of remuneration, etc.), and
- the right to anonymity and confidentiality.

---

[2] It is important to organize and present the details of a user study in a way that is clear and predicable for readers. More on this in Chapter 8 (section 8.2.5, Method).

The last point is particularly important. Participants have the right to privacy and confidentiality. Any information gathered that can identify participants must be protected. And so, the ethics review process often requires researchers to explain in excruciating detail how data will be handled and stored, both during the research and for years after. One tip to consider is this: Instead of concocting a complex lock-and-key protocol to protect confidential information, avoid gathering any such information at all. When a person agrees to participate in a research project, it is often sufficient just to identify them with a code (e.g., P01) and to avoid recording or storing their name or any other identifying information.

Details for ethics approval vary according to local guidelines. Special attention is given for vulnerable participants, such as pregnant women, children, or the elderly. The basis for approving the research, where human participants are involved, is striking a balance between the risks to participants and the benefits to society.

5.3 Experiment design

Experiment design is the process of bringing together all the pieces necessary to test hypotheses on a user interface or interaction technique. It involves deciding on and defining which variables to use, what tasks and procedure to use, how many participants to use and how to solicit them, and so on.

One of the most difficult steps in designing an HCI experiment is just getting started. Ideas about a novel interface or interaction technique take shape well before thoughts of doing an experiment. There may even be an existing prototype that implements a research idea. Perhaps, there is no prototype – yet. Regardless, there is an idea about an interface or interaction technique, and it seems new and interesting. Doing an experiment to test the idea seems like a good idea, but it is difficult to transition from the creative and exciting work of developing a novel idea to the somewhat mechanical and mundane work of doing an experiment. Here is a question that will focus the mind more than any other in getting off and running with an HCI experiment:

What are the experimental variables?

This seems like an odd place to begin. After all, experimental variables are in a distant world from the creative effort invested thus far. Well, not really. Thinking about experimental variables is an excellent exercise. Here's why. The process forces us to transition from well-intentioned, broad yet untestable questions (e.g., *Is my idea any good?*) to narrower yet testable questions (e.g., *Can a task be performed more quickly with my new interface compared to an existing interface?*). If necessary, review the discussion in the preceding chapter on research questions and internal and external validity.

Thinking about experimental variables forces us to craft narrow and testable questions. The two most important experimental variables are *independent variables* and *dependent variables*. In fact, these variables are found in the example question in the preceding paragraph. Expressions like "more quickly" or "fewer steps" capture the essence of dependent variables: human behaviours that are measured. The expression "with my new interface compared to an existing interface" captures the essence of an independent variable: an interface that is compared with an alternative interface. In fact, a testable research question inherently expresses the relationship between an independent variable and a dependent variable. Let's examine these two variables in more detail.

5.4 **Independent variables**

An *independent variable* is a circumstance or characteristic that is manipulated or systematically controlled to elicit a behavioural response while a human interacts with an interface or technology of some sort. An independent variable is also called a *factor*. Experiments designed with independent variables are often called *factorial experiments*. The variable is manipulated across two or more levels of the circumstance or characteristic. The variable is "independent" because it is independent of participant behaviour, which means there is nothing a participant can do to influence an independent variable.

The variable manipulated is typically a nominal-scale attribute, often related to a property of an interface. Review any HCI research paper that presents a factorial experiment, or user study, and examples of independent variables are easily found. They are anything that might affect users' proficiency in using a computer system. Below are some independent variables, as found in the HCI literature. The levels of the independent variable are in parentheses.

- Device (mouse, trackball, stylus) [318]
- Feedback mode (auditory, visual, tactile) [5]
- Cross-display technique (stitching, mouse ether, ether+halo) [365]
- Transfer function (constant gain, pointer acceleration) [68]
- Tree visualization (traditional, list, multi-column) [461]
- Navigation technique (standard pan, zoom, poly-zoom) [222]
- Scrolling method (kinetic scroll, tap scroll, fingerprint scroll) [140]
- Entry mode (eyes-free, eyes-on) [534]
- Input method (touch-only, touch+gaze, touch-gaze-path) [259]
- Input method (finger, stylus) [70].

These variables are easy to manipulate because they are attributes of the apparatus (i.e., the computer or software). The idea of "manipulating" simply refers to systematically giving one interface, then another, to participants as part of the experimental procedure.

However, an independent variable needn't be an attribute of a computer system. It can be characteristics of people, such as age [77,78,258,285], gender [476,541], hand preference [235,396], expertise in assessing web pages [39], mobility [124], preferred operating system, first language, political viewpoint, religious viewpoint, highest level of education, income, height, weight, hair colour, shoe size, and so on. It is not clear that these human characteristics necessarily relate to HCI, but who knows.

Note that human characteristics, such as gender or first language, are naturally occurring attributes. Although such attributes are legitimate independent variables, they cannot be "manipulated" in the same way as an attribute of an interface. On this point, see also the discussion in Chapter 4 (section 4.8, Relationships, Circumstantial and Causal, p. 190).

An independent variable can also be an environmental circumstance, such as background noise (quiet, noisy), room lighting (sun, incandescent, fluorescent), vibration level (calm, in a car, in a train), and so on.

Here are two tips to consider. First, when formulating an independent variable, express it both in terms of the circumstance or characteristic itself and as the levels of the circumstance or characteristic chosen for testing. (The levels of an independent variable are often called *test conditions* or in statistics textbooks *treatments*.) So, we might have an independent variable called interaction stance with levels sitting, standing, and walking. This might seem like an odd point; however, in reading HCI research papers, it is surprising how often an independent variable is not explicitly named.

As an example, a paper in the CHI proceedings [421] presents an experiment comparing marking menus [263] with a novel technique that combines a marking menu with a unistroke gesture. The authors call the technique "augmented letters." It was noted in the method section that the experiment compared augmented letters (AL) to marking menus (MM). Although AL and MM are the levels of an independent variable, the write-up does not name the independent variable. In fact, the write-up does not even mention that the experiment includes an independent variable or factor. The statistical result is given along with a statement that participants took more time to complete their tasks using AL compared to MM. While there is nothing strictly wrong with the authors' descriptions, there is room for improvement. A better approach is to note that the experiment has an independent variable and to give it a name. In the method section, this could appear as "The independent variable was gesture technique with levels augmented letters (AL) and marking menus (MM)." The results are then given citing the statistical effect of the independent variable (gesture technique) on the dependent variable (task completion time). Of course, means, effect sizes, and other data may be provided, as appropriate. The point here is clarity: Help for the reader. A valuable technique is to provide a clear big-picture summary of the design of the experiment by identifying and naming independent variables and the levels for each independent variable. See also student exercise 5-1 at the end of this chapter.

The second tip is related to the first: Once the name of the independent variable and the names of the levels are decided, stick with these terms consistently throughout a paper. These terms hold special meaning within the experiment and any deviation in form is potentially confusing to the reader. Switching to terms like interaction

| Independent | Effects | | | | | Total |
Variables	Main	2-way	3-way	4-way	5-way	
1	1	-	-	-	-	1
2	2	1	-	-	-	3
3	3	2	1	-	-	7
4	4	6	4	1	-	15
5	5	10	10	5	1	31

FIGURE 5.2

The number of effects (main and interaction) increases with the number of independent variables.

position (cf. interaction stance), upright (cf. standing), sound (cf. audio), or vibration (cf. tactile) is potentially confusing.

As an example on the point above is also found in the CHI proceedings [399]. The authors describe an experiment with a single independent variable. In the method section, the reader is informed that "the independent variable is cueing intensity" [399, p. 1272]. However, the term "cueing intensity" does not appear elsewhere in the paper. In the results section, a significant statistical effect is reported for "type of cueing" [399, p. 1273]. Reading carefully, it is evident that "cueing intensity" and "type of cueing" are the same, but the change in terminology is potentially confusing. Again, clarity is the goal: Help for the reader. See also student exercise 5-3 at the end of this chapter.

Are the points above just minor, nit-picky musings? No. At times, it is a struggle to follow the discussions in a research paper. The fault is in the write-up, not in one's ability to follow or understand. The onus is on the researcher writing up the results of their work to deliver the rationale, methodology, results, discussion, and conclusions is the clearest way possible. Writing in a clear, consistent, and concise voice cannot be overemphasized. Further tips on writing for clarity are elaborated in Chapter 8.

Although it is reasonable to design and conduct an HCI experiment with a single independent variable, experiments often have more than one independent variable. Since considerable work is invested in designing and executing an experiment, there is a tendency to pack in additional variables so that more research questions are posed and, presumably, answered. However, including too many variables may compromise the entire experiment. With every additional independent variable, more effects exist between the variables. Fig. 5.2 illustrates. Given k independent variables, there are $2^k - 1$ effects, consisting of k main effects and $2^k - k - 1$ interaction effects.

A design with a single independent variable only includes a *main effect* – the effect of the independent variable on the dependent variable. A design with two independent variables includes two main effects and one *interaction effect*, for a total of three effects. The interaction effect is a *two-way interaction*, since it is the combined effect of the two independent variables on the dependent variable. For example, an experiment with independent variables device and task includes main effects for device and task as well as a Device × Task interaction effect.[3] To be clear, the effect is on the dependent variable. (The interpretation of interaction effects is discussed in Chapter 6 on Hypothesis Testing.)

Once a third independent variable is introduced, the situation expands: There are seven effects. With four and five independent variables, there are 15 and 31 effects, respectively. Too many variables! It is difficult to find meaningful interpretations for all the effects, where there are so many. Furthermore, variability in the human responses is added with each independent variable, so all may be lost if too many variables are included. Interaction effects that are three-way, or higher, are extremely difficult to interpret, and are best avoided. A good design limits the number of independent variables to one or two, three at most.[4]

5.5 Dependent variables

A *dependent variable* is a measured human behaviour. In HCI the most common dependent variables relate to speed or accuracy, with speed often reported in its reciprocal form, time – task completion time. Accuracy is often reported as the percentage of trials or other actions performed correctly or incorrectly. In the latter case, accuracy is called error rate.

The "dependent" in dependent variable refers to the variable being dependent on the human. The measurements *depend on* what the participant does. If the dependent variable is, for example, task completion time, then clearly the measurements are highly dependent on the participant's behaviour.

Besides speed and accuracy, many other dependent variables are used in HCI experiments. Others include preparation time, action time, throughput, gaze shifts, mouse-to-keyboard hand transitions, presses of BACKSPACE, target re-entries, retries, key actions, gaze shifts, wobduls, etc. The possibilities are limitless.

If you are wondering about "wobduls," then you are following the discussion. So, what is a wobdul? Well, nothing, really. It's just a made-up word. It is mentioned to highlight something important in dependent variables: Any observable, measurable aspect of human behaviour is a potential dependent variable. Provided the behaviour has the ability to tease out performance differences between test conditions, to shed light on the strengths or weaknesses of one condition over another, then it is a legitimate dependent variable. So, for a dependent variable, it is acceptable to "roll

---

[3] As a matter of style in a research paper, the names of independent variables, such as device or task, are not capitalized unless they appear with multiplication signs, for example, when referring to the Device × Task interaction effect [10, p. 169].

[4] Independent variables are sometimes added simply to ensure the testing covers a representative range of behaviours. For example, a Fitts' law experiment primarily interested in device and task might also include movement distance and target size as independent variables. The latter two are often not of research interest but are included to ensure the trials encompass a typical range of target selection conditions [318].

your own." Of course, all dependent variables must be clearly defined to ensure the research is replicable.

An example of a novel dependent variable is *read text events*. In pilot testing an eye tracking system for text entry (eye typing), Majaranta et al. observed that users frequently shifted their point of gaze from the on-screen keyboard to the typed text to monitor their progress [334]. There was a sense that this behaviour was particularly prominent for one of the test conditions. Thus, RTE (read text events) was defined and used as a dependent variable. The same research also used *re-focus events* (RFE) as a dependent variable. RFE was the number of times a participant re-focused on a key to select it.

Another example is *negative facial expressions* defined by Duh et al. [108] in a comparative evaluation of three mobile phones used for gaming. Participants were videotaped playing games on different mobile phones. A post-test analysis of the videotape was performed to count negative facial expressions, such as frowns, confusion, frustration, and head shaking. The counts were entered in an analysis of variance to determine whether participants had different degrees of difficulty with any of the interfaces.

One more example. In research on gaming, Negini et al. used a dependent variable named *kills*, defined as the number of zombies killed during game play [366]. The experiment used four levels of an independent variable called *condition* (adjustments to game parameters). Participants played a first-person shooter game and killed as many zombies as possible. For each test condition, the number of zombies killed was logged as a count. Follow-on analyses tested whether the dependent variable, kills, differed by condition.

Unless one is investigating eye typing or mobile gaming, it is unlikely that read text events, negative facial expressions, or zombie kills are used as dependent variables. They are mentioned only to emphasize the merit in defining, measuring, and analyzing any human behaviour that might expose differences in the interfaces or interaction techniques under investigation. See also student exercise 5-5.

As with independent variables, it is often helpful to name the variable separate from its units. For example, in a text entry experiment there is likely a dependent variable called *text entry speed* with units "words per minute." Experiments on computer pointing devices often use a Fitts' law paradigm for testing. There is typically a dependent variable named *throughput* with units "bits per second." The most common dependent variable is "task completion time" with units "seconds" or "milliseconds." If the measurement is a simple count of events, there is no unit per se.

When contriving a dependent variable, it is important to consider how the measurements are gathered and the data collected, organized, and stored. The most efficient method is to design the experimental software to gather the measurements based on time stamps, key presses, or other interactions detectable through software events. The data should be organized and stored in a manner that facilitates follow-up analyses. Fig. 5.3 shows an example for a text entry experiment. There are two data files. The first contains low-level timestamps and key presses, while the second summarizes entry of a complete phrase, one line per phrase.

```
my bike has a flat tire
my bike has a flat tire
16 3
891 2
1797 3 m
3656 2
4188 1
4672 2 y
5750 3
5938 3 [Space]
6813 3
6984 2
7219 0
8656 3 b
...
```
(a)

```
min_keystrokes,keystrokes,presented_characters,transcribed_characters, ...
55, 59, 23, 23, 29.45, 0, 9.37, 0.0, 2.5652173913043477, 93.22033898305085
61, 65, 26, 26, 30.28, 0, 10.3, 0.0, 2.5, 93.84615384615384
85, 85, 33, 33, 48.59, 0, 8.15, 0.0, 2.5757575757575757, 100.0
67, 71, 28, 28, 33.92, 0, 9.91, 0.0, 2.5357142857142856, 94.36619718309859
61, 70, 24, 24, 39.44, 0, 7.3, 0.0, 2.9166666666666665, 87.14285714285714
```
(b)

FIGURE 5.3

Example data files from a text entry experiment. (a) The summary data one (.sd1) file contains timestamps and keystroke data. (b) The summary data two (.sd2) file contains one line for each phrase of entry.

The data files in Fig. 5.3 were created by the experiment software. Pilot testing is crucial. It is a rough test of the user interface – with modifications to get the interaction right. And that's true. But pilot testing is also important to ensure the data collected are correct and available in an appropriate format for follow-on analyses. So, pilot test the experiment software and perform preliminary analyses on the data collected. A spreadsheet application is often sufficient for this.

To facilitate follow-up analyses, the data should also include codes to identify the participants and test conditions. Typically, this information appears in added columns in the data or in the filenames, or both. For example, the filename for the data in Fig. 5.3a is TextInputHuffman-P01-D99-B06-S01.sd1 and identifies the experiment (TextInputHuffman), the participant (P01), the device (D99), the block (B06) and the session (S01). The suffix is .sd1 for "summary data one." Note that the .sd2 file in Fig. 5.3b is comma-delimited, to facilitate importing, and contains a header line identifying the data in each column below.

If the experiment uses a commercial product, it is usually not possible to collect data through the software. Participants are observed externally, rather than through software. In such cases, data collection is problematic and requires a creative approach. Methods include manual timing by the experimenter, using a log sheet and pencil to record events, or taking photos or screen snaps of the interaction as entry proceeds. A photo is useful, for example, if results are visible on the display at the end of a trial. Videotaping is another option, but follow-up analyses of video data are time consuming. Companies such as Noldus[5] offer complete systems for videotaping interaction and performing timeline analyses on the recordings.

5.6 **Other variables**

Besides independent and dependent variables, there are three other variables: control, random, and confounding. These receive less attention and are rarely mentioned in research papers. Nevertheless, understanding each is important for experimental research.

5.6.1 **Control variables**

There are many circumstances or factors that might influence a dependent variable, but are not under investigation. These need to be understood and accommodated in some way. One method is to control them – to treat them as *control variables*. Examples include room lighting, room temperature, background noise, display size, mouse shape, mouse cursor speed, keyboard angle, chair height, and so on. Mostly, researchers don't think about these conditions. But, they exist and they might influence a dependent variable. Controlling them means that they are fixed at a nominal setting during the experiment – so they don't interfere. But, they might interfere if set at an extreme value. If the background noise level is very high or if the room is too cold, these factors might influence the outcome. Allowing such circumstances to exist at a fixed, nominal value is typical in experiment research. The circumstances are control variables.

Consider an experiment investigating on-line reading comprehension, and in particular whether there is an effect due to font colour or background colour. The independent variables are font colour and background colour. The dependent variable is score on a comprehension test. To avoid undue sources of variation, the setup for all test combinations uses the same font family (e.g., Times) and the same font size (e.g., 12 pt.). The researchers also do all the testing in a room with fluorescent lighting. In this example, font family, font size, and room lighting are control variables.

As an example in the HCI literature, McIntire et al. [351] describe an experiment where participants performed a task simulating the sustained vigilance demanded of air traffic controllers. As the authors noted, "laboratory vigilance tasks are very sensitive to outside stimuli" (p. 168). And so, they worked to control circumstances that might influence the participants' behaviour. The testing room was isolated from noise and participants were required to wear ear plugs. Participants were positioned

---

[5] https://www.noldus.com/.

behind a half wall and could not see the experimenter. There were no clocks, watches, or cell phones visible to participants. The room lighting was adjusted to be consistent and with minimum glare on the task screen. Clearly, McIntire and colleagues were concerned about the possible influence of these circumstances on the behaviour of participants. The circumstances were held constant – they were treated as control variables.

Sometimes it is desirable to control characteristics of the participants. The type of interface or the objectives of the research might necessitate testing participants with certain attributes, for example, right-handed participants, participants with 20-20 vision, or participants with certain experience. Having lots of control variables reduces the variability in the measured behaviours, but yields results that are less generalizable.

5.6.2 Random variables

Instead of controlling circumstances or factors, some might be allowed to vary randomly. Such circumstances are *random variables*. There is a cost since more variability is introduced in the measures, but there is a benefit since results are more generalizable.

Typically, random variables pertain to characteristics of the participants, including biometrics (e.g., height, weight, hand size, grip strength), social disposition (e.g., conscientious, relaxed, nervous), or even genetics (e.g., gender, IQ). Generally, these characteristics are allowed to vary at random.

Consider research investigating whether user stance affects performance while playing Guitar Hero, Beat Saber, or another rhythm game or music performance game. The independent variable is stance (standing, sitting). The dependent variable is score on a song. When recruiting participants, the researchers did not screen for musical ability. They also did not give the participants any instructions on the consumption of coffee before testing. Here, musical ability and coffee consumption are random variables.

Before proceeding, it is worth summarizing the trade-off noted above for control and random variables. The comparison is best presented juxtaposed with the experimental properties of internal validity and external validity, as discussed in the preceding chapter. Fig. 5.4 shows the trade-off.

5.6.3 Confounding variables

Any circumstance or condition that changes systematically with the levels an independent variable is a *confounding variable*. Unlike control or random variables, confounding variables are usually problematic in experimental research: Is the effect observed due to the independent variable or to the confounding variable? Researchers must attune to the possible presence of a confounding variable and eliminate it, adjust for it, or consider it in some way. Otherwise, the effects observed may be incorrectly interpreted.

Variable	Advantage	Disadvantage
Random	Improves external validity by using a variety of situations and people	Compromises internal validity by introducing additional variability in the measured behaviours
Control	Improves internal validity since variability due to a controlled circumstance is eliminated	Compromises external validity by limiting responses to specific situations and people

FIGURE 5.4

Relationship between random and control variables and internal validity and external validity.

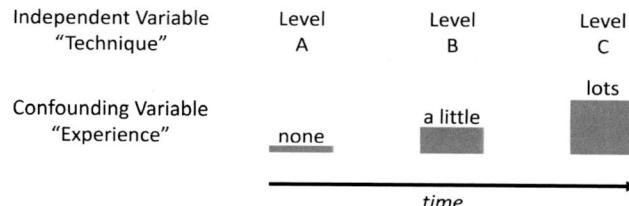

FIGURE 5.5

The confounding variable "experience" varies systematically with the levels of the independent variable "technique."

The most obvious example of a confounding variable is "experience." This confound occurs in experiments using a within-subjects design. Although easily avoided through counterbalancing (see section 5.11), discussion is warranted here. Consider an experiment where a group of participants is tested on three variations of an interaction technique. The independent variable is "technique" with levels A, B, and C. If testing begins with technique A and then proceeds to technique B, there is a chance participants will perform better with technique B because of their experience with technique A. While using technique A, they get comfortable with the experiment procedure and gather skill with the technique. This might contribute to better performance with technique B. If testing then proceeds with technique C, they may perform better still, since they have experience with techniques A and B. Here, "experience" is a confounding variable since it varies systematically with the levels of the independent variable. The idea of "varies systematically" is illustrated in Fig. 5.5, where experience increases from "none" to "a little" to "lots" over levels of the independent variable, technique.

Since there is a confounding variable in the example, it is possible the performance differences observed between the techniques are not due to inherent properties of the techniques. If technique A performed poorly, perhaps this occurred because participants were tested with technique A first, and therefore lacked experience with the experimental procedure, the task, and with the techniques in general. The solution for this example is simple (see section 5.11). In other cases, dealing with a confounding variable is more problematic.

Here's another example where the presence of a confounding variable is not so obvious. Consider an eye-tracking experiment seeking to determine if *camera distance* affects users ability to select on-screen buttons using the gaze of their eyes. In the experiment, camera distance – the independent variable – has two levels, near and far. For the near condition, a small camera (A) is mounted on a bracket attached to the user's eye glasses. For the far condition, a commercial eye tracking system is used with the camera (B) positioned above the system's display. Here, camera is a confounding variable since it varies systematically across the levels of the independent variable: camera A for the near condition and camera B for the far condition. If the experiment shows a significant effect of camera distance on human performance, there is the possibility that the effect has nothing to do with camera distance. Perhaps the effect is simply the result of using one camera for the near condition and a different camera for the far condition. The confound is avoided by using the same camera (and same system) in both the near and far conditions. Another possibility is simply to rename the independent variable. The new name could be "setup," with levels "near setup" and far setup." The new labels acknowledge that the independent variable encompasses multiple facets of the interface, in this case, camera distance, camera, and system. The distinction is important if for no other reason than to ensure the conclusions speak broadly to the different setups, rather than to camera distance alone.

Sometimes a confounding variable is deliberately used. This is fine provided the variable is acknowledged and the results are correctly interpreted. An example is found in an evaluation of a scanning ambiguous keyboard (SAK) for text entry [306]. The evaluation sought to measure the progression of learning, so participants entered text over five blocks of testing. Thus, "block" was an independent variable with five levels. With scanning keyboards, the rate of scanning impacts performance: Fast scanning promotes fast input, but accurate input is difficult, particularly for novices. Slow scanning rate is easier for novices, but limits the text entry rate. To accommodate the effect of scanning interval and to promote learning, the scanning interval was set at 1100 ms for block 1 and then decreased by 100 ms for each subsequent block, finishing at 700 ms in block 5. Here, "scanning interval" was a confounding variable, since it varied systematically with the levels of the independent variable. In the write-up, the chart showing "entry speed by block" acknowledged the systematic change in the scanning interval over the 5 blocks. See Fig. 5.6. Since there was a confounding variable, care is warranted on interpreting the statistical test for the effect of block on entry speed. This was handled in the write-up as follows: "Although the main effect of block on entry speed was significant ($F_{4,44} = 7.58$, $p < .0001$), this is expected in view of the confounding influence of scanning interval" [306, p. 96].

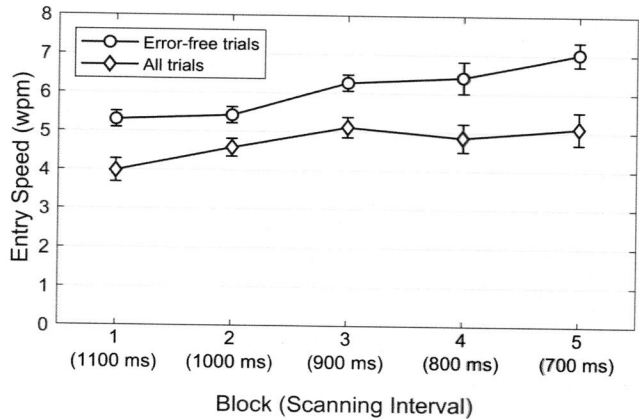

FIGURE 5.6

Scanning interval as a confounding variable. The scanning interval changed systematically with the levels of the independent variable, block [306, Fig. 10].

5.7 **Task and procedure**

Let's revisit the definition of an independent variable: "a circumstance or characteristic that is manipulated in an experiment to *elicit a change in a human response* while interacting with a computer." Emphasis is added to "elicit a change in a human response." When participants are given a test condition, they are asked to do a task while their performance is measured. Later, they are given a different test condition – another level of the independent variable – and asked to do the task again. Clearly, the choice of task is important.

There are two objectives in designing a good task: *represent* and *discriminate*. A good task is representative of the activities people do with the interface. A task that is similar to actual or expected usage will improve the external validity of the research – the ability to generalize results to other people and other situations. A good task is also one that can discriminate the test conditions. Obviously, there is something in the interaction that differentiates the test conditions, otherwise there is no research to conduct. A good task attunes to the points of differentiation in order to elicit behavioural responses that expose benefits or problems among the test conditions. This should surface as a difference in the measured responses across the test conditions. A difference might occur if the interfaces or interaction techniques are sufficiently distinct in the way the task is performed.

Often, the choice of a task is self-evident. If the research idea is a graphical method for inserting functions in a spreadsheet, a good task is inserting functions into a spreadsheet – using the graphical method vs. the traditional typing method. If the research idea is an auditory feedback technique while programming a GPS tracker, a good task is programming a destination in a GPS tracker – aided with auditory feedback vs. visual feedback.

Making a task representative of actual usage will improve external validity, but there is a downside. The more representative the task, the more the task is likely to include behaviours not directly related to the interface or interaction method under test. Such behaviours may compromise the ability of the task to discriminate among the test conditions. There is nothing sinister in this. It is simply a reflection of the complex way humans go about their business while using computers. When we enter text, we also think about what to enter. We might pause, think, enter something, think again, change our mind, delete something, enter some more, and so on. This is actual usage. If the research goal is to evaluate a new text entry method, a task that mimics actual usage includes secondary tasks – lots of them. If the task involves, for example, measuring text entry speed in words per minute, the measurement is seriously compromised if tasks unrelated to the entry method are present.

While using a task that is representative of actual usage improves external validity, the downside is decreased internal validity. Recall that high internal validity means the effects observed (i.e., the differences in means on a dependent variable) are due to the test conditions. The additional sources of variation introduced by secondary tasks reduce the likelihood that the differences observed are actually due to, or caused by, the test conditions. The differences may simply be an artefact of the secondary tasks. Furthermore, the additional variation may bring forth a non-significant statistical result. This is unfortunate if indeed there are inherent differences between the test conditions – differences that should have produced a statistically significant outcome.

A good task is natural yet limited to the core aspects of the interaction: the points of differentiation between the test conditions. Points of similarly, while true to actual usage, introduce variability. Consider two different text entry techniques compared in an experimental evaluation. If the techniques include the same method of capitalization, then capitalization does not serve to discriminate the techniques and can be excluded from the experimental task. Including capitalization will improve external validity but will also compromise internal validity due to the added variability.

The tasks considered above are mostly performance-based or skill-based. Sometimes, an independent variable necessitates using a *knowledge-based task*. For example, if the research is comparing two search methods, a reasonable task is to locate an item of information in a database or on the Internet (e.g., "Find the date of birth of Albert Einstein."). Performance is still measured; however the participant acquires knowledge of the task goal and, therefore, is precluded from further exposure to the same task. This is a problem if the independent variable is assigned within-subjects (discussed below). When the participant is tested with the other search method, the task must be changed (e.g., "Find the date of birth of William Shakespeare."). This is tricky, since the new task must be more or less the same (so the search methods are fairly compared), but also different enough that the participant does not benefit from exposure to the earlier, similar task.

The experimental procedure includes the task, but also the instructions, demonstration, or practice given to the participants. The procedure encompasses everything the participant did or was exposed to. If a questionnaire was administered before or after testing, this is also part of the experimental procedure and deserves due consideration – and explanation in the write-up of the experiment.

5.8 Participants

Researchers often assume their results apply to people not tested. Applying results to people other than those tested is possible; however, two conditions are required. First, the people actually tested must be members of the same population of people to whom results are assumed to hold. For example, results are unlikely to apply to children if the participants in the experiment were drawn exclusively from the local university campus. Second, a sufficient number of participants must be tested. This requirement has more to do with statistical testing than with the similarly of participants to the population.[6] Within any population, or any sample drawn from a population, variability is present. When performance data are gathered on participants, the variability in the measurements affects the likelihood of obtaining statistically significant results. Increasing the number of participants (large n) increases the likelihood of achieving statistically significant results.

In view of the point above, we might ask:

How many participants should be used in an experiment?

Although the answer might seem peculiar, it goes something like this: Use the same number of participants as in similar research [342, p. 234]. Using more participants seems like a good idea, but there is a downside. As the number of participants increases, the likelihood of achieving statistical significance approaches 100% [447, p. 63]. Sometimes the inherent difference is slight, and therein lays the problem. To explain, here is a research question to consider: Is there a speed difference between left-handed and right-handed users in performing point-select tasks using a mouse? There may be a slight difference; but, it likely would surface only if a very large number of left- and right-handed participants were tested. Use enough participants and statistically significant results will appear. But, the difference may be miniscule, and of no practical value. Therein is the problem of using a large number of participants: statistically significant results for a small difference of no practical significance.

The converse is also problematic. If not enough participants are used, statistical significance may fail to appear. There might be a substantial experimental effect, but the variance combined with a small sample size (not enough participants) might prevent statistical significance from appearing.

It is possible to compute the power of statistical tests and therein determine the number of participants required. The analysis may be done a priori – before an experiment is conducted. In practice, a priori power analysis is rarely done because it

---

[6] Participants drawn from a population are, by definition, similar to the population, since they (collectively) define the population.

hinges on knowing the variance in a sample before the data are collected.[7] The recommendation, again, is to study published research. If a similar published experiment reported statistically significant results with, say, 15 participants, then the use of 15 participants is a reasonable choice.

In HCI, we often hear of researchers doing a *usability evaluation* or *usability testing*. These exercises typically seek to assess a prototype system with users to determine problems with the interface. Such evaluations are generally not organized as factorial experiments. So, the question of how many participants is not relevant in a statistical sense. In usability evaluations, it is known that a small number of participants is sufficient to expose a high percentage of the problems in an interface. There is evidence that about five participants (often usability experts) are sufficient to expose about 80 percent of the usability problems [281,373].

It is worth reflecting on the term *participants*. When referring specifically to the experiment, use the term participants (e.g., "all participants exhibited a high error rate"). General comments on the topic or conclusions drawn may use other terms (e.g., "these results suggest that users are less likely to . . .").

When recruiting participants, it is important to consider how the participants are selected. Are they solicited by word of mouth, through an e-mail list, using a notice posted on a wall, or through some other means? Ideally, participants are drawn at random from a population. In practice, this is rarely done, in part because of the need to obtain participants that are close by and available.

More typically, *convenience sampling* is used. Participants are solicited from a convenient pool of individuals (e.g., members in the workplace, children at a school, or students from the local university campus). Strictly speaking, convenience sampling compromises the external validity of the research, since the true population is somewhat narrower than the desired population.

To help identify the population, participants are typically given a brief questionnaire (discussed shortly) at the beginning or end of the experiment to gather demographic data, such as age and gender. Other information is gathered as relevant to the research, such as daily computer usage or experience with certain applications, devices, products, or tasks. For example, Zinck and Vogel [557] researched non-verbal vocal interaction (NVVI) and conducted a user study where participants performed simple interactions by vocalizing musical intervals and melodies. Before testing began, participants were asked a variety of questions, including on their musical background, such as "How many years of private music lessons have you had?" and "How often do you sing?" For the latter question, responses were on a seven-point scale, from 1 (*rarely*) to 7 (*multiple times a day*).

HCI experiments often require participants with specific skills. Perhaps candidates are screened to ensure only appropriate participants are used. For example,

---

[7] Calculating statistical power in advance of an experiment also requires the researcher to know the size of the experimental effect (the difference in the means on the dependent variable) that is deemed relevant. Usually, the researcher simply wants to know if there is a statistically significant difference without committing in advance to a particular difference being of practical significance.

an experiment investigating a new gaming input device might want a participant pool with specific skills, such a minimum of 15 hours per week playing computer games. Or, perhaps participants without gaming experience are desired. Whatever the case, the selection criteria should be clear and should be stated in the write-up of the methodology, in a section labelled "Participants."

Depending on the agency or institution overseeing the research, ethics approval for the research usually requires participants to sign a consent form prior to testing. The goal is to ensure participants know that their participation is voluntary, they will incur no physical or psychological harm, they can withdraw at any time, and their privacy, anonymity, and confidentiality will be protected.

5.9 Questionnaire design

Questionnaires are a part of most HCI experiments. There are two purposes: (i) to gather information about the participants, such as demographics (e.g., age, gender, income, level of education) and experience related to the research, and (ii) to solicit participants' opinions on the devices or interaction tasks with which they were tested.

Questionnaires are the primary instrument for survey research, a form of research seeking to query a large number of people for their opinions and behaviours on a subject, such as politics, spending habits, or use of technology. Such questionnaires are often lengthy, spanning many pages. See also section 4.3.3, Correlational Method (p. 174). Questionnaires administered in HCI experiments are more modest, generally taking just a few minutes complete.

Before testing begins, participants are often given a brief Welcome Questionnaire, soliciting demographic information and details on their experience with technology or interaction techniques relevant to the research.

5.9.1 Demographics and experience

As suggested earlier (see Ethics Approval, p. 205), it is preferable, if possible, to avoid gathering information that might identify participants. To distinguish participants, usually only a code is needed:

> Participant code: _____ (fill in, as instructed)

If the experiment uses a within-subjects design, the Welcome Questionnaire provides a good opportunity to assign participants to groups for counterbalancing:

> Group code: _____ (fill in, as instructed)

See also the use of a group code in the experiment worksheet in Fig. 5.11 (p. 231).

Age can be solicited as an open-ended item:

> Please indicate your age: _____

Collected in this manner, age is a ratio-scale response, so the mean and standard deviation are easily calculated. Ratio-scale responses are also useful to look for relationships in data. For example, if the same questionnaire also includes a ratio-scale item on the number of text messages sent per day, then it is possible to examine if the responses are correlated (e.g., *Is the number of text messages sent per day related to age?*).

Age can also be solicited as an ordinal response:

> Please indicate your age:
> ☐ < 20   ☐ 20-29   ☐ 30-39
> ☐ 40-49   ☐ 50-59   ☐ 60+

In this case, the counts in each category are tabulated. Such data are particularly useful if there are a large number of respondents. However, ordinal data are inherently lower quality than ratio-scale data, since it is not possible to compute the mean or standard deviation.

"Sex" and "gender" have different meanings, but are often used interchangeably. Sex is a set of biological attributes in humans and animals with "female" or "male" as the usual categories. Gender refers to socially constructed roles and behaviours. It reflects how people perceive themselves and how they interact with others.

When collecting information on sex or gender, questionnaires should use inclusive language that supports gender non-conforming individuals. Depending on ethical or legal requirements, and as local circumstances suggest, any of the following questions are reasonable in gathering information on participants' gender or sex:

> What is your gender?   ☐ Female   ☐ Male

> What is your birth sex?   ☐ Female   ☐ Male

> What is your birth sex?
> ☐ Female
> ☐ Male
> ☐ Intersex
> ☐ Prefer not to say

```
What is your gender identity?
    □ Woman
    □ Man
    □ Transgender
    □ Non-binary/non-conforming
    □ Prefer not to say
```

Additional information relevant to the research may be collected in several ways, depending on the nature of the information sought and the intended use. Closed-ended questions are convenient, since they constrain a participant's response to small set of options. For example,

```
Do you use a GPS device while driving?   □ Yes   □ No
```

```
Please indicate your computer usage:
    □ < 2 hrs/day      □ 2-5 hrs/day
    □ 5-10 hrs/day     □ > 10 hrs/day
```

```
How many text messages do you send each day?
    □ 0             □ 1-10
    □ 11-25         □ 26-50
    □ 51-100        □ > 100
```

```
Which browser do you use?
    □ Mozilla Firefox  □ Google Chrome
    □ Apple Safari     □ Other (_____)
```

The question above includes an open-ended category, "Other." Of course, the entire question could be open-ended:

```
Which browser do you use? _____
```

Closed-end questions simplify follow-on analyses, since it is straightforward to tally counts of responses.

5.9.2 **Participant opinions**

Questionnaires are also used after testing to obtain qualitative feedback: participants' opinions and feelings about the interfaces or interaction techniques. Items are often formatted using a Likert scale (see also Fig. 4.12, p. 182) to facilitate summarizing and analysing the responses. One example is the NASA-TLX (task load index), which assesses perceived workload on six subscales: mental demand, physical demand, temporal demand, performance, effort, and frustration [179]. An item on frustration may be presented as follows:

Frustration: I felt a high level of insecurity, discouragement, irritation, stress, or annoyance.

1	2	3	4	5	6	7
Strongly			Neutral			Strongly
disagree						agree

The ISO 9241-411 standard for non-keyboard input devices includes a questionnaire with 12 items to assess the comfort and fatigue experienced by participants [210]. The items are similar to those in the NASA-TLX but are directed to interaction with devices such as mice, joysticks, pens, fingers, or eye trackers. The items are tailored to the device under test. For example, an evaluation of an eye tracker for computer control might include the following item (see also [551, Fig. 7]):

Eye fatigue:

1	2	3	4	5	6	7
Very						None
high						

Note that the preferred response above is 7, whereas the preferred response in the NASA-TLX example is 1. In the event the mean is computed over several response items, it is important that the items are consistently constructed or the scoring adjusted as needed.

Another common questionnaire is the System Usability Scale (SUS), developed by Brooke in the 1990s [42]. SUS is a 10-item set with Likert-scale responses from 1 (*strongly disagree*) to 5 (*strongly agree*). See Fig. 5.7. The goal is to assess the usability of an entire system. As such, SUS is well aligned with usability evaluations, as distinguished from user studies in Chapter 4 (see p. 176). User studies typically focus on interaction techniques or one aspect of a system in a research prototype. When using SUS in this manner, some modifications are warranted. For example, "system" in Fig. 5.7 could be replaced with "*xyz* input method," as appropriate.

SUS overall yields a summary score out of 100 with a high score indicating good overall usability. For items 1, 3, 5, 7, and 9, higher scores are better. Each item is scored from 0 to 4 by subtracting 1 from the number circled. Items 2, 4, 6, 8, and 10, use reverse scoring, so lower scores are better. Each item is scored by subtracting the number circled from 5, also yielding a score from 0 to 4. The sum of the scores is multiplied by 2.5 to get a score out of 100.

For interpreting the summary SUS score, verbal tags are often used with scores of about 71 or 86 considered "good" or "excellent," respectively [22, Table 3]. Or,

	Strongly disagree	Mildly disagree	Neutral	Mildly agree	Strongly agree
1. I think I would like to use this system frequently,	1	2	3	4	5
2. I found the system unnecessarily complex.	1	2	3	4	5
3. I thought the system was easy to use.	1	2	3	4	5
4. I think I would need technical support to use this system.	1	2	3	4	5
5. I found the functions in this system well integrated.	1	2	3	4	5
6. I thought there was too much inconsistency in this system.	1	2	3	4	5
7. I would imagine that most people would learn to use this system very quickly.	1	2	3	4	5
8. I found the system very cumbersome to use.	1	2	3	4	5
9. I felt very confident using the system.	1	2	3	4	5
10. I needed to learn a lot of things before I could get going with this system.	1	2	3	4	5

FIGURE 5.7

System Usabilitly Scale (SUS) questionnaire items [42].

the scores can be mapped to student letter grades, where an SUS score in the range of 77.2 to 78.8 merits a usability grade of B+ [282, Table 1].

There are a few precautions to consider when scoring a system or interaction technique using SUS. As Brooke notes,

Usability ... can only be defined with reference to particular contexts. This, in turn, means there are no absolute measures of usability, since, if the usability of

an artefact is defined by the context in which that artefact is used, measures of usability must of necessity be defined by that context too.

[42, p. 189]

The implication is that SUS scores, while valid within a study, cannot be compared across studies unless the methodology and context of the research are the same. Such is rarely the case. It has also been noted that SUS items 4 and 10 pertain to learnability, not usability [283].

5.10 Within-subjects, between-subjects

The administering of test conditions (levels of a factor) is either *within-subjects* or *between-subjects*. *Within-subjects*, also called *repeated measures*, means each participant was tested on all levels of a factor, because the measurements on each test condition are repeated on each participant. Assigning conditions *between-subjects* means each participant was tested on only one level of a factor. In this case a separate group of participants is used for each test condition. Fig. 5.8 provides a simple illustration of the difference. The figure assumes a single factor with three levels: A, B, and C. Fig. 5.8a shows a within-subjects assignment because each participant is tested on all three levels of the factor (but see section 5.11, Counterbalancing). Fig. 5.8b shows a between-subjects assignment, since each participant is tested on only one level of the factor. There are three groups of participants, with two participants in each group.

There is a trade-off. For a between-subjects design, more participants are needed to obtain the same number of observations (Fig. 5.8b). For a within-subjects design, fewer participants are needed; however, more testing is required for each participant (Fig. 5.8a). Given this trade-off, it is reasonable to ask: Is it better to assign a factor within-subjects or between-subjects? Let's examine the possibilities.

Sometimes a factor must be between-subjects. For example, if investigating whether males or females are more adept at texting, the experiment task is entering text messages on a mobile phone. The independent variable is gender with two levels, male and female. The variable gender is between-subjects. There is no choice! A participant cannot be male for half the testing, then female for the other half. Another example is hand preference. Research investigating performance differences between left-handed and right-handed users requires a group of left-handed participants and a group of right-handed participants. Hand preference, then, is a between-subjects factor. Again, no choice.

Sometimes a factor must be within-subjects. The most obvious example is practice, since the acquisition of skill occurs within people, not between people. Practice is usually investigated by testing participants over multiple blocks of trials. For such designs, block is an independent variable, or factor, and there are multiple levels, such as block 1, block 2, block 3, and so on. Clearly, block is within-subjects since each participant is exposed to multiple blocks of testing. There is no choice.

	Participant	Test Condition		
(a)	1	A	B	C
	2	A	B	C

(b)	Participant	Test Condition
	1	A
	2	A
	3	B
	4	B
	5	C
	6	C

FIGURE 5.8

Assigning test conditions to participants. (a) Within-subjects (b) Between-subjects. See text for discussion.

Sometimes there is a choice. An important trade-off was noted above. That is, a within-subjects design requires fewer participants but requires more testing for each participant. There is a significant advantage to using fewer participants, since recruiting, scheduling, briefing, demonstrating, practising, and so on, is easier if there are fewer participants.

Another advantage of a within-subjects design is that the variance due to participants' pre-dispositions will be approximately the same across test conditions. Pre-disposition, here, refers to any aspect of a participant's personality, mental condition, or physical condition that might influence performance. In other words, a participant who is pre-disposed to be meticulous (or sloppy!) is likely to carry their disposition in the same manner across the test conditions. For a between-subjects design, there are more participants and, therefore, more variability due to differences between participants.

Yet another advantage of within-subjects designs is that is not necessary to balance groups of participants – because there is only one group! Between-subjects designs include a separate group of participants for each test condition. In this case, balancing is needed to ensure the groups are approximately equal in characteristics that might introduce bias in the measurements. Balancing is typically done through random assignment, but may also be done by explicitly placing participants in groups according to reasonable criteria (e.g., ensuring levels of computer experience are similar among the groups).

Given the within-subjects advantages just cited,

- Fewer participants
- Less variation due to participants
- No need to balance groups

experiments in HCI tend to favour within-subjects designs over between-subjects designs.

However, there is an advantage to a between-subjects design. Between-subjects designs avoid interference between test conditions. Interference, here, refers to conflict that arises when a participant is exposed to one test condition and then switches to another test condition. As an example, consider an experiment comparing two game controllers on "enemy kills" in a first-person shooter game. The controllers have different arrangements of buttons and thumbsticks. The motor skills required to use one game controller are likely to conflict with those required for the other controller. Participants cannot "unlearn" one condition before testing on another condition. A between-subjects design avoids this because each participant is tested on one, and only one, of the game controllers.

As an example from a CHI paper, Castellucci and MacKenzie [71] compared two pen-based gesture sets for text entry, Unistrokes and Graffiti. The gesture shapes differed significantly in the two sets, so the motor skill required to learn one set was likely to interfere with the motor skill for the other set. To avoid this, a between-subjects design was used.

When using a between-subjects assignment, as in the game controller and gesture examples above, it is important to randomly assign participants to conditions. Avoid allowing participants to choose their condition for testing, as this introduces the potential for self-selection bias. In the presence of self-selection bias, it is not possible to know whether the differences observed were due to the conditions tested or to preexisting characteristics of the individuals.

If the interference between conditions is minimal or can be mitigated with a few warm-up trials, then the benefit of a between-subjects design is diminished and a within-subjects design is the best choice. In fact the majority of factors that appear in HCI experiments are like this; so, levels of factors tend to be assigned within-subjects. We will say more about interference in the next section.

It is worth noting that in some areas of research, within-subjects designs are rarely used. Research testing new drugs, for example, would not use a within-subjects design because of interference effects. Between-subjects designs are typically used.

For an experiment with two factors it is possible to assign the levels of one factor within-subjects and the levels of the other factor between-subjects. This is a *mixed design*. Consider the example of an experiment seeking to compare learning of a text entry method between left-handed and right-handed users. The experiment has two factors: Block is within-subjects with perhaps 10 levels (block 1, block 2 ... block 10) and hand preference is between-subjects with two levels (left, right).

5.11 Order effects, counterbalancing, and Latin squares

When the levels of a factor (test conditions) are assigned within-subjects, participants are tested with one condition, then another condition, and so on. In such cases, interference between the test conditions may result due to the order of testing, as noted above. In most within-subjects designs, it is possible – in fact, likely – that participants' performance will improve as they progress from one test condition to the next. Thus, participants may perform better on the second condition simply because they benefited from practice on the first. They are getting familiar with the apparatus and procedure, and they are learning to do the task more effectively. Practice, then, is a confounding variable, because the amount of practice increases systematically from one condition to the next. This is referred to as a *practice effect* or a *learning effect*.

(a)

A	B
B	A

(b)

A	B	C
B	C	A
C	A	B

(c)

A	B	C	D
B	C	D	A
C	D	A	B
D	A	B	C

(d)

A	B	C	D	E
B	C	D	E	A
C	D	E	A	B
D	E	A	B	C
E	A	B	C	D

FIGURE 5.9

Latin squares. (a) 2 × 2. (b) 3 × 3. (c) 4 × 4. (d) 5 × 5.

It is also possible that performance will worsen on conditions that follow other conditions. This may follow from mental or physical fatigue – a *fatigue effect*. In a general sense, the phenomenon is an *order effect* or *sequence effect*, and may surface either as improved performance or degraded performance, depending on the nature of the task, the inherent properties of the test conditions, and the order of testing conditions in a within-subjects design.

If the goal of the experiment is to compare test conditions in terms of performance on a dependent variable, then the confounding influence of practice is a problem. The usual method of compensating for an order effect is to divide participants into groups and administer the conditions in a different order for each group. The compensatory ordering of test conditions to offset practice effects is called *counterbalancing*.

In the simplest case of a factor with two levels, A and B, participants are divided into two groups. If there are 12 participants overall, then group 1 has 6 participants and group 2 has 6 participants. Group 1 is tested on first on condition A then on condition B. Group 2 is given the test conditions in the reverse order. This is the simplest case of a *Latin square*. In general, a Latin square is an $n \times n$ table filled with n different symbols (e.g., A, B, C, etc.).[8] The defining property is that each symbol occurs exactly once in each row and each column. Examples of Latin square tables are shown in Fig. 5.9. Look carefully and the pattern is easily seen. The first column is in order, starting at A. The entries in each row are in order, with wrap-around.

A deficiency in Latin squares of order 3 and higher is that conditions precede and follow other conditions an unequal number of times. In the 4 × 4 Latin square, for example, B follows A three times, but A follows B only once. Thus an A-B sequence effect, if present, is not fully compensated for. A solution to this is a *balanced Latin square*, which can be constructed for even-order tables. Fig. 5.10 shows 4 × 4 and 6 × 6 balanced Latin squares. The pattern is a bit peculiar. The 1st column is in order, starting at A. The top row has the sequence, A, B, n, C, n - 1, D, n - 2, etc. Entries in the 2nd and subsequent columns are in order, with wrap around.

When designing a within-subjects counterbalanced experiment, the number of levels of the factor must divide equally into the number of participants. If a factor has three levels, then the experiment requires multiple-of-3 participants, for example,

[8] The name "Latin" in Latin square refers to the habit of Swiss mathematician Leonhard Euler (1707-1783) who used Latin symbols in exploring the properties of multiplication tables.

(a)

A	B	D	C
B	C	A	D
C	D	B	A
D	A	C	B

(b)

A	B	F	C	E	D
B	C	A	D	F	E
C	D	B	E	A	F
D	E	C	F	B	A
E	F	D	A	C	B
F	A	E	B	D	C

FIGURE 5.10

Balanced Latin squares where each condition precedes and follows other conditions an equal number of times. (a) 4 × 4. (b) 6 × 6.

9, 12, or 15 participants. If there are 12 participants, then there are three groups, 4 participants per group. The conditions are assigned to group 1 in order ABC, to group 2 in order BCA, and to group 3 in order CAB (see Fig. 5.9b). Let's explore this design with a hypothetical example.

An experimenter seeks to determine if three editing methods (A, B, C) differ in the time to do common editing tasks. The evaluation used the following task:[9]

> Replace one 5-letter word with another, starting one line away.

Three editing methods are compared (details omitted):

- Method A – arrow keys
- Method B – search and replace
- Method C – mouse pointing

Twelve participants are recruited. To counterbalance for learning effects, participants are divided into three groups with the tasks administered according to a Latin square (see Fig. 5.9b). Each participant does the task five times with one editing method, then again with the second editing method, then again with the third.

To aid in administering the experiment, the researcher creates and prints a worksheet identifying the participants and revealing the order of administering the conditions. See Fig. 5.11. The worksheet is useful to avoid confusion. Each participant is assigned a code and group and is given the test conditions in the order noted in the worksheet. After each condition is administered, the experimenter strikes through or checks the entry in the worksheet and proceeds to the next condition.

When the data are tabulated later, it is convenient to organize the conditions in straight columns, without reflecting the order of testing. This helps in calculating means and standard deviations, as seen in Fig. 5.12. The table shows the mean task

[9] This is the same as task T1 in Card, Moran, and Newell's experiment to validate the keystroke-level model (KLM) [63]).

Participant	Notes	1st Condition	2nd Condition	3rd Condition	Group
P01		Arrow Keys	Search/replace	Mouse pointing	
P02		Arrow Keys	Search/replace	Mouse pointing	
P03		Arrow Keys	Search/replace	Mouse pointing	G1
P04		Arrow Keys	Search/replace	Mouse pointing	
P05		Search/replace	Mouse pointing	Arrow keys	
P06		Search/replace	Mouse pointing	Arrow keys	
P07		Search/replace	Mouse pointing	Arrow keys	G2
P08		Search/replace	Mouse pointing	Arrow keys	
P09		Mouse pointing	Arrow keys	Search/replace	
P10		Mouse pointing	Arrow keys	Search/replace	
P11		Mouse pointing	Arrow keys	Search/replace	G3
P12		Mouse pointing	Arrow keys	Search/replace	

FIGURE 5.11

Worksheet to assist with experiment. The conditions are counterbalanced over 12 participants in 3 groups using a 3 × 3 Latin square.

Participant	Test Condition A	B	C	Group	Mean	SD
1	12.98	16.91	12.19			
2	14.84	16.03	14.01			
3	16.74	15.15	15.19	G1	14.7	1.84
4	16.59	14.43	11.12			
5	18.37	13.16	10.72			
6	15.17	13.09	12.83			
7	14.68	17.66	15.26	G2	14.6	2.46
8	16.01	17.04	11.14			
9	14.83	12.89	14.37			
10	14.37	13.98	12.91			
11	14.40	19.12	11.59	G3	14.4	1.88
12	13.70	16.17	14.31			
Mean	15.2	15.5	13.0			
SD	1.48	2.01	1.63			

FIGURE 5.12

Example data for an experiment with one within-subjects factor having three levels (A, B, C). Values are the mean task completion time (s) for five repetitions of an editing task.

completion time for each participant using each editing method as well as the overall means and standard deviations for each editing method and for each group. Note that the left-to-right order of the test conditions in the figure applies only to group 1. The order for group 2 was BCA and for group 3 CAB (see Fig. 5.9b).

At 13.0 s, the mouse method (C) was fastest. The arrow-key method (A) was 17.4% slower at 15.2 s, while the search-and-replace method (B) was 19.3% slower

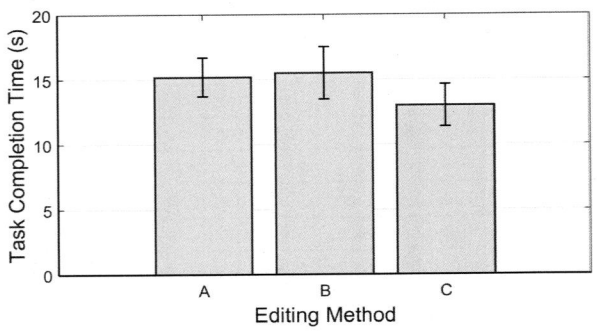

FIGURE 5.13

Task completion time (s) by editing method for the data in Fig. 5.12. Error bars show ±1 *SD*.

A	B	C
A	C	B
B	A	C
B	C	A
C	A	B
C	B	A

FIGURE 5.14

Counterbalancing an odd number of conditions using all (*n*!) combinations.

at 15.5 s. (Testing for statistical significance in the differences is discussed in the next chapter.) Evidently, counterbalancing worked, as the group means are very close, within 0.3 s. The tabulated data in Fig. 5.12 are not typically provided in a research report. More likely, the results are presented in a chart, similar to that in Fig. 5.13.

Although counterbalancing worked in the above hypothetical example, there is a potential problem for the 3 × 3 Latin square. Note in Fig. 5.9b that B follows A twice, but A follows B only once. So, there is an imbalance. This occurs in Latin squares with an odd number of conditions. One solution is to counterbalance by using all sequences. The 3 × 3 case is shown in Fig. 5.14. There are 3! = 6 combinations. Balancing is complete (e.g., B follows A three times, A follows B three times). MacKenzie and Isokoski [312] used such an arranged in an experiment with 18 participants, with 3 participants assigned to each order.

Yet another way to offset learning effects is to randomize the order of conditions. This is most appropriate where (a) the task is very brief, (b) there are many repetitions of the task, and (c) there are many test conditions. For example, experiments that use point-select tasks often include movement direction, movement distance, or target size as factors (Fig. 5.15).

The test conditions in Fig. 5.15 might appear as factors in an experiment even though the experiment is primarily directed at something else. For example, research

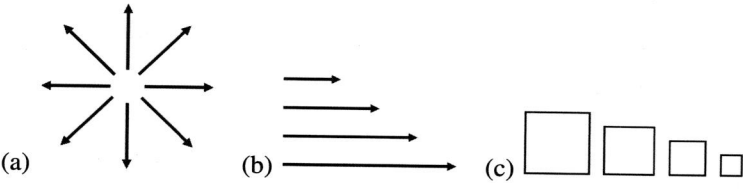

FIGURE 5.15

Test conditions suitable for random assignment. (a) Movement direction. (b) Movement distance. (c) Target size.

comparing the performance of different pointing devices might include device as a factor with, say, three levels (mouse, trackball, stylus). Movement direction, movement distance, and target size might be varied to ensure the tasks cover a typical range of conditions. Treating these conditions as factors ensures they are handled in a systematic manner. To ensure equal treatment, the conditions are chosen at random without replacement. Once all conditions have been used, the process may repeat if multiple blocks of trials are desired.

5.12 Group effects and asymmetric skill transfer

If the learning effect is the same from condition to condition in a within-subjects design, then the group means on a dependent variable should be approximately equal.[10] This was demonstrated above (see Fig. 5.12). In other words, the advantage due to practice for a condition tested later in the experiment is offset equally by the disadvantage when the same condition is tested earlier in the experiment. That's the point of counterbalancing. However, there are occasions where different effects appear for one order (e.g., A → B) compared to another (e.g., B → A). In such cases there may be a *group effect* – differences across groups in the mean scores on a dependent variable. When this occurs, it is a problem. In essence, counterbalancing did not work. A group effect is typically due to *asymmetric skill transfer* – differences in the amount of improvement, depending on the order of testing.

We could develop an example of asymmetric skill transfer with hypothetical data, as with the counterbalancing example above; however, there is an example data set in a research report where an asymmetric transfer effect is evident. The example provides a nice visualization of the effect, plus an opportunity to understand why asymmetric skill transfer occurs. So, we'll use that data.

The experiment compared two types of single-switch scanning keyboards for text entry [252]. Scanning keyboards use an on-screen virtual keyboard and a single button or switch for input. Rows of keys are highlighted in sequence one by one

---

[10] There is likely some difference, but the difference should not be statistically significant.

(a) LO keyboard

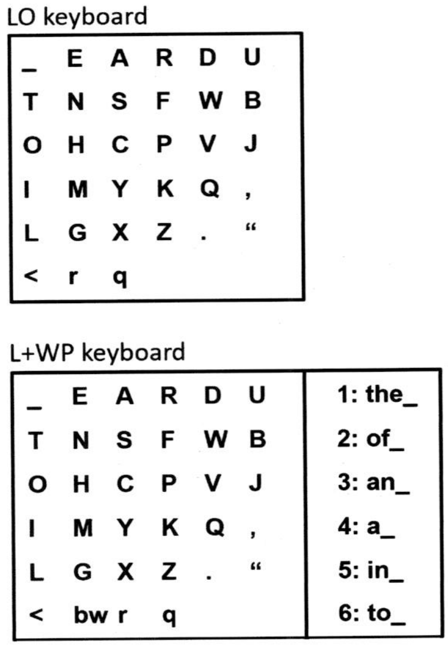

(b)

	Testing Half		Group
	First (trials 1-10)	Second (trials 11-20)	
	20.42	27.12	
	22.68	28.39	
	23.41	32.50	
	25.22	32.12	
	26.62	35.94	1
	28.82	37.66	
	30.38	39.07	
	31.66	35.64	
	32.11	42.76	
	34.31	41.06	
	19.47	24.97	
	19.42	27.27	
	22.05	29.34	
	23.03	31.45	
	24.82	33.46	2
	26.53	33.08	
	28.59	34.30	
	26.78	35.82	
	31.09	36.57	
	31.07	37.43	

FIGURE 5.16

Experiment comparing two scanning keyboards. (a) LO (letters-only) and L+WP (letters plus word prediction) (b) Results for entry speed in characters per minute (cpm). Shaded cells are for the LO keyboard.

("scanned"). When the row bearing the desired letter is highlighted, it is selected. Scanning enters the row and advances left to right. When the key bearing the desired letter is highlighted it is selected and the letter is added to the text message. Additional details are in Chapter 3 (section 3.1.5, Single-switch Scanning). Scanning keyboards provided a convenient text entry method for many users with a physical disability.

The experiment compared two keyboards: a letters-only (LO) scanning keyboard and a similar keyboard that added word prediction (L+WP). The keyboards are shown in Fig. 5.16a. Six participants entered 20 phrases of text, 10 with one keyboard, followed by 10 with the other. To compensate for learning effects, counterbalancing was used. Participants were divided into two groups. Group 1 entering text with the LO keyboard first, then with the L+WP keyboard. Group 2 used the keyboards in the reverse order. Although not usually provided in a report, the results were given in a table showing the entry speed in characters per minute (cpm). The data are reproduced in Fig. 5.16b, as they appeared in the original report [252, Table 2]. The two columns show the sequence of testing; first half, then second half. The shaded and un-shaded cells show the results for the LO and L+WP keyboards, respectively, thus revealing the counterbalanced order.

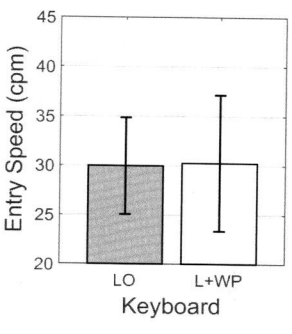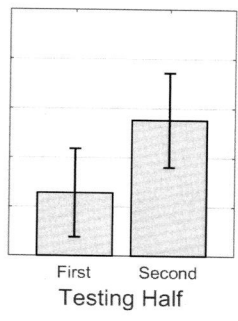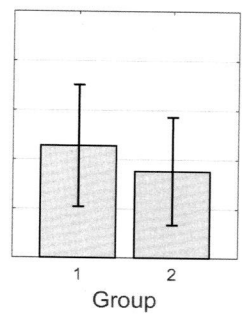

FIGURE 5.17

Three ways to summarize the results in Fig. 5.16b, by keyboard (left), by testing half (centre), and by group (right). Error bars show ±1 *SD*.

There are at least three ways to summarize the data in Fig. 5.16b. The overall result showing the difference between the LO and L+WP keyboards is shown in the left-side chart in Fig. 5.17. Clearly, there was very little difference between the two keyboards: 30.0 cpm for the LO keyboard vs. 30.3 cpm for the L+WP keyboard. The L+WP keyboard was just 1% faster. The error bars are large, mostly due to the improvement from trial to trial, as seen in Fig. 5.16b.

The centre chart in Fig. 5.17 shows another view of the results, comparing the first half and second half of testing. A learning effect is clearly seen. The overall entry speed was 26.4 cpm in the first half of testing (trials 1 to 10) and 33.8 cpm, or 28% higher, in the second half of testing (trials 11 to 20). Learning is fully expected, so this result is not surprising.

Now consider the right-side chart in Fig. 5.17. Counterbalancing only works if the order effects are the same or similar. This implies that the performance benefit of an LO → L+WP order is the same as the performance benefit of an L+WP → LO order. If so, the group means will be approximately equal. This was demonstrated earlier in the counterbalancing example. See Fig. 5.12. The right-side chart in Fig. 5.17 reveals a different story. The means for group 1 and group 2 were 31.4 cpm and 28.8 cpm, respectively. For some reason, there was an 8% performance disadvantage for group 2. This is an example of asymmetric skill transfer. Fig. 5.18 illustrates. The figure reduces the data in Fig. 5.16b to four points, one for each quadrant of 10 trials. Asymmetry is clearly seen in the cross-over of the lines connecting the LO points and L+WP points between the first half and second half of testing. If counterbalancing worked, the lines in Fig. 5.18 would be approximately parallel. They are not parallel because of the asymmetry in the LO → L+WP order vs. the L+WP → LO order.

Asymmetric skill transfer is usually explainable by considering the test conditions or the experimental procedure. For this experiment, the effect occurs because of the inherent differences in entering text with the letters-only (LO) keyboard vs.

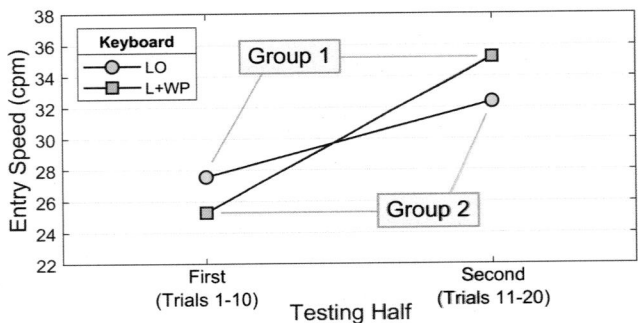

FIGURE 5.18

Demonstration of asymmetric skill transfer. The chart uses the data in Fig. 5.16b.

entering text with the letters plus word prediction (L+WP) keyboard. In fact, this is example provides an excellent opportunity to understand why asymmetric skill transfer sometimes occurs. Here's the explanation. The L+WP keyboard is an enhanced version of the LO keyboard. The basic method of entering letters is the same with both keyboards; however, the L+WP keyboard adds word-prediction, allowing words to be entered before all letters in the word are entered. It is very likely that entering text first with the LO keyboard served as excellent practice for the more difficult subsequent task of entering text with the L+WP keyboard. To appreciate this, examine the two points labelled Group 1 in Fig. 5.18. Group 1 participants performed better overall because they were tested initially with the easier LO keyboard before moving on the enhanced L+WP keyboard. Group 2 participants fared less well because they were tested initially on the more difficult L+WP keyboard.

The simplest way to avoid asymmetric skill transfer is to use a between-subjects design. Clearly, if participants are exposed to only one test condition, they cannot experience skill transfer from another test condition. There are other possibilities, such as practicing participants on a condition prior to data collection. The practice trials seek to overcome the benefit of practice in the earlier condition, so that the measured performance accurately reflects the inherent properties of the test condition. It is not clear that this would work in the example. Participants cannot "unlearn."

In the end, the performance difference between the LO and L+WP keyboards remains an outstanding research question. The practice effect (28%) was much greater than the group effect (8%); so, it is difficult to say whether word prediction in the L+WP keyboard offers a performance advantage. Clearly, there is a benefit with the L+WP keyboard, because words can be entered before all the letters are entered. However, there is also a cost, since users must attend to the on-going prediction process, and this slows entry. To determine whether the costs outweigh the benefits, in the long run, a longitudinal study is required. This is examined in the next section.

5.13 **Longitudinal studies**

The preceding discussion focused on the confounding influence of learning in experiments where an independent variable is assigned within-subjects. Learning effects – more generally, order effects – are problematic and must be accommodated in some way, such as counterbalancing. However, sometimes the research has a particular interest in learning, or the acquisition of skill. In this case, participants are tested over multiple sessions while their improvement in performance is measured. Instead of eliminating learning, the research seeks to observe it, measure it, and perhaps model it. An experimental evaluation where participants practice over a prolonged period is called a *longitudinal study*.

In a longitudinal study, "amount of practice" is an independent variable. Participants perform the task over multiple units of testing, while their improvement with practice is observed and measured. Each unit of testing is a level of the independent variable. Various names are used for the independent variable, but a typical example is "session" with levels session 1, session 2, session 3, and so on. An example is an experiment comparing two text entry methods for mobile phones: multi-tap and LetterWise [315]. At the time, multi-tap was the standard input method for sending SMS text messages on mobile phones. LetterWise was a new method offering a 44% reduction in keystrokes. Although potentially faster, a performance benefit might not appear immediately, since users must learn the technique. Furthermore, learning occurs with both methods, as participants become familiar with the experimental procedure and task. However, it was felt that the reduction in keystrokes with LetterWise would eventually produce higher text entry speeds. To test this, a longitudinal study was conducted, with entry method assigned between-subjects. The results are shown in Fig. 5.19. Indeed, the conjectured improvement with practice was observed. Initial entry speeds were about 7.3 wpm for both methods in Session 1. With practice, both methods improved; however, the improvement was greater with LetterWise because of the ability to produce English text with fewer keystrokes on average. By Session 20, text entry speed with LetterWise was 21.0 wpm, about 36% higher than the rate of 15.5 wpm for multi-tap.

Performance trends in longitudinal studies, as shown in Fig. 5.19, are often accompanied with an equation and best-fitting curve demonstrating the power law of learning. Examples are given in Chapter 7, section 7.2.5 (Skill Acquisition).

In many situations, the goal of a longitudinal study is to compare the viability of a new technique against current practice. Here, "current practice" is any conventional interaction that is quantifiable using a performance measure. Examples include text entry, editing, pointing, selecting, searching, panning, zooming, rotating, drawing, scrolling, menu access, and so on. If users are experienced with a current interaction technique, then relatively poorer initial performance is expected with the new technique. But, as learning progresses, the performance trends may eventually crossover, wherein performance with the new technique exceeds that with current practice. This is illustrated in Fig. 5.20.

The ubiquitous Qwerty keyboard is an excellent example. Although improved designs are known, users experienced with a Qwerty keyboard are unlikely to demon-

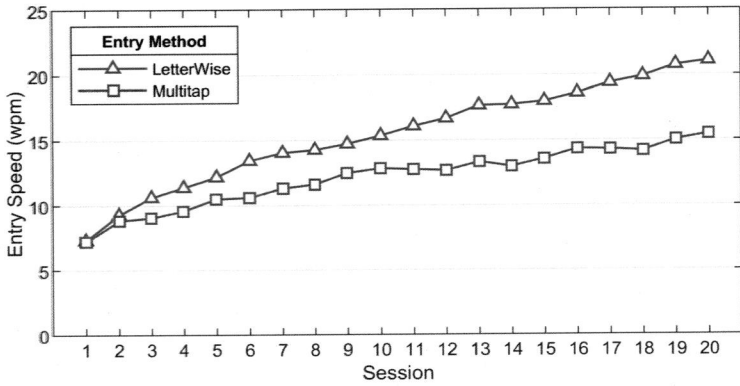

FIGURE 5.19

Example of a longitudinal study. Two text entry methods were tested and compared over 20 sessions of input. Each session involved about 30 minutes of text entry.

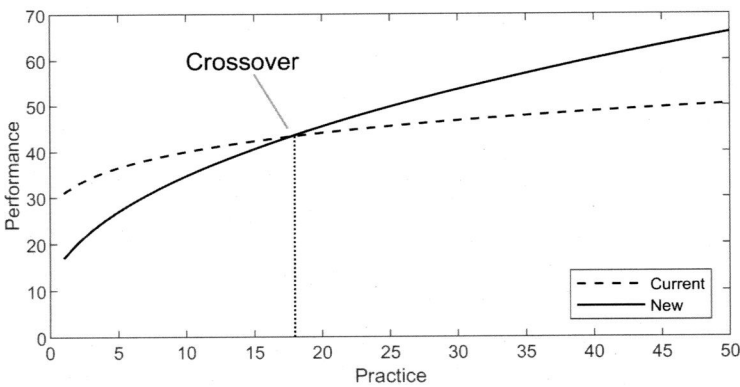

FIGURE 5.20

Crossover point. With practice, human performance with a new interaction technique may exceed human performance using a current technique (from [333]).

strate an immediate improvement in performance with an alternative design. Considerable practice may be required before performance on the new keyboard exceeds that with the Qwerty keyboard. The Dvorak simplified keyboard (DSK), for example, has been demonstrated in longitudinal studies to provide a speed advantage over Qwerty (see [377] for a review). Yet, Qwerty remains the dominant form factor for computer keyboards. From a practical standpoint, learning a new technique bears a cost, since performance is initially superior with the current technique. However, after the crossover point is reached, the new technique provides a benefit, since per-

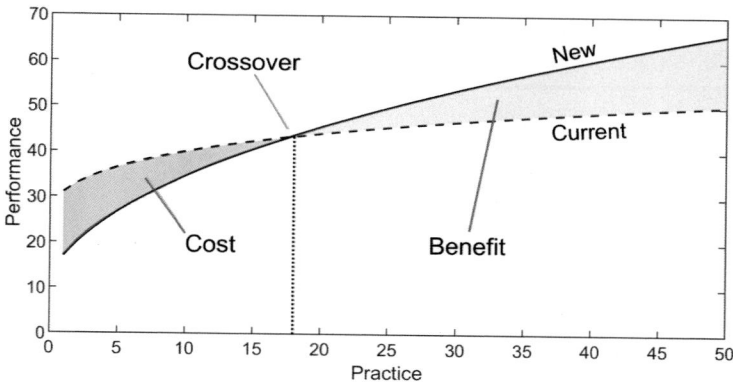

FIGURE 5.21

Cost-benefit progression in learning a new interaction technique where there is existing skill with current practice.

formance is superior compared to current practice. The cost-benefit trade-off is shown in Fig. 5.21.

Despite the long-term benefits evident in Fig. 5.21, new technologies often languish in the margins while established but less-optimal designs continue to dominate the marketplace. Evidently, the benefits are insufficient to overcome the costs. With respect to the Qwerty debate, there are two such costs. One is the cost of manufacturing and re-tooling. Keyboards are electro-mechanical devices; so, new designs require ground-up re-engineering and new manufacturing materials and procedures. This is expensive. The other cost lies in overcoming user perceptions and attitudes. By and large, users are change-adverse: They are reluctant to give up habits they have acquired and are comfortable with. Noyes notes that users are "unwilling to change to a new keyboard layout because of the retraining required" [377, p. 278].

One interesting example is a soft or virtual keyboard, as commonly used on smartphones or tablets. Input is typically with a finger or stylus. Most such keyboards use the Qwerty letter arrangement. However, since the keyboard is created in software, there is no re-tooling cost for an alternative design. Thus, there is arguably a better chance for an optimized design to enter the marketplace. One idea to increase text entry speed is to rearrange letters with common letters clustered near the centre of the layout and less common letters around the perimeter. The increase in speed results from the reduction in finger or stylus movement. However, since users are unfamiliar with the optimized letter arrangement, performance is initially dominated by visual search (i.e., finding the next letter). If learning the new technique is likely to take several hours, or more, then the evaluation requires a longitudinal study, where users are tested over multiple sessions of input. Eventually, the crossover point may appear. This idea is explored further in Chapter 7 (section 7.2.5, Skill Acquisition).

> Perform the task as quickly and accurately as possible, but at a pace that is comfortable.

FIGURE 5.22

Instructions to participants (example wording).

5.14 Running the experiment

When the experiment is designed, the apparatus built and tested, the participants recruited and scheduled, testing begins. But wait! Are you sure the time to begin testing has arrived? It is always useful to have a pilot test (yes, one more pilot test) with one or two participants. This will help smooth out the protocol for briefing and preparing the participants. It will serve as a check on the amount of time needed for each participant. If the testing is scheduled for one hour, it is important that the all the testing combined with briefing, practice, etc., comfortably fit in one hour. A final tweak to the protocol may be necessary. Better now, than to have regrets later on.

The experiment begins. The experimenter greets each participant and introduces the experiment, and usually asks the participant to sign a consent form. Often, a brief questionnaire is administered to gather demographic data and information on the participant's experience in the research topic. This takes just a few minutes. The apparatus is revealed, the task explained and demonstrated. Practice trials are allowed, as appropriate.

An important aspect of the experiment is the instructions given to participants. The instructions depend on the nature of the experiment and the task. For most interaction tasks, the participant is expected to proceed quickly and accurately. These terms – quickly and accurately – are subject to interpretation and to the capabilities of participants. What is reasonably quick for one participant may be unattainable by another. Performing tasks reasonably quick and with high accuracy, but at a rate comfortable to the individual, is usually the goal. See Fig. 5.22 for an example. Additional instructions might be necessary, for example, on whether errors that are noticed should be corrected or ignored.

Whatever the goals, the instructions must be carefully considered and must be given to all participants in the same manner. If a participant asks for clarification, exercise caution in elaborating on the instructions. Any additional explanation that might motivate a participant to act differently from other participants is to be avoided.

The experimenter (aka investigator) plays a special role, as the public face of the experiment. Remaining neutral is important. If you've created a really neat something-or-other and you're hoping the experiment reveals this, that's fine. But, don't sell your idea to the participants. Keep your demeanour flat to avoid introducing bias in participants' behaviour. Participants should not feel under pressure to produce a specific outcome. Deliberately attempting to perform better on one test condition, compared to another, is to be avoided. As well, participants should not sense a particular attitude in the experimenter. An overly attentive experimenter may make participants nervous. Conveying indifference or disregard may carry over to the participants. A neutral manner is best.

*****

This chapter introduced the key elements in designing an HCI experiment. Although the process may seem straight forward, HCI experiments (and other experiments) are difficult to design and conduct properly. In the next chapter, we examine the statistical tests used to determine if the experiment's independent variables significantly impact the dependent variables.

A web site is available as a resource accompanying this book's second edition:

* http://www.yorku.ca/mack/HCIbook2e

Student exercises

5-1 It was noted in section 5.4 (Independent Variables) that independent variables in research papers are sometimes identified without being named. Review some experimental research papers in HCI and find three examples of this. Propose a name for the independent variable and give examples of how to improve the paper. Present your findings in a brief report or slide show presentation.

5-2 It was noted in section 5.4 (Independent Variables) that the name of an independent variable sometimes changes within a research paper. This is also the case for the names of the levels of independent variables. The effect is potentially confusing to readers. Find three examples of HCI research papers where an independent variable or a level of an independent variable was referred to using different names in different parts of the paper. Prepare a brief report or slide show presentation that identifies the issues and offers ways to improve the write-up.

5-3 Review some HCI experimental research papers and find three examples where an independent variable was assigned between-subjects. Briefly describe the rationale in a report or slide show presentation.

5-4 Find an example of an HCI research paper describing an experiment that included three (or more) independent variables. Construct a chart similar to Fig. 5.2, labelling the independent variables. Indicate which effects were reported and which effects (if any) were not reported.

5-5 Find an example of an HCI research paper describing an experiment that included an unusual and unique dependent variable (i.e., something unlike task completion time or error rate). Prepare a brief report or slide show presentation on the dependent variable, indicating the name, the units, the definition, the analysis used, and how the write-up referred to and justified the use of the measurement as a dependent variable.

5-6 Users and computers (Part I). Design and administer a simple questionnaire to solicit four items of information: gender, age, hours per day using a computer, and preferred brand of computer (Mac vs. PC). Use a ratio-scale questionnaire item to solicit the respondent's age. Prepare a brief report or slide show presentation on the findings. This student exercise continues in Chapter 6 (Part II) and Chapter 7 (Part III).

5-7 Find an example of an HCI paper not cited in this book that describes a longitudinal study. Prepare a brief report or slide show presentation describing the testing procedure. Over what period of time did testing extend, and how were the trials organized? Identify the main independent variable (and levels) and discuss how it was administered. Note features such as counterbalancing, within-subjects or between-subjects assignment, and whether practice trials were administered.

Hypothesis testing

6

At a cocktail party, it is best to avoid discussions on religion or politics. The reason is that people tend to have strong and divergent opinions on these thorny topics. Let's add statistics to the list. Few topics raise more controversy than the application of statistical techniques to the data and hypotheses in experimental research. Fortunately, the reader is not dragged into the debate here.[1] Instead, our approach is to describe and present common statistical tests and techniques, as typically used in HCI research. In the pages ahead we will work hard to minimize theory and controversy while maximizing practical value.

Statistical procedures for hypothesis testing come in two flavours: *parametric tests* and *non-parametric tests*. Both are examined in this chapter. The distinguishing feature is that parametric tests operate on data from a probability distribution, such as the normal distribution or the t-distribution, whereas non-parametric tests are "distribution free," which is to say, they make no assumption about the distribution of the underlying data.

A useful way to distinguish parametric tests and non-parametric tests is by the scale of measurement in the data tested [447, p. 109] [451, Table 1]. Fig. 6.1 illustrates. The figure shows the four scales of measurement discussed in Chapter 4 (section 4.9, Measurement Scales) with ratio data as the most sophisticated and nominal data as the least sophisticated.

Parametric tests are applicable to ratio data and interval data, although they are most commonly used with ratio data. The analysis of variance (ANOVA), discussed in detail in this chapter, is the most widely used parametric procedure. For experi-

---

[1] The footnotes in this chapter add detail and rigour to the discussions, which, taken alone, explain in the simplest way possible. Readers new to statistical techniques for hypothesis testing are invited to ignore these footnotes, at least initially. No doubt, readers with statistical training will place a discerning eye on the footnotes. While the footnotes add detail, the presentation as a whole is introductory. Many topics are omitted or only briefly presented, such as the assumptions and tests on the distribution of data, and the corrections and alternative techniques to apply when assumptions are violated. The best sources for these topics are the user manuals and guides that accompany advanced statistical tools, such as SPSS, SAS, or R. A notable comprehensive source is Sheskin's *Handbook of Parametric and Nonparametric Statistical Procedures* [447].

Human-Computer Interaction. https://doi.org/10.1016/B978-0-44-314096-9.00012-9

Measurement Scale	Defining Relations	Examples of Appropriate Statistics	Appropriate Statistical Tests
Ratio	• Equivalence • Order • Ratio of intervals • Ratio of values	• Geometric mean • Coeff. of variation	• Parametric • Non-parametric
Interval	• Equivalence • Order • Ratio of intervals	• Mean • Standard deviation	
Ordinal	• Equivalence • Order	• Median • Percentile	• Non-parametric
Nominal	• Equivalence	• Mode • Frequency	

FIGURE 6.1

Measurement scales of data, properties of data, and appropriate statistical tests.

mental research in HCI, ratio data are typically human performance measurements, such as the time, speed, or accuracy in doing tasks or counts for events such as key presses, finger flicks, gaze shifts, or target re-entries.

Non-parametric tests are applicable to any scale of data, although they are most commonly used for nominal data or ordinal data. The non-parametric procedures examined in this chapter include the chi-square (χ^2) test for nominal data and the Mann-Whitney U, Wilcoxon Signed-Ranks, Kruskal-Wallis, and Friedman tests for ordinal data. Typically, the data used in non-parametric tests are nominal categories, questionnaire responses, rating scores, or assessments on a scale. There is limited use of non-parametric tests for ratio data, a topic we will return to later in this chapter.

Since non-parametric tests span the right-hand column in Fig. 6.1, they are more generally applicable than parametric tests. However, by the criterion of statistical power, parametric tests are superior to non-parametric tests. That is, parametric tests have a greater likelihood of detecting a true effect if there is one. This is a by-product of the strong assumptions and requirements of parametric tests. Provided the assumptions are reasonably adhered to, parametric tests bring greater ability (power) to draw correct conclusions in the statistical tests undertaken.

The initial part of this chapter is directed at the ANOVA. However, most researchers who use an ANOVA have little knowledge of the calculations and assumptions underpinning the "F-test" in the ANOVA. And that's fine. Understanding what the test is, how to do it, and how to interpret and explain it is important, however. Therefore our approach here is more cookbook-like than academic.

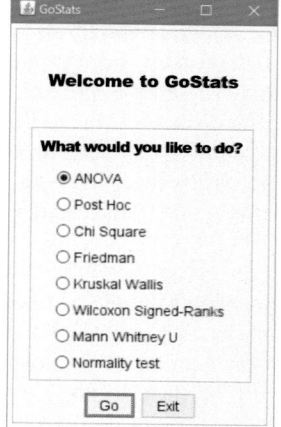

FIGURE 6.2

Launch screen for GoStats. Select the desired test and click "Go."

6.1 Utility software: GoStats

All the analyses in this chapter can be performed using the GoStats utility software available as a free download on this book's website.[2] GoStats is a single executable `.jar` file that will run on any computer that can run Java applications. All the example data files in this chapter are included as well. When the utility is launched, the supported statistical tests appear in a UI window. The user selects the desired test and clicks "Go." See Fig. 6.2.

Upon first launch, the example data files are extracted and placed in a directory called GoStatsExamples. We will say more about GoStats later in this chapter.

6.2 Analysis of variance

An ANOVA, or F-test, is a parametric test. It is the main statistical procedure for hypothesis testing in factorial experiments. The majority of HCI research papers that describe experiments include the results of an ANOVA, giving the F-statistic, the degrees of freedom for the F-statistic, and the associated p-value. The ANOVA result is typically reported in parentheses, as support for a statement indicating whether or not the outcome of the test was statistically significant.

The goal of an ANOVA is to determine if an independent variable – the test conditions – had a significant impact on a dependent variable – the measured responses. The ANOVA determines this by partitioning the variances in the measurements on

---

[2] Direct link: https://www.yorku.ca/mack/GoStats/.

a dependent variable into components attributable to the variance. The "components attributable" are the test conditions (factors and levels) and the participants.

The F-statistic is a ratio. The numerator is the variance due to the "effect" (of the test conditions) and the denominator is all the remaining variance (due to other test combinations and participants). If the variance due to the effect is large relative to the remaining variance, it is often possible to conclude that the distinguishing properties of the test conditions *caused* the observed differences in the measurements on the dependent variable. If so, the factor is said to have had a statistically significant effect on the dependent variable.

There are different ways to set up an ANOVA, depending in the design of the experiment. Our discussion begins with a simple one-factor design with two test conditions. We then progress to a one-factor design with four test conditions. A post hoc comparisons test is often used if there are more than two test conditions, and we give an example of such a test as well. We then discuss more complex designs with two or more factors, each having two or more levels.

The initial examples assume a within-subjects assignment of test conditions to participants. This means each participant was tested on all levels of a factor. Some designs have test conditions assigned between-subjects, meaning a separate group of participants is recruited and assigned to each test condition. A few examples of between-subjects ANOVAs are also given.

6.2.1 Why analyse the variance?

We noted earlier that research questions are usually comparative. Typically, the goal is to compare two or more interfaces or interaction techniques to determine which is better. By "better" we mean superior performance on one or more dependent variables, such as task completion time, error rate, task re-tries, presses of the BACKSPACE key, target re-entries, and so on. It is interesting that the test is called the "analysis of variance" yet our interest is in overall performance:

> Is the time to complete a task less using method A than using method B?

The question above refers to time – the overall, average, or mean, time that was observed and measured. Little can be inferred from a single observation made on one participant for one trial under one test condition. So, the mean is calculated for each test condition over multiple users and often over multiple trials of a representative task. The mean is a more stable measure since it represents the central tendency in a collection of measurements.

In some situations, multiple trials of a task are administered to investigate learning effects (see Chapter 5, Longitudinal Studies); but, often, multiple trials are used just to obtain stable and representative measurements. Nevertheless, it is the difference in the means, not the variances, that interests us. Note that while the above research question is certainly important, the statistical question pursued is not a question. It is a statement known as the *null hypothesis*:

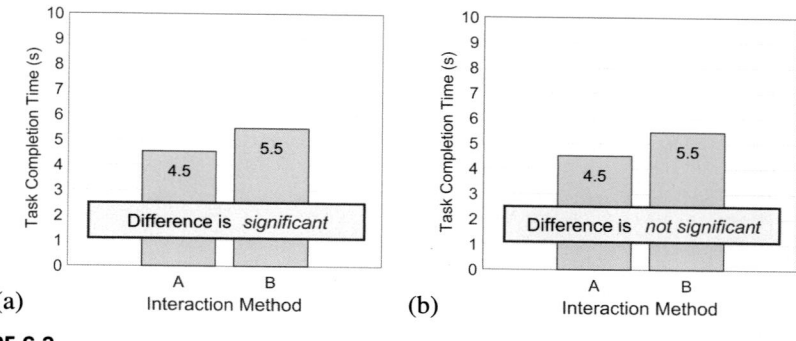

FIGURE 6.3

Difference in task completion time (in seconds) across two interaction methods, A and B. Two hypothetical outcomes are shown: (a) The difference is statistically significant. (b) The difference is not statistically significant. See text for discussion.

> There is no difference in the mean time to complete a task using method A vs. method B.

There is an assumption of "no difference," which is a reasonable starting point. The ANOVA tests the data to determine the likelihood that the null hypothesis is true (tenable) or false (rejected). In most cases, the researcher seeks to reject the null hypothesis. By convention, a statistically significant result means there is little likelihood the null hypothesis is true. The conclusion in such case is that (i) there is a difference in the means, (ii) the difference is statistically significant, and (iii) the difference was caused by distinguishable properties in the test conditions. Let's see how this is done.

Consider a hypothetical experiment where 10 participants perform a few repetitions of a task using two interaction techniques. The techniques could be anything, for example, use of a finger vs. a stylus for input on a smartphone. A task is chosen that is representative of common interactions, yet likely to expose inherent differences. An example might be entering an appointment in a calendar application. How long does this take using finger input? How long does it take using stylus input? For this discussion, we'll just refer to the interaction methods as A and B. Bear in mind that the experiment has a single factor (interaction method) with two levels (A and B).

Performance is measured on a dependent variable such as task completion time (in seconds) and the means are computed for each participant over a few trials. Then the means are computed for each method. Two example outcomes for this hypothetical experiment are shown in the bar charts in Fig. 6.3.

The mean task completion times are the same in Fig. 6.3a and Fig. 6.3b. However, the annotations proclaim vastly different outcomes. In Fig. 6.3a, the difference in the means is statistically significant. This implies that in all likelihood the difference

(a)

Participant	Interaction Method	
	A	B
1	5.3	5.7
2	3.6	4.8
3	5.2	5.1
4	3.5	4.5
5	4.6	6.0
6	4.1	6.8
7	4.0	6.0
8	4.8	4.6
9	5.2	5.5
10	5.1	5.6
Mean	4.5	5.5
SD	0.68	0.72

(b)

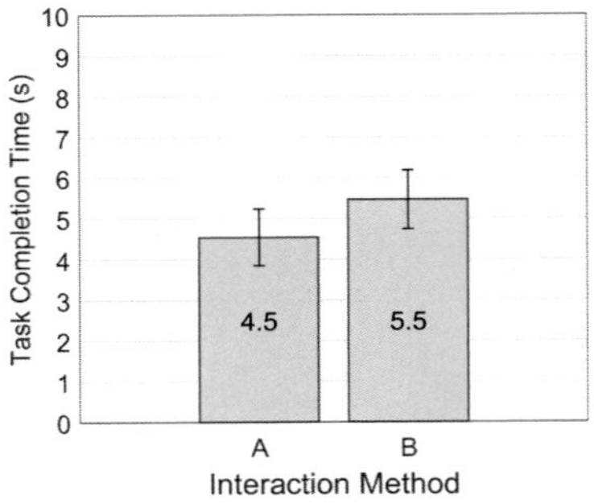

FIGURE 6.4

Simulation in Fig. 6.3a. (a) Data. (b) Bar chart. Error bars show ± 1 standard deviation about the means.

observed was real and was due to distinguishing properties of method A vs. method B. Simply put, method A is faster than method B. Do the test again, and there is a pretty good chance the result will be similar.

In Fig. 6.3b, the difference in the means is not statistically significant. This implies the difference in the means is likely due to chance. There is no reasonable basis to suggest that either method is faster than the other. Do the test again and the outcome could very well be reversed. Despite the dramatically different interpretations, the two examples seem the same: a task completion time of 4.5 seconds for method A vs. 5.5 seconds for method B. How is this? The answer lies in the variability in the observations – the variance. Let's have a closer look.

Fig. 6.4a gives the data for the simulation in Fig. 6.3a as the mean task completion time (in seconds) for each participant for each method along with the overall mean and standard deviation for each method. Fig. 6.4b shows the corresponding bar chart embellished with error bars. The error bars show ± 1 standard deviation about the means. The variance is the square of the standard deviation; however, it is more common in research papers to report standard deviations because the units of the standard deviation and the mean are the same ("seconds" in this case).

The step-by-step process of doing an ANOVA on the data in Fig. 6.4a depends on the statistics app used. The result is a table similar to that shown in Fig. 6.5.[3]

The most important statistic in the table is the "p-Value." The p-value is the probability of obtaining the observed data if the null hypothesis is true. A low probability

---

[3] The analysis in Fig. 6.5 was done using SAS's StatView 5.0 running on a Lenovo T480 with Windows 10.

ANOVA Table for Task Completion Time

	DF	Sum of Squares	Mean Square	F-Value	P-Value
Subject	9	5.080	.564		
Interaction Method	1	4.232	4.232	9.796	.0121
Interaction Method * Subject	9	3.888	.432		

FIGURE 6.5

Analysis of variance table for data in Fig. 6.4a.

indicates that the differences in the means are unlikely to have occurred in view of the null hypothesis. A high probability indicates that the differences in the means may simply be a chance outcome. With $p = .0121$, there is a fairly low probability – less than 2% – that the difference is simply a chance outcome. In all likelihood, there are distinguishing properties in the methods that caused the difference. Note the term "caused" in the preceding sentence. One reason experimental research is so valuable is that conclusions of a cause-and-effect nature are possible.

At the same time, it is important to acknowledge an important limitation in statistical procedures such as the ANOVA, and statistics in general. Statistics can determine the probability of an event – in this case, the probability that observed data are consistent with the null hypothesis – but statistics do not explain or interpret. For this, the researcher draws upon insight and other resources, such as examinations of the behaviours and responses involved.

It is common in experimental research that significance, in a statistical sense, requires p less than .05, or a 1 in 20 probability.[4] That is, we consider the null hypothesis tenable unless there is a 1 in 20 chance, or less, that it is not. As well as the probability, important statistics in the ANOVA are the F-statistic (the ratio of sample variances) and the degrees of freedom for the main effect (Interaction Method) and the residual effect (Interaction Method * Subject).[5] The relevant statistics come together in a statement that declares the outcome of the research question. An example of how this might appear in a research paper for the hypothetical experiment is shown in Fig. 6.6 (with F rounded to three significant figures).

---

[4] The significance level is also called alpha (α). Alpha is the probability of committing a Type I error or false positive. A Type I error occurs when the null hypothesis is incorrectly rejected. Beta (β) is the probability of committing a Type II error or false negative. A Type II error occurs when the test fails to reject a false null hypothesis. These explanations are confusing because of the double-negative wording ("incorrectly rejected") and the built-in assumption of "no difference" in the null hypothesis. Medical examples are more straightforward: A false positive (Type I error) occurs when a test indicates that a patient has a disease when in fact the patient does not. A false negative (Type II error) occurs when a test indicates that a patient does not have a disease when in fact the patient does.

[5] The F-statistic in Fig. 6.5 is the ratio of the variance (mean square) for the Interaction Method to the Interaction Method * Subject: $4.232 / 0.432 = 9.796$. The numerator is the variance due to the effect of the methods, or test conditions. The denominator is all the remaining variance. If there is no experimental effect this ratio should be approximately 1. The amount F rises above 1 is an indication of the impact of the

> The mean task completion time for interaction method A was 4.5 s. This was 18.2% less than the mean of 5.5 s observed for interaction method B. The difference was statistically significant ($F_{1,9} = 9.80$, $p < .05$).

FIGURE 6.6

Example text to report the results of an analysis of variance in a research paper.

Note that the probability is not precisely cited. Instead, p is cited as less than a more conservative threshold from the set {.05, .01, .005, .001, .0005, .0001}. So, p is cited as $p < .05$ rather than $p = .0121$.[6]

The language in Fig. 6.6 includes both the means for the test conditions and the difference in the means. The difference in the means is the *effect size*. The effect size is usually conveyed in HCI research giving the means and the absolute difference (1 second, in this case) or the relative difference (18.2%, in this case). Of course, whether the effect size is of practical significance is not within the scope of the ANOVA.[7]

F-statistics are often poorly formatted in research papers, so is it worthwhile to pause for a moment and observe the following in Fig. 6.6:

- ANOVA result in parentheses
- Uppercase for F
- Lowercase for p
- Italics for F and p
- Space on both sides of the equal sign
- Space after the comma
- Space on both sides of the less than sign
- Degrees of freedom are subscript, plain, smaller font[8]

---

test conditions on the differences in the means observed across the test conditions. Statistical significance depends on the value of F, the degrees of freedom, and the threshold for p that is deemed significant.

[6] The APA's Publication Manual has a different recommendation: "It is best to provide the exact probabilities to two or three decimal places (e.g., $p = .023$). However, when p values are less than .001, it is acceptable to write the value as '$< .001$'" [10, p. 204]. This practice is not (yet) generally followed in human-computer interaction.

[7] Here, and in most HCI research, the reported effect size is unstandardized. The unstandardized effect size is useful since it conveys the practical importance of the results and allows direct comparisons with other research using the same dependent variable. Statisticians generally prefer a standardized effect size, such as Cohen's d or partial η^2, which normalize for the standard deviation in the sample. A standardized effect size is unitless and, therefore, more difficult to interpret in terms of the differences in measurements on the dependent variable. Standardized effect sizes are generally not reported in HCI research, although there are exceptions (e.g., [23,298,512]).

[8] Alternatively, the degrees of freedom may be set in parentheses in a plain style. In this case, a space follows the comma.

Participant	Interaction Method	
	A	B
1	2.4	6.9
2	2.7	7.2
3	3.4	2.6
4	6.1	1.8
5	6.4	7.8
6	5.4	9.2
7	7.9	4.4
8	1.2	6.6
9	3.0	4.8
10	6.6	3.1
Mean	4.5	5.5
SD	2.23	2.45

(a)

(b)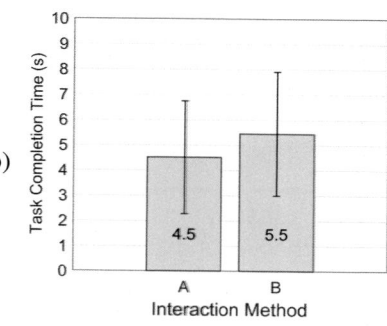

FIGURE 6.7

Simulation in Fig. 6.3b. (a) Data. (b) Bar chart. Error bars show ±1 standard deviation about the means.

- Three or four significant figures for the F-statistic
- No zero before the decimal point for the p-statistic (because it is constrained between 0 and 1)[9]

6.2.2 Non-significant ANOVA results

Turning now to the second example – the simulation in Fig. 6.3b – the data and corresponding bar chart embellished with error bars are shown in Fig. 6.7.

As noted, the results for the second simulation are not statistically significant. A hint of this is the large error bars in Fig. 6.7b. The ANOVA reveals and confirms the lack of significance with a high p-value. See Fig. 6.8. There is about a 45% chance the difference in the means is simply a chance outcome. Even though the means are the same as in the first simulation, there was a large variation in the performance of participants – enough that the difference in the means between the test conditions is perhaps just due to chance. Observe in Fig. 6.7a for example that participant #8 completed the task in 1.2 seconds using method A while participant #10 took 6.6 seconds. Evidently, there is something going on that falls outside the explanatory power of the two interaction methods under test.

In a research paper, non-significant results are also important to report. Fig. 6.9 is an example for the second simulation of how this might appear in a research paper.

For non-significant results, the ANOVA result is reported in one of two ways:

---

[9] Some journals include a zero before the decimal point.

ANOVA Table for Task Completion Time

	DF	Sum of Squares	Mean Square	F-Value	P-Value
Subject	9	37.372	4.152		
Interaction Method	1	4.324	4.324	.626	.4491
Interaction Method * Subject	9	62.140	6.904		

FIGURE 6.8

Analysis of variance for data in Fig. 6.7a. See text for discussion.

> The mean task completion times were 4.5 s for interaction method A and 5.5 s for interaction method B. As there was substantial variation in the observations across participants, the difference was not statistically significant as revealed in an analysis of variance ($F_{1,9} = 0.644$, ns).

FIGURE 6.9

Reporting an ANOVA result that is not statistically significant.

- If $p > .05$ and $F > 1$, report as "$p > .05$"
- If $p > .05$ and $F \leq 1$, report as "ns" (for "not significant")

The latter style is used because it is impossible for the differences to be significant if $F \leq 1$.

Sometimes, a non-significant ANOVA result is the preferred outcome. An example is Roig-Maimó et al.'s comparison of three sizes of mobile devices for camera-based monitoring of neck movements for rehabilitation following an injury [420]. They devised an exergame that required participants to move their head and neck in various patterns. The independent variable was device type with three levels: iPhone X4 (small), iPad Mini 4 (medium), and iPad Air (large). In testing the effect of device type on range of motion (ROM) as a dependent variable, the ANOVA revealed no significant difference by device type on six movement directions. This was considered a positive result and lead to a conclusion that the rehabilitation exergame could be used on different devices.

Another example is MacKenzie and Isokoski's user study testing the hypothesis that Fitts' throughput is independent of the speed-accuracy trade-off [312]. The independent variable was cognitive set with three levels: speed emphasis, nominal, and accuracy emphasis. An ANOVA revealed that the effect of cognitive set on throughput was not statistically significant. This was interpreted as evidence in support of the hypothesis.

Bear in mind that a non-significant ANOVA does not imply that the null hypothesis is true. A non-significant ANOVA indicates only that the evidence is insufficient to reject the null hypothesis: The null hypothesis remains tenable. This is analogous to a decision in a criminal trial, where the assumption of innocence is the default, or null, hypothesis. When the jury concludes their deliberations, they bring forth a verdict of guilty or not guilty. A verdict of not guilty does not mean that the crime did not occur or that the accused did not commit a crime. A not-guilty verdict only implies the evidence did not meet the stringent requirements to reject the assumption of innocence (e.g., beyond a reasonable doubt). The null hypothesis – in this case, innocence – remains tenable.

6.2.3 More than two test conditions

The example above involves one factor with two levels (test conditions).[10] In practice, a factor often has more than two levels. Although the idea is similar, an example is worthwhile. Fig. 6.10 gives the data and bar chart for a hypothetical experiment where four interaction methods are compared. The data are the observed, measured responses on a dependent variable.

An ANOVA on the data produces the table in Fig. 6.11. Right off, we see that p is less than .05, the accepted threshold for significance. Plainly put, there was a significant effect of interaction method on the dependent variable ($F_{3,45} = 4.95$, $p < .005$). In the parentheses, the relevant statistics are pulled from the table, as before. The degrees of freedom are different in this example.

If n is the number of interaction methods and m is the number of participants, the degrees of freedom are $(n - 1)$ for the variance due to the factor (the interaction methods) and $(n - 1)(m - 1)$ for the remaining variance.

Since the p-value in the ANOVA table is .0047, there is less than a 0.5% chance the difference in the means is a chance outcome. It is likely that the difference was caused by distinguishing properties among the interaction methods. In other words, the effect of the interaction methods on the dependent variable was statistically significant.

6.2.4 Post hoc comparisons

The ANOVA in Fig. 6.11 only reveals that at least one of the means is significantly different from at least one other mean. A quick glance at the bar chart in Fig. 6.10b leaves us wondering which interaction methods differ from which other interaction methods. To determine this, *post hoc comparisons* are performed. Several post hoc comparisons tests are available, including Fisher PLSD, Bonferroni/Dunn, Dunnett, Scheffé, Tukey/Kramer, Games/Howell, Student-Newman-Keuls, and orthogonal contrasts. The results are generally the same or similar between the different tests. There are statistical assumptions inherent in each, but these are not discussed here.

An example using the Scheffé test is shown in Fig. 6.12. Among the four interaction methods, six comparisons are possible. Of these, only the A-C and B-C comparisons are significant. In other words, the means are significantly different between interaction methods A and C and between interaction methods B and C. The other four comparisons did not meet the 5% threshold for significance.

---

[10] A *t*-test is the same as an analysis of variance if only two test conditions are compared.

Participant	Interaction Method			
	A	B	C	D
1	11	11	21	16
2	18	11	22	15
3	17	10	18	13
4	19	15	21	20
5	13	17	23	10
6	10	15	15	20
7	14	14	15	13
8	13	14	19	18
9	19	18	16	12
10	10	17	21	18
11	10	19	22	13
12	16	14	18	20
13	10	20	17	19
14	10	13	21	18
15	20	17	14	18
16	18	17	17	14
Mean	14.25	15.13	18.75	16.06
SD	3.84	2.94	2.89	3.23

(a)

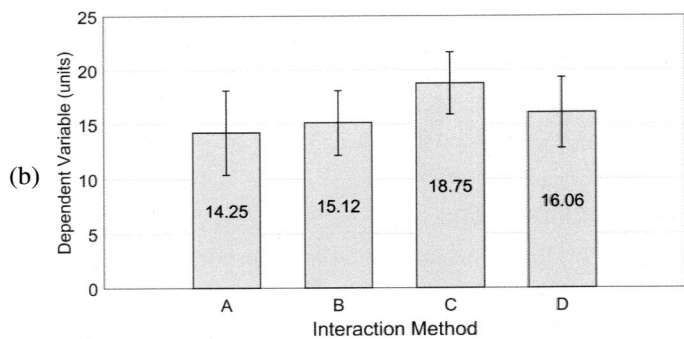

(b)

FIGURE 6.10

Experiment comparing four interaction methods. (a) Data. (b) Bar chart. Error bars show ±1 standard deviation about the means.

ANOVA Table for Dependent Variable

	DF	Sum of Squares	Mean Square	F-Value	P-Value
Subject	15	81.109	5.407		
Interaction Method	3	182.172	60.724	4.954	.0047
Interaction Method * Subject	45	551.578	12.257		

FIGURE 6.11

ANOVA for data in Fig. 6.10a.

Scheffe for Dependent Variable
Effect: Interaction Method
Significance Level: 5 %

	Mean Diff.	Crit. Diff	P-Value	
A, B	-.875	3.302	.9003	
A, C	-4.500	3.302	.0032	S
A, E	-1.813	3.302	.4822	
B, C	-3.625	3.302	.0256	S
B, E	-.938	3.302	.8806	
C, E	2.688	3.302	.1520	

FIGURE 6.12

Scheffé post hoc comparisons for data in Fig. 6.10a. "S" identifies comparisons that meet the $p < .05$ threshold for significance.

Since each comparison is between two values, post hoc comparisons are sometimes called *pairwise comparisons* or *multiple comparisons*. In general, if there are k conditions, there are $k \times (k - 1) / 2$ comparisons.

Several HCI research papers using a Scheffé post hoc analysis are hereby cited [74,95,123,135,261,266].

6.2.5 Between-subjects designs

The examples above use a within-subjects design: Each participant was tested on all interaction methods (levels of the factor). While within-subjects designs are common in HCI, between-subjects designs are also used. When performing an ANOVA on the data for either design, it is important to set up the analysis properly, as the variances are partitioned differently for within-subjects data vs. between-subjects data.

Let's consider an example experiment on the differences between left-handed and right-handed users in using a stylus to add calendar entries on a smartphone. Depending on the screen layout, occlusion may occur when, for example, a left-handed user interacts with widgets on the right side of the display. Does occlusion affect performance? Maybe, maybe not. For the experiment, 16 participants were recruited. Hand preference was a between-subjects factor with two levels. There were eight left-handed participants and eight right-handed participants. Each participant performed a few iterations of an "add calendar entry" task. The mean times to complete the task for each participant are tabulated in Fig. 6.13a.

While tables such as Fig. 6.13a are generally not provided in research papers, the data are given here to illustrate the organization for between-subjects ANOVAs. Many ANOVA applications operate on a matrix of data where the number of rows equals the number of participants. And so, the data in Fig. 6.13a are organized in 16 rows. The between-subjects factor appears as an added column of nominal data encoding the levels of the factor. "L" and "R" identify the participants who were left handers vs. right handers.

(a)

Participant	Task Completion Time (s)	Hand Preference
1	23	L
2	19	L
3	22	L
4	21	L
5	23	L
6	20	L
7	25	L
8	23	L
9	17	R
10	19	R
11	16	R
12	21	R
13	23	R
14	20	R
15	22	R
16	21	R
Mean	20.9	
SD	2.38	

(b)

Hand Preference	Task Completion Time (s)	
	Mean	SD
Left	22.0	1.93
Right	19.9	2.42

(c)

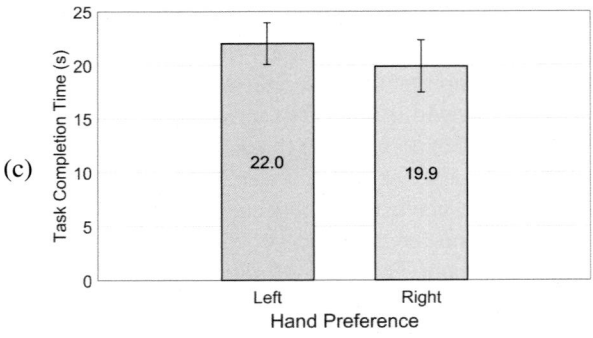

FIGURE 6.13

Experiment with hand preference as a between-subjects factor. (a) Data by participant and hand preference. (b) Data by hand preference. (c) Bar chart.

Fig. 6.13b summarizes the results by hand preference, while Fig. 6.13c presents the same information in a bar chart, as might appear in a research paper. The ANOVA is performed on the 16 × 2 matrix in the right two columns in Fig. 6.13a. The result

ANOVA Table for Task Completion Time (s)

	DF	Sum of Squares	Mean Square	F-Value	P-Value
Hand Preference	1	18.063	18.063	3.781	.0722
Residual	14	66.875	4.777		

FIGURE 6.14

Between-subjects ANOVA for data in Fig. 6.13a.

is shown in Fig. 6.14. The degrees of freedom are $(n-1)$ for the variance due to hand preference and $(m-n)$ for the residual variance.

Since the p-value in Fig. 6.14 is greater than .05, the difference between left handers and right handers was not statistically significant. Even though there was about a 10% difference between the groups – 22.0 s for left handers, 19.9 s for right handers – there was considerable variability in the observations. Based on the results of this experiment, we consider the null hypothesis tenable and conclude that there is no performance difference between left and right handed users in performing the add calendar entry task on the system under test.

6.2.6 Two-way analysis of variance

An experiment with two independent variables, or two factors, is a *two-way design*. For such experiments, the analysis of variance tests for the main effects of each factor on the dependent variable, as well as an interaction effect. A significant interaction effect means the factors in combination influence, or have an effect on, the dependent variable. Let's see how these effects are revealed in a two-way analysis of variance.

If an experiment has two factors, there are three possibilities for assigning conditions to participants. The assignments may be within-subjects for both factors, between-subjects for both factors, or within-subjects for one factor and between-subjects for the other. The latter is referred to as a *mixed-design*, as noted earlier (p. 228).

Let's consider an example experiment with two within-subjects factors. The experiment compared pointing and dragging operations on a smartphone with input using a finger, a finger while wearing a conductive glove, and a stylus. The factors were input method with three levels (finger, finger+glove, stylus) and task with two levels (pointing, dragging).

For the example, each participant was tested on all three input methods and for both tasks in a simple target acquisition task. In this case, the experiment is referred to as a "3 × 2 within-subjects design." We assume as well that the order of administering conditions was counterbalanced (see Chapter 5, section 5.11). Fig. 6.15 gives the results. The data show the measured responses on the dependent variable, task completion time in seconds.

In Fig. 6.15a, the data are given by participant, input method, and task. Evidently, participant #12 performed dragging with the stylus in 9 seconds. The means and standard deviations are shown in the bottom rows, calculated across the 12 participants

(a)

Participant	Finger		Finger+Glove		Stylus	
	Pointing	Dragging	Pointing	Dragging	Pointing	Dragging
1	11	18	15	13	20	14
2	10	14	17	15	11	13
3	10	23	13	20	20	16
4	18	18	11	12	11	10
5	20	21	19	14	19	8
6	14	21	20	11	17	13
7	14	16	15	20	16	12
8	20	21	18	20	14	12
9	14	15	13	17	16	14
10	20	15	18	10	11	16
11	14	20	15	16	10	9
12	20	16	16	16	20	9
Mean	15.4	18.5	15.8	15.3	15.4	12.2
SD	4.01	2.94	2.69	3.50	3.92	2.69

(b)

Condition	Pointing	Dragging	Mean
Finger	15.4	18.5	17.0
Finger+Glove	15.8	15.3	15.6
Stylus	15.4	12.2	13.8
Mean	15.6	15 3	15.4

(c)

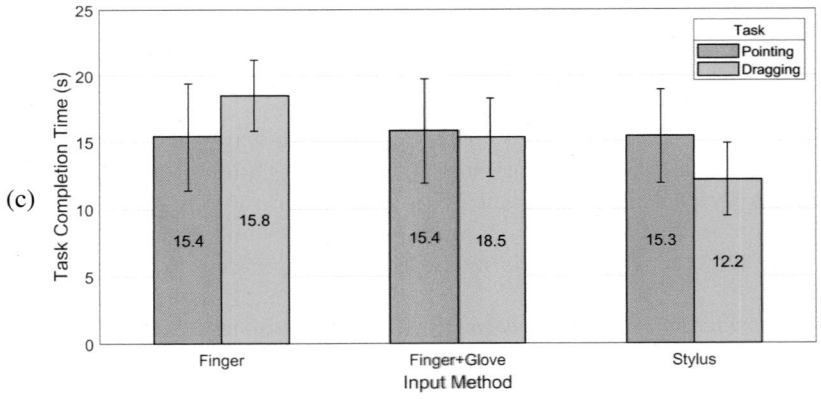

FIGURE 6.15

Hypothetical experiment with two within-subjects factors. The factors are input method with three levels and task with two levels. (a) Task completion time (s) by participant, input method, and task. (b) Task completion time (s) by input method and task. (c) Bar chart with error bars showing ±1 standard deviation about the means.

for each input method by task condition. Fig. 6.15b reorganizes the data to more clearly demonstrate the input method and task effects. As seen, the stylus was the fastest, the finger the slowest. Dragging was performed slightly faster than pointing. Fig. 6.15c shows the mean scores for each input method and task in a bar chart, as

ANOVA Table for Task Completion Time (s)

	DF	Sum of Squares	Mean Square	F-Value	P-Value
Subject	11	134.778	12.253		
Input Method	2	121.028	60.514	5.865	.0091
Input Method * Subject	22	226.972	10.317		
Task	1	.889	.889	.076	.7875
Task * Subject	11	128.111	11.646		
Input Method * Task	2	121.028	60.514	5.435	.0121
Input Method * Task * Subject	22	244.972	11.135		

FIGURE 6.16

Two-way analysis of variance for data in Fig. 6.15a.

might appear in a research paper. The error bars show ±1 standard deviation about the means.

While there were differences between the three input methods and two tasks, there was also variability in the responses, as evident along the bottom row in Fig. 6.15a. So, the question remains: Were the observed differences significant and attributable to inherent properties of the input methods or tasks, or were the differences simply a chance outcome? This question is answered by an analysis of variance. The ANOVA is performed on the core 12×6 matrix in Fig. 6.15a. In preparing the data for analysis, it is important to properly assign the factors and levels. As organized in Fig. 6.15a, the columns are ordered by input method, with task nested within input method. The results are shown in Fig. 6.16.

There are three results in Fig. 6.16: (i) the input method main effect, (ii) the task main effect, and (iii) the input method by task interaction effect. Let's see how these results are pulled from the analysis of variance table and presented in a research paper. An example is given in Fig. 6.17.

It is a challenge to create interest in presenting statistical results. A reader who confronts a tedious, sterile, recitation of statistic after statistic will quickly lose interest. The goal in reporting results is to selectively pull interesting and revealing measures and statistics from the data that emerge in experimental research. Note in Fig. 6.17 expressions like "difference was modest," "slightly faster," and "due solely to." These are minor embellishments intended to improve the readability of the results. Further discussion is needed to explain the results (e.g., "The improved performance with the stylus while dragging is attributed to ...").

It is, of course, the observations and measurements that are important, not the statistics. Statistical tests help assess hypotheses, but they are not the results per se. Day and Gastel [99, p. 63] further emphasize this point: "Generally, a lengthy description of statistical methods indicates that the writer has recently acquired this information and believes that the readers need similar enlightenment." Don't feel compelled to explain the analysis of variance, or any other statistical test. Give the results in terms of the data, with supporting statistical tests conveyed plainly and without elaboration.

The grand mean for task completion time was 15.4 seconds. Stylus input was the fastest at 13.8 seconds, while finger input was the slowest at 17.0 seconds. The main effect of input method on task completion time was statistically significant ($F_{2,22} = 5.865$, $p < .01$). The task effect was modest, however. Task completion time was 15.6 seconds for pointing. Dragging was slightly faster at 15.3 seconds; however, the difference was not statistically significant ($F_{1,11} = 0.076$, ns). The results by input method and task are shown in Figure x. There was a significant Input Method × Task interaction effect ($F_{2,22} = 5.435$, $p < .05$), which was due solely to the difference between the finger and stylus while dragging, as determined by a Scheffé post hoc analysis.

FIGURE 6.17

Results of the two-way analysis of variance in Fig. 6.16, as might appear in a research paper.

6.2.7 Doing an ANOVA with GoStats

An ANOVA is easy to do using the GoStats utility software available through this book's web site. Just launch GoStats and click "Go." See Fig. 6.2. This brings up the Anova utility within GoStats. See Fig. 6.18a.

The GoStats Anova utility includes an extensive tutorial with many ANOVA examples, etc. These are online and viewable in a browser through the API link in the Anova GUI (arrow in figure). Let's work through an example.

The file `dix-example-10x2.txt` contains the data from a hypothetical experiment on icon recognition, as described by Dix et al. [103, p. 337]. To load the data, click "Open ...," navigate to the GoStatsExamples folder and select the file. This loads the data into the data pane in the Anova GUI. See Fig. 6.18b.

The data in `dix-example-10x2.txt` form a 10×2 matrix. There were 10 participants and a single within-subjects factor, icon design, with two levels, natural and abstract. The data are the measurements for task completion time, the dependent variable. The first column contains the task completion times for the natural icons, the second column for the abstract icons. Each row contains the measurements for one participant.

The mean task completion times (not shown) are 697.7 s for the natural icons and 750.3 s for the abstract icons. Evidently the recognition time for the natural icons was about 7% less than for the abstract icons. An analysis of variance determines if the difference was statistically significant or if it was likely due to chance. To do this, first enter "2" in the F1 box. This indicates that the first within-subjects factor, F1, has two levels. Click "Analyse" and the ANOVA table appears. See Fig. 6.18c.

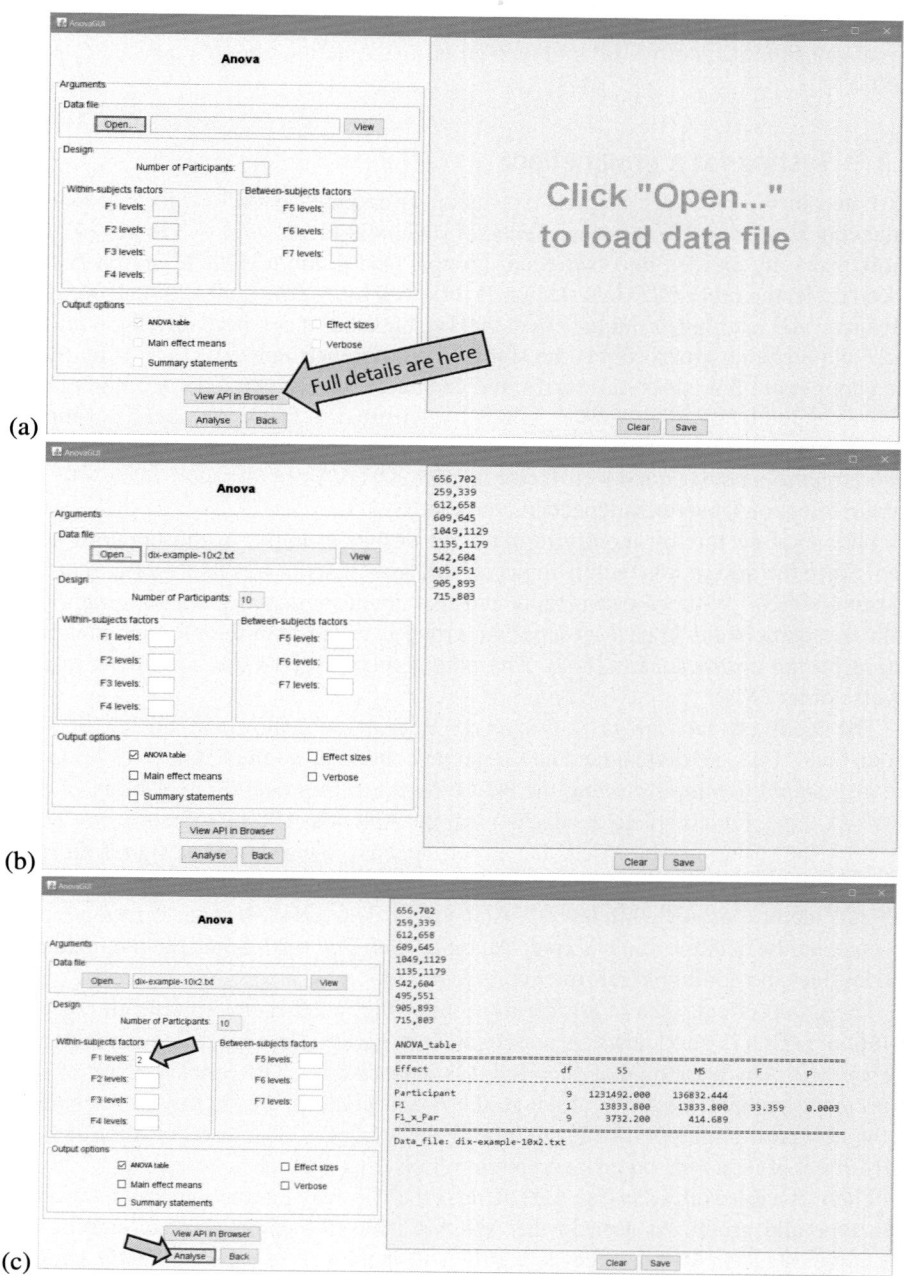

FIGURE 6.18

GoStats. (a) Anova GUI. (b) Data in file `dix-example-10x2.txt` loaded into the data pane.
(c) ANOVA table for data in `dix-example-10x2.txt`.

As seen in the table, and as might appear in a research paper, "The experiment revealed a significant effect of icon type on task completion time ($F_{1,9} = 33.36$, $p < .0005$)."

6.2.8 Testing for a group effect

As noted in the previous chapter, if a factor is assigned within-subjects, counterbalancing is used to offset order effects. For a single factor with two levels (A, B), participants are divided into two equal groups. One group (G1) is tested on A followed by B, the other (G2) is tested on B followed by A. The goal is to balance out, or cancel, any learning or fatigue effect that might occur. If counterbalancing worked, there should be no group effect – no significant difference between G1 and G2. Simple enough, but how does one verify that counterbalancing worked? A group effect is investigated by treating "group" as a between-subjects factor. Of course, group is not a factor in the sense of a research topic. Nevertheless, the data can be organized with group as a between-subjects factor and the ANOVA can test for a *group effect* – a main effect of group on a dependent variable.

Let's explore this by modifying the icon design example in the previous section. Since the design was within-subjects, counterbalancing was likely used to offset learning effects. With 10 participants and two conditions, two groups are required with five participants in each group. One group is tested with the natural icons followed by the abstract icons (NA). The other group is given the conditions in the reverse order (AN).

The modified data are in `dix-example-h10x2b.txt`, shown in Fig. 6.19. The group codes (NA, AN) are added as a separate column of nominal data. Header lines are also added to simplify doing the ANOVA and to improve the readability of the ANOVA table. For complete details, consult the ANOVA API in GoStats.

With the group codes added, the experiment is now a 2 × 2 design with one within-subjects factor ("icon type" with levels natural and abstract) and one between-subjects factor ("group" with levels NA and AN). The ANOVA is performed simply by opening the data file and clicking "Analyse." See Fig. 6.20. Since the file includes header lines, no additional information is required.

The group effect, seen along the top row in Fig. 6.20, is not significant ($F_{1,8} = 0.466$, ns). This is good news. A non-significant group effect means counterbalancing worked. Any learning that occurred was balanced out. The primary result of the experiment remains the same, although the F and p values are slightly different due to the new partitioning of data in computing the variances. The result is still a significant effect of icon type on task completion time ($F_{1,8} = 30.68$, $p < .001$).

There is a third effect in Fig. 6.20. This is the two-way interaction effect between icon type and group. As seen in the ANOVA table, the effect was not significant ($F_{1,8} = 0.277$, ns). If this effect is significant, it represents a phenomenon known as *asymmetric skill transfer* [406], meaning there was a learning effect and it was different transitioning from A to N than from N to A (see also Chapter 5, section 5.12, p. 233).

```
DV: Completion Time (s)
F1: Icon Type, Natural, Abstract
F2: .
F3: .
F4: .
F5: Group
F6: .
F7: .
656,702,NA
259,339,NA
612,658,NA
609,645,NA
1049,1129,NA
1135,1179,AN
542,604,AN
495,551,AN
905,893,AN
715,803,AN
```

FIGURE 6.19

Contents of the file `dix-example-h10x2b.txt`. The data are for the icon recognition experiment modified to illustrate counterbalancing and the use of header lines with GoStats.

ANOVA_table_for_Completion Time (s)

Effect	df	SS	MS	F	p
Group	1	67744.800	67744.800	0.466	0.5142
Participant(Group)	8	1163747.200	145468.400		
Icon Type	1	13833.800	13833.800	30.680	0.0005
Icon Type_x_Group	1	125.000	125.000	0.277	0.6128
Icon Type_x_P(group)	8	3607.200	450.900		

Data_file: dix-example-h10x2b.txt

FIGURE 6.20

ANOVA for data in Fig. 6.19.

One unique feature of GoStats is worth noting. If the "Summary statements" output option is selected, GoStats will pull the relevant statistics from the ANOVA table and organize them into generic summary statements. Statements are output for the main effects and two-way interaction effects. If the data file contains header lines, as in Fig. 6.19, the summary statements include the names of the independent variables and the dependent variables. See Fig. 6.21. These statements, or something similar, are commonly found in research papers where the ANOVA results are presented.

In many research experiments, counterbalancing is used for within-subjects factors without actually testing for a group effect. This is largely a matter of choice.

Consult the student exercises at the end of this chapter for practice examples on the analysis of variance.

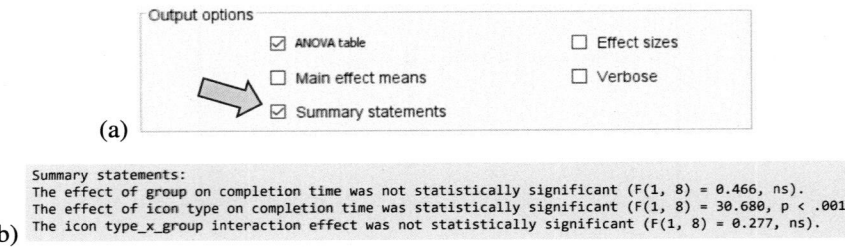

(a)

(b)

Summary statements:
The effect of group on completion time was not statistically significant (F(1, 8) = 0.466, ns).
The effect of icon type on completion time was statistically significant (F(1, 8) = 30.680, p < .001).
The icon type_x_group interaction effect was not statistically significant (F(1, 8) = 0.277, ns).

FIGURE 6.21

Generating summary ANOVA statements with GoStats. (a) Output option. (b) Summary ANOVA statements for table in Fig. 6.20.

6.3 Chi-square test

A common statistical procedure for investigating relationships is the chi-square test, also known as the Pearson chi-square test, and sometimes using "squared" instead of "square." The pronunciation is $k\bar{i}$ (to rhyme with *sky*). The relationships are between categorical, or nominal-scale, variables representing attributes of people, interaction methods, systems, etc. The data are commonly summarized in a *contingency table* – a cross tabulation organizing data in rows and columns with each cell containing a count, the number of observations in the category. A chi-square test compares the observed values – the counts in the table – against expected values. The expected values are developed under the assumption that there is no difference among the categories in the table. The chi-square test is a non-parametric test since the categories are nominal-scale attributes and do not have a probability distribution associated with them. A hypothetical example will illustrate.

6.3.1 Example 1

A researcher is interested in knowing if males or females differ in their method of scrolling when using a desktop computer system. To study this, a large number of users are observed. For each user it is noted whether they are male or female and whether they scroll using the mouse wheel (MW), the scrollbar by clicking and dragging (CD), or the keyboard (KB). The categories are gender (male, female) and scrolling method (MW, CD, KB). Fig. 6.22a shows the data in a 2 × 3 contingency table. Over 100 users were observed, including 56 males and 45 females. Counts for usage of the scrolling methods were 49 (MW), 24 (CD), and 28 (KB). Fig. 6.22b shows the data in a bar chart, as might appear in a research paper.

A quick glance at the data and chart suggests there may indeed be a difference between males and females in their method of scrolling on desktop computer systems. Only 9 females used clicking and dragging, compared to 15 males. However, more males were observed overall; so the difference is not as dramatic as it seems. The issue then is whether the differences observed are real or simply due to random

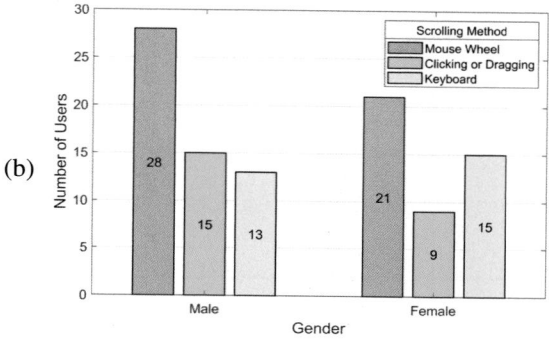

Gender	Scrolling Method			Total
	MW	CD	KB	
Male	28	15	13	56
Female	21	9	15	45
Total	49	24	28	101

(a)

(b)

FIGURE 6.22

Contingency table example. (a) Data. (b) Bar chart. See text for discussion.

effects. To determine this, the chi-square test is used. The test statistic is χ^2, using the lowercase Greek letter *chi*.[11] Like the analysis of variance, the underlying assumption is "no difference" with the test often seeking to reject the assumption. Unlike the analysis of variance, however, a chi-square test is simple. The calculations are easily done by hand or using a spreadsheet application. Let's work through the details for this example.

6.3.2 Chi-square calculations

The chi-square test is a comparison between the observed values and the expected values, with the expected values accounting for the different row and column totals. Fig. 6.23a shows the expected values for the data in Fig. 6.22a, under the no-difference assumption. Each expected value is the row total multiplied by the column total, divided by the grand total. For example, the Male-MW expected value is $(56 \times 49) / 101 = 27.2$. From the observed and expected values, a table of chi-squares is created, as shown in Fig. 6.23b. Each chi-square is the square of the observed value minus the expected value, divided by the expected value. For example, the Male-MW chi-square is $(28.0 - 27.2)^2 / 27.2 = 0.025$.

The final chi-square value is the sum of the individual chi-squares in the table. For the example, $\chi^2 = 1.462$, shown in the bottom-right cell in Fig. 6.23b. Determining if there is a statistically significant difference among the cell entries involves com-

---

[11] As a matter of style in a research paper, Greek letters are not set in italics [10, p. 171].

Gender	Scrolling Method			Total
	MW	CD	KB	
(a) Male	27.2	13.3	15.5	56.0
Female	21.8	10.7	12.5	45.0
Total	49.0	24.0	28.0	101

Gender	Scrolling Method			Total
	MW	CD	KB	
(b) Male	0.025	0.215	0.411	0.651
Female	0.032	0.268	0.511	0.811
Total	0.057	0.483	0.922	1.462

FIGURE 6.23

Expected values and chi-squares for the data in Fig. 6.22. (a) Expected number of users. (b) Chi squares.

Significance Threshold (α)	Degrees of Freedom							
	1	2	3	4	5	6	7	8
.1	2.71	4.61	6.25	7.78	9.24	10.65	12.02	13.36
.05	3.84	5.99	7.82	9.49	11.07	12.59	14.07	15.51
.01	6.64	9.21	11.35	13.28	15.09	16.81	18.48	20.09
.001	10.83	13.82	16.27	18.47	20.52	22.46	24.32	26.13

FIGURE 6.24

Chi-square critical values.

paring the final chi-square with values in a table of critical values. If the chi-square exceeds the critical value, the differences in the contingency table are statistically significant, implying there is a significant difference in the nominal-scale variables in the table. Two additional details are required: (a) the degrees of freedom, and (b) the required alpha level, or p-value, for significance. The degrees of freedom for the chi-square statistic is $(r-1)(c-1)$, where r is the number of rows and c is the number of columns. For the example, $df = (2-1)(3-1) = 2$. The alpha level is chosen prior to testing. We'll use $\alpha = .05$ for the example. The critical value for significance is looked-up in a table. Fig. 6.24 gives the chi-square critical values for $df = 1$ to $df = 8$ using four common alpha levels. At $\alpha = .05$ and $df = 2$, the critical value is $\chi^2 = 5.99$. Since the computed value of $\chi^2 = 1.462$ is less than the critical value, the differences in the observed values (see Fig. 6.22) are not statistically significant. The conclusion is that there is no difference in the way males and females scroll using desktop computer systems.

6.3.3 Chi-square in GoStats

Doing a chi-square test in GoStats is a simple. From the launch screen, select Chi Square (see Fig. 6.2, p. 245) and click "Go." The ChiSquare utility appears. Click "Open ..." to bring up the file chooser. The data for this example are in

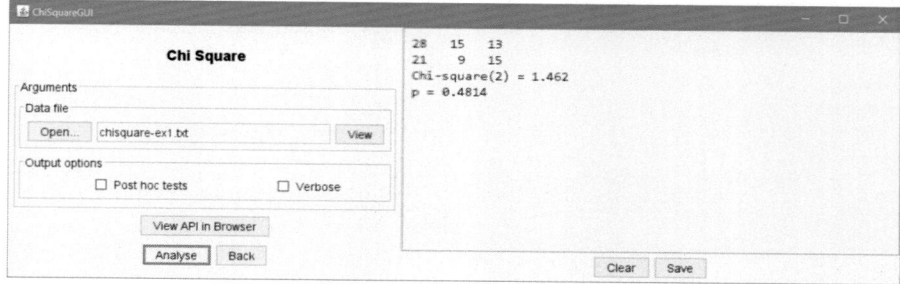

FIGURE 6.25

GoStats utility to compute chi-square statistic and probability, *p*.

Opinion	Category of Person			Total
	Student	Professor	Parent	
Agree	10	12	98	120
Disagree	30	48	102	180
Total	40	60	200	300

FIGURE 6.26

Contingency table showing the number of responses to a question about mobile phone usage during classroom lectures.

the GoStatsExamples folder. Navigate to the folder and open `chi-square-ex1.txt`. Click "Analyse." See Fig. 6.25. The result is the same, $\chi^2 = 1.462$. However, with GoStats and other statistics programs, probabilities are computed directly, thus avoiding the need to compare the test statistic with values in a look-up table. In Fig. 6.25, we find $p = .4814$. Since $p > .05$, the conclusion is the same: no difference in the way males and females scroll using desktop computer systems.

6.3.4 Example 2

In this example, the outcome is statistically significant with post hoc comparisons used to determine which conditions are significantly different from one another.

A researcher wishes to investigate whether students, professors, and parents have the same opinion on the subject of mobile phone usage during classroom lectures. To study this, a large number of students, professors, and parents are randomly sampled and asked if they agree that students should be allowed to use mobile phones during classroom lectures. The categories are opinion (agree, disagree) and person (student, professor, parent). In all, 300 people were sampled, including 40 students, 60 professors, and 200 parents. The responses were 120 agree and 180 disagree. The contingency table in Fig. 6.26 shows the number of responses organized by opinion and person.

Evidently, respondents overall feel that the use of mobile phones during classroom lectures should not be allowed. Furthermore, the responses are in the same direction

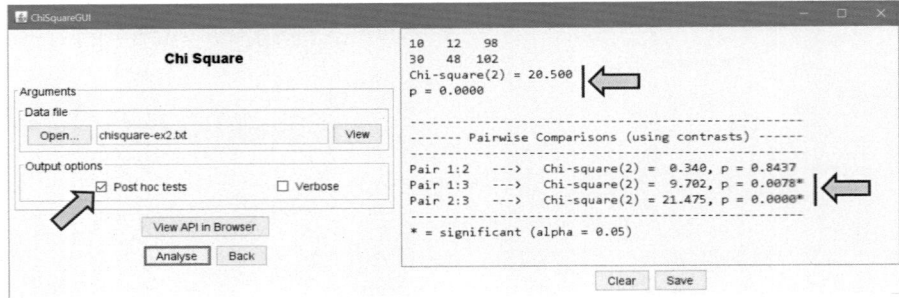

FIGURE 6.27

Chi-square test including post hoc pairwise comparisons.

for all three categories of people. However, a closer look at the table reveals some variation among the categories. Although three times more students disagreed than agreed, only a few more parents disagreed than agreed. To determine if the differences in response are statistically significant, a chi-square test is used.

The calculations leading to the chi-square statistic are identical to those demonstrated for the last example. The result in this case is $\chi^2 = 20.5$ with $df = 2$. With reference to Fig. 6.24, the chi-square statistic exceeds the critical value both for $\alpha = .05$ (5.99) and for $\alpha = .001$ (13.82). Clearly, there is a difference in opinions among students, professors, and parents on the question of interest. However, since there were three categories of people, a post hoc pairwise comparisons test is required to determine which categories differ from one another.

The ChiSquare utility within GoStats includes a "Post hoc tests" option to perform the comparisons. See Fig. 6.27. The comparisons indicate statistical significance ($p < .05$) for the 1:3 and 2:3 comparisons. Thus, on the question at issue there is a difference in opinion between students and parents and between professors and parents. However, there is no difference in opinion between students and professors.[12]

6.3.5 Example 3

This example uses data published in the ACM SIGCHI conference proceedings. Ayyavu and Jensen [15] researched tools to assist users in determining if web sites are considered trustworthy (free of spam, predators, etc.). In particular, they were interested in differences in the ratings provided by community-based tools vs. heuristics-based tools. They examined Web Of Trust (WOT) as a community-based tool and McAfee's Site Advisor (MSA) as a heuristics-based tool. The tools were presented

---

[12] The calculations for the pairwise comparisons are not described here. Interested readers are directed to Glass and Hopkins [146, pp. 391-392]. The data in this example are from a chi-square test described by Glass and Hopkins pertaining to the attitude of school superintendents, teachers, and principals toward collective bargaining.

System	Set	Sample Size	Samples
WOT	Good	16,968	90.79%
	Bad	1,722	9.21%
MSA	Good	18,062	96.21%
	Bad	628	3.36%

(a)

```
16968    1722
18062     628
Chi-square(1) = 543.458
p = 0.0000
```

(b)

FIGURE 6.28

Comparison of web site assessments between Web Of Trust (WOT) and McAfee's Site Advisor (MSA). (a) Data (from Table 1 in [15]). (b) GoStats chi-square test.

with 20,000 web sites and for each site the tools provided an assessment of good (safe), bad (not safe), or unsure.

After removing sites for which WOT or MSA gave an unsure rating, 18,690 remained. Ayyavu and Jensen presented the results for these sites in a contingency table, as shown in Fig. 6.28a. Thankfully, most of the sites were deemed good, or safe. WOT rated 9.21% of the sites bad, or not safe. The figure was 3.36% for MSA. That seems like a substantial difference. To determine if the difference was statistically significant, a chi-square test was used. The result was $\chi^2 = 543.5$ with $df = 1$. This is confirmed in GoStats (see Fig. 6.28b). That's above the critical value of $\chi^2 = 3.84$ for $p < .05$ (see Fig. 6.24). Ayyavu and Jensen concluded that there was a statistically significant difference between the assessments provided by the tools. In fact, they reported that the difference was "highly significant," noting that the chi-square statistic exceeded the $p < .0001$ critical value [15, p. 2309].

*****

A contingency table combined with a chi-square test is a simple and effective way to study relationships in HCI research. The relationships are frequently between naturally occurring attributes of people (males vs. females, Mac users vs. PC users, etc.) and their behaviours (e.g., preferred scrolling method, texting habits, etc.). But, as the last example illustrates, the attributes may also involve systems and the behaviours of systems. A few additional examples of chi-square tests in the HCI literature are hereby cited [26,236,247,407]. See also student exercises 6-6, 6-7, and 6-8.

6.4 Lilliefors test for normality

In HCI research, it is sometimes assumed or desired that participant responses follow a distribution, usually the normal distribution. Many responses are of interest, such as task completion times, selections coordinates, scores on a test, and so on. Given data for the responses, it would be useful to have a statistical procedure to test the hypothesis that the data are normally distributed. In this section, we present such a test.

There are several statistical procedures to test the assumption of normality in a data set. A well-known example is the Kolmogorov-Smirnov (K-S) test for normality. However, the calculations for the K-S test use the population mean and variance. Often, the researcher wishes to test the assumption of normality without specifying a particular normal distribution. A variation of the K-S test is the Lilliefors tests which uses the sample mean and variance in the calculations. Both tests evaluate the null hypothesis that a sample of data points is normally distributed. If the goal is to test the assumption of normality, without prior knowledge of the population mean and variance, then the Lilliefors test is a good option.

The calculation of the test statistic (M) is the same for the K-S test and the Lilliefors test, except in the latter case the calculation uses the sample mean and standard deviation.[13] Therefore, the Lilliefors test is more conservative and bears a greater likelihood of accepting the null hypothesis. To compensate for this and to maintain the desired alpha, the Lilliefors test uses a more stringent set of critical values in assessing the test statistic.

As with the chi-square test, the Lilliefors test compares observed and expected values. However, the comparisons are not between the counts among nominal-scale attributes of people, systems, interaction techniques, or such. Instead, the comparisons are between the observed and expected cumulative probabilities in two distributions. The expected distribution is the normal distribution, as represented in standardized z-scores. The observed distribution is developed from the sample data. The Lilliefors test is now described through examples in the HCI literature.

6.4.1 **Example 1**

A researcher is studying relationships among friends on social networking sites. As part of the research, users are given a questionnaire that includes the Big Five Inventory to assess personality traits [228]. The summary responses for 15 users to the item on "agreeableness" are as follows:

33, 28, 31, 33, 33, 32, 34, 33, 41, 43, 42, 34, 36, 37, 25

The mean of the responses is 34.3 ($SD = 4.9$).[14] The researcher wishes to determine if the distribution of the responses is normally distributed. This is demonstrated in

---

[13] The calculations are not presented here. Interested readers are directed to numerous online sources, such as Wikipedia. A recommended published source is Sheskin [447, pp. 261-275]. Additional information is in the API for the Lilliefors test in GoStats.

[14] This example is based on Staiano et al.'s [468] research on the relationship between social network structure and personality. They administered the Big Five Inventory to 53 users. Using the Lilliefors test for normality, they concluded that the responses were normally distributed for all five personality traits (agreeableness, conscientiousness, extroversion, neuroticism, and openness).

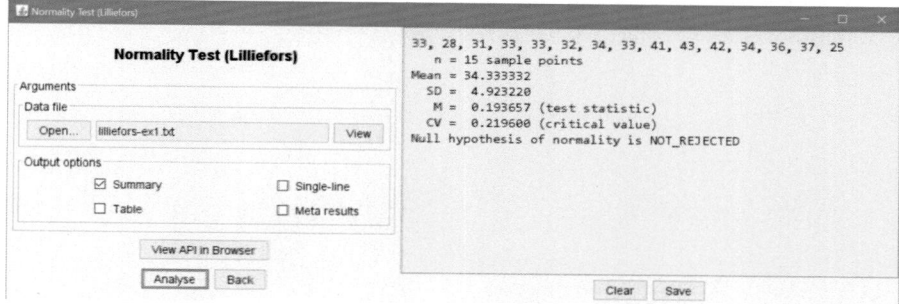

FIGURE 6.29

Lilliefors test for normality on responses from 15 users on a questionnaire item on personality.

Fig. 6.29 using the Lilliefors test in GoStats. The test statistic is $M = 0.1937$. This is compared against a critical value extracted from a look-up table built-in to the GoStats utility. For $n = 15$ and $\alpha = .05$, the critical value $CV = 0.2196$. Since $M < CV$, the null hypothesis of normality is not rejected: It is concluded that the responses follow a normal distribution.

6.4.2 Example 2

A researcher is investigating target selection using fingers on smartphones. In an experiment with 16 participants, targets are selected by tapping back and forth 20 times between pairs of targets presented on the display. This is an example of the reciprocal tapping task introduced by Fitts [125]. See Fig. 6.30. Over the course of the experiment, multiple sequences of 20 trials are performed using different movement amplitudes and target widths.

For one sequence, the following data are logged:

-13.9, -13.9, -26.6, -7.5, -14.6, -13.5, -15.2, 33.1, -10.7, 36.8
2.4, -12.2, -1.5, -24.5, 21.8, 17.3, 1.9, 23.7, -6.7, -11.0

The data are the x-coordinates of selection, mapped so that 0.0 is the centre of the target. Negative values are selections on the near side, positive values are selections on the far side. Although the data include selections near the centre of the target and selections on either side, the researcher questions whether the data follow a normal distribution. To determine this, the Lilliefors test is used. See Fig. 6.31. As seen in the last three lines of output, the test statistic ($M = 0.2054$) exceeds the critical value ($CV = 0.1920$); therefore, the null hypothesis is rejected. The conclusion is that the selection coordinates for the sequence of trials are not normally distributed.

One issue to consider in this example is whether the selection coordinates include outliers. Were the responses, as a whole, just slightly deviate – enough to yield a non-normal distribution? Or, were there one or two particular responses that were so

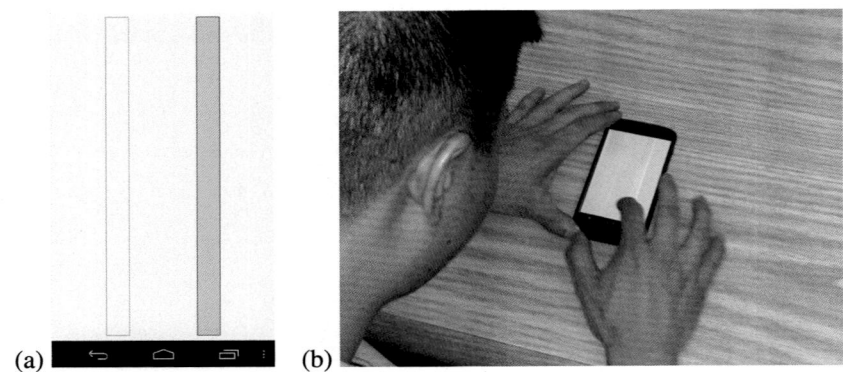

FIGURE 6.30

Target selection using the finger on a touchscreen smartphone (from [302]). (a) Screen snap. (b) A participant performing the task.

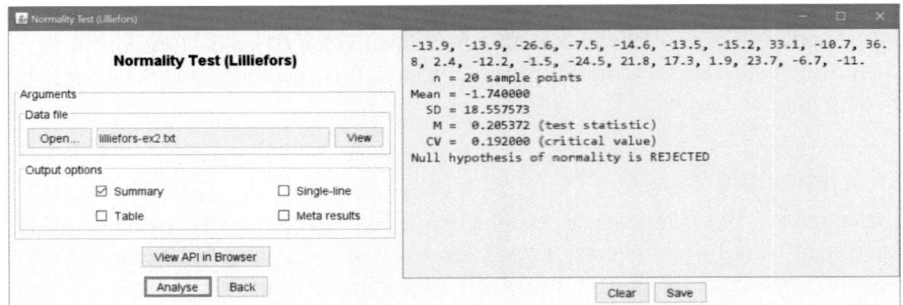

FIGURE 6.31

Lilliefors test for normality on selection coordinates from a target selection task.

deviate, or abnormal, as to be deemed outliers? This issue was studied in Chapter 2 (The Human Factor). See section 2.7.6 (p. 83).

Most sources detailing the K-S or Lilliefors tests include graphs contrasting the observed and expected cumulative probabilities. Fig. 6.32 is an example for the analysis in Fig. 6.31. The test statistic (M) is the largest vertical distance between the observed and expected cumulative distributions.

6.4.3 Example 3

Example 2 tested the normality assumption for a single sequence of 20 trials. However, the experiment included several independent variables and multiple blocks for each condition [302]. In all, there were 1920 sequences of trials. The Lilliefors utility in GoStats has options to analyse and summarize many data sequences in one pass.

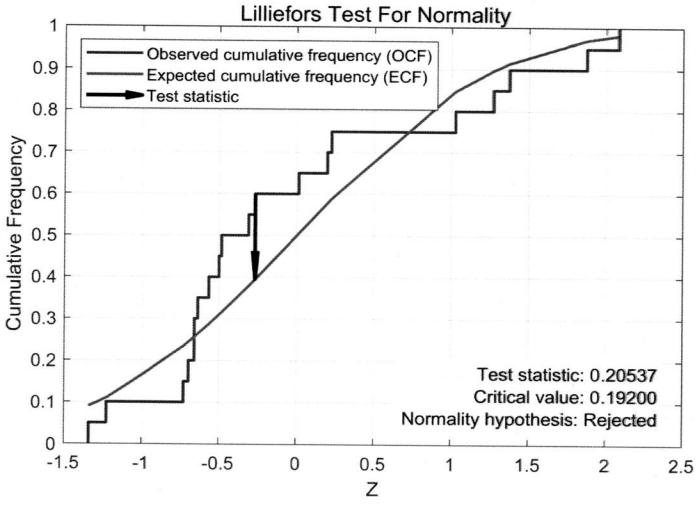

FIGURE 6.32

Observed vs. expected cumulative probability distributions for Example 2 (Fig. 6.31). The test statistic (*M*) is the largest vertical distance between the two lines.

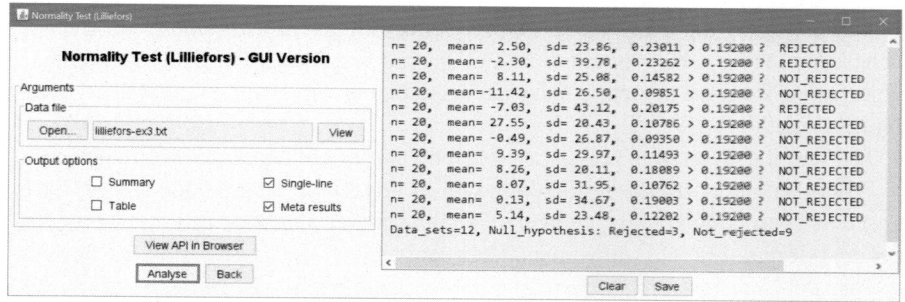

FIGURE 6.33

Lilliefors test for multiple sequences of data.

As an example, the file `lilliefors-ex3.txt` contains the data for 12 sequences of trials from this experiment. If the utility is run using the "Single-line" and "Meta results" options, the output summarizes the analyses over all sequences. See Fig. 6.33. The single-line output option gives, for each sequence, the number of samples, the mean, the standard deviation, the test statistic, and the critical value. These are followed by the result of the test of the null hypothesis: REJECTED or NOT_REJECTED. The Meta results option (last line in Fig. 6.33) summarizes the analyses. In the example, nine sequences were deemed normally distributed and three sequences were deemed not normally distributed.

Design	Conditions	
	2	3 or more
Between-subjects (independent samples)	Mann-Whitney U	Kruskal-Wallis
Within-subjects (correlated samples)	Wilcoxon Signed-Ranks	Friedman

FIGURE 6.34

Choosing a non-parametric test based on experiment design and number of conditions.

Other HCI research using the Lilliefors test is hereby cited [70,165,182]. See also student exercises 6-10 and 6-11 at the end of this chapter.

6.5 Non-parametric tests for ordinal data

Non-parametric tests make no assumptions about the probability distribution of the population from which the underlying data are obtained. In the examples ahead, non-parametric tests are described as they are typically used in HCI research – to analyse ordinal (and sometimes interval) data. The data are typically obtained through questionnaires (e.g., using a Likert scale), preference ratings, or assessments on a scale. Rather than using direct measurement of human responses, the data are obtained subjectively, from participants, or using heuristics or other non-empirical or semi-empirical methods.

The four most common non-parametric procedures are the Mann-Whitney U test, the Wilcoxon Signed-Ranks test, the Kruskal-Wallis test, and the Friedman test. Each is used in a particular context, depending on the number of test conditions and the experiment design. Fig. 6.34 illustrates. Between-subjects and within-subjects designs generate data that are from *independent samples* and *correlated samples*, respectively, as shown in the figure. Between-subjects designs generate independent samples because different participants are tested with each condition. Within-subjects designs generate correlated samples (aka dependent samples) because the same participants are tested with each condition. Bear in mind that the conditions are levels of a single independent variable (factor) in the experiment.

The non-parametric tests in Fig. 6.34 are demonstrated below through a series of hypothetical examples. As the problems are described and the data presented, it will be apparent which test is appropriate. Since the Kruskal-Wallis and Friedman tests operate on three or more conditions, a statistically significant outcome is usually followed with post hoc pairwise comparisons. This is also demonstrated.

For each example, two versions of the data analysis are provided. One uses a commercial statistics application. The other uses the GoStats utility available on this book's web site. The results are identical for both analyses. Let's begin.

Mac Users	PC Users
2	4
3	6
2	5
4	4
9	8
2	3
5	4
3	2
4	4
3	5

FIGURE 6.35

Assessments of the political leanings for 10 Mac users and 10 PC users. See text for discussion.

6.5.1 Mann-Whitney U test

A researcher seeks to determine if there is a difference in the political leaning of Mac users vs. PC users. Are Mac or PC users more likely to have political views leaning to the "left" or "right?" The experimenter randomly selects 10 Mac users and 10 PC users.[15] The participants are interviewed and asked a variety of questions about their political views. Each participant is assessed on a linear scale from 1 (*very left*) to 10 (*very right*) with the results stored in a file as a table with 10 rows and 2 columns. The first column contains the assessments for the Mac users, the second column for the PC users. The data are given in Fig. 6.35.

The mean scores (not shown) are 3.7 for the Mac users and 4.5 for the PC users. Evidently, the PC users are a little more "right-leaning." But, is the difference real or is it just an artefact of the variability in responses? The data are potentially interval-scale, but the researcher senses that the intervals between successive codes are not equal – because they are based on a qualitative assessment. The data are at least ordinal; so, a non-parametric test is chosen to answer this question. There are two conditions and the assignment is between-subjects, therefore the appropriate test is Mann-Whitney U (see Fig. 6.34). The results are shown in Fig. 6.36 using a commercial app and using GoStats. There are numerous behind-the-scenes data manipulations and calculations leading to the test statistic, U.[16] The output also includes a normalized z-score (calculated from U) and p, the probability of obtaining the observed data under the null hypothesis of "no difference." Two z and p values are

---

[15] For simplicity, the number of participants in the examples is on the low side. Research where only questionnaire data are collected often includes substantially more participants or respondents than used in the examples.

[16] For readers interested in the details, there are many sites providing the step-by-step calculations leading to U. A good published source for all the tests described herein is Sheskin's *Handbook of Parametric and Nonparametric Statistical Procedures* [447].

Mann-Whitney U for Response
Grouping Variable: Category for Political_Leaning

U	31.000
U Prime	69.000
Z-Value	-1.436
P-Value	.1509
Tied Z-Value	-1.469
Tied P-Value	.1418
# Ties	4

(a)

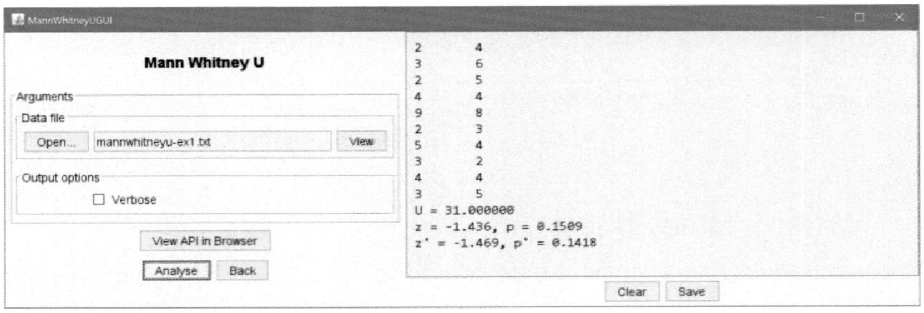

(b)

FIGURE 6.36

Mann-Whitney U test for the political leanings of Mac and PC users. (a) Commercial app. (b) GoStats.

provided. The second set includes a "correction for ties." In most cases, the difference with the corrected values is minor.

For the example, $U = 31.0$ with $p = .1418$ (corrected for ties). Since p is greater than .05, the differences in the assessments fail to meet the customary threshold for statistical significance. The conclusion is that there is no difference in the political leanings of Mac users and PC users ($U = 31.0$, $p > .05$).

6.5.2 Wilcoxon Signed-Ranks test

A researcher is interested in comparing two new designs for media players. There is a particular interest in knowing if the designs differ in "cool appeal" for young users. Ten young tech-savvy participants are recruited and given demos of the two media players (MPA, MPB). The participants are asked to rate the designs for "cool appeal" on a linear scale from 1 (*not cool at all*) to 10 (*really cool*). The results are given in Fig. 6.37.

The mean ratings (not shown) are 6.4 for media player A and 3.7 for B. It seems media player A fares quite well compared to media player B. However, there was some variability in the responses, so perhaps the difference was just a chance outcome. To test if the differences in the ratings are real, a statistical test is used. Since the data are interval-scale (see discussion for Example 1), a non-parametric test is chosen. There are two test conditions and the design is within-subjects, therefore the

Participant	Media Player	
	MPA	MPB
1	3	3
2	6	6
3	4	3
4	10	3
5	6	5
6	5	6
7	9	2
8	7	4
9	6	2
10	8	3

FIGURE 6.37

Ratings for "cool appeal" of two media players. See text for discussion.

Wilcoxon Signed Rank Test for MPA, MPB

# 0 Differences	2
# Ties	2
Z-Value	-2.240
P-Value	.0251
Tied Z-Value	-2.254
Tied P-Value	.0242

(a)

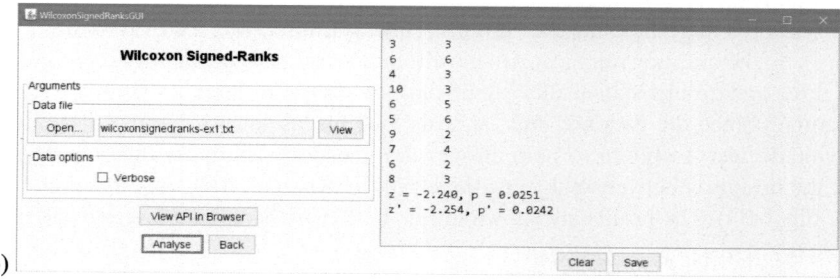

(b)

FIGURE 6.38

Wilcoxon Signed-Ranks test for the "cool appeal" ratings for two media players. (a) Commercial app. (b) GoStats.

Wilcoxon Signed-Ranks test is appropriate (see Fig. 6.34). The results are shown in Fig. 6.38 using a commercial app and using GoStats.

The test statistic for the Wilcoxon Signed-Ranks test is a normalized z score. For the example, $z = -2.254$ with $p = .0242$ (corrected for ties). Since p is less than .05, the customary threshold for statistical significance is exceeded. The conclusion is that the two media players differ in "cool appeal" ($z = -2.254$, $p < .05$).

Age Group		
20-29	30-39	40-49
9	7	4
9	3	5
4	5	5
9	3	2
6	2	2
3	1	1
8	4	2
9	7	2

FIGURE 6.39

Acceptability scores by three age groups for a GPS tracker. See text for discussion.

6.5.3 Kruskal-Wallis test

The designers of a new vehicle GPS tracker are wondering if age will be a factor in the acceptance of the product. They decide to conduct a small experiment to find out. Eight participants are recruited from each of three age groups: 20-29 years, 30-39 years, and 40-49 years. The participants are given a demo of the new GPS tracker, and then asked if they liked it enough to consider purchasing it for personal use. They respond on a linear scale from 1 (*definitely no*) to 10 (*definitely yes*). The results are given in Fig. 6.39.

The mean scores by age group (not shown) are 7.1 (20-29), 4.0 (30-39), and 2.9 (40-49). There is a difference, since the 20-29 year age group gave higher acceptability scores than the other two groups. However, there was also variability in the scores. So the question remains: Are the differences in the acceptability scores among the three age groups statistically significant, or are the differences simply a chance outcome? Since the data are interval-scale (see discussion for Example 1), a non-parametric test is chosen to help answer the question. There are three age groups and the design is between-subjects, therefore the Kruskal-Wallis test is appropriate (see Fig. 6.34). The results are shown in Fig. 6.40 using a commercial app and using GoStats.

The test statistic is H, which follows a chi-square distribution with $df = k - 1$ (k is the number of groups). In the example, $H = 9.605$ with $p = .0082$ (corrected for ties). Since p is below the customary threshold for statistical significance (.05), the test shows a significant effect of age group on the acceptability of the GPS tracker design ($\chi^2 = 9.605$, $df = 2$, $p < .05$).

There are three age groups, therefore post hoc pairwise comparisons are needed to determine which age groups differ significantly from one another. This is available in GoStats by checking the "Post hoc tests" box in Fig. 6.40b.[17] As evident, only the 1:3 pair was deemed statistically significant. The acceptability scores for the three

---

[17] The pairwise comparisons test was implemented using the procedure described by Siegel and Castellan [452, pp. 213-214].

Kruskal-Wallis Test for Acceptability
Grouping Variable: Category for Age_Group

DF	2
# Groups	3
# Ties	7
H	9.421
P-Value	.0090
H corrected for ties	9.605
Tied P-Value	.0082

(a)

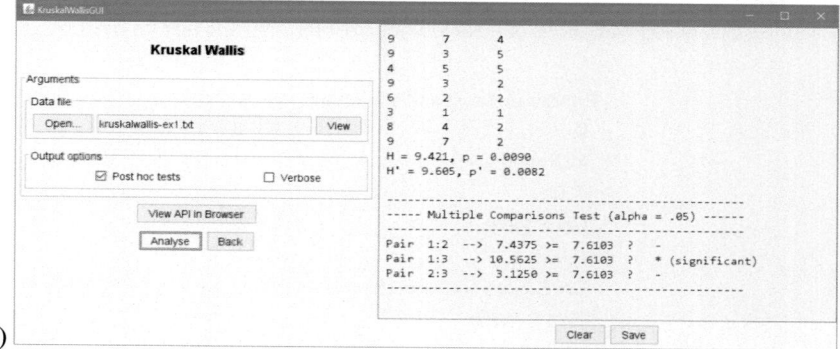

(b)

FIGURE 6.40

Kruskal-Wallis test for acceptability of a GPS tracker by three age groups. (a) Commercial app. (b) GoStats (with post hoc comparisons).

GPS trackers differed significantly only between the 20-29 year group and the 40-49 year group.

6.5.4 Friedman test

A researcher implemented four variations of a search engine interface (A, B, C, and D). Each uses a different dialogue for users to build queries. The researcher wishes to know if the interfaces differ in the quality of results they produce. Eight participants are recruited and are given a demonstration of each interface and then asked to do a series of search tasks. The "quality of results" is assessed for each participant and for each search engine. The assessment uses a linear scale from 1 (*very poor*) to 100 (*very good*). A Latin square was used to balance the order of conditions, but this isn't important here. The results are given in Fig. 6.41.

The mean scores (not shown) for the search engines A to D were 71.0, 68.1, 60.9, and 69.8, respectively. The spread is only about ten points between the highest and lowest assessments, so it is unclear if there is any difference in the quality of results between the four interfaces. Nevertheless, it is worthwhile testing for significant

Participant	Search Interface			
	A	B	C	D
1	66	80	67	73
2	79	64	61	66
3	67	58	61	67
4	71	73	54	75
5	72	66	59	78
6	68	67	57	69
7	71	68	59	64
8	74	69	69	66

FIGURE 6.41

Quality of results for four variations of a search engine interface. See text for discussion.

Friedman Test for 4 Variables

DF	3
# Groups	4
# Ties	2
Chi Square	8.475
P-Value	.0372
Chi Square corrected for ties	8.692
Tied P-Value	.0337

(a)

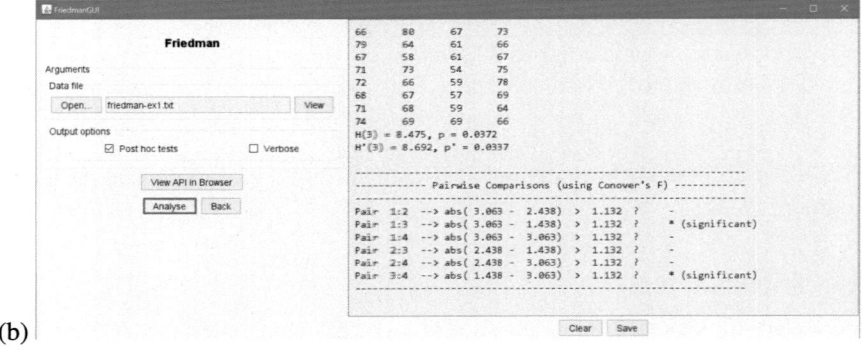

(b)

FIGURE 6.42

Friedman test for quality of results for four search engine interfaces. (a) Commercial app. (b) GoStats (with post hoc comparisons).

differences. Since the data are interval-scale (see discussion for Example 1), a nonparametric test is chosen to investigate further. There are four test conditions and the conditions were assigned within-subjects, therefore the Friedman test is appropriate (see Fig. 6.34). The results are shown in Fig. 6.42 using a commercial app and using GoStats.

The Friedman test statistic is H, which follows the chi-square distribution with $k - 1$ degrees of freedom (k = number of conditions). As seen in the figure, there is indeed a difference in the quality of results between the four search engine interfaces ($\chi^2 = 8.692$, $df = 3$, $p < .05$).

Post hoc pairwise comparisons are needed to determine which search engine interfaces are significantly different from one another. This is available in GoStats by checking the "Post hoc tests" box in Fig. 6.42b.[18] With four conditions, there are six pairwise comparisons. Only two were significant: 1:3 and 3:4. So, significant differences in the search results were found between interfaces C and A and between interfaces C and D.

6.6 **Discussion**

In the examples above, the data were summarized using the means (averages) for each condition. This is common in HCI research for data of this sort. It is also valid. Since the assessment scales were described as "linear," the data are interval-scale. Therefore, the mean is the correct statistic for central tendency. However, many HCI experiments use questionnaires with responses on a Likert-scale or some other combination of numbers and verbal tags. Since the response items are subject to human interpretation, the data may not be interval scale in the strictest sense (cf. temperature). If the scales are non-linear, then the quality of the data is compromised. In the worst case, the data degrade to ordinal and the appropriate statistic for central tendency is the median (middle value) or mode (most common value). In some research papers, questionnaire responses are summarized using the mean, while in other papers the median is used. On this subject, we enter a gray area, with different opinions on which measure is the correct measure. Some claim outright that Likert-scale responses are ordinal and that it is simply wrong to report means (e.g., [418]). The truth is likely somewhere in the middle (i.e., between interval and ordinal).

The non-parametric tests demonstrated above are limited to single-factor analyses. The Friedman test, for example, can analyse many conditions; but, the conditions are all levels of a single factor. The test cannot be used for multi-factor analyses, such as a 2×3 design or a $4 \times 2 \times 2$ design. (Of course, the parametric ANOVA is applicable to multi-factor experiments.) Although there are extensions of non-parametric tests to multi-factor experiments [240,521], the value of these tools to HCI research is limited. Non-parametric tests are most commonly used to analyse questionnaire data or ratings, as in the examples above. Questionnaires are rarely administered for each condition in a multi-factor experiment (e.g., $4 \times 2 \times 2 = 16$ times). Typically, a single questionnaire is used when testing is finished, with the goal of gathering participants' comments and preference ratings on the conditions tested (perhaps in a multi-factor experiment). In this case, the non-parametric tests demonstrated above are fine. One

---

[18] The test was implemented using Conover's F at $\alpha = .05$ for a two-tailed test.

possible exception is the use of non-parametric tests for ratio-scale data, which we discuss in the next section.

This section demonstrated the use of non-parametric procedures for hypothesis testing, as typically used in HCI research. An example was provided for each of the most common non-parametric tests: Mann-Whitney U, Wilcoxon Signed-Ranks, Kruskal-Wallis, and Friedman (see Fig. 6.34). See as well the student exercises at the end of this chapter.

6.7 Parametric vs. non-parametric tests

When alternative tests are available to study data in an experiment, a rationale is needed to choose among the possibilities. For statistical tests, the guiding principle is that of power. Statistical power is about improving the odds of getting it right with the null hypothesis: rejecting the null hypothesis when it should be rejected and not rejecting it when there is insufficient basis to. However there are other issues to consider. Sheskin [447, p. 109] suggests that an appropriate test is one where the measurement requirements of the test are consistent with the measurement scale of the data gathered. Of the four scales of measurement – nominal, ordinal, interval, ratio (see Fig. 4.9, p. 179) – the pairings are simple. If the research data are ordinal, then a statistical test that operates on ordinal data is a good choice. Similarly, if the experimental data are ratio, then a statistical test that operates on ratio data is a good choice. In HCI, there is a common practice that cuts across this simple principle. In this final section on hypothesis testing in HCI research, we venture into territory that was declared off-limits in this chapter's introduction: controversy. The incursion will be brief, however.

Parametric tests, such as the analysis of variance, assume the data are sampled from a probability distribution, such as the normal distribution. Provided this assumption and a few others are met, parametric tests have more statistical power and are more accurate and more precise than non-parametric tests. However, if the assumptions are not met, then the researcher must decide on the appropriate course of action. There are three possibilities: (i) proceed with the parametric test, (ii) transform or clean the data in some manner to correct the violations and then proceed with the parametric test, or (iii) use a non-parametric test. All three options have advantages and disadvantages. Proceeding with a parametric test on data that potentially violate underlying assumptions is a common approach. This may occur because researchers don't understand or don't have access to statistical tools that test the assumptions. As well some researchers feel parametric tests are reasonably robust to violations and, in any event, the underlying assumptions are rarely met when analysing real data [117]. Researchers with a particular concern for violations in assumptions are likely to choose one of the latter two options. However, both come at a cost.

Transforming data using a log or power function is an effective way to correct the violations in assumptions. However, as Siegel asks, "will the process of 'normalizing' the distribution by altering the numerical values of the scores cause a distortion in the experimental effect under investigation?" [451, p. 14]. He notes that this is a question the investigator may not be able to answer. Sheskin adds "one might view a data transformation as little more than a convenient mechanism for 'cooking' data until it allows a researcher to achieve a specific goal," while allowing "when used judiciously, data transformation can be a valuable tool" [447, p. 483]. So, the issues in transforming data are a matter for deeper consideration.

The third option is to proceed with a non-parametric test. Conveniently, this approach sidesteps questions about the probability distribution of the underlying data. However, the decision to use a non-parametric test on ratio-scale data is not to be entered into lightly. Let's consider this point further.

For ordinal data, such as rankings or qualitative assessments on a scale, non-parametric tests are the logical choice. For ratio data, such as measurements of human performance, parametric tests are preferred, in part due to their increased power (the ability to reject a false null hypothesis) but also by the simple standard that the test-to-data pairing is correct. But, do ratio-scale human performance measurements meet the requirements for parametric data? Put another way, are measurements such as the time or errors in completing tasks normally distributed? The answer to this question is never "yes" in a precise way. The data are samples and therefore inherit a multitude of haphazard, even capricious, tendencies. If the samples are expected to bring forth precise properties of a probability distribution, such as normality, then disappointment looms.

There are numerous tests for normality, skewness, etc., and small sets of empirically sampled data will frequently fail. If the data are measures on a dependent variable collected in an experiment, a researcher may conclude that the data are not parametric and then proceed with a non-parametric test. But, this may be unnecessary or unwise.

We noted above that non-parametric tests collapse data into ranks. As Sheskin notes "when a researcher elects to transform a set of interval/ratio data into ranks, information is sacrificed" [447, p. 531]. Let's demonstrate through an example. Consider research comparing the accuracy of three eye tracking methods, A, B, and C. In an experiment, participants do some gaze-select trials while their accuracy is measured. The accuracy was 94% for method A, 17% for method B, and 15% for method C. There is clearly a large difference in the measures: Method A was much more accurate than methods B or C. But, only a few participants were tested and there was variability in the data. It is decided to test the data to determine if the differences are statistically significant. Fig. 6.43a illustrates the ratio data that are compared if a parametric test is used. Fig. 6.43b illustrates the rank-ordered data that are compared if the researcher proceeds with a non-parametric test. Clearly, information is lost when ratio data are downgraded to ranks.

So, choosing a non-parametric test for ratio-scale measurements that deviate from normality is to replace one deficiency with another. Restraint is advised. The procedures and instrumentation put in place to collect ratio-scale human performance data in experimental research should not be muted so casually – as occurs if ratio data are downgraded to ordinal data (ranks). Let's examine a few related points.

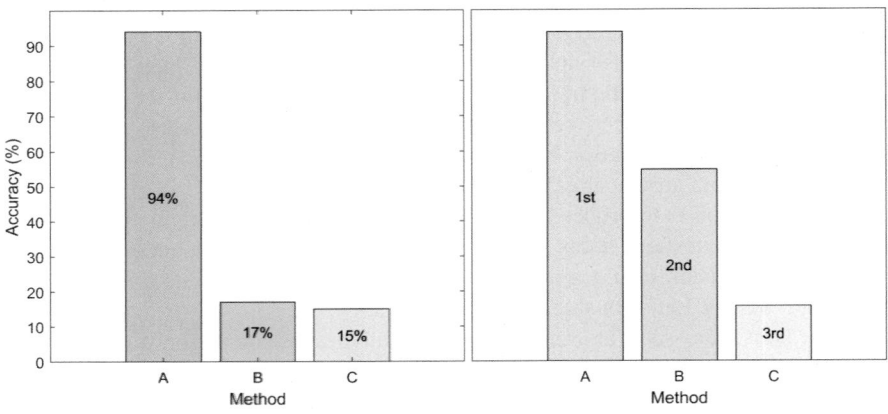

FIGURE 6.43

Loss of information. Method A fared much better than methods B or C (left). However, this is lost if the data are converted to ranks (right).

In the 1950s and early 1960s, applied statistics in the social sciences experienced a broad migration to non-parametric tests. However, abandoning parametric tests – mainly the parametric ANOVA – in favour of non-parametric tests was largely unnecessary, as noted by Glass et al. [147]. The shift occurred because researchers asked the wrong question. They asked "Are the assumptions of the parametric ANOVA met?" instead of "What are the consequences of the inevitable violations in the parametric ANOVA?" The first of these two questions is easy to answer, as there are numerous "assumption tests" for parametric data.[19] However, the second question presents formidable challenges. For one, standards of rigour necessarily degrade when a researcher moves from studying a mathematical model under defined assumptions to studying that same model under violations to the assumptions. Examining the consequences of violations in assumptions requires empirical data, which are deviate, or simulated data, which are deviate by design. It is a difficult and highly complex assignment. But, all is not lost. Considerable research into these issues exists (although not in HCI). In the end, there is evidence that the parametric ANOVA is reasonably robust to violations in the underlying assumptions [250].[20] Even with small sample sizes (e.g., $n = 3$), the consequences of violations in the assumptions underpinning the ANOVA are usually minor.

---

[19] Tests commonly used include the Kolmogorov-Smirnov test, the χ^2 goodness-of-fit test, Levene's test, Bartlett's test, the Shapiro-Wilk test, and Mauchly's test for sphericity. It is worth noting that these tests are themselves subject to assumptions. Some statisticians claim the implementation of assumptions tests in commercial software (e.g., SPSS) is fatally flawed and recommend these tests never be used [117, p. 594].

[20] Readers interested in examining this point further are directed to the survey of related studies by Glass et al. [147, p. 246-255]. Of course, there are contrary opinions (see [117] for a summary).

In eschewing a parametric test, some researchers are clearly hesitant in fully adopting a non-parametric approach. Munteanu et al. reported,

> *Although we tested the data for normalcy, a non-parametric (distribution-free) test, Friedman's Rank Test for correlated samples, was also run and chi-square scores were computed, in order to confirm the validity of the F-scores obtained through ANOVA.*

[361, p. 497]

The results of both the parametric and non-parametric tests were given. As it turns out, the tests lead to the same conclusion. Perugini et al. reported,

> *Since the distribution of task completion times was significantly different from a normal distribution, we also used the Mann-Whitney U test for non-parametric statistical significance. However, since the patterns of significant differences ($p <$ .05) of the eight tasks were the same for the ANOVA and the Mann-Whitney U, we present the results for the ANOVA.*

[394, p. 968]

In both of these examples, we see a hint of caution – that there is an issue around the use of a non-parametric test on ratio-scale data. So, which is the correct test? At this juncture, it would be remiss to recommend strict testing of ratio data using a parametric test (despite violations in assumptions) or a non-parametric test (despite loss of information and a reduction in statistical power). Arguably, the balance tips in favour of parametric tests due to the added precision and statistical power. However, the practice of Munteanu et al. [361] and Perugini et al. [394] is laudable: Examine both avenues, consider the outcome for each, and attune for possible contradictions.

*****

This chapter introduced hypothesis testing, as typically used in HCI experiments. Our treatment of these subjects was limited but practical, with the intent to demonstrate the basic ideas underlying the tests and the mechanisms for doing them. The next chapter examines descriptive and predictive models of human-computer interaction.

A web site is available as a resource accompanying this book's second edition:

- http://www.yorku.ca/mack/HCIbook2e

Student exercises

6-1 The data in Fig. 6.44 are from a hypothetical experiment comparing texting speeds on a smartphone while sitting vs. walking. Eight participants were

Participant	Texting Speed (wpm)	
	Sitting	Walking
P1	13	10
P2	14	11
P3	12	9
P4	9	13
P5	15	14
P6	11	8
P7	18	9
P8	9	11

FIGURE 6.44

Student exercise on texting speed.

tested.[21] Instead of counterbalancing, learning effects were offset by administering a practice session before testing. Perform an ANOVA on the data to determine if there is a difference in texting speed while sitting or walking. Prepare a brief report or slide show presentation on your findings.

6-2 A research project investigated the effect of distraction on driving. A driving simulator was used with the mean driving error (in pixels) measured under three distraction conditions: no distraction, call answering, and texting. Twelve participants were tested. The participants were divided into three groups with the distraction conditions administered according to a Latin square to offset order effects. The data are shown in Fig. 6.45. Perform an ANOVA on the data to determine if there is an effect of distraction condition on driving error. Also, determine if counterbalancing using a Latin square adequately offset any order effect that might have occurred. Prepare a brief report or slide show presentation on your findings. Include a chart to illustrate the result and post hoc multiple comparisons, if appropriate.

6-3 Are gamers more adept than non-gamers in manipulating objects in 3D graphics environments? This question was investigated in an experiment with 10 participants, including 5 non-gamers and 5 gamers. Participants performed five object-manipulation trials with task completion times logged for follow-on analyses. The five tasks were of equal difficulty. The data are in Fig. 6.46. Perform an ANOVA on the data to determine if there is an effect of participant background on task completion time. As well, investigate whether learning occurred over the five tasks and whether the progress in learning, if any, was the same for both groups of participants. Prepare a brief report or slide show presentation on your findings. Include a chart to illustrate the results.

---

[21] To minimize the data transcription requirements, the number of participants in the student exercises is generally less than what is expected for real experiments.

Participant	Mean Driving Error (pixels)			Group
	No Distraction	Call Answering	Texting	
P1	10	10	17	G1
P2	14	11	13	G1
P3	11	9	14	G1
P4	9	13	11	G1
P5	13	14	10	G2
P6	11	8	18	G2
P7	14	9	14	G2
P8	9	11	16	G2
P9	7	14	15	G3
P10	9	11	17	G3
P11	10	9	11	G3
P12	12	14	15	G3

FIGURE 6.45

Student exercise on distracted driving.

Participant	Task Completion Time (s)					Background
	T1	T2	T3	T4	T5	
P1	23	21	16	17	15	Non-gamer
P2	24	21	20	17	14	Non-gamer
P3	24	20	21	15	13	Non-gamer
P4	26	21	20	17	16	Non-gamer
P5	17	18	20	15	14	Non-gamer
P6	19	16	15	14	15	Gamer
P7	20	16	15	13	14	Gamer
P8	16	16	14	13	11	Gamer
P9	15	15	12	14	12	Gamer
P10	17	16	13	14	12	Gamer

FIGURE 6.46

Student exercise on 3D object manipulation over five trials for gamers and non-gamers.

6-4 An experiment with 12 participants sought to determine if interaction with touchscreen phones is improved using the flick gesture and whether the improvement, if any, is related to one-handed vs. two-handed interaction. A variety of map-locating tasks were devised. All tasks were of equal difficulty. For each task, participants were presented with a starting location and were required to navigate to a final location using finger gestures on the map image. To avoid visual search in the task, the map and locations were familiar to participants. The system was configured to have a drag-only mode (flick disabled) and a drag-flick mode. The twelve participants were divided into two groups, counterbalancing the one-handed vs. two-handed conditions. The data for task completion time are shown in Fig. 6.47. Perform an ANOVA on the

Participant	Task Completion Time (s)				Group
	One-handed		Two-handed		
	Drag-only	Drag+flick	Drag-only	Drag+flick	
P1	12	11	7	6	G1
P2	11	7	6	8	G1
P3	9	8	8	7	G1
P4	9	9	7	6	G1
P5	13	5	6	5	G1
P6	6	6	5	9	G1
P7	7	7	8	8	G2
P8	9	8	8	5	G2
P9	8	8	9	7	G2
P10	7	8	9	5	G2
P11	11	10	8	11	G2
P12	12	8	8	11	G2

FIGURE 6.47

Student exercise on touchscreen interaction.

data to determine if there is an effect of hand use (one-handed, two-handed) or interaction method (drag-only, drag+flick) on task completion time for the map-locating task. Prepare a brief report or slide show presentation on your findings.

6-5 Using Google Scholar, locate and examine some HCI research papers. Find examples of factorial experiments where the F-statistics were poorly reported or poorly formatted. Indicate what is wrong and suggest an improved way to report the result. Present your findings in a brief report or slide show presentation.

6-6 The data in Fig. 4.10 (p. 180) show observations on male and female university students in their mobile phone usage habits. Use a chi-square test to determine if the data reveal a statistically significant difference between males and females in their tendency to use or not use a mobile phone while walking about campus. Perform the calculations using a spreadsheet application and the method shown for the data in Fig. 6.22. Verify the results using the GoStats utility available on this book's web site.

6-7 Verify the chi-square statistic of $\chi^2 = 543.5$ reported for the data in Fig. 6.28 comparing the Web of Trust (WOT) and McAfee's Site Advisor (MSA) tools for assessing the safety of web sites. Perform the calculations using a spreadsheet application and the method shown for the data in Fig. 6.22.

6-8 A researcher is interested in investigating whether Mac or PC users differ in their habits for using "wallpaper" on their desktop. (Wallpaper is a personalized background picture.) A number of users on a university campus were approached and asked to provide two items of information. First, they were asked whether their main system was a Mac or PC. Second, they were asked

System	Wallpaper Habit		
	None	Static	Dynamic
Mac	13	8	25
PC	25	21	18

FIGURE 6.48

Student exercise on wallpaper habits.

about their wallpaper habits and, in particular, whether they (a) did not use wallpaper, (b) used personalized wallpaper but changed it less than once per month (<12 times in the last year), or (c) used personalized wallpaper and changed it more than once per month. The responses were coded as *none*, *static*, and *dynamic*, respectively. The data are shown in Fig. 6.48. Each cell contains the number of users in each category. Perform a chi-square test on the data above to determine if Mac or PC users differ in their wallpaper habits. Prepare a brief report or slide show presentation on your findings.

6-9 Users and computers (Part II). Extend the report for Part I of this exercise (see Chapter 5, p. 242) to examine if user preference for a Mac or a PC differs by gender, according to a chi-square test. Perform a similar test by age. For the age test, divide the respondents into equally sized nominal-scale groups: younger and older. (Use the median age to divide the groups.) This student exercise continues in Chapter 7 (Part III).

6-10 Below are the selection coordinates for one sequence of trials in a target selection experiment.

-29, 8, 3, 7, 4, -19, 44, -15, -8, -1, -27, 18, 26, 22, 21, 31, -16, 45, 71, 63

Are the selection coordinates normally distributed? Prepare a brief report or slide show presentation on your findings.

6-11 One of the examples in Chapter 2 examined performance scores for 15 participants on a search task. See Fig. 2.46 (p. 84). Revisit the example and do a Lilliefors test for normality on the scores. Prepare a brief report or slide show presentation on your findings.

6-12 Conduct a small self-experiment to determine if the measurements over repeated trials in a simple reaction time task are normally distributed. Use the ReactionTimeSoftware provided on this book's web site. Perform 5 to 10 sequences (blocks) of 16 trials each and perform a Lilliefors normality test on each sequence. Data are automatically collected and stored by the utility. Consult the API for details. Prepare a brief report or slide show presentation on your findings.

6-13 A telecommunications company has developed a new texting interface for their latest smartphone. They are wondering if the phone will be equally acceptable

Gender	
Female	Male
25	18
25	14
19	13
21	15
22	17
19	19
15	18
18	20

FIGURE 6.49

Student exercise on the acceptance of a texting interface for eight females and eight males.

to female and male users and decide to investigate by conducting a small experiment. Nine female and nine male participants (all experienced texters) are recruited and given a demo of the texting interface. The participants are then given the phone and asked to test the texting feature for a period of one week. Afterword, they rate the texting interface on a 25-point linear scale from 1 (*really bad*) to 25 (*really good*). The data are in Fig. 6.49. Is there a difference in the ratings of the texting interface between females and males? Prepare a brief report or slide show presentation on your findings.

6-14 A software company has developed a tool for personal project planning. The tool includes a variety of features that the company wishes to test with potential users. Eight participants are recruited and given a demonstration of the personal project planner and then tested the tool using four features: drag & link, integration, in-context create, and outline. After, the participants rated the features on a 5-point scale on their expected frequency of use (1 = *will never use*, 5 = *will use daily*). The data are shown in Fig. 6.50. Is there a difference in the estimated frequency of use for the features in the personal project planner? Prepare a brief report or slide show presentation on your findings.[22]

6-15 A robotics company with a focus on children's toys has designed and prototyped two computerized electro-mechanical pet dogs: Waggy and Sniffy. Through the wonder of software,[23] the dogs have different "personalities." The company is interested in evaluating the toy dogs with children to assess the level of engagement. Eight children are recruited. The children are introduced separately to Waggy and Sniffy and then play with each dog for thirty minutes. (Counterbalancing is used, but this is not important here.) "Verbal engagement"

---

[22] This student exercise was inspired by the evaluation of a personal project planner by Jones et al. [232]. Their study used 21 participants who evaluated seven features of a personal project planner.

[23] Of course, for marketing, instead of "software," the term "AI" is more likely to be used.

Participant	Tool Feature			
	Drag & Link	Integration	In-context Use	Outline
P1	3	5	3	2
P2	5	4	2	1
P3	5	4	1	3
P4	4	4	1	4
P5	3	3	2	3
P6	4	4	2	5
P7	3	5	1	4
P8	3	3	3	2

FIGURE 6.50

Student exercise on participant ratings for a project planning tool.

Participant	Toy Dog	
	Waggy	Sniffy
P1	189	75
P2	189	130
P3	222	135
P4	178	143
P5	205	98
P6	278	125
P7	231	156
P8	177	213

FIGURE 6.51

Student exercise on children's verbal engagement with toy dogs.

is considered important so the sessions are videotaped. Afterward, the tapes are analysed to tally the number of words spoken by each child while playing with each dog. The data are shown in Fig. 6.51. Is there a difference between Waggy and Sniffy based on the level of verbal engagement with the children? Since the data are ratio-scale, consider the merits of using a parametric vs. a non-parametric testing procedure. Prepare a brief report or slide show presentation on your findings.[24]

---

[24] This student exercise was inspired by a similar evaluation by Stanton et al. [469]. Their study used 11 autistic children. Five measures of behavioural interaction were analysed (including verbal engagement).

Modelling interaction

A model is a simplification of reality. Consider an architect's scale model of a building or a physicist's equation for the trajectory of a tossed ball. Both are reductions or simplifications of more complex phenomena. They are useful because they allow us to explore the phenomena, think about them, make changes, and so on – without actually constructing the building or throwing the ball. A great many problems in HCI are explored in this manner. This chapter is about modelling interaction – building models, testing models, using models, and thinking about interaction through models.

The term "model" is often used loosely, without a clear and simple definition. A mathematician's model is probably quite distant from a psychologist's or sociologist's model. To the mathematician, a model is a formal calculus tested through computer simulation. To the psychologist or sociologist it is often a verbal-analytic description of behaviour. Pew and Baron elaborate:

> *There is a continuum along which models vary that has loose verbal analogy and metaphor at one end and closed-form mathematical equations at the other.*
>
> **[398, p. 664]**

This seems like a useful way to organize our discussion. Models using "loose verbal analogy and metaphor" describe phenomena. Let's called them *descriptive models*. Models using "closed-form mathematical equations" predict phenomena. Let's call them *predictive models*. This chapter opened with an example of each. An architect's model of a building is a descriptive model. A physicist's equation for the trajectory of a tossed ball is a predictive model.

There are many examples of descriptive and predictive models in HCI. The rest of this chapter is organized in two parts. In the next section, we present descriptive models. Examples are presented, along with discussion on how each can provide insight into a design or interaction problem. Following this, we present a few examples of predictive models, with a similar organization.

7.1 Descriptive models

Descriptive models are everywhere. They emerge from a process so natural it barely seems like modelling. Look in any HCI paper and there is a good chance you'll find a descriptive model, perhaps without knowing it. There are many examples in the preceding pages, such as Card et al.'s model human processor in Chapter 1 (Fig. 1.11,

p. 19). In many cases, the word "model" isn't even used. Such was the case in Chapter 2 where we met Newell's time scale of human action (Fig. 2.1, p. 33) and a human factors view of the human operator in a work environment (Fig. 2.2, p. 34). Likewise for the analysis in Chapter 3 of the cost vs. frequency of errors (Fig. 3.67, p. 154) or the comparison in Chapter 4 of form and function (Fig. 4.2, p. 167). Make no mistake: These are models, descriptive models. And they provide a powerful mechanism to study any facet of human-computer interaction. The general idea is developed in the next section.

7.1.1 Delineating a problem space

A descriptive model divides up a problem space. Taken as a whole, without divisions, the problem space is ... well, that's what it is, a space – vast and uncharted, a "big fuzzy cloud" perhaps. However, with a little thought and organization it becomes a partitioned domain. With partitions, we are empowered to think differently about the problem space, to get inside it and see the constituent parts or processes. We can focus on certain parts of the problem space, consider how one part differs from, or relates to, another, and weigh strengths, weaknesses, advantages, or disadvantages of certain parts over others.

Here is a non-HCI example, just to get started. Consider politics, a subject we all know a little about. Fig. 7.1a gives the "big fuzzy cloud" model of politics. Of course, there is no model! It's just the thing itself, without delineation. If we really want to study politics, it would be useful to break it down, delineate it, categorize it, structure it, or whatever – to get inside the problem, to identify and label the constituent parts, and begin the process of charting out a corner of the problem space as a research area. In Fig. 7.1b, we see Johnston's delineation of the problem space for politics [231, p. 19]. This is a descriptive model for politics. Open any textbook on any subject and you are likely to find similar diagrams.

Johnston's chart in Fig. 7.1b is beautifully crafted. It is organized as a semi-circular spoked wheel, with politics at the centre. Do you like the organization? Is there a different organization that might work better? Note the symmetry between "State/Government" (left) and "Citizens/Communities" (right). Nice. "Ideas/Interests" is mirrored with "Processes." Is that reasonable? What about "Federalism" under Institutions? That seems odd. Is federalism an institution? Perhaps Federalism, like Democracy, should be under Ideas/Interests. Enough said. The descriptive model in Fig. 7.1b adds insight into politics. It empowers us not only to think about the problem, but to think critically about it. With every tweak, refinement, and improvement, we get a better model and, more importantly we get a better understanding of the problem. That's the goal with descriptive models.

In HCI, researchers often approach problems in a similar way. Let's have a look at a few descriptive models in HCI and examine how they are used to analyse a problem space and inform interaction design.

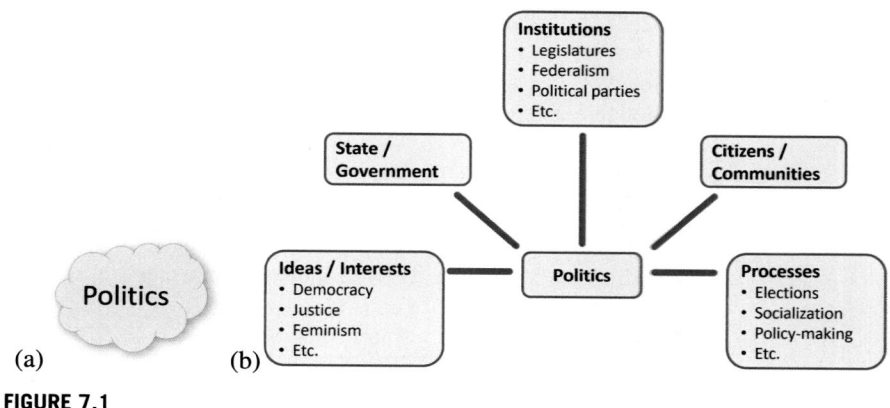

FIGURE 7.1

Politics. (a) The "big fuzzy cloud" model. (b) A descriptive model delineating the problem space (after [229, p. 19]).

7.1.2 Quadrant model of groupware

An important area of research within HCI is computer-supported cooperative work (CSCW). Computer applications to support collaboration are known as *groupware*. There are many facets to groupware, including teleconferencing, team writing, group voting, and so on. Is it possible to delineate the problem space of groupware into a descriptive model? Of course it is. And there are many ways to do this. The starting point, as always, is just to think about groupware, to consider aspects of it that differ in some way. These differences can assist in dividing the problem space into simpler components or processes.

One such possibility for groupware is to consider collaboration in terms of space and time. Spatially, users might collaborate in the same physical place or in different physical places. Temporally, users might collaborate at the same time or at different times. The spatial and temporal aspects of the collaboration are illustrated in Johansen's *quadrant model of groupware* [227,239]. See Fig. 7.2. The model presents groupware as a 2 × 2 matrix with four cells, each representing a distinct quality of interaction. A group of colleagues co-authoring a report involves people working in different places and different times. This is labelled group writing and appears in the bottom-right cell. A team meeting where members use computer technology to present and discuss ideas involves people working in the same place and at the same time. This is labelled PC projectors and appears in the top-left cell.

The examples in Fig. 7.2 are from a report published in 1991 [227]. There are numerous forms of collaboration today that didn't exist in 1991. Think of sharing selfies, web cams, social networking, tweeting, Zoom meetings, FaceTime, Overleaf, and so on. All involve people collaborating or interacting with other people in some manner. Can these interactions be positioned in the quadrant model of groupware? Probably. See also student exercise 7-2.

	Same Time	Different Times
Same Place	Copy Boards PC Projectors Facilitation Services Group Decision Room Polling Systems	Shared Files Shift Work Kiosks Team Rooms Group Displays
Different Places	Conference Calls Graphics and Audio Screen Sharing Video Teleconferencing Spontaneous Meetings	Group Writing Computer Conferencing Conversational Structuring Forms Management Group Voice Mail

FIGURE 7.2

Quadrant model of groupware (after [227, Figure 1]).

Consider Zoom meetings, which entered the mainstream of computing in 2020 with the shift to remote work due to the Covid-19 pandemic. Attendees in a Zoom meeting are in difference places at the same time – the bottom-left quadrant in Fig. 7.2. Taking this further, some attendees have their camera on while other have their camera off. Some meetings are recorded, to be viewed later, others not. Zoom meetings often involve screen sharing or breakout rooms for sub-meetings. And there are chat comments, reactions, whiteboards, etc. So, we might ask whether the bottom-left quadrant of the model is sufficient in capturing the full spectrum of collaboration in Zoom meetings. The nuances just mentioned suggest a need for refinements to the model or a new model.

Our goal is not to engage in this exercise for groupware or Zoom meetings, but only to suggest that descriptive models provide a context for these analyses and this type of thinking.

Examples of HCI research using the quadrant model of groupware include the following:

- Investigating groupware opportunities between humans and artificial teammates or cyber-agents [130]
- Exploring issues in cloud-based tools for group support systems [535]
- Proposal for a design pattern classification for mobile groupware [139]

7.1.3 Key-action model (KAM)

Computer keyboards today contain a vast array of buttons, or keys. Most desktop keyboards have a row of function keys across the top and a numeric keypad on the right. Have you ever thought about the operation and organization of keys on a keyboard? Here's a descriptive model for this purpose: the *key-action model* (KAM). KAM includes three categories of keys:

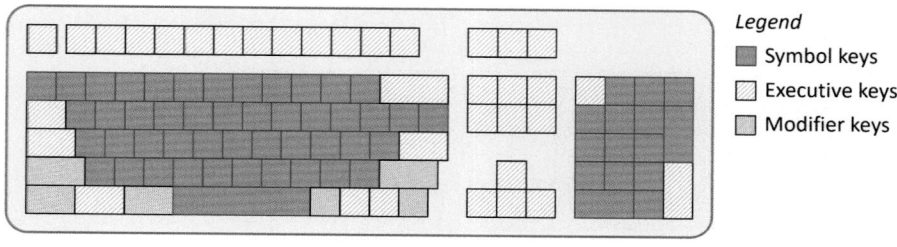

FIGURE 7.3

The key-action model (KAM) illustrated.

- Symbol keys
- Executive keys
- Modifier keys

Symbol keys deliver graphic symbols to an application such as a text editor. Generally, these are letters, numbers, or punctuation symbols. Executive keys invoke actions in the application or at the system-level. Examples include ENTER, F1, or ESC. Modifier keys do not generate symbols or invoke actions. Instead, they set up a condition that modifies the effect of a subsequently pressed key. Examples include SHIFT or ALT. That's about it. KAM is a simple model. It has a name, it delineates a problem space, and it identifies three categories of keys and for each category provides a name, a definition, and examples. There is no chart like Fig. 7.1b for politics. Perhaps you can do that. What do you think of KAM? Is it correct? Is it flawed? Do all keyboard keys fit the model? Can you think of additional categories or subcategories to improve the model or to make it more accurate or more comprehensive? Do some keys have features of more than one category? Is the model useful?

The questions above – by their very nature – are evidence of the value of descriptive models such as the KAM. The model piques our interest and suggests aspects of keyboard operation that merit consideration, particularly if a new design is contemplated. The most important question is the last. The merit of a model is its ability to tease out critical arguments on the potential, the capabilities, and the limitations in an interaction domain. Can the KAM do that? Let's see.

Fig. 7.3 illustrates a keyboard, with keys highlighted according to the KAM. It's a typical desktop keyboard with a wide space bar along the bottom, function keys along the top, a numeric keypad on the right, and non-alpha keys in various locations.

Is there anything unusual in Fig. 7.3? Think about this in terms of left-hand and right-hand usage. Consider the executive keys, such as ENTER. On the keyboard's left we find four executive keys: TAB, CAPS_LOCK, ESC, and WINDOWS. On the keyboard's right, ... My gosh, there's a lot happening over there on the right. A

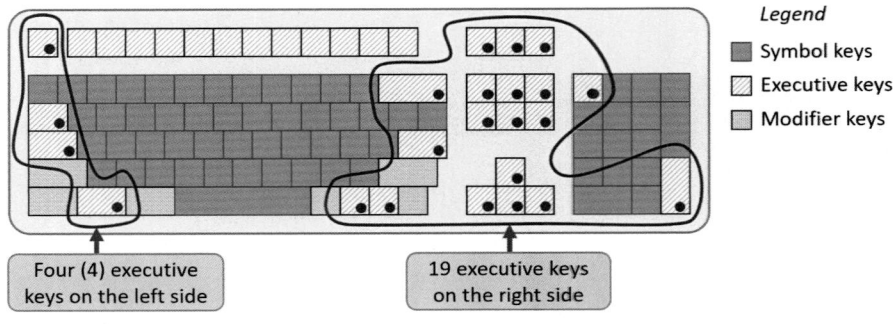

Legend

■ Symbol keys
▨ Executive keys
■ Modifier keys

Four (4) executive keys on the left side

19 executive keys on the right side

FIGURE 7.4

The key-action model (KAM) reveals a right-side bias for executive keys.

quick tally reveals 19 executive keys:[1] ENTER (×2), WINDOWS, RIGHT_CLICK, BACKSPACE, INSERT, DELETE, HOME, END, PAGE_UP, PAGE_DOWN, ←, ↑, →, ↓, PRNT_SCRN, SROLL_LOCK, PAUSE, and NUM_LOCK.

The numbers for executive keys are 4 on the left, 19 on the right. These are grouped together and identified by dots in Fig. 7.4. Clearly, there is a right-side bias for executive keys.

Before continuing, let's remember our goal. We're not here to deliver a tutorial on keyboards, but to develop a descriptive model with the ability to delineate a problem space and potentially expose problems and suggest opportunities. The analysis in the preceding paragraph is a good example of this. Using the key-action model, we identified a peculiar bias in desktop keyboards. Let's continue.

With a 4:19 left-to-right ratio of executive keys, the desktop keyboard is clearly entrenched with a right-side bias. Simply put, our right hand is busy. Furthermore, with the emergence of the mouse in the 1980s, the right hand is even busier. Is it possible, the right hand is, in fact, overloaded?

Interactions that juxtapose executive-key activation and point-click operations are problematic for right-handed users. The right hand is just too busy. If the right hand is gripping the mouse and there is a need to press a right-side executive key, the options are (a) to "reach over" with the left hand, or (b) to release the mouse and acquire and activate the executive key with the right hand. Not so good in either case. For users who manipulate the mouse with their left hand, the situation is quite different.[2] For "lefties," left-hand mouse operations efficiently mix with right-hand executive-key operations. In fact, an analysis of common GUI tasks reveals an inter-

---

[1] For this analysis, we exclude the function keys along the top, as they do not pose a left- or right-side bias.

[2] Numerous straw votes by the author at presentations and lectures reveal that the majority of left-handed users operate a mouse with their right hand. The reason, it seems, is that most users learned to use a computer at school, where the mouse is positioned, and often anchored, on the right side of the keyboard.

Hand	Role and Action
Non-preferred	• Leads the preferred hand • Sets the spatial frame of reference for the preferred hand • Performs coarse movements
Preferred	• Follows the non-preferred hand • Works within the established frame of reference set by the non-preferred hand • Performs fine movements

FIGURE 7.5

Model of bimanual control (from [234]).

esting phenomenon: The desktop interface is biased to favour left-hand mouse usage! But, that's another story. Details are provided elsewhere [305].

The key-action model only captures one aspect of keyboards, namely the actions associated with each key. Another way to think about keyboards is in the ambiguity of key presses. If pressing a symbol key always produces to the same symbol, then the situation is simple. But, if a key can produce two or more symbols, then this is worth thinking about. For this, a "key-ambiguity" descriptive model might be useful [322, Fig. 5].

The key-action model delineates a design space for keyboards and allows for analyses to tease out design issues. Let's move on to another descriptive model.

7.1.4 Bimanual control model

Humans are not only two-handed, they use their hands differently. This human behaviour has undergone considerable study in a specialized area of human motor control known as bimanual control or laterality [244,395,404,520]. Studying the between-hand division of labour in everyday tasks reveals that most tasks are asymmetric: Our hands work together but play different roles. Given this, and the knowledge that people are considered right-handed or left-handed, examining the assignment of tasks to hands is a useful exercise. Guiard undertook such an exercise, and proposed what he described as "a simple model, based on a non-quantitative physical approach, which aims at describing the logic of the division of labour that appears to govern the variety of human bimanual asymmetrical actions" [166]. This is the essence of a descriptive model. The result is Guiard's *model of bimanual control* – a simple three-part descriptive model identifying the roles and actions of the non-preferred and preferred hands. See Fig. 7.5.

The points in Fig. 7.5 are best explained through an exemplary illustration and narrative. In Fig. 7.6, a right-handed graphic artist is sketching the design of a new car. The artist acquires the template with the left hand (non-preferred hand leads).

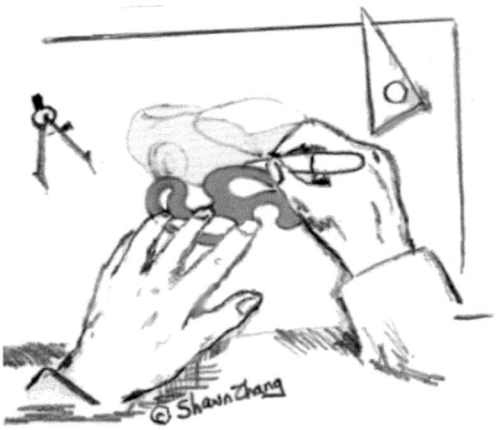

FIGURE 7.6

Two-handed interaction paradigm (sketch courtesy of Shawn Zhang).

The template is manipulated over the workspace (coarse movement, sets the frame of reference). The stylus is acquired in the right hand (preferred hand follows) and brought into the vicinity of the template (works within frame of reference set by the non-preferred hand). Sketching takes place (preferred hand makes precise movements).[3]

The roles and actions just described provide a provocative and fresh way to describe how humans approach common tasks. This is true both for every-day tasks and in the specialized context of human-computer interaction.

Guiard's research was published in a journal article in experimental psychology, not HCI. As originally published, no context for HCI was provided. Watershed moments in multi-disciplinary fields like HCI often occur when researchers through due diligence locate and adopt relevant research in other fields – research that can inform and guide their own discipline.[4] Guiard's work was located and studied by Paul Kabbash, a graduate student at the University of Toronto in the early 1990s. The paper by Kabbash, Buxton, and Sellen [234] was the first in HCI to cite Guiard's 1987 work and adapt it to analyse two-handed computer input. Since then, Guiard's model has been widely adopted for HCI research in two-handed interaction (e.g., [94,129,134,265,337,360,427,511,531,536]). An example follows.

---

[3] Also see Fig. 3.45 (p. 133) which shows the non-preferred hand performing a mode-switch on a tablet computer with the preferred hand acting in accordance with the new mode.

[4] There are examples in HCI, for example, Card, English, and Burr's [60] first use of Fitts' law [125], or Norman's [376, pp. 9-11] introduction of Gibson's affordances [143].

Task	Characteristics
Scrolling	• Precedes/overlaps other tasks • Sets the frame of reference • Minimal precision needed (coarse)
Selecting, editing, reading, drawing, etc.	• Follows/overlaps scrolling • Works within the frame of reference set by scrolling • Demands precision (fine)

FIGURE 7.7

Relationship between scrolling and common GUI tasks.

7.1.4.1 Bimanual control and scrolling

Scrolling on desktop system is typically performed by dragging the elevator of the scrollbar on the side of an application's window. Acquiring the elevator is a target acquisition task taking up to two seconds per trial [305]. However, this action is in conflict with a basic goal of good user interfaces: unobtrusiveness and transparency. That is, users should not be required to divert their attention from the primary task (reading, editing, drawing, etc.) to acquire and manipulate a user interface widget for scrolling.

Desktop affordances for scrolling changed dramatically in 1996 with the introduction of Microsoft's IntelliMouse, which included a scrolling wheel between the mouse buttons. Numerous copycat variations appeared after from other manufacturers. The so-called "wheel mouse" puts scrolling in the preferred hand. This is arguably bad for right-handed users because it increases the right-side bias noted in the preceding section. This insight – revealed in Guiard's descriptive model of bimanual control – presents an opportunity for design. An analysis of scrolling and the accompanying tasks reveals that scrolling is well suited to the non-preferred hand. Evidence of this is in Fig. 7.7, which juxtaposes the properties of scrolling with tasks typically performed in concert with scrolling. (The reader is invited to compare the organization of bullets in Fig. 7.7 with that in Fig. 7.5, which presents the guiding principles for bimanual control.)

Fig. 7.8 presents a scrolling concept for a right-handed user. On the keyboard's left, a touch strip is shown, but a wheel is just as appropriate. There are many implementation issues, such as scrolling sensitivity and support for up/down paging, but these are not explored here. Our point is simply that scrolling is an appropriate task for the non-dominant hand and that this is revealed in the model of bimanual control. See also Buxton and Myers [52].

On a personal note, the idea of non-dominant hand scrolling was sufficiently appealing that I decided to re-engineer a Microsoft Intellimouse, separating the wheel assembly from the mouse. The new setup allowed operation of the mouse with the dominant hand while scrolling with the non-dominant hand, as seen in Fig. 7.9a for

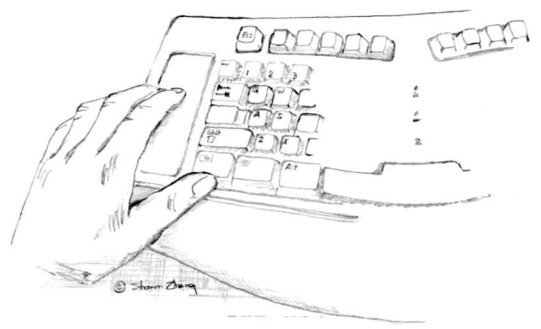

FIGURE 7.8

Scrolling interface example (sketch courtesy of Shawn Zhang).

a right-handed user. This setup was used for numerous demos and presentations. Two such presentations were given in February 1998 during a visit to Microsoft in Redmond, Washington. The first audience was the "mouse group" of Microsoft's Hardware Ergonomics Group. The idea seemed provocative, so the team arranged an impromptu meeting later that day for the "keyboard group." I gave the same presentation again. The idea of non-dominant hand scrolling, as suggested in the model of bimanual control, was convincing. A new project was initiated within Microsoft. About two years later, Microsoft released the Office Keyboard. See Fig. 7.9b. On the left side, the device includes some power keys and a scrolling wheel (see arrow) – perfect for right-handed users.

Variations of keyboards with left-side scrolling were subsequently released by Microsoft and other keyboard manufacturers, including Logitech. In the end, however, the momentum and popularity of the wheel mouse was just too much. The benefit of non-dominant-hand scrolling was insufficient to overcome the cost of learning a new interaction method. A satisfied user community could not be swayed toward a new interface paradigm.[5] Today, most computer mice continue to include a wheel for scrolling while most keyboards do not.

In this section, we examined common GUI tasks and patterns of bimanual skill. Two important observations emerged: First, current desktop systems favour left-hand mouse use, and, second, scrolling is well supported by delegation to the non-dominant hand. These insights are examples of how a descriptive model can inform the analysis and design of human-computer interactions.

---

[5] On the challenges in introducing changes to established practice, see also the cost-benefit analysis in Fig. 5.21 (p. 239).

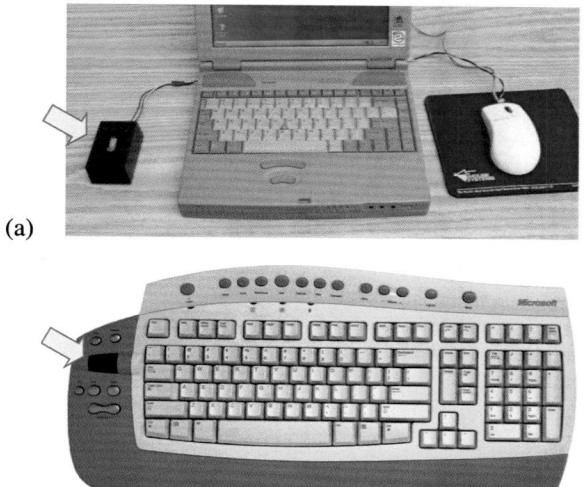

(a)

(b)

FIGURE 7.9

Non-dominant-hand scrolling. (a) The author's re-engineered Microsoft Intellimouse with the wheel on left side of the keyboard. (b) Microsoft Office Keyboard with scrolling wheel on the left side.

7.1.5 Circumplex model of affect

The *circumplex model of affect* (CMA), presented by Russell [424] in 1980, is a two-dimensional descriptive model of human affect or emotion. The visualization positions affect in a 2D space with degrees of pleasure vs. displeasure along the horizontal axis and arousal vs. sleep along the vertical axis. See Fig. 7.10. The term "valence" is commonly used for the pleasure-displeasure axis. One can image that at any moment each of us is positioned somewhere in the 2D space of the model.

Like Guiard's model of bimanual control, the circumplex model of affect originated outside HCI, in this case in social psychology. The first use of the CMA in HCI was Schiano et al.'s [435] application of the model to the evaluation of human facial expressions, presented at the SIGCHI conference in 2000. There have been many applications since.

Griffiths et al. [159,160] used the model to generate musical playlists. The emotional state of the user was assessed using acquired physiological and contextual data and fuzzy logic inferencing. Musical preferences were also considered. The goal was to position the user in the 2D space of the CMA. A separate process analysed music files through extracted audio features such as rhythm structure and melody features to also position songs in the CMA. Music was deemed appropriate for the playlist if the position in the CMA was close to the user position. Users were also given the option to reclassify music to a different location according to their personal sense of the music's position in the CMA.

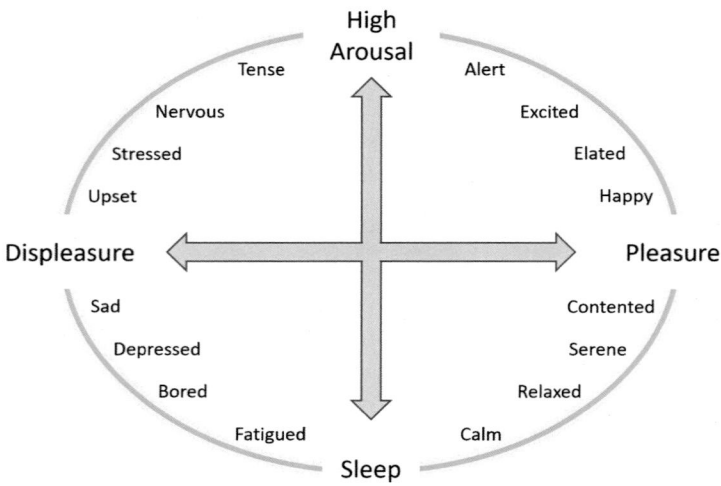

FIGURE 7.10

The circumplex model of affect (CMA) (after [424]).

Song and Yamada [462] used the CMA in human-robot research noting that in-situ motion and expressive lighting in a robot can convey emotions. Yoshida and Yonezawa [539] suggest, in the context of the CMA, that a robot's artificial respiratory rate and heart rate can express emotion.

An interesting extension to the CMA is converting what is mostly a qualitative assessment of valence and arousal to numeric scores. For this, Russell et al. [425] recast the CMA into a 9 × 9 "affect grid" with valence and arousal along the horizontal and vertical dimensions, respectively. Assessments involve placing a check in the grid according to the estimated position for valence and arousal of a mood, facial expression, or something else. The check location yields a 1-to-9 numeric score for valence (horizontal position) and arousal (vertical position).

A related tool is Bradley and Lang's self-assessment manikin (SAM) [38]. Participants are shown sketches of manikin figures with expressions of affect. There is a set for valence (Fig. 7.11a) and another for arousal (Fig. 7.11b). Words appear representing each pole, with participants asked to select a position from 1 to 9. They might be assessing themselves, or they might be assessing some other situation, such as a music sample, a facial expression, or a robot's behaviour.

There is an implication for models when using SAM or the affect grid to assign numeric codes for emotional states. The process shifts the CMA model from descriptive to analytic. It is not quite a predictive model, since no predictions are generated, but it is more than a "partition of a problem space," since the assessment is numeric. It becomes an analytic model.

Other uses of the circumplex model of affect in HCI include the following:

- Conveying emotion through shape-changing interfaces [473]

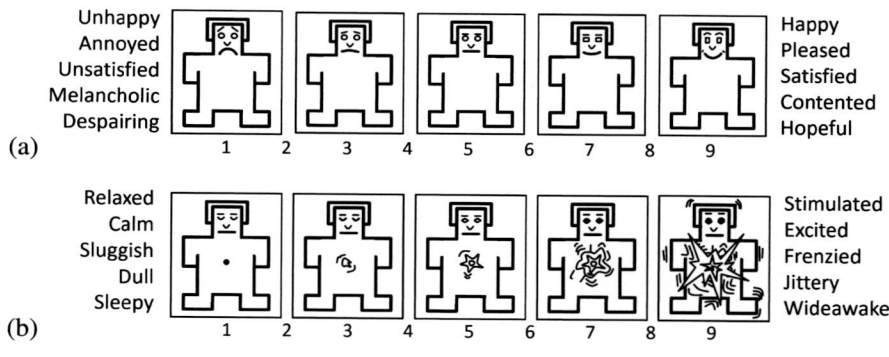

FIGURE 7.11

Presentation sheet for self-assessment manikin (SAM) responses (after [552]). (a) Valence items. (b) Arousal items.

- With wearable devices, adding visual cues to vibrotactile signals to convey emotion [552]
- In VR, studying the emotional associations of colour and music on the evaluation of cold brew coffee [374]
- Evaluating the emotional expressions of a robot that communicates using skin texture and human touch [202]
- Evaluating emotionally resonant vibrotactile stimuli for real-world sensations such as animal purring or running water [297]
- Evaluating a user's emotional state in an interactive play environment [338]

7.1.6 Three-state model of graphical input

Another descriptive model is the *three-state model of graphical input*, presented by Buxton in 1990 for mouse, stylus, and finger input [49] and earlier by Newman for light-pen input [370]. The model characterizes the operation of computer pointing devices in terms of state transitions. It is described as "a vocabulary to recognize and explore the relationship between pointing devices and the interaction techniques they afford" [49, p. 449]. In this sense, it is a paradigm of descriptive modelling. The three states are identified in Fig. 7.12, annotated for mouse interaction.

Left-to-right in Fig. 7.12, the states are *Out of Range* (State 0) for clutching or repositioning a mouse on a desktop, *Tracking* (State 1) for moving a tracking symbol on a display, and *Dragging* (State 2) for moving an object on the display or for grouping a set of objects or a range of text. The model seems simple and obvious, and we might question its ability to add insight to the existing body of pointing device research. Yet, the model can be extended to capture additional aspects of pointing device interaction such as multi-button interaction and direct vs. indirect input. See Buxton [49] for further details.

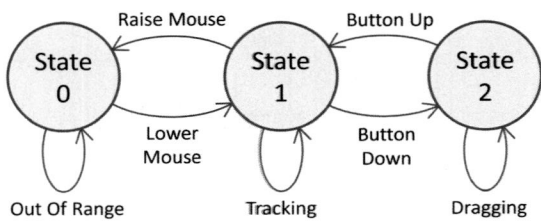

FIGURE 7.12

Three-state model of graphical input (after [49]).

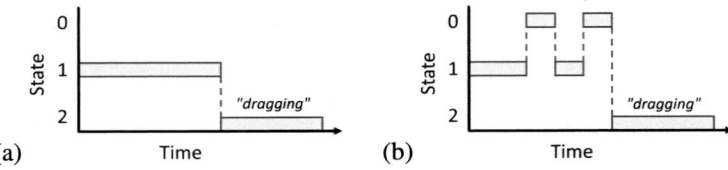

FIGURE 7.13

State transitions for dragging tasks. (a) Mouse. (b) Touchpad using lift-and-tap. Dragging begins upon entering State 2 (after [316]).

As further evidence of this work, MacKenzie and Oniszczak [316] used the three-state model to help characterize an interaction technique that didn't exist when the model was introduced. The insight lead to a redesign of an interaction technique that later appeared in RIM's Blackberry Storm and Apple's MacBook. This work is briefly recounted here.

Never shy of innovation, Apple took a bold step in 1994 by commercializing a new pointing device in its PowerBook 500 notebook computer: the TrackPoint touchpad [330]. Today, touchpads are the dominant pointing device for laptop computers. One of the interaction techniques supported by touchpads is "lift-and-tap," where primitive operations like clicking, double-clicking, or dragging, are implemented without a button. These new interaction primitives are easily represented in the three-state model. Fig. 7.13 provides a simple comparison of the state transitions for dragging tasks (a) using a mouse, and (b) using lift-and-tap on a touchpad.

Diagrams like this are evidence of the value of descriptive models such as the three-state model. Two observations follow: (1) lift-and-tap necessitates extra state transitions in comparison to a mouse, and (2) the use of state 1-0-1 transitions for lift-and-tap is confounded with clutching (not shown) which uses the same state transitions.[6] Among users' frustrations in using touchpads is that these primitives are difficult, awkward, or error prone. For example, if a touch following a lift is spatially

---

[6] Clutching refers to lifting the mouse to reposition it within its operating space.

 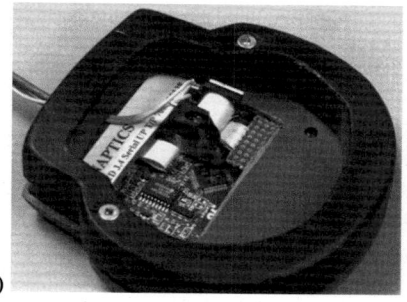

(a)   (b)

FIGURE 7.14

The tactile touchpad [316,324]. (a) Top view. (b) Bottom view showing relay.

displaced from the point of lifting, the system sometimes enters the Tracking state (State 1) instead of the Dragging state (State 2).

Armed with a deeper understanding of touchpad interaction, the state transitions on touchpads were re-designed. The additional pressure sensing capability of touchpads was used to implement state 1-2 transitions by "pressing harder."[7] A relay was added to provide both tactile and auditory feedback to inform the user of state transitions, much like the feedback in pressing a mouse button. See Fig. 7.14.

With the tactile touchpad operations such as clicking, double clicking, and dragging were implemented without a button, yet using the same state transitions as on a mouse. The complete details are presented in the 1997 and 1998 proceedings of the ACM's SIGCHI conference [316,324].

Despite being introduced in 1990, the three state model of graphical input continues to serve as a descriptive model for interactive systems. Recent applications include the following:

- Selection of moving targets [170]
- Indirect touch input [506]
- Clutching in remote manipulation tasks [137]
- Modelling the physical manipulation of digital content via touch-aware tangible objects [505]
- Modelling smartphone ray casting for 3D environments on public displays [400]
- For large interactive displays, modelling interactions on the display and in the air in front of the display [91]

Let's move across the continuum of the modelling space to models that work with closed-form mathematical equations – predictive models.

---

[7] The pressure sensing capability of a touchpad exists within the firmware as a separate mode of operation. In this mode, the device provides absolute x, absolute y, and z-axis data. The z-axis data corresponds to finger pressure on the touchpad surface.

7.2 **Predictive models**

A predictive model is an equation. The equation predicts the outcome on a variable based on the value of one or more other variables (predictors). The outcome or response variable is often a dependent variable such as the time or speed in doing a task. It could also be accuracy, represented as spatial variability, error rate, or any other measure of human behaviour. The only requirement is that the variable use continuous, or ratio-scale, data.

Many statistics sources call the predictor variable the independent variable. While correct, the terminology is problematic here. In experimental research, independent variable has a special meaning: It is a circumstance or characteristic that is manipulated. The vast majority of independent variables are nominal-scale attributes (e.g., device, feedback modality, display type, gender). That poses a problem, since a nominal-scale variable cannot serve as a predictor in a prediction equation (e.g., $3 \times$ device = ?). Of course, independent variables in experimental research can also be ratio-scale attributes. Such variables can serve as a predictor in prediction equations. Examples include distance to target, size of target, number of targets, angle of movement, system lag, joystick force, angle of tilt, decibel (dB) level of background noise, word size, number of choices, and so on. A predictor variable can also be a ratio-scale attribute of users, such as age, years of computer experience, number of e-mails received per day, hours per day playing video games, geographical distance from a friend, and so on.[8]

Predictive models are useful in HCI. Like descriptive models, they allow a problem space to be explored. However, with a predictive model, we are dealing with numbers, not concepts. Card, English, and Burr [60] presented in 1978 what is likely the first predictive model in HCI. They conducted an experiment comparing the effect of four input devices (mouse, joystick, text keys, step keys) on users' speed and accuracy in selecting text on a CRT display. In many respects, their work is straightforward; the methodology is as expected for an experiment with human participants. However, Card et al. went beyond a typical user study. Here are the first are two sentences in the Discussion:

> *While these empirical results are of direct use in selecting a pointing device, it would obviously be of greater benefit if a theoretical account of the results could be made. For one thing, the need for some experiments might be obviated; for another, ways of improving pointing performance might be suggested.*

[60, p. 608]

This is an inspired preamble to their discussion on building models – models of interaction that (a) embed a theoretical account of the underlying human processes and (b) serve as prediction tools for follow-up analyses of design alternatives. The remainder

---

[8] "Geographical distance from friend" is an excellent example of the diverse and multi-disciplinary nature of HCI research. This ratio-scale circumstance was used both as an independent variable and as a predictor in a prediction equation for research on maintaining on-line friendships when people move apart [448].

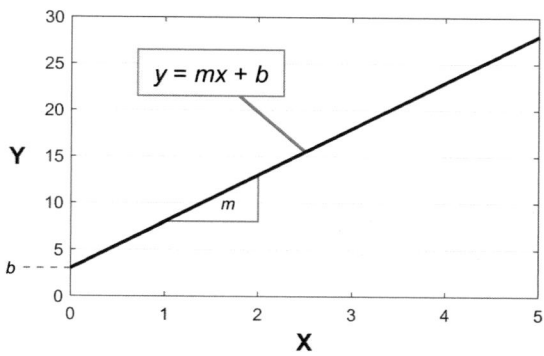

FIGURE 7.15

Linear relationship between a predictor variable (x) and a response variable (y).

of their paper is about modelling using Fitts' law. They built and compared Fitts' law models for the mouse and joystick. Many dozens of HCI papers on Fitts' law have followed in the same vein. We will visit Fitts' law shortly, but first let's examine how a prediction equation is built.

7.2.1 **Linear regression model**

The basic prediction equation expresses a linear relationship between an predictor variable (x) and a criterion or response variable (y):

$$y = mx + b \qquad (7.1)$$

where m is the slope of the relationship and b is the y-intercept. See Fig. 7.15.

To build this equation, we first need a set of x-y sample points. Although any two ratio-scale variables will do, most commonly the x-y points combine the setting on a predictor or independent ratio-scale variable (x) with the measured value of a human response on a dependent variable (y). Since we are dealing with humans, variability is unavoidable; so, the sample points are unlikely to lie on the line. They will scatter about. If the model is good, the points will be reasonably close to a straight line. How close is a key question.

Finding the best-fitting straight line involves a process known in statistics as linear regression. The objective is to find coefficients m and b in Eq. (7.1) for the line that minimizes the squared distances (least squares) of the points from the line.[9] The result is the prediction equation – an equation that gives the best estimate of y in terms of x. Of course, the model is based on the sample points used in building the equation. If the data are valid and the model is correct, a good prediction equation should

---

[9] Enter "linear regression" or "least squares" into Google or Wikipedia, and you will find all the details.

Participant	Entry Speed (wpm)	
	Stylus Tapping	Touch Typing
P1	18.2	14
P2	23.5	44
P3	26.0	32
P4	20.3	50
P5	20.3	36
P6	17.1	33
P7	24.0	74
P8	14.7	22
P9	20.3	31
P10	19.7	33
P11	22.4	25
P12	13.1	19

(a)

(b)

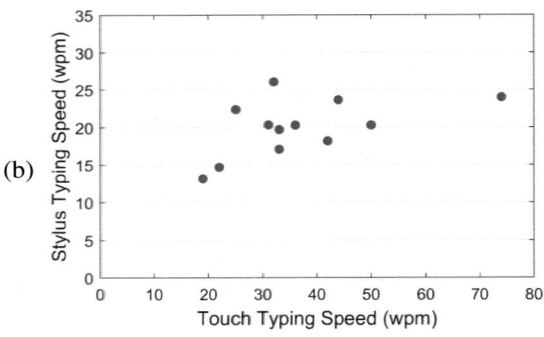

FIGURE 7.16

Relationship between stylus-tapping speed and touch-typing speed. (a) Data. (b) Scatter plot (adapted from [328, Fig. 4]).

emerge. There is also a built-in assumption that the relationship is linear, which is not necessarily the case. Let's visit an example in HCI.

As part of an experiment investigating text entry using a stylus on soft keyboards, MacKenzie and Zhang [328] also wondered whether entry speed by stylus-tapping could be predicted from user's speed in touch-typing with a standard keyboard. The experiment involved 12 participants. Each participant was given a pretest to measure their touch-typing speed. During the experiment, participants entered text using a stylus and a Qwerty soft keyboard displayed on an LCD tablet. The pretest touch-typing speed (predictor variable) and experimentally measured stylus-tapping speed (response variable) are given in Fig. 7.16a for each participant. As customary, the predictor variable is along the x-axis and the response variable is along the y-axis.

As a precursor to building a prediction equation, a simpler question is often posed: Is there a relationship between the two variables? For this example, the question is this: Are fast touch typists also fast at stylus tapping?[10] Visualizing the data as a scatter plot helps. See Fig. 7.16b. Yes, there seems to be a relationship. For example the slowest touch typist, P12 at 19 wpm, was also rather slow at stylus tapping (13.1 wpm). For the 12 points in the figure, the coefficient of correlation is $r = .5228$.[11] That's a modest positive correlation.

The next step is to build the prediction equation – the best-fitting straight-line equation predicting stylus-tapping speed (y) from touch-typing speed (x). This is easily done using a spreadsheet application such as Microsoft Excel.[12] For the data in Fig. 7.16a, the prediction equation is

$$y = 0.1342\,x + 15.037 \tag{7.2}$$

Fig. 7.17 is an embellished version of the chart in Fig. 7.16b. As well as the scatter of points, it shows the line for the prediction equation along with the equation and the squared coefficient of correlation, $R^2 = .2733$. (By convention, R^2 is set in uppercase, r in lowercase.) R^2 is interpreted as "the amount of variation in the data that is explained by the model." It is commonly articulated as a percent. So, the model in Eq. (7.2) explains about 27% of the variation of the data in Fig. 7.16a. That's not very high, so, in this case, the model is at best a modest predictor of stylus-tapping speed from touch-typing speed.[13]

One of the benefits of a predictive model is the potential to predict the outcome on a value of the predictor never actually visited. Note in Fig. 7.16a that no participant had a touch-typing speed in the range of 60 wpm. Even so, we might conjecture that a user with a touch-typing speed of 60 wpm would have a stylus-tapping speed of

$$y = 0.1342 \times 60 + 15.037 = 23.1 \text{ wpm}. \tag{7.3}$$

Given the scatter of points in Fig. 7.16b, there is clearly some uncertainty surrounding this prediction. The standard error (SE) is a useful statistic for gauging this uncertainty. SE establishes confidence intervals around a prediction. For the data in Fig. 7.16a, $SE = 3.39$ wpm.[14] Values within $-1.96\,SE$ and $+1.96\,SE$ of a prediction

---

[10] The motivation is that proficient typists have a good visual image of letter positions on a Qwerty keyboard, and, therefore, may require less visual scan time when using a stylus on a soft keyboard. Perhaps, this phenomenon only applies to hunt-and-peck typists – typists who visually attend to the keyboard when typing. True touch typists tend to use muscle memory and do not visually attend to their keyboard. Perhaps they will exhibit a reverse phenomenon. More research is needed!

[11] The coefficient of correlation is computed in Microsoft Excel using the CORREL function.

[12] First, the points are plotted as a "(XY) scatter" chart. With the points selected, the "Add Trendline" option from the Chart menu is used to add a linear regression line (trendline) to the chart. Options are available to include the equation and the squared correlation (R^2). If the goal is just to compute the slope (m) and intercept (b), then the SLOPE and INTERCEPT functions may be used.

[13] Low values of R^2 are common in the literature. Yin and Zhai [538] report a linear regression model with $R^2 = .013$. As they noted "the model accounted for very little of the variance in the actual selection (1.3%)."

[14] The standard error (SE) is calculated in Microsoft Excel using the STEYX function. The formula assumes the data are from a sample, rather than the population.

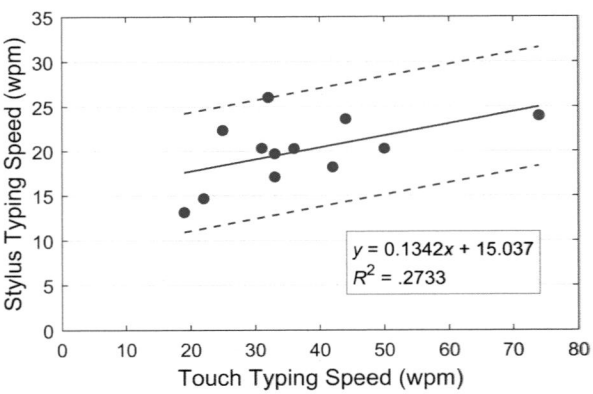

FIGURE 7.17

Scatter plot from Fig. 7.16b embellished with linear regression line, prediction equation, squared coefficient of correlation (R^2) and dashed lines showing the 95% confidence interval.

are within a 95% confidence interval. So, for the model developed here, there is 95% confidence that a user whose touch-typing speed is 60 wpm will have a stylus-tapping speed between $23.1 + (1.96 \times 3.39) = 16.4$ wpm and $23.1 + (1.96 \times 3.39) = 29.7$ wpm. Dashed lines showing the 95% confidence window are included in Fig. 7.17.

Usually linear regression models are reported giving the equation and R^2. Confidence intervals and *SE* are generally not given, although there are exceptions [80,309]. Sometimes, the standard error is given separately for the slope and intercept coefficients in a linear regression model [2,57,387]. Let's move on to a popular prediction model in HCI, Fitts' law.

7.2.2 Fitts' law

One of the most widely used models in HCI is Fitts' law. If an interaction involves a rapid-aimed movement, such a moving a finger or cursor to a target and selecting the target, there's a good chance someone has experimented with the interaction and used Fitts' law to model it. Fitts' law has three uses in HCI:

- To learn if a device or interaction technique conforms to the model by building the prediction equation and examining the correlation for "goodness of fit"
- To use the prediction equation in analysing design alternatives
- To use Fitts' index of performance (now throughput) as a dependent variable in a comparative evaluation

We'll visit each of these in the discussions that follow.

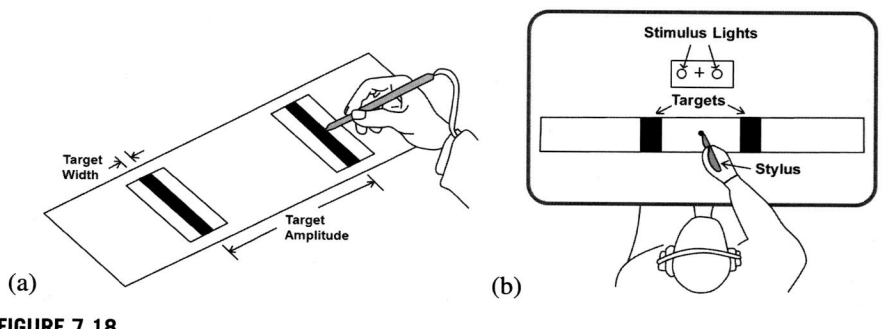

(a)   (b)

FIGURE 7.18

Experiment paradigms for Fitts' law. (a) Serial task [125]. (b) Discrete task [126].

Since Fitts' law comes to HCI by way of basic research in experimental psychology, we begin with some background. Detailed reviews are provided elsewhere [301,356,466,514].

7.2.2.1 Background

Fitts was an experimental psychologist interested in applying information theory to human behaviour. This was a common theme of research in the 1950s as it merged the idea of human performance with the contemporary and emerging mathematical concept of "information" in electronic communications. Fitts argued that the amplitude of an aimed movement was analogous to the information in an electronic signal and that the spatial accuracy of the move was analogous to electronic noise. Furthermore, he proposed that the human motor system is like a communications channel, where movements are like the transmission of signals. Fitts' analogy emerged from Shannon's Theorem 17, expressing the information capacity C (in bits/s) of a communications channel of bandwidth B (in s^{-1} or Hz) as

$$C = B \log_2 \left(\frac{S}{N} + 1 \right)$$ (7.4)

where S is the signal power and N is the noise power [444, p. 100-103].

Fitts presented his analogy – now his "law" – in two highly celebrated papers, one in 1954 [125], the second in 1964 [126]. The 1954 paper described a serial, or reciprocal, target acquisition task where participants alternately tap on targets of width W separated by amplitude A (see Fig. 7.18a). The 1964 paper described a similar experiment using a discrete task, where subjects selected one of two targets in response to a stimulus light (see Fig. 7.18b). It is easy to imagine how to update Fitts' apparatus with computer input devices and targets rendered on a computer display.

The relationship Fitts examined is that between the amplitude of the movement task, the time taken, and the width, or tolerance, of the region within which the move terminates. In what may be the most understated conclusion in all of experimental psychology, Fitts summarized his findings as follows: "The results are sufficiently uniform to indicate that the hypothesized relation between speed, amplitude, and tolerance may be a general one" [125, p. 389]. Indeed, the robustness of Fitts' law is extraordinary. In the decades since Fitts' seminal work, the relationship has been verified countless times and in remarkably diverse settings, whether under a microscope or under water.

Fitts proposed to quantify a movement task's difficulty – ID, the index of difficulty – using information theory by the metric "bits." Specifically,

$$ID = \log_2\left(\frac{2A}{W}\right) \qquad (7.5)$$

The amplitude (A) and width (W) are analogous to Shannon's signal (S) and noise (N) in Eq. (7.4). Note the offsetting influences of A and W in the equation. Doubling the distance to a target has the same effect as halving its size. An important thesis in Fitts' work was that the relationship between task difficulty and the movement time (MT) is linear. The following expression for ID was introduced later to improve the information-theoretic basis for the relationship [301]:

$$ID = \log_2\left(\frac{A}{W} + 1\right) \qquad (7.6)$$

Because A and W are both measures of distance, the term in parentheses in Eq. (7.6) is unitless. The unit "bits" emerges from the use of base 2 for the logarithm.

Fitts also proposed to quantify the human rate of information processing in aimed movements using "bits per second" as the units. This is a provocative idea, based purely on analogy, without a basis in human psychomotor behaviour. Fitts' *index of performance*, now called *throughput* (TP, in bits/s), is calculated by dividing ID (bits) by the mean movement time, MT (seconds), computed over a sequence of trials:

$$TP = \frac{ID_e}{MT} \qquad (7.7)$$

The subscript "e" in ID_e reflects a small but important adjustment, which Fitts endorsed in his 1964 paper. An adjustment for accuracy involves first computing the effective target width as

$$W_e = 4.133 \times SD_x \qquad (7.8)$$

where SD_x is the standard deviation in a participant's selection coordinates.[15] Computed in this manner, W_e includes the spatial variability, or accuracy, in responses. In essence, it captures what a participant actually did, rather than what he or she

---

[15] The effective target width (W_e) adjusts W to reflect a 4% error rate. Full details are provided by Fitts and others [126,300,301,466] [514, pp. 145-149].

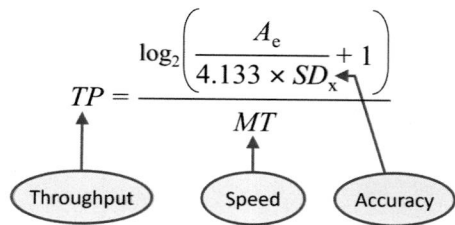

FIGURE 7.19

Throughput equation showing speed and accuracy.

was asked to do. This adjustment necessitates a similar adjustment to *ID*, yielding an "effective index of difficulty:"

$$ID_e = \log_2 \left(\frac{A}{W_e} + 1 \right) \tag{7.9}$$

Calculated using the adjustment for accuracy, *TP* is a human performance measure that embeds both the speed and accuracy of responses. Because of this, *TP* is a more stable measure than speed or accuracy alone [167,312,546]. Fig. 7.19 presents an expanded version of Eq. (7.7) showing the connection to speed and accuracy in participant responses.

Throughput is most useful as a dependent variable in factorial experiments using pointing devices or pointing techniques as independent variables.

If using Fitts' law as a predictive model is the goal, then the movement time (*MT*) to complete a task is predicted using a simple linear equation:[16]

$$MT = a + b \times ID \tag{7.10}$$

The slope and intercept coefficients in the prediction equation are determined through empirical tests, typically using linear regression. The tests are undertaken in a controlled experiment using a group of participants and one or more input devices and task conditions.

7.2.2.2 Example

In this section we demonstrate how to build a Fitts' law predictive model using a subset of the data from an experiment comparing two pointing devices [313]. One device was an Interlink Electronics RemotePoint. The RemotePoint is a cordless pointing device operated in the air, for example, while giving a presentation using

---

[16] It is important to distinguish between building a Fitts' law model and using a Fitts' law model. In building the model, ID_e should be used, so the model reflects both the speed and accuracy of participants' responses. In using the model, *ID* is used. The predictions will carry a 4% error probability.

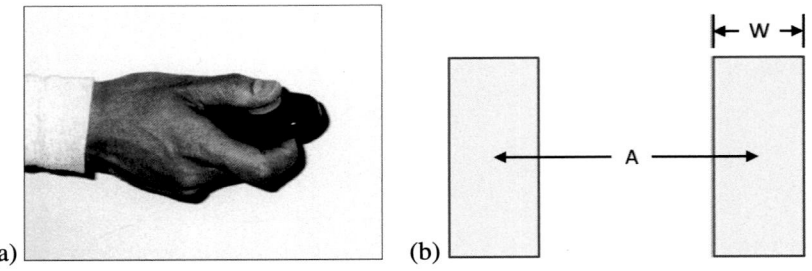

FIGURE 7.20

Fitts' law example. (a) RemotePoint pointing device. (b) Experiment task.

a large interactive vertical display. Cursor position is controlled by a thumb-activated isometric joystick. Selection uses a trigger-like switch operated with the index finger. See Fig. 7.20a. A Microsoft Mouse 2.0 served as a baseline condition. Twelve participants performed a series of reciprocal point-select tasks across nine target conditions: $A = 40, 80, 160$ pixels crossed with $W = 10, 20, 40$ pixels. Using Eq. (7.6), the target conditions spanned a range of difficulties from

$$ID = \log_2 \left(\frac{40}{40} + 1 \right) = 1.00 \text{ bits} \tag{7.11}$$

to

$$ID = \log_2 \left(\frac{160}{10} + 1 \right) = 4.09 \text{ bits.} \tag{7.12}$$

See Fig. 7.20b.

The data for the mouse and RemotePoint conditions are given in Fig. 7.21. There are nine rows, one for each A-W target condition. The three columns on the left are the target conditions (A, W, and the calculated index of task difficulty, ID). The remaining columns are the participants' responses. W_e is the effective target width (Eq. (7.8)). ID_e is the effective index of difficulty (Eq. (7.9)). MT is the mean movement time in milliseconds. TP is the throughput in bits/s (Eq. (7.7)).

A Fitts' law model can be built for both device conditions in Fig. 7.21. The prediction equations use MT as the dependent variable and either ID or ID_e as the predictor variable. The advantage in using ID_e is that the model includes both the speed and accuracy of responses and therefore more accurately reflects participant behaviour.

The easiest way to build and demonstrate the models is using a spreadsheet application. Fig. 7.22 provides a visualization of the data as a scatter plot for each device. The chart also includes the regression lines, the prediction equations, and R^2. Both R^2 values are very high. The mouse model, for example, explains 97% of the variance in the observations.

The format of the prediction equations in Fig. 7.22 can be improved. For the RemotePoint, the predicted time to move a cursor over a distance A to select a target

A (pixels)	W (pixels)	ID (bits)	Mouse				RemotePoint			
			W_e (pixels)	ID_e (bits)	MT (ms)	TP (bits/s)	W_e (pixels)	ID_e (bits)	MT (ms)	TP (bits/s)
40	10	2.32	11.23	2.19	665	3.29	13.59	1.98	1587	1.25
40	20	1.58	19.46	1.61	501	3.21	21.66	1.51	1293	1.17
40	40	1.00	40.20	1.00	361	2.76	37.92	1.04	1001	1.04
80	10	3.17	10.28	3.13	762	4.11	10.08	3.16	1874	1.69
80	20	2.32	18.72	2.40	604	3.97	25.21	2.06	1442	1.43
80	40	1.58	35.67	1.70	481	3.53	37.75	1.64	1175	1.40
160	10	4.09	10.71	3.99	979	4.08	10.33	4.04	2353	1.72
160	20	3.17	21.04	3.11	823	3.77	19.09	3.23	1788	1.81
160	40	2.32	41.96	2.27	615	3.69	35.97	2.45	1480	1.65
		Mean:	23.25	2.38	644	3.60	23.51	2.35	1555	1.46

FIGURE 7.21

Experiment conditions (A, W, ID) and participant responses (W_e, ID_e, MT, TP) for the standard mouse and the RemotePoint.

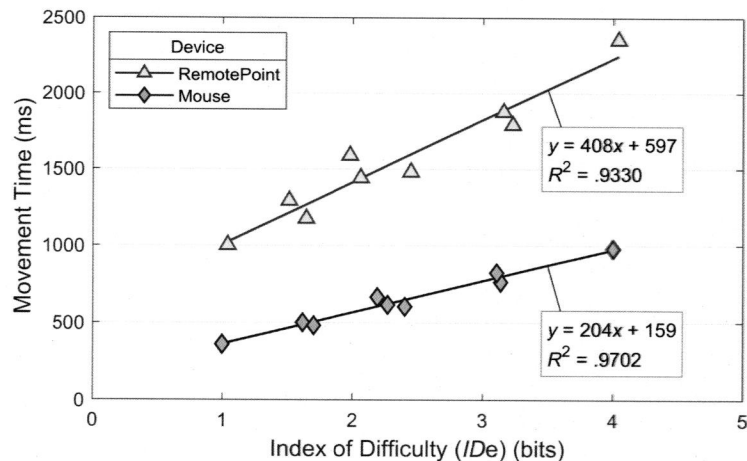

FIGURE 7.22

Scatter plot and regression lines for data in Fig. 7.21 (adapted from [313]).

of width W is

$$MT = 597 + 408 \times \log_2\left(\frac{A}{W} + 1\right) \text{ ms.} \tag{7.13}$$

For the mouse, the prediction equation is

$$MT = 159 + 204 \times \log_2\left(\frac{A}{W} + 1\right) \text{ ms.} \tag{7.14}$$

What insight is found in the Fitts' law models in Fig. 7.22? An initial observation is that point-select operations with both devices conform to Fitts' law, as evident by the high values of R^2. This is the first use of Fitts' law, noted earlier. Also, it is apparent that the RemotePoint performed poorly compared to the mouse. The movement time was substantially longer for the RemotePoint, for all target conditions. The slopes of the regression lines demonstrate a substantially lower rate of information processing for the RemotePoint. The slope has units ms/bit. The slope reciprocal, with a conversion to seconds, has units bits/s. Thus, a lower slope is a higher rate of information processing (throughput). The mouse is clearly a better device.[17] As an overall measure, the preferred calculation for throughput uses a division of means (Eq. (7.7)), as proposed by Fitts [125]. These values are along the bottom row in Fig. 7.21. The throughput for the RemotePoint (1.46 bits/s) is less than half that for the mouse (3.60 bits/s).

There is also some debate on the method of calculating throughput. For example, the throughput for the mouse is 3.60 bits/s using the division of means (Fig. 7.21) or $\frac{1}{204}$ = 4.90 bits/s using the slope reciprocal in the regression equation (Fig. 7.22). See Soukoreff and MacKenzie [466] or Zhai et al. [546] for further discussion.

There are many dozens of scatter plots in the HCI literature that include Fitts' law prediction models. Some examples are summarized in Fig. 7.23. Although R^2 > .8 for all models in the figure, there is a significant spread in the slope coefficients. This is partly due to the use of different methodologies in collecting data and building the models. Consequently, across-study comparisons for Fitts' law research are often difficult.

In the 1950s, when Fitts proposed his model of human movement, graphical user interfaces and computer pointing devices did not exist. Yet, throughout the history of HCI, since Card et al. [60], research on computer pointing is inseparable from Fitts' law. The initial studies focused on device comparisons and model conformity. As the field evolved and matured, however, Fitts' law found its way into diverse topics – topics only peripherally related to pointing devices. Examples include expanding targets, hidden targets, fish-eye targets, crossing-based interfaces, path following, steering, pointing on the move, eye tracking, force feedback, gravity wells, multi-monitor displays, magic lenses, and so on. Research in these topics, and more, has thrived on the theory and predictive modelling techniques inspired and guided by Fitts' law. This is Fitts' legacy to research in human-computer interaction.

In looking back, the success of Fitts' law in HCI is due in no small measure to the endorsement the model received early on from Card, Moran, and Newell in *The Psychology of Human-Computer Interaction* [64]. Their model human processor (MHP) included two general psychological information-theoretic models as guiding principles for the field [64, pp. 26-27]. One was Fitts' law. The other was the Hick-Hyman law for choice reaction time.

---

[17] "Better," here, refers to performance measured using task completion time or Fitts' throughput. If the interaction involves standing in front of an audience, the RemotePoint is likely a better choice.

First Author (reference)	ID range (bits)	Inter-cept, b (ms)	Slope, m (ms/bit)	1/m (bits/s)	R^2	Notes
Kim [246, Fig. 12]	1.9-4.3	297	357	2.80	.9230	12 participants, standing, face tracking using camera on phone
Kyian [267, Fig. 8]	1.1-3.6	511	483	2.07	.9494	12 participants, direct touch on smartphone, viewed in VR
Lin [285, Fig. 2]	2.0-4.1	433	104	9.6	.9483	38 participants ages 60-69 yrs, tapping targets on tablet
Triantafyllidis [493, Fig. 1]	0.9-4.3	660	270	3.70	.9060	1 participant, target clicking, 20 trial repetitions per condition
Woodward [529, Fig. 2]	1.9-3.8	471	83	12.1	.9282	54 children ages 5-10 yrs, 2D task on a touchscreen
Yamanaka [532, Fig. 5a]	1.5-5.0	133	90	11.1	.9813	12 participants, 1D task, touch input on smartphone
Zhou [554, Fig. 11]	2.3-7.8	710	230	4.35	.8200	16 participants, VR 3D pointing with depth-adaptive cursor

FIGURE 7.23

Examples of Fitts' law regression models.

7.2.3 Choice reaction time

The Hick-Hyman law for choice reaction time, like Fitts' law, arrived in HCI by way of basic research in experimental psychology – research seeking to model human behaviour according to information processing principles [189,205]. The model also takes the form of a prediction equation. Given n stimuli, associated one-for-one with n responses, the time to react (RT) to the onset of a stimulus and make the correct response is given by

$$RT = a + b \log_2(n + 1) \qquad (7.15)$$

where a and b are empirically determined constants. Reasonable values for the constants are $a = 200$ ms and $b = 150$ ms/bit [64, pp. 27, 75].[18] Fig. 7.24 shows a typical setup for a choice reaction time experiment. At random intervals, a stimulus light is activated and the human responds by pressing the associated key as quickly as possible.

As with Fitts' law, the log term is analogous to the information content of the task, with units "bits." There is an interesting twist to this for choice reaction time. If some

---

[18] The model is sometimes expressed as $RT = a + b \log_2(n)$ and sometimes without an intercept. See Card et al. [64, pp. 71-76] and Welford [514, pp. 61-70]) for detailed discussions.

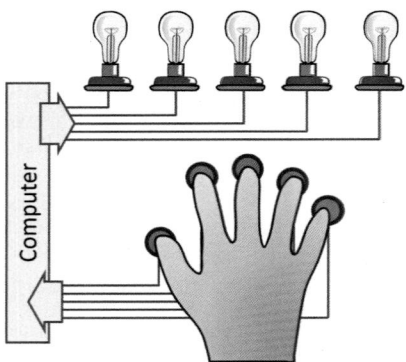

FIGURE 7.24

Paradigm for choice reaction time experiments.

choices are more probable than others, the information content of the task is reduced. This in turn reduces the choice reaction time. Let's explore this idea.

For a set of alternatives with different probabilities, the information (H) is

$$H = \sum_i p_i \log_2 \left(\frac{1}{p_i} + 1 \right) \tag{7.16}$$

where p_i is the probability of occurrence of the ith item in the set. Consider a choice selection task with 26 alternatives. If the alternatives appear with equal probability, the information content of the task is simply

$$H = \log_2 (26) = 4.70 \text{ bits} \tag{7.17}$$

If the alternatives appear with different probabilities, the information is reduced according to Eq. (7.16). This occurs, for example, if the 26 stimuli are letters of the English alphabet and they appear with the expected frequency for English. For example, "e" is common, "z" uncommon. An example set of letter frequencies and probabilities for English is shown in Fig. 7.25. The data were obtained from the British National Corpus[19] using the word-frequency list of Silfverberg et al. [454].

Since "e" appears with greater frequency than, for example, "z", the task is slightly easier because there is a small opportunity to anticipate the choices at the onset of a stimulus. In so doing, the reaction time is reduced. Overall, there is less

---

[19] www.natcorp.ox.ac.uk/.

Letter	Frequency	Probability (p)	$p \, log_2(1/p + 1)$
a	24373121	0.0810	0.3028
b	4762938	0.0158	0.0950
c	8982417	0.0299	0.1525
d	10805580	0.0359	0.1742
e	37907119	0.1260	0.3981
f	7486889	0.0249	0.1335
g	5143059	0.0171	0.1008
h	18058207	0.0600	0.2486
i	21820970	0.0725	0.2819
j	474021	0.0016	0.0147
k	1720909	0.0057	0.0427
l	11730498	0.0390	0.1846
m	7391366	0.0246	0.1322
n	21402466	0.0711	0.2783
o	23215532	0.0772	0.2935
p	5719422	0.0190	0.1092
q	297237	0.0010	0.0099
r	17897352	0.0595	0.2471
s	19059775	0.0633	0.2578
t	28691274	0.0954	0.3358
u	8022379	0.0267	0.1404
v	2835696	0.0094	0.0636
w	6505294	0.0216	0.1203
x	562732	0.0019	0.0170
y	5910495	0.0196	0.1119
z	93172	0.0003	0.0036
		H (bits) =	4.2500

FIGURE 7.25

Letters of the English alphabet, with frequency counts and probabilities from a corpus. Information H, in bits, is calculated using Eq. (7.16).

uncertainty, or information, in the task. The information content of the task is reduced from 4.70 bits (Eq. (7.17)) to 4.25 bits (Eq. (7.16), illustrated in Fig. 7.25).

The Hick-Hyman law has surfaced in a few contexts in HCI research. Card et al. [64, p. 74] describe an example of a telephone operator selecting among ten buttons when the light behind a button comes on.

Landauer and Nachbar [271] applied the Hick-Hyman law in measuring and predicting the time to select items in hierarchical menus. Besides confirming the suitability of the law to this category of task, they also found empirical support that breadth should be favoured over depth in hierarchical menus. Note that choice reaction is different from visual search, which is a linear function of the number of items. Landauer and Nachbar eliminated visual scanning in the task by ensuring that "the sets of choice alternatives were well practiced and well-ordered so that it was not necessary to search them sequentially to find the target location" [271, p. 73].

Roy et al. [421] discuss the impact of learning on choice reaction time, as modelled by the Hick-Hyman law. Ruiz et al. [422] used the Hick-Hyman law to model the perception, planning, and activation time for users to switch modes with their non-dominant hand in a tablet interface.

Despite these efforts, and a few others, the Hick-Hyman law has failed to gain the same momentum in HCI as Fitts' law [442]. One reason is that the model alone is of limited use [288]. In many situations there are additional behaviours concurrent with choice reaction, such as movement or visual search, and these complicate applying the model.

7.2.4 The keystroke-level model

One of the earliest and certainly one of the most comprehensive predictive models in the HCI literature is the keystroke-level model (KLM) by Card, Moran, and Newell [63][64, chap. 8]. Unlike Fitts' law and the Hick-Hyman law, the KLM was developed specifically for analysing human performance in interactive computing systems. It was offered as a practical design tool, or as the authors' called it, an engineering model. The model predicts expert error-free task completion times using the following elements:

- Task (or series of sub-tasks)
- Method used
- Command language of the system
- Motor skill parameters of the user
- Response time parameters of the system

The model is useful in situations where the sequence of interactions in performing a task is known. For example, if the task is "delete a file," the KLM can predict the time to do the task provided the interactions (operators) can be specified. If there are two or three different methods to do the task (e.g., mouse + menu selection vs. keyboard + command entry) then the KLM can predict the time for each method. If used at the design stage, then design alternatives may be considered and compared.

The KLM is not useful if the details of the interactions are not known. A related model, GOMS (Goals, Operators, Methods, Selection rules), operates at a higher level and attempts, among other things, to predict the method the user will adopt [64, chap. 5]. This is complicated as it builds upon the cognitive information processing activities of the user and assumes also that users act rationally in attaining their goals.

A KLM prediction divides a task down into subtasks, or primitive operations. The total predicted time is the sum of the subtask times. The model works with four motor-control operators (K = keystroking, P = pointing, H = homing, D = drawing),

Operator	Description	Time (s)
K	PRESS A KEY OR BUTTON Pressing a modifier key (e.g., shift) counts as a separate operation. Time varies with typing skill: Best typist (135 wpm) Good typist (90 wpm) Average skilled typist (55 wpm) Average non-secretary typist (40 wpm) Typing random letters Typing complex codes Worst typist (unfamiliar with keyboard)	 0.08 0.12 0.20 0.28 0.50 0.75 1.20
P	POINT WITH A MOUSE Empirical value based on Fitts' law. Range from 0.8 to 1.5 seconds. Operator does *not* include the button click at the end of a pointing operation	1.10
H	HOME HAND(S) ON KEYBOARD OR OTHER DEVICE	0.40
$D(n_D.l_D)$	DRAW n_D STRAIGHT-LINE SEGMENTS OF TOTAL LENGTH l_D. Drawing with the mouse constrained to a grid.	$.9\,n_D + .16\,l_D$
M	MENTALLY PREPARE	1.35
$R(t)$	RESPONSE BY SYSTEM Different commands require different response times. Counted only if the user must wait.	t

FIGURE 7.26

Keystroke-level model (KLM) operators and values (from [64, p. 264]).

one mental operator (M), and one system response operator (R):

$$t_{\text{EXECUTE}} = t_K + t_P + t_H + t_D + t_M + t_R \qquad (7.18)$$

Some operations are omitted or repeated, depending on the task. For example, if a keying subtask requires n keystrokes, t_K becomes $n \times t_K$. Each t_K operation is assigned a value according to the skill of the user, with values ranging from $t_K = 0.08$ s for highly skilled typists to $t_K = 1.20$ s for a novice working with an unfamiliar keyboard. The pointing operator, t_P, is a constant based on Fitts' law. The operators and their values from the original KLM are given in Fig. 7.26.

7.2.4.1 Original KLM experiment

To validate the KLM, Card, Moran, and Newell conducted an experiment using fourteen tasks performed using various methods. Task T1, for example, was "Replace one 5-letter word with another (one line from previous task)." It was performed on three different systems, each with a unique command set. On one system, POET, the required sequence of subtasks was as follows:

Jump to next line	**M K** LINEFEED
Issue Substitute command	**M K** [S]
Type new word	5**K** [word]
Terminate new word	**M K** RETURN
Type old word	5**K** [word]
Terminate old word	**M K** RETURN
Terminate command	**K** RETURN

The operators for each subtask are shown on the right. The task required 4 mental operations (M) and 15 keystroking operations (K):

$$t_{\text{EXECUTE}} = 4 \times t_{\text{M}} + 15 \times t_{\text{K}} \tag{7.19}$$

t_{M} was set to 1.35 s (Fig. 7.26). t_{K} was set to 0.23 s, based on the mean keystroking time of the participants, determined in a five-minute pretest. The predicted execution time for task T1 on POET was therefore

$$t_{\text{EXECUTE}} = 4 \times 1.35 + 15 \times 0.23 = 8.58 \text{ s}. \tag{7.20}$$

In the experiment, twelve users preformed the task an average of 27 times each. The mean execution time was 7.8 s ($SE = 0.9$ s). So, the observation deviated from the prediction by ~11%. The results were similar for the other tasks. Fig. 7.27 shows the observed vs. predicted task execution times for all 14 tasks (32 tasks, counting method variations). The coalescing of points about the diagonal is clear. This provides a general validation of the model. An arrow identifies the result for task T1 discussed above.

7.2.4.2 Parametric analysis

A model is a malleable tool that researchers can and should mould to tease out issues or opportunities in a problem space – opportunities to build a better interface or better interaction technique. A teaching of this by Card, Moran, and Newell is their parametric analysis or sensitivity analysis of the KLM. A predictive model is built on parameters. If parameters become variables, and slide up and down, what is the effect on the model's outcome? How sensitive are the predictions to changes in the parameters? This was explored in a series of arguments and demonstrations [64, pp. 287-293]. Fig. 7.28 is an example for an editing task. The figure charts t_{EXECUTE} for three interaction methods as a function of n – the distance in words from an initial location to the location of a misspelled word to correct. Viewing from left to right, optimal performance is achieved with Method W for $n < 2.7$ Method S for $2.7 < n < 10.2$, and Method R for $n > 10.2$. If the designer is choosing among candidate methods, and it is known that certain values of n are common, then the parametric analysis in Fig. 7.28 provides precisely the information needed. A design choice is made, supported by evidence obtained from a model of the interaction. Similar sensitivity analyses have appeared since Card et al.'s original KLM publication (e.g., [2,84,156,320]).

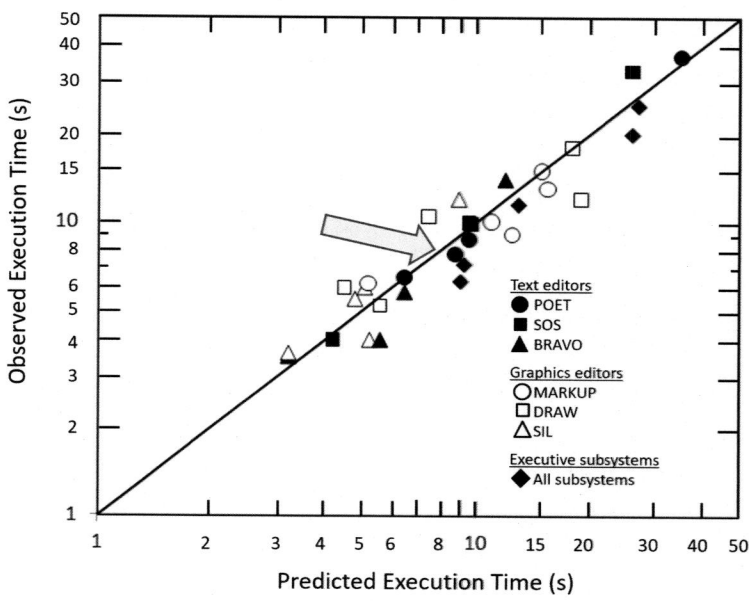

FIGURE 7.27

Observed vs. predicted execution times for tasks in the KLM validation experiment. The arrow shows task T1 with POET (adapted from [64, p. 277]).

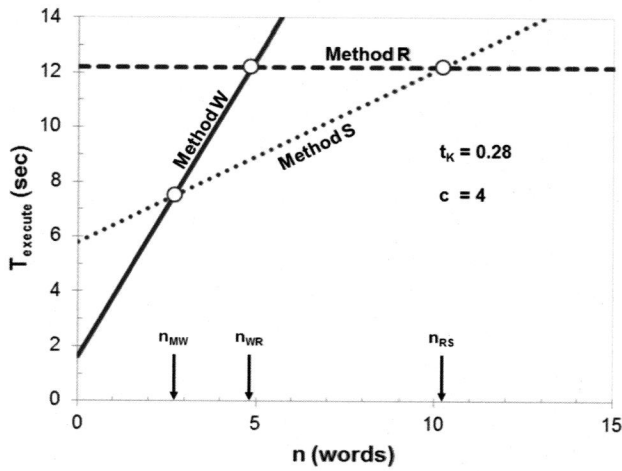

FIGURE 7.28

Parametric analysis showing the sensitivity of predictions for three methods based on changes in *n* – the location of an edit relative to the current location (adapted from [64, p. 290]).

Early experiments with the KLM related primarily to text editing and document management. The tasks were things like "delete a line of text," "add a label to a box," or "transfer a file to another computer, renaming it" [64, p. 272]. These tasks are just as common today as in the early 1980s; however, the available task methods are quite different. Transferring a file to another computer is good example. Today, this task is likely to involve a mix of mouse and keyboard operations with a GUI-based FTP (file transfer protocol) application. In the original experiment, the task involved FTP as well; but the method only involved a keyboard. The subtask coding included 31 keystroking operations and 0 pointing operations.

7.2.4.3 Updating the pointing operator (P)

Considering that the KLM dates to the 1980s, it is not surprising that some of the operators need updating. The pointing operator (P), for example, is a constant of 1.10 seconds. With the ubiquity of the mouse in today's graphical user interfaces (GUIs), this operator could benefit from the additional fidelity afforded with a Fitts' law prediction. Using the mouse model from Fig. 7.22, for example, a reasonable substitute for P is

$$t_P = 0.159 + 0.204 \times \log_2 \left(\frac{A}{W} + 1 \right). \tag{7.21}$$

If there are numerous mouse operations in a task undergoing KLM predictions, then the added precision in Eq. (7.21) will improve the analysis. For example, if a subtask involves clicking a 1.2 cm wide toolbar button, having just clicked a neighbouring button 3.2 cm away, then the pointing time is[20]

$$t_P = 0.159 + 0.204 \times \log_2 \left(\frac{3.2}{1.2} + 1 \right) = 0.45 \text{ s}. \tag{7.22}$$

Alternatively, if the mouse pointer must move, say, 44.6 cm to reach the same toolbar button, the pointing time is

$$t_P = 0.159 + 0.204 \times \log_2 \left(\frac{44.6}{1.2} + 1 \right) = 1.22 \text{ s}. \tag{7.23}$$

The predictions above include the terminating mouse-button click to select the target, unlike the original P operator.

As an example of applying the KLM to current GUI interaction, consider the editing operations to change the font style and font family for text while word processing. Fig. 7.29 shows the operations to change "M K" to boldface in the Arial font. The image is a screen snap for the editing performed above using Microsoft Word to characterise task T1. Four pointing operations are required: select the text, select Bold, select the drop-down arrow in the Font list, and select Arial. See Fig. 7.30.

---

[20] For Fitts' law studies with the mouse, pointing times of 500 ms or less are common for easy tasks (*ID* ~ 3 bits). The minimum mouse pointing time in the original KLM was 800 ms (see Fig. 7.26) which seems high.

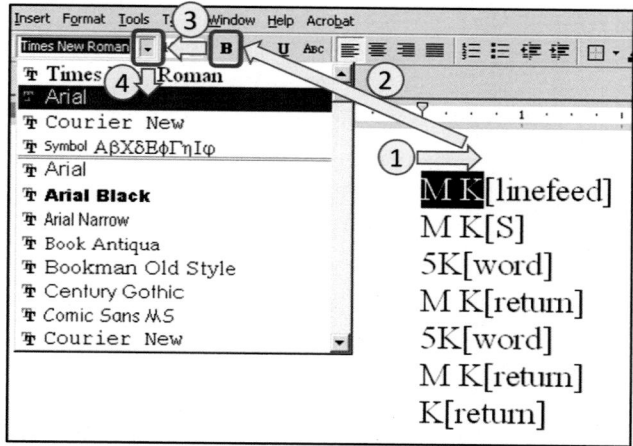

FIGURE 7.29

Mouse operations to change "M K" to boldface in the Arial font. The application is MS Word.

Mouse Subtasks	KLM Operators	t_P (s)
1. Drag across text to select "M K"	**M P**[2.5, 0.5]	0.686
2. Move pointer to Bold button and click	**M P**[13, 1]	0.936
3. Move pointer to Font drop-down button and click	**M P**[3.3, 1]	0.588
4. Move pointer down list to "Arial" and click	**M P**[2.2, 1]	0.501
	$\Sigma t_P =$	2.71

FIGURE 7.30

Mouse subtasks and KLM operators for editing operations in Fig. 7.29.

Here, the pointing operator appears as P[A,W] to specify the movement amplitude and target width of the pointing task. The values shown were obtained using a ruler applied to Fig. 7.29.[21] The execution time for each P operation is given in the right-hand column, computed using Eq. (7.21). As there are four distinct subtasks, each is coded with a mental operator (M) as well as a pointing operator. The predicted task execution time is

$$t_{\text{EXECUTE}} = 4 \times t_M + \sum t_P = 4 \times 1.35 + 2.71 = 8.11 \text{ s}. \quad (7.24)$$

---

[21] If the measurements are done on a display, they vary according to the display size and the zoom-factor of the document view. Since target amplitude and width appear as a ratio in Fitts' index of difficulty, scaling up or down does not affect the Fitts' law predictions.

Keyboard Subtasks	KLM Operators
Select text	**M K**[shift] 3**K**[→]
Convert to boldface	**M K**[ctrl] **K**[b]
Activate Format menu and enter Font sub-menu	**M K**[alt] **K**[o] **K**[f]
Type *a* ("Arial" appears at top of list)	**M K**[a]
Select "Arial"	**K**[↓] **K**[enter]

FIGURE 7.31

Keyboard subtasks and KLM operators for task in Fig. 7.29.

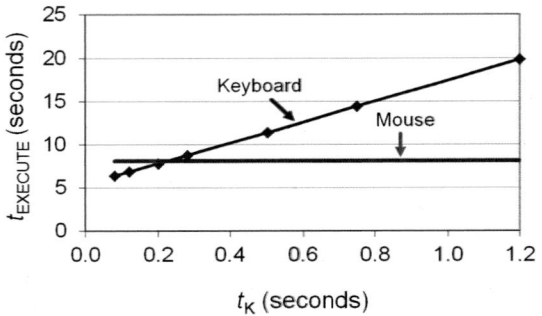

FIGURE 7.32

Sensitivity of prediction to keystroking time, t_K.

As with the keystroking operator (K) in the original KLM, applications of the model using P[A,W] should use a pretest to determine the coefficients in the Fitts' law model for the pointing device and method involved.

Of course, the same task can be done using the keyboard. A set of keyboard subtasks achieving the same effect is shown in Fig. 7.31.

Here, we see the same four mental operators; however, there is an assortment of keystroking actions, as per Microsoft Word. The KLM uses a separate keystroking value for pressing a modifier key, such as SHIFT. The predicted execution time using the keyboard is

$$t_{EXECUTE} = 4 \times t_M + 12 \times t_K = 4 \times 1.35 + 12 \times 0.75 = 14.40 \text{ s.} \qquad (7.25)$$

This prediction uses the "typing complex codes" setting for t_K (0.75 s, see Fig. 7.26). Depending on the user, this value might be too high or too low. Fig. 7.32 explores this by showing the sensitivity of the prediction to changes in the keystroking time, t_K. Markers on the keyboard line show the t_K settings from Fig. 7.26. Of course, changes in t_K do not affect the mouse prediction. The keyboard is slower than the mouse over all but the fastest three settings for t_K. Given that these settings correspond to keystroking times while typing at 55+ wpm, it is unlikely the keyboard method would be faster than the mouse method for any user, including experts.[22]

Of course, the mouse model deserves the same scrutiny as the keystroking operations. The mouse predictions are sensitive to the slope and intercept coefficients in the Fitts' law model. The first subtask was a dragging operation. Strictly speaking, a separate Fitts' law dragging model is required, since it is known that dragging operations are less efficient than pointing operations [301].

7.2.4.4 Other applications and extensions

The example above is a common task on today's GUI systems. Other tasks offer a great range of possibilities for keystroke-level modelling. Examples include scrolling a document with a mouse wheel, finger, or thumb input on a mobile phone (perhaps while walking), two-thumb input on a mini-Qwerty keyboard, or stylus input on a PDA. How are these tasks modelled with a keystroke-level model? Clearly, there are many issues to consider in contemporary applications of the KLM. Despite this – or should we say, motivated by this – researchers continue to use the KLM to model interactions in novel HCI contexts.

Other KLM applications include the following:

- Models for attention shifts with mobile phones [197]
- Stylus-based circling gestures [190]
- Managing folders and messages in e-mail applications [21]
- Predictive text entry on mobile phones [12,110,289]
- Task switching in multi-monitor systems [180]
- Mode switching on tablet PCs [422]
- Distractions with in-vehicle information systems (IVIS) [397]
- Nutritionists use of eHealth food plans to assist patients [92]
- Interactions in mixed-reality (MR) systems [54]
- Interfaces using multiple pointing methods [132]
- Exploring visualizations of multi-dimensional graphs [355]
- Task analysis for touch-based smart watches [353]
- Estimating KLM parameters using reinforcement learning [278]

In other cases, the KLM is an embedded component of a comprehensive yet general-purpose modelling tool. An example is CogTool-Explorer [488].

Much of the work just cited extends the KLM by adding or refining operators to suit the application. For example, Ruiz et al. [422] defined a new operator t_{INT}, the interval between a mode switch with the non-dominant hand and the beginning the next action. Pettitt et al. [397] define t_{RF} for "reach far," the time to reach from a

---

[22] The KLM applies to expert users doing a task for the first time. It is not intended for highly over-learned actions (Bonnie John, personal communication, January 2005). If a human operator were to repeatedly perform the task in this example, the task becomes over-learned. It could be modelled using the KLM; however, in such case, there are no mental operators and the key stroking time is substantially reduced.

car's steering wheel to an IVIS (in-vehicle information system). As mentioned above, a model is a malleable tool. Use it, modify it, to suit the problem.

In all cases, use of the KLM entails breaking a task into subtasks and building an overall prediction using Eq. (7.18), perhaps updated with new or refined operators. If the particular KLM implementation is known to work, then the predictions may be used in a true design or engineering setting – the original intention. However, if the model is being extended or applied in a novel research initiative, validation is required. This is typically done in a formal or semi-formal experiment, where the task is performed with users while task completion times are observed and measured. The predicted and observed times are compared. If they are the same or similar, the KLM is validated. Deviations between predictions and observations signal a problem, but not necessarily a problem in the KLM. The discrepancy may indicate a problem in the task coding. The insight can be valuable. As Hinckley et al. [190] note,

> *[The discrepancy] shows where the techniques deviate from the model, indicating the presence of hidden costs. These costs might include increased reaction time resulting from planning what to do next, mental pauses, or delays while the user attends to visual feedback after performing an action. Our methodology cannot attribute these costs to a specific cause. It just lets us deduce that a hidden cost must exist in a specific portion of the task. This is sufficient to generate many insights as to where the bottlenecks to performance lie and what parts of a technique might be improved.*

[190, p. 187]

So, as with descriptive models, predictive models like the KLM are tools for thinking, for generating insight.

Hinckley et al. refer to reacting, planning, pausing, and attending as hidden costs contributing to deviations between predictions and observations. These intangibles are problematic: It is difficult to get inside a user's mind to know what he or she is contemplating, let alone attribute a time cost to mental processes in a model. Arguably, the mental operator (M) in the KLM is its Achilles heel. It is a single operator, pegged at 1.35 s, and is used for all mental processes. The human mind is simply too rich to be distilled so uniformly.

For this reason, researchers often do not model or predict execution time but, instead, model or predict only the keystrokes, or other primitive actions. This is a much simpler problem. Actions, such as keystrokes, stylus taps, finger gestures, button clicks, gaze shifts, menu accesses, and so on, often capture important aspects of an interaction method apart from the human performance element. And modelling such actions is relatively straightforward. The end result is a model that is accurate, but limited. While optimizing an "action parameter" is a noble cause, the connection to user performance is tenuous at best. Hidden costs are real costs, and the earlier they are accounted for – that is, at the modelling or design stage – the better.

7.2.4.5 The KLM and predictive text entry

A classic HCI example of keystroke-level modelling, minus the hidden costs, is text entry, particularly with ambiguous keyboards, such as a phone-style keypad. The relevant statistic for this is KSPC (keystrokes per character). KSPC is both an analytic metric and an empirical measure.[23] As an analytic metric, KSPC is the number of keystrokes required, on average, for each character of text produced using a given input method in a given language. It is known for, example, that a phone-style keypad has KSPC $\approx$ 2.023 for multi-tap and KSPC $\approx$ 1.007 for predictive text entry [303]. If word completion or word prediction is added, KSPC < 1. However, these figures do not account for the performance costs of visually attending to the interface. Let's consider how these costs might be accommodated in a keystroke-level model.

The original KLM experiment did not include a task such as "enter a 43-character phrase of text." The task was likely considered too trivial to bother with, since the prediction reduces to $43 \times t_K$, where t_K is the keystroking time of the participant, based on a pretest for typing speed. In essence, the task would just confirm the pretest.

However, if the target system used a phone-style keypad and the text-entry method was multi-tap, the task seems appropriate for a KLM prediction. Or is it? Consider the 43-character phrase "the quick brown fox jumps over the lazy dog." Entering it using multi-tap requires 88 keystrokes.[24] In this case, the KLM prediction reduces to $88 \times t_K$, where t_K is the keystroking time of the participant, based on a pretest. Of course, the pretest is on a phone keypad using multi-tap. Once again, the task simply confirms the pretest. It is important to remember that the KLM is a model for expert users. The participants would be experts with phone-style keypads.

However, interaction with a phone-style keypad is distinctly different from two-handed typing on a computer keyboard. A phone-style keypad is typically held in the hand with keys pressed either by the thumb of the supporting hand or by the index finger of the opposite hand, as illustrated in Fig. 7.33a and Fig. 7.33b, respectively. Since only a single digit is used for input, the time for each key press can be modelled by Fitts' law, as suggested in Fig. 7.33c for pressing "h" preceded by "t". Many multi-tap key presses are on the same key, but this too is a Fitts' law task (with $A = 0$; $MT \approx$ 160 ms). So, a more refined prediction for multi-tap text entry can use the KLM pointing operator, with Fitts' law coefficients determined in a pretest. Silfverberg et al. [454] developed this approach, presenting separate Fitts' law models for the thumb and index finger.

For touch typing on a Qwerty keyboard or multi-tapping on a phone-style keypad, the KLM's mental operator (M) is not needed. The user knows what to do, and does it – according to his or her keystroking expertise. This is not the case for predictive text entry. Systems that involve word completion, word prediction, phrase prediction, or other language-based adaptive or predictive features are well known to tax the

---

[23] The use of KSPC as an empirical measure was discussed in Chapter 2 (p. 81).

[24] The words (keystrokes) are as follows: the (84433S) quick (778844422255S) brown (22777666966S) fox (33366699S) jumps (58867N7777S) over (66688833777S) the (84433S) lazy (55529999N999S) dog (36664S). S is the SPACE key. N is a NEXT key (e.g., ↓) to segment consecutive letters on the same key.

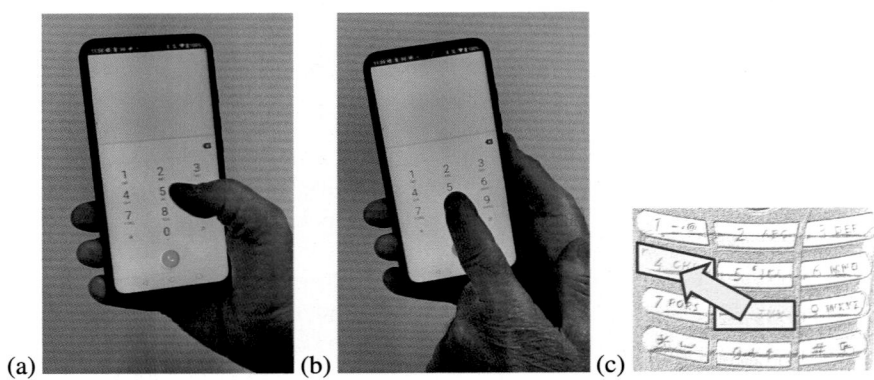

(a)   (b)   (c)

FIGURE 7.33

Interaction with a phone-style ambiguous keypad. (a) Thumb. (b) Index finger. (c) "h" preceded by "t".

attention of users (e.g., [243,253,454]). Predictive text entry techniques require the user to attend to and consider the system's behaviour. Modelling this requires the KLM's mental operator (M) – or something similar. Let's consider the possibilities.

Predictive text entry on a phone-style keypad requires only one keystroke per character as a word is entered.[25] The system uses an internal dictionary to map candidate words to the key sequence. When the user finishes the keystrokes for a word, there is a good chance the desired word is displayed.[26] Unfortunately, "a good chance" isn't good enough; the uncertainty keeps the user on guard, monitoring the system's display. This creates an on-going attention demand ("Has the word appeared?"). Input sometimes generates *collisions* – multiple words matching the key sequence. The words are presented in order of their probability in English and the user cycles through the possibilities to select the desired word. So, there is an additional attention demand to navigate the list.

To further develop this idea, Fig. 7.34a shows the key sequences (left) and display progress (right) for inputting "beep" on a phone-style keypad using predictive entry. For reference, a phone-style keypad is shown in Fig. 7.34b. The key sequence includes pressing *n* for NEXT (e.g., ↓) to navigate the candidate list when collisions occur. After entering 2337, "beer" appears on the display. Four presses of NEXT are required to reach the desired word. When the desired word appears, 0 is pressed to select it and append a space.

How are the interactions in Fig. 7.34a modelled using the KLM? Clearly a raw breakdown using only the keystroking operator (K) or the pointing operator (P) is in-

---

[25] The method is commonly called "T9" since letters on a phone keypad are on eight keys with an additional key for SPACE.

[26] For English, one estimate is that 95% of the words can be entered unambiguously [454].

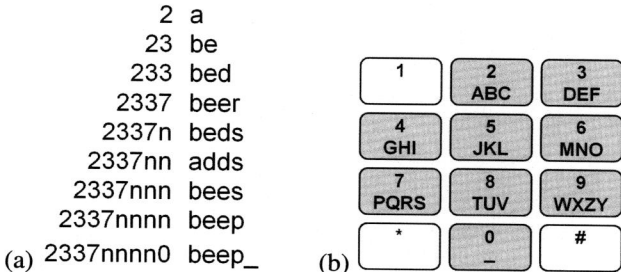

2	a
23	be
233	bed
2337	beer
2337n	beds
2337nn	adds
2337nnn	bees
2337nnnn	beep
(a) 2337nnnn0	beep_

(b)

FIGURE 7.34

Entering "beep" on a phone-style keypad using predictive input. (a) Key sequence and display progress. Note: *n* is the NEXT key (e.g., ↓). (b) Phone-style keypad (for reference).

$$\boxed{2}\ \boxed{3}\ \boxed{3}\ \boxed{7}\ \text{M}_\text{P}\ \boxed{n}\ \text{M}_\text{P}\ \boxed{n}\ \text{M}_\text{P}\ \boxed{n}\ \text{M}_\text{P}\ \boxed{n}\ \text{M}_\text{P}\ \boxed{0}$$

FIGURE 7.35

Key sequences and mental operators for input of "beep" (see Fig. 7.34).

appropriate. The interactions require mental processing as well as keying or pointing. The KLM's mental operator (M) is for mentally preparing to take the next action [64, p. 263]. This is inadequate here, since the user must perceive, decide, and react. Yet, a variant of M is clearly needed. Fig. 7.35 proposes a task coding with nine keying operations and five mental operations. M is coded as M_P, for performing a physical match between a stimulus (the presented word) and a code stored in the user's short-term memory (the desired word). After keying 2337, the user sees the wrong word. The user reacts by pressing NEXT (*n*). A similar M_P occurs after each press of NEXT until the desired word appears, whereupon the user presses 0 to select the word and append space. An assumption here is that the candidate words are presented to the user one at a time, as typical of most mobile phones.

Here is a question in applying KLM principles to predictive interfaces: What is an expert user? The question is not as odd as one might think. Remember, the original KLM used a sliding scale for expertise. The keystroking operator (K) was tuned according to the typing skill of the user. Is there a similar sliding scale for the mental operator? Perhaps. Consider entering "the" (843), "of" (63), "and" (263), or other common words in English. Novices might view the display after entering 843 to confirm that the word is displayed; but, with a little practice, monitoring isn't necessary. 8430 produces 'the" – no need to monitor the display! So, the issue is not about tuning the value of M_P according to expertise, but in deciding when and where the mental operator is present.

The presence of, or need for, the M_P operator can be explored by examining a ranked list of English words and considering each word's position within ambiguous word sets. For this analysis, a ranked list of 64,000 unique words in English was

Rank	Word	Keystrokes	Higher Ranking Colliding Word (rank)
47	if	43n0	he (15)
51	no	66n0	on (13)
63	then	8436n0	them (57)
72	me	63n0	of (2)
78	these	84373n0	there (35)
105	go	46n0	in (6)
118	us	87n0	up (56)
159	home	4663n0	good (115)
227	night	64448n0	might (141)
298	war	927n0	was (10)

FIGURE 7.36

Top ten ambiguous words requiring one press of NEXT.

drawn from the British National Corpus.[27] As it turns out, the top 46 words are either unambiguous or are at the front of the candidate list (if there are collisions). They are entered without pressing NEXT. The 47th ranked word is "if" which is ambiguous with "he" at rank 15. So, while "he" is entered with keys 430, "if" requires 43n0. The top ten such words are shown in Fig. 7.36. The issue is whether users adopt behaviours that negate or reduce the presence of mental operations. No doubt, experts expeditiously enter top-ranked words without hesitating. Such behaviour may also extend to top-ranked words that require presses of NEXT. While empirical evidence is lacking, anecdotal evidence suggests that experienced users press NEXT without hesitation while entering words such as *if* and *no*.[28] But, how far down the list do such behaviours extend, and at what level of expertise do they begin? These are potential research questions. It is unlikely that any level of expertise would negate the need to monitor the display while entering "beep," which is at rank 20,767 in the list. The word is simply too infrequent for sufficient skilled behaviour to develop that would allow entry without mental operators.[29]

To move beyond keystroke-only modelling, heuristics are needed for the hidden costs – the mental operators. Two simple possibilities are "all-in" or "all-out." An all-in model includes mental operators at every reasonable juncture (e.g., Fig. 7.35). An all-out model recognizes an all-knowing absolute expert and excludes all mental operators. Assuming a reasonable value for the keystroking operator (K), the two approaches produce upper-bound (all-in) and lower-bound (all-out) execution time

---

[27] The list is an expanded version of that used by Silfverberg et al. [454]. It is available on this book's web site.

[28] The author knows this from personal experience as well as from conversations with other mobile phone users on this subject.

[29] Of course, an obscure word that just happens to be entered frequently by a user would be expeditiously entered (i.e., no mental operators).

predictions. Neither is likely to occur in practice. More accurate predictions require a smarter heuristic, perhaps obtained through a creative pretest.

Predictive text entry on a mobile phone is but one point in a rich and diverse problem space for text entry. Word completion adds to the mix by allowing entry of a full word after entering only part of it. This is particularly interesting with a phone keypad since, with 26 letters on 8 keys, the keypad is ambiguous for text entry. A candidate list of complete words is generated with each key selection. If the desired word appears early, it is selected immediately, thus saving keystrokes. To explore mobile phone text entry involving word prediction and word completion, an application named PhoneKeypadExperiment was developed to test and demonstrate several setups.[30] The GUI simulation for word completion is shown in Fig. 7.37. Keys are pressed by mouse clicks tapping with a stylus or finger. The entry of "vegetables" is shown. With each key press, a ten-word candidate list is generated.[31] After three key presses (834), "vegetables" appears in the 3rd position in the candidate list. Clicking on it selects it, delivering it to the edit buffer. So, 4 key actions produce 11 characters of text (*vegetables_*).

While there are fewer key actions, it is not certain that execution time or text entry speed will improve. What is a reasonable model for this interaction? Two possibilities are shown in Fig. 7.38. If the candidate list is not generated until the third key action, or if the user chooses not to look until the third key action, the pattern in Fig. 7.38a applies. The key action W is a selection on the candidate word. The mental operator M is coded as M_V representing the time to visually scan the candidate words. It is clearly a different process than M_P – performing a physical match between a stimulus and a code in short-term memory. The visual search equation developed in Chapter 2 (section 2.7.2) is a logical substitute for M_V, but this is not explored here.

Fig. 7.38b models a different scenario where the user is presented with and views the candidate list after each key action. Which behaviour produces better performance? The behaviour in Fig. 7.38a is faster for the example (fewer operations), but what about English in general? This is where an enhanced KLM can help. There are many design issues. A long candidate list bears a cost since it takes longer to visually scan but brings benefit since the desired word appears sooner. Viewing the list after each key action adds time to the interaction (cost), but allows entry of the intended word at the earliest opportunity (benefit).

The methods also differ between stylus or finger input and keyed input. For stylus or finger input, once the desired word appears and is located, it is selected directly. For keyed input, selecting the nth word in the candidate list takes an extra $n - 1$ key actions, assuming arrows keys are required to navigate the list. And, as noted earlier, for mobile phone keyboards or stylus input, the pointing operator (P), in the form of a Fitts' law prediction, is more appropriate than the keystroking operator (K). Clearly

---

[30] The app, including an API and supporting files, is available on this book's web site.

[31] For convenience, discussions here speak of key presses. Since the interface uses soft keys, each key action involves a point-select operation using a mouse, finger, or stylus.

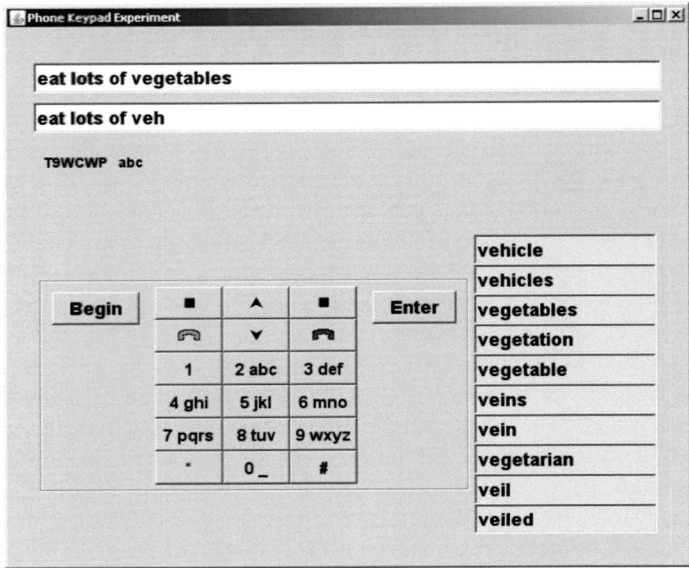

FIGURE 7.37

Input of "vegetables" using a GUI simulation of an ambiguous phone keypad with word completion. After three key presses (834), "vegetables" appears as the third entry in the candidate list.

(a) 8 3 4 M_V W (b) 8 M_V 3 M_V 4 M_V W

FIGURE 7.38

Key sequences and mental operators for input of "vegetables" (see Fig. 7.37). (a) Visual check after third keystroke. (b) Visual check after each keystroke.

there are many design choices and modelling issues that are ripe for a KLM analysis – one that includes a revised set of mental operators.

Models of predictive text entry in the HCI literature generally do not account for mental operations. The focus is usually on modelling or reducing keystrokes [109,110,152,303,389,426]. Models that predict text entry speed generally do so by incorporating only keystroking (K) or pointing (P) operators [322,454].

7.2.4.6 Updating the mental operator (M)

Earlier, we advocated updating the KLM's pointing operator (P) to include a Fitts' law prediction (P[A,W]). Perhaps the mental operator (M) also needs revisiting. Can the KLM's single mental operator (M) be replaced with a set of operators for the diverse interactions requiring user attention and cognition? M_P and M_V were suggested above as mental operations where the cognitive process involves physical matching

Proposed Mnemonic	Task	Execution Time (ms)	
		Card et al.	Chapter 2
M_S	Simple Reaction	240 [105 - 470]	277[±44]
M_P	Physical Matching	310 [130 - 640]	510[±59]
M_N	Name Matching	380 [155 - 810]	485[±52]
M_L	Class Matching	450 [180 - 980]]	566[±96]
M_C	Choice Reaction	$200 + 150 \log_2(N + 1)$	-
M_V	Visual Search	-	$498 + 41\,N$

FIGURE 7.39

Mental operators and proposed mnemonics for simple decision tasks, along with the nominal value and the range of execution times (ms). For Chapter 2 values, see Fig. 2.36 and Fig. 2.38. See text for discussion.

or visual searching. But, what are the execution times? What is the theory supporting these and other mental operators? Interestingly enough, the KLM's mental operator was not supported by any theory. The placement of the KLM's mental operator involved heuristics to analyse the operations in a task and deduce where a mental operation was likely to occur [64, p. 265]. There was no theory offered on the cognitive processes or on the execution times expected for the operations, as gleaned from experimental work in psychology or elsewhere. As noted, "the use of a single mental operator is a deliberate simplification" [64, p. 263].

M was estimated from the experimental data "by removing the predicted time for all physical operations from the observed execution time" [64, p. 274]. Then, t_M was estimated by a least-squares fit of the time removed vs. the estimated number of mental operations. The result was $t_M = 1.35$ s ($SD = 1.1$ s).[32] The standard deviation was quite large (81% of the mean), suggesting that the method of estimating M was rough, at best.

M_P, physical matching, was motivated by Card et al.'s model human processor [64, chap. 2], which includes a range of human behaviours called "simple decisions." Notably, these behaviours are not included in the KLM. The behaviours each involve a stimulus that is connected to a response through one or more cycles of cognitive processing. The behaviours are given in Fig. 7.39 along with a proposed mnemonic. There are two sets of nominal execution times, one provided by Card et al. and another from the experiment described in Chapter 2 (see Fig. 2.36 and Fig. 2.38). The range appears in brackets as the upper-bound and lower-bound from Card et al.'s values or as ±1 standard deviation for the values in Chapter 2. The execution times include the time for the motor response (e.g., a button or key press).

Card et al.'s values were obtained by reviewing a large body of literature on human sensory-motor responses. The range of execution times in brackets is large because of

---

[32] The value $t_M = 1.35$ s was used to calculate the predicted execution times in validating the KLM. Given that t_M was estimated from observed data in the same experiment, the observed vs. predicted comparison in Fig. 7.27 is of questionable value – because the predictions are derived from the observations.

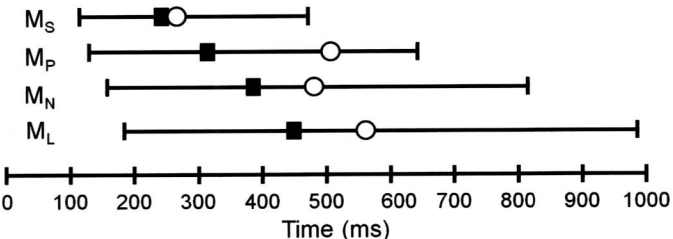

FIGURE 7.40

Mental operators. Nominal values and ranges (ms) for M_S, M_P, M_N, and M_L. Times are from Card et al. [64, pp. 65-76]. Circles are means from experiment results in Fig. 2.36 and summarized in Fig. 7.39.

the variety of experimental procedures and task conditions included in their review. Some conditions increase execution time, while others decrease execution time. For example, reaction times are known to vary by the intensity of the stimulus: Increase the loudness (auditory) or brightness (visual) of a stimulus and the reaction time decreases. The values from Chapter 2 are offered as an example. They are considered accurate, but limited to the task, apparatus, and procedure used in the experiment. For M_S, M_P, M_N, and M_L, the values fall within the range provided by Card et al., although in all cases the value is greater than Card et al.'s nominal value.

For a simple reaction (M_S), the user is attending to the system, waiting for the onset of a stimulus. When the stimulus appears, the user reacts by pressing a key or button. For physical matching (M_P), the user compares the stimulus to a code stored in short-term memory. When the stimulus appears and a match is deduced between the stimulus and the code in memory, the user presses a key or button. An example was given earlier (see Fig. 7.35). Name matching (M_N) is similar to physical matching except the user abstracts the stimulus in some manner, deducing equivalence. For example, the user might press a key or button in response to the stimulus of a "key" regardless of its appearance (e.g., "key" vs. "**KEY**," vs. 🔑. For class matching (M_L), the user makes multiple references from long-term memory. An example is responding to the stimulus of a letter regardless of which letter appears.

The nominal execution times for the top-four mental operators in Fig. 7.39 are in the range 240-566 ms. All values are well below 1.35 seconds, the value for the KLM's original mental operator (M) (see Fig. 7.26, p. 323). At the very least, the addition of new operators – more aligned with a user's perceptual and cognitive processes – should help with KLM modelling of interfaces that include adaptive or predictive features. There is also considerable overlap in the execution times, in view of the lower and upper bounds. These are illustrated in Fig. 7.40. So, predictions of tasks or sub-tasks enhanced with these operators, while behaviourally correct, will vary considerably.

The visual search operator (M_V) cannot be expressed as a nominal value, or even a range of values. The time depends on the number of choices the user must scan. For the example in Fig. 7.38, where the user is searching for a word among ten choices,

$$t_{M_V} = 498 + 41 \times 10 = 908 \text{ ms.} \tag{7.26}$$

If this delay is unacceptable, it can be lowered by reducing the size of the candidate list to five words:

$$t_{M_V} = 498 + 41 \times 5 = 703 \text{ ms.} \tag{7.27}$$

This time includes a match or no-match key press, which might be an over-simplification, depending on the interface. The difference of 205 ms is substantial and illustrates the kind of design trade-off that is possible if the range of interactions is analysed and compared using a keystroke-level model.

In this section, we reviewed Card, Moran, and Newell's keystroke-level model (KLM) as an example of a predictive model. We also suggested an update to the original pointing operator (P) as P[A,W] with A and W representing the movement amplitude and target width of a pointing operation. As well, an enhanced set of mental operators (M_S, M_P, M_N, M_L, and M_C) was offered to augment the single mental operator (M) in the original KLM. Let's consider another predictive model.

7.2.5 Skill acquisition

Not surprisingly, there is a relationship between skill and practice. Whether learning to play a musical instrument, fly an airplane, search a database, navigate a menu system, or touch type on a keyboard, we begin as novices. Initial performance is poor, but with practice we acquire skill. With continued practice, we become proficient, perhaps experts. If skill or proficiency can be measured by a ratio-scale variable, then the transition from novice to expert is well suited to predictive modelling.[33] In the model, the predicted or dependent variable is performance or skill, typically the time to do a specified task or the speed in doing the task. The independent variable is the amount of practice, typically in hours, days, years, trials, blocks, or sessions.

The relationship between skill and practice is non-linear. In the beginning, a small amount of practice yields substantial improvement. Later, the same "small amount" produces only a slight improvement. It seems the best mathematical expression of the relationship is a power function of the form

$$y = b \times x^a \tag{7.28}$$

where x is the regressor or independent variable (amount of practice), y is the dependent variable (performance), and a and b are constants that determine the shape of the relationship. Represented in this form the relationship between skill and practice

---

[33] This is generally not the case for playing a musical instrument or flying a plane. However, one can imagine unit tasks within these skills that are measurable with a ratio-scale variable and suitable for predictive modelling.

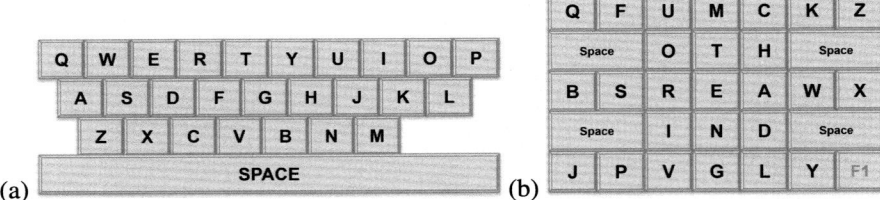

FIGURE 7.41

Soft keyboards layouts. (a) Qwerty. (b) Opti.

is often called the *power law of learning* or the *power law of practice* [64,368, p. 27]. The law dates at least to the 1920s [369, p. 6].

If the dependent variable is the time to do a task, T, then Eq. (7.28) can be recast as

$$T_n = T_1 \times n^a \tag{7.29}$$

where T_n is the time to do the task on the nth trial, T_1 is the time on the first trial. n is the trial number and a is a constant setting the shape of the curve. *Trial* is any practice indicator, such as repetition number, hours of practice, session number, etc. Note that a is negative, because the acquisition of skill means task completion time decreases with practice.

Alternatively, the dependent variable can be speed (S), the reciprocal of time. In this case, the model predicts "tasks per unit time," rather than "time per task." An example for speed might be text entry speed, in "words per minute." Predicting speed, Eq. (7.28) is recast as

$$S_n = S_1 \times n^a \tag{7.30}$$

where S_n is the speed on the nth trial, S_1 is the speed on the first trial, n is the trial number, and a is a constant setting the shape of the curve. In this form, a is positive since speed increases with practice. Furthermore, $0 < a < 1$, to reflect the diminishing return with practice. Let's develop an example.

7.2.5.1 Example

An experiment compared two soft keyboard layouts for text entry using a stylus. See Fig. 7.41. One layout had the familiar Qwerty letter arrangement. The other was Opti, a design intended to minimize stylus or finger movement for English text entry. The Opti layout was new to all participants. Because participants were familiar with the Qwerty layout, better performance was expected for the Qwerty condition, at least initially. To test the potential of the Opti layout, a longitudinal study was conducted. With the acquisition of skill, would Opti eventually outperform Qwerty? If so, how much practice is required to reach a crossover point? The experiment involved 20 sessions of text entry. (See [329] for complete details.)

(a)

Session	Layout	
	Qwerty	Opti
1	28.44	16.98
2	29.98	21.06
3	31.56	24.80
4	32.62	27.26
5	33.20	29.18
6	34.52	31.04
7	34.14	33.08
8	34.68	34.16
9	35.66	34.72
10	36.77	35.89
11	36.95	37.22
12	37.36	38.75
13	38.50	39.95
14	38.65	40.73
15	39.12	40.68
16	39.00	41.85
17	39.20	42.74
18	39.85	43.55
19	40.16	43.91
20	40.30	44.29

(b)

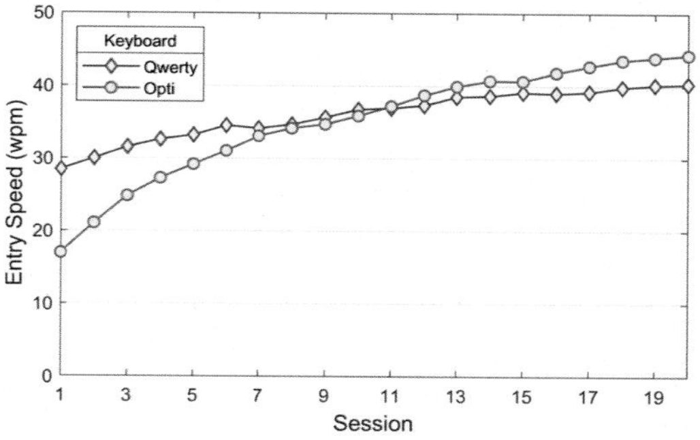

FIGURE 7.42

Experiment demonstrating skill acquisition in a text entry task comparing two soft keyboard layouts over 20 sessions of testing. (a) Data. (b) Chart.

Fig. 7.42a gives the summary data from the experiment. The independent variables are practice, labelled "Session" in the table, and layout (Qwerty and Opti). The dependent variable is text entry speed in words per minute (wpm). Since two layouts were compared, there are two patterns of learning to consider. These are shown in Fig. 7.42b. The improvement with practice in both cases follows the conjectured non-linear pattern. The crossover point – where Opti becomes faster than Qwerty – occurred at session 11.

The curve for the Qwerty layout is more flat because participants were well along the learning curve at the beginning of the experiment, due to familiarly with the letter arrangement. Curve fitting each set of points to Eq. (7.28) is easily done with a spreadsheet application, such as Microsoft Excel. The result is shown in Fig. 7.43. Both curves show a power function with the observed points clustered close to the line.

The prediction equation for each layout is shown in the chart. The equations appear in their default power form (see Eq. (7.28)), as produced by Microsoft Excel. The goodness-of-fit is given by the squared correlation coefficient (R^2), commonly articulated as the percentage of the variance explained by the model. For Opti, 99.7% of the variance is explained by the model, and for Qwerty, 98.0%. These high figures attest that both models are excellent predictors.

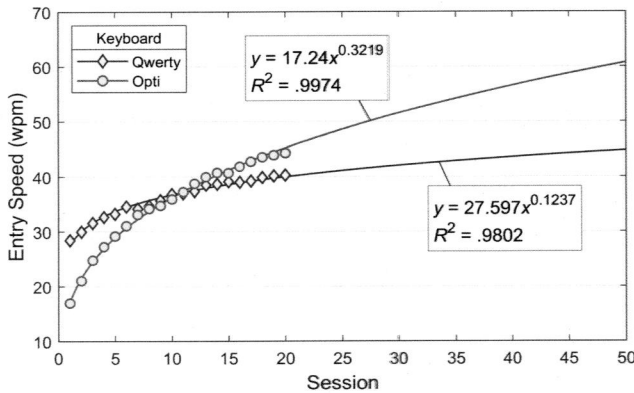

FIGURE 7.43

Power law of learning for Opti and Qwerty showing extrapolation to session 50.

Fig. 7.43 also shows an extrapolation of the models to session 50. However, extrapolating beyond the testing range is risky. Although the correlations are high for both models, the ability to predict text entry speed diminishes the farther one ventures from the range of testing. For example, at session 50 the predicted text entry speed for Opti is

$$S_{50} = 17.24 \times 50^{0.3219} = 60.7 \text{ wpm.} \tag{7.31}$$

That's fast! Too fast, perhaps. Here's a simple exercise to demonstrate a model's ability (or inability!) to extrapolate. Using only the data for sessions 1-10 for Opti, the prediction equation is

$$S_n = 17.03 \times n^{0.3319} \tag{7.32}$$

Using this equation to predict the text entry speed at session 20 yields

$$S_{20} = 17.03 \times 20^{0.3319} = 46.03 \text{ wpm.} \tag{7.33}$$

But the observed text entry speed at session 20 was 44.29 wpm (see Fig. 7.42a). The prediction is generous by (46.03 − 44.29) / 44.28 = 4.0%. So, perhaps the prediction for session 50 is generous as well.[34]

---

[34] Perhaps the prediction for Opti at session 50 for (60.7 wpm) is realistic. In the experiment, text phrases were drawn at random from a small set of just 70 phrases (~25 characters/phrase). The number of phrases per session was 50-60 early on, and 90-110 in later sessions. In view of this, participants were likely developing muscle memory with the phrases as the experiment progressed. This is similar to the highly over-learned motor skill one develops in other activities, such as buttoning a shirt, tying shoelaces, or entering a password (for people who never change their password). While this argument may have merit, it also means that the predicted text entry speed for session 50, while accurate, may apply only to the phrase set, not to English.

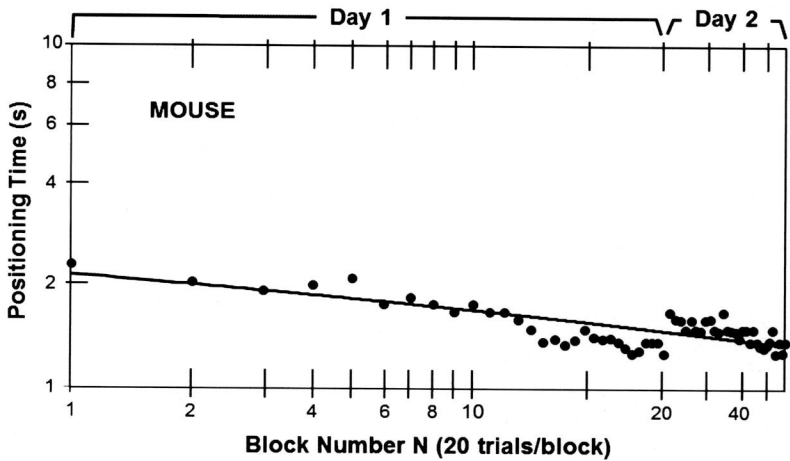

FIGURE 7.44

Skill acquisition for the mouse in a text selection task (adapted from [60]).

7.2.5.2 Skill acquisition research in HCI

Besides the experiment summarized above, there are other examples of the power law of learning in the HCI literature. The earliest is by Card, English, and Burr [60] who compared a mouse, a joystick, and two keyboard techniques for selecting text on a CRT display. In building a learning model, they performed a log transformation on both the x-axis data (block) and the y-axis data (positioning time). With this change, the relationship is linear. The relationship for the mouse is shown in Fig. 7.44. Similar log-log (linear) models are reported by Recker and Pitkow [409] for mapping document access to document storage in a multi-media database, and by Seibel for a choice reaction task (reported in [369, p. 7]).

Additionally, in *The Psychology of Human-Computer Interaction* there are skill acquisition models for reaction time [64, pp. 57-59] and execution time [64, pp. 284-285]. Numerous other sources in the HCI literature report predictive models of skill acquisition. Text entry is the predominant theme [30,71,83,121,212,254,295,296,315, 329,352,363,516,517,525,526,549]. There are also examples in the literature where the progression of learning is presented in a plot but without including a model of the behaviour (e.g., [213,336]).

7.2.6 More than one predictor

The equations above predict the outcome on a dependent variable from a single predictor variable (independent variable). It is also possible to build a model where the outcome is predicted from multiple predictors. In statistics the technique is called

Participant	Time To Reach Criterion (hours)	Age (years)	Computer Use (hours/day)
P1	2.3	16	8
P2	2.1	17	7
P3	2.5	18	8
P4	3.6	23	6
P5	2.6	25	7
P6	5.3	26	5
P7	4.8	29	6
P8	6.1	31	4
P9	7.2	32	5
P10	7.3	35	3
P11	6.4	37	4
P12	8.1	38	2
P13	7.9	40	4

FIGURE 7.45

Data for a hypothetical experiment testing the relationship between the time to learn a computer game and the age and daily computer use of players.

multiple regression and takes the form

$$y = a + b_1x_1 + b_2x_2 + b_3x_3 + \dots \qquad (7.34)$$

7.2.6.1 Example

A researcher is interested in the relationship between the time to learn a computer game and the age and computing habits of players. Is age a factor in learning the game? Is the amount of daily computer use a factor? Can the time to learn the game be predicted from a player's age and daily computer use? This last question suggests a prediction equation with multiple predictors. The dependent variable is y, the time to reach a performance criterion in playing the game. The two independent variables (predictors) are x_1, a player's age, and x_2, a player's daily computer use in hours.

To explore the research questions above, an experiment was conducted. Thirteen participants were recruited. Their ages ranged from 16 to 40 years, and their use of computers ranged from 2 to 8 hours per day. The participants were given basic instructions on the operation of the game. Then they were observed playing and learning the game in 15-20 minute segments over a period of one week. They continued to play until they reached a criterion score. The data are shown in Fig. 7.45.

It is difficult to visually scan raw data and see patterns; so, the first step is to import the data into a spreadsheet or statistics application and build scatter plots and other charts. Two scatter plots are shown in Fig. 7.46.[35] In both cases, a strong relationship is seen. Older participants generally took longer to reach the criterion in playing the game (Fig. 7.46a). At $r = .9448$, the coefficient of correlation is high.

---

[35] The data, charts, and regression models are available in an Excel spreadsheet on this book's web site.

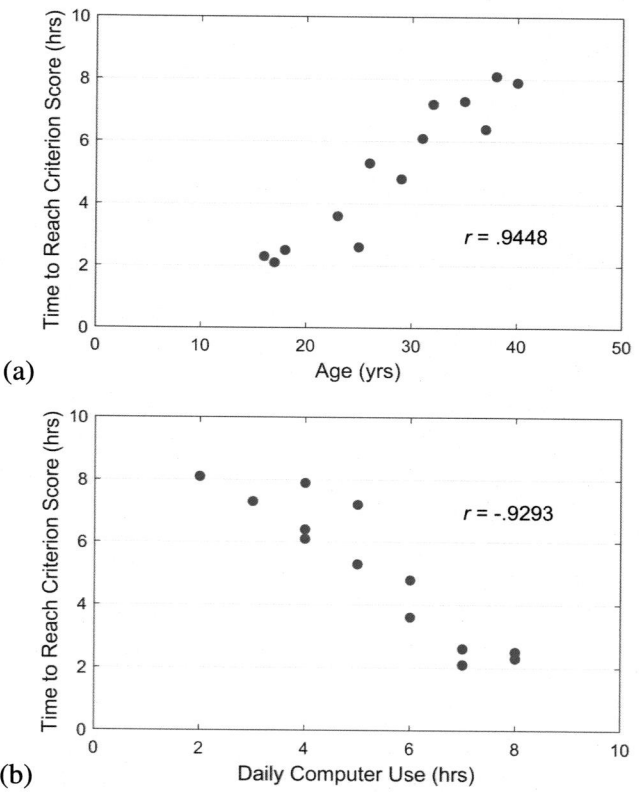

FIGURE 7.46

Relationships in the data between the time to reach a criterion score and (a) age and (b) daily computer use. The coefficient of correlation (r) is high in both cases.

The relationship is similarly strong between the time to reach the criterion score and players' daily use of computers. In this case, however, the relationship is negative. Players who self-report spending a lot of time each day using computers generally took less time learning the game (Fig. 7.46b). The coefficient of correlation is $r = -.9292$, indicating a strong negative relationship.

Building a prediction equation using multiple regression is straightforward using any statistics application. Spreadsheet applications can also be used, depending on the features available. Microsoft Excel supports multiple regression using its Analysis ToolPak, available as an add-in. Regardless of the tool, a multiple prediction equation for the data in Fig. 7.45 yields

$$y = 3.274 + 0.158\, x_1 - 0.495\, x_2 \qquad (7.35)$$

Model for MT (ms)[a]	Fit[b]	Variance Explained
$MT = 435 + 190\ ID_e$	$r = .560$	31.3%
$MT = 894 + 46\ LAG$	$r = .630$	39.8%
$MT = -42 + 246\ ID_e + 3.4\ LAG$	$R = .948$	89.8%
$MT = 230 + (169 + 1.03\ LAG)\ ID_e$	$R = .967$	93.5%

[a] LAG in ms, ID_e in bits

[b] $n = 48$, $p < .0001$ for all models

FIGURE 7.47

Models for movement time (MT) based on index of difficulty (ID_e) and system lag (LAG) (from [327]).

where y is the time to reach the criterion score, x_1 is a player's age, and x_2 is a player's daily computer usage in hours. The equation is accompanied with $R^2 = .9249$, meaning the model explains about 92.5% of the variance in the data. All in all, it's a very good model. Typically, other statistics are provided, such as the standard error of estimate for the prediction equation overall ($SE = 0.6769$, for the example above) and for each regression coefficient, and the p-value for each coefficient.

7.2.6.2 Example

As an example in the literature, MacKenzie and Ware [327] studied the effect of lag (aka system delay or latency) on human performance while using a mouse in point-select tasks. The experiment followed a Fitts' law paradigm, manipulating target amplitude (A) and target width (W) in the usual manner. Lag was also manipulated by buffering mouse samples. Processing was delayed by multiples of the screen refresh period. The factors were target amplitude ($A = 96$, 192, and 384 pixels), target width ($W = 6$, 12, 24, and 48 pixels), and lag (8.3, 25, 75, and 225 ms). The A-W conditions yielded six levels of index of task difficulty (ID), ranging from 1.58 bits to 6.02 bits. The dependent variable was the movement time (MT, in ms) to complete point-select tasks. They presented four models for MT. See Fig. 7.47. The first model in the figure is the traditional Fitts' law model with a single predictor, ID_e. The correlation is quite low, perhaps due to the additional variance introduced by the lag. The second model also used a single predictor, LAG. The fit was slightly better. The third model uses two predictors, ID_e and LAG. With $R = .948$, the fit is quite good.[36] The model explains 89.8% of the variance.

The final model in Fig. 7.47 reorganizes the independent variables to demonstrate an observed interaction effect between lag and task difficulty. Indeed, there is an improvement in the model: $R = .967$, explaining 93.5% of the variance. At lag = 0 ms, the fourth model reduces to

$$MT = 230 + 169 \times ID_e \tag{7.36}$$

[36] It is a convention for multiple regression to use uppercase R for the correlation coefficient.

which is consistent with other Fitts' law models for the mouse. Each millisecond of lag in the fourth model adds 1 ms/bit to the slope of the prediction line. This is the sort of additional explanation that motivates adding extra predictors to regression models.

Similar uses of multiple regression in the HCI literature are hereby cited [2,57, 419,436,490].

$$*****$$

HCI researchers with a social science perspective tend to use multiple regression with a slightly different motivation. Social scientists are more interested in observing and explaining human behaviour, rather than in measuring and predicting human performance. Typically the research seeks to determine the relative impact of several behavioural factors (independent variables) on a dependent variable. A common method is stepwise linear regression. All variables are tested individually to determine which has the greatest explanatory power (highest R^2) on the variance in the dependent variable. A linear model is built using that variable. Then, the remaining variables are tested one at a time against the model to determine which has the greatest explanatory power on the remaining variance. The process is repeated until all variables are added.

As an example, Dabbish et al. [97] describe a model using "probability of replying to an e-mail message" as a dependent variable. The model was built using 12 predictor variables. Some contributed significantly and positively to the dependent variable (e.g., number of e-mails with only one recipient), some contributed significantly and negatively to the dependent variable (e.g., number of e-mails from close colleagues), while others had little or no effect (e.g., number of e-mails about scheduling). Even with 12 variables the model had a modest $R^2 = .37$. However, behavioural variables are in general less stable than performance variables, so overall Dabbish et al.'s model was good. Other researchers describe similar stepwise multiple regression models [80,208,270,379,430,437,448,475].

One property of multiple regression deserves mention. When an additional predictor is added to the model, the correlation (R) always increases. It cannot decrease. Thus, caution is warranted in declaring the new model a "better model" simply because of a higher correlation.[37] The true test is whether the new predictor offers additional explanatory power relevant to the intended application of the model. MacKenzie and Ware's work was motivated to model interaction in virtual reality systems, where lag is common, thus adding lag to the model makes sense.

7.3 **A model continuum model**

We finish with modelling interaction by returning to Pew and Baron's model continuum noted at the beginning. In this chapter, we treated the problem space of

---

[37] For example, if participants' shoe sizes were measured, then shoe size (SS) could be added as a predictor. The model's correlation would increase!

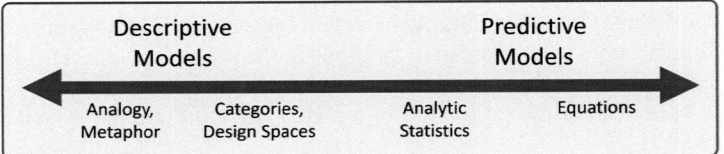

FIGURE 7.48

Model Continuum Model (MCM) with descriptive models at one end and predictive models at the other end.

modelling as a dichotomy – a space with two mutually exclusive zones: descriptive models and predictive models. While useful, this is in conflict with the continuum suggested by Pew and Baron. If the space is a continuum, rather than a dichotomy, there will be identifiable points along the way. Let's finish by proposing another model, a Model Continuum Model (MCM). See Fig. 7.48.

Fig. 7.48 is at best a suggestion, a work in progress. Certainly, it lacks the organization and clarity of the descriptive model of politics in Fig. 7.1. The model shows a continuum, and places descriptive and predictive models at opposite ends. It suggests positions along the continuum where certain kinds of activities or processes are placed according to their descriptive or predictive emphasis. Are there ways to improve the model? Perhaps the terms qualitative and quantitative should be added at each end.

This chapter presented the core ideas of descriptive and predictive models of human-computer interaction. The student exercises that follow take up and extend many of the ideas presented above.

*****

At this juncture, we have examined many aspects of empirical research for human-computer interaction, including the place for descriptive models and predictive models. The final step in research is writing it up for publication. This is the topic for our next and final chapter.

A web site is available as a resource accompanying this book's second edition:

- http://www.yorku.ca/mack/HCIbook2e

Student exercises

7-1 Fig. 7.49 shows a "big fuzzy cloud" model of human-computer interaction. Improve on this by proposing a descriptive model of human-computer interaction, as per the discussions in section 7.1.1, Delineating a Problem Space. Present your findings in a brief report or slide show presentation.

FIGURE 7.49

Student exercise on descriptive modelling.

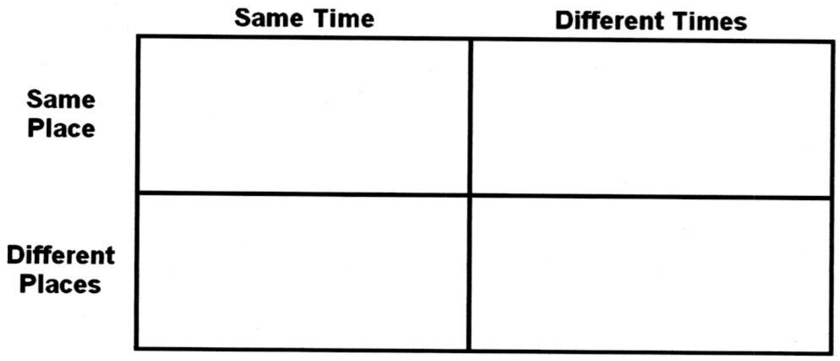

	Same Time	**Different Times**
Same Place		
Different Places		

FIGURE 7.50

Student exercise on the quadrant model of groupware.

7-2 Fig. 7.50 shows a blank version of the quadrant model of groupware from Fig. 7.2 (p. 296). Identify two current groupware activities for each quadrant of the model and redraw the figure to include the activities. Do not use any of the examples from Fig. 7.2. Prepare a brief report or slide show presentation summarizing each activity and justifying its position in the model.

7-3 Propose a descriptive model of text entry. (Hint: Do not try to encompass all aspects of text entry. Work only with two or three aspects of text entry that suggest a delineation of the problem space.) Present your model in a brief report or slide show presentation.

7-4 Propose a descriptive model of _____. (Fill in with any HCI research topic.)

7-5 Review published papers in HCI to find a descriptive model. Remember, in some cases, researchers present a breakdown of a problem space without actually calling it a descriptive model or even using the term "model." Summarize the model. Identify at least one weakness or limitation in the model and propose at least one improvement or extension to the model. Present your findings in a brief report or slide show presentation.

7-6 At a conference on human-computer interaction, a presenter used a Venn diagram to demonstrate the relationship between the disciplines of computer science (CS), human-computer interaction (HCI), and interaction design (ID). See Fig. 7.51. Critique this descriptive model. Suggest a revision to the model. Perhaps add one more circle to the Venn diagram to include an additional

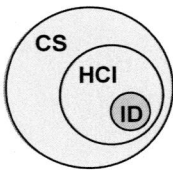

FIGURE 7.51

Student exercise on a three-part descriptive model for HCI.

FIGURE 7.52

Student exercise on design thinking.

discipline or activity. Present your findings in a brief report or slide show presentation.

7-7 Fig. 7.52 shows a descriptive model for the design process (from [489]). The model shows a continuum of activities that encompass design according to the philosophy of *design thinking* [45,343]. Prepare a brief report or slide show presentation on this model considering the following. What is design thinking? What is meant by mystery, heuristic, algorithm, and binary code as applied to design thinking? Why do the labels appear in two groups? Are there activities beyond each end of the continuum, as inferred by the arrows? (Hint: Search Google Scholar using the phrase "design thinking.")

7-8 Fig. 7.53 shows a descriptive model of multitasking (from [432]). The model shows a series of task pairings along a time continuum with concurrent multitasking at one end and sequential multitasking at the other end. Prepare a brief report or slide show presentation with an analysis of this model considering the following. What is multitasking? What are concurrent multitasking and sequential multitasking? Identify at least three additional task pairings, where at least one of the tasks involves humans interacting with technology, and place each in the model. Also, identify a task pairing that is positioned beyond the left extreme of the model and another beyond the right extreme of the model.

7-9 Besides the desktop keyboard, the key-action model (KAM) applies to physical or soft keyboards on mobile devices. See Fig. 7.54. Create an illustration similar to Fig. 7.3 (p. 297) for a mobile phone keyboard, such as above. Preferably, use your own device. Propose some changes to the model to make it more representative of the keyboard. Present your findings in a brief report or slide show presentation.

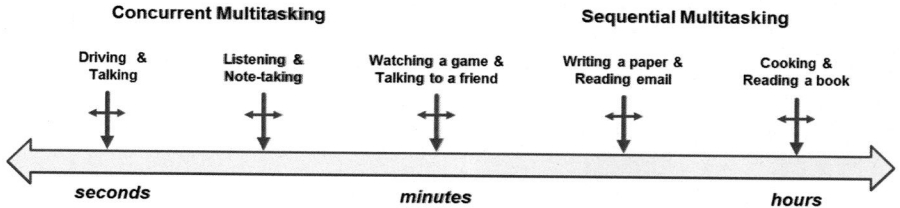

FIGURE 7.53

Student exercise on multitasking.

FIGURE 7.54

Student exercise on the key-action model (KAM).

7-10 Consider the exemplary diagram in Fig. 7.6 (p. 300) for Guiard's model for bi-manual control. Create a similar diagram for some other common task that illustrates asymmetric but cooperative use of the preferred hand and non-preferred hand. Write a brief description of the task using language as in Fig. 7.5 (p. 299). Create the diagram as a sketch, a photograph, or using a graphics application of your choosing. Present your findings in a brief report or slide show presentation.

7-11 Beaudouin-Lafon defines an interaction model as "a set of principles, rules, and properties, that guide the design of an interface" [28, p. 446]. Where are interaction models positioned in the "model continuum model" in Fig. 7.48? Prepare a brief report or slide show presentation on both models and propose a revised pictorial of the model continuum model that includes interaction models and other models reviewed by Beaudouin-Lafon.

7-12 Jacob et al. [216] propose a framework for a category of interaction styles called *reality-based interaction* (RBI). Their framework is a descriptive model. Summarize RBI and demonstrate how it meets the criteria described above for a descriptive model. Give examples. Present your findings in a brief report or slide show presentation.

Participant	Entry Speed (wpm)	
	Stylus Tapping	Touch Typing
P1	21.4	42
P2	23.6	44
P3	22.0	32
P4	24.0	50
P5	23.0	36
P6	17.1	33
P7	29.0	55
P8	14.7	22
P9	20.3	31
P10	19.7	33

FIGURE 7.55

Student exercise on linear prediction equations.

7-13 The data in Fig. 7.55 show the text entry speed (wpm) for 10 participants. The entry methods are stylus tapping on a tablet and touch typing on a desktop computer. What is the coefficient of correlation (r) between the two entry methods? What is the linear prediction equation for stylus tapping speed, given touch tapping speed? What percentage of the variation (R^2) is explained by the prediction model? Create a chart showing a scatter plot of the points, the prediction equation, and R^2. Present your findings in a brief report or slide show presentation.

7-14 Fig. 7.56 shows a chart adapted from a Fitts' law study comparing target selection times for stationary and expanding targets [545]. (Note: Expanding targets increase in virtual size when the cursor is close, thus potentially improving interaction.) The authors did not build predictive models for the data sets, but they could have. Use a ruler or some other apparatus (e.g., Microsoft PowerPoint or Adobe PhotoShop) to reverse engineer the chart and create data sets for the expanding and stationary conditions. Enter the data into a spreadsheet application, such as Microsoft Excel or use a programming language of your choice. Create a new chart that includes for each condition the regression line, prediction equation, and R^2. Which condition is better in terms of throughput? Explain. Present your findings in a brief report or slide show presentation.

7-15 Fig. 7.57 is adapted from a study measuring the selection time for menu items based on the serial position of an item within the menu [53, Fig. 1]. The scatter plot appeared without a regression line. Reverse engineer the chart and build a data set for the plot. Recreate the chart, showing the scatter points, a regression line, regression equation, and R^2. What is the predicted time to select the fifth item in the menu? What is the 95% confidence interval for the prediction? Present your findings in a brief report or slide show presentation.

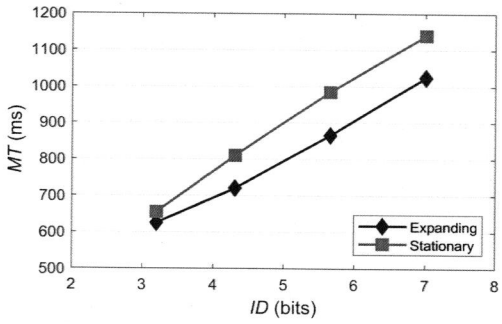

FIGURE 7.56

Student exercise on modelling selection times for stationary and expanding targets.

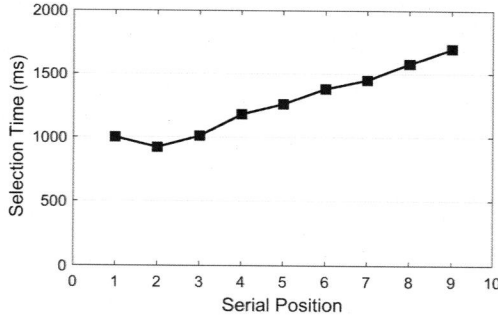

FIGURE 7.57

Student exercise on modelling selection times for items in a menu.

7-16 The data in Fig. 7.58 are from a Fitts' law study using a mouse. Using a spreadsheet, create a chart showing the scatter plot, regression line, prediction equation, and R^2. (Note: These data were used for Figure 4a in [526].)

7-17 Users and computers (Part III). Extend the report for Part II of this exercise (see Chapter 6, p. 289) to examine if there is a relationship between the age of respondents and the number of hours per day of computer use. Since both variables are ratio-scale, the relationship may be explored using a scatter plot, regression line, and the coefficient of correlation (r). For the purpose of the report, consider the relationship strong, mild, or weak, according to the criteria in Fig. 7.59. If the relationship is strong, propose a prediction equation that gives the number of hours per day of computer use as a function of a user's age. Present your findings in a brief report or slide show presentation.

7-18 The data in Fig. 7.60 are from a choice reaction time experiment. Plot the data and build regression models using a few different relationships (e.g., linear, power). What model explains the most variation in the data? (Note: These data

A (pixels)	W (pixels)	ID (bits)	MT (ms)
192	16	3.70	654
192	32	2.81	518
192	64	2.00	399
320	16	4.39	765
320	32	3.46	613
320	64	2.58	481
512	16	5.04	872
512	32	4.09	711
512	64	3.17	567

FIGURE 7.58

Student exercise on building a Fitts' law regression model.

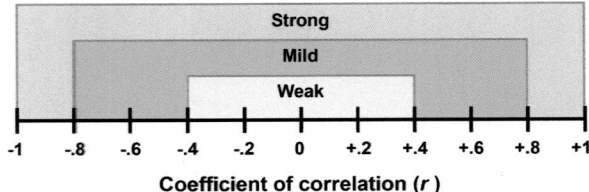

FIGURE 7.59

Student exercise on linear regression.

Choices (n)	Reaction Time (ms)
1	155
2	265
3	310
4	365
5	400
6	425
8	505
10	530

FIGURE 7.60

Student exercise on choice reaction time.

were reverse engineered from Figure 4 in [442].) Present your findings in a brief report or slide show presentation.

7-19 The chart in Fig. 7.61 was adapted from an experiment showing the relationship between error rate and target width in a target selection task using a smartphone camera [419, Fig. 5]. As expected, smaller targets are incorrectly selected more often than larger targets. The relationship seems well suited to curve fitting using a power formula. Reverse engineer the chart and generate a set of x-y points, where x = target width and y = error rate. Use a spreadsheet application

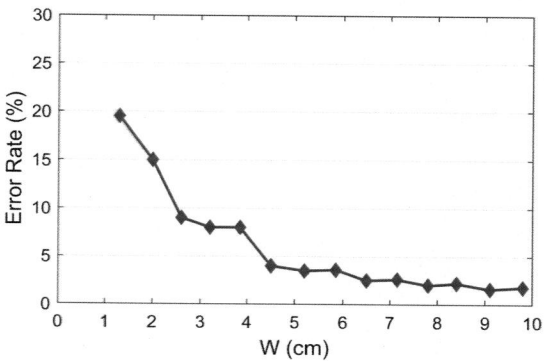

FIGURE 7.61

Student exercise on target selection using a smartphone camera.

to re-create the chart showing the scatter of points and the best-fitting curve. What percent of the variation in the observations is explained by the model? Present your findings in a brief report or slide show presentation.

7-20 In a choice reaction time experiment, a human operator attends to eight stimulus lights and presses one of eight keys when the corresponding light turns on. Two of the lights turn on more frequently than the others, accounting for 40% and 30% of all activations, respectively. The other light bulbs activate with the same frequency. What is the information content of the task? Present your findings in a brief report or slide show presentation.

7-21 Fig. 7.62 shows the layouts for the Qwerty and Dvorak keyboards, as well as an alphabetic layout proposed by Card et al. [64, p. 63]. Assuming the layouts are implemented as standard physical keyboards, which design provides the most even split between left-hand and right-hand keying? (See Fig. 7.25.) Propose a new design where the split is more even between hands. Present your findings in a brief report or slide show presentation.

7-22 If the Qwerty keyboard in Fig. 7.62 is implemented as a soft keyboard on a desktop computer, the keys can be accessed (pressed) using a mouse. Use a spreadsheet and the Fitts' law mouse model in Eq. (7.14) (p. 317) to compute the time to enter "the quick brown fox jumps over the lazy dog." Convert the time to an entry speed in words per minute (wpm). Repeat for the Dvorak and Alphabetic layouts. In digitizing the keyboards, ignore the small gaps between keys in the images. Present your findings in a brief report or slide show presentation.

7-23 Repeat the exercise above for the Opti soft keyboard layout in Fig. 7.41b. Of the four SPACE keys on Opti, assume the user chooses the one that minimizes

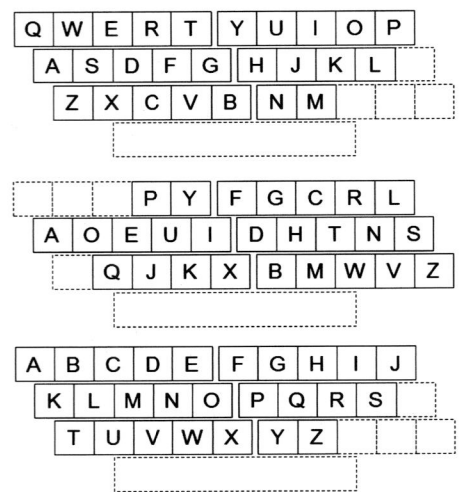

FIGURE 7.62

Student exercise on keyboard usage by hand.

the movement distances (e.g., for C_W, the user chooses the SPACE key at the top right). Present your findings in a brief report or slide show presentation.

7-24 Fig. 7.63 illustrates a sequence of mouse operations to set "Small caps" as the formatting style for a word of text. The screen snap is from MS Word. What is the predicted execution time for the task? What is the predicted execution time if the keyboard is used instead of the mouse? For this question, assume t_K = 0.4 seconds. For both questions, provide a KLM breakdown of all operations. Present your findings in a brief report or slide show presentation.

7-25 Use the KLM to predict the time to enter "I hate baking pies" on a mobile phone. Provide three predictions: one for multi-tap, one for predictive input using an "all-in" assumption for mental operators, and one using an "all-out" assumption for mental operations. In building the models, assume the keystroking operator (K) is nominally t_K = 0.4 seconds. For predictive input, the ordered collision sets at the end of the words are I = {I}, hate = {have, gave, gate, hate}, baking = {baking, baling, caking}, and pies = {pier, pies, rids}. Present your findings in a brief report or slide show presentation.

7-26 Build a multiple regression model for the data in student exercise 7-16 (p. 353). Treat *MT* as the dependent variable and *A* and *W* as predictors. What is the multiple regression equation? What percent of the variance is explained by the model? Experiment with some transformations on *A* and *W* to obtain a better model (higher R^2). What transformation produces the highest R^2? Present your findings in a brief report or slide show presentation.

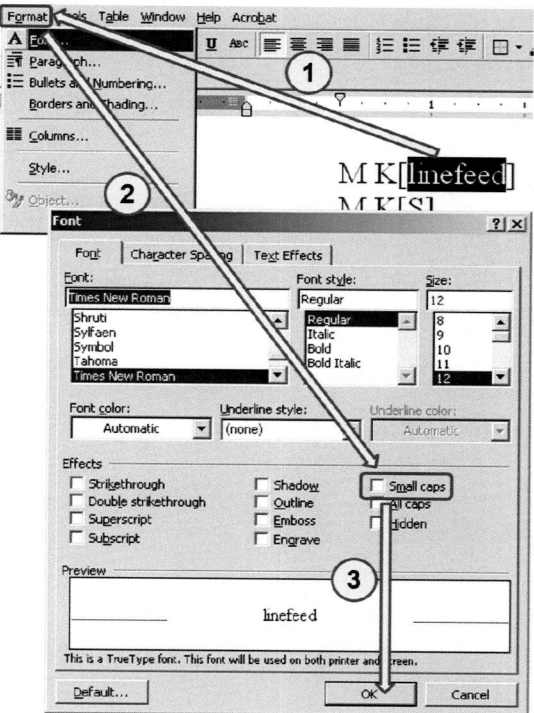

FIGURE 7.63

Student exercise on mouse operations in a graphical user interface.

7-27 Fig. 7.64 is a chart showing the relationship between text entry speed in characters per minute (cpm) over seven blocks of testing for three entry methods: GazeTalk (standard), GazeTalk (centred), and Dasher (adapted from [213, Fig. 4]). The power law of learning is clearly evident in the chart; however, no model was provided in the publication. Reverse engineer the chart and generate a set of x-y points for each of three entry methods. Using a spreadsheet, re-create the chart showing the scatter of points and the best-fitting curve and prediction equation for each method. What percent of the variation in the observations does each model explain? Present your findings in a brief report or slide show presentation.

7-28 Conduct an experiment investigating two input methods for pointing and selecting. Use the GoFitts software from this book's web site. Use any two methods of input. Consider using two input devices or a single input device operated in different ways. The setup dialog is shown in Fig. 7.65a.

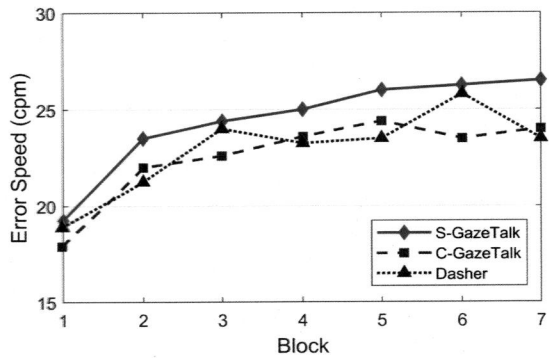

FIGURE 7.64

Student exercise comparing three methods for text entry.

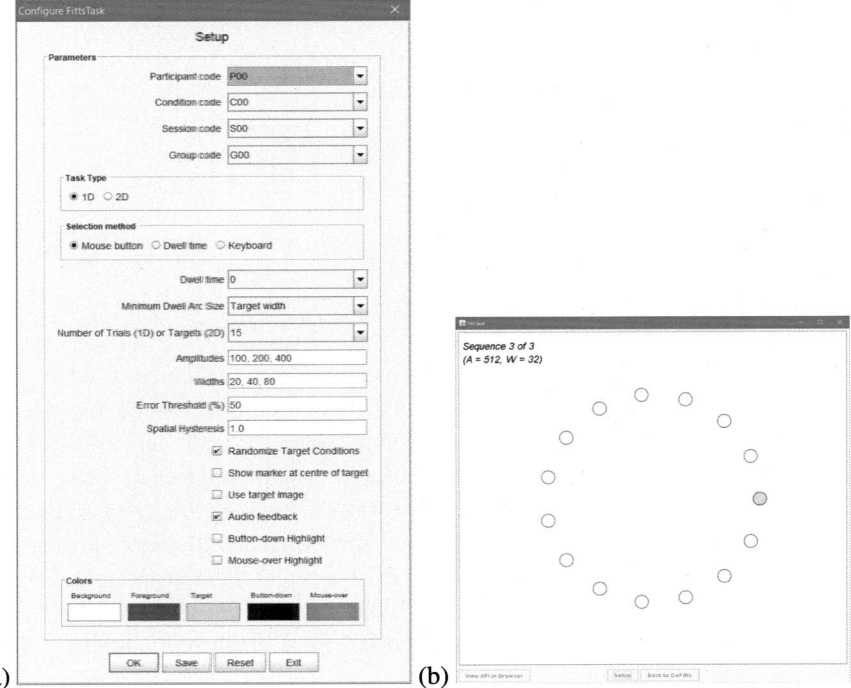

FIGURE 7.65

Student exercise using GoFitts software to compare two methods of input. (a) Setup dialog.
(b) Experiment screen.

Recruit an even number of participants, about 12, and divide them into two groups to counterbalance the order of testing the input methods. Assign each participant a code (P01, P02, etc.). Also, assign each participant a Group Code to identify their counterbalancing group (G01 or G02). Before testing, enter these codes in the setup dialog and click "Save."

The software implements the ISO 9241-411 protocol for evaluating non-keyboard input devices. Consult the API for complete details. Configure the software for the 2D task. Enter three movement amplitudes (128, 256, 512), three target widths (32, 64, 128), and set the number of targets to 15. Click "Save." An example experiment screen is shown in Fig. 7.65b.

Ask the participants to perform five blocks of trials for each input method. With three amplitudes and three widths, a block consists of nine sequences of trials with 15 target selections (trials) in each sequence. Testing takes about 15 minutes per participant per input method. Consider other aspects of the experiment design, as per discussions in Chapter 5 (Designing HCI Experiments). Prepare a brief report or slide show presentation on your findings. For the results, use ANOVAs to test for statistical significance for the effects of input method, block, and group on movement time, error rate, throughput, and other dependent variables. Include bar charts or line charts, as appropriate. Also include a chart with scatter data, regression lines, prediction equations, and squared correlations, as per Fig. 7.22 (p. 317).

7-29 Let's revisit the relationship between CD gain and gross and fine movement times in selecting targets. This was presented in Chapter 3 showing the relationship in general terms. See Fig. 3.32 (p. 119). In this student exercise, we'll give this figure an empirical twist.

Using the GoFitts software and a mouse or touchpad for input, design and run an experiment to verify the effect shown in Fig. 3.32. Use five settings for pointer speed: VL (*very low*), L (*low*), N (*nominal*), H (*high*), VH (*very high*). These are shown in Fig. 7.66a. The CD gain setting is changed from the system control panel.

Recruit 10 or 15 participants and divide them into five groups. Administer the CD gain settings using a 5 × 5 Latin square to offset order effects.

For the GoFitts setup, use the 2D task with 15 targets per sequence. To keep the experiment small, only use one value for movement amplitude (e.g., 500) and one value for target width (e.g., 75). For each CD gain setting, give three to five blocks of testing, as time permits. A block is a single sequence of 15 trials (target selections). The first block can be considered practice trials.

Each participant is given a code (P01, P02, etc.) Ensure the code is entered and saved in the setup dialog before testing begins. As well, use the Condition Code setting in the setup dialog to represent the CD gain setting, as in Fig. 7.67. Very important: Remember to change and save the Condition Code each time

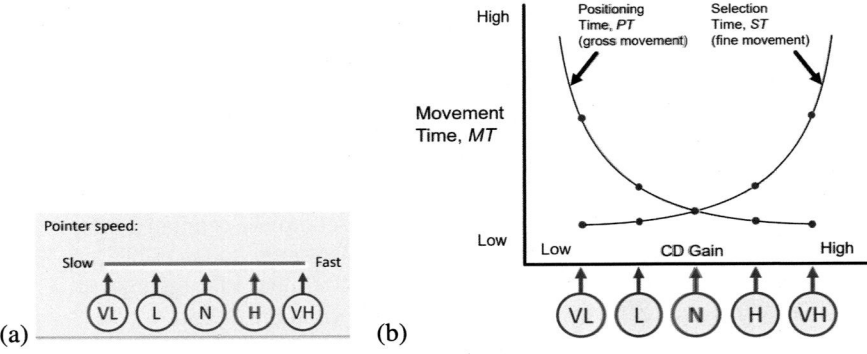

FIGURE 7.66

Student exercise exploring the relationship between CD gain and gross and fine movement times for target selection tasks. (a) Five CD gain settings for pointer speed. (b) Trade-off between gross and fine movement times for five settings of CD gain. Note: CD gain settings are VL (very low), L (low), N (nominal), H (high), and VH (very high).

Condition Code	CD Gain
C01	VL
C02	L
C03	N
C04	H
C05	VH

FIGURE 7.67

Condition codes for CD gain settings.

CD gain is changed. This happens five times for each participant. To avoid confusion, prepare and use an experiment worksheet. See Fig. 5.11 (p. 231) for an example.

The GoFitts software records and logs many user performance measures. One is movement time (*MT*) which is the positioning time (*PT*) plus the selection time (*ST*). Remember, *PT* is the gross movement time and *ST* is the fine movement time. Analyse the data and create a chart showing the fine vs. gross movement time trade-off. There are 10 points of interest: 5 for gross movement time and 5 for fine movement time. These appear as red dots in Fig. 7.66b. Create other charts, as appropriate, for other performance measures, such as error rate. Prepare a brief report or slide show presentation on your findings.

Writing and publishing a research paper

In Chapter 4, we noted that publication is the final step in research (section 4.1.1, p. 163). It is fitting, then, to make our final step a chapter on writing and publishing a research paper.

A typical HCI research paper presents a novel interface idea along with an evaluation of the idea in a user study. User studies are designed (or should be designed!) according to accepted standards for experiments with human participants, as laid out in Chapter 5. Adhering to accepted standards is important in HCI and other fields since the practice brings consistency to the body of work that defines the field. This practice extends to the final step in research – preparing and publishing the results.

8.1 Conference papers, journal papers

The main venues for publishing HCI research papers are conference proceedings and journals. Journals are considered the top tier for research publications. There are two primary reasons. First, journal submissions undergo a tightly controlled peer review to ensure the research is novel, correct, and carried out according to accepted standards in the field. The reviewers are experts in the subject matter and are enlisted by the journal's editor or by a member of the editorial board. Second, journals are archived in major libraries around the world. Thus, research published in a journal is readily available to other researchers. For some disciplines, such as physics, journal publications are virtually all that matter, with conference contributions viewed as little more than a summary of one's presentation at a meeting, the content of which appears (or will appear) in a journal publication. And so, the review of submissions to physics conferences is cursory, at best.

HCI is different. HCI conferences bring together researchers and practitioners, as noted in Chapter 1. The practitioners are the engineers and designers of products, and they are there to learn about the latest research in HCI. Life cycles and timelines for such products are short. The big players, like IBM, Apple, Microsoft, or Google, announce new products regularly, and with great fanfare. So, reaching and influencing the designers and engineers of products requires HCI research to also have a short timeline.[1] The timeline from submission to publication in a journal is

---

[1] On timelines, see Research vs. Engineering vs. Design (p. 167) for a contrary view.

longer – typically one to two years, sometimes more. For conferences, the timeline is short – typically eight months, sometimes less. It is no surprise, then, that conferences and conference publications have emerged as an important vehicle for presenting and publishing research in HCI. Simply put, publishing in a conference proceedings is the quickest way to get one's work "out there." Furthermore, the archival advantage for journals no longer exists. Today, the term "archive" extends to online databases maintained by organizations such as the ACM or IEEE. The review process is also different. For some HCI conferences, the peer review process is as rigorous as with many journals. So, the prestige of publishing in some HCI conferences, such as the ACM's annual SIGCHI conference, equals that of publishing in some journals.

Prior to publication, a research paper is a manuscript. In some cases, the venue for submitting is decided before writing begins. The decision will depend on many factors, such as the subject matter, the timing and scope of the research, and the prestige of the conference or journal. An additional factor for a conference is location and travel costs, since acceptance of the manuscript implies attending the conference and presenting the research.

Journals generally have relaxed requirements for the format of submissions. This is reasonable since a journal submission, if accepted, undergoes a round or two of revision before publication. Revisions are introduced to improve the manuscript based on the referees' suggestions. Acceptance is often conditional on final approval by the journal editor or referees. Publication in a journal often includes professional copy-editing by the journal staff. Hence, the formatting of the initial manuscript is not so important.

Conferences, on the other hand, have strict requirements on the format of submissions, including page length. There are a few reasons. For one, the timeline is short. The entire process is deadline-driven, with dates for the initial submission, reviewer feedback, notification (accept or reject), and final submission. The initial submissions usually have formatting requirements (see below), since there is little time to rework a rough manuscript into the final camera-ready copy that is published.

Another reason for formatting the initial submission is that the responsibility lies with the author(s) to provide the final camera-ready copy that is published. Acceptance usually includes a request for "minor revisions," again, based on referees' suggestions. However, there is little or no vetting of the revisions or of the formatting within the manuscript, in part due to the short timelines. So, formatting lies with the author and precedes the initial submission.

Before delving into formatting and presentation, we examine the major parts of a research paper. The discussion that follows applies to conference or journal submissions that describe a user study.

8.2 Parts of a research paper

In this section, we decompose a research paper into its constituent parts. For each part, we examine the objectives and requirements. Fig. 8.1 shows the major sections

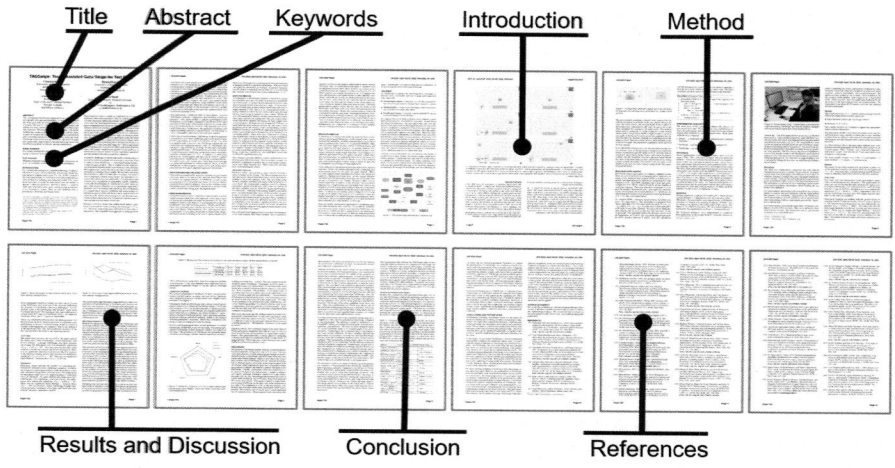

FIGURE 8.1

Parts of a research paper. The backdrop paper is a 12-page conference contribution by Kumar et al. [259].

using a 12-page conference paper by Kumar et al. [259] as a backdrop. The text is seen in two columns, as typical for conference papers. However, this is irrelevant from the perspective of the major sections and the content.

The sections in Fig. 8.1 apply to the majority, but not all, research papers in HCI. The backdrop paper describes a novel interface idea, which was evaluated in a user study. The user study is elaborated in the "Method" and "Results and Discussion" sections. Some HCI research papers do not describe a user study. The annual ACM SIGCHI conference, for example, welcomes other types of submissions, such as Late-Breaking Work, Interactivity, HCI in Practice, or Case Studies.[2] Such contributions are also important to HCI. And they may not include a user study (although they could). It is worth re-iterating the important role of non-experimental research in HCI. However, our discussion here focuses on a traditional HCI research paper with a user study. Let's proceed.

8.2.1 **Title**

Every word tells! A title is short, so every word must contribute. The title must identify the subject area of the paper while at the same time narrowing the scope of the work. The backdrop paper in Fig. 8.1 is titled "TAGSwipe: Touch Assisted Gaze Swipe for Text Entry." The title is in two parts with a separator (typically a colon)

---

[2] These contribution types were noted in the CHI 2023 submissions web site (https://chi2023.acm.org/for-authors/).

between the main title and a secondary title. There are no rules here. Either part can serve to broaden or narrow the scope of the work.

The main title is "TAGSwipe," the name of a novel interaction technique presented and evaluated in the paper. This is expand in the secondary title to "Touch Assisted Gaze Swipe," appended with "for Text Entry." The seven-word title sufficiently identifies the topic, broadly speaking, while narrowing in on text entry as the application.

Sometimes, the title strives to catch the attention of the reader, perhaps with a provocative claim or phrase. Examples include "Rock 'n' Scroll is here to stay" [25], "You're In Control: A Urinary User Interface" [347], "To Kill a Mockingbird Robot" [26], or "Are We All in the Same 'Bloat'" [349].

Have you developed a novel interaction technique? The authors of the backdrop paper believe they did. And they contrived a name for the technique and included the name in the title: TAGSwipe. With a contrived name, a new keyword is created for future searches. If the aforementioned TAGSwipe is adopted or cited in subsequent research, the source is easily retrieved using "TAGSwipe" as a search keyword. Examples of contrived terms in the titles of HCI research papers include EdgeWrite [524], TwitInfo [341], NaviRadar [423], QB-Gest [534], GIMIS [199], BlinkWrite [308], BubbleBoard, [90], PinchText [225], TapGazer [184], GazeBar [113], OddEyeCam [246], TiltWalker [542], TiltWriter [72], VisualTouch [552], PizzaText [540], SliceType [31], SurfAirs [91], etc.

In short, any title is fine provided it is concise, identifies the subject area, and narrows the scope of the work.

The title is followed by the names, affiliations, and contact information for the authors. This information is provided and positioned according to the submission requirements of the conference or journal.

8.2.2 Abstract

The abstract is written last. There is often a size limit, such as 150 words, so the abstract must be concise. No room to expound! The abstract is a single paragraph, without citations. After the title, the abstract is likely the first part of the research paper that is read. The title has caught someone's interest; the abstract then delivers a succinct summary of the story within. After reading the abstract, the reader will decide if the rest of the paper is relevant and worth reading.

If the abstract is poorly written and fails to deliver on its essential objective (see next paragraph), then the paper has little chance of being read, or, even worse, being accepted for publication. So, edit, edit, edit. The abstract should be the best-written section of the paper. The English and grammar should be perfect, the content succinct and clear. A poorly written abstract foretells of a tough slog ahead for anyone with the patience to continue reading.

In writing an abstract, there are two objectives: Tell the reader *what you did* and *what you found*. Both themes are highly condensed since the abstract is constrained in size. Nevertheless, this is the abstract's mission. An example of a well-crafted abstract is provided by Zinck and Vogel [557] in their paper "Evaluating Singing for Computer Input Using Pitch, Interval, and Melody":

> *In voice-based interfaces, non-verbal features represent a simple and underutilized design space for hands-free, language-agnostic interactions. We evaluate the performance of three fundamental types of voice-based musical interactions: pitch, interval, and melody. These interactions involve singing or humming a sequence of one or more notes. A 21-person study evaluates the feasibility and enjoyability of these interactions. The top performing participants were able to perform all interactions reasonably quickly (<5 s) with average error rates between 1.3% and 8.6% after training. Others improved with training but still had error rates as high as 46% for pitch and melody interactions. The majority of participants found all tasks enjoyable. Using these results, we propose design considerations for using singing interactions as well as potential use cases for both standard computers and augmented reality glasses.*

[557, p. 213.1]

The abstract contains 130 words in eight sentences:

- Introduction – 1 sentence
- What was done – 3 sentences
- What was found – 3 sentences
- Design considerations – 1 sentence

The first sentence conveys the topic of the research. Introducing the topic creates context and gives the abstract a nice flow. But, introductory material should be minimized – one sentence at most. Unfortunately, treating the abstract as an introduction is a common flaw. This point deserves emphasis: The abstract is not an introduction! The reader has read the title and is now examining the abstract for further details. It is reasonable to assume that the reader is familiar with the subject matter, broadly speaking. Save the introductory material for the Introduction.

The example abstract continues with seven more sentences. In clear and simple terms, the authors inform the reader what done ("We evaluate the performance of ...") and what was found ("The top performing participants were able to ...").

It is important to convey specific quantitative results in the abstract and to do so without including results from statistical tests. All too often, an abstract conveys general outcomes only. Instead of "A was faster than B," something like "A was 15% faster than B" is always better. And the authors deliver: "...with average error rates between 1.3% and 8.6% after training." So, convey the most salient findings in the abstract. See also student exercise 8-1.

To round out the example abstract, the authors mention that in the paper they propose some "design considerations" and offer some "use cases" for their work. This sort of comment is common in abstracts for HCI research papers, and it gives a sense of closure. But, it does not contain any information. It would perhaps be better to omit this and give more results or actually give a design recommendation or use-case for the work.

```
CCS Concepts
● Human-centred computing → Text input; Interaction devices; Accessi-
bility technologies; Interaction paradigms
```

FIGURE 8.2

Example of the ACM Computing Classification System.

8.2.3 Keywords

Keywords are used for database indexing and searching. They allow people interested in the work to find it. Keywords are chosen by the author(s). They identify the subject matter and the scope of the work. For the backdrop paper in Fig. 8.1, the keywords are "Eye typing; multimodal interaction; touch input; dwell-free typing; word-level text entry; swipe; eye tracking."

Since 1998, and with revisions in 2012, research papers published in ACM conference proceedings or journals are required to also include indexing and retrieval information according to the ACM's Computing Classification System (CCS). As noted, "this is beneficial to [authors] because accurate categorization provides the reader with quick content reference, facilitating the search for related literature, as well as searches for your work in ACM's Digital Library and on other online resources" [3].

In applying the CCS, research papers include "Categories and Subject Descriptors" and "General Terms." For conference submissions, these are shortened to "CCS Concepts," as seen in Fig. 8.2 for the backdrop paper. The formatting (e.g., brackets, bold, italics) is required and must be strictly followed. Although choosing the terms is a challenge, there is an easy way. Just find a paper on the same or similar topic in the same proceedings or journal as the paper in preparation and mimic that paper's descriptors and terms. In fact, the ACM recommends this [3]. Of course care is warranted, in the event of an inappropriate descriptor in a published paper.

8.2.4 Introduction

The opening section of a research paper is typically called Introduction, although other labels, such as Background, are fine. The introduction gives the context for the research. Usually opening comments characterise the state of the art and indicate why the subject matter is interesting and relevant. A user interface problem or challenge is identified and the reader is alerted, early on, to the solution or approach that is developed in the rest of the paper.

It is common practice to give an overview of the contents of the entire paper – perhaps the overall results – usually at a convenient place within the first page or so of the introduction. Fig. 8.3 is an excerpt from the 5th paragraph of the backdrop paper (Fig. 8.1).

It is also desirable to state the contribution of the work. This is tricky, since it entails laying down the bragging rights, so to speak, for a novel aspect of the work.

> Our experiment, conducted with 12 participants, assessed TAGSwipe's efficacy compared to gaze-based text entry approaches. The result yielded a superior performance with TAGSwipe (15.46 wpm) compared to Eye-Swipe (8.84 wpm) and Dwell (8.48 wpm). Participants achieved an average entry rate of . . .

FIGURE 8.3

Introduction section. Provide an overview of the entire paper.

A statement like, "The approach presented here is the first example of . . ." is strong but, in most cases, should be avoided. Usually, it is sufficient to note that the idea improves on existing practice, or something similar.

The introduction may span several sections. Any reasonable organization is fine. Other sections may use the same level of heading as the introductory section and subsections may be added, as appropriate. It's your story to tell! Take liberties to prepare and organize the introduction as you see fit.

Usually a literature review is expected. This is typically organized in a separate section, with an appropriate heading (e.g., Related Work). The literature review discusses published work related to the current research. Points relevant are presented and contrasted with the current research. A citation is included for each publication mentioned. Include figures, charts, or tables, as appropriate.

It is useful to include a table in the literature review that summarizes the papers reviewed. The process is tricky since common elements from different papers must be extracted and organized to facilitate comparisons. But, the result is worthwhile and helpful to readers. And example was provided in Chapter 4 (p. 197).

In describing the new interaction method, you might need to include a lot of technical details, for example, of an algorithm or on the design of a complex prototype. If so, it is best to do this in a dedicated section in the Introduction, rather that in the Apparatus subsection of the Method (see below).

The main ideas developed in the paper should be laid out in detail in the introductory sections. Use formulas, screen snaps, sketches, or any appropriate visual aid to help the reader understand the solution to a problem that the research presents. The introduction usually finishes with a statement indicating the need to test the idea in an empirical evaluation. This sets the stage for the method section.

8.2.5 Method

The method section of a research paper tells the reader how the experiment was designed and carried out. Although the heading Method or Methodology is most common, this section is sometimes given other titles, such as Evaluation, Experiment, User Study, etc.

The method section should be written in an entirely straightforward and predictable fashion. Any creative flair conveyed in the introduction should come to a full stop here. The method section should read like a recipe. The reader wants to know what you did and how you did it. And this information must be delivered in a style that is simple, clear, and predictable.

We noted earlier that a critical requirement of research is that it must be replicable (see section 4.1.3, p. 166). It is the method section that delivers this crucial property. After reading the method section, a reader might ask, "Could this research be reproduced?" If the reader is reviewing the manuscript for a conference or journal and the answer is "no" or "I'm not sure," there is little chance of acceptance.

Predictability is important. It allows a reader to scour papers quickly to find key points and results. A reader will lose patience if it is a struggle to determine the independent variables, the dependent variables, the number of participants, or the tasks performed by participants, and other important details of the experiment. So, keep it simple, make it predictable. On predictability, convention dictates that the method section is divided into the following subsections and in the following order:

- Participants
- Apparatus
- Procedure
- Design

Let's examine each of these.

8.2.5.1 Participants

The participants subsection states the number of participants and how they were selected. Relevant demographic information is also given, such as age, gender, and related experience. Other details might be useful, such as level of education, first language, hand preference, or whether the participants wore eye glasses or corrective lenses. The details to provide depend on the task and apparatus used in the experiment.

The information on participants identifies the population of people used and, therefore, the population to which the results apply. It is reasonable to limit the participant pool to people with certain skills or attributes, if it makes sense for the research. An experiment on gaming devices, for example, might only enlist college-age users who play computer games more than 10 hours per week. That's fine, but the results may not generalize to other people.

The participants subsection is usually short – just a couple of sentences. However, if a property of the user (cf. the interface) is an independent variable, then the participants section is often more detailed. For example, Brajnik et al. [39] describe an experiment where an independent variable was "expertise in judging web sites for accessibility." The experiment included a group of experts and a group of non-experts. The participants section of the paper is quite detailed, as it is necessary to quantify the degree of expertise for both groups and to describe how such was determined and applied.

8.2.5.2 Apparatus

The apparatus subsection describes the hardware and software. Other titles for this section include Materials, Interface, or Hardware and Software. Think of reproducibility when preparing this section. Give all the details necessary so that a skilled researcher could replicate the apparatus if he or she chooses. Of course, needless details can be excluded. Mention, perhaps, that the test computer was a Lenovo Thinkpad T80 running Microsoft Windows 10, but the amount of memory or the capacity of the hard drive is likely of no consequence. Some discretion is warranted. If the experimental task involved finger input on a touchscreen, then the make and model of the touchscreen are relevant. Other details might include the screen resolution, the screen size, sampling rate, how the screen was held, or even the participants' finger size.

If the experiment used a custom interface, the development language (e.g., Java) and other relevant details should be given. It is always helpful to provide screen snaps or photos of the interface. If comprehensive details of the interface were disclosed prior to the method section, then it is reasonable just to refer the reader to the earlier material, for example, "The software included the algorithm described in the preceding section."

8.2.5.3 Procedure

The procedure subsection tells exactly what happened with each participant. State the instructions given, and indicate if demonstration or practice was used, etc. If participants completed a questionnaire before or after testing (or both), indicate this in the procedure section. It is also common to indicate if participants were paid, volunteered without pay, or were required to participate, for example, as part of a university course.

Typically, participants are tested over multiple conditions and, perhaps, multiple trials for each condition. Give the details. Usually, there is a specific task that participants performed. Ensure the task is properly defined. What was the task? What was the goal of the task? When did timing begin and end? Were errors recorded? Give a precise definition of what constituted an error? Were participants allowed and instructed to correct errors? Did they correct all errors or only at their discretion? How were errors corrected? Were rest breaks allowed or encouraged? What was the total time for testing with each participant? And so on. Again, a screen snap of the interface may help. It is also common to include a photograph of a participant performing the task.

If participants need to be prepared for testing in any special way, give the details in the procedure subsection. As an example, Mandryk et al. [338] describe a user study where participants played a game while their emotional state was measured through physiological sensors. It was important for the participants to be calm and relaxed before testing began. Fig. 8.4, from the procedure subsection, reveals how this was done.

> Before each experimental condition, participants rested
> for five minutes while listening to a CD containing nature
> sounds. The resting period allowed the physiological mea-
> sures to return to baseline levels prior to each condition.

FIGURE 8.4

Procedure subsection. Preparing participants for testing [338, p. 1031].

> The total number of trials was 14 participants × 2 key-
> boards × 5 blocks × 5 phrases = 700.

FIGURE 8.5

Design subsection. A calculation reveals the total number of trials in the experiment (from [181]).

8.2.5.4 Design

The design subsection summarizes the experiment in terms of the independent variables (factors and levels), the dependent variables (measures and units), trial repetitions, and other relevant details. For short papers, this information is sometimes given in the procedure subsection.

Many of the details in the design of the user study are revealed implicitly in earlier information. Mostly, the goal of the design subsection is to deliver – in a predictable place – a compact summary of the user study. This all-important summary is a perfect and necessary prelude to the results section that follows.

It is common to begin the design subsection with a statement such as, "The experiment was a 2 × 5 within-subjects design." If counterbalancing was used, the way the conditions were administered to participants should be stated. Be thorough and clear! It's important that your research is reproducible.

A good way to conclude the design subsection is to state the total number of trials in the experiment. This can be revealed by a calculation that includes the number of participants and the variables and repetitions in the study. Fig. 8.5 provides an example. The reader is left with a clear summary of what took place in the user study.

8.2.6 Results and discussion

Following the method section, the results of the experiment are given. It is common in HCI to combine the results with discussion, although it is also acceptable to present the results first, followed by a discussion. Note, also, that the heading "Results and Discussion" is at the same level as "Method." Results are not part of the method!

If there were problems in the data collection, state this up front and give details on any data that were eliminated before analysis. Such data are often referred to as outliers, as discussed earlier (see section 2.7.6, p. 83). Outliers may also occur through wildly deviate behaviour in participants. Either way, it is important to (a) state the cri-

> Some participants accidentally pressed the ENTER key during a trial. This caused the trial to end prematurely and potentially compromised the data. Trials with an incomplete phrase and with >50% error rate were deemed outliers. Eleven such trials (1.6%) were identified and removed from the analyses.

FIGURE 8.6

Results section. Removing outlier data [181, p. 6].

> The mean task completion time for method A was 2.7 seconds. Method B was 9.1% slower with a mean task completion time of 3.0 seconds.

FIGURE 8.7

Reporting results in absolute and relative terms.

teria for classifying data as outliers, (b) describe the root cause and rationalize why some data were deviate, and (c) indicate the amount of data eliminated. An example is shown in Fig. 8.6.

Although, there are no strict rules, it is common to use sub-sections that organize the results by dependent measures, beginning with the most important dependent variable. Often, this is speed or task completion time. Then, results are presented for accuracy or error rate, followed by results for other dependent variables.

For each dependent variable, begin with a broad observation, such as the overall mean, often called the "grand mean," then move to finer details such as the means for each test condition. The difference in the means between test conditions is the effect size. In HCI, effect size is typically given either as an absolute difference or as a relative difference, expressing the percent difference between one condition and another. Providing the means as absolute values and the difference as a percent is useful to expose the practical implications of results. For example, if the mean task completion time was 3.0 seconds for method A and 2.7 seconds for method B, then the result can be presented as in Fig. 8.7.

It is important to explain the results through discussion: What caused the differences in the measurements across experimental conditions. What detail in the interaction caused one method to be slower? Did one condition require more input actions? Were participants confused? Was the method hard to learn? Did participants experience fatigue or discomfort? Were corrective actions required as the task was carried out? Obviously, the answers lie in the interactions used in the experiment and the observations made by the experimenter or obtained through a post-experiment questionnaire or interview.

There is very likely a difference in the observed dependent measures across experimental conditions. The difference may be real or it may be an artefact of the variability that occurs in experiments with human participants. Of course, finding a real difference is often the goal of the research: A novel interaction method improves on an existing interaction method. "Improves on" usually implies interaction that is faster, more accurate, more efficient, or better in some other quantifiable manner (e.g., fewer re-tries, less movement, higher quality results, etc.).

Testing for a real difference typically involves doing an analysis of variance on the data, as described in Chapter 6. The results of this test are given in a succinct statement indicating the outcome. See Fig. 6.6 (p. 250) for an example where the difference is real (i.e., statistically significant). See Fig. 6.9 (p. 252) for an example where the difference is deemed a random effect (i.e., not statistically significant).

In conveying results, bear in mind that the results of statistical tests are not the results per se. The results lie in the observations and measurements. This point deserves special emphasis. It is a common weakness in research papers that undue attention is directed at the statistical tests. This is likely a by-product of the significant effort young researchers invest in learning how to analyse data using statistical tools and procedures. This may lead to a skewed sense that the statistical results *are the results*. They are not! The results of statistical procedures, such as the ANOVA, only play a supporting role. Results are best framed in terms of the actual measurements obtained and the differences in measurements across the test conditions. Where a difference is deemed statistically significant, say so and give the supporting evidence – the results of statistical tests – in parentheses.

An example where this was not done is found in a study comparing three methods for performing touchless mid-air gestures [168]. The user study included a target selection task performed using each of three gesture methods. One of the dependent variables was throughput (in bits per second). In the results section, a statistically significant difference was reported between the throughput values for the three gesture methods. The results of a post-hoc pairwise comparisons test were also given. But, the actual values for throughput were not given. The reader is left with no sense of the magnitude of throughput for any of the gesture methods. To conclude and emphasize: The results lie in the observations and measurements, with statistical tests playing a supporting role.

Experimental software can log a considerable amount of data and statistics software can pump out a lot of charts and analyses on that data. A key challenge, then, is deciding which results to present and which to exclude. Giving too many results or too much data is an indication that you can't distinguish what is important from what is unimportant. The advice here is to limit the presentation to a minimum set of revealing results – results that shed light on the goals of the research. And never give results "just for the record." If there is no insight to offer, leave it out.

Another way to make results interesting for the reader is through visuals. Bar charts, line graphs, 3D plots, or the like, appear in most research papers in HCI, with examples appearing throughout this book.

The results and discussion section should compare the results with those in other research papers on a similar topic, citing prior work as appropriate. Is the new technique faster, slower, more accurate, less accurate?

The results and discussion section also summarizes information obtained through questionnaires or interviews given at the end of testing. Participant feedback is often enlightening. Include it. Discuss it. What does participant feedback suggest in terms of improvements to the interaction?

8.2.7 Conclusion

The conclusion summarizes what you did, restates the important findings, and restates the contribution. It is common to identify topics for future work, although developing new ideas is to be avoided in the concluding section.

The conclusion is often followed by an acknowledgement thanking funding sources as well as people who assisted in some way with the research.

8.2.8 References

The last section of a research paper is the reference list. The list contains the full bibliographic details on papers cited earlier in the paper. Only papers cited in the paper are included in the reference list. References should be formatted as stipulated by the conference or journal. Formatting details are discussed in the next section.

8.3 Preparing the manuscript

The experience in reading a research paper should be like the experience in listening to music. Hopefully, the music is creative, interesting, and well executed. Hopefully, as well, the playback system is free of static, noise, distractions, or other annoying sounds. Music that is creative and well executed might fail to engage the listener due to extraneous factors.

Similarly, a research paper seeks to present ideas that are creative and interesting. And the research must rise to the expected standards in the field as described throughout this book. But, there is more. Research that is creative and well executed might fail to engage the reader due to factors aside from the quality of the research. If the reader is distracted due to flaws in the delivery and presentation, he or she may have difficulty following and understanding the ideas. Soon enough, the reader's patience wears thin. So, presenting ideas that are creative and well executed is not enough. The story must be properly assembled and presented.

In this section, we present ideas and suggestions on preparing a manuscript. The process is more about simplicity than flair: writing in a straightforward style, constructing figures, tables, and other visuals that are simple, clear, and consistent. Easier said than done. But, resist any temptation to jazz-up the presentation. A research paper is a product of scholarship, not a marketing brochure.

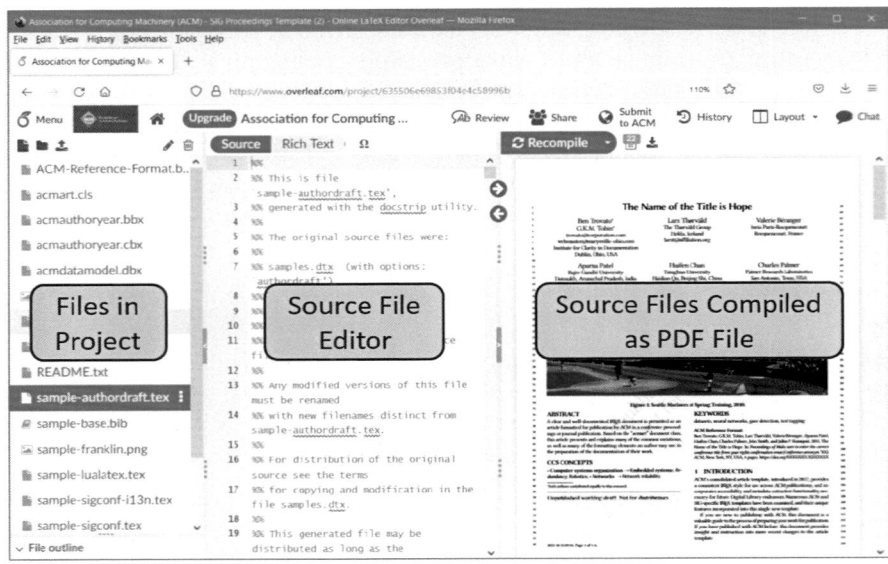

FIGURE 8.8

Overleaf web-based front-end for LaTeX.

8.3.1 Environment

For many years, most researchers used either Microsoft Word or LaTeX for preparing research papers, technical reports, theses, books, and other scholarly documents. The same is true today. However, since about 2017, Overleaf (formerly WriteLaTeX) has emerged as a popular platform for writing research papers.[3] Overleaf is web-based. Researchers create an account, log on, and open a "project" wherein a research paper is prepared. The result is generated as a PDF file.

Project owners can invite other researchers to join the project – perfect for multi-author papers. Beyond that, Overleaf is simply a web-based front-end for LaTeX with an expansive user interface that includes many project management features. Overleaf can be used for free, with certain limitations, or through a paid subscription with extra features.

Most conferences offer templates to help researchers get started in preparing their submissions. The ACM's annual SIGCHI conference, for example, offers MS/Word and LaTeX templates with the LaTeX template also available pre-loaded in Overleaf.

Fig. 8.8 shows Overleaf in a web browser with the ACM SIGCHI conference template loaded and open as a project. The UI includes three panels: (i) left, a file-tree panel showing the files in the project, (ii) middle, an editor panel where a file, such as a source .tex LaTeX file, is edited, and (iii) right, a PDF panel showing the

---

[3] https://www.overleaf.com/.

compiled project as a downloadable PDF file. Readers new to Overleaf and LaTeX are advised to begin at the Overleaf Documentation Home page.[4]

8.3.2 **Formatting**

Formatting is the minutia, but don't be fooled. What every successful researcher knows is this: *details matter!* Formatting covers many details in a manuscript: fonts, columns, margins, caption position, punctuation, spelling, capitalization, italics, quotations, abbreviations, numbers, variables, and so on. These properties of a manuscript are important for clarity and flow. The goal is to get the formatting right, actually ...*perfect!* In fact, get it so perfect that the reader won't even notice. Remember, one of the first persons to read the paper will be a reviewer, who will make a recommendation for accepting or rejecting the paper. Will the reviewer critique the paper based on its value and novelty and put aside a confusing presentation or poor formatting that causes him or her to read, then re-read? Perhaps, but this is a chance you don't want to take. It is distinctly possible that a reviewer who struggles with formatting flaws and other distractions will eventually lose focus and patience and render a negative opinion. The goal is to let the story of the research come through.

Formatting rules are too numerous to set out here. Fortunately, there are many sources to assist. *The Publication Manual of the American Psychological Association* (APA) is recommended [10]. Chapter 6 in the 7th edition is "The Mechanics of Style" – a 39-page *tour de force* containing a wealth of tips, actually rules, for formatting manuscripts. There are subsections on small details – proper use of the period, comma, semicolon, colon, quotation marks, double or single quotation marks, parentheses, brackets, slash – and subsections on broader details, like capitalization, hyphenation, italics, abbreviations, statistics, and spelling.

A dictionary is also a valuable asset. Reputable dictionaries, such as Merriam-Webster's *Collegiate Dictionary*, are considered the final authority on spelling.[5] For some words there are differences in the American and British spellings (labor vs. labour). Either form is generally accepted provided the choices are applied consistently throughout a manuscript. Dictionaries teach in other ways. A dictionary is a good source to determine if a word is capitalized (Internet), hyphenated (e-mail), not hyphenated (smartphone), set as two words (screen snap), or set as a single word (database).

The template file provided by conferences embeds many of the formatting requirements, such as the margin sizes, fonts for headings and text, line spacing, paragraph spacing, and so on. Generally, the manuscript is prepared directly in a renamed copy of the template file.

The template file also provides instructions and guidance on aspects of the paper under control of the author. These include writing style, the preparation of figures and other visual aids, formatting for citations and references, etc.

---

[4] https://www.overleaf.com/learn.

[5] Online version: http://www.merriam-webster.com/.

> This sentence cites examples of common research publications, including a conference paper [3], a journal paper [4], a book [1], a chapter in an edited book [2], an article in a magazine [6], and an online document [5].
>
> **REFERENCES**
> [1] Andrew T. Duchowski. 2017. *Eye tracking methodology: Theory and practice* (3rd ed.). Springer, London.
> [2] Jonathan T. Grudin. 1983. Error patterns in novice and skilled transcription typing. In *Cognitive aspects of skilled typing*, W. E. Cooper (Ed.). Springer, New York, 121–143.
> [3] Zhenyi He, Christof Lutteroth, and Ken Perlin. 2022. TapGazer: Text entry with finger tapping and gaze-directed word selection. In *Proceedings of the ACM SIGCHI Conference on Human Factors in Computing Systems - CHI '22*. ACM, New York, Article 337, 16 pages. https://doi.org/10.1145/3491102.3501838
> [4] Calvin A. Liang, Sean A. Munson, and Julie A. Kientz. 2021. Embracing four tensions in human-computer interaction research with marginalized people. *ACM Transactions on Computer-Human Interaction* 28, 2, Article 14 (2021), 47 pages. https://doi.org/10.1145/3443686
> [5] Taylor_&_Francis. 2012. HCI Style Guidelines for Final Submissions. http://www.tandf.co.uk/journals/authors/HHCIguidelines.pdf Accessed October 21, 2022.
> [6] Mark Weiser. 1991. The computer for the 21st century. *Scientific American* 265, 1 (September 1991), 94–105.

FIGURE 8.9

Formatting examples for papers published in the CHI conference proceedings.

8.3.3 Citations and references

Citations and references are the connections that tie research together. Research submissions (e.g., for CHI) have formatting requirements for citations and reference lists. This is one area where HCI conferences generally deviate from the APA guidelines. The following is a quick view into the formatting of citations and references for conference submissions to CHI and many other HCI conferences.

8.3.3.1 Reference list

The most common types of publications cited in HCI research papers are conference papers, journal papers, books, chapters in edited books, magazine articles, and online documents. Fig. 8.9 illustrates the formatting for each of these as they might appear in a CHI conference proceedings. The example was prepared using the Overleaf template for submissions to the CHI conference. The entries are numbered and in alphabetical order by first author's surname.

Citing web pages or documents downloaded from the Internet as the primary source for research is discouraged. However, if a relevant source is only available on the web or as a downloadable document, then it is reasonable to cite it. The formatting tends to vary here. The example in Fig. 8.9 includes four items: the source (e.g., author or organization), the title, the URL, and the date the document was accessed. Citing web pages for product information is usually best done through a footnote.

The following is a checklist of common formatting rules for reference lists in the CHI conference proceedings.

- Number the references: 1, 2, 3, etc.
- Order the entries alphabetical by first author's surname.
- Include all authors, but beyond about eight authors, use "et al.".
- For each author, give the first name(s) following by the surname, as they appear in the publication (e.g., "John A. Smith").
- Set the title plain using sentence case. That is, only capitalize the first word, the first word in a secondary title (e.g., after a colon), and proper nouns. Set plain.
- Include the year. Substitute "in press" for accepted but not-yet-published papers.
- For papers, include pages. Give the number of pages (for online papers) or the page sequence (e.g., "pp. 25-35"), as available.
- Set the name of the publication in italics and capitalize all keywords (e.g., *Proceedings of the ACM SIGCHI Conference on Human Factors in Computing Systems – CHI '22*).
- For journal papers, include the volume number following by the issue number. Set plain.
- If space permits, use the full name for conferences and journals. If space is tight, use abbreviated names for conferences (e.g., *Proc CHI '22*) and journals (e.g., *ACM Trans Comput-Hum Interact*). Do not mix full and abbreviated names; use one style or the other.
- Give the name and address of the publisher for conference papers and books (e.g., "ACM, New York"). It is best practice to use the most economical yet understandable expression of the publisher (e.g., "IEEE" not "Institute for Electrical and Electronics Engineers") and address (e.g., "New York" not "New York, NY, U.S.A.").
- Only include works cited in the paper.
- Be consistent.

8.3.3.2 Citations

Citations connect current research with prior research or other sources. Most commonly for conference submissions, citations appear as numbers in brackets. The following are examples and tips for correctly citing prior work.

Basic citation:

> A previous experiment [5] confirmed that . . .

Group multiple citations together. Separate the numbers with a comma. Preface with "e.g.," if there are additional known sources supporting the same point:

> These results are consistent with previous findings [e.g., 5, 7, 12].

Do not treat citations as nouns:

> INCORRECT:
> It was proposed in [5] that . . .
>
> CORRECT:
> It was proposed by Smith and Jones [5] that . . .

Exception: Within parentheses, a citation may serve as a noun:

> There are many user studies on this topic (see [6] for a review).

Quotations require a citation with a page number:

> Smith and Jones argue, "the primary purpose of research is publication" [14, p. 123].

If citing a specific point from a book, include the page number. If the point spans several pages, indicate the range:

> Norman defines six categories of slips [15, pp. 105-110].

If a publication is referred to by author(s), cite the first author followed by "et al." if there are three or more authors:

> Douglas et al. [5] describe an empirical evaluation using an isometric joystick.

Alternatively, include all the authors' names for the first appearance of the citation and use "et al." for subsequent appearances. All the authors' names (up to about eight) appear in the reference list.

It is worth the effort get the citations and references correct. Clarivate's End-Note[6] is a tool to simplify that task. It works with a bibliographic database and a plug-in for word processors, such as Microsoft Word. With EndNote, inserting a citation is as simple as copy (from the database) and paste (at the desired location in the manuscript). Formatting the bibliography is typically done by an option in the Tools menu or EndNote ribbon. The process formats both the citations within the manuscript and the references list at the end. Numerous styles are included and they

---

[6] http://www.endnote.com/.

```
@inproceedings{he2022a,
    author = {He, Zhenyi and Lutteroth, Christof and Perlin, Ken},
    title = {{TapGazer}: Text entry with finger tapping and gaze-
        directed word selection},
    year = {2022},
    publisher = {ACM},
    address = {New York},
    doi = {10.1145/3491102.3501838},
    booktitle = {Proceedings of the ACM SIGCHI Conference on Human
        Factors in Computing Systems - CHI '22},
    articleno = {337},
    numpages = {16},
    type = {Conference Proceedings}
}
```

FIGURE 8.10

BibTeX entry for a conference paper.

are easy to customize according to the submission requirements of a conference or journal. See also student exercise 8-2 at the end of this chapter.

Overleaf and LaTeX have the ability to automatically format the citations and build the reference list when the document is compiled. The citations and reference list in Fig. 8.9 were created from a .tex file in an Overleaf project using the template for ACM SIGCHI conference papers. The papers were included in a separate .bib file in BibTeX format. As an example, Fig. 8.10 shows the BibTeX entry for the conference paper in Fig. 8.9. See the Wikipedia entry for "bibtex" for further details.[7]

8.3.4 Visual aids

Visual aids are powerful tools for conveying ideas and results. Few areas in experimental research have gained more by technological advances than the methods and tools for displaying results. Charts, tables, graphs, drawings, and photographs are now fully in the digital domain, with sophisticated tools for editing and stylizing the presentation.[8]

A common result to present is the effect of an independent variable on a dependent variable. A bar chart is usually the most appropriate format, since most independent variables are nominal-scale attributes. See Fig. 8.11a. The chart shows the results of Zhu et al.'s experiment on teleoperation [555]. Participants used a scene camera while manipulating a robot arm to nudge rocks into a hole. The independent variable was camera control model (manual, natural, auto). The dependent variable was the

---

[7] For readers interested in exploring further, the Overleaf project generating the list in Fig. 8.9 is included as a zip file on this book's web site.

[8] Of course, hand-drawn sketches maintain a special appeal (see Fig. 3.67 or Fig. 7.6).

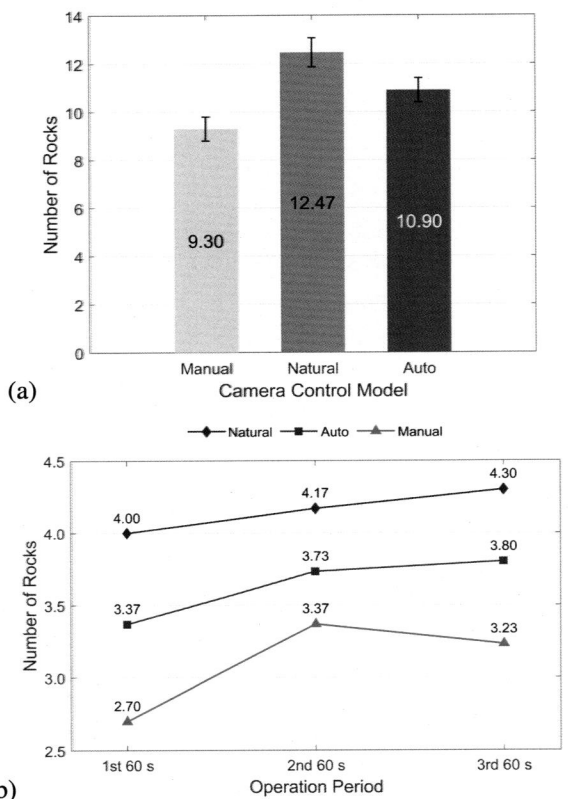

FIGURE 8.11

Charts presenting research results. (a) Bar chart for categorical data. (b) Line chart for continuous data (adapted from [555]).

number of rocks sunk in a specified time interval. As seen in the figure, the natural model performed best. (This was confirmed in an analysis of variance.)

Note the presence of error bars in Fig. 8.11a. Error bars are an important reminder of the variability in human responses. However, error bars add little insight unless they are appropriately labelled in the figure's caption (which was not the case in Zhu et al.'s paper). A typical label is "Error bars shows ± 1 SD." Instead of the standard deviation (SD), the standard error (SE) is sometimes used to reduce the size of the bars.[9]

If the variable shown along the x-axis is continuous, then a line chart is appropriate. In Zhu et al.'s experiment on teleoperation, participants proceeded under a time

---

[9] Standard error (SE) is calculated as $\frac{SD}{\sqrt{n}}$, where n is the number of sample points.

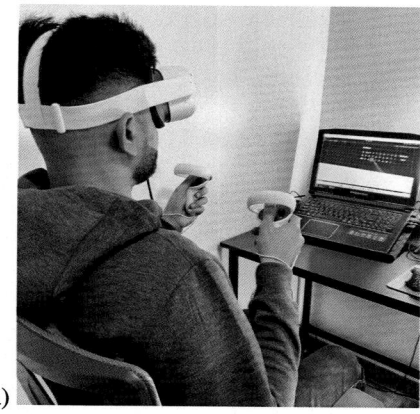

(a)

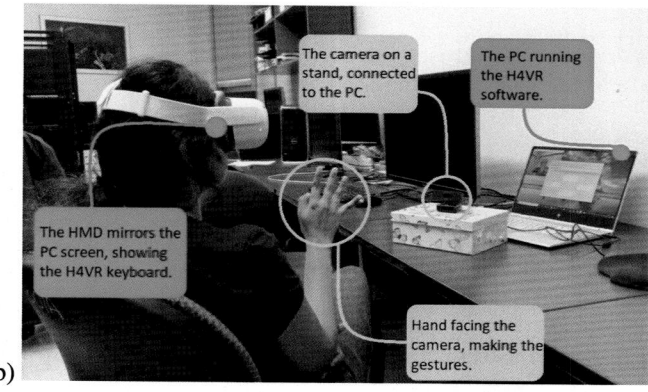

(b)

FIGURE 8.12

Photographs showing experiment task and apparatus. (a) Using hand controllers [181]. (b) Using hand gestures [121] (photos used with permission).

constraint. An additional result was provided on the number of rocks sunk in each of three 60-second intervals. See Fig. 8.11b. The lines between intervals convey a sense of continuity as the experiment trials progressed.

Well before the Results and Discussion section, visuals are an important adjunct to text. Visuals can clarify concepts about the research or details of an apparatus. In preparing a manuscript, try to find opportunities to assist the reader wherever possible. The methodology, in particular, can benefit from a judicious and targeted use of visuals. A powerful way to augment the procedure section of a research paper is through a photograph of a participant performing the experiment task. Two examples are shown in Fig. 8.12. Part (a) shows a participant in VR performing text input using handheld controllers and raycasting [181].

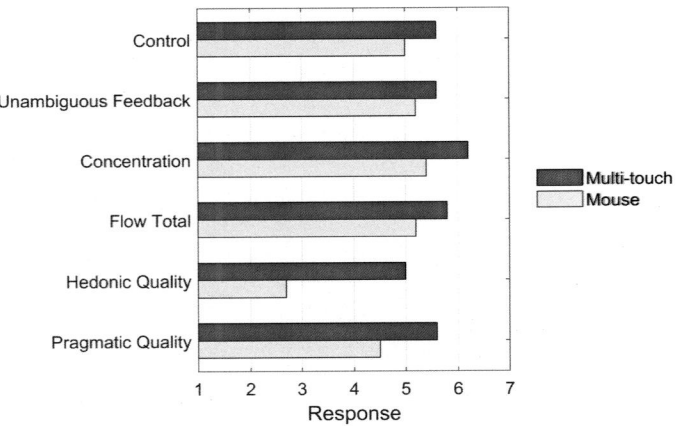

FIGURE 8.13

A chart summarizing participant responses from a questionnaire on target acquisition using multi-touch vs. a mouse (adapted from [277]). Higher scores are better.

Part (b) is an experiment that also involves VR text entry using hand gestures [121]. The photos help a reader understand the nuisances of the experiment task and apparatus. Note the annotations in Fig. 8.12b. These engage the reader and add interest. As further examples, see the annotations in Fig. 3.7 (p. 100) and Fig. 3.10b (p. 102) – very helpful.

Summaries of Likert-scale questionnaire items used to obtain qualitative feedback may be presented as shown in Fig. 8.13 [277]. The chart shows participants' impressions in a target acquisition task using multi-touch and a mouse. Seven is the most favourable response. Clearly participants preferred multi-touch, as this condition was rated higher on all items. The difference was particularly pronounced in the item about hedonic quality (pleasure) with scores of 5.1 for multi-touch compared to 2.8 for the mouse. A visual presentation, as here, helps the reader understand the results both in absolute and in relative terms.

8.3.5 Writing for clarity

The goal in writing a research paper is communication. Effective communication demands clarity: "a clear mind attacking a clearly stated problem and producing clearly stated conclusions" [99, pp. 3-4]. Clarity comes with economy – saying what needs to be said, and little else. This seems straightforward. But, it isn't. Writing with clarity and economy is a challenge that is never fully achieved. Even the most seasoned researcher struggles continually to express ideas in the clearest and most succinct way possible. The guard must never be down, lest the prose enlarge and swell.

Writing with clarity is both a craft and an art. The craft is driven by rules, rigour, and precision. The art is creative, engaging human qualities such as imagination, inspiration, ingenuity, and originality. Succeeding at both, and with a balance that retains economy while delivering style, is a challenge. However, unlike fictional writing, the balance for scholarly writing leans toward craft. In scholarly writing, clarity trumps all.

It is outside the scope of this book to teach either the craft or art of scholarly writing. The topics include sentence structure, grammar, tense, flow, tone, continuity, economy of expression, and so on. It is a huge assignment. Besides, excellent sources on these and related themes already exist. Four sources are recommended below. The first three address scholarly writing and also the methodology in experimental research. The fourth is the classic "Strunk and White," first published in 1919. At 105 pages, it packs more punch per page than any other source on writing style. It is not to be passed over.

- The APA's *Publication Manual of the American Psychological Association* [10]
- Day and Gastel's *How to Write and Publish a Scientific Paper* [99]
- Martin's *Doing Psychology Experiments* [342]
- Strunk and White's *The Elements of Style* [474]

There is one strategy leading to clarity of expression that we will dwell on in our closing paragraphs. It is, in this author's view, the single most powerful technique for transforming a loosely written manuscript into a succinct and clear research paper. The technique is simple: *Get rid of clutter.*

If clarity is the prize, clutter is the curse. A profusion of words that fill space, but add nothing, is certain to suffocate any research paper. Without doubt, the reader who faces a stream of added, useless words will quickly tire. The superfluous words draw in the reader's attention, but in the end they encumber, rather than enlighten. Every source on writing style has a take on this point. Strunk and White's Rule 17 is to Omit Needless Words:

> *A sentence should contain no unnecessary words, a paragraph no unnecessary sentences, for the same reason that a drawing should have no unnecessary lines and a machine no unnecessary parts.*

[474, p. 23]

The APA's Publication Manual gives similar advice:

> *Say only what needs to be said. The author who is more concise – that is, more frugal with words – writes a more readable paper.*

[10, p. 113]

Humourist Mark Twain has a different angle, but the same message:

> *I apologize for such a long letter – I didn't have time to write a short one.*[10]

---

[10] American humourist and author Mark Twain (1835-1910) is best known for adventure novels such as *The Adventures of Tom Sawyer* or *Adventures of Huckleberry Finn*.

Original	Revised
In order to do this	To do this
Should be able to understand	Should understand
The software used was our	The software was our
Stacking objects one on top of the other	Stacking objects
Prior gaming experience	Gaming experience
With this goal in mind	With this in mind
Two paths that can be taken to reach the	Two paths to the
The selection was made based on	The selection was based on
The use of the homing keys helps	Homing keys help
The top five most frequent letters	The five most frequent letters
The rate at which the cursor moves	The rate the cursor moves
The ESC key on the keyboard	The ESC key
Each of the participants	Each participant
Can be used to show	Can show
The average value can be calculated as	The average is
When they were ready	When ready
It is worth mentioning that the number of	Notably, the number of
For the sake of consistency	For consistency
The number of keys the user has to press	The number of key presses
The time it takes to compose a message	The time to compose a message
Users who prefer to use the keyboard	Users who prefer the keyboard
This is not a recommended idea	This is not recommended
Three types of interaction techniques	Three interaction techniques
Should be able to quickly adapt	Should quickly adapt
At any given time	At any time
To the best of our knowledge	To our knowledge
The movement time required to	The movement time to
For the purpose of improving	For improving
Because the selection operation requires	Because selection requires
Sorted in the order of their similarity	Sorted by similarity
The time taken to complete the task	The time to complete the task
Was developed in an attempt to	Was developed to
One point to note is that	Note that
Two different methods of input are	Two methods of input are
We ran an exploratory pilot study	We ran a pilot study
At their own discretion	At their discretion
Studies conducted in the past have found	Studies have found

FIGURE 8.14

Omit needless words.

Twain's point is simple: Writing with economy takes more effort than scribbling down rambling verbose prose.

Fig. 8.14 offers a few edits in view of Strunk and White's Rule 17. The examples are real. They are from a larger collection compiled by this book's author while editing, co-authoring, or reviewing HCI manuscripts. In each case, redundant words are removed. The revised phrase is succinct. It delivers the same point with less energy demanded of the reader.

There is little to gain in analysing each revision in Fig. 8.14. Perhaps one observation is worthwhile, however: User studies that are written about in the past tense have already been conducted. Furthermore, they were conducted in a previous time, before now ... ☺ See the last example in the figure. Yes, every sentence should be parsed in this manner. Break it down. Get rid of every needless word. The result is clarity and economy – a better manuscript.

When preparing the initial draft of a manuscript, relax. First and foremost, get the words and ideas down and into the manuscript. It would be nice if the editing that produced the revisions in Fig. 8.14 surfaced in the first draft. But, this is not likely and it isn't necessary. Few writers are gifted enough to produce crisp prose in the first pass. So, don't struggle to make the initial draft the final draft. But, before submitting the manuscript, give it every ounce of editing that time permits. The reviewers will appreciate it, and the result may ultimately – and hopefully – achieve that final and essential step in research – a publication. Congratulations and good luck.

*****

A web site is available as a resource accompanying this book's second edition:

- http://www.yorku.ca/mack/HCIbook2e

Student exercises

8-1 Use Google Scholar or the ACM Digital Library to locate several research papers from a recent conference proceedings. Study the abstracts to determine if they are succinctly and clearly written and if they convey "what was done" and "what was found" in the research. Choose two of the abstracts (perhaps the best and worst) and prepare a brief report or slide show presentation on your analysis. Suggest improvements, as appropriate.

8-2 Do a Google Scholar search on "tactile feedback" (or some other topic of interest). Examine the papers returned, starting at the beginning of the list. Find two examples each of conference papers, journal papers, and book chapters. Write a brief report (just a paragraph or two) citing each source and summarizing the central theme and findings. Also, use a table to present the papers with one paper per row and important details in columns. See Fig. 4.19 (p. 197) for an example. Include a reference list at the end. Format the citations and reference list as per the recommendations in section 8.3.3, Citations and References.

8-3 Design and administer a questionnaire to a group of people (participants). Collect data on characteristics of the participants and aspects of their interaction with technology. Analyse the data and write a report outlining the topic (Introduction), the methodology (Method) and the results (Results and Discussion).

Participants are drawn (ideally, at random) from a population. For this exercise, use convenience sampling. Recruit local university students or other adult computer users conveniently available, such as people at a local shopping mall or metro station or in the neighbourhood where you live.

Narrow the population as appropriate. For example, if there is an interest in Apple Mac users, WhatsApp users, Instagram users, or people over the age of 50, then screen candidates and use only those from the desired population. Use at least 25 participants.

Create the questionnaire following the guidelines in section 5.9, Questionnaire Design (p. 221).

The participants may be given the questionnaire to complete. Alternatively, use an interview style and directly ask the participants questions. In the latter case, more reliable information is obtained since participants are more engaged and can ask for clarification.

So, what data are of interest? A questionnaire usually begins by asking simple demographic information such as age and gender. Also solicit more specific information relevant to the topic, such as first-language spoken, number of hours per day using a computer, hours per day playing video games, preferred browser (Chrome vs. Firefox), preferred computer type (Mac vs. PC), number of tweets sent per day, preferred method for messaging (text message vs. voice input), estimated typing speed, and so on. There are numerous possibilities. Try to think of interesting relationships and ways to summarize, group, and graph the data?

Venture beyond the examples above. Remember, this is your research project! What other relationships are there? Do Faculty of Arts students differ from Faculty of Science students in ...? Does age or gender make a difference in ...? Do left-handed people prefer ...? Is the number of text messages sent per day related to ...? Are tablet users more likely to ...? Which pointing device do users of laptop computers prefer? Are people more likely to answer a phone call from a friend, a sibling, or co-worker? Is the latter behaviour different for males vs. females? Is there an age effect? Are Starbucks devotees more likely to drive a sports car than clients at Dunkin' Donuts? Are people with body piercings more likely to be Mac users or PC users?

Looking for any relationship is fine, but a plausible explanation is needed. For example, it is unlikely people who wear glasses differ from people who don't wear glasses in their texting habits. But, who knows. If a relationship such as this is investigated, that's fine, but develop a plausible reason and include it in your report. If, in the end, the relationship sought doesn't surface, that's fine too. But, an explanation is necessary. Hint: Use Google Scholar to determine if other researchers have investigated a similar topic. You may be surprised by what you find.

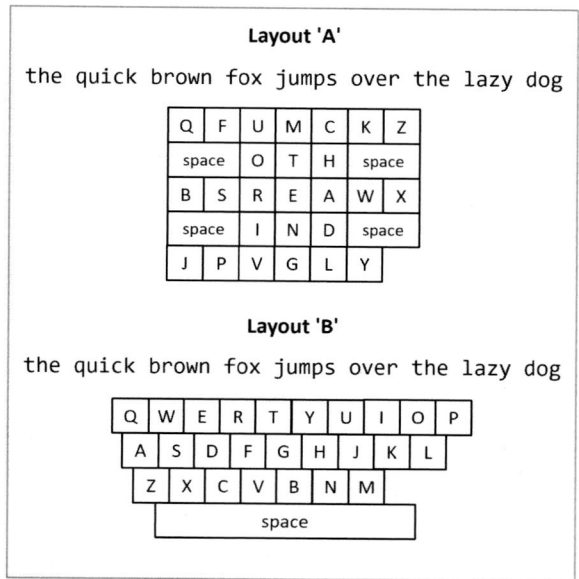

FIGURE 8.15

Student exercise on a text entry experiment using a paper mock-up of two keyboard layouts.

For the report, use the standard two-column conference format. Preferably, use LaTeX or Overleaf, along with the ACM template for conference submissions. The final formatted report should be 5-10 pages and include citations and references to at least four papers.

8-4 Recruit some participants for a study on text entry using paper mock-ups of two keyboard layouts.[11] Prepare a handout sheet containing images of the keyboards. The top-half of the sheet contains the heading "Layout A," with a phrase of text below. Use "the quick brown fox jumps over the lazy dog." Below the phrase appears the keyboard. The bottom-half of the sheet contains the heading "Layout B," with same phrase below, and with a different keyboard below that. The general idea is shown in Fig. 8.15.

For the two keyboards, use Opti (A) and Qwerty (B), as shown in Fig. 8.15, or any other layouts of interest, such as the Metropolis layout by Hunter et al. [204] or the Fitaly layout by Textware Solutions.[12]

---

[11] This student exercise is used in the author's course "Empirical Research Methods for Human-Computer Interaction" presented numerous times at the ACM's annual SIGCHI conference [317].
[12] https://textware.com/.

Ask participants to enter the phrase by tapping on the keyboard image using a non-marking stylus, such as a pen held upside-down. They are to enter the phrase five times on one keyboard, then five times on the other keyboard. Use a watch or other timing device to record to the entry time for each phrase. Enter the times on a log sheet. Divide the participants into two groups and counterbalance the order of testing (see section 5.11, p. 228).

After testing is complete, enter the data into a spreadsheet. Convert the entry time t (in seconds) to entry speed s (in words per minute) using

$$s = \frac{43/5}{t/60} \qquad (8.1)$$

where $\frac{43}{5}$ is the number of words and $\frac{t}{60}$ is the number of minutes.[13] Analyse the data for significant effects using an analysis of variance, as outlined in Chapter 6. For the purpose of the ANOVA, the experiment has three independent variables: layout (A, B), phrase iteration (1, 2, 3, 4, 5), and group (AB, BA). Layout and phrase iteration are within-subjects, group is between-subjects.

Write a research paper for the experiment, following the guidelines in this chapter and book. Use the standard two-column conference format. Preferably, use LaTeX or Overleaf, along with the ACM template for conference submissions. The final formatted report should be 6-8 pages and include citations and references to at least four papers.

8-5 Recruit some participants for a study on text entry. Use a procedure similar to the previous student exercise. However, instead of using paper mock-ups, use the SoftKeyboardExperiment software on this book's web site. Many options are set via the setup dialog (Fig. 8.16a) including a choice from seven pre-configured keyboard layouts. See Fig. 8.16b. Use any two. The software also supports custom layouts and word completion. Consult the API for further details. Fig. 8.16c shows the experiment task. Data collection is automated in the software and includes dependent measures such as entry speed (wpm), error rate (%), and keystrokes per character (KSPC).

Write a research paper for the experiment following the guidelines in this chapter and book. Use the standard two-column conference format and the ACM template for conference submissions. Include citations and references to at least four papers (e.g., research papers on soft keyboards).

8-6 How accurate are users in estimating their typing speed? Conduct a small experiment investigating this question. Recruit some participants and administer a brief questionnaire to each. Include a question asking them to estimate their typing speed in words per minute on a desktop computer. Then measure their

---

[13] See footnote 31 on p. 87.

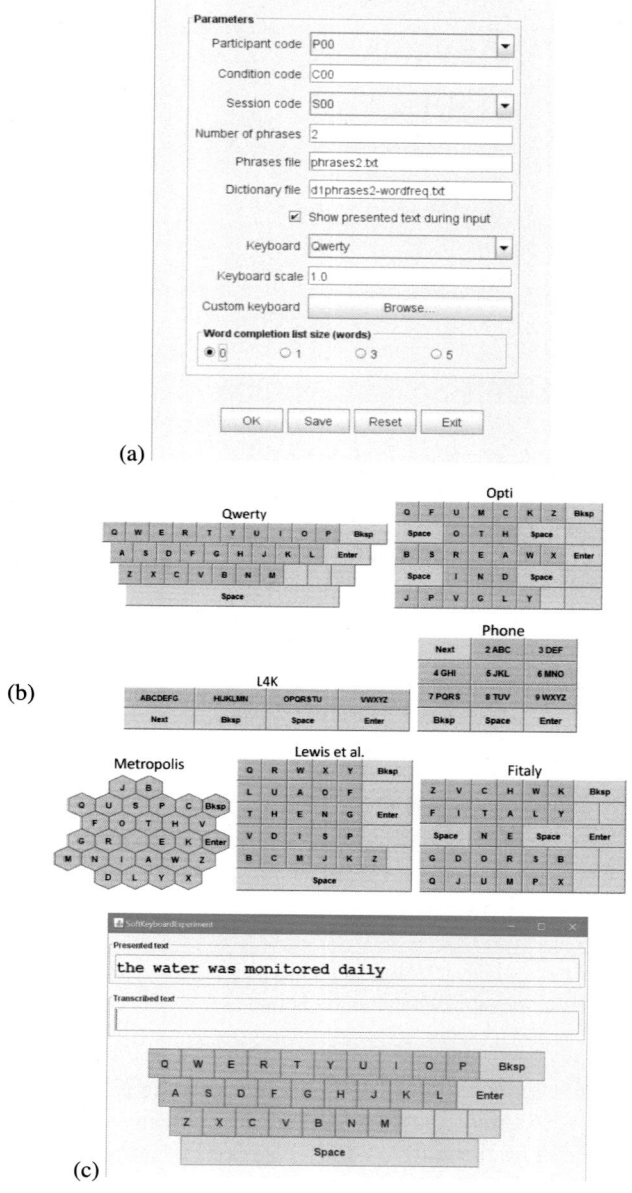

FIGURE 8.16

Student exercise using the SoftKeyboardExperiment software. (a) Setup dialog. (b) Keyboard options. (c) Experiment task.

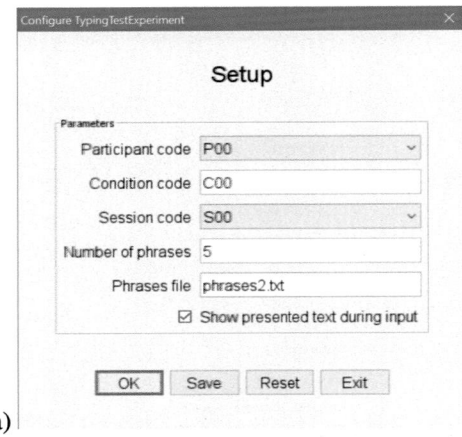

(a)

(b)

FIGURE 8.17

Student exercise on users' ability to estimate their typing speed using the TypingTestExperiment software. (a) Setup dialog. (b) Experiment screen.

typing speed using the TypingTestExperiment software provided on this book's web site. Fig. 8.17 shows the setup dialog and a screen snap of the experiment procedure. Configure the software for ten phrases of entry. Compare the users' estimates with the observed typing speeds. Do users tend to overestimate or underestimate their typing speed? Is the discrepancy different for female and male participants? Try to think of additional questions to consider. Present your findings in a brief report or slide show presentation.

Bibliography

[1] Y. Abdrabou, M. Mostafa, M. Khamis, A. Elmougy, Calibration-free text entry using smooth pursuit eye movements, in: Proceedings of the 2019 Symposium on Eye Tracking Research & Applications - ETRA '19, ACM, New York, 2019, pp. 35.1–35.5, https://doi.org/10.1145/3314111.3319838.

[2] J. Accot, S. Zhai, Refining Fitts' law models for bivariate pointing, in: Proceedings of the ACM SIGCHI Conference on Human Factors in Computing Systems - CHI '03, ACM, New York, 2003, pp. 193–200, https://doi.org/10.1145/642611.642646.

[3] ACM, ACM computing classifiction system, https://dl.acm.org/ccs, 2012. (Accessed 20 March 2023).

[4] ACM, TOCHI author guidelines, https://dl.acm.org/journal/tochi/author-guidelines, 2021. (Accessed 15 March 2023).

[5] M. Akamatsu, I.S. MacKenzie, T. Hasbrouq, A comparison of tactile, auditory, and visual feedback in a pointing task using a mouse-type device, Ergonomics 38 (4) (1995) 816–827, https://doi.org/10.1080/00140139508925152.

[6] R. Almeida, P. Cubaud, Supporting 3D window manipulation with a yawing mouse, in: Proceedings of the 4th Nordic Conference on Human-Computer Interaction - NordiCHI '06, ACM, New York, 2006, pp. 477–480, https://doi.org/10.1145/1182475.1182541.

[7] J. Alvina, C. Qu, J. McGrenere, W.E. Mackay, MojiBoard: Generating parametric emojis with gesture keyboards, in: Extended Abstracts of the ACM SIGCHI Conference on Human Factors in Computing Systems - CHI '19, ACM, New York, 2019, pp. 1–6, https://doi.org/10.1145/3290607.3312771.

[8] A.S. Anggaira, Linguistic errors on narrative text translation using Google Translate, Pedagogy: Journal of English Language Teaching 5 (1) (2017) 1–14.

[9] M. Annett, F. Anderson, W.F. Bischof, A. Gupta, The pen is mightier: Understanding stylus behaviour while inking on tablets, in: Proceedings of Graphics Interface - GI '14, Canadian Information Processing Society, Toronto, 2014, pp. 193–200.

[10] APA, Publication Manual of the American Psychological Association, 7th ed., APA, Washington, DC, 2020.

[11] F. Argelaguet, C. Andujar, Improving 3D selection in VEs through expanding targets and forced disocclusion, in: Proceedings of the 9th International Symposium on Smart Graphics - SG '08 (LNIP 5116), Springer, Berlin, 2008, pp. 45–57, https://doi.org/10.1007/978-3-540-85412-8_5.

[12] A.S. Arif, W. Stuerzlinger, Predicting the cost of error correction in character-based text entry technologies, in: Proceedings of the ACM SIGCHI Conference on Human Factors in Computing Systems - CHI '10, ACM, New York, 2010, pp. 5–14, https://doi.org/10.1145/1753326.1753329.

[13] L.Y. Arnault, J.S. Greenstein, Is display/control gain a useful metric for optimizing an interface? Human Factors 32 (6) (1990) 651–663, https://doi.org/10.1177/001872089003200604.

[14] C. Asakawa, H. Takagi, Text entry for people with visual impairments, in: I.S. MacKenzie, K. Tanaka-Ishii (Eds.), Text Enty Systems: Mobility, Accessibility, Universality, Morgan Kaufmann, San Francisco, 2007, pp. 305–318, https://doi.org/10.1016/B978-012373591-1/50016-4.

[15] P. Ayyavu, C. Jensen, Integrating user feedback with heuristic security and privacy management systems, in: Proceedings of the ACM SIGCHI Conference on Human Factors in Computing Systems - CHI '11, ACM, New York, 2011, pp. 2305–2314, https://doi.org/10.1145/1978942.1979281.

[16] R.M. Baecker, J. Grudin, W.A.S. Buxton, S. Greenberg, A historical and intellectual perspective, in: R.M. Baecker, J. Grudin, W.A.S. Buxton, S. Greenberg (Eds.), Readings in Human-Computer Interaction: Toward the Year 2000, 2nd ed., Morgan Kaufmann, San Francisco, 1995, pp. 35–47.

[17] R.W. Bailey, Human Performance Engineering: Designing High Quality, Professional User Interfaces for Computer Products, Applications, and Systems, 3rd ed., Prentice Hall, Upper Saddle River, NJ, ISBN 978-0131496347, 1996.

[18] R. Balakrishnan, T. Baudel, G. Kurtenbach, G. Fitzmaurice, The Rockin'Mouse: Integral 3D manipulation on a plane, in: Proceedings of the ACM SIGCHI Conference on Human Factors in Computing Systems - CHI '97, ACM, New York, 1997, pp. 311–318, https://doi.org/10.1145/258549.258778.

[19] R. Balakrishnan, I.S. MacKenzie, Performance differences in the fingers, wrist, and forearm in computer input control, in: Proceedings of the ACM SIGCHI Conference on Human Factors in Computing Systems - CHI '97, ACM, New York, 1997, pp. 303–310, https://doi.org/10.1145/258549.258764.

[20] R. Balakrishnan, P. Patel, The PadMouse: Facilitating selection and spatial positioning for the non-dominant hand, in: Proceedings of the ACM SIGCHI Conference on Human Factors in Computing Systems - CHI '98, ACM, New York, 1998, pp. 9–16, https://doi.org/10.1145/274644.274646.

[21] O. Bälter, Keystroke level analysis of email message organization, in: Proceedings of the ACM SIGCHI Conference on Human Factors in Computing Systems - CHI '00, ACM, New York, 2000, pp. 105–112, https://doi.org/10.1145/332040.332413.

[22] A. Bangor, P. Kortum, J. Miller, Determining what individual SUS scores mean: Adding an adjective rating scale, Journal of Usability Studies 4 (3) (May 2009) 114–123.

[23] N. Banovic, F.C.Y. Li, D. Dearman, K. Yatani, K.N. Truong, Design of unimanual multi-finger pie menu interaction, in: Proceedings of the ACM International Conference on Interactive Tabletops and Surfaces – ITS '11, ACM, New York, 2011, pp. 120–129, https://doi.org/10.1145/2076354.2076378.

[24] R.C. Barrett, E.J. Selker, J.D. Rutledge, R.S. Olyha, Negative inertia: A dynamic pointing function, in: Companion Proceedings of the ACM SICGHI Conference on Human Factors in Computing Systems - CHI '95, ACM, New York, 1995, pp. 316–317, https://doi.org/10.1145/223355.223692.

[25] J.F. Bartlett, Rock 'n' Scroll is here to stay, IEEE Computer Graphics and Applications 20 (3) (May 2000) 40–45, https://doi.org/10.1109/38.844371.

[26] C. Bartneck, M. Verbunt, O. Mubin, A.A. Mahmud, To kill a mockingbird robot, in: Proceedings of the ACM/IEEE International Conference on Human-Robot Interaction - HRI '07, ACM, New York, 2007, pp. 81–87, https://doi.org/10.1145/1228716.1228728.

[27] A.U. Batmaz, X. Sun, D. Taskiran, W. Stuerzlinger, Eye-hand coordination training for sports with mid-air VR, in: Proceedings of the 26th ACM Symposium on Virtual Reality Software and Technology - VRST '20, ACM, New York, 2020, pp. 19.1–19.10, https://doi.org/10.1145/3385956.3418971.

[28] M. Beaudouin-Lafon, Instrumental interaction: An interaction model for designing post-WIMP user interfaces, in: Proceedings of the ACM SIGCHI Conference in Human Factors on Computing Systems - CHI '00, ACM, New York, 2000, pp. 446–453, https://doi.org/10.1145/332040.332473.

[29] S. Belia, F. Fidler, J. Williams, G. Cumming, Researchers misunderstand confidence intervals and standard error bars, Psychological Methods 10 (4) (2005) 389–396, https://doi.org/10.1037/1082-989X.10.4.389.

[30] T. Bellman, I.S. MacKenzie, A probabilistic character layout strategy for mobile text entry, in: Proceedings of Graphics Interface - GI '98, Canadian Information Processing Society, Toronto, 1998, pp. 168–176, https://doi.org/10.20380/GI1998.21.

[31] B. Benligiray, C. Topal, C. Akinlar, SliceType: Fast gaze typing with a merging keyboard, Journal on Multimodal User Interfaces 13 (4) (2019) 321–334, https://doi.org/10.1007/s12193-018-0285-z.

[32] S. Bhattacharya, D. Samanta, A. Basu, Performance models for automatic evaluation of virtual scanning keyboards, IEEE Transactions on Neural Systems and Rehabilitation Engineering 16 (5) (2008) 510–519, https://doi.org/10.1109/TNSRE.2008.2003377.

[33] R. Blanch, Y. Guiard, M. Beaudouin-Lafon, Semantic pointing: Improving target acquisition with control-display ratio adaptation, in: Proceedings of the ACM SIGCHI Conference on Human Factors in Computing Systems - CHI '04, ACM, New York, 2004, pp. 519–526, https://doi.org/10.1145/985692.985758.

[34] A. Bodnar, R. Corbett, D. Nekrasovski, AROMA: Ambient awareness through olfaction in a messaging application, in: Proceedings of the 6th International Conference on Multimodal Interfaces - ICMI '04, ACM, New York, 2004, pp. 183–190, https://doi.org/10.1145/1027933.1027965.

[35] R.A. Bolt, "Put-That-There": Voice and gesture at the graphics interface, in: Proceedings of the 7th Annual Conference on Computer Graphics and Interactive Techniques - SIGGRAPH '80, ACM, New York, 1980, pp. 262–270, https://doi.org/10.1145/800250.807503.

[36] L. Borman, SIGCHI: The early years, SIGCHI Bulletin 28 (1) (Jan. 1996) 4–6, https://doi.org/10.1145/249170.249172.

[37] A. Bouch, A. Kuchinsky, N. Bhatti, Quality is in the eye of the beholder: Meeting users' requirements for Internet quality of service, in: Proceedings of the ACM SIGCHI Conference on Human Factors in Computing Systems - CHI '00, ACM, New York, 2000, pp. 297–304, https://doi.org/10.1145/332040.332447.

[38] M.M. Bradley, P.J. Lang, Measuring emotion: The self-assessment manikin and the semantic differential, Journal of Behavior Therapy and Experimental Psychiatry 25 (1) (1994) 49–59, https://doi.org/10.1016/0005-7916(94)90063-9.

[39] G. Brajnik, Y. Yesilada, S. Harper, The expertise effect of web accessibility evaluation methods, Human-Computer Interaction 26 (3) (2011) 246–283, https://doi.org/10.1080/07370024.2011.601670.

[40] S.A. Brewster, D. McGookin, C. Miller, Olfoto: Designing a smell-based interaction, in: Proceedings of the ACM SIGCHI Conference on Human Factors in Computing Systems - CHI '06, ACM, New York, 2006, pp. 653–662, https://doi.org/10.1145/1124772.1124869.

[41] S.A. Brewster, P.C. Wright, A.D.N. Edwards, The design and evaluation of an auditory-enhanced scrollbar, in: Proceedings of the ACM SIGCHI Conference on Human Factors in Computing Systems - CHI '94, ACM, New York, 1994, pp. 173–179, https://doi.org/10.1145/191666.191733.

[42] J. Brooke, SUS: A 'quick and dirty' usability scale, in: P.W. Jordan, B. Thomas, I.L. McClelland, B. Weerdmeester (Eds.), Usability Evaluation in Industry, CRC Press, London, 1996, pp. 189–194, https://doi.org/10.1201/9781498710411.

[43] F.P. Brooks Jr., M. Ouh-Young, J.J. Batter, P.J. Kilpatrick, Project GROPE: Haptic displays for scientific visualization, Computer Graphics 24 (2) (1990) 177–185, https://doi.org/10.1145/97880.97899.

[44] M.A. Brown, I.S. MacKenzie, Evaluating video game controller usability as related to user hand size, in: Proceedings of the International Conference on Multimedia and Human-Computer Interaction - MHCI '13, ASET, Ottawa, Canada, 2013, pp. 114.1–114.8.

[45] T. Brown, Change by Design: How Design Thinking Transforms Organizations and Inspires Innovation, HarperBusiness, New York, ISBN 978-0061766084, 2009.

[46] T. Brown, Design thinking, Harvard Business Review 86 (6) (June 2008) 84–92.

[47] V. Bush, As we may think, The Atlantic Monthly 176 (1) (July 1945) 101–108, reprinted in the ACM's Interactions (March 1996) 35–46, https://doi.org/10.1145/227181.227186.

[48] B. Buxton, The long nose of innovation (revised), Business Week Electronic Article, Jan. 2008, https://www.billbuxton.com/01%20The%20Long%20Nose%20of%20Innovation%20Revised.pdf. (Accessed 15 March 2023).

[49] W. Buxton, A three-state model of graphical input, in: Proceedings of the IFIP TC13 Third International Conference on Human-Computer Interaction - INTERACT '90, Elsevier, Amsterdam, 1990, pp. 449–456.

[50] W. Buxton, There's more to interaction than meets the eye: Some issues in manual input, in: D.A. Norman, S.W. Draper (Eds.), User Centered System Design: New Perspectives on Human-Computer Interaction, Erlbaum, Hillsdale, NJ, 1986, pp. 319–337.

[51] W. Buxton, R. Hill, P. Rowley, Issues and techniques in touch-sensitive tablet input, in: Proceedings of SIGGRAPH '85, ACM, New York, 1985, pp. 215–224, https://doi.org/10.1145/325334.325239.

[52] W. Buxton, B.A. Myers, A study in two-handed input, in: Proceedings of the ACM SIGCHI Conference on Human Factors in Computing Systems - CHI '87, ACM, New York, 1986, pp. 321–326, https://doi.org/10.1145/22339.22390.

[53] M.D. Byrne, J.R. Anderson, S. Douglass, M. Matessa, Eye tracking the visual search of click-down menus, in: Proceedings of the ACM SIGCHI Conference on Human Factors in Computing Systems - CHI '99, ACM, New York, 1999, pp. 402–409, https://doi.org/10.1145/302979.303118.

[54] F. Cabric, E. Dubois, M. Serrano, A predictive performance model for immersive interactions in mixed reality, in: 2021 IEEE International Symposium on Mixed and Augmented Reality (ISMAR), IEEE, New York, 2021, pp. 202–210, https://doi.org/10.1109/ISMAR52148.2021.00035.

[55] J.R. Callahan, D. Hopkins, M.D. Weiser, B. Shneiderman, An empirical comparison of pie vs. linear menus, in: Proceedings of the ACM SIGCHI Conference on Human Factors in Computing Systems - CHI '88, ACM, New York, 1988, pp. 95–100, https://doi.org/10.1145/57167.57182.

[56] T. Canham, I.S. MacKenzie, R.F. Murray, M.S. Brown, The effect of perceptual optimization on color space navigability, in: Proceedings of Graphics Interface - GI '23, Canadian Information Processing Society, Toronto, 2023, pp. 14.1–14.10.

[57] X. Cao, J.J. Li, R. Balakrishnan, Peephole pointing: Modeling acquisition of dynamically revealed targets, in: Proceedings of the ACM SIGCHI Conference on Human Factors in Computing System - CHI '08, ACM, New York, 2008, pp. 1699–1708, https://doi.org/10.1145/1357054.1357320.

[58] S.K. Card, User perceptual mechanisms in the search of computer command menus, in: Proceedings of Human Factors in Computer Systems, ACM, New York, 1982, pp. 190–196, https://doi.org/10.1145/800049.801779.

[59] S.K. Card, The model human processor: A model for making engineering calculations of human performance, in: Proceedings of the 25th Annual Meeting of the Human Factors Society, Human Factors Society, Santa Monica, CA, 1981, pp. 301–305, https://doi.org/10.1177/107118138102500180.

[60] S.K. Card, W.K. English, B.J. Burr, Evaluation of mouse, rate-controlled isometric joystick, step keys, and text keys for text selection on a CRT, Ergonomics 21 (8) (1978) 601–613, https://doi.org/10.1080/00140137808931762.

[61] S.K. Card, J.D. Mackinlay, G.G. Robertson, A morphological analysis of the design space of input devices, ACM Transactions on Office Information Systems 9 (2) (1991) 99–122, https://doi.org/10.1145/123078.128726.

[62] S.K. Card, T.P. Moran, A. Newell, Computer text-editing: An information-processing analysis of a routine cognitive skill, Cognitive Psychology 12 (1) (1980) 32–74, https://doi.org/10.1016/0010-0285(80)90003-1.

[63] S.K. Card, T.P. Moran, A. Newell, The keystroke-level model for user performance time with interactive systems, Communications of the ACM 23 (7) (July 1980) 396–410, https://doi.org/10.1145/358886.358895.

[64] S.K. Card, T.P. Moran, A. Newell, The Psychology of Human-Computer Interaction, Erlbaum, Hillsdale, NJ, 1983.

[65] J.M. Carroll, J.C. Thomas, Metaphor and the cognitive representation of computing systems, IEEE Transactions on Systems, Man and Cybernetics 12 (2) (1982) 107–116, https://doi.org/10.1109/TSMC.1982.4308795.

[66] S.M. Casey, Set Phasers on Stun: And Other True Tales of Design, Technology, and Human Error, 2nd ed., Aegean Publishing Company, Santa Barbara, CA, 1998, https://doi.org/10.1080/00140139408964936.

[67] S.M. Casey, The Atomic Chef: And Other True Tales of Design, Technology, and Human Error, Aegean Publishing Company, Santa Barbara, CA, 2006, https://doi.org/10.1097/01.HP.0000238602.11156.a7.

[68] G. Casiez, D. Vogel, Q. Pan, C. Chaillou, RubberEdge: Reducing clutching by combining position and rate control with elastic feedback, in: Proceedings of the ACM Symposium on User Interface Software and Technology - UIST '07, ACM, New York, 2007, pp. 129–138, https://doi.org/10.1145/1294211.1294234.

[69] B. Cassidy, J.C. Read, I.S. MacKenzie, An evaluation of radar metaphors for providing directional stimuli using non-verbal sound, in: Proceedings of the ACM SIGCHI Conference on Human Factors in Computing Systems - CHI '19, ACM, New York, 2019, pp. 59:1–59:8, https://doi.org/10.1145/3290605.3300289.

[70] B. Cassidy, J.C. Read, I.S. MacKenzie, FittsFarm: Comparing children's drag-and-drop performance using finger and stylus input on tablets, in: Human-Computer Interaction – INTERACT '19 (LNCS 11748), Springer, Berlin, 2019, pp. 656–668, https://doi.org/10.1007/978-3-030-29387-1_38.

[71] S.J. Castellucci, I.S. MacKenzie, Graffiti vs. unistrokes: An empirical comparison, in: Proceedings of the ACM SIGCHI Conference on Human Factors in Computing Systems - CHI '08, ACM, New York, 2008, pp. 305–308, https://doi.org/10.1145/1357054.1357106.

[72] S.J. Castellucci, I.S. MacKenzie, M. Misra, L. Pandey, A.S. Arif, TiltWriter: Design and evaluation of a no-touch tilt-based text entry method for handheld devices, in: Proceed-

ings of the 18th International Conference on Mobile and Ubiquitous Multimedia - MUM '19, ACM, New York, 2019, pp. 7.1–7.8, https://doi.org/10.1145/3365610.3365629.

[73] A. Chapanis, Man-Machine Engineering, Wadsworth, Belmont, CA, 1965.

[74] C.-H. Chen, Y.-H. Chien, Reading Chinese text on a small screen with RSVP, Displays 26 (3) (2005) 103–108, https://doi.org/10.1016/j.displa.2005.02.004.

[75] D.K.Y. Chen, J.-B. Chossat, P.B. Shull, HaptiVec: Presenting haptic feedback vectors in handheld controllers using embedded tactile pin arrays, in: Proceedings of the ACM SIGCHI Conference on Human Factors in Computing Systems - CHI '19, ACM, New York, 2019, pp. 171.1–171.11, https://doi.org/10.1145/3290605.3300401.

[76] M. Chignell, L. Wang, A. Zare, J. Li, The evolution of HCI and human factors: Integrating human and artificial intelligence, ACM Transactions on Computer-Human Interaction 30 (2) (Mar. 2023) 17.1–17.30, https://doi.org/10.1145/3557891.

[77] J. Chin, W.-T. Fu, Interactive effects of age and interface difference on search strategies and performance, in: Proceedings of the ACM SIGCHI Conference on Human Factors in Computing Systems - CHI '10, ACM, New York, 2010, pp. 403–412, https://doi.org/10.1145/1753326.1753387.

[78] J. Chin, W.-T. Fu, T. Kannampallil, Adaptive information search: Age-dependent interactions between cognitive profiles and strategies, in: Proceedings of the ACM SIGCHI Conference on Human Factors in Computing Systems - CHI '09, ACM, New York, 2009, pp. 1683–1692, https://doi.org/10.1145/1518701.1518961.

[79] M. Choi, D. Sakamoto, T. Ono, Kuiper Belt: Utilizing the "out-of-natural angle" region in the eye-gaze interaction for virtual reality, in: Proceedings of the ACM SIGCHI Conference on Human Factors in Computing Systems - CHI '22, ACM, New York, 2022, https://doi.org/10.1145/3491102.3517725.

[80] K. Chung, L. Hossain, Network structure, position, ties and ICT use in distributed knowledge-intensive work, in: Proceedings of the ACM Conference on Computer Supported Cooperative Work - CSCW '08, ACM, New York, 2008, pp. 545–554, https://doi.org/10.1145/1460563.1460649.

[81] L.D. Clark, M. El Iskandarani, S.L. Riggs, The effect of movement direction, hand dominance, and hemispace on reaching movement kinematics in virtual reality, in: Proceedings of the ACM SIGCHI Conference on Human Factors in Computing Systems - CHI '23, ACM, New York, 2023, pp. 407.1–407.18, https://doi.org/10.1145/3544548.3581191.

[82] L.D. Clark, S.L. Riggs, VR-based kinematic assessments: Examining the effects of task properties on arm movement kinematics, in: Extended Abstracts of the ACM SIGCHI Conference on Human Factors in Computing Systems - CHI '22, ACM, New York, 2022, pp. 413.1–413.8, https://doi.org/10.1145/3491101.3519841.

[83] E. Clarkson, J. Clawson, K. Lyons, T. Starner, An empirical study of typing rates on mini-QWERTY keyboards, in: Proceedings of the ACM SIGCHI Conference on Human Factors in Computing Systems - CHI '05, ACM, New York, 2005, pp. 1288–1291, https://doi.org/10.1145/1056808.1056898.

[84] J. Clawson, K. Lyons, A. Rudnick, R.A. Iannucci, T. Starner, Automatic whiteout++: Correcting mini-QWERTY typing errors using keypress timing, in: Proceedings of the ACM SIGCHI Conference on Human Factors in Computing Systems - CHI '08, ACM, New York, 2008, pp. 573–582, https://doi.org/10.1145/1357054.1357147.

[85] A. Cockburn, C. Gutwin, S. Greenberg, A predictive model of menu performance, in: Proceedings of the ACM SIGCHI Conference on Human Factors in Computing Systems - CHI '07, ACM, New York, 2007, pp. 627–636, https://doi.org/10.1145/1240624.1240723.

[86] C.I. Constantin, I.S. MacKenzie, Tilt-controlled mobile games: Velocity-control vs. position-control, in: Proceedings of the 6th IEEE Consumer Electronics Society Games, Entertainment, Media Conference - GEM '14, IEEE, New York, 2014, pp. 1–7, https://doi.org/10.1109/GEM.2014.7048091.

[87] A. Cooper, The Inmates Are Running the Asylum, Sams, Indianapolis, 1999, https://doi.org/10.1007/978-3-322-99786-9_1.

[88] A. Cooper, R. Riemann, About Face 2.0: The Essentials of Interaction Design, Wiley, Indianapolis, 2003.

[89] L. Coretti, D. Pica, Facebook's communication protocols, algorithmic filters, and protest: A critical socio-technical perspective, in: M. Mortensen, C. Neumayer, T. Poell (Eds.), Social Media Materialities and Protest: Critical Reflections, Routledge, London, 2018, https://doi.org/10.4324/9781315107066.

[90] G. Costagliola, M. De Rosa, V. Fuccella, B. Martin, BubbleBoard: A zoom-based text entry method on smartwatches, in: Proceedings of the International Conference on Human-Computer Interaction - HCII '22 (LNCS 13303), Springer, Berlin, 2022, pp. 14–27, https://doi.org/10.1007/978-3-031-05409-9_2.

[91] E. Courtoux, C. Appert, O. Chapuis, SurfAirs: Surface + mid-air input for large vertical displays, in: Proceedings of the ACM SIGCHI Conference on Human Factors in Computing Systems - CHI '23, ACM, New York, 2023, https://doi.org/10.1145/3544548.3580877.

[92] C.A.S. Cunha, R.P. Duarte, Multi-device nutrition control, Sensors 22 (7) (2022) 1–24, https://doi.org/10.3390/s22072617.

[93] H.A. Cunningham, Aiming error under transformed spatial mappings suggest a structure for visual-motor maps, Journal of Experimental Psychology: Human Perception and Performance 15 (3) (1989) 493–506, https://doi.org/10.1037/0096-1523.15.3.493.

[94] L.D. Cutler, B. Fröhlich, P. Hanrahan, Two-handed direct manipulation on the responsive workbench, in: Proceedings of the 1997 Symposium on Interactive 3D Graphics - I3D '97, ACM, New York, 1997, pp. 107–114, https://doi.org/10.1145/253284.253315.

[95] M. Czerwinski, S. Dumais, G. Robertson, S. Dziadosz, S. Tiernan, M. van Dantzich, Visualizing implicit queries for information management and retrieval, in: Proceedings of the ACM SIGCHI Conference on Human Factors in Computing Systems - CHI '99, ACM, New York, 1999, pp. 560–567, https://doi.org/10.1145/302979.303158.

[96] M. Czerwinski, E. Horvitz, S. Wilhite, A diary study of task switching and interruptions, in: Proceedings of the ACM SIGCHI Conference on Human Factors in Computing Systems - CHI '04, ACM, New York, 2004, pp. 175–182, https://doi.org/10.1145/985692.985715.

[97] L.A. Dabbish, R.E. Kraut, S. Fussell, S. Kiesler, Understanding email use: Predicting action on a message, in: Proceedings of the ACM SIGCHI Conference on Human Factors in Computing Systems - CHI '05, ACM, New York, 2005, pp. 591–700, https://doi.org/10.1145/1054972.1055068.

[98] P.T. Daniels, W. Bright, The World's Writing Systems, Oxford University Press, New York, 1996.

[99] R.A. Day, B. Gastel, How to Write and Publish a Scientific Paper, 6th ed., Greenwood Publishing, Westport, CT, 2006, https://doi.org/10.1017/S095026880003079X.

[100] W. Delamare, M. Daniel, K. Hasan, MultiFingerBubble: A 3D bubble cursor variation for dense environments, in: Extended Abstracts of the ACM SIGCHI Conference on Human Factors in Computing Systems - CHI '22, ACM, New York, 2022, pp. 453.1–453.6, https://doi.org/10.1145/3491101.3519692.

[101] L. Diana, P. Pilastro, E.N. Aiello, A.K. Eberhard-Moscicka, R.M. Müri, N. Bolognini, Saccades, attentional orienting and disengagement: The effects of anodal TDCS over right posterior parietal cortex (PPC) and frontal eye field (FEF), in: Proceedings of the 2021 Symposium on Eye Tracking Research & Applications - ETRA '21, ACM, New York, 2021, pp. 20.1–20.7, https://doi.org/10.1145/3448018.3457995.

[102] P. Dietz, D. Leigh, DiamondTouch: A multi-user touch technology, in: Proceedings of the ACM Symposium on User Interface Software and Technology - UIST '01, ACM, New York, 2001, pp. 219–226, https://doi.org/10.1145/502348.502389.

[103] A. Dix, J. Finlay, G. Abowd, R. Beale, Human-Computer Interaction, 3rd ed., Prentice Hall, London, 2004.

[104] M. Dragovic, Towards an improved measure of the Edinburgh Handedness Inventory, Laterality 9 (4) (2004) 411–419, https://doi.org/10.1080/13576500342000248.

[105] M.H. Draper, E.S. Viire, T.A. Furness, V.J. Gawron, Effects of image scale and system time delay on simulator sickness within head-coupled virtual environments, Human Factors 43 (1) (2001) 120–146, https://doi.org/10.1518/001872001775992552.

[106] T.J. Dube, Y. Ren, H. Limerick, I.S. MacKenzie, A.S. Arif, Push, tap, dwell, and pinch: Evaluation of four mid-air selection methods augmented with ultrasonic haptic feedback, Proceedings of the ACM on Human–Computer Interaction 6 (ISS) (Nov. 2022) 565.1–565.19, https://doi.org/10.1145/3567718.

[107] A.T. Duchowski, Eye Tracking Methodology: Theory and Practice, 3rd ed., Springer, London, 2017.

[108] H.B.-L. Duh, V.H.H. Chen, C.B. Tan, Playing different games on different phones: An empirical study on mobile gaming, in: Proceedings of MobileHCI '08, ACM, New York, 2008, pp. 391–394, https://doi.org/10.1145/1409240.1409296.

[109] M.D. Dunlop, Watch-top text-entry: Can phone-style predictive text entry work with only 5 buttons? in: Proceedings of MobileHCI '04, Springer, Heidelberg, 2004, pp. 342–346.

[110] M.D. Dunlop, A. Crossan, Predictive text entry methods for mobile phones, Personal and Ubiquitous Computing 4 (2000) 134–143, https://doi.org/10.1007/BF01324120.

[111] R. Eg, K. Raaen, M. Claypool, Playing with delay: With poor timing comes poor performance, and experience follows suit, in: Proceedings of the 10th International Conference on Quality of Multimedia Experience - QoMEX '18, IEEE, New York, 2018, pp. 1–6, https://doi.org/10.1109/QoMEX.2018.8463382.

[112] L.A. Elkin, J.-B. Beau, G. Casiez, D. Vogel, Manipulation, learning, and recall with tangible pen-like input, in: Proceedings of the ACM SIGCHI Conference on Human Factors in Computing Systems - CHI '20, ACM, New York, 2020, pp. 1–12, https://doi.org/10.1145/3313831.3376772.

[113] C. Elmadjian, C.H. Morimoto, GazeBar: Exploiting the Midas touch in gaze interaction, in: Extended Abstracts of the ACM SIGCHI Conference on Human Factors in Computing Systems - CHI '21, ACM, New York, 2021, pp. 248.1–248.7, https://doi.org/10.1145/3411763.3451703.

[114] D. Engelbart, X-Y position indicator for a display system (U.S. Patent 3,541,541), 1970.

[115] W.K. English, D.C. Engelbart, M.L. Berman, Display selection techniques for text manipulation, IEEE Transactions on Human Factors in Electronics HFE-8 (1) (1967) 5–15, https://doi.org/10.1109/THFE.1967.232994.

[116] N. Enns, I.S. MacKenzie, Touch-based remote control devices, in: Extended Abstracts of the ACM SIGCHI Conference on Human Factors in Computing Systems - CHI '98, ACM, New York, 1998, pp. 229–230, https://doi.org/10.1145/286498.286717.

[117] D.M. Erceg-Hurn, V.M. Mirosevich, Modern robust statistical methods: An easy way to maximize the accuracy and power of your research, American Psychologist 63 (7) (2008) 591–601, https://doi.org/10.1037/0003-066X.63.7.591.

[118] T. Erickson, D.W. McDonald, HCI Remixed: Reflections on Works That Have Influenced the HCI Community, MIT Press, Cambridge, MA, 2007.

[119] Ericsson, 10 hot consumer trends 2030: The Internet of senses, Ericsson ConsumerLab, Dec. 2019, https://www.ericsson.com/4ac661/assets/local/reports-papers/consumerlab/reports/2019/10hctreport2030.pdf. (Accessed 1 March 2023).

[120] K.B. Evans, P.P. Tanner, M. Wein, Tablet based valuators that provide one, two, or three degrees of freedom, Computer Graphics 15 (3) (1981) 91–97, https://doi.org/10.1145/965161.806794.

[121] S. Fallah, I.S. MacKenzie, H4VR: One-handed gesture-based text entry in virtual reality using a four-key keyboard, in: Extended Abstracts of the ACM SIGCHI Conference on Human Factors in Computing Systems - CHI '23, ACM, New York, 2023, pp. 151.1–151.7, https://doi.org/10.1145/3544549.3585876.

[122] D. Fallman, Design-oriented human-computer interaction, in: Proceedings of the ACM SIGCHI Conference on Human Factors in Computing Systems - CHI '03, ACM, New York, 2003, pp. 225–232, https://doi.org/10.1145/642611.642652.

[123] R. Fang, J.Y. Chai, F. Ferreira, Between linguistic attention and gaze fixations in multimodal conversational interfaces, in: Proceedings of the '09 International Conference on Multimodal Interfaces - ICMI '09, ACM, New York, 2009, pp. 143–150, https://doi.org/10.1145/1647314.1647339.

[124] D. Fitton, I.S. MacKenzie, J.C. Read, M. Horton, Exploring tilt-based text input for mobile devices with teenagers, in: Proceedings of the 27th International British Computer Society Human-Computer Interaction Conference – HCI '13, British Computer Society, London, 2013, pp. 1–6, https://doi.org/10.14236/ewic/HCI2013.34.

[125] P.M. Fitts, The information capacity of the human motor system in controlling the amplitude of movement, Journal of Experimental Psychology 47 (6) (1954) 381–391, https://doi.org/10.1037/h0055392.

[126] P.M. Fitts, J.R. Peterson, Information capacity of discrete motor responses, Journal of Experimental Psychology 67 (2) (1964) 103–112, https://doi.org/10.1037/h0045689.

[127] P.M. Fitts, M.I. Posner, Human Performance, Brooks/Cole Publishing Company, Belmont, CA, 1968.

[128] G.W. Fitzmaurice, Situated information spaces and spatially aware palmtop computers, Communications of the ACM 36 (7) (1993) 39–49, https://doi.org/10.1145/159544.159566.

[129] G.W. Fitzmaurice, H. Ishii, W.A.S. Buxton, Bricks: Laying the foundation for graspable user interfaces, in: Proceedings of the ACM SIGCHI Conference on Human Factors in Computing Systems - CHI '95, ACM, New York, 1995, pp. 442–449, https://doi.org/10.1145/223904.223964.

[130] C. Flathmann, B. Schelble, B. Tubre, N. McNeese, P. Rodeghero, Invoking principles of groupware to develop and evaluate present and future human-agent teams, in: Proceedings of the 8th International Conference on Human-Agent Interaction - HAI '20, ACM, New York, 2020, pp. 15–24, https://doi.org/10.1145/3406499.3415072.

[131] J.D. Foley, A. van Dam, S.K. Feiner, J.F. Hughes, Computer Graphics: Principles and Practice, 2nd ed., Addison-Wesley, Reading, MA, 1987.

[132] M.J. Foley, Q. Roy, D.-Y. Huang, W. Li, D. Vogel, Switching between standard pointing methods with current and emerging computer form factors, in: Proceedings of the ACM

SIGCHI Conference on Human Factors in Computing Systems - CHI '22, ACM, New York, 2022, pp. 212.1–212.14, https://doi.org/10.1145/3491102.3517433.

[133] C. Forlines, R. Balakrishnan, Evaluating tactile feedback and direct vs. indirect stylus input in pointing and crossing selection tasks, in: Proceedings of the ACM SIGCHI Conference on Human Factors in Computing Systems - CHI '08, ACM, New York, 2008, pp. 1563–1572, https://doi.org/10.1145/1357054.1357299.

[134] C. Foucoult, M. Micaux, D. Bonnet, M. Beaudouin-Lafon, SPad: A bimanual interaction technique for productivity applications on multi-touch tablets, in: Extended Abstracts of the ACM SIGCHI Conference on Human Factors in Computing Systems - CHI '14, ACM, New York, 2014, pp. 1879–1884, https://doi.org/10.1145/2559206.2581277.

[135] M. Freeman, A. Norris, P. Hyland, Usability of online grocery systems: A focus on errors, in: Proceedings of OzCHI '06, ACM, New York, 2006, pp. 269–275, https://doi.org/10.1145/1228175.1228222.

[136] A. Fuentes-Luque, An approach to analysing the quality of menu translations in southern Spain restaurants, Journal of Multilingual and Multicultural Development 38 (2) (2017) 177–188, https://doi.org/10.1080/01434632.2016.1187154.

[137] Z. Gao, H. Wang, A. Ge, H. Lv, G. Feng, Effects of clutching mechanism on remote object manipulation tasks, in: Proceedings of the IEEE Conference on Virtual Reality and 3D User Interfaces Abstracts and Workshops – VRW '22, IEEE, New York, 2022, pp. 538–539, https://doi.org/10.1145/1357054.1357250.

[138] M. Garau, M. Slater, V. Vinayagamoorthy, A. Brogni, A. Steed, M.A. Sasse, The impact of avatar realism and eye gaze control on perceived quality of communication in a shared immersive virtual environment, in: Proceedings of the ACM SIGCHI Conference on Human Factors in Computing Systems - CHI '03, ACM, New York, 2003, pp. 529–536, https://doi.org/10.1145/642611.642703.

[139] H.L. Garcia, R.M. Gonzalez, M.V. Martin, J.M. Arteaga, F.J.A. Rodriguez, L.C.R. Martinez, A classification of design patterns to support mobile groupware systems, in: Proceedings of the 5th Mexican Conference on Human-Computer Interaction - MexIHC '14, ACM, New York, 2014, pp. 46–52, https://doi.org/10.1145/2676690.2676691.

[140] S. Garg, I.S. MacKenzie, Fingerprint Scroll: A comparison of touchless and touch-based scroll navigation techniques, in: Proceedings of the 18th IFIP TC 13 International Conference on Human-Computer Interaction - INTERACT '21 (LNCS 12932), Springer, Berlin, 2021, pp. 139–150, https://doi.org/10.1007/978-3-030-85613-7_10.

[141] A. Geven, R. Sefelin, M. Tschelig, Depth and breadth away from the desktop: The optimal information hierarchy for mobile use, in: Proceedings of MobileHCI '06, ACM, New York, 2006, pp. 157–164, https://doi.org/10.1145/1152215.1152248.

[142] C.B. Gibbs, Controller design: Interactions of controlling limbs, time-lags and gains in positional and velocity systems, Ergonomics 5 (2) (1962) 383–402, https://doi.org/10.1080/00140136208930602.

[143] J.J. Gibson, The Ecological Approach to Visual Perception, Erlbaum, Hillsdale, NJ, 1979, https://doi.org/10.4324/9781315740218.

[144] W.G. Gillick, C.C. Lam, Roller mouse for implementing scrolling in windows applications (U. S. Patent 5,530,455), 1994.

[145] M. Gladwell, Outliers: The Story of Success, Little Brown, New York, 2008.

[146] G.V. Glass, K.D. Hopkins, Statistical Methods in Education and Psychology, 2nd ed., Prentice Hall, Englewood Cliffs, NJ, 1984.

[147] G.V. Glass, P.D. Peckham, J.R. Sanders, Consequences of failure to meet assumptions underlying the fixed effects analyses of variance and covariance, Review of Educational Research 42 (3) (1972) 237–288, https://doi.org/10.3102/00346543042003237.

[148] D. Goldberg, C. Richardson, Touch-typing with a stylus, in: Proceedings of the INTER-ACT '93 and CHI '93 Conference on Human Factors in Computing Systems - INTER-CHI '93, ACM, New York, 1993, pp. 80–87, https://doi.org/10.1145/169059.169093.

[149] J.H. Goldberg, J.I. Helfman, Visual scanpath representation, in: Proceedings of the 2010 Symposium on Eye Tracking Research & Applications - ETRA '10, ACM, New York, 2010, pp. 203–210, https://doi.org/10.1145/1743666.1743717.

[150] E.B. Goldstein, J.R. Brockmole, Sensation and Perception, 10th ed., Cengage Learning, Boston, 2017.

[151] M. Goldstein, D. Chincholle, M. Backström, Assessing two new wearable input paradigms: The finger-joint-gesture palm-keypad glove and the invisible phone clock, Personal and Ubiquitous Computing 4 (2000) 123–133, https://doi.org/10.1007/BF01324119.

[152] J. Gong, P. Tarasewich, Alphabetically constrained keypad designs for text entry on mobile phones, in: Proceedings of the ACM SIGCHI Conference on Human Factors in Computing Systems - CHI '05, ACM, New York, 2005, pp. 211–220, https://doi.org/10.1145/1054972.1055002.

[153] J. Gong, P. Tarasewich, I.S. MacKenzie, Improved word list ordering for text entry on ambiguous keyboards, in: Proceedings of the Fifth Nordic Conference on Human-Computer Interaction - NordiCHI '08, ACM, New York, 2008, pp. 152–161, https://doi.org/10.1145/1463160.1463177.

[154] J. Gray, The role of menu title as a navigational aid in hierarchical menus, SIGCHI Bulletin 17 (3) (Jan. 1986) 33–40, https://doi.org/10.1145/15671.15674.

[155] W.D. Gray, D.A. Boehm-Davis, Milliseconds matter: An introduction to microstrategies and to their use in describing and predicting interactive behaviour, Journal of Experimental Psychology: Applied 6 (4) (2000) 322–335, https://doi.org/10.1037/1076-898X.6.4.322.

[156] W.D. Gray, B.E. John, M.E. Atwood, Project Ernestine: Validating a GOMS analysis for predicting and explaining real-world task performance, Human-Computer Interaction 8 (3) (1993) 237–309, https://doi.org/10.1207/s15327051hci0803_3.

[157] J. Greene, J. Haidt, How (and where) does moral judgment work? Trends in Cognitive Sciences 6 (1) (2002) 517–523, https://doi.org/10.1016/S1364-6613(02)02011-9.

[158] A. Greif, Devon Allen's storybook ending wiped out in 0.001 of a second at world championships, Los Angeles Times, 2022, https://www.latimes.com/sports/olympics/story/2022-07-17/devon-allen-disqualified-110-hurd%20les-%20false-start?_amp=true (visited on 09/22/2022).

[159] D. Griffiths, S. Cunningham, J. Weinel, A discussion of musical features for automatic music playlist generation using affective technologies, in: Proceedings of the 8th Audio Mostly Conference - AM '14, ACM, New York, 2013, pp. 13.1–13.4, https://doi.org/10.1145/2544114.2544128.

[160] D. Griffiths, S. Cunningham, J. Weinel, R. Picking, A multi-genre model for music emotion recognition using linear regressors, Journal of New Music Research 50 (4) (2021) 355–372, https://doi.org/10.1080/09298215.2021.1977336.

[161] R. Grinter, M. Eldridge, Wan2tlk? Everyday text messaging, in: Proceedings of the ACM SIGCHI Conference on Human Factors in Computing Systems - CHI '03, ACM, New York, 2003, pp. 441–448, https://doi.org/10.1145/642611.642688.

[162] T. Grossman, R. Balakrishnan, The Bubble Cursor: Enhancing target acquisition by dynamic resizing of the cursor's activation area, in: Proceedings of the ACM SIGCHI Conference on Human Factors in Computing Systems - CHI '05, ACM, New York, 2005, pp. 281–290, https://doi.org/10.1145/1054972.1055012.

[163] J. Grudin, A moving target: The evolution of human-computer interaction, in: J.A. Jacko (Ed.), The Human-Computer Interaction Handbook: Fundamentals, Evolving Technologies, and Emerging Applications, 3rd ed., CRC Press, Boca Raton, FL, 2012, pp. xxvii–lxi.

[164] J. Grudin, From Tool to Partner: The Evolution of Human-Computer Interaction, Springer, Berlin, 2017, https://doi.org/10.1007/978-3-031-02218-0.

[165] F. Grzeskowiak, M. Babel, J. Bruneau, J. Pettre, Toward virtual reality-based evaluation of robot navigation among people, in: 2020 IEEE Conference on Virtual Reality and 3D User Interfaces, IEEE, New York, 2020, pp. 766–774, https://doi.org/10.1109/VR46266.2020.00100.

[166] Y. Guiard, Asymmetric division of labor in human skilled bimanual action: The kinematic chain as a model, Journal of Motor Behavior 19 (4) (1987) 486–517, https://doi.org/10.1080/00222895.1987.10735426.

[167] Y. Guiard, H.B. Olafsdottir, S.T. Perrault, Fitt's law as an explicit time/error trade-off, in: Proceedings of the ACM SIGCHI Conference on Human Factors in Computing Systems - CHI '11, ACM, New York, 2011, pp. 1619–1628, https://doi.org/10.1145/1978942.1979179.

[168] D. Guiness, A. Jude, G.M. Poor, A. Dover, Models for rested touchless gestural interaction, in: Proceedings of the 3rd ACM Symposium on Spatial User Interfaces - SUI '15, ACM, New York, 2015, pp. 34–43, https://doi.org/10.1145/2788940.2788948.

[169] A. Hafizi, J. Henderson, A. Neshati, W. Zhou, E. Lank, D. Vogel, In-vehicle performance and distraction for midair and touch directional gestures, in: Proceedings of the ACM SIGCHI Conference on Human Factors in Computing Systems - CHI '23, ACM, New York, 2023, pp. 316.1–316.12, https://doi.org/10.1145/3544548.3581335.

[170] A.A. Hajri, S. Fels, G. Miller, M. Ilich, Moving target selection in 2D graphical user interfaces, in: Proceedings of the IFIP Conference on Human-Computer Interaction – INTERACT '11, Springer, Berlin, 2011, pp. 141–161, https://doi.org/10.1007/978-3-642-23771-3_12.

[171] D. Halbhuber, N. Henze, V. Schwind, Increasing player performance and game experience in high latency systems, Proceedings of the ACM on Human–Computer Interaction 5 (CHI PLAY) (Oct. 2021) 283.1–283.20, https://doi.org/10.1145/3474710.

[172] P.W. Halligan, A. Zemen, A. Berger, Phantoms in the brain: Question the assumption that the adult brain is 'hard wired', British Medical Journal 319 (1999) 587–588, https://doi.org/10.1136/bmj.319.7210.587.

[173] M.S. Hancock, K.S. Booth, Improving menu placement strategies for pen input, in: Proceedings of Graphics Interface - GI '04, Canadian Information Processing Society, Toronto, 2004, pp. 221–230, https://doi.org/10.14288/1.0051221.

[174] J. Hannagan, TwistMouse for simultaneous translation and rotation, B. Comm. Dissertation, University of Otego, Dunedin, New Zealand, 2007.

[175] J.P. Hansen, V. Rajanna, I.S. MacKenzie, P. Bækgaard, A Fitts' law study of click and dwell interaction by gaze, head and mouse with a head-mounted display, in: Proceedings of the Workshop on Communication by Gaze Interaction - COGAIN '18, ACM, New York, 2018, pp. 7.1–7.5, https://doi.org/10.1145/3206343.3206344.

[176] S. Harada, J.A. Landay, J. Malkin, X. Li, J.A. Bilmes, The vocal joystick: Evaluation of voice-based cursor control techniques, in: Proceedings of the ACM Conference on Computers and Accessibility - ACCESS '06, ACM, New York, 2006, pp. 187–204, https://doi.org/10.1145/1168987.1169021.

[177] B. Harrison, K.P. Fishkin, A. Gujar, C. Mochon, R. Want, Squeeze me, hold me, tilt me! An exploration of manipulative user interfaces, in: Proceedings of the ACM SIGCHI

Conference on Human Factors in Computing Systems - CHI '98, ACM, New York, 1998, pp. 17–24, https://doi.org/10.1145/274644.274647.

[178] C. Harrison, S.E. Hudson, Providing dynamically changeable physical buttons on a visual display, in: Proceedings of the ACM SIGCHI Conference on Human Factors in Computing Systems - CHI '09, ACM, New York, 2009, pp. 299–308, https://doi.org/10.1145/1518701.1518749.

[179] S.G. Hart, L.E. Staveland, Development of NASA-TLX (Task Load Index): Results of empirical and theoretical research, in: P.A. Hancock, N. Meshkati (Eds.), Human Mental Workload, in: Advances in Psychology, vol. 52, Elsevier, Amsterdam, 1988, pp. 139–183, https://doi.org/10.1016/S0166-4115(08)62386-9.

[180] A. Hashizume, M. Kurosu, T. Kaneko, Multi-window system and the working memory, in: Proceedings of International Conference on Engineering Psychology and Cognitive Ergonomics - EPCE '07 (LNAI 4562), Springer, Berlin, 2007, pp. 297–305.

[181] A. Hassan, G. Sohn, I.S. MacKenzie, Comparison of one-handed and two-handed text entry in virtual reality using handheld controllers, in: Proceedings of the 14th International Conference on Applied Human Factors and Ergonomics - AHFE '23, AHFE International, New York, 2023, pp. 101–111, https://doi.org/10.54941/ahfe1003872.

[182] M. Hassan, J. Magee, I.S. MacKenzie, A Fitts' law evaluation of hands-free and hands-on input on a laptop computer, in: Proceedings of the 21st International Conference on Human-Computer Interaction – HCII '19 (LNCS 11572), Springer, Berlin, 2019, pp. 234–249, https://doi.org/10.1007/978-3-030-23563-5_20.

[183] A.G. Hauptmann, Speech and gestures for graphic image manipulation, in: Proceedings of the ACM SIGCHI Conference on Human Factors in Computing Systems - CHI '89, ACM, New York, 1989, pp. 241–246, https://doi.org/10.1145/67449.67496.

[184] Z. He, C. Lutteroth, K. Perlin, TapGazer: Text entry with finger tapping and gaze-directed word selection, in: Proceedings of the ACM SIGCHI Conference on Human Factors in Computing Systems - CHI '22, ACM, New York, 2022, pp. 337.1–337.16, https://doi.org/10.1145/3491102.3501838.

[185] R. Hedeshy, C. Kumar, R. Menges, S. Staab, Hummer: Text entry by gaze and hum, in: Proceedings of the ACM SIGCHI Conference on Human Factors in Computing Systems - CHI '21, ACM, New York, 2021, pp. 741.1–741.11, https://doi.org/10.1145/3411764.3445501.

[186] K. Hemenway, Psychological issues in the use of icons in command menus, in: Proceedings of the Conference on Human Factors in Computing Systems, ACM, New York, 1982, pp. 20–23, https://doi.org/10.1145/800049.801748.

[187] C.F. Herot, G. Weinzapfel, One-point touch input of vector information for computer displays, in: Proceedings of SIGGRAPH '78, ACM, New York, 1978, pp. 210–216, https://doi.org/10.1145/800248.807392.

[188] S.R. Herring, A.E. Trejo, M.S. Hallbeck, Evaluation of four cursor control devices during a target acquisition task for laparoscopic tool control, Applied Ergonomics 41 (1) (2010) 47–57.

[189] W.E. Hick, On the rate of gain of information, Quarterly Journal of Experimental Psychology 4 (1) (1952) 11–36, https://doi.org/10.1080/17470215208416600.

[190] K. Hinckley, F. Guimbretière, P. Baudisch, R. Sarin, M. Agrawala, E. Cutrell, The springboard: Multiple modes in one spring-loaded control, in: Proceedings of the ACM SIGCHI Conference on Human Factors in Computing Systems - CHI '06, ACM, New York, 2006, pp. 181–190, https://doi.org/10.1145/1124772.1124801.

[191] K. Hinckley, R. Pausch, D. Proffitt, J. Patten, N. Kassell, Cooperative bimanual action, in: Proceedings of the ACM SIGCHI Conference on Human Factors in Computing Systems - CHI '97, ACM, New York, 1997, pp. 27–34, https://doi.org/10.1145/258549. 258571.

[192] K. Hinckley, J. Pierce, M. Sinclair, E. Horvitz, Sensing techniques for mobile interaction, in: Proceedings of the ACM Symposium on User Interface Software and Technology - UIST '00, ACM, New York, 2000, pp. 91–100, https://doi.org/10.1145/354401. 354417.

[193] K. Hinckley, M. Sinclair, E. Hanson, R. Szeliski, M. Conway, The VideoMouse: A camera-based multi-degree-of-freedom input device, in: Proceedings of the ACM Symposium on User Interface Software and Technology - UIST '99, ACM, New York, 1999, pp. 103–112, https://doi.org/10.1145/320719.322591.

[194] K. Hinckley, J. Tullio, R. Pausch, D. Proffitt, N. Kassell, Usability analysis of 3D rotation techniques, in: Proceedings of the ACM Symposium on User Interface Software and Technology - UIST '97, ACM, New York, 1997, pp. 1–10, https://doi.org/10.1145/ 263407.263408.

[195] J.E. Hirsch, An index to quantify an individual's scientific research output, Proceedings of the National Academy of Sciences 102 (46) (2005) 16568–16572.

[196] G.M. Hodgson, S.R. Ruth, The use of menus in the design of on-line systems: A retrospective view, SIGCHI Bulletin 17 (1) (July 1985) 16–22, https://doi.org/10.1145/ 378965.378969.

[197] P. Holleis, F. Otto, H. Hussmann, A. Schmidt, Keystroke-level model for advanced mobile phone interaction, in: Proceedings of the ACM SIGCHI Conference on Human Factors in Computing Systems - CHI '07, ACM, New York, 2007, pp. 1505–1514, https://doi.org/10.1145/1240624.1240851.

[198] A.J. Hornof, D.E. Kieras, Cognitive modeling reveals menu search is both random and systematic, in: Proceedings of the ACM SIGCHI Conference on Human Factors in Computing Systems - CHI '97, ACM, New York, 1997, pp. 107–114, https:// doi.org/10.1145/258549.258621.

[199] B.J. Hou, P. Bækgaard, I.S. MacKenzie, J.P. Hansen, S. Puthusserypady, GIMIS: Gaze input with motor imagery selection, in: Proceedings of the 2020 Symposium on Eye Tracking Research & Applications – ETRA '20 Adjunct, ACM, New York, 2020, pp. 18:1–18:10, https://doi.org/10.1145/3379157.3388932.

[200] B.J. Hou, J.P. Hansen, C. Uyanik, P. Bækgaard, S. Puthusserypady, J.M. Araujo, I.S. MacKenzie, Feasibility of a device for gaze interaction by visually-evoked brain signals, in: Proceedings of the 2022 Symposium on Eye Tracking Research & Applications - ETRA '22, ACM, New York, 2022, pp. 62.1–62.7, https://doi.org/10.1145/3517031. 3529232.

[201] A. Howes, S.J. Payne, Display-based competence: Towards user models for menudriven interfaces, International Journal of Man-Machine Studies 33 (6) (1990) 637–655, https://doi.org/10.1016/S0020-7373(05)80067-7.

[202] Y. Hu, G. Hoffman, Using skin texture change to design emotion expression in social robots, in: Proceedings of the 14th ACM/IEEE International Conference on Human-Robot Interaction - HRI '20, IEEE, New York, 2020, pp. 2–10.

[203] D.A. Huffman, A method for the construction of minimum redundancy codes, Proceedings of the IRE 40 (9) (1952) 1098–1101, https://doi.org/10.1109/JRPROC.1952. 273898.

[204] M. Hunter, S. Zhai, B.A. Smith, Physics-based graphical keyboard design, in: Extended Abstracts of the ACM SIGCHI Conference on Human Factors in Computing Systems - CHI '00, ACM, New York, 2000, pp. 157–158, https://doi.org/10.1145/633292.633380.

[205] R. Hyman, Stimulus information as a determinant of reaction time, Journal of Experimental Psychology 45 (3) (1953) 188–196, https://doi.org/10.1037/h0056940.

[206] IAAF, Competition rules 2018-2019, Monaco, 2017, https://www.worldathletics.org/. (Accessed 10 December 2022).

[207] T. Igarashi, J.F. Hughes, Voice as sound: Using non-verbal voice input for interactive control, in: Proceedings of the ACM Symposium on User Interface Software and Technology - UIST '01, ACM, New York, 2001, pp. 155–156, https://doi.org/10.1145/502348.502372.

[208] S.T. Iqbal, B.P. Bailey, Leveraging characteristics of task structure to predict the cost of interruption, in: Proceedings of the ACM SIGCHI Conference on Human Factors in Computing Systems - CHI '06, ACM, New York, 2006, pp. 741–750, https://doi.org/10.1145/1124772.1124882.

[209] H. Ishii, B. Ullmer, Tangible bits: Towards seamless interfaces between people, bits, and atoms, in: Proceedings of the ACM SIGCHI Conference on Human Factors in Computing Systems - CHI '97, ACM, New York, 1997, pp. 234–241, https://doi.org/10.1145/258549.258715.

[210] ISO, Ergonomics of human-system interaction — Part 411: Evaluation methods for the design of physical input devices, Report Number ISO/TS 9241-411:2012, International Organisation for Standardisation, 2012.

[211] P. Isokoski, M. Käki, Comparison of two touchpad-based methods for numeric entry, in: Proceedings of the ACM SIGCHI Conference on Human Factors in Computing Systems - CHI '02, ACM, New York, 2002, pp. 25–32, https://doi.org/10.1145/503376.503382.

[212] P. Isokoski, R. Raisamo, Quikwriting as a multi-device text entry method, in: Proceedings of the Third Nordic Conference on Human-Computer Interaction - NordiCHI '04, ACM, New York, 2004, pp. 105–108, https://doi.org/10.1145/1028014.1028031.

[213] K. Itoh, H. Aoki, J.P. Hansen, A comparative usability study of two Japanese gaze typing systems, in: Proceedings of the 2006 Symposium on Eye Tracking Research & Applications - ETRA '06, ACM, New York, 2006, pp. 59–66, https://doi.org/10.1145/1117309.1117344.

[214] M.Y. Ivory, M.A. Hearst, The state of the art in automating usability evaluation of user interfaces, ACM Computing Surveys 33 (4) (2001) 470–516, https://doi.org/10.1145/503112.503114.

[215] R.J.K. Jacob, What you look at is what you get: Eye movement-based interaction techniques, in: Proceedings of the ACM SIGCHI Conference on Human Factors in Computing Systems - CHI '90, ACM, New York, 1990, pp. 11–18, https://doi.org/10.1145/97243.97246.

[216] R.J.K. Jacob, A. Girouard, L.M. Hirshfield, M.S. Horn, O. Shaer, E.T. Solovey, J. Zigelbaum, Reality-based interaction: A framework for post-WIMP interfaces, in: Proceedings of the ACM SIGCHI Conference on Human Factors in Computing - CHI '00, ACM, New York, 2008, pp. 201–210, https://doi.org/10.1145/1357054.1357089.

[217] R.J.K. Jacob, L.E. Sibert, D.C. McFarlane, M.P. Mullen Jr., Integrality and separability of input devices, ACM Transactions on Computer-Human Interaction 1 (1) (1994) 3–26, https://doi.org/10.1145/174630.174631.

[218] M. Jain, R. Balakrishnan, User learning and performance with bezel menus, in: Proceedings of the ACM SIGCHI Conference on Human Factors in Computing Systems - CHI '12, ACM, New York, 2012, pp. 2221–2230, https://doi.org/10.1145/2207676.2208376.

[219] G. Jalal, N. Maudet, W.E. Mackay, Color portraits: From color picking to interacting with color, in: Proceedings of the ACM SIGCHI Conference on Human Factors in Computing Systems - CHI '15, ACM, New York, 2015, pp. 4207–4216, https://doi.org/10.1145/2702123.2702173.

[220] I. Jamil, K. O'Hara, M. Perry, A. Karnik, S. Subramanian, The effects of interaction techniques on talk patterns in collaborative peer learning around interactive tables, in: Proceedings of the ACM SIGCHI Conference on Human Factors in Computing Systems - CHI '11, ACM, New York, 2011, pp. 3043–3052, https://doi.org/10.1145/1978942.1979393.

[221] R. Javanovic, I.S. MacKenzie, MarkerMouse: Mouse cursor control using a head-mounted marker, in: Proceedings of the 12th International Conference on Computers Helping People with Special Needs - ICCHP '10, Springer, Berlin, 2010, pp. 49–56.

[222] W. Javed, S. Ghani, N. Elmaqvist, PolyZoom: Multiscale and multifocus exploration in 2D visual spaces, in: Proceedings of the ACM SIGCHI Conference on Human Factors in Computing Systems - CHI '12, ACM, New York, 2010, pp. 287–296, https://doi.org/10.1145/2207676.2207716.

[223] H.D. Jellinek, S.K. Card, Powermice and user performance, in: Proceedings of the ACM SIGCHI Conference on Human Factors in Computing Systems - CHI '90, ACM, New York, 1990, pp. 213–220, https://doi.org/10.1145/97243.97276.

[224] W.L. Jenkins, M.B. Connor, Some design factors in making settings on a linear scale, Journal of Applied Psychology 33 (4) (1949) 395–409, https://doi.org/10.1037/h0056573.

[225] H. Jiang, D. Weng, X. Dongye, Y. Liu, PinchText: One-handed text entry technique combining pinch gestures and hand positions for head-mounted displays, International Journal of Human–Computer Interaction 0 (0) (2022) 1–17, https://doi.org/10.1080/10447318.2022.2115333 (Open Access).

[226] M.A. Jiménez-Crespo, Translation and Web Localization, Routledge, London, ISBN 978-0-203-52002-8, 2013.

[227] R. Johansen, Groupware: Future directions and wild cards, Journal of Organizational Computing and Electronic Commerce 1 (2) (1991) 219–227, https://doi.org/10.1080/10919399109540160.

[228] O.P. John, S. Srivastava, The Big Five trait taxonomy: History, measurements, and theoretical perspectives, in: L.A. Pervin, O.P. John (Eds.), Handbook of Personality, 2nd ed., Guilford Publications, New York, 1999, pp. 102–138.

[229] J. Johnson, GUI Bloopers 2.0, Morgan Kaufmann, San Francisco, 2007.

[230] J. Johnson, T.L. Roberts, W. Verplank, D.C. Smith, C. Irby, M. Beard, K. Mackey, The Xerox Star: A retrospective, IEEE Computer 22 (9) (Sept. 1989) 11–29, https://doi.org/10.1109/2.35211.

[231] L. Johnston, Politics: An Introduction to the Modern Democratic State, 3rd ed., Broadview Press, Peterborough, ON, Canada, 2007.

[232] W. Jones, P. Klasnja, A. Civan, M.L. Adcock, The personal project planner: Planning to organize personal information, in: Proceedings of the ACM SIGCHI Conference on Human Factors in Computing Systems - CHI '08, ACM, New York, 2008, pp. 681–684, https://doi.org/10.1145/1357054.1357162.

[233] A. Joshi, A. Ajikumar, K. Umaraiya, P. Chavan, Fitts' throughput and "absolute" finger precision by handedness, hand, digit and target width, in: Proceedings of the Nordic Human-Computer Interaction Conference - NordiCHI '22, ACM, New York, 2022, pp. 57.1–57.11, https://doi.org/10.1145/3546155.3546644.

[234] P. Kabbash, W. Buxton, A. Sellen, Two-handed input in a compound task, in: Proceedings of the ACM SIGCHI Conference on Human Factors in Computing Systems - CHI '94, ACM, New York, 1994, pp. 417–423, https://doi.org/10.1145/191666.191808.

[235] P. Kabbash, I.S. MacKenzie, W. Buxton, Human performance using computer input devices in the preferred and non-preferred hands, in: Proceedings of the INTERACT '93 and CHI '93 Conference on Human Factors in Computing Systems - INTERCHI '93, ACM, New York, 1993, pp. 474–481, https://doi.org/10.1145/169059.169414.

[236] S.K. Kane, J.O. Wobbrock, R.E. Ladner, Usable gestures for blind people: Understanding preference and performance, in: Proceedings of the ACM SIGCHI Conference on Human Factors in Computing Systems - CHI '11, ACM, New York, 2011, pp. 413–422, https://doi.org/10.1145/1978942.1979001.

[237] B.H. Kantowitz, G.C. Elvers, Fitts' law with an isometric controller: Effects of order of control and control-display gain, Journal of Motor Behavior 20 (1) (1988) 53–66, https://doi.org/10.1080/00222895.1988.10735432.

[238] B.H. Kantowitz, R.D. Sorkin, Human Factors: Understanding People-System Relationships, Wiley, New York, 1983.

[239] S. Kaplan, The CSCW column: The quadrant model of GroupWare, SIGGROUP Bulletin 18 (2) (Aug. 1997) 11–14, https://doi.org/10.1145/265665.265669.

[240] M. Kaptein, C. Nass, M. Markopoulos, Powerful and consistent analysis of likert-type rating scales, in: Proceedings of the ACM SIGCHI Conference on Human Factors in Computing Systems - CHI '10, ACM, New York, 2010, pp. 466–472, https://doi.org/10.1145/1753326.1753686.

[241] A. Kay, A. Goldberg, Personal dynamic media, IEEE Computer 10 (3) (Mar. 1977) 31–41, https://doi.org/10.1109/C-M.1977.217672.

[242] S. Keates, S. Trewin, Effect of age and Parkinson's disease on cursor positioning using a mouse, in: Proceedings of the 7th International ACM SIGACCESS Conference on Computers and Accessibility - ASSETS '05, ACM, New York, 2005, pp. 68–75, https://doi.org/10.1145/1090785.1090800.

[243] S.W. Keele, Attention and Human Performance, Goodyear Publishing Company, Inc., Pacific Palisades, CA, 1973, p. 184.

[244] J.A.S. Kelso, D.L. Southard, D. Goodman, On the coordination of two-handed movements, Journal of Experimental Psychology: Human Perception and Performance 5 (2) (1979) 229–238, https://doi.org/10.1037/0096-1523.5.2.229.

[245] J.I. Kiger, The depth/breadth trade-off in the design of menu-driven user interfaces, International Journal of Human-Computer Studies 20 (2) (1984) 201–213, https://doi.org/10.1016/S0020-7373(84)80018-8.

[246] D. Kim, K. Park, G. Lee, OddEyeCam: A sensing technique for body-centric peephole interaction using WFoV RGB and NFoV depth cameras, in: Proceedings of the ACM Symposium on User Interface Software and Technology - UIST '20, ACM, New York, 2020, pp. 85–97, https://doi.org/10.1145/3379337.3415889.

[247] T. Kindberg, E. O'Neill, C. Beven, V. Kostakos, D.S. Fraser, T. Jay, Measuring trust in Wi-Fi hotspots, in: Proceedings of the ACM SIGCHI Conference on Human Factors in Computing Systems - CHI '08, ACM, New York, 2008, pp. 173–182, https://doi.org/10.1007/978-3-030-64357-7_6.

[248] A. Kitaoka, A brief classification of colour illusions, Color: Design and Creativity 5 (3) (2010) 1–9.

[249] C. Klochek, I.S. MacKenzie, Performance measures of game controllers in a three-dimensional environment, in: Proceedings of Graphics Interface - GI '12, Canadian Information Processing Society, Toronto, 2006, pp. 73–79.

[250] U. Knief, W. Forstmeier, Violating the normality assumption may be the lesser of two evils, Behavior Research Methods 53 (6) (2021) 2576–2590, https://doi.org/10.3758/s13428-021-01587-5.

[251] M. Kobayashi, T. Igarashi, Ninja cursors: Using multiple cursors to assist target acquisition on large screens, in: Proceedings of the ACM SIGCHI Conference on Human Factors in Computing Systems - CHI '08, ACM, New York, 2008, pp. 949–958, https://doi.org/10.1145/1357054.1357201.

[252] H.H. Koester, S.P. Levine, Modeling the speed of text entry with a word prediction interface, IEEE Transactions on Rehabilitation Engineering 2 (3) (1994) 177–187, https://doi.org/10.1109/86.331567.

[253] H.H. Koester, S.P. Levine, Validation of a keystroke-level model for a text entry system used by people with disabilities, in: Proceedings of the First ACM Conference on Assistive Technologies, ACM, New York, 1994, pp. 115–122, https://doi.org/10.1145/191028.191061.

[254] T. Költringer, T. Grechenig, Comparing the immediate usability of Graffiti 2 and virtual keyboard, in: Extended Abstracts of the ACM SIGCHI Conference on Human-Factors in Computing Systems - CHI '04, ACM, New York, 2004, pp. 1175–1178, https://doi.org/10.1145/985921.986017.

[255] W.A. Konig, J. Gerken, S. Dierdorf, H. Reiterer, Adaptive pointing: Design and evaluation of a precision enhancing technique for absolute pointing devices, in: Proceedings of INTERACT '09, Springer, Berlin, 2009, pp. 659–671, https://doi.org/10.1007/978-3-642-03655-2_73.

[256] P.-O. Kristensson, S. Zhai, SHARK^2: A large vocabulary shorthand writing system for pen-based computers, in: Proceedings of the ACM Symposium on User Interface Software and Technology - UIST '04, ACM, New York, 2004, pp. 43–52, https://doi.org/10.1145/1029632.1029640.

[257] A. Królak, P. Strumiłło, Eye-blink controlled human-computer interface for the disabled, in: Z.S. Hippe, J.L. Kulikowski (Eds.), Human-Computer Systems Interaction: Advances in Intelligent and Soft Computing, vol. 60, Springer, Berlin, 2009, pp. 123–133, https://doi.org/10.1007/978-3-642-03202-8_10.

[258] E. Kuang, R. Chen, M. Fan, Enhancing older adults' gesture typing experience using the T9 keyboardon small touchscreen devices, in: Proceedings of the ACM SIGCHI Conference on Human Factors in Computing Systems - CHI '23, ACM, New York, 2023, pp. 1–14, https://doi.org/10.1145/3544548.3581105.

[259] C. Kumar, R. Hedeshy, I.S. MacKenzie, S. Staab, TAGSwipe: Touch assisted gaze swipe for text entry, in: Proceedings of the ACM SIGCHI Conference on Human Factors in Computing Systems - CHI '20, ACM, New York, 2020, pp. 1–12, https://doi.org/10.1145/3313831.3376317.

[260] N. Kumar, J.A. Adams, B. Buxton, L. Candy, P. Cesar, L. Clark, B.R. Cowan, A. Dey, P.O.T. Dugas, E. Edmonds, M.A. Goodrich, M. Green, J. Grudin, Y. Kitamura, J. Konstan, C. Latulipe, M. Lee, T. Malone, R. Mandryk, P. Markopoulos, M. Muller, L. Nacke, Y. Nakano, M. Obrist, M. Porcheron, A. Sarcevic, J. Schöning, S. Scott, B. Sharif, F. Steinicke, S. Stumpf, E. Tse, V. Vinayagamoorthy, A chronology of SIGCHI conferences: 1983 to 2022, Interactions 29 (6) (Nov. 2022) 34–41, https://doi.org/10.1145/3568732.

[261] K. Kurihara, D. Vronay, T. Igarashi, Flexible timeline user interface using constraints, in: Extended Abstracts of the ACM SIGCHI Conference on Human Factors in Computing Systems - CHI '05, ACM, New York, 2005, pp. 1581–1584, https://doi.org/10.1145/1056808.1056971.

[262] G.P. Kurtenbach, The design and evaluation of marking menus, Doctoral Dissertation, University of Toronto, 1993.

[263] G.P. Kurtenbach, A.J. Sellen, W.A.S. Buxton, An empirical evaluation of some articulatory and cognitive aspects of marking menus, Human-Computer Interaction 8 (1) (1993) 1–23, https://doi.org/10.1207/s15327051hci0801_1.

[264] G. Kurtenbach, B. Buxton, GEdit: A test bed for editing by contiguous gestures, SIGCHI Bulletin 23 (2) (Mar. 1991) 22–26, https://doi.org/10.1145/122488.122490.

[265] G. Kurtenbach, G. Fitzmaurice, T. Baudel, B. Buxton, The design of a GUI paradigm based on tablets, two-hands, and transparency, in: Proceedings of the ACM SIGCHI Conference on Human Factors in Computing Systems - CHI '97, ACM, New York, 1997, pp. 35–42, https://doi.org/10.1145/258549.258574.

[266] H. Kuzuoka, J. Kosaka, K. Yamazaki, Y. Suga, A. Yamazaki, P. Luff, C. Heath, Mediating dual ecologies, in: Proceedings of the ACM Conference on Computer Supported Cooperative Work - CSCW '04, ACM, New York, 2004, pp. 478–486, https://doi.org/10.1145/1031607.1031686.

[267] S. Kyian, R. Teather, Selection performance using a smartphone in VR with redirected input, in: Proceedings of the ACM Symposium on Spatial User Interaction - SUI '21, ACM, New York, 2021, pp. 6.1–6.12, https://doi.org/10.1145/3485279.3485292.

[268] J. Lai, D. Zhang, ExtendedThumb: A target acquisition approach for one-handed interaction with touch-screen mobile phones, IEEE Transactions on Human-Machine Systems 45 (3) (2015) 362–370, https://doi.org/10.1109/THMS.2014.2377205.

[269] D.R. Lamichhane, J.R. Read, I.S. MacKenzie, When children chat with machine translated text: Problems, possibilities, potential, in: Proceedings of the 22nd Annual ACM Interaction Design and Children Conference - IDC '23, ACM, New York, 2023, pp. 198–209, https://doi.org/10.1145/3585088.3589369.

[270] C.A.C. Lampe, N. Ellison, C. Steinfield, A familiar face(book): Profile elements as signals in an online social network, in: Proceedings of the ACM SIGCHI Conference on Human Factors in Computing Systems - CHI '07, ACM, New York, 2007, pp. 435–444, https://doi.org/10.1145/1240624.1240695.

[271] T.K. Landauer, D.W. Nachbar, Selection from alphabetic and numeric menu trees using a touch screen: Breadth, depth, and width, in: Proceedings of the ACM SIGCHI Conference on Human Factors in Computing Systems - CHI '85, ACM, New York, 1985, pp. 73–77, https://doi.org/10.1145/1165385.317470.

[272] M. Langner, N. Aßfalg, P. Toreini, A. Maedche, EyeLikert: Eye-based interactions for answering surveys, in: Proceedings of the 2022 Symposium on Eye Tracking Research & Applications - ETRA '22, ACM, New York, 2022, pp. 16.1–16.3, https://doi.org/10.1145/3517031.3529776.

[273] B. Laurel, Computers as Theatre, Addison-Wesley, Reading, MA, 1991.

[274] B. Lee, M. Nancel, S. Kim, A. Oulasvirta, AutoGain: Gain function adaptation with submovement efficiency optimization, in: Proceedings of the ACM SIGCHI Conference on Human Factors in Computing Systems - CHI '20, ACM, New York, 2020, pp. 1–12, https://doi.org/10.1145/3313831.3376244.

[275] S.K. Lee, W. Buxton, K.C. Smith, A multi-touch three dimensional touch-sensitive tablet, in: Proceedings of the ACM SIGCHI Conference on Human Factors in Computing Systems - CHI '85, ACM, New York, 1985, pp. 21–25, https://doi.org/10.1145/1165385.317461.

[276] S. Lee, J. Lee, G. Lee, Diagnosing and coping with mode errors in Korean-English dual-language keyboard, in: Proceedings of the ACM SIGCHI Conference on Human

Factors in Computing Systems - CHI '19, ACM, New York, 2019, pp. 1–12, https://doi.org/10.1145/3290605.3300255.

[277] I. Leftheriotis, K. Chorianopoulos, User experience quality in multi-touch tasks, in: Proceedings of the ACM Conference in Engineering Interactive Computing Systems - EICS '11, ACM, New York, 2011, pp. 161–164, https://doi.org/10.1145/1996461.1996536.

[278] K. Leino, A. Oulasvirta, M. Kurimo, RL-KLM: Automating keystroke-level modeling with reinforcement learning, in: Proceedings of the 24th International Conference on Intelligent User Interfaces - IUI '19, ACM, New York, 2019, pp. 476–480, https://doi.org/10.1145/3301275.3302285.

[279] G. Lesher, B. Moulton, D.J. Higginbotham, Techniques for augmenting scanning communication, Augmentative and Alternative Communication 14 (2) (1998) 81–101, https://doi.org/10.1080/07434619812331278236.

[280] S. Levy, Insanely Great: The Life and Times of Macintosh, the Computer That Changed Everything, Penguin, New York, 1995.

[281] J.R. Lewis, Sample sizes for usability studies: Additional considerations, Human Factors 36 (2) (1994) 366–378, https://doi.org/10.1177/001872089403600215.

[282] J.R. Lewis, J. Sauro, Item benchmarks for the system usability scale, Journal of Usability Studies 13 (3) (May 2018) 158–167.

[283] J.R. Lewis, J. Sauro, The factor structure of the system usability scale, in: International Conference on Human-Centered Design - HCD '09 (LNISA 5619), Springer, Berlin, 2009, pp. 94–103.

[284] J. Liang, C. Shaw, M. Green, On temporal-spatial realism in the virtual reality environment, in: Proceedings of the ACM Symposium on User Interface Software and Technology - UIST '91, ACM, New York, 1991, pp. 19–25, https://doi.org/10.1145/120782.120784.

[285] C.J. Lin, S.-H. Ho, Prediction of the use of mobile device interfaces in the progressive aging process with the model of Fitts' law, Journal of Biomedical Informatics 107 (2020) 1–18, https://doi.org/10.1016/j.jbi.2020.103457.

[286] C. Lindholm, T. Keinonen, H. Kiljander, Mobile Usability: How Nokia Changed the Face of the Mobile Phone, McGraw Hill, New York, 2003.

[287] O.W. Linzmayer, Apple Confidential 2.0: The Definitive History of the World's Most Colorful Company, No Starch Press, San Francisco, 2004.

[288] W. Liu, J. Gori, O. Rioul, M. Beaudouin-Lafon, Y. Guiard, How relevant is Hick's Law for HCI? in: Proceedings of the ACM SIGCHI Conference on Human Factors in Computing Systems - CHI '20, ACM, New York, 2020, pp. 1–11, https://doi.org/10.1145/3313831.3376878.

[289] Y. Liu, K.-J. Räihä, Predicting Chinese text entry speeds on mobile phones, in: Proceedings of the ACM SIGCHI Conference on Human Factors in Computing Systems - CHI '10, ACM, New York, 2010, pp. 2183–2192, https://doi.org/10.1145/1753326.1753657.

[290] M. Long, C. Gutwin, Effects of local latency on game pointing devices and game pointing tasks, in: Proceedings of the ACM SIGCHI Conference on Human Factors in Computing Systems - CHI '19, ACM, New York, 2019, pp. 1–12, https://doi.org/10.1145/3290605.3300438.

[291] S.K. Long, J.P. Bliss, The effect of control device on performance in a robotic arm task, in: Proceedings of the Human Factors and Ergonomics Sociecy Annual Meeting - HFES '16, HFES, Washington, DC, 2016, pp. 795–799, https://doi.org/10.1177/1541931213601182.

[292] O.H. Lowry, N.J. Rosenbrough, A.L. Farr, R.J. Randall, Protein measurement with the folin phenol reagent, Journal of Biological Chemistry 193 (1951) 265–275.

[293] X. Lu, D. Yu, H.-N. Liang, W. Xu, Y. Chen, X. Li, K. Hasan, Exploration of hands-free text entry techniques for virtual reality, in: Proceedings of the IEEE International Symposium on Mixed and Augmented Reality - ISMAR '20, IEEE, New York, 2020, pp. 344–349, https://doi.org/10.1109/ISMAR50242.2020.00061.

[294] E. Lyakso, O. Frolova, E. Kleshnev, N. Ruban, A.M. Mekala, K.V. Arulalan, Approbation of the child's emotional development method (CEDM), in: Proceedings of the International Conference on Multimodal Interaction - ICMI '22, ACM, New York, 2022, pp. 1–10, https://doi.org/10.1145/3536220.3563371.

[295] K. Lyons, T. Starner, B. Gane, Experimental evaluation of the Twiddler one-handed chording mobile keyboard, Human-Computer Interaction 21 (4) (2006) 343–392, https://doi.org/10.1207/s15327051hci2104_1.

[296] K. Lyons, T. Starner, D. Plaisted, J. Fusia, A. Lyons, A. Drew, E.W. Looney, Twiddler typing: One-handed chording text entry for mobile phones, in: Proceedings of the ACM SIGCHI Conference on Human Factors in Computing Systems - CHI '04, ACM, New York, 2004, pp. 671–678, https://doi.org/10.1145/985692.985777.

[297] S.A. Macdonald, S. Brewster, F. Pollick, Eliciting emotion with vibrotactile stimuli evocative of real-world sensations, in: Proceedings of the 2020 International Conference on Multimodal Interaction - ICMI '20, ACM, New York, 2020, pp. 125–133, https://doi.org/10.1145/3382507.3418812.

[298] K.F. MacDorman, T.J. Whalen, C.-C. Ho, H. Patel, An improved usability measure based on novice and expert performance, International Journal of Human–Computer Interaction 27 (3) (2011) 280–302, https://doi.org/10.1080/10447318.2011.540472.

[299] I.S. MacKenzie, Citedness, uncitedness, and the murky world between, in: Extended Abstracts of the ACM SIGCHI Conference on Human Factors in Computing Systems - CHI '09, ACM, New York, 2009, pp. 2545–2554, https://doi.org/10.1145/1520340.1520360.

[300] I.S. MacKenzie, Fitts' law, in: K.L. Norman, J. Kirakowski (Eds.), Handbook of Human-Computer Interaction, Wiley, Hoboken, NJ, 2018, pp. 349–370, https://doi.org/10.1002/9781118976005.

[301] I.S. MacKenzie, Fitts' law as a research and design tool in human-computer interaction, Human-Computer Interaction 7 (1) (1992) 91–139, https://doi.org/10.1207/s15327051hci0701_3.

[302] I.S. MacKenzie, Fitts' throughput and the remarkable case of touch-based target selection, in: Proceedings of the 16th International Conference on Human-Computer Interaction - HCII '15 (LNCS 9170), Springer, Berlin, 2015, pp. 238–249, https://doi.org/10.1007/978-3-319-20916-6_23.

[303] I.S. MacKenzie, KSPC (keystrokes per character) as a characteristic of text entry techniques, in: Proceedings of the Fourth International Symposium on Human-Computer Interaction with Mobile Devices - MobileHCI '02, Springer, Berlin, 2002, pp. 195–210, https://doi.org/10.1007/3-540-45756-9_16.

[304] I.S. MacKenzie, Modeling text input for single-switch scanning, in: Proceedings of the 13th International Conference on Computers Helping People with Special Needs – ICCHP 2012 (LNCS 7383), Springer, Berlin, 2012, pp. 423–430, https://doi.org/10.1007/978-3-642-31534-3_63.

[305] I.S. MacKenzie, Motor behaviour models for human computer interaction, in: J.M. Carroll (Ed.), HCI Models, Theories, and Frameworks: Toward a Multidisciplinary Science, Morgan Kaufmann, San Francisco, 2003, pp. 27–54.

[306] I.S. MacKenzie, The one-key challenge: Searching for an efficient one-key text entry method, in: Proceedings of the ACM Conference on Computers and Accessibility

- ASSETS '09, ACM, New York, 2009, pp. 91–98, https://doi.org/10.1145/1639642. 1639660.

[307] I.S. MacKenzie, User studies and usability evaluations: From research to products, in: Proceedings of Graphics Interface - GI '15, Canadian Information Processing Society (CIPS), Toronto, 2015, pp. 1–8.

[308] I.S. MacKenzie, B. Ashtiani, BlinkWrite: Efficient text entry using eye blinks, Universal Access in the Information Society 10 (2011) 69–80, https://doi.org/10.1007/s10209-010-0188-6.

[309] I.S. MacKenzie, W. Buxton, Prediction of pointing and dragging times in graphical user interfaces, Interacting with Computers 6 (2) (1994) 213–227, https://doi.org/10.1016/0953-5438(94)90025-6.

[310] I.S. MacKenzie, J. Chen, A. Oniszczak, Unipad: Single-stroke text entry with language-based acceleration, in: Proceedings of the Fourth Nordic Conference on Human-Computer Interaction - NordiCHI '06, ACM, New York, 2006, pp. 78–85, https://doi.org/10.1145/1182475.1182484.

[311] I.S. MacKenzie, T. Felzer, SAK: Scanning ambiguous keyboard for efficient one-key text entry, ACM Transactions on Computer-Human Interaction 17 (3) (2010) 11:1–11:39, https://doi.org/10.1145/1806923.1806925.

[312] I.S. MacKenzie, P. Isokoski, Fitts' throughput and the speed-accuracy tradeoff, in: Proceedings of the ACM SIGCHI Conference on Human Factors in Computing Systems - CHI '08, ACM, New York, 2008, pp. 1633–1636, https://doi.org/10.1145/1357054.1357308.

[313] I.S. MacKenzie, S. Jusoh, An evaluation of two input devices for remote pointing, in: Proceedings of the Eighth IFIP Working Conference on Engineering for Human-Computer Interaction - EHCI '01 (LNCS 2254), Springer, Berlin, 2001, pp. 235–249, https://doi.org/10.1007/3-540-45348-2_21.

[314] I.S. MacKenzie, T. Kauppinen, M. Silfverberg, Accuracy measures for evaluating computer pointing devices, in: Proceedings of the ACM SIGCHI Conference on Human Factors in Computing Systems - CHI '01, ACM, New York, 2001, pp. 9–16, https://doi.org/10.1145/365024.365028.

[315] I.S. MacKenzie, H. Kober, D. Smith, T. Jones, E. Skepner, LetterWise: Prefix-based disambiguation for mobile text entry, in: Proceedings of the ACM Symposium on User Interface Software and Technology - UIST '01, ACM, New York, 2001, pp. 111–120, https://doi.org/10.1145/502348.502365.

[316] I.S. MacKenzie, A. Oniszczak, A comparison of three selection techniques for touch-pads, in: Proceedings of the ACM SIGCHI Conference on Human Factors in Computing Systems - CHI '98, ACM, New York, 1998, pp. 336–343, https://doi.org/10.1145/274644.274691.

[317] I.S. MacKenzie, J.R. Read, M. Horton, Empirical research methods for human-computer interaction, in: Proceedings of ACM SIGCHI Conference on Human Factors in Computing Systems - CHI '23, ACM, New York, 2023, https://doi.org/10.1145/3544549.3574165.

[318] I.S. MacKenzie, A. Sellen, W. Buxton, A comparison of input devices in elemental pointing and dragging tasks, in: Proceedings of the ACM SIGCHI Conference on Human Factors in Computing Systems - CHI '91, ACM, New York, 1991, pp. 161–166, https://doi.org/10.1145/108844.108868.

[319] I.S. MacKenzie, R.W. Soukoreff, A character-level error analysis technique for evaluating text entry methods, in: Proceedings of the Second Nordic Conference on Human-

Computer Interaction - NordiCHI '02, ACM, New York, 2002, pp. 243–246, https://doi.org/10.1145/572020.572056.

[320] I.S. MacKenzie, R.W. Soukoreff, A model of two thumb text entry, in: Proceedings of Graphics Interface - GI '02, Canadian Information Processing Society, Toronto, 2002, pp. 117–124, https://doi.org/10.20380/GI2002.14.

[321] I.S. MacKenzie, R.W. Soukoreff, Phrase sets for evaluating text entry techniques, in: Extended Abstracts of the ACM SIGCHI Conference on Human Factors in Computing Systems - CHI '03, ACM, New York, 2003, pp. 754–755, https://doi.org/10.1145/765891.765971.

[322] I.S. MacKenzie, R.W. Soukoreff, Text entry for mobile computing: Models and methods, theory and practice, Human-Computer Interaction 17 (2) (2002) 147–198, https://doi.org/10.1080/07370024.2002.9667313.

[323] I.S. MacKenzie, R.W. Soukoreff, C. Pal, A two-ball mouse affords three degrees of freedom, in: Extended Abstracts of the ACM SIGCHI Conference on Human Factors in Computing Systems - CHI '97, ACM, New York, 1997, pp. 303–304, https://doi.org/10.1145/1120212.1120405.

[324] I.S. MacKenzie, A. Oniszczak, The tactile touchpad, in: Extended Abstracts of the ACM SIGCHI Conference on Human Factors in Computing Systems - CHI '97, ACM, New York, 1997, pp. 309–310, https://doi.org/10.1145/1120212.1120408.

[325] I.S. MacKenzie, K. Tanaka-Ishii, Text entry using a small number of buttons, in: I.S. MacKenzie, K. Tanaka-Ishii (Eds.), Text Entry Systems: Mobility, Accessibility, Universality, Morgan Kaufmann, San Francisco, 2007, pp. 105–121, https://doi.org/10.1016/B978-012373591-1/50005-X.

[326] I.S. MacKenzie, R.J. Teather, FittsTilt: The application of Fitts' law to tilt-based interaction, in: Proceedings of the 7th Nordic Conference on Human-Computer Interaction - NordiCHI '12, ACM, New York, 2012, pp. 568–577, https://doi.org/10.1145/2399016.2399103.

[327] I.S. MacKenzie, C. Ware, Lag as a determinant of performance in interactive systems, in: Proceedings of the INTERACT '93 and CHI '93 Conference in Human Factors in Computing Systems - INTERCHI '93, ACM, New York, 1993, pp. 488–493, https://doi.org/10.1145/169059.169431.

[328] I.S. MacKenzie, S.X. Zhang, An empirical investigation of the novice experience with soft keyboards, Behaviour & Information Technology 20 (6) (2001) 411–418, https://doi.org/10.1080/01449290110089561.

[329] I.S. MacKenzie, S.X. Zhang, The design and evaluation of a high-performance soft keyboard, in: Proceedings of the ACM SIGCHI Conference on Human Factors in Computing Systems - CHI '99, ACM, New York, 1999, pp. 25–31, https://doi.org/10.1145/302979.302983.

[330] D. MacNeill, C.H. Blickenstorfer, Trackpads: Alternative input technologies, Pen Computing 3 (10) (May 1996) 42–45.

[331] J. Magee, T. Felzer, I.S. MacKenzie, Camera mouse + ClickerAID: Dwell vs. single-muscle click actuation in mouse-replacement interfaces, in: Proceedings of the 16th International Conference on Human-Computer Interaction - HCII '15 (LNCS 9175), Springer, Switzerland, 2015, pp. 74–84, https://doi.org/10.1007/978-3-319-20678-3_8.

[332] C. Magerkurth, R. Stenzel, A pervasive keyboard: Separating input from display, in: Proceedings of the 1st IEEE Conference on Pervasive Computing and Communications - PerCom '03, IEEE, New York, 2003, pp. 388–395.

[333] P. Majaranta, U.-K. Ahola, O. Špakov, Fast gaze typing with an adjustable dwell time, in: Proceedings of the ACM SIGCHI Conference on Human Factors in Computing Systems - CHI '09, ACM, New York, 2009, pp. 357–360, https://doi.org/10.1145/1518701. 1518758.

[334] P. Majaranta, I.S. MacKenzie, A. Aula, K.-J. Räiha, Effects of feedback and dwell time on eye typing speed and accuracy, Universal Access in the Information Society (UAIS) 5 (2006) 199–208, https://doi.org/10.1007/s10209-006-0034-z.

[335] P. Majaranta, K.-J. Räihä, Twenty years of eye typing: Systems and design issues, in: Proceedings of the 2002 Symposium on Eye Tracking Research & Applications - ETRA '02, ACM, New York, 2002, pp. 15–22, https://doi.org/10.1145/507072.507076.

[336] S. Malacria, G. Bailly, J. Harrison, A. Cockburn, C. Gutwin, Promoting hotkey use through rehearsal with ExposeHK, in: Proceedings of the ACM SIGCHI Conference on Human Factors in Computing Systems - CHI '13, ACM, New York, 2013, pp. 573–582, https://doi.org/10.1145/2470654.2470735.

[337] S. Malik, J. Laszlo, Visual touchpad: A two-handed gestural input device, in: Proceedings of the 6th International Conference on Multimodal Interfaces - ICMI '04, ACM, New York, 2004, pp. 289–296, https://doi.org/10.1145/1027933.1027980.

[338] R.L. Mandryk, M.S. Atkins, K.M. Inkpen, A continuous and objective evaluation of emotional experience with interactive play environments, in: Proceedings of the ACM SIGCHI Conference on Human Factors in Computing Systems - CHI '06, ACM, New York, 2006, pp. 1027–1036, https://doi.org/10.1145/1124772.1124926.

[339] J. Mankoff, G.D. Abowd, Cirrin: A word-level unistroke keyboard for pen input, in: Proceedings of the ACM Symposium on User Interface Software and Technology - UIST '98, ACM, New York, 1998, pp. 213–214, https://doi.org/10.1145/288392.288611.

[340] R.E. Mankowski, Predicting communication rates: Efficacy of a scanning model, MSc Thesis, University of Pittsburg, Pittsburgh, PA, 2009.

[341] A. Marcus, M.S. Berstein, O. Badar, D.R. Karger, S. Madden, R.C. Miller, TwitInfo: Aggregating and visualizing microblogs for event exploration, in: Proceedings of the ACM SIGCHI Conference on Human Factors in Computing Systems - CHI '11, ACM, New York, 2011, pp. 227–236, https://doi.org/10.1145/1978942.1978975.

[342] D.W. Martin, Doing Psychology Experiments, 7th ed., Wadsworth, Belmont, CA, 2007.

[343] R.L. Martin, The Design of Business: Why Design Thinking Is the Next Competitive Advantage, Harvard Business School, Boston, MA, 2009.

[344] D.V. Martinec, P. Gatta, B. Zheng, P.M. Denk, L.L. Swanstrom, The trade-off between flexibility and maneuverability: Task performance with articulating laparoscopic instruments, Surgical Endoscopy 23 (2009) 2697–2701, https://doi.org/10.1007/s00464-009-0462-y.

[345] J. Matejka, T. Grossman, G. Fitzmaurice, Citeology: Visualizing paper genealogy, in: Extended Abstracts of the ACM SIGCHI Conference on Human Factors in Computing Systems - CHI '12, ACM, New York, 2012, pp. 181–190, https://doi.org/10.1145/ 2212776.2212796.

[346] E. Matias, I.S. MacKenzie, W. Buxton, One-handed touch typing on a QWERTY keyboard, Human-Computer Interaction 11 (1) (1996) 1–27, https://doi.org/10.1207/ s15327051hci1101_1.

[347] D. Maynes-Aminzade, H. Raffle, You're in control: A urinary user interface, in: Extended Abstracts of the ACM SIGCHI Conference on Human Factors in Computing Systems - CHI '03, ACM, New York, 2003, pp. 986–987, https://doi.org/10.1145/ 765891.766108.

[348] D.C. McCallum, P. Irani, ARC-Pad: Absolute+relative cursor positioning for large displays with a mobile touchscreen, in: Proceedings of the ACM Symposium on User Interface Software and Technology - UIST '09, ACM, New York, 2009, pp. 153–156, https://doi.org/10.1145/1622176.1622205.

[349] J. McGrenere, G. Moore, Are we all in the same "bloat"? in: Proceedings of Graphics Interface - GI '00, Canadian Information Processing Society, Toronto, 2000, pp. 187–196, https://doi.org/10.20380/GI2000.25.

[350] M. McGuffin, R. Balakrishnan, Acquisition of expanding targets, in: Proceedings of the ACM SIGCHI Conference on Human Factors in Computing Systems - CHI '02, ACM, New York, 2002, pp. 57–64, https://doi.org/10.1145/503376.503388.

[351] L.K. McIntire, J.P. McIntire, A. McKinley, C. Goodyear, Detection of vigilance performance with pupillometry, in: Proceedings of the 2014 Symposium on Eye Tracking Research & Applications - ETRA '14, ACM, New York, 2014, pp. 167–174, https://doi.org/10.1145/2578153.2578177.

[352] C. McQueen, I.S. MacKenzie, S.X. Zhang, An extended study of numeric entry on pen-based computers, in: Proceedings of Graphics Interface - GI '95, Canadian Information Processing Society, Toronto, 1995, pp. 215–222, https://doi.org/10.20380/GI1995.25.

[353] S. Al-Megren, A predictive fingerstroke-level model for smartwatch interaction, Multimodal Technologies and Interaction 2 (3) (2018) 1–23, https://doi.org/10.3390/mti2030038.

[354] B. Mehlenbacher, T.M. Duffy, J. Palmer, Finding information on a menu: Linking menu organizaton onto the user's goals, Human-Computer Interaction 4 (3) (1989) 231–251, https://doi.org/10.1207/s15327051hci0403_3.

[355] A. Menin, R. Cava, C.M.D.S. Freitas, O. Corby, M. Winckler, Towards a visual approach for representing analytical provenance in exploration processes, in: 25th International Conference on Information Visualisation - IV '21, IEEE, New York, 2021, pp. 21–28, https://doi.org/10.1109/IV53921.2021.00014.

[356] D.E. Meyer, J.E.K. Smith, S. Kornblum, R.A. Abrams, C.E. Wright, Speed-accuracy tradeoffs in aimed movements: Toward a theory of rapid voluntary action, in: M. Jeannerod (Ed.), Attention and Performance XIII, Erlbaum, Hillsdale, NJ, 1990.

[357] D.P. Miller, The depth/breadth tradeoff in hierarchical computer menus, in: Proceedings of the Human Factors Society, Human Factors Society, Santa Monica, CA, 1981, pp. 12–16, https://doi.org/10.1177/107118138102500179.

[358] G.A. Miller, The magical number seven plus or minus two: Some limits on our capacity for processing information, Psychological Review 63 (2) (1956) 81–97.

[359] M. Moritz, The Little Kingdom: The Private Story of Apple Computer, William Morrow, New York, 1984.

[360] M.R. Morris, A. Huang, A. Paepcke, T. Winograd, Cooperative gestures: Multi-user gestural interactions for co-located groupware, in: Proceedings of the ACM SIGCHI Conference on Human Factors in Computing Systems - CHI '06, ACM, New York, 2006, pp. 1201–1210, https://doi.org/10.1145/1124772.1124952.

[361] C. Munteanu, R. Baecker, G. Penn, E. Toms, D. James, The effect of speech recognition accuracy rates on the usefulness and usability of webcast archives, in: Proceedings of the ACM SIGCHI Conference on Human Factors in Computing Systems - CHI '06, ACM, New York, 2006, pp. 493–502, https://doi.org/10.1145/1124772.1124848.

[362] L.R.D. Murthy, A. Mukhopadhyay, V. Yellheti, S. Arjun, P. Thomas, M. Dilli Babu, K.P. Singh Saluja, D.V. JeevithaShree, P. Biswas, Evaluating accuracy of eye gaze controlled interface in military aviation environment, in: Proceedings of the 2020 IEEE Aerospace

Conference, IEEE, New York, 2020, pp. 1–12, https://doi.org/10.1109/AERO47225.2020.9172480.

[363] A.K. Mutasim, A.U. Batmaz, M.H. Mughrabi, W. Stuerzlinger, Does repeatedly typing the same phrase provide a good estimate of expert text entry performance? in: Extended Abstracts of the ACM SIGCHI Conference on Human Factors in Computing Systems - CHI '23, ACM, New York, 2023, pp. 90.1–90.8, https://doi.org/10.1145/3544549.3585647.

[364] B.A. Myers, A brief history of human-computer interaction technology, Interactions 5 (2) (Mar. 1998) 44–54, https://doi.org/10.1145/274430.274436.

[365] M.A. Nacenta, R.L. Mandryk, C. Gutwin, Targeting across displayless space, in: Proceedings of the ACM SIGCHI Conference on Human Factors in Computing Systems - CHI '08, ACM, New York, 2008, pp. 777–786, https://doi.org/10.1145/1357054.1357178.

[366] F. Negini, R.L. Mandryk, K.G. Stanley, Using affective state to adapt characters, NPCs, and the environment in a first-person shooter game, in: Proceedings of the IEEE Games, Entertainment, Media Conference - IEEE-GEM '14, IEEE, New York, 2014, pp. 109–116, https://doi.org/10.1109/GEM.2014.7048094.

[367] B. New, C. Pallier, M. Brysbaert, L. Ferrand, Lexique 2: A new French lexical database, Behavior Research Methods, Instruments, & Computers 36 (2004) 516–524, https://doi.org/10.3758/BF03195598.

[368] A. Newell, P.S. Rosenbloom, Mechanisms of skill acquisition and the law of practice, in: J.R. Anderson (Ed.), Cognitive Skills and Their Acquisition, Erlbaum, Hillsdale, NJ, 1981, pp. 1–55.

[369] A. Newell, Unified Theories of Cognition, Harvard University Press, Cambridge, MA, 1990.

[370] W.M. Newman, A graphical technique for numerical input, The Computer Journal 11 (1) (1968) 63–64, https://doi.org/10.1093/comjnl/11.1.63.

[371] M. Nguyen, M. Laly, B.C. Kwon, C. Mougenot, J. McNamara, Moody Man: Improving creative teamwork through dynamic affective recognition, in: Extended Abstracts of the ACM SIGCHI Conference on Human Factors in Computing Systems - CHI '22, ACM, New York, 2022, pp. 465.1–465.14, https://doi.org/10.1145/3491101.3519656.

[372] H. Nicolau, J. Jorge, Touch typing using thumbs: Understanding the effect of mobility and hand posture, in: Proceedings of the ACM SIGCHI Conference on Human Factors in Computing Systems - CHI '12, ACM, New York, 2012, pp. 2683–2686, https://doi.org/10.1145/2207676.2208661.

[373] J. Nielsen, Estimating the number of subjects needed for a thinking aloud test, International Journal of Human-Computer Studies 41 (3) (1994) 385–397, https://doi.org/10.1006/ijhc.1994.1065.

[374] A. Nivedhan, L.A. Mielby, Q.J. Wang, The influence of emotion-oriented extrinsic visual and auditory cues on coffee perception: A virtual reality experiment, in: Companion Proceedings of the 2020 International Conference on Multimodal Interaction - ICMI '21, ACM, New York, 2021, pp. 301–306, https://doi.org/10.1145/3395035.3425646.

[375] D.A. Norman, Design rules based on analyses of human error, Communications of the ACM 26 (4) (1983) 254–258, https://doi.org/10.1145/2163.358092.

[376] D.A. Norman, The Design of Everyday Things, Basic Books, New York, 1988.

[377] J. Noyes, Chord keyboards, Applied Ergonomics 14 (1) (1983) 55–59, https://doi.org/10.1016/0003-6870(83)90221-1.

[378] S. O'Meara, Single-site surface electromyography for human-machine interfaces, Doctoral Dissertation, University of California, Davis, 2021.

[379] P. O'Toole, D. Glowinski, I. Pitt, M. Mancini, When emotions are triggered by single musical notes: Revealing the underlying factors of auditory-emotion associations, in: Companion Publication of the '21 International Conference on Multimodal Interaction, ACM, New York, 2021, pp. 291–298, https://doi.org/10.1145/3461615.3485419.

[380] M. Obrist, A.N. Tuch, K. Hornbaek, Opportunities for odor: Experiences with smell and implications for technology, in: Proceedings of the ACM SIGCHI Conference on Human Factors in Computing Systems - CHI '14, ACM, New York, 2014, pp. 2843–2852, https://doi.org/10.1145/2556288.2557008.

[381] R.C. Oldfield, The assessment and analysis of handedness: The Edinburgh inventory, Neuropsycholologia 9 (1) (1971) 97–113, https://doi.org/10.1016/0028-3932(71)90067-4.

[382] C. Oswald, K. Adjikari, A. Mohan, Effect of front-of-package labels on consumer product evaluation and preferences, Current Research in Food Science 5 (2022) 131–140, https://doi.org/10.1016/j.crfs.2021.12.016.

[383] A. Oulasvirta, S. Tamminen, V. Roto, J. Kuorelahti, Interaction in 4-second bursts: The fragmented nature of attentional resources in mobile HCI, in: Proceedings of the ACM SIGCHI Conference on Human Factors in Computing Systems - CHI '05, ACM, New York, 2005, pp. 919–928, https://doi.org/10.1145/1054972.1055101.

[384] K. Palin, A.M. Feit, S. Kim, P.O. Kristensson, A. Oulasvirta, How do people type on mobile devices? Observations from a study with 37,000 volunteers, in: Proceedings of the 21st International Conference on Human-Computer Interaction with Mobile Devices and Services - MobileHCI '19, ACM, New York, 2019, https://doi.org/10.1145/3338286.3340120.

[385] B. Pan, H.A. Hembrooke, G.K. Gay, L.A. Granka, M.K. Feusner, J.K. Newman, The determinants of web page viewing behavior: An eye-tracking study, in: Proceedings of the 2004 Symposium on Eye Tracking Research & Applications - ETRA '04, ACM, New York, 2004, pp. 147–154, https://doi.org/10.1145/968363.968391.

[386] V. Pandey, N.C. Khan, A.S. Gupta, K.Z. Gajos, Accuracy and reliability of at-home quantification of motor impairments using a computer-based pointing task with children with Ataxia-Telangiectasia, ACM Transactions on Accessible Computing (Jan. 2023) 1–25, https://doi.org/10.1145/3581790.

[387] R. Pastel, Measuring the difficulty of steering through corners, in: Proceedings of the ACM SIGCHI Conference on Human Factors in Computing Systems - CHI '06, ACM, New York, 2006, pp. 1087–1096, https://doi.org/10.1145/1124772.1124934.

[388] R. Pausch, Virtual reality on five dollars a day, in: Proceedings of the ACM SIGCHI Conference on Human Factors in Computing Systems - CHI '91, ACM, New York, 1991, pp. 265–269, https://doi.org/10.1145/108844.108913.

[389] A. Pavlovych, W. Stuerzlinger, Less-tap: A fast and easy-to-learn text input technique for phones, in: Proceedings of Graphics Interface - GI '03, Canadian Information Processing Society, Toronto, 2003, pp. 97–104, https://doi.org/10.20380/GI2003.12.

[390] G. Pearson, M.D. Weiser, Of moles and men: The design of foot controls for workstations, in: Proceedings of the ACM SIGCHI Conference on Human Factors in Computing Systems - CHI '86, ACM, New York, 1986, pp. 333–339, https://doi.org/10.1145/22627.22392.

[391] G.L. Pellecchia, Figure-of-eight method of measuring hand size: Reliability and concurrent validity, Journal of Hand Therapy 14 (4) (2003) 300–304, https://doi.org/10.1197/S0894-1130(03)00154-6.

[392] W. Penfield, T. Rasmussen, The Cerebral Cortex of Man: A Clinical Study of Localization of Function, Macmillan, New York, 1990.

[393] K. Perlin, Quikwriting: Continuous stylus-based text entry, in: Proceedings of the ACM Symposium on User Interface Software and Technology - UIST '98, ACM, New York, 1998, pp. 215–216, https://doi.org/10.1145/288392.288613.

[394] S. Perugini, T.J. Anderson, W.F. Moroney, A study of out-of-turn interaction in menu-based, IVR, voicemail systems, in: Proceedings of the ACM SIGCHI Conference on Human Factors in Computing Systems - CHI '07, ACM, New York, 2007, pp. 961–970, https://doi.org/10.1145/1240624.1240770.

[395] M. Peters, Constraints in the performance of bimanual tasks and their expression in unskilled and skilled subjects, Quarterly Journal of Experimental Psychology 37 (2) (1985) 171–196, https://doi.org/10.1080/14640748508400929.

[396] M. Peters, J. Ivanoff, Performance asymmetries in computer mouse control of right-handers, and left-handers with left- and right-handed mouse experience, Journal of Motor Behavior 31 (1) (1999) 86–94, https://doi.org/10.1080/00222899909601894.

[397] M. Pettitt, G. Burnett, A. Stevens, An extended keystroke level model (KLM) for predicting the visual demand of in-vehicle information systems, in: Proceedings of the ACM SIGCHI Conference on Human Factors in Computing Systems - CHI '07, ACM, New York, 2007, pp. 1515–1524, https://doi.org/10.1145/1240624.1240852.

[398] R.W. Pew, S. Baron, Perspectives on human performance modelling, Automatica 19 (1983) 663–676, https://doi.org/10.1016/B978-0-08-029348-6.50008-7.

[399] B. Pfleging, N. Henze, A. Schmidt, D. Rau, B. Reitschuster, Influence of subliminal cueing on visual search tasks, in: Extended Abstracts of the ACM SIGCHI Conference on Human Factors in Computing Systems - CHI '13, ACM, New York, 2013, pp. 1269–1274, https://doi.org/10.1145/2468356.2468583.

[400] K. Pietroszek, A. Kuzminykh, J.R. Wallace, E. Lank, Smartcasting: A discount 3D interaction technique for public displays, in: Proceedings of the 26th Australian Computer-Human Interaction Conference - OzCHI '14, ACM, New York, 2014, pp. 119–128, https://doi.org/10.1145/2686612.2686629.

[401] A. Pino, E. Tzemis, N. Ioannou, G. Kouroupetroglou, Using Kinect for 2D and 3D pointing tasks: Performance evaluation, in: M. Kurosu (Ed.), Human-Computer Interaction. Interaction Modalities and Techniques, Springer, Berlin, 2013, pp. 358–367, https://doi.org/10.1007/978-3-642-39330-3_38.

[402] M. Ploner, J. Gross, L. Timmermann, A. Schnitzler, Pain processing is faster than tactile processing in the human brain, Journal of Neuroscience 26 (42) (2006) 10879–10882, https://doi.org/10.1523/JNEUROSCI.2386-06.2006.

[403] M.F. Poller, S.K. Garter, The effects of modes on text editing by experienced editor users, Human Factors 26 (4) (1984) 449–462, https://doi.org/10.1177/001872088402600408.

[404] C. Porac, S. Coren, Lateral Preference and Human Behaviour, Springer, New York, 1981.

[405] R.L. Potter, L.J. Weldon, B. Shneiderman, Improving the accuracy of touch screens: An experimental evaluation of three strategies, in: Proceedings of the ACM SIGCHI Conference on Human Factors in Computing Systems - CHI '88, ACM, New York, 1988, pp. 27–32, https://doi.org/10.1145/57167.57171.

[406] E.C. Poulton, Tracking Skill and Manual Control, Academic Press, New York, 1974, p. 427.

[407] P. Qvarfordt, A. Jönsson, N. Dahlbäck, The role of spoken feedback in experience multimodal interfaces as human-like, in: Proceedings of the 5th International Conference on Multi-modal Interfaces - ICMI '03, ACM, New York, 2003, pp. 250–257, https://doi.org/10.1145/958432.958478.

[408] M. Raynal, I.S. MacKenzie, TBS[3]: Two-bar single-switch scanning for target selection, in: Proceedings of the 18th International Conference on Computers Helping People with Special Needs – ICCHP '22 (LNCS 13341), Springer, Cham, 2022, pp. 338–346, https://doi.org/10.1007/978-3-031-08648-9_39.

[409] M.M. Recker, J.E. Pitkow, Predicting document access in large multimedia repositories, ACM Transactions on Computer-Human Interaction 3 (4) (1996) 352–375, https://doi.org/10.1145/235833.236058.

[410] J. Rekimoto, Pick-and-drop: A direct manipulation technique for multiple computer environments, in: Proceedings of the ACM Symposium on User Interface Software and Technology - UIST '97, ACM, New York, 1997, pp. 31–39, https://doi.org/10.1145/263407.263505.

[411] J. Rekimoto, Tilting operations for small screen interfaces, in: Proceedings of the ACM Symposium on User Interface Software and Technology - UIST '96, ACM, New York, 1996, pp. 167–168, https://doi.org/10.1145/237091.237115.

[412] V. Remizova, A. Sand, I.S. MacKenzie, O. Špakov, K. Nyyssönen, I. Rakkolainen, A. Kylliäinen, V. Surakka, Y. Gizatdinova, Mid-air gestural interaction with a large fogscreen, Multimodal Technologies and Interaction 7 (63) (2023) 1–18, https://doi.org/10.3390/mti7070063.

[413] M.A. Renom, B. Caramiaux, M. Beaudouin-Lafon, Exploring technical reasoning in digital tool use, in: Proceedings of the ACM SIGCHI Conference on Human Factors in Computing Systems - CHI '22, ACM, New York, 2022, pp. 579.1–579.17, https://doi.org/10.1145/3491102.3501877.

[414] R.E. Rider, Position indicator for a display system (U.S. Patent 3,835,464, 1973), 1973.

[415] D. Roberts, T. Duckworth, C. Moore, R. Wolff, J. O'Hare, Comparing the end to end latency of an immersive collaborative environment and a video conference, in: Proceedings of the 13th Symposium on Distributed Simulation and Real Time Applications, ACM, New York, 2009, pp. 89–94, https://doi.org/10.1109/DS-RT.2009.43.

[416] M. Roberts, Humans sense 10 basic types of smell, scientists say, BBC Online News, Sept. 2021, http://www.bbc.co.uk/news/health-24123676. (Accessed 23 October 2022).

[417] S.K. Roberts, A look at NCC '81, Byte (Sept. 1981) 36–37.

[418] J. Robertson, Likert-type scales, statistical methods, and effect sizes, Communications of the ACM 55 (5) (2012) 6–7, https://doi.org/10.1145/2160718.2160721.

[419] M. Rohs, A. Oulasvirta, Target acquisition with camera phones when used as magic lenses, in: Proceedings of the ACM SIGCHI Conference on Human Factors in Computing Systems - CHI '08, ACM, New York, 2008, pp. 1409–1418, https://doi.org/10.1145/1357054.1357275.

[420] M.F. Roig-Maimó, I. Salinas-Bueno, R. Mas-Sansó, J. Varona, P. Martínez-Bueso, The influence of mobile device type on camera-based monitoring of neck movements for cervical rehabilitation, Sensors 23 (5) (2023) 2481.1–2482.13, https://doi.org/10.3390/s23052482.

[421] Q. Roy, S. Malacria, Y. Guiard, E. Lecolinet, J. Eagan, Augmented letters: Mnemonic gesture-based shortcuts, in: Proceedings of the ACM SIGCHI Conference on Human Factors in Computing Systems - CHI '13, ACM, New York, 2013, pp. 2325–2328, https://doi.org/10.1145/2470654.2481321.

[422] J. Ruiz, A. Bunt, E. Lank, A model of non-preferred hand mode switching, in: Proceedings of Graphics Interface - GI '08, Canadian Information Processing Society, Toronto, 2008, pp. 49–56, https://doi.org/10.1145/1375714.1375724.

[423] S. Rümelin, E. Rukzio, R. Hardy, NaviRadar: A tactile information display for pedestrian navigation, in: Proceedings of the ACM Symposium on User Interface Software and Technology - UIST '11, ACM, New York, 2011, pp. 293–302, https://doi.org/10.1145/2047196.2047234.

[424] J.A. Russell, A circumplex model of affect, Journal of Personality and Social Psychology 39 (6) (1980) 1161–1178, https://doi.org/10.1037/h0077714.

[425] J.A. Russell, A. Weiss, G.A. Mendelsohn, Affect grid: A single-item scale of pleasure and arousal, Journal of Personality and Social Psychology 57 (3) (1989) 493–502, https://doi.org/10.1037/0022-3514.57.3.493.

[426] H. Ryu, K. Cruz, LetterEase: Improving text entry on a handheld device via letter reassignment, in: Proceedings of the 19th Conference of the Computer-Human Interaction Special Interaction Group (CHISIG) of Australia - OZCHI '05, ACM, New York, 2005, pp. 1–10.

[427] N. Ryu, H.-Y. Jo, M. Pahud, M. Sinclair, A. Bianchi, GamesBond: Bimanual haptic illusion of physically connected objects for immersive VR using grip deformation, in: Proceedings of the ACM SIGCHI Conference on Human Factors in Computing Systems - CHI '21, ACM, New York, 2021, pp. 125.1–125.10, https://doi.org/10.1145/3411764.3445727.

[428] A. Saad, U. Gruenefeld, L. Mecke, M. Koelle, F. Alt, S. Schneegass, Mask removal isn't always convenient in public! The impact of the Covid-19 pandemic on device usage and user authentication, in: Extended Abstracts of the ACM SIGCHI Conference on Human Factors in Computing Systems - CHI '22, ACM, New York, 2022, pp. 218.1–218.7, https://doi.org/10.1145/3491101.3519804.

[429] M. Sáenz, J. Sánchez, Indoor position and orientation for the blind, in: Proceedings of Human-Computer Interaction International - HCII '07 (LNCS 5616), Springer, Berlin, 2009, pp. 236–245, https://doi.org/10.1007/978-3-642-02713-0_25.

[430] S. Sallam, Y. Sakamoto, J. Leboe-McGowan, C. Latulipe, P. Irani, Towards design guidelines for effective health-related data videos: An empirical investigation of affect, personality, and video content, in: Proceedings of the ACM SIGCHI Conference on Human Factors in Computing Systems - CHI '22, ACM, New York, 2022, pp. 342.1–342.22, https://doi.org/10.1145/3491102.3517727.

[431] G. Salvendy (Ed.), Handbook of Human Factors, Wiley, New York, 1987.

[432] D. Salvucci, N.A. Taatgen, J.P. Borst, Toward a unified theory of the multitasking continuum: From concurrent performance to task switching, interruption, and resumption, in: Proceedings of the ACM SIGCHI Conference on Human Factors in Computing Systems - CHI '09, ACM, New York, 2009, pp. 1819–1828, https://doi.org/10.1145/1518701.1518981.

[433] A. Sand, V. Remizova, I.S. MacKenzie, O. Špakov, K. Nieminen, I. Rakkolainen, A. Kylliäinen, V. Surakka, J. Kuosmanen, Tactile feedback on mid-air gestural interaction with a large fogscreen, in: Proceedings of the 23rd International Conference on Academic Mindtrek - AcademicMindtrek '20, ACM, New York, 2020, pp. 161–164, https://doi.org/10.1145/3377290.3377316.

[434] F.E. Sandnes, F.O. Medola, Effects of optimizing the scan-path on scanning keyboards with QWERTY-layout for English text, in: P. Cudd, L. de Witte (Eds.), Harnessing the Power of Technology to Improve Lives, IOS Press, Amsterdam, 2017, pp. 930–938.

[435] D.J. Schiano, S.M. Ehrlich, K. Rahardja, K. Sheridan, Face to interface: Facial affect in (hu)man and machine, in: Proceedings of the ACM SIGCHI Conference on Human Factors in Computing Systems - CHI '00, ACM, New York, 2000, pp. 193–200, https://doi.org/10.1145/332040.332430.

[436] A. Sears, B. Shneiderman, High precision touchscreens: Design strategies and comparisons with a mouse, International Journal of Man-Machine Studies 34 (4) (1991) 593–613, https://doi.org/10.1016/0020-7373(91)90037-8.

[437] A.F. Seay, R.E. Kraut, Project massive: Self-regulation and problematic use of online gaming, in: Proceedings of the ACM SIGCHI Conference on Human Factors in Computing Systems - CHI '07, ACM, New York, 2007, pp. 829–838, https://doi.org/10.1145/1240624.1240749.

[438] T. Selker, Touching the future, Communications of the ACM 51 (12) (Dec. 2008) 14–16, https://doi.org/10.1145/1409360.1409366.

[439] A.J. Sellen, G.P. Kurtenbach, W.A.S. Buxton, The prevention of mode errors through sensory feedback, Human-Computer Interaction 7 (2) (1992) 141–164, https://doi.org/10.1207/s15327051hci0702_1.

[440] A. Sellen, R. Eardley, S. Iazdl, R. Harper, The whereabouts clock: Early testing of a situated awareness device, in: Extended Abstracts of the ACM SIGCHI Conference on Human Factors in Computing Systems - CHI '06, ACM, New York, 2006, pp. 1307–1312, https://doi.org/10.1145/1125451.1125694.

[441] K. Sengupta, S. Bhattarai, S. Sarcar, I.S. MacKenzie, S. Staab, Leveraging error correction in voice-based text entry by talk-and-gaze, in: Proceedings of the ACM SIGCHI Conference on Human Factors in Computing Systems - CHI '20, ACM, New York, 2020, pp. 1–11, https://doi.org/10.1145/3313831.3376579.

[442] S.C. Seow, Information theoretic models of HCI: A comparison of the Hick-Hyman law and Fitts' law, Human-Computer Interaction 20 (3) (2005) 315–352, https://doi.org/10.1207/s15327051hci2003_3.

[443] C.E. Shannon, Prediction and entropy of printed English, Bell System Technical Journal 30 (1) (1951) 50–64, https://doi.org/10.1002/j.1538-7305.1951.tb01366.x.

[444] C.E. Shannon, W. Weaver, The Mathematical Theory of Communications, University of Illinois Press, Urbana, IL, 1949.

[445] F. Shein, G. Hamann, N. Brownlow, J. Treviranus, M. Milner, P. Parnes, WiViK: A visual keyboard for Windows 3.0, in: Proceedings of the Annual Conference of the Rehabilitation Engineering Society of North America - RESNA '91, RESNA, Arlington, VA, 1991, pp. 160–162.

[446] T.B. Sheridan, W.R. Ferrell, Remote manipulation control with transmission delay, IEEE Transactions on Human Factors in Electronics HFE-4 (1) (1968) 25–29, https://doi.org/10.1109/THFE.1963.231283.

[447] D. Sheskin, Handbook of Parametric and Nonparametric Statistical Procedures, 5th ed., CRC Press, Boca Raton, FL, 2011, https://doi.org/10.1201/9781420036268.

[448] I. Shklovski, R. Kraut, J. Cummings, Routine patterns of Internet use and psychological well-being: Coping with a residential move, in: Proceedings of the ACM SIGCHI Conference on Human Factors in Computing Systems - CHI '06, ACM, New York, 2006, pp. 969–978, https://doi.org/10.1145/1124772.1124917.

[449] B. Shneiderman, Direct manipulation: A step beyond programming languages, IEEE Computer 16 (8) (Aug. 1983) 57–69, https://doi.org/10.1145/800276.810991.

[450] B. Shneiderman, C. Plaisant, Designing the User Interface: Strategies for Effective Human-Computer Interaction, 4th ed., Pearson, New York, 2005.

[451] S. Siegel, Nonparametric statistics, American Statistician 11 (3) (1957) 13–19, https://doi.org/10.1080/00031305.1957.10501091.

[452] S. Siegel, N.J. Castellan, Nonparametric Statistics for the Behavioral Sciences, McGraw-Hill, London, 1988.

[453] M. Silfverberg, P. Korhonen, I.S. MacKenzie, Zooming and panning content on a display screen (International Patent WO 03021568 (A1)), 2003.

[454] M. Silfverberg, I.S. MacKenzie, P. Korhonen, Predicting text entry speed on mobile phones, in: Proceedings of the ACM SIGCHI Conference on Human Factors in Computing Systems - CHI '00, ACM, New York, 2000, pp. 9–16, https://doi.org/10.1145/332040.332044.

[455] D. Small, H. Ishii, Design of spatially aware graspable displays, in: Proceedings of the ACM SIGCHI Conference on Human Factors in Computing Systems - CHI '97, ACM, New York, 1997, pp. 367–368, https://doi.org/10.1145/1120212.1120437.

[456] D.C. Smith, C.H. Irby, Xerox Star live demonstration, in: Proceedings of the ACM SIGCHI Conference on Human Factors in Computing Systems - CHI '98, vol. 2, ACM, New York, 1998, p. 17, https://doi.org/10.1145/286498.286507.

[457] D.C. Smith, C. Irby, R. Kimball, E. Harslem, The Star user interface: An overview, in: Proceedings of the AFIPS Joint Computer Conference, ACM, New York, 1982, pp. 515–528, https://doi.org/10.1145/1500774.1500840.

[458] D.K. Smith, R.C. Alexander, Fumbling the Future: How Xerox Invented, then Ignored, the First Personal Computer, William Morrow, New York, 1988.

[459] K. Snowberry, S.R. Parkinson, N. Sisson, Computer display menus, Ergonomics 26 (7) (1983) 699–712, https://doi.org/10.1080/00140138308963390.

[460] K.M. Snyder, Y. Ashitaka, H. Shimada, J.E. Ulrich, G.D. Logan, What skilled typists don't know about the QWERTY keyboard, Attention, Perception, & Psychophysics 76 (2014) 162–171, https://doi.org/10.3758/s13414-013-0548-4.

[461] H. Song, B. Kim, B. Lee, J. Seo, A comparative evaluation on tree visualization methods for hierarchical structures with large fan-outs, in: Proceedings of the ACM SIGCHI Conference on Human Factors in Computing Systems - CHI '10, ACM, New York, 2010, pp. 223–232, https://doi.org/10.1145/1753326.1753359.

[462] S. Song, S. Yamada, Designing expressive lights and in-situ motions for robots to express emotions, in: Proceedings of the 6th International Conference on Human-Agent Interaction - HAI '18, ACM, New York, 2018, pp. 222–228, https://doi.org/10.1145/3284432.3284458.

[463] D. Sonnenschein, Sound Design: The Expressive Power of Music, Voice, and Sound Effects in Cinema, Michael Weiser Productions, Studio City, CA, ISBN 0-941188-26-4, 2001.

[464] R.W. Soukoreff, I.S. MacKenzie, Measuring errors in text entry tasks: An application of the Levenshtein string distance statistic, in: Extended Abstracts of the ACM SIGCHI Conference on Human Factors in Computing Systems - CHI '01, ACM, New York, 2001, pp. 319–320, https://doi.org/10.1145/634067.634256.

[465] R.W. Soukoreff, I.S. MacKenzie, Metrics for text entry research: An evaluation of MSD and KSPc, and a new unified error metric, in: Proceedings of the ACM SIGCHI Conference on Human Factors in Computing Systems - CHI '03, ACM, New York, 2003, pp. 113–120, https://doi.org/10.1145/642611.642632.

[466] R.W. Soukoreff, I.S. MacKenzie, Towards a standard for pointing device evaluation: Perspectives on 27 years of Fitts' law research in HCI, International Journal of Human-Computer Studies 61 (6) (2004) 751–789, https://doi.org/10.1016/j.ijhcs.2004.09.001.

[467] A.J. Sporka, T. Felzer, S.H. Kurniawan, P. Ondrej, P. Haiduk, I.S. MacKenzie, CHANTI: Predictive text entry using non-verbal vocal input, in: Proceedings of the ACM SIGCHI Conference on Human Factors in Computing Systems - CHI '11, ACM, New York, 2011, pp. 2463–2472, https://doi.org/10.1145/1978942.1979302.

[468] J. Staiano, B. Lepri, N. Aharony, F. Pianesi, N. Sebe, A. Pentland, Friends don't lie: Inferring personality traits from social network structure, in: Proceedings of the ACM Conference on Ubiquitous Computing - UbiComp '12, ACM, New York, 2012, pp. 321–330, https://doi.org/10.1145/2370216.2370266.

[469] C.M. Stanton, P.H. Kahn Jr., R.L. Severson, J.H. Ruckert, B.T. Gill, Robotic animals might aid in the social development of children with autism, in: Proceedings of Human Robot Interaction - HRI '08, ACM, New York, 2008, pp. 271–278, https://doi.org/10.1145/1349822.1349858.

[470] J. Stasko, J. Choo, Y. Han, M. Hu, H. Pileggi, R. Sadana, C.D. Stolper, CiteVis: Exploring conference paper citation data visually, in: Posters of IEEE InfoVis '13, vol. 2, IEEE, New York, 2013, pp. 2–3.

[471] A. Steed, A simple method for estimating the latency of interactive, real-time graphics simulations, in: Proceedings of the ACM Symposium on Virtual Reality Software and Technology - VRST '08, ACM, New York, 2008, pp. 123–129, https://doi.org/10.1145/1450579.1450606.

[472] C.E. Steriadis, P. Constantinou, Designing human-computer interfaces for quadriplegic people, ACM Transactions on Computer-Human Interaction 10 (2) (2003) 87–118, https://doi.org/10.1145/772047.772049.

[473] P. Strohmeier, J.P. Carrascal, B. Cheng, M. Meban, R. Vertegaal, An evaluation of shape changes for conveying emotions, in: Proceedings of the ACM SIGCHI Conference on Human Factors in Computing Systems - CHI '16, ACM, New York, 2016, pp. 3781–3792, https://doi.org/10.1145/2858036.2858537.

[474] W. Strunk Jr., E.B. White, The Elements of Style, 4th ed., Pearson, Needham Heights, MA, 2000.

[475] N.M. Su, G. Mark, Communication chains and multitasking, in: Proceedings of the ACM SIGCHI Conference on Human Factors in Computing Systems - CHI '08, ACM, New York, 2008, pp. 83–92, https://doi.org/10.1145/1357054.1357069.

[476] X. Sun, Q. Zhang, S. Wiedenbeck, T. Chintakovid, Gender differences in trust perception when using IM and video, in: Extended Abstracts of the ACM SIGCHI Conference on Human Factors in Computing Systems - CHI '06, ACM, New York, 2006, pp. 1373–1378, https://doi.org/10.1145/1125451.1125705.

[477] H.B. Surale, F. Matulic, D. Vogel, Experimental analysis of mode switching techniques in touch-based user interfaces, in: Proceedings of the ACN SIGCHI Conference on Human Factors in Computing Systems - CHI '17, ACM, New York, 2017, pp. 3267–3280, https://doi.org/10.1145/3025453.3025865.

[478] I.E. Sutherland, Sketchpad: A man-machine graphical communication system, in: Proceedings of the AFIPS Spring Joint Computer Conference, vol. 23, ACM, New York, 1963, pp. 329–346, https://doi.org/10.1177/003754976400200514.

[479] R.G. Swensson, The elusive tradeoff: Speed vs accuracy in visual discrimination tasks, Perception & Psychophysics 12 (1A) (1972) 16–32, https://doi.org/10.3758/BF03212837.

[480] A.Y.J. Szeto, E.J. Allen, M.C. Littrell, Comparison of speed and accuracy for selected electronic communication devices and input methods, Augmentative and Alternative Communication 9 (4) (1993) 229–242, https://doi.org/10.1080/07434619312331276651.

[481] M. Talbot, W. Cowan, On the audio representation of distance for blind users, in: Proceedings of the ACM SIGCHI Conference on Human Factors in Computing Systems - CHI '09, ACM, New York, 2009, pp. 1839–1848, https://doi.org/10.1145/1518701.1518984.

[482] B.W. Tatler, N.J. Wade, H. Kwan, J.M. Findlay, B.M. Velichkovsky, Yarbus, eye movements, and vision, i-Perception 1 (1) (2010) 7–27, https://doi.org/10.1068/i0382.

[483] Taylor and Francis, HCI guidelines for final submissions, https://files.taylorandfrancis.com/hhciguidelines.pdf, 2021. (Accessed 15 March 2023).

[484] R.J. Teather, I.S. MacKenzie, Comparing order of control for tilt and touch games, in: Proceedings of the 2014 Conference on Interactive Entertainment – IE '14, ACM, New York, 2014, pp. 1–10, https://doi.org/10.1145/2677758.2677766.

[485] R.J. Teather, I.S. MacKenzie, Position vs. velocity control for tilt-based interaction, in: Proceedings of Graphics Interface - GI '14, Canadian Information Processing Society, Toronto, 2014, pp. 51–58.

[486] R.J. Teather, A. Pavlovych, W. Stuerzlinger, I.S. MacKenzie, Effects of tracking technology, latency, and spatial jitter on object movement, in: Proceedings of the IEEE Symposium on 3D User Interfaces - 3DUI '09, IEEE, New York, 2009, pp. 43–50, https://doi.org/10.1109/3DUI.2009.4811204.

[487] R.J. Teather, A. Roth, I.S. MacKenzie, Tilt-touch synergy: Input control for "dual-analog" style mobile games, Entertainment Computing 21 (2017) 33–43, https://doi.org/10.1016/j.entcom.2017.04.005.

[488] L. Teo, B.E. John, Comparisons of keystroke-level model predictions to observed data, in: Extended Abstracts of the ACM SIGCHI Conference on Human Factors in Computing Systems - CHI '06, ACM, New York, 2006, pp. 1421–1426, https://doi.org/10.1145/1125451.1125713.

[489] P. Thornton, Design thinking in stereo: Brown and Martin, Interactions 17 (2) (Mar. 2010) 12–15, https://doi.org/10.1145/1699775.1699778.

[490] G. Tisza, K. Sharma, S. Papavlasopoulou, P. Markopoulos, M. Giannakos, Understanding fun in learning to code: A multi-modal data approach, in: Proceedings of Interaction Design and Children - IDC '22, ACM, New York, 2022, pp. 274–287, https://doi.org/10.1145/3501712.3529716.

[491] M. Tohidi, W. Buxton, R. Baecker, A. Sellen, Getting the right design and the design right: Testing many is better than one, in: Proceedings of the ACM SIGCHI Conference on Human Factors in Computing Systems - CHI '06, ACM, New York, 2006, pp. 1243–1252, https://doi.org/10.1145/1124772.1124960.

[492] K. Tominaga, S. Fujita, R. Takakura, B. Shizuki, Investigating the effects of position and angle of virtual keyboard on text entry performance and workload, in: Proceedings of the Asian CHI Symposium 2021, ACM, New York, 2021, pp. 25–27, https://doi.org/10.1145/3429360.3468174.

[493] E. Triantafyllidis, Z. Li, The challenges in modeling human performance in 3D space with Fitts' law, in: Extended Abstracts of the ACM SIGCHI Conference on Human Factors in Computing Systems - CHI '21, ACM, New York, 2021, pp. 56.1–56.9, https://doi.org/10.1145/3411763.3443442.

[494] T.S. Tullis, Designing a menu-based interface to an operating system, in: Proceedings of the ACM SIGCHI Conference on Human Factors in Computing Systems - CHI '85, ACM, New York, 1985, pp. 70–84, https://doi.org/10.1145/317456.317471.

[495] H.P. Van Cott, R.G. Kinkade, Human Engineering Guide to Equipment Design, U.S. Government Printing Office, Washington, DC, 1972.

[496] L. Vanacken, T. Grossman, K. Coninx, Exploring the effects of environment density and target visibility on object selection in 3D virtual environments, in: Proceedings of the IEEE Symposium on 3D User Interfaces - 3DUI '07, IEEE, New York, 2007, pp. 117–124, https://doi.org/10.1109/3DUI.2007.340783.

[497] N. Vanderschantz, C. Timpany, A. Hinze, Design exploration of ebook interfaces for personal digital libraries on tablet devices, in: Proceedings of the 15th New Zealand Conference on Human-Computer Interaction - CHINZ '15, ACM, New York, 2015, pp. 21–30, https://doi.org/10.1145/2808047.2808054.

[498] E. Velloso, J. Alexander, A. Bulling, H. Gellersen, Interactions under the desk: A characterisation of foot movements for input in a seated position, in: Proceedings of the 15th IFIP TC13 Conference on Human-Computer Interaction - INTERACT '15, Springer, Berlin, 2015, pp. 384–401, https://doi.org/10.1007/978-3-319-22701-6_29.

[499] D. Venolia, Facile 3D manipulation, in: Proceedings of the INTERACT '93 and CHI '93 Conference on Human Factors in Computing Systems - INTERCHI '93, ACM, New York, 1993, pp. 31–36, https://doi.org/10.1145/169059.169065.

[500] D.S. Venolia, S. Ishikawa, Three degree of freedom graphic object controller (U. S. Patent 5,313,230), 1994.

[501] D. Venolia, F. Neiberg, T-Cube: A fast, self-disclosing pen-based alphabet, in: Proceedings of the ACM SIGCHI Conference on Human Factors in Computing Systems - CHI '94, ACM, New York, 1994, pp. 265–270, https://doi.org/10.1145/191666.191761.

[502] K. Vertanen, P.-O. Kristensson, Parakeet: A continuous speech recognition system for mobile touch-screen devices, in: Proceedings of the ACM Conference on Intelligent User Interfaces - IUI '09, ACM, New York, 2009, pp. 237–246, https://doi.org/10.1145/1502650.1502685.

[503] K. Vertanen, H. Memmi, J. Emge, S. Reyal, P.O. Kristensson, VelociTap: Investigating fast mobile text entry using sentence-based decoding of touchscreen keyboard input, in: Proceedings of the ACM SIGCHI Conference on Human Factors in Computing Systems - CHI '15, ACM, New York, 2015, pp. 659–668, https://doi.org/10.1145/2702123.2702135.

[504] N. Villar, S. Izadi, D. Rosenfeld, H. Benko, J. Helmes, J. Westhues, S. Hodges, E. Ofek, A. Butler, X. Cao, B. Chen, Mouse 2.0: Multi-touch meets the mouse, in: Proceedings of the ACM Symposium on User Interface Software and Technology - UIST '09, ACM, New York, 2009, pp. 33–42, https://doi.org/10.1145/1622176.1622184.

[505] S. Voelker, C. Corsten, N.A.-h. Hamdan, K.I. Overgaard, J. Borchers, An interaction model for touch-aware tangibles on interactive surfaces, in: Extended Abstracts of the ACM SIGCHI Conference on Human Factors in Computing Systems - CHI '04, ACM, New York, 2014, pp. 1873–1878, https://doi.org/10.1145/2559206.2581273.

[506] S. Voelker, C. Wacharamanotham, J. Borchers, An evaluation of state switching methods for indirect touch systems, in: Proceedings of the ACM SIGCHI Conference on Human Factors in Computing Systems - CHI '13, ACM, New York, 2013, pp. 745–754, https://doi.org/10.1145/2470654.2470759.

[507] D. Vogel, R. Balakrishnan, Direct pen interaction with a conventional graphical user interface, Human-Computer Interaction 25 (4) (2010) 324–388, https://doi.org/10.1080/07370024.2010.499839.

[508] D. Vogel, P. Baudisch, Shift: A technique for operating pen-based interfaces using touch, in: Proceedings of the ACM SIGCHI Conference on Human Factors in Computing Systems - CHI '07, ACM, New York, 2007, pp. 657–666, https://doi.org/10.1145/1240624.1240727.

[509] Y. Wang, C. Shi, L. Li, H. Tong, H. Qu, Visualizing research impact through citation data, ACM Transactions on Interactive Intelligent Systems 8 (1) (2018) 5.1–5.24, https://doi.org/10.1145/3132744.

[510] C. Ware, H.H. Mikaelian, An evaluation of an eye tracker as a device for computer input, in: Proceedings of the CHI+GI Conference on Human Factors in Computing Systems

- CHI+GI '87, ACM, New York, 1987, pp. 183–188, https://doi.org/10.1145/30851. 275627.

[511] A.M. Webb, M. Pahud, K. Hinckley, B. Buxton, Wearables as context for Guiard-abiding bimanual touch, in: Proceedings of the ACM Symposium on User Interface Software and Technology - UIST '16, ACM, New York, 2016, pp. 287–300, https://doi.org/10.1145/2984511.2984564.

[512] S. Weisband, S. Kiesler, Self disclosure on computer forms: Meta-analysis and implications, in: Proceedings of the ACM SIGCHI Conference on Human Factors in Computing Systems - CHI '96, ACM, New York, 1996, pp. 3–10, https://doi.org/10.1145/238386. 238387.

[513] M. Weiser, The computer for the 21st century, Scientific American 265 (3) (Sept. 1991) 94–105, https://doi.org/10.1145/329124.329126.

[514] A.T. Welford, Fundamentals of Skill, Methuen, London, 1968.

[515] C.D. Wickens, Engineering Psychology and Human Performance, Harper Collins, New York, 1987, https://doi.org/10.4324/9781003177616.

[516] D. Wigdor, R. Balakrishnan, A comparison of consecutive and concurrent input text entry techniques for mobile phones, in: Proceedings of the ACM SIGCHI Conference on Human Factors in Computing Systems - CHI '04, ACM, New York, 2004, pp. 81–88, https://doi.org/10.1145/985692.985703.

[517] D. Wigdor, R. Balakrishnan, TiltText: Using tilt for text input to mobile phones, in: Proceedings of the ACM Symposium on User Interface Software and Technology - UIST '03, ACM, New York, 2003, pp. 81–90, https://doi.org/10.1145/964696.964705.

[518] D. Wigdor, C. Forlines, P. Baudisch, J. Barnwell, C. Shen, LucidTouch: A see-through mobile device, in: Proceedings of the ACM Symposium on User Interface Software and Technology - UIST '07, ACM, New York, 2007, pp. 269–278, https://doi.org/10.1145/1294211.1294259.

[519] D. Wigdor, C. Shen, C. Forlines, R. Balakrishnan, Effects of display position and control space orientation on user preference and performance, in: Proceedings of the ACM SIGCHI Conference on Human Factors in Computing Systems - CHI '06, ACM, New York, 2006, pp. 309–318, https://doi.org/10.1145/1124772.1124819.

[520] A. Wing, Timing and coordination of repetitive bimanual movements, Quarterly Journal of Experimental Psychology 34 (3) (1982) 339–348, https://doi.org/10.1080/14640748208400847.

[521] J.O. Wobbrock, L. Findlater, D. Gergle, J.J. Higgins, The aligned rank transform for nonparametric factorial analyses using only anova procedures, in: Proceedings of the ACM SIGCHI Conference on Human Factors in Computing Systems - CHI '11, ACM, New York, 2011, pp. 143–146, https://doi.org/10.1145/1978942.1978963.

[522] J.O. Wobbrock, J. Fogarty, S.-Y. Liu, S. Kimuro, S. Harada, The angle-mouse: Target-agnostic dynamic gain adjustment based on angular deviation, in: Proceedings of the ACM SIGCHI Conference on Human Factors in Computing Systems - CHI '09, ACM, New York, 2009, pp. 1401–1410, https://doi.org/10.1145/1518701.1518912.

[523] J.O. Wobbrock, K.Z. Gajos, A comparison of area pointing and goal crossing for people with and without motor impairments, in: Proceedings of the ACM SIGACCESS Conference in Computers and Accessibility - ASSETS '07, ACM, New York, 2007, pp. 3–10, https://doi.org/10.1145/1296843.1296847.

[524] J.O. Wobbrock, B.A. Myers, J.A. Kembel, EdgeWrite: A stylus-based text entry method designed for high accuracy and stability of motion, in: Proceedings of the Annual ACM Symposium on User Interface Software and Technology - UIST '03, ACM, New York, 2003, pp. 61–70, https://doi.org/10.1145/964696.964703.

[525] J.O. Wobbrock, B.A. Myers, B. Rothrock, Few-key text entry revisited: Mnemonic gestures on four keys, in: Extended Abstracts of the ACM SIGCHI Conference on Human Factors in Computing Systems - CHI '06, ACM, New York, 2006, pp. 489–492, https://doi.org/10.1145/1124772.1124846.

[526] J.O. Wobbrock, J. Rubinstein, M.W. Sawyer, A.T. Duchowski, Longitudinal evaluation of discrete consecutive gaze gestures for text entry, in: Proceedings of the 2008 Symposium on Eye Tracking Research & Applications - ETRA '08, ACM, New York, 2008, pp. 11–18, https://doi.org/10.1145/1344471.1344475.

[527] C. Wong, People with paralysis navigate a room via a mind-controlled wheelchair, New Scientist, Nov. 2022, https://www.newscientist.com/article/2347757. (Accessed 6 December 2022).

[528] N. Wong, C. Gutwin, Controlling an avatar's pointing gestures in desktop collaborative virtual environments, in: Proceedings of the ACM International Conference on Supporting Group Work - GROUP '12, ACM, New York, 2012, pp. 21–30, https://doi.org/10.1145/2389176.2389180.

[529] J. Woodward, J. Cato, J. Smith, I. Wang, B. Benda, L. Anthony, J. Ruiz, Examining Fitts' and FFitts' law models for children's pointing tasks on touchscreens, in: Proceedings of the International Conference on Advanced Visual Interfaces - AVI '20, ACM, New York, 2020, pp. 56.1–56.5, https://doi.org/10.1145/3399715.3399844.

[530] H. Yamada, A historical study of typewriters and typing methods: From the position of planning Japanese parallels, Journal of Information Processing (ISSN 0387-6101) 2 (4) (1980) 175–202.

[531] M. Yamagami, S. Junuzovic, M. Gonzalez-Franco, E. Ofek, E. Cutrell, J.R. Porter, A.D. Wilson, M.E. Mott, Two-in-one: A design space for mapping unimanual input into bimanual interactions in VR for users with limited movement, ACM Transactions on Accessible Computing 15 (3) (July 2022) 23.1–23.25, https://doi.org/10.1145/3510463.

[532] S. Yamanaka, H. Usuba, Computing touch-point ambiguity on mobile touchscreens for modeling target selection times, in: Proceedings of the ACM Conference on Interactive, Mobile, Wearable, and Ubiquitous Technologies - IMWUT '21, ACM, New York, 2021, pp. 186.1–186.21, https://doi.org/10.1145/3494976.

[533] S. Yanisky-Ravid, C. Martens, From the myth of Babel to Google Translate: Confronting malicious use of artificial intelligence: Copyright and algorithmic biases in online translations systems, Seattle University Law Review 43 (2019) 99, https://doi.org/10.2139/ssrn.3345716.

[534] L. Ye, F.E. Sandnes, I.S. MacKenzie, QB-Gest: Qwerty bimanual gestural input for eyes-free smartphone text input, in: Proceedings of the International Conference on Human-Computer Interaction – HCII '20 (LNCS 12188), Springer, Berlin, 2020, pp. 223–242, https://doi.org/10.1007/978-3-030-49282-3_16.

[535] M. Yearworth, L. White, Group support systems: Experiments with an online system and implications for same-time/different places working, in: D.M. Kilgour, C. Eden (Eds.), Handbook of Group Decisions and Negotiation, 2nd ed., Springer, Cham, 2019, pp. 1–28, https://doi.org/10.1007/978-3-030-49629-6_48.

[536] K.-P. Yee, Two-handed interaction on a tablet display, in: Extended Abstracts of the ACM SIGCHI Conference on Human Factors in Computing Systems - CHI '04, ACM, New York, 2004, pp. 1493–1496, https://doi.org/10.1145/985921.986098.

[537] H.-S. Yeo, J. Lee, A. Bianchi, A. Quigley, WatchMI: Pressure touch, twist and pan gesture input on unmodified smartwatches, in: Proceedings of the 18th International Conference on Human-Computer Interaction with Mobile Devices and Services - Mo-

bileHCI '16, ACM, New York, 2016, pp. 394–399, https://doi.org/10.1145/2935334. 2935375.

[538] M. Yin, S. Zhai, The benefits of augmenting telephone voice menu navigation with visual browsing and search, in: Proceedings of the ACM SIGCHI Conference on Human Factors in Computing Systems - CHI '06, ACM, New York, 2006, pp. 319–328, https://doi.org/10.1145/1124772.1124821.

[539] N. Yoshida, T. Yonezawa, Arousal and valence in robot's emotional expression of breathing and heartbeat, in: Proceedings of the 6th International Conference on Human-Agent Interaction - HAI '18, ACM, New York, 2018, pp. 330–332, https://doi.org/10.1145/3284432.3287176.

[540] D. Yu, K. Fan, H. Zhang, D. Monteiro, W. Xu, H.-N. Liang, PizzaText: Text entry for virtual reality systems using dual thumbsticks, IEEE Transactions on Visualization and Computer Graphics 24 (11) (2018) 2927–2935, https://doi.org/10.1109/TVCG.2018. 2868581.

[541] C. Zanbaka, P. Goolkasian, L. Hodges, Can a virtual cat persuade you? The role of gender and realism in speaker persuasiveness, in: Proceedings of the ACM SIGCHI Conference on Human Factors in Computing Systems - CHI '06, ACM, New York, 2006, pp. 1153–1162, https://doi.org/10.1145/1124772.1124945.

[542] G. Zand, Y. Ren, A.S. Arif, TiltWalker: Operating a telepresence robot with one-hand by tilt controls on a smartphone, Proceedings of the ACM on Human–Computer Interaction 6 (ISS) (Nov. 2022) 572.1–572.26, https://doi.org/10.1145/3567725.

[543] P. Zaphiris, S.H. Kurniawan, R.D. Ellis, Age related differences and the depth vs. breadth tradeoff in hierarchical online information systems, in: Proceedings of the 7th ERCIM International Workshop on User Interfaces for All - UI4ALL '02 (LNCS 2615), Springer, Berlin, 2002, pp. 23–42, https://doi.org/10.1007/3-540-36572-9_2.

[544] S. Zhai, Human performance in six degree of freedom input control, Doctoral Dissertation, University of Toronto, 1995.

[545] S. Zhai, S. Conversy, M. Beaudouin-Lafon, Y. Guiard, Human on-line response to target expansion, in: Proceedings of the ACM SIGCHI Conference on Human Factors in Computing Systems - CHI '03, ACM, New York, 2003, pp. 177–184, https://doi.org/10.1145/642611.642644.

[546] S. Zhai, J. Kong, X. Ren, Speed-accuracy tradeoff in Fitts' law tasks: On the equivalency of actual and nominal pointing precision, International Journal of Human-Computer Studies 61 (6) (2004) 823–856, https://doi.org/10.1016/j.ijhcs.2004.09.007.

[547] S. Zhai, P.O. Kristensson, The word-gesture keyboard: Reimagining keyboard interaction, Communications of the ACM 55 (9) (Sept. 2012) 91–101, https://doi.org/10.1145/2330667.2330689.

[548] S. Zhai, P.-O. Kristensson, Shorthand writing on a stylus keyboard, in: Proceedings of the ACM SIGCHI Conference on Human Factors in Computing Systems - CHI '03, ACM, New York, 2003, pp. 97–104, https://doi.org/10.1145/642611.642630.

[549] S. Zhai, A. Sue, J. Accot, Movement mode, hits distribution and learning in virtual keyboarding, in: Proceedings of the ACM SIGCHI Conference on Human Factors in Computing Systems - CHI '02, ACM, New York, 2002, pp. 17–24, https://doi.org/10.1145/503376.503381.

[550] M.R. Zhang, S. Zhai, J.O. Wobbrock, TypeAnywhere: A QWERTY-based text entry solution for ubiquitous computing, in: Proceedings of the ACM SIGCHI Conference on Human Factors in Computing Systems - CHI '22, ACM, New York, 2022, pp. 339.1–339.16, https://doi.org/10.1145/3491102.3517686.

[551] X. Zhang, I.S. MacKenzie, Evaluating eye tracking with ISO 9241 – Part 9, in: Proceedings of HCI International - HCII '07 (LNCS 4552), Springer, Heidelberg, 2007, pp. 779–788, https://doi.org/10.1007/978-3-540-73110-8_85.

[552] Z. Zhang, R. Héron, E. Lecolinet, F. Detienne, S. Safin, VisualTouch: Enhancing affective touch communication with multi-modality stimulation, in: Proceedings of the 2019 International Conference on Multimodal Interaction - ICMI '19, ACM, New York, 2019, pp. 114–123, https://doi.org/10.1145/3340555.3353733.

[553] S. Zhao, P. Dragicevic, M. Chignell, R. Balakrishnan, P. Baudisch, EarPod: Eyes-free menu selection using touch input and reactive audio feedback, in: Proceedings of the ACM SIGCHI Conference on Human Factors in Computing Systems - CHI '07, ACM, New York, 2007, pp. 1395–1404, https://doi.org/10.1145/1240624.1240836.

[554] Q. Zhou, G. Fitzmaurice, F. Anderson, In-depth nouse: Integrating desktop mouse into virtual reality, in: Proceedings of the ACM SIGCHI Conference on Human Factors in Computing Systems - CHI '22, ACM, New York, 2022, pp. 354.1–354.17, https://doi.org/10.1145/3491102.3501884.

[555] D. Zhu, T. Gedeon, K. Taylor, Exploring camera viewpoint control models for a multitasking setting in teleoperation, in: Proceedings of the ACM SIGCHI Conference on Human Factors in Computing Systems - CHI '11, ACM, New York, 2011, pp. 53–62, https://doi.org/10.1145/1978942.1978952.

[556] T.G. Zimmerman, J. Lanier, C. Blanchard, S. Bryson, Y. Harvill, A hand gesture interface device, in: Proceedings of the ACM SIGCHI Conference on Human Factors in Computing Systems - CHI+GI '87, ACM, New York, 1987, pp. 189–192, https://doi.org/10.1145/1165387.275628.

[557] G. Zinck, D. Vogel, Evaluating singing for computer input using pitch, interval, and melody, in: Proceedings of the ACM SIGCHI Conference on Human Factors in Computing Systems - CHI '22, ACM, New York, 2022, pp. 213.1–213.15, https://doi.org/10.1145/3491102.3517691.

Glossary

This glossary is limited to terms relevant to empirical research following an experimental, observational, or correlational paradigm, particularly as used in HCI.

alpha in an experiment, the likelihood of incorrectly rejecting the null hypothesis; that is, the probability of rejecting a true null hypothesis (i.e., committing a Type I error). Alpha is chosen by the investigator based on what is deemed acceptable for the experiment, with $\alpha = .05$ commonly used.

analysis of variance (ANOVA) a statistical procedure for studying the effect of a set of conditions (such as the levels of an independent variable) on a dependent variable.

apparatus in an experiment, the instrument or equipment used (including hardware and software).

balanced Latin square a Latin square whereby each condition precedes and follows each other condition an equal number of times. Only for even-order Latin squares (e.g., 4×4).

between-subjects an experiment design whereby each participant is tested on just one level of an independent variable. A separate group of participants is required for each level.

categorical data *see* nominal scale data.

convenience sampling in an experiment, a process for selecting participants that is governed by availability.

correlated samples *see* dependent samples.

correlation coefficient (*r*) a numeric index between -1 and $+1$ reflecting the degree of linear relationship between two variables, with -1 indicating a perfect negative relationship, $+1$ indicating a perfect positive relationship, and 0 indicating no relationship.

correlational research a research methodology in which relationships between variables are observed and studied without controlling the setting in which those relationships exist.

counterbalancing arranging experiment conditions to minimize the influence of order effects, such as due to practice or fatigue.

degrees of freedom in statistics, the number of elements that can vary in a calculation. Generally, one less than the number of scores.

dependent samples in an experiment, sets of data collected from the single group of participants. *See also* within-subjects.

dependent variable (DV) in an experiment, an outcome that is observed across levels of an independent variable.

ecological validity the extent to which the methodology in an experiment is representative of conditions in the wider world.

effect size a measure of the magnitude or meaningfulness of a relationship between two variables, with the intent to convey the practical significance of a research finding.

empirical 1: originating in or based on observation or experience; 2: relying on experience or observation alone often without due regard for system and theory; 3: capable of being verified or disproved by observation or experiment.

empirical research research using observation as the basis for conclusion or determination, as opposed to speculative, theoretical, or exclusively reason-based approaches.

experiment a series of observations conducted under controlled conditions with the purpose of drawing causal inferences about the relationship between variables. An experiment involves manipulating one or more independent variables, the measurement of a dependent variable, and the exposure of participants the conditions being studied.

experimental research a research methodology whereby participants are randomly assigned to conditions and with variables that are systematically manipulated with the goal of drawing causal conclusions.

external validity in an experiment, the extent to which the results can be generalized beyond the sample of participants and circumstances that were tested.

F-statistic in an analysis of variance, the ratio of the amount of variance due to the groups or conditions being compared (numerator) and all the remaining variance (denominator). The value determines whether to accept the null hypothesis of no difference between the groups or conditions being compared, with a large value indicating the presence of a significant effect.

factorial experiment an experiment in which categorical variables (factors) are manipulated in order to study their separate influence (main effects) or combined influence (interaction effects) on a dependent variable.

factor *see* independent variable.

fatigue effect a decline in performance on a task that is attributed to the participant becoming tired or bored.

group effect in a counterbalanced design, the effect of the groups on a dependent variable. Group is a contrived between-subjects variable which, ideally, is not statistically significant.

independent samples in an experiment, sets of data collected whereby each set is from a different group of participants. *See also* between-subjects.

independent variable (IV) in an experiment, a variable that is manipulated to assess its effect on a dependent variable.

interaction effect in an experiment, the combined effect of two or more independent variables on a dependent variable.

internal validity the degree to which an experiment is free from compromises in its internal structure and therefore yields accurate results.

interval-scale data data on a scale with equal intervals and with equivalent differences between any two consecutive values.

Latin square an $n \times n$ matrix filled with n Latin letters (A, B, ...) with each letter occurring exactly once in each row and each column. In an experiment, each row corresponds to a group of participants and the letters in the columns along each row correspond to test conditions.

law a statement of a relationship that is invariable under given conditions.

learning effect an improvement in performance on a task that is attributed to the participant gaining familiarity with the task as testing proceeds.

level in an experiment, a category of the independent variable.

Likert scale an attitude measure consisting of a statement along with responses reflecting the degree of positive or negative sentiment toward the statement. Commonly using a five-point scale with a neutral middle point which may or may not be included.

linear regression a regression analysis whereby the predictor variable x is related to the criterion or dependent variable y such that increases in x result in consistent increases or decreases in y.

longitudinal user study a type of experiment design where the responses on a dependent variable are observed and measured over an extended period of time. Typically, time-sequenced units of practice, such as "session" or "block," are the levels of the independent variable.

main effect in an experiment, the consistent total effect of a single independent variable on a dependent variable.

measurement the act of assigning a figure, amount, or extent on some dimension, property, or criterion.

mixed design an experiment design with at least one within-subjects independent variable and at least one between-subjects independent variable.

multiple comparisons test *see* post hoc test.

multiple regression a statistical technique for examining the linear relationship between two or more predictor variables (x_1, x_2, ...) and a criterion or dependent variable (y).

nominal-scale data data or codes whereby the values do not indicate order, magnitude, or a true zero point but instead identify items in mutually exclusive categories.

non-parametric test a statistical test on data with no assumptions (e.g., of the distribution) about the population from which the data are drawn.

null hypothesis a statement that an experiment will find no meaningful differences between the conditions under test.

observation the careful, close examination of an object, process, or other phenomenon for the purpose of collecting data about it or drawing conclusions.

observational research a research methodology whereby the experimenter passively observes the behaviour of participants without intervention or manipulation of circumstances influencing the behaviours.

order effect in a within-subjects design, the influence of the order in which conditions are administered, such as the effect of being administered first vs. second.

ordinal-scale data data whereby the values do not indicate magnitude or a true zero point but instead reflect a rank ordering on the attribute measured.

pairwise comparisons test *see* post hoc test.

parametric test a statistical test on data with assumptions on the distribution or other properties of the population from which the data are drawn.

participant a person who takes part in an investigation, study, or experiment, such as by performing tasks or by answering questions.

post hoc test a statistical procedure conducted after an analysis of variance has revealed a significant effect, with the goal of determining which pairs of conditions significantly differ from each other.

power *see* statistical power

practice effect *see* learning effect.

precision-relevance tradeoff *see* relevance-precision tradeoff.

probability (p-value) in hypothesis testing, the likelihood of obtaining the observed data if the null hypothesis is true.

procedure in an experiment, the step-by-step directions on what occurred with each participant, including briefing, informed consent, instructions, demonstration, practice, performing tasks, rest breaks, completing questionnaires, interviews, renumeration, time involved, and so on.

random sampling in an experiment, a process for selecting participants from a larger group of people, such that each person has the same chance of being included.

ratio-scale data data on a measurement scale having a true zero (indicating absence of the property) and a meaningful ratio of values.

relevance-precision tradeoff in an experiment, the balance struck between measuring dependent variables specifically and accurately (precision) vs. obtaining results that apply beyond the limited setting of the experiment (relevance).

repeated measures *see* within-subjects.

research 1: careful or diligent search; 2: collecting information about a subject; 3: investigation or experimentation aimed at the discovery and interpretation of facts, revision of accepted theories or laws in the light of new facts.

scientific method principles and procedures for the systematic pursuit of knowledge involving the recognition and formulation of a problem, the collection of data through observation and experiment, and the formulation and testing of hypotheses.

self-selection bias a type of bias that is introduced when study participants choose their own conditions for testing, rather than being randomly assigned.

statistical power the likelihood of a hypothesis test detecting a true effect if there is one. A statistically powerful test is more likely to reject a false negative (i.e., commit a Type II error).

statistical significance in an experiment, the degree to which the differences between conditions (e.g., the levels of an independent variable) cannot reasonably be attributed to chance or random effects.

t-test a statistical procedure used to determine if there is a significant difference between the means of two populations or groups.

test condition the level of an independent variable (or a combination of levels for a multi-factor experiment) presented to participants when conducting an experiment. *See also* level.

theory 1: a hypothesis assumed for the sake of argument; 2: abstract or speculative thought; 3: a scientifically accepted body of principles that explain phenomena.

Type I error occurs when the null hypothesis is rejected when it is in fact true.

Type II error occurs when the null hypothesis is not rejected when it is in fact not true.

usability evaluation a test to determine how well users can learn and use a product, focusing on ease of learning, efficiency of use, errors (including frequency and severity), overall satisfaction, and so on. The products are typically prototypes, interfaces, websites, software products, computer applications, or commercial systems.

user study an experiment with human participants. *See also* experiment.

within-subjects an experiment design whereby each participant is tested on all levels of an independent variable.

Index

Printed in the United States
by Baker & Taylor Publisher Services